October 22–24, 2012
Boulder, Colorado, USA

 Association for Computing Machinery

Advancing Computing as a Science & Profession

ASSETS'12

Proceedings of the14th International ACM SIGACCESS Conference on

Computers and Accessibility

Sponsored by:
ACM SIGACCESS

Supported by:
National Science Foundation, Microsoft Research, Coleman Institute & The University of Rochester

Association for
Computing Machinery

Advancing Computing as a Science & Profession

The Association for Computing Machinery
2 Penn Plaza, Suite 701
New York, New York 10121-0701

ISBN: 978-1-4503-1321-6

Additional copies may be ordered prepaid from:

ACM Order Department
PO Box 30777
New York, NY 10087-0777, USA

Phone: 1-800-342-6626 (USA and Canada)
+1-212-626-0500 (Global)
Fax: +1-212-944-1318
E-mail: acmhelp@acm.org
Hours of Operation: 8:30 am – 4:30 pm ET

ACM Order No: 444120

Printed in the USA

ASSETS 2012 General Chair's Welcome

It is my pleasure to welcome you to ASSETS 2012, the Fourteenth International ACM SIGACCESS Conference on Computers and Accessibility, in Boulder, Colorado, USA. At the base of the foothills of the Rocky Mountains, Boulder is known for its beautiful views, wide-open spaces, and its open-mindedness. Long a destination for freethinkers, Boulder is a modern center for higher education. We are fortunate to be near the main campus of the University of Colorado, which has been a hub of accessibility and assistive technology research. The university is also the home of the Coleman Institute for Cognitive Disabilities, which has partnered with our conference to organize special events for our attendees, including a tour of a local smart home with technologies for people with disabilities.

We are happy to continue the tradition of the ASSETS conference being the premier forum for presenting innovative research on mainstream and specialized assistive technologies, accessible computing, and assistive applications of computer, network, and information technologies. Our Program Chair, Sri Kurniawan, and our Posters and Demo Chair, Faustina Hwang, have assembled an impressive program. As a highlight of our conference program, we are delighted to welcome Emeritus Professor John Gardner, who is the 2012 winner of the ACM SIGACCESS Award for Outstanding Contribution to Computing and Accessibility, to present our keynote.

In addition, we are also pleased to continue the tradition of the ASSETS conference as a welcoming venue for student researchers. I would like to thank Simon Harper for chairing our Student Research Competition (SRC) this year, with event sponsorship from Microsoft Research. In addition, I would like to thank Jeff Bigham for his work in chairing the Doctoral Consortium event for Ph.D. students this year, with generous support from the National Science Foundation.

I would also like to thank the other members of our organizing committee for their contributions to making the ASSETS 2012 conference a reality: Ravi Kuber (Treasurer and Registration Chair) for work on the conference budget and registration system, Enrico Pontelli (Mentoring Chair) for continuing the ASSETS tradition of supporting new members of the community, Jeff Hoehl (Local Arrangements Chair) for organizing events in Boulder and local preparations, Barbara Morris (Logistics Chair) for her work in ensuring the on-site conference details are executed flawlessly, Raja Kushalnagar (Accessibility Chair) for ensuring that ASSETS continues to be a model how an accessible conference should be run, Tiago Guerreiro (Web Chair) for designing and maintaining our beautiful website, and Kyle Montague (Publicity Chair) for engaging in a variety of media to spread the word and build excitement for ASSETS 2012. I'm also grateful for the guidance of our steering committee for the conference (Armando Barreto, Kathy McCoy, Enrico Pontelli, Andrew Sears, and Shari Trewin), which includes general chairs from prior ASSETS conferences, for their valuable advice during the planning of ASSETS 2012.

Welcome to Boulder and to ASSETS 2012!

Matt Huenerfauth
ASSETS'12 General Chair
City University of New York, USA

ASSETS 2012 Program Chair's Welcome

On behalf of the ASSETS 2012 Program Committee, it is my pleasure to welcome you to an exciting technical program offered by the Fourteenth International ACM SIGACCESS Conference on Computers and Accessibility.

The technical program of 25 podium presentations and 46 posters and demonstrations has been selected through peer-review by a distinguished international program committee. This committee had the very difficult job of assembling a conference program from the diverse set of very high-quality submissions. We received submissions from more than 20 different countries. The podium presentations were selected from 88 full-length submissions (a 28% acceptance rate), and have been organized into 9 themes including designing for older adults, understanding aging performance, accessibility at large, shared work, screen reader usage, interactions without sight, visual impairment simulation, communication aids and sign language. The accepted papers address a variety of assistive technology users including older adults, people who use sign language, and people with visual, intellectual, mobility and speech impairments. The Program Committee was also involved in the poster and demonstration program, which was chaired by Faustina Hwang. These 46 presentations were selected from 65 submissions (a 70% acceptance rate). The posters and demonstrations provide an opportunity to showcase late-breaking results as well as work in progress and practical implementations.

Posters and demonstrations and selected ACM Student Research Competition entries are represented by abstracts in these proceedings and in two poster sessions during the conference. The winners of the ACM Student Research Competition will go on to compete in the ACM-wide grand finals, where ASSETS entrants have established a strong track record.

The poster sessions will also showcase participants in the Doctoral Consortium. This one-day workshop preceding the main conference brought together 10 emerging researchers working on accessibility to discuss their ideas with a panel of established experts. A special edition of the SIGACCESS newsletter will feature extended abstracts from these doctoral students.

Putting together the technical program of ASSETS 2012 was a team effort. I first thank the authors for providing the content of the program. I would also like to extend my deepest appreciation to the session chairs as well as the entire program committee and additional reviewers who worked very hard in reviewing papers and providing feedback for authors. The success of the technical program would not have been possible without their tremendous effort.

Welcome to the technical program of ASSETS 2012!

Sri Kurniawan
ASSETS'12 Program Chair
University of California Santa Cruz, USA

Table of Contents

Session 1: Screen Reader Usage
Session Chair: Jeff Bigham *(University of Rochester)*

Session 2: Designing for Older Adults
Session Chair: Vicki Hanson *(University of Dundee)*

Session 3: Communication Aids
Session Chair: Adam Sporka *(Czech Technical University)*,

Session 4: Accessibility at Large
Session Chair: Simon Harper *(University of Manchester)*,

Session 9: Sign Language
Session Chair: Raja Kushalnagar *(Rochester Institute of Technology)*

Posters and Demonstrations

Student Research Competition Abstracts

ASSETS 2012 Conference Organization

General Chair: Matt Huenerfauth *(City University of New York, USA)*

Program Chair: Sri Kurniawan *(University of California Santa Cruz, USA)*

Treasurer & Registration Chair: Ravi Kuber *(University of Maryland Baltimore County, USA)*

Poster & Demo Chair: Faustina Hwang *(University of Reading, UK)*

Doctoral Consortium Chair: Jeff Bigham *(University of Rochester, USA)*

Student Research Competition Chair: Simon Harper *(University of Manchester, UK)*

Mentoring Chair: Enrico Pontelli *(New Mexico State University, USA)*

Local Arrangements Chair: Jeffery Hoehl *(University of Colorado, USA)*

Logistics Chair: Barbara Morris *(University of Maryland Baltimore County, USA)*

Accessibility Chair: Raja Kushalnagar *(Rochester Institute of Technology, USA)*

Web Chair: Tiago Guerreiro *(Instituto Superior Técnico, Portugal)*

Publicity Chair: Kyle Montague *(University of Dundee, UK)*

Steering Committee Chair: Andrew Sears *(Rochester Institute of Technology, USA)*

Steering Committee: Armando Barreto *(Florida International University, USA)*

Kathy McCoy *(University of Delaware, USA)*

Enrico Pontelli *(New Mexico State University, USA)*

Shari Trewin *(IBM T.J. Watson Research Center, USA)*

Program Committee: Julio Abascal *(University of Basque Country, Spain)**
** = Organizing Committee Member Ray Adams *(University of Middlesex, UK)*
* = Associate Program Chair Chieko Asakawa *(IBM Research Japan, Japan)**
Armando Barreto *(Florida International University, USA)**
Jeffrey P. Bigham *(University of Rochester, USA)***
Giorgio Brajnik *(University of Udine, Italy)**
Ruth Campbell *(University College London, UK)*
Anna Cavender *(Google, USA)**
Alistair D. N. Edwards *(University of York, UK)**
Harriet Fell *(Northeastern University, USA)*
Torsten Felzer *(Darmstadt University of Technology, Germany)*
Jinjuan Heidi Feng *(Towson University, USA)*
Leah Findlater *(University of Maryland, USA)*

ASSETS 2012 Sponsor & Supporters

Sponsor:

Special Interest Group on Accessible Computing

Doctoral
Consortium
Supporter:

Student Research
Competition
Supporter:

Partners:

The 2012 SIGACCESS Award for Outstanding Contribution to Computing and Accessibility

John Gardner, Professor Emeritus, Oregon State University

John Gardner is a Professor Emeritus of Physics at Oregon State University, whose professional career has spanned over 46 years. Dr. Gardner has had a very successful academic career in the field of physics. As a recognized expert on the physics of defects in materials, he has received research funding from the National Science Foundation, the Department of Energy, the Office of Naval Research, the Department of Defense, NASA, and several other sources.

After many years of scientific publications in the field of physics, Dr. Gardner became blind in the 1980s. He not only continued his contribution to physics after his blindness, but he also pioneered an entirely new area of accessibility in math and science. Half of Dr. Gardner's more than 130 publications are devoted to accessibility. He has contributed to incorporating accessibility into Microsoft's operating systems, developed the DotsPlus Braille mathematics notation, and contributed to the MathML mark-up language. He and his group developed the Tiger embosser, the IVEO audiohaptic display technology, an accessible graphing calculator, and collaborated with American Physical Society (APS) to develop technology and infrastructure needed for APS to publish its journals in the DAISY format. He is also the founder and president of ViewPlus Technologies, Inc.

Dr. Gardner has received several professional awards, including the Humboldt Prize, Distinguished Service Awards from Oregon State University and the University of Illinois, and the Oregon Governor's Award for his accessibility contributions. He received his B.A. from Rice University in 1961, his M.S. from the University of Illinois in 1963, and his Ph.D. from the University of Illinois in 1966.

Keynote Presentation at ASSETS 2012

Dr. Gardner will deliver the keynote presentation at the ASSETS 2012 conference, entitled "Creating the Future." Two essential developments have led to textual information becoming largely accessible today to people with print disabilities. One is the development of access technologies such as screen readers and computer braille displays. The other development is that mainstream electronic text is largely distributed as Unicode characters, a format that is more compact, more searchable, more editable, and therefore more accessible to everybody than other formats such as bit-map images. It is clear that in a few short years, more complex information – math, static graphics, and simple interactive graphics – will increasingly be created and distributed in more compact, more flexible formats than what is typical today. It would be excellent for everybody if this complex information were also highly accessible, but that future is not automatic. Dr. Gardner will discuss his vision of how that future might be created.

About the Award

The SIGACCESS Award for Outstanding Contributions to Computing and Accessibility recognizes individuals who have made significant and lasting contributions to the development of computing technologies that improve the accessibility of media and services to people with disabilities. Outstanding contributions through research, practice, or advocacy are recognized. Towards this goal, contributions are considered from academia, industry, as well as other professions that focus on computer users with disabilities and the application of computing technology to improve access. The award recognizes members of the community for long-term accomplishments or those who have made a notable impact through a significant innovation.

Candidates' contributions can include innovative ideas, influence in the community, and/or the social impact of their work.

The award includes a $1000 honorarium, an award certificate of recognition, and an invitation for the recipient to present a keynote talk at the ASSETS Conference. A public citation for the award will be placed on the SIGACCESS website.

Table 1. Proposed usage scenarios for context-aware AAC, based on our early design meetings, including the contextual data needed, and possible sources of this data.

	Scenario	*Context*	*Data sources*
1	When I am at the supermarket, I want to talk about food.	Location	GPS; GSM; Wi-Fi
2	When I am with my coworker, I want to talk about the office.	Conversation partner	Face recognition; tagged ID card
3	When my friend mentions her family, I want to discuss my family.	Partner's speech	Speech recognition
4	I want to ask about some object or landmark in the environment.	Objects in environment	Tagged objects; computer vision-based object recognition
5	I want to talk about recent news and the local sports team.	Current events	Web-based news; social networks

4.1 Hardware and Software

We developed TalkAbout for touch screen tablets, as tablets are commonly used at the aphasia center where we conducted this research. Our prototype was tested on a 2012 Apple iPad.

The TalkAbout software was developed using the PhoneGap application framework[1] and Google App Engine (GAE)[2]. TalkAbout's application logic was written in Python. User data such as saved locations and phrases were stored in the online GAE database, and could be accessed from multiple devices. The OpenCV library[3] was used for image processing.

TalkAbout's user interface was written in HTML and JavaScript. Creating a web-based user interface enabled the research team to make quick adjustments to the interface, even during site visits.

4.2 User Interface

Similar to many other AAC systems, TalkAbout's purpose is to enable users to store, organize, browse, and speak stored words and phrases. The current prototype enables users to *browse* items, to *add* new items, and to *filter* items based on the current context.

Browsing items. TalkAbout's main interface (Figure 1) comprises a scrollable grid of words and phrases. Each item comprises a picture and an associated word or phrase. Touching an on-screen item speaks the associated text using the iPad's built-in speech synthesizer. In its most basic form, the interface is similar to commercially available AAC software such as Proloquo2Go[4], but with additional features related to the user's context. A *context bar* at the top of each screen shows the current context as detected by TalkAbout. Currently, the context bar displays the current user, their location, and their conversation partner.

Like other AAC systems, words and phrases may be assigned to hierarchical groups. While many AAC systems organize words by topic (*e.g.,* food, vehicles, parts of the body), TalkAbout enables users to organize words and phrases by the *location* that they are spoken or the *partner* that they are discussed with. TalkAbout also enables the user to view a master list of all saved words and phrases. Items that are associated with a specific context are tagged with an image of that context, as shown in Figure 2.

Adding new items. Users may add new words or phrases to TalkAbout's catalog, by themselves or with the assistance of an aide. Adding a new item requires the user to: 1) input the text to be spoken; and 2) add an associated image. This process is similar to how users add content to existing AAC systems, although TalkAbout takes steps to streamline the process. Words and phrases may be entered using the iPad's keyboard (with optional error correction), or may be spoken and recognized automatically.

The associated image may be captured by the user via the iPad's camera, selected by the user from a set of previously captured images, or chosen automatically. If the user does not provide an image, TalkAbout uses Microsoft's Bing Image Search API[5] to automatically select an image from the web. Newly added phrases can optionally be associated with a specific location or conversation partner. This combination of speech input and automatic image selection enabled the research team and study participants to quickly create sets of conversation topics.

Figure 2. Topics in TalkAbout's user interface are tagged with their contextual associations. The topic *piano* is associated with a specific conversation partner, while the topic *garden* is associated with a specific location. The accompanying images were chosen automatically via a web image search.

Filtering items by context. We experimented with several methods of adapting to context in TalkAbout. Initially, we thought that it would be best for the system to automatically adapt to the current context. However, participants seemed to have difficulty understanding when and why the interface was adapting. Furthermore, taking a picture of the user's conversation partner sometimes required the user to reposition the device, and thus could not always occur automatically. In the current prototype, users press an *Update* button to capture a picture of the user's conversation partner and update the device location. If TalkAbout identifies a previously seen location or conversation partner, the associated words and phrases are moved to the top of the word list. The user may also manually select their location or conversation partner if they wish, or if automatic recognition fails.

4.3 Detecting Context

TalkAbout provides the ability to detect the user's context and to adapt the user interface to that context. Currently, TalkAbout can automatically recognize the *current user* via the front-facing device camera, the user's *location* via GPS, and the user's *conversation partner* via the rear-facing camera.

TalkAbout detects the user's location using PhoneGap's location API, which relies upon GPS and Wi-Fi localization. The user may add a new location, attach a name and image to that location, and associate words and phrases with that location.

---

[1] http://phonegap.com
[2] https://developers.google.com/appengine
[3] http://opencv.willowgarage.com
[4] http://www.assistiveware.com/product/proloquo2go
[5] http://www.bing.com/toolbox/bingdeveloper

TalkAbout can also identify the current user and his or her conversation partner using automatic face recognition and the device cameras. TalkAbout uses the Viola–Jones algorithm [24] to detect faces, which are then matched using eigenfaces [22]. The user may also select his or her partner from a list of photos. We chose to include face recognition for several reasons. First, we were interested in exploring multiple ways to automatically detect useful context. Second, our research participants expressed interest in the idea of face recognition during early design sessions. Third, face recognition may improve TalkAbout's usability for individuals with comorbid conditions, such as visual impairment or prosopagnosia (face blindness), which is sometimes a side effect of stroke [10].

5. PARTICIPATORY DESIGN

The TalkAbout prototype, introduced in the previous section, was developed through a process of participatory design. In this section, we describe our process of researching, developing, and testing TalkAbout with adults who have aphasia.

5.1 The Aphasia Center

Our research was conducted at an aphasia center located in Baltimore, MD, USA. The center serves approximately 40 adults who previously experienced a stroke and currently experience some level of aphasia. Members attend classes for approximately four hours per day, two times per week. Classes are taught by trained facilitators, and cover such topics as reading, news, music, yoga, gardening, travel, and exotic animals.

Members also meet one-on-one with professional speech language pathologists and student volunteers. During these meetings, members practice conversations, learn to use or customize their current AAC devices, or work on creating scripted stories for future conversations using their AAC devices.

5.2 Participants

We conducted the majority of our design activities with a group of 5 research participants (4 male, 1 female), all adults with aphasia. These 5 were selected from the larger group of members based on their enthusiasm for the research activity, and diversity of ability. While we considered the possibility of choosing participants with the highest language abilities, we were strongly encouraged by our colleagues at the aphasia center to include people with a range of language abilities. Our participants are described here:

P1 (M, age 47, time post stroke onset (TPSO): 2 years). P1 presents with right-sided hemiparesis and severe expressive aphasia due to stroke. He is able to walk independently, but uses his left hand for most motor tasks. His comprehension of language is mildly impaired, and his expressive language abilities are severely impaired. He is able to speak in short phrases fraught with semantic and grammatical errors (telegraphic speech). Functionally, he has significant difficulty retrieving words (names, places, objects) that accurately convey his thoughts. P1 frequently uses software on his mobile phone (Apple iPhone) and laptop to share photos and to assist with reading and writing.

P2 (M, 43, 7 years). P2 presents with right-sided hemiparesis and moderate expressive aphasia due to stroke. He is able to speak fluently, but has significant difficulty retrieving names and personal information. Although most of his sentences are well formed, the content is often incorrect. He substitutes words and leaves out words that he cannot retrieve. His comprehension of language is also moderately impaired. He is unable to follow complex commands or lengthy material. His functional

communication abilities are fair, but he benefits greatly from the use of pictures and written words to facilitate comprehension. He is able to walk independently but uses his left hand for most motor tasks. He did not use assistive technology during our meetings.

P3 (F, 63, 7 months). P3's functional communication abilities are severely impaired due to aphonia (loss of voice due to vocal cord paralysis) caused by stroke. Her receptive and expressive language abilities are within normal limits. She communicates using gestures and by writing with pen and paper. However, her writing is limited to short phrases due to right-sided weakness secondary to her stroke. She is able to operate a computer mouse and keyboard, but has difficulty typing lengthy messages.

P4 (M, 72, 12 years). P4 presents with right-sided hemiparesis and severe expressive aphasia due to stroke. He also presents with severe apraxia of speech (a motor speech disorder). He is able to walk independently but uses his left hand for most motor tasks. His comprehension of language is mildly impaired. He has significant difficulty retrieving words. When he is able to produce a word, it is often unintelligible due to apraxia. His functional communication is limited to single words and gestures. He sometimes uses photos on his iPhone or laptop to support communication.

P5 (M, 73, 17 years). P5 presents with right-sided hemiparesis and severe expressive aphasia due to stroke. He walks using a cane and uses his left hand for most motor tasks. His language skills are globally impaired. He is unable to read or write and has severely impaired comprehension. His expressive language is limited to a few single words. He uses gestures, drawing, and pictures (often displayed on an iPad) to communicate.

5.3 Design Activities

Over the course of 6 weeks, we conducted several design activities intended to introduce our participants to the project, to solicit information about how participants might use a context-aware communication device, and to gather feedback about early versions of our prototype. These activities took place at the aphasia center, and were conducted by members of our research team, which included both HCI researchers and a speech language pathologist.

Due to variations in our participants' ability to communicate, and due to the variability of the schedule at the aphasia center, not all participants were able to take part in each study session. However, each participant took part in multiple sessions, and provided substantive feedback on the development of our prototype.

5.3.1 Interviews and Observations

During the first several weeks of our research, we conducted a series of preliminary interviews and observations with members of the aphasia center. During the interview sessions, participants demonstrated the technology that they currently used and provided feedback about what they liked and did not like about their current technology. Our research team also observed class meetings and one-on-one sessions between members and staff. These interviews were intended to introduce members to our research team, to sensitize our research team to working with people with aphasia, and to learn about the technologies currently used by people with aphasia at the aphasia center.

5.3.2 Focus Groups

Based on our initial site visits, we identified a group of 8 potential participants. These participants were chosen based on their enthusiasm for participating in research and because they represented a range of language ability. Following our initial

Figure 3. Storyboards used to introduce TalkAbout's proposed usage scenarios. Left: introducing the tablet's ability to detect information about the environment. Center: Adapting the word list based on location. Right: Adapting the word list based on conversation partner. Each drawing was accompanied with an interactive demonstration by the research team.

interviews, we conducted 2 focus group sessions (4 participants each), in which we introduced the concept of context-aware AAC and solicited feedback about our proposed usage scenarios.

As we had not yet identified the scenarios that we would develop for the initial prototype, a major goal of the focus groups was to identify the scenarios that were most compelling to our participants. We introduced the 5 scenarios described in Table 1, and asked the focus groups to consider the scenarios and provide feedback. As focus groups can present communication challenges for people with aphasia, a speech language pathologist (the fourth author) facilitated the meetings. The facilitator asked clarifying questions, wrote key terms on an easel, and paused the session if any of the participants seemed confused. To further reduce the difficulty of participating in the focus group, we created *storyboard diagrams* for each of the scenarios, as well as an overview diagram describing the broader goals of the project, and posted them on the wall during the focus group session. A selection of these storyboard diagrams is shown in Figure 3.

We began the session with an introduction to the idea of context-aware computing. We presented a diagram of the iPad hardware and its associated sensors. While participants had seen the iPad before, they had not previously considered its ability to sense context. We stated that the iPad is a computer that can gather information about the environment, and that it contains sensors that could see, hear, identify its location, and identify who is around. To demonstrate the iPad's image capture capability, we took a photo of the focus group and displayed it to the group. To demonstrate the iPad's ability to detect location, we opened the native Maps application and used GPS to locate the aphasia center. All participants were able to follow this demonstration, but some participants were surprised that the iPad could identify its own location or identify people from photographs.

Following this introduction, we walked through each of the scenarios presented in Table 1. For each scenario, we presented the relevant storyboard diagram and talked through the scenario. Once the focus group had examined the storyboard diagram, the research team play-acted the scenario using low-fidelity user interface sketches presented on the iPad. These *play-acted scenarios* emphasized the relationship between the users and the software, and the adaptation of the software to the current context. For example, to show how the software could adapt to different conversation partners (scenario #2 in Table 1), we introduced the "Friends" diagram shown in Figure 3. The diagram shows that Bob talks to Carol about food, but talks to Alice about baseball. One member of our research group portrayed Bob, while others portrayed Carol and Alice. In our play-acted scenario, Bob first talked to Carol. At this point, the researcher showed the iPad

screen, which displayed a series of food-related terms, to the participants. Bob then turned to Alice. Again, the researcher showed the iPad screen to the participants, which had transformed to display baseball-related terms. The facilitator narrated the scene as it was acted out. Following each scenario, participants were given time to ask questions and provide feedback.

Overall, the focus group participants seemed to understand the scenarios we presented, although not all participants provided feedback. Participants seemed to gain the most information from the facilitator's narration and from the play-acting of the scenarios. In several cases, participants seemed confused about a specific scenario, but then indicated their understanding during or after the demonstration.

5.3.3 Prioritizing Usage Scenarios

In general, the focus group participants were enthusiastic about the concept of producing "smarter" AAC technologies, and were eager to test this new technology. Of the scenarios we presented (summarized in Table 1), participants were most excited about an AAC that could adapt to location (#1), an AAC that could adapt to conversation partner (#2), and an AAC that could recognize the speech of others (#3). As the Converser project [25] previously combined automatic speech recognition with AAC, but suffered from low recognition accuracy, we decided that our initial prototype would support the other two popular scenarios: adapting based on location and adapting based on conversation partner.

5.3.4 Gathering Contextual Data

After deciding to focus on two usage scenarios (adapting to location and adapting to conversation partner), we began to develop those features of the prototype, as well as to consider how to evaluate our prototypes of this system. Evaluating context-aware and adaptive technologies can be difficult, as these systems must gather sufficient data about the user's context in order to function, and are susceptible to recognition and other errors. Furthermore, as our participants already experienced significant challenges when communicating with others in everyday life, conducting a field study with early prototypes could be stressful.

As a result of these concerns, we decided to evaluate the TalkAbout prototype via a Wizard of Oz study at the aphasia center. We selected 5 participants (described in Section 5.2) to continue testing the prototype. As we decided to evaluate the system using Wizard of Oz techniques, our research team began to collect the contextual data needed to construct the prototype. Over the next several visits, we collected data about our participants' favorite conversation topics, commonly visited locations, and common conversation partners.

We used two methods to collect this contextual data. As we were still developing the interactive prototype, we first created a *paper-based questionnaire* that asked participants about what they talked about, or wished to talk about, in specific contexts (Figure 4). Each page of the questionnaire focused on a single location or conversation partner. As most of our participants experienced some difficulties in reading and writing, participants worked through the questionnaire with assistance from the research team[6].

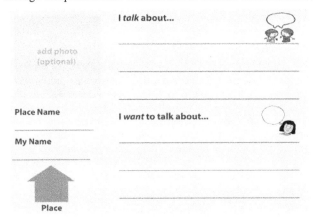

Figure 4. The contextual data questionnaire captured topics that the participant liked to discuss in a specific location.

Unfortunately, participants had difficulty understanding the motivation behind this activity, and thus had difficulty completing the questionnaire. P4 and P5 required significant amounts of coaching in order to complete the questionnaire, and the participants only filled out between 1 and 3 pages of the questionnaire each, providing little contextual data.

Overall, the limited information we collected using the paper forms did not provide us with enough data to configure the TalkAbout prototype. In our second visit, we performed a similar data collection activity, but instead used an early version of the TalkAbout prototype. This version of the prototype allowed users to add items, but did not provide context-aware adaptation. We met with each of the participants, introduced the prototype, and showed how it could be used to group together important people and places. We then gave the participants an opportunity to enter data into the prototype, or to instruct the researcher to enter data, depending on their motor ability and confidence.

Participants responded much more positively to the interactive prototype than to the paper forms, perhaps because the prototype was similar to AAC software that they had previously seen. Participants were eager to add new content to the prototype and to use the prototype to explore this new content. However, the level of interaction with the prototype did vary with the participant's level of ability. P1, P2, and P3 were relatively independent in adding content, and added content that related both to conversation partners and frequently visited places. P4 and P5, having lower linguistic ability, were less independent. For P4 and P5, the researchers suggested topics that had been discussed in prior meetings, and the participant indicated which should be added. Figure 5 shows example words and phrases added by P3 to a word list related to the doctor's office.

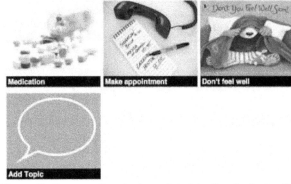

Figure 5. Conversation topics related to the doctor's office, added to the prototype by a study participant (P3).

In addition to providing data needed to configure the prototype, this contextual data collection provided useful information about the people and places that were most important to our participants. Not surprisingly, all five participants wished to create content relevant their friends and conversation partners at the aphasia center. In addition to this content, P1 added content relevant to his alma mater; P3 added content relevant to the supermarket, doctor, and paratransit; and P5 added content relevant to his family, to visiting restaurants, and to riding in taxis.

5.3.5 Prototype Testing

Once we had gathered enough contextual data to customize the prototype, we imported this data into TalkAbout and presented the customized prototype to each participant. This version of the prototype contained the features described in Section 4, but used the Wizard of Oz method to set the location and conversation partner.

The researcher introduced the participant to the prototype and explained that the data shown in the prototype had been gathered in prior sessions. The participant was given an opportunity to explore the prototype for as long as he or she wished, and was able to both explore existing content and add new content. The researcher provided verbal guidance and help using the touch screen as needed. Because the evaluation occurred at the aphasia center, participants were unable to test the location-based adaptation in the real world. Instead, the researcher manually changed the device location, and asked the participant to imagine using the device in the other location. As participants were familiar with how the system could adapt to different locations, they understood the instructions and were able to complete this portion of the study.

Following their use of the prototype, the participants completed a brief questionnaire about the current prototype[7]. The questionnaire contained 4 questions, each accompanied by a picture-based, 9-point Likert-type scale designed for people with aphasia [12]. The questionnaire contained the following questions:

1. How much did you like the software?
2. Is the software better or worse than technology you use now?
3. Would you use this software?
4. Where would this software be most helpful?

---

[6] P3 was unable to complete the questionnaire due to scheduling conflicts, but provided similar feedback using the interactive prototype later.

[7] P5 found the questionnaire activity difficult, and asked to be excused from this activity.

Numerical responses are provided in Table 2. Given the small sample size and the early stage of the technology, we have omitted a deep quantitative analysis of the scores. Instead, we note general trends in the data. P1, P3, and P4 were strongly positive about the prototype. P2 was less enthusiastic about the prototype, but noted that he had not had much success in using technology in the past, and was thus cautious about adopting new technology. P1 and P3 were especially enthusiastic. P3 said that the software was "cool," and indicated that it could help her act more independently. When asked where she might use the prototype, P3 indicated that it would be most helpful at the doctor, and wrote, "I could go myself." When asked where he might use it, P1 stated that he wanted to use it "all the places."

Table 2. Evaluation of the TalkAbout prototype, rated on a 9-point scale (1=negative, 9=positive).

	Liked software	Better than current	Would use
P1	7	7	9
P2	6	7	5
P3	9	9	9
P4	8	9	8

6. DISCUSSION

In this section, we reflect upon lessons learned in developing TalkAbout and provide recommendations for designing context-aware communication tools for people with aphasia.

6.1 Benefits of Context-Aware AAC

We began this research with the belief that context-aware adaptation could improve the usability of AAC devices. While we have not yet conducted a rigorous performance comparison between adaptive and non-adaptive AAC, we observed our participants struggling with several specific challenges that may be addressed by an adaptive user interface:

1. *Motor impairments.* Most of our participants had some motor impairment due to their stroke (especially P3, P4, and P5). This impairment sometimes made it difficult for participants to navigate using the touch screen. Context-based adaptation could reduce the amount of search needed to find commonly used words and phrases.

2. *Lack of organization.* Participants often experienced challenges organizing content on their mobile devices, including photos (P5), AAC phrases (P1, P5), and applications on their device's home screen (P1, P4, P5). Often these items were not sorted into categories, but were instead stored as a single-level list. Finding items in this list was sometimes frustrating. Context-based adaptation could improve users' ability to find AAC phrases hidden in long lists by hiding irrelevant content.

3. *Encouraging recognition over recall.* Participants often experienced difficulty when attempting to produce words or phrases extemporaneously. Recalling a word was much easier if the participant was presented with a photo, text, or spoken audio of the word. Context-based adaptation could help in such situations by identifying appropriate words and phrases and automatically presenting them to the user, increasing the likelihood that the user would see the desired word or phrase.

6.2 Designing with People with Aphasia

Active involvement from our research participants was key to the success of this work. However, participatory design with people with aphasia presents many challenges. While prior research has offered guidelines for conducting participatory design with people

with aphasia [6,16], we encountered unexpected challenges during this work and gained additional insights about how to collaborate with this population. Over the course of this research, we identified several strategies that were especially helpful:

1. *Prepare alternative activities.* Due to the diversity of our participant group, not all participants were able to participate fully in each research activity. For example, P4 was unable to provide much feedback in the written questionnaire due to his limited vocabulary. As an alternative, we asked P4 to show us photos that he had stored on his computer, and together identified locations of the photos using the iPad's Maps app. This activity provided an alternate means for learning about the people and places that were most important to our participant.

2. *Support rapid prototyping and UI tweaks.* Our study sessions were conducted during and between class sessions. Because participants often had limited time, it was important that we be able to quickly generate, test, and tweak prototypes. We designed TalkAbout to make it easy to add new content and to make UI changes in the field, enabling us to discover problems, fix them, and evaluate the fix in a single site visit.

3. *Balance focus groups by communication ability.* Some research sessions required us to meet with two or more participants simultaneously. In one such instance, a participant with high language ability (P1) was paired with a participant with low language ability (P5). Even though a facilitator was present, P5 had difficulty sharing his opinion in the session, and became frustrated. In subsequent sessions, we made sure to group participants with similar levels of communication ability.

Conducting participatory design with people with aphasia can be quite challenging. Our experience has shown that these challenges may be magnified when designing context-aware technologies, as these may be more difficult to explain or understand. We found the following techniques helpful in communicating the nuances of context-aware technology to our participants:

4. *Present scenarios using multiple formats.* We presented our usage scenarios verbally, as storyboards, as low-fidelity prototypes, as acted-out demonstrations, and as interactive prototypes. Participants were sometimes slow to engage with the material, but often became more interested and responsive after experiencing the information in multiple formats.

5. *Make demonstrations concrete and personalized.* Participants seemed to respond best to the most concrete demonstrations, specifically play-acting with low-fidelity prototypes and testing the interactive prototypes. Participants also responded with enthusiasm when testing prototypes that contained content that they themselves had entered in previous sessions.

6. *Clearly illustrate changes in the user interface.* Our early prototypes provided minimal feedback when adapting to the current context. Some participants did not understand what changes were happening to the interface, or that a change had happened at all. Our later prototypes announced changes to the interface with an audible camera click (when snapping a photo) and a clear visual refresh, which helped participants understand how the user interface was adapting.

7. FUTURE WORK

A major limitation of the current work is that we have not conducted a rigorous comparison between adaptive and non-adaptive AAC. We intend to continue to develop the TalkAbout software, and to evaluate it with the community at the aphasia center. We intend to distribute our prototype to more participants, and to test it in the lab as well as in the field.

The current version of TalkAbout considers only two contextual factors: the user's location and conversation partner. Future versions may incorporate additional contextual factors to further improve the adaptability of the user interface. Furthermore, while the current TalkAbout prototype uses contextual information only to retrieve previously added phrases, future versions could use contextual information to suggest new words and phrases. For example, TalkAbout could identify that the user is at a bank and present common words and phrases used in banking, even if the user did not pre-program them.

Finally, some study participants experienced difficulty when using the touch screen and aiming the tablet camera due to comorbid motor impairments. While other researchers have explored touch screen accessibility for people with motor impairments (*e.g.,* [8]), we hope to build upon this work and explore new methods for creating more accessible touch screens and camera interfaces.

8. CONCLUSION
In this paper, we have explored how context-aware computing may improve the usability of AAC for people with aphasia. We created a framework for designing context-aware AAC technologies, developed a prototype of a context-aware AAC device, and tested this prototype through a series of participatory design activities with a group of adults with aphasia. Our participants enjoyed using the prototype and preferred it to their existing technology solutions. We hope this work will encourage the development of a new generation of smarter, more aware, and more adaptive communication devices.

9. ACKNOWLEDGMENTS
For assistance with this project, we thank Brian Frey, Amy Hurst, Chinedu Okeke, and the members and staff of SCALE Baltimore.

10. REFERENCES
1. Al Mahmud, A. and Martens, J.-B. Re-connect: designing accessible email communication support for persons with aphasia. *Proc. CHI EA '10,* ACM Press (2010), 3505-3510.
2. Allen, M., McGrenere, J., and Purves, B. The design and field evaluation of PhotoTalk: a digital image communication application for people with aphasia. *Proc. ASSETS '07,* ACM Press (2007), 187-194.
3. Baecker, R.M., Moffatt, K., and Massimi, M. Technologies for aging gracefully. *interactions 19,* 3 (2012), 32-36.
4. Beukelman, D.R. and Mirenda, P. *Augmentative & Alternative Communication: Supporting Children & Adults With Complex Communication Needs.* Paul H Brookes Pub Co, 2006.
5. Boyd-Graber, J.L., Nikolova, S.S., Moffatt, K.A., Kin, K.C., Lee, J.Y., Mackey, L.W., Tremaine, M.M., and Klawe, M.M. Participatory design with proxies: developing a desktop-PDA system to support people with aphasia. *Proc. CHI '06,* ACM Press (2006), 151-160.
6. Davies, R., Marcella, S., McGrenere, J., and Purves, B. The ethnographically informed participatory design of a PD application to support communication. *Proc. ASSETS '04,* ACM Press (2004), 153-160.
7. Fenwick, K., Massimi, M., Baecker, R., Black, S., Tonon, K., Munteanu, C., Rochon, E., and Ryan, D. Cell phone software aiding name recall. *Proc. CHI '09 EA,* ACM Press (2009), 4279-4284.
8. Guerreiro, T., Nicolau, H., Jorge, J., and Gonçalves, D. Towards accessible touch interfaces. *Proc. ASSETS '10,* ACM Press (2010), 19-26.
9. Hailpern, J., Danilevsky, M., Harris, A., Karahalios, K., Dell, G., and Hengst, J. ACES: promoting empathy towards aphasia through language distortion emulation software. *Proc. CHI '11,* ACM Press (2011), 609-618.
10. Hier, D.B., Mondlock, J., and Caplan, L.R. Behavioral abnormalities after right hemisphere stroke. *Neurology 33,* 3 (1983), 337–344.
11. Hightower, J. and Borriello, G. Location systems for ubiquitous computing. *Computer 34,* 8 (2001), 57-66.
12. Kagan, A., Simmons-Mackie, N., Rowland, A., Huijbregts, M., Shumway, E., McEwen, S., Threats, T., and Sharp, S. Counting what counts: a framework for capturing real-life outcomes of aphasia interventions. *Aphasiology 22,* 3 (2008), 258-280.
13. Kane, S.K., Jayant, C., Wobbrock, J.O., and Ladner, R.E. Freedom to roam: a study of mobile device adoption and accessibility for people with visual and motor disabilities. *Proc. ASSETS '09,* ACM Press (2009), 115-122.
14. Krishna, S., Little, G., Black, J., and Panchanathan, S. iCARE interaction assistant: a wearable face recognition system for individuals with visual impairments. *Proc. ASSETS '05,* ACM Press (2005), 216-217.
15. McGrenere, J., Davies, R., Findlater, L., Graf, P., Klawe, M., Moffatt, K., Purves, B., and Yang, S. Insights from the aphasia project: designing technology for and with people who have aphasia. *Proc. CUU '03,* ACM Press (2003), 112-118.
16. Moffatt, K., McGrenere, J., Purves, B., and Klawe, M. The participatory design of a sound and image enhanced daily planner for people with aphasia. *Proc. CHI '04,* ACM Press (2004), 407-414.
17. Sohlberg, M.M., Fickas, S., Ehlhardt, L., and Todis, B. The longitudinal effects of accessible email for individuals with severe cognitive impairments. *Aphasiology 19,* 7 (2005), 651-681.
18. Piper, A.M., Weibel, N., and Hollan, J.D. Write-N-Speak: authoring multimodal digital-paper materials for speech-language therapy. *ACM Transactions on Accessible Computing 4,* 1 (2011), 1-20.
19. Schilit, B., Adams, N., and Want, R. Context-aware computing applications. *IEEE Workshop on Mobile Computing Systems and Applications,* IEEE (1994), 85-90.
20. Sánchez, J. and de la Torre, N. Autonomous navigation through the city for the blind. *Proc. ASSETS '10,* ACM Press (2010), 195-202.
21. Tee, K., Moffatt, K., Findlater, L., MacGregor, E., McGrenere, J., Purves, B., and Fels, S.S. A visual recipe book for persons with language impairments. *Proc. CHI '05,* ACM Press (2005), 501-510.
22. Turk, M.A. and Pentland, A.P. Face recognition using eigenfaces. *Computer Vision and Pattern Recognition,* IEEE (1991), 586-591.
23. Vance, A. Insurers fight speech-impairment remedy. *The New York Times,* September 15 2009.
24. Viola, P. and Jones, M. Robust real-time face detection. *International Journal of Computer Vision 57,* 2, (2004), 137-154.
25. Wisenburn, B. and Higginbotham, D. An AAC application using speaking partner speech recognition to automatically produce contextually relevant utterances: objective results. *Augmentative and Alternative Communication 24,* 2, (2008), 100-109.

iSCAN: A Phoneme-based Predictive Communication Aid for Nonspeaking Individuals

Ha Trinh[1], Annalu Waller[1], Keith Vertanen[2], Per Ola Kristensson[3], Vicki L. Hanson[1]

[1]School of Computing
University of Dundee
{hatrinh,awaller,vlh}@
computing.dundee.ac.uk

[2]Department of Computer Science
Montana Tech of the University of Montana
kvertanen@mtech.edu

[3]School of Computer Science
University of St Andrews
pok@st-andrews.ac.uk

ABSTRACT

The high incidence of literacy deficits among people with severe speech impairments (SSI) has been well documented. Without literacy skills, people with SSI are unable to effectively use orthographic-based communication systems to generate novel linguistic items in spontaneous conversation. To address this problem, phoneme-based communication systems have been proposed which enable users to create spoken output from phoneme sequences. In this paper, we investigate whether prediction techniques can be employed to improve the usability of such systems. We have developed iSCAN, a phoneme-based predictive communication system, which offers phoneme prediction and phoneme-based word prediction. A pilot study with 16 able-bodied participants showed that our predictive methods led to a 108.4% increase in phoneme entry speed and a 79.0% reduction in phoneme error rate. The benefits of the predictive methods were also demonstrated in a case study with a cerebral palsied participant. Moreover, results of a comparative evaluation conducted with the same participant after 16 sessions using iSCAN indicated that our system outperformed an orthographic-based predictive communication device that the participant has used for over 4 years.

Categories and Subject Descriptors

H.5.2 [**Information Interfaces and Presentation**]: User Interfaces – *input devices and strategies.* K.4.2 [**Computers and Society**]: Social Issues – *assistive technologies for persons with disabilities.*

General Terms

Performance, Design, Human Factors.

Keywords

Augmentative and Alternative Communication, Phoneme-based Communication, Phoneme Prediction, Word Prediction.

1. INTRODUCTION

The United States Census Bureau has estimated that 2.5 million Americans had difficulty having their speech understood, of

which 0.5 million had severe speech impairments (SSI) [3]. Not only are these individuals unable to communicate using natural speech, many of them have motor impairments which restrict access to other communication channels, such as signing or writing. Thus, they often require Augmentative and Alternative Communication (AAC) strategies to meet their communication needs. The majority of existing AAC systems employ graphical symbols to encode a limited set of commonly used words and messages, thereby allowing for quick retrieval of reusable conversational content. However, users of these systems are limited to pre-programmed items rather than being able to create novel words and messages in spontaneous conversation. To overcome this limitation, a number of orthographic-based AAC systems have been developed to enable users to spell out their own messages. Prediction techniques, such as character or word prediction, are often applied to improve the usability and accessibility of these systems. However, these systems are only applicable to people with literacy skills; skills that many children and adults with SSI struggle to acquire [17].

In an effort to empower nonspeaking users to generate spontaneous, unique words and messages without the need for literacy skills, previous research has proposed the use of a phoneme-to-speech approach. This approach allows users to access a limited set of phonemes (i.e. speech sounds). By combining sequences of phonemes, novel conversational items can be generated without knowledge of orthographic spelling. This approach has been used in several communication aids [7] and literacy tools [1]. It has also been adopted as an alternative typing method for people with spelling difficulties [16].

To date, research on phoneme-based AAC systems is very limited. The few published reports on existing phoneme-based systems have highlighted a number of usability issues, including poor communication rate [4, 24], difficult access methods to target phonemes [1, 4, 24], and high learning demands [4, 8]. This past work demonstrates the need for rate enhancement strategies to facilitate phoneme entry and word creation processes. We began to address this issue in our previous work by applying prediction methods to phoneme-based AAC systems [19]. We developed a phoneme-based prediction model, which employed statistical language modeling techniques to perform context-dependent phoneme prediction and word prediction. Theoretical evaluation demonstrated that our prediction model could potentially lead to substantial keystroke savings when applied to a hypothetical 12-key phoneme keyboard [19]. However, we did not conduct any empirical studies on how the prediction model could be integrated into an actual phoneme-based AAC system to improve user performance.

Thus, our current work aims to demonstrate empirical evidence of the potential of our prediction methods. We have developed a novel phoneme-based predictive communication system. Our system performs prediction at both phoneme and word levels. Our model's phoneme predictions are used to dynamically rearrange the phoneme interface layout to allow for faster access to the most probable next phonemes. The word creation process is further supported by a phoneme-based word auto-completion feature. This feature predicts the word being entered based on the current phoneme prefix and prior words.

Before evaluating our system with representative AAC users, we first wanted to assess the usability of our predictive methods. For this purpose, we tested our system in a three-session study with 16 able-bodied participants measuring their entry rates, error rates, and user experience. We then validated the benefits of our predictive methods in a longitudinal case study with a cerebral palsied adult and report evaluation results of 16 training and practice sessions. In addition, we discuss the results of a study comparing the usability of our phoneme-based predictive system with two orthographic-based predictive communication systems already familiar to the participant. Finally, we propose a number of further studies to extend our current work.

2. RELATED WORK
2.1 Phoneme-based AAC Systems
The history of phoneme-based AAC systems dates back in 1978 with the development of the HandiVoice by Phonic Ear [7]. The device contained a set of 45 phonemes, each of which was assigned a three-digit code. Users could access these phonemes using a numeric keypad and blend them into synthetic speech. Reports from a few HandiVoice users [4, 24] highlighted the system's slow communication rate as well as the high physical and cognitive efforts required to select target phonemes and produce intended words and sentences.

In an effort to enhance the communication rate of phoneme-based AAC systems, Goodenough-Trepagnier and Prather [8] developed the SPEEC system. The SPEEC system provided users with a combined set of spoken phonemes and frequently used phoneme sequences, each of which was represented by a letter or a letter combination. The size of the selection set ranged from 256 to 400 items. The authors reported that one nonspeaking individual trained in a 400-item version of the system achieved a speed of 8.2 words per minute, a 30% increase over an alphabet system [9]. However, the amount of training was not specified. Results of an evaluation with five cerebral palsied adolescents, including one pre-reader as well as beginning and proficient readers, showed that the participants required from 4 to 8 months of training to achieve some degree of proficiency [8]. This highlights the high learning demands imposed on the users of this system.

Black et al. [1] explored the potential of phoneme-based AAC systems to support language play and phonics teaching for children with SSI. The researchers developed the PhonicStick™ talking joystick, which enables users to access the 42 phonemes used in the Jolly Phonics literacy program [13] using a joystick interface. A prototype of the PhonicStick™, using a subset of 6 phonemes, has been evaluated with seven children without and with SSI. Results of the evaluations showed that the participants could create short words using the phonemes. However, some participants with severe motor impairments experienced difficulties in using the joystick to access target phonemes [1].

Schroeder [16] developed the REACH Sound-It-Out Phonetic Keyboard™, a phoneme-based typing interface for individuals with spelling difficulties. This on-screen keyboard consists of 40 phonemes and 4 phoneme combinations, each of which is represented by a letter or a digraph and optionally a picture. It utilizes a dictionary-based phoneme prediction method to remove improbable next phonemes from the keyboard, thereby aiding users in visually locating the next phoneme in the intended word. The system also employs a dictionary-based word prediction method to present users with a list of the most frequently used words that phonetically match the current phoneme prefix. Evaluations conducted with children and adults both with and without learning disabilities demonstrated that the system led to an increased text input accuracy compared to conventional letter-based keyboards [16]. To our knowledge, REACH Sound-It-Out Phonetic Keyboard™ is the only currently available system that provides phoneme-based predictions. However, these predictions rely on a simple dictionary-based algorithm, which does not take into account contextual information, such as prior text. To date, little research has been done on how more advanced prediction techniques can be employed to improve phoneme-based predictions.

2.2 Phonological Awareness
We start with the assumption that in order to use phoneme-based AAC systems without support of predictive features, users must have adequate phonological awareness (PA) skills. PA refers to the explicit attention to the sound structure of language and encompasses a wide range of skills, from rhyming recognition, phoneme blending, to phoneme segmentation and phoneme manipulation [2]. These skills are essential prerequisites for literacy acquisition [2], even in populations of profoundly deaf readers who do not use speech as their primary means of communication [10]. Previous research has shown that individuals with SSI can develop their PA skills despite the absence of speech production [5]. This implies that phoneme-based AAC systems are potentially usable to these individuals. However, many individuals with SSI demonstrate PA deficits compared to their typical developing peers and hence would require focused PA training to acquire these skills [12]. This suggests that users with poor PA skills stand to benefit from phoneme-based predictive interfaces.

2.3 Prediction Techniques
Prediction is a rate enhancement strategy widely used in orthographic-based AAC systems [6]. A number of prediction strategies have been developed for AAC users, of which the most commonly used are character prediction and word prediction. Character prediction anticipates probable next characters based on the previously selected characters. Word prediction anticipates the word being entered on the basis of the prefix of the current word and possibly prior words, thereby saving the user the effort of entering every character of a word. Prediction results are typically presented in a horizontal or vertical list, requiring the users to scan the list to select the desired item. While these techniques often result in keystroke savings, previous work has suggested that these savings might not be translated into increased communication rates due to the cognitive and perceptual workload of navigating the prediction list to search for target items [11].

Most existing prediction systems employ statistical language modelling techniques to perform prediction tasks. These techniques often use a large collection of training text to construct n-gram language models, which can be used to predict next most probable items (such as characters or words) based on (n-1) preceding items. A number of advanced language modelling techniques have also been investigated, which utilize additional information such as word recency, syntactic information, semantic information, and topic modelling [6]. These techniques have the potential to improve prediction performance at the cost of increased computational complexity.

3. SYSTEM DESIGN

Little work has been done on how well statistical prediction models can be adapted to phoneme-based AAC systems. In this section, we provide an overview of our phoneme-based prediction model. Our model employs statistical language modeling techniques to perform single phoneme prediction and phoneme-based word prediction. Readers are referred to [19] for a more detailed description of our model. We then present the design of iSCAN (**I**nteractive **S**ound-based **C**ommunication **A**id for **N**on-speakers), which uses the prediction model to implement two predictive features, namely dynamic phoneme layout and word auto-completion.

3.1 Phoneme-based Prediction Model

Our prediction model uses a set of 42 phonemes (17 vowels and 25 consonants) used in the Jolly Phonics, a systematic synthetic phonics program widely used in the UK for literacy teaching [13]. By using a literacy-based phoneme set, our model can readily be incorporated into both literacy learning tools (such as the PhonicStick™ joystick [1]) and communication aids.

The prediction model uses a 6-gram phoneme mixture model and a 3-gram word mixture model to provide predictions at both phoneme and word levels. The 6-gram phoneme model is used to predict the next probable phonemes based on up to five preceding phonemes, while the 3-gram word model is used to predict the word currently being entered based on up to two words of prior context. Ideally, these models would be constructed from a large corpus of transcribed conversations of real AAC users on various topics. However, such a corpus has been unavailable to date. We addressed this problem by creating a large corpus of fictional AAC data via crowdsourcing [22]. This crowdsourced corpus was then used to intelligently select a much larger set of AAC-like sentences from Twitter, Blog, and Usenet datasets. To generate the phoneme language model, we converted our fictional AAC word corpus to a phoneme-based corpus using a pronunciation dictionary. We trained a 6-gram phoneme language model for each of the phoneme-based Twitter, Blog and Usenet datasets. We then created a 6-gram mixture model using linear interpolation with mixture weights optimized on our crowdsourced development set. The same approach was applied to construct the 3-gram word mixture language model. In previous work, we demonstrated that word language models generated using this approach outperformed other models trained on telephone transcripts, which were often used in previous research on AAC prediction [22].

3.2 iSCAN Design

We incorporated our prediction model into the design of iSCAN. iSCAN uses the 6-gram phoneme language model to dynamically optimize the phoneme layout after each phoneme selection to allow for easier access to highly probable next phonemes. Each time the user has selected a phoneme, the system also attempts to automatically complete the word currently being entered using the word language model. This allows users to complete a word without entering every single phoneme. Our design was motivated by the following principles:

Small number of selection targets. Many individuals with SSI also have severe motor impairments and hence often experience difficulties in accessing interfaces containing a large number of selection targets (e.g. buttons or keys). For example, many motor-impaired users are unable to use a direct selection method to access physical or on-screen keyboards, due to the lack of fine motor skills required to precisely point over small targets among a large set of keys. Although alternative access methods, such as scanning, can be employed to facilitate target acquisition, the efficiency of these methods tends to decrease as the number of selection targets increases. Therefore, in our interface design, we aimed to enable the users to access the phoneme set using a minimal number of selection targets.

Support various input devices. Individuals with SSI and motor impairments utilize a wide range of input devices, such as touch screen, joysticks, trackballs, eye tracking devices, or switches, to control their AAC systems Our design, therefore, should be easily adapted to effectively support the use of those devices.

Avoid using separate lists to present prediction results. Predictive systems that display vertical or horizontal lists can create perceptual and cognitive demands that may outweigh the keystroke savings offered by prediction [11]. We therefore aimed to find an appropriate method of displaying the prediction results without using a list-based presentation.

3.2.1 Interface Design

In iSCAN, the Jolly Phonics's phoneme set is arranged onto an eight-slice two-layer pie menu adapted from the PhonicStick™ joystick interface [1]. This design provides the users with access to the 42 phonemes by using only 9 selection targets, including the 8 slices and the center circle of the pie menu. In addition, this 8-direction gestural interface design can also be easily adapted for various input devices, such as joysticks, touch-screens, or eye-tracking systems.

The 42 spoken phonemes are classified into 7 groups and mapped onto 7 directions on the front layer of the pie menu (Figure 1a). The phoneme groups consist of 3 vowel groups and 4 consonant groups, each of which contain from 5 to 7 phonemes. The groups are formed according to the manner of articulation and are color coded, with warm colors for vowels and cool colors for consonants (Figure 1a). Each phoneme is represented by a picture selected from the Jolly Phonics' resources and optionally a letter or digraph. The remaining direction of the front layer of the menu (i.e. West direction) is reserved for the functional group, which contains 5 functions, including 'Speak current word', 'Delete current word', 'Delete last phoneme', 'Speak current sentence', and 'Delete current sentence'. Selecting a phoneme or functional group on the front layer switches the pie menu to the secondary layer, which displays all items within the group. Each secondary layer contains a maximum of 7 item slices and at least one empty slice, which is treated as an 'escape' route to allow the user to leave the layer without selecting any items (Figure 1b).

3.2.1.1 Phoneme Entry Method

The phoneme entry consists of three steps, including: (1) selecting the correct phoneme group from the front layer; (2) navigating the secondary layer to search for the intended phoneme; (3) moving back to the center circle of the menu to confirm the selection and redisplay the front layer. Our design supports phoneme entry via either tapping or continuous gestures, thereby accommodating both novice and expert users.

Figure 1 depicts an example of the transition of the pie menu through four stages in the process of selecting phoneme /g/, the initial phoneme of 'good', assuming that 'good' is the first word of the user's new sentence. Before the user starts creating a new sentence, the phonemes within each group are initially ordered based on their probabilities of being the first phoneme in a sentence (calculated from the phoneme language model). The phoneme with the highest probability of entry within each group is chosen as the representative of the group and displayed on the corresponding slice on the front layer (Figure 1a).

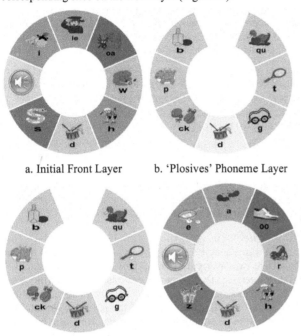

a. Initial Front Layer   b. 'Plosives' Phoneme Layer

c. Navigating to '/g/'   d. Updated Front Layer

Figure 1. Four stages of the pie menu in the process of selecting the phoneme '/g/' in 'good'

To enter phoneme '/g/', the user first selects the 'Plosives' group located at the South direction of the front layer of the pie menu. This can be done either by tapping the corresponding slice or by sliding from the center circle towards the South direction. Once the user has entered the 'Plosives' group, the menu switches to the phoneme layer displaying all phonemes within the group (Figure 1b). The user navigates counterclockwise to access phoneme '/g/' using tapping or sliding gestures (see Figure 1c). Auditory and visual feedback is provided to facilitate the navigation process. Once the target phoneme has been found, the user navigates back to the center circle to confirm the selection and switches back to the front layer (Figure 1d).

3.2.1.2 Dynamic Phoneme Layout

After each phoneme selection, the system recalculates the probability of entry of each phoneme based on the previously entered phonemes and rearranges the phonemes within each group accordingly. The phoneme with the highest probability of entry in each group is chosen as the new representative of the group and placed on the front layer of the pie menu. The remaining phonemes in the group are relocated in such a way that phonemes with higher probabilities are closer to the representative phoneme and hence require fewer movements to navigate to from the representative phoneme. The location of the groups on the front layer, however, remains unchanged, thereby reducing the cognitive overhead associated with dynamic layouts. Figure 1d shows the updated front layer displayed after the user has selected phoneme '/g/'. Phoneme '/oo/', the next phoneme in the target word 'good', has appeared on the front

layer as the new representative of the 'Rounded back vowels' group and can be selected by simply tapping or sliding to the slice at NE direction then moving back to the center circle.

3.2.1.3 Phoneme-based Word Auto-completion

After each phoneme selection, the system inputs the current phoneme prefix into a basic auto-correction function to generate alternative phoneme prefixes. The auto-correction function employs a limited set of phoneme insertion and replacement rules to deal with the *schwa* phoneme [19] and some common mistakes in phonetic spelling. For example, in our previous study on PA intervention for nonspeaking adults [18], we observed that our participants often had difficulties in distinguishing between phonemes '/s/' and '/z/' in word-ending position. Thus, we added a rule to generate alternative prefixes by replacing '/s/' with '/z/' in this position. The alternative prefixes and the original prefix are then used to look up a list of matching words in our pronunciation dictionary. If there is no matching word, the system simply blends the selected phonemes together using a speech synthesizer to generate speech output. Otherwise, the matching words are input into the 3-gram word language model to calculate their probabilities based on up to two prior words. The word with the highest probability is spoken out to the user for selection. If prediction is correct, the user can add the predicted word and a following whitespace to the current sentence by selecting the 'Speak word' function located at the west direction on the front layer (see Figure 1d) and then moving back to the center circle. The phoneme layout is updated thereafter based on the newly added word. If the prediction is incorrect, the user can simply ignore the predicted word and continue entering the next phoneme of the intended word. By offering only one spoken prediction, we eliminated the cognitive and perceptual load imposed on the user to scan a multi-word prediction list to search for the desired word.

3.2.2 Computational Experiments

We evaluated the accuracy of our dynamic phoneme arrangement using hit rate. Hit rate (HR) is defined as the percentage of times that the desired phoneme appears *within* a specified distance D in a group, wherein D is defined as the distance between a phoneme in the group and the group's representative phoneme. The representative phoneme is located at distance D=0 while the two phonemes next to the representative phonemes are located at distance D=1. A phoneme is said to be *within* a distance D if its distance to the representative phoneme is smaller than or equal to D. We calculated the hit rates on three AAC-like test sets:

- *Specialists*: A collection of context specific conversational phrases recommended by AAC professionals[1]. 966 sentences, 3814 words.

- *Communication*: A collection of sentences written by students in response to 10 hypothetical communication situations [21]. 251 sentences, 1789 words.

- *SwitchTest*: Three telephone transcripts taken from the Switchboard corpus, used in Trnka et al. [20]. 59 sentences, 508 words.

For each sentence in the test sets, we generated its pronunciation string using our pronunciation dictionary. During this generation, any time we encountered a word with multiple

---

[1] http://aac.unl.edu/vocabulary.html, accessed 4 September 2011

pronunciations, we chose a pronunciation at random. We manually added pronunciations for out-of-vocabulary words.

Figure 2 shows the hit rates of the dynamic phoneme layout for distances D=0 and D=1 on the three test sets. At D=0, the average hit rate for the three test sets was 70.8%, which means that the user has a 70.8% chance of seeing the desired phoneme on the front layer of the pie menu. At D=1, the average hit rate increased to 93.2%. This shows that in most cases the intended phoneme is either the first phoneme or next to the first phoneme that the user encounters after entering the phoneme group.

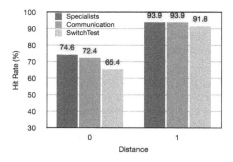

Figure 2. Hit rates of the dynamic phoneme layout for distances D=0 and D=1 on the three test sets.

3.2.2.1 Word Auto-completion

We estimated the accuracy of our word auto-completion feature using hit rate for 1-4 phoneme prefixes. Figure 3 shows the hit rates of word auto-completion on the *Specialists*, *Communication*, and *SwitchTest* test sets. The average hit rate for the three test sets for 1-phoneme prefix was 55.6%, which means that the user has a 55.6% chance of having the intended word autocompleted after entering just the initial phoneme of the word. The average hit rate substantially increased to 80.4% after the first two phonemes are entered, and rose to 90.0% and 96.3% for 3-phoneme and 4-phoneme prefixes respectively.

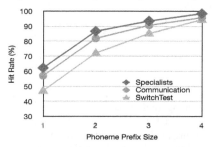

Figure 3. Hit rates of the word auto-completion for 1-4 phoneme prefixes on the three test sets.

4. FORMATIVE STUDY

To evaluate the usability of our predictive features, we conducted a lab study with able-bodied participants.

4.1 Participants and Apparatus

16 university students (9 male, 7 female, aged from 19-42, M=24, SD=5.3) participated study. All participants were native speakers of English with no severe speech, physical, perceptual, or intellectual impairments. Participants were compensated £15.

We developed a prototype of iSCAN on the Apple's iPad 2 providing the users with touch screen access method. Speech output is generated using the CereProc's speech synthesizer. The prototype supports two settings, namely predictive and non-predictive settings. In the predictive setting, the dynamic

phoneme layout and word auto-completion features are switched on. The participants select phonemes from the dynamic phoneme layout and are offered one predicted spoken word per entered phoneme. In the non-predictive setting, these two features are switched off. The participants enter phonemes using a static phoneme layout and can hear the blending of all the selected phonemes after each phoneme selection.

To aid the transition between the non-predictive and predictive settings, we used the same starting phoneme layout in both settings, i.e. the phoneme layout is initially optimized based on their probabilities of being the first phoneme in a new sentence. This layout remains unchanged in the non-predictive setting while it is dynamically updated in the predictive setting. As all participants are literate, we decided *not* to associate phonemes with letters in both settings to minimize potential confusion between phonetic spelling and orthographic spelling.

The prototype was instrumented to present a randomly generated set of spoken test phrases to each participant, one at a time, during the experiment. These phrases were short conversational phrases derived from the *Specialists* test set and were pre-recorded using a Scottish English voice. Each phrase consists of 3-5 words (10-12 phonemes). The prototype also contained a logging function to record all user input, including all time-stamped phoneme input and touch information.

4.2 Procedure

The study was a within-subjects design and consisted of three sessions. Each session lasted between 30-45 minutes, with at least 2 hours and at most 2 days between sessions, and was videotaped. Sessions 1 and 2 were training sessions and session 3 was the testing session:

Session 1: Participants were given instructions on the phoneme layout and the key functionality of the prototype using the non-predictive setting. The phoneme groups were given more 'user-friendly' names when introduced to the participants (e.g. plosive consonants were called 'poppy' sounds). At the end of the session, participants were instructed to create two spoken phrases using the non-predictive setting.

Session 2: At the beginning of the session, the participants were instructed to create three spoken phrases using the non-predictive setting. Thereafter, they were introduced to the predictive setting and were instructed to create five spoken phrases spoken by the prototype using this setting.

Session 3: Participants were asked to create a set of spoken phrases in both non-predictive and predictive settings. For each setting, they were given one practice phrase and five test phrases. They were instructed to create the phrases as quickly and accurately as possible. After the prototype spoke a phrase, the participants could repeatedly listen to the phrase by tapping a button on the screen. The order of settings was counterbalanced. At the end of the session, the participants took part in a brief interview about the two settings.

4.3 Entry Speeds

We measured entry speed in both words per minute (WPM) and phonemes per minute (PPM). Results of the entry speeds (see Table 1) showed that the use of predictive features led to a 108.4% increase in average PPM and a 109.2% increase in average WPM. Data analysis using the repeated measures ANOVA test showed that there was a significant difference between the entry speeds of the non-predictive and the predictive settings, both in terms of PPM ($F_{1,15} = 79.35$, p <

.0001, partial $\eta^2=0.84$), and WPM ($F_{1,15} = 90.10$, $p < .0001$, partial $\eta^2=0.86$).

Table 1. Average phoneme entry rate and average word entry rate for the non-predictive and predictive settings.

Setting	PPM		WPM	
	Mean	SD	Mean	SD
Non-predictive	11.07	2.74	3.0	0.82
Predictive	23.07	6.07	6.29	1.67

4.4 Error Rates

We measured error rate using the phoneme error rate (PER) and word error rate (WER). Results of the error rates (see Table 2) show that the predictive features led to a 79.0% reduction in average PER and a 78.8% reduction in average WER. Data analysis using the repeated measures ANOVA test showed that the use of the predictive features had a significant effect on both PER ($F_{1,15} = 16.12$, $p = .001$, partial $\eta^2=0.52$), and WER ($F_{1,15} = 12.07$, $p = .003$, partial $\eta^2=0.45$).

Table 2. Average phoneme error rate and average word error rate for the non-predictive and predictive settings.

Setting	PER		WER	
	Mean	SD	Mean	SD
Non-predictive	9.19%	6.76	17.15%	13.83
Predictive	1.93%	1.91	3.63%	4.63

4.5 Subjective Preferences

At the end of session 3, the participants were asked to provide feedback on the system and specify their preferences for the two settings. Overall, all participants preferred the predictive setting to the non-predictive setting. 13 of 16 participants reported that the dynamic phoneme layout was useful, stating that in most cases they found the intended phonemes on the front layer. 3 of 16 participants, however, commented that this dynamic layout was distracting. 15 of 16 participants stated that the word auto-completion was useful; many of them highly praised the accuracy of this feature. Only one participant found this feature frustrating, stating that it frequently gave her incorrect suggestions. This happened because there were a few instances that the participant chose incorrect phonemes and thus the system repeatedly offered her incorrect predictions without detecting her mistakes. The two features well complemented each other, as all participants liked at least one of the two features. This explains their overall preference for prediction.

In summary, this study demonstrated the usability of iSCAN with a group of able-bodied individuals whose cognitive, physical, and PA abilities might be different from those of our target users. The next step is to test with representative users.

5. CASE STUDY

We evaluated the usability of iSCAN in a longitudinal case study with a nonspeaking adult. We had two goals: (1) to compare the usability of the non-predictive and predictive settings, and (2) to investigate whether our system could provide effective communication support for nonspeaking people with limited literacy.

5.1 Participant

Our participant, who we will call 'Alex', was a 41-year-old male with severe speech and motor impairments due to cerebral palsy. Results of a literacy and phonological awareness test conducted four months prior to the study confirmed that he has significant spelling difficulties, as he only scored 30% for the spelling real words tasks. Alex demonstrated relatively good phoneme blending and phoneme analysis skills. However, he performed poorly on the phoneme-counting task, which requires him to count the number of phonemes in a spoken word. Prior to the study, he indicated that he had difficulty saying sounds in his head, which suggests that he might have problems with subvocal rehearsal. Alex's cognitive ability was assessed using the Raven's Colored Progressive Matrices test [15] and an adapted version of the Digit Span test from the Wechsler Adult Intelligence Scale-III [23]. Results of these tests revealed that he possibly has working memory deficits.

Alex has been using a 400-word paperboard for more than 30 years as his primary means of communication. He reported infrequent use of voice output communication aids (VOCAs), primarily for telephone conversation and occasionally for group discussion. He has used two VOCAs, including the Say-It! Sam™ communicator and the Assistive Chat application on Apple's iPad. Alex is an experienced prediction user, as he heavily relies on word prediction to generate messages in both of those systems. Prior to this study, Alex had no experience using a phoneme-based system for communication.

5.2 Study 1: Predictive vs. Non-predictive

The aim of this study was to compare the usability of the non-predictive and the predictive settings. The study used the same procedure described in our formative study and included two training sessions and one testing session. Each session lasted 45-70 minutes and was videotaped. These sessions were conducted at Alex's home over two consecutive days. On day one, we conducted the first training session. On day two, we conducted the second training session and the final test session, separated by about 2 hours. In the testing session, Alex used the predictive setting first followed by the non-predictive setting. We used the prototype from the formative study, but changed three phoneme pictures based on the user feedback from the formative study. Letters were *not* included in phoneme representations.

Alex completed the transcription task using the predictive setting but not in the non-predictive setting. After creating one practice and one test phrase in the non-predictive setting, Alex expressed a strong preference for the predictive setting and stated that he did not want to proceed with the non-predictive setting. Using the predictive setting, Alex achieved an average entry speed of 6.04 PPM (3.35% PER) and 1.72 WPM (0.0% WER) (note that the difference between PER and WER was due to our auto-correction mechanism described in Section 3.2.1.3). For comparison, Alex's entry speed for the one completed test phrase in the non-predictive setting was 2.35 PPM (21.43% PER) and 0.74 WPM (75.0% WER).

5.3 Study 2: Extended Training

To determine whether Alex's entry rate could be improved, we conducted additional sessions with him using the predictive setting to assess his performance after extended hours of practice. Previous research has also reported that long-term use is critical for accurate evaluations of prediction [14].

We conducted 13 additional sessions over an 11-day period using the predictive setting. Each session lasted 20-40 minutes, with at least two hours and at most two days between sessions and no more than two sessions per day. Each session began with a 5-minute warm-up during which Alex was asked to create his own words and sentences. Thereafter, Alex was asked to transcribe ten test phrases as quickly and accurately as possible. We used the same prototype from Study 1.

Entry speeds. Figure 4 shows Alex's improvement in phoneme entry speed over the 13 sessions. His word entry speed followed a similar trend. His speeds for session 1 were 4.45 PPM and 1.22 WPM. On the 13th session, his speeds increased to 18.53 PPM and 4.82 WPM. A speed of 4.82 WPM is not an improvement compared to the frequently cited communication rate of 2-10 words per minute of AAC users. However, it is noteworthy considering the small number of practice hours Alex required to reach this speed.

Error rates. Figure 5 shows Alex's phoneme error rates over the 13 sessions. His word error rates followed a similar trend. Overall, his error rates were extremely low as he corrected almost all errors. The average PER over the sessions was 0.66% (SD=0.65) and the average WER was 1.31% (SD=2.23). The effect of our auto-correction mechanism was clearly shown in sessions 2, 3, 7, 8 in which incorrect phonemes were auto-corrected, resulting in 0.0% WER.

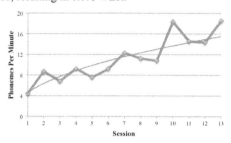

Figure 4. Alex's entry speeds as PPM over sessions 1-13.

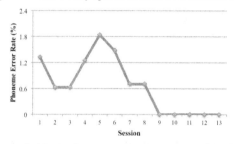

Figure 5. Alex's phoneme error rates over sessions 1-13.

5.4 Study 3: Comparative Evaluation

In this study we aimed to compare the usability of our phoneme-based predictive system with the two orthographic-based predictive systems that Alex has been using for communication. We evaluated Alex's performance using the Say-It!Sam™ and Assistive Chat systems in a transcription task. Alex has used the Say-It!Sam™ communication device for over 4 years and started using Assistive Chat at around the same time of the commencement of Study 1. Say-It!Sam™ provides 8 word predictions, organized into 2 columns of 4 predictions each, after each character entry. Assistive Chat provides 4 word predictions after each character entry. Both systems offer word predictions even before the first character of a new word is entered. The study consisted of two sessions, each of which lasted 40-60 minutes and was videotaped:

Session 1: The session started with a 5-minute warm-up during which Alex was asked to create his own words and sentences using Say-It! Sam™. He was then asked to transcribe a set of 10

test phrases as quickly and accurately as possible. These test phrases were the same test phrases used in the 13th session of Study 2 and were spoken by the iSCAN prototype. This session was conducted approximately two hours after the completion of the 13th session of Study 2.

Session 2: The session was conducted 6 days after session 1. Following a 5-minute warm-up, Alex was asked to transcribe 10 test phrases used in session 1 as quickly and accurately as possible using Assistive Chat. At the end of this session, Alex took part in a brief interview in which he ranked Say-It!Sam™, Assistive Chat, and iSCAN in his order of preferences.

The time taken by Alex to enter each test phrase was recorded using a stopwatch and was verified using the video recordings. As this study commenced only two hours after the 13th session of Study 2, we did not conduct a separate session to re-evaluate iSCAN. Instead, we compared the entry speeds and error rates of the Say-It!Sam™ and Assistive Chat with those reported in the 13th session of Study 2.

Entry speeds. We only calculated Alex's average entry speeds as WPM over the 10 test phrases as it was not suitable to measure PPM for Say-It!Sam™ and Assistive Chat. In this task, Alex achieved the following entry speeds: Assistive Chat (M=5.44, SD=3.37), iSCAN (M=4.82, SD=2.63), and Say-It!Sam™ (M=2.78, SD=1.78).

Error rates. Average WER over the 10 test phrases was as follows: iSCAN (M=0.0%, SD=0.0), Assistive Chat (M=11.67%, SD=21.94), Say-It!Sam™ (M=19.17%, SD=20.81).

As Alex has learned orthographic spelling through memorization, he struggled to derive the spellings of unfamiliar words. Therefore, whenever he encountered an unfamiliar word in the test phrases, he either skipped it by choosing a random word from the prediction list or attempted to replace it with a familiar word of similar meanings. This explains his high error rates for the two orthographic-based systems. With iSCAN, however, he has developed a strategy of listening to target words and sounding the words out using his dysarthric speech to identify the target phonemes, rather than relying on memorization. He was also able to confirm whether his phoneme selection was correct by listening to the blending of all selected phonemes. As a result, he showed greater confidence dealing with unfamiliar words using our system and thus attempted to complete all the target words.

User preference. At the end of the study, Alex was asked to rank the three evaluated communication systems in his order of preference. He placed the Say-It!Sam™ last, which was not surprising considering its low entry speed and high error rate. Alex ultimately chose iSCAN over Assistive Chat, stating that he would like to use it for learning new words. This decision can partly be explained by his positive experience using iSCAN to produce many novel words during his 16 sessions. He also reported that difficulties in selecting the intended words from the prediction list in the two orthographic-based systems resulted from his reading problems and thus he preferred our word auto-completion feature.

6. CONCLUSIONS & FUTURE WORK

In this paper we have described how prediction techniques can be employed to improve the usability of phoneme-based communication systems. To our knowledge, this is the first empirical research on phoneme-based prediction. We developed a novel phoneme-based predictive system employing robust statistical language modeling techniques to provide users with single phoneme prediction and phoneme-based word prediction. Results of the evaluations demonstrated that our predictive methods led to significant improvements in user performance, both in terms of entry rate and accuracy. Through a series of studies with a nonspeaking adult, we showed that our phoneme-based predictive communication system had the potential to provide an effective means of generating novel words and messages for a large proportion of AAC users who have literacy difficulties.

We are in the process of analyzing usage data of this participant who has been using our system in the field for four months. Results of this data analysis will allow us to evaluate our predictive methods in real-time spontaneous conversational settings. Our second case study with a nonspeaking female participant who has very limited literacy skills is also underway.

We outline a number of further studies based on this work. First, we plan to investigate whether the use of such a phoneme-based predictive system like iSCAN could have any positive effects on the phonological awareness and literacy development of nonspeaking individuals. Second, results of our longitudinal case study showed that our participant had significant difficulties in identifying vowels in spoken words. Therefore, we aim to explore a more robust auto-correction mechanism to accommodate this issue and facilitate users in vowel selection. Finally, we plan to conduct further empirical studies on how our prediction system can be incorporated into different interfaces and input devices, such as joysticks and eye-tracking systems.

7. ACKNOWLEDGMENTS

We thank the Scottish Informatics and Computer Science Alliance and the University of Dundee's School of Computing for funding this project. This work was supported by a Royal Society Wolfson Merit Award, by RCUK EP/G066091/1 "RCUK Hub: Social Inclusion in the Digital Economy", and by EPSRC grant number EP/H027408/1.

8. REFERENCES

[1] Black, R., Waller, A., Pullin, G., and Abel, E., 2008. Introducing the PhonicStick: Preliminary evaluation with seven children. In *13th Biennial Conference of the International Society for Augmentative and Alternative Communication*, Montreal, Canada.

[2] Brady, S.A. and Shankweiler, D.P., 1991. *Phonological processes in literacy*. Erlbaum, Hillsdale, NJ.

[3] Brault, M.W., 2008. *Americans with disabilities: 2005 Household Economic Studies*. U.S. Census Bureau Ed., Washington, DC, USA.

[4] Creech, R., 2004. Rick Creech, 2004 Edwin and Esther Prentke AAC Distinguished Lecturer, ASHA Convention Ed., Philadelphia, USA.

[5] Foley, B.E. and Pollatsek, A., 1999. Phonological processing and reading abilities in adolescents and adults with severe congenital speech impairments. *Augmentative and Alternative Communication 15*, 156-173.

[6] Garay-Victoria, N. and Abascal, J., 2005. Text prediction systems: a survey. *Universal Access in the Information Society 4*, 188-203.

[7] Glennen, S.L. and DeCoste, D.C., 1997. *The Handbook of Augmentative and Alternative Communication*. Thomson Delmar Learning.

[8] Goodenough-Trepagnier, C. and Prather, P., 1981. Communication systems for the nonvocal based on frequent phoneme sequences. *Journal of Speech and Hearing Research 24*, 322-329.

[9] Goodenough-Trepagnier, C., Tarry, E., and Prather, P., 1982. Derivation of an efficient nonvocal communication system. *Human Factors: The Journal of the Human Factors and Ergonomics Society 24*, 2, 163-172.

[10] Hanson, V.L., Goodell, E., and Perfetti, C., 1991. Tongue-twister effects in the silent reading of hearing and deaf college students. *Journal of Memory and Language 30*, 319-330.

[11] Koester, H.H. and Levine, S.P., 1996. Effect of a word prediction feature on user performance. *Augmentative and Alternative Communication 14*, 25-35.

[12] Light, J. and McNaughton, D., 2009. Addressing the literacy demands of the curriculum for conventional and more advanced readers and writers who require AAC. In *Practically Speaking: Language, Literacy, and Academic Development for Students with AAC Needs*, G.S.C. ZANGARI Ed. Paul H. Brookes Publishing Co, Baltimore, MD, 217-245.

[13] Lloyd, S.M., 1998. *The Phonics Handbook*. Jolly Learning Ltd., Chigwell.

[14] Magnuson, T. and Hunnicutt, S., 2002. Measuring the effectiveness of word prediction: The advantage of long-term use. *Speech, Music, and Hearing 43*, 57-67.

[15] Raven, J. and Court, J.H., 1998. *Manual for Raven's progressive matrices and vocabulary scales*. Oxford Psychologists Press Ltd., Oxford, UK.

[16] Schroeder, J.E., 2005. Improved spelling for persons with learning disabilities. In *The 20th Annual International Conference on Technology and Persons with Disabilities*, California, USA.

[17] Smith, M., 2005. *Literacy and augmentative and alternative communication*. Elsevier Academic Press.

[18] Trinh, H., 2011. Using a computer intervention to support phonological awareness development of nonspeaking adults. In *The 13th International ACM SIGACCESS Conference on Computers and Accessibility*, Dundee, UK.

[19] Trinh, H., Waller, A., Vertanen, K., Kristensson, P.O., and Hanson, V.L., 2012. Applying prediction techniques to phoneme-based AAC systems. In *NAACL-HLT 2012 Workshop on Speech and Language Processing for Assistive Technologies (SLPAT)*, Montreal, Canada.

[20] Trnka, K., McCaw, J., Yarrington, D., McCoy, K.F., and Pennington, C., 2009. User interaction with word prediction: The effects of prediction quality. *ACM Transactions on Accessible Computing 1*, 3, 1-34.

[21] Venkatagiri, H.S., 1999. Efficient keyboard layouts for sequential access in augmentative and alternative communication. *Augmentative and Alternative Communication 15*, 2, 126-134.

[22] Vertanen, K. and Kristensson, P.O., 2011. The imagination of Crowds: Conversational AAC language modelling using crowdsourcing and large data sources. In *International Conference on Empirical Methods in Natural Language Processing (EMNLP)*, Edinburgh, UK, 700-711.

[23] Wechsler, D., 1997. *WAIS-III administration and scoring manual*. Psychological Corp.

[24] Williams, M.B., 1995. Transitions and transformations. In *9th Annual Minspeak Conference* Prentke Romich Company, Wooster, OH.

Detecting Linguistic HCI Markers in an Online Aphasia Support Group

Yoram M Kalman
The Open University of Israel
yoramka@openu.ac.il

Kathleen Geraghty, Cynthia K Thompson, Darren Gergle
Northwestern University
k-geraghty, ckthom, dgergle
@northwestern.edu

ABSTRACT

Aphasia is an acquired language disorder resulting from trauma or injury to language areas of the brain. Despite extensive research on the impact of aphasia on traditional forms of communication, little is known about the impact of aphasia on computer-mediated communication (CMC). In this study we asked whether the well-documented language deficits associated with aphasia can be detected in online writing of people with aphasia. We analyzed 150 messages (14,754 words) posted to an online aphasia support forum, by six people with aphasia and by four controls. Significant linguistic differences between people with aphasia and controls were detected, suggesting five putative linguistic HCI markers for aphasia. These findings suggest that interdisciplinary research on communication disorders and CMC has both applied and theoretical implications.

Categories and Subject Descriptors

H.1.2 [Information Systems]: Models and Principles – *human factors*

General Terms

Measurement, Human Factors.

Keywords

Aphasia, computer-mediated communication, HCI markers, human factors, online support groups, unobtrusive monitoring, user modeling.

1. INTRODUCTION

HCI markers are signals created during human-computer interaction (HCI) which might provide information about the cognitive, mental, psychological or physiological state of the user [24]. The concept of HCI markers is analogous to the concept of biomarkers, which are indicators of physiological or disease processes. Some widely known biomarkers used for health assessment include physical measures such as body temperature or blood pressure, as well as biochemical measures such as hormone levels. Changes in these biomarkers have been linked to a diverse set of conditions including cancer, Alzheimer's disease, metabolic disorders, stress, and cardiovascular disease [12, 14, 17, 21]. In

this paper, we study messages posted by users with aphasia who contribute to an online support forum, and present evidence for the presence of HCI markers for aphasia, a language disorder resulting from neurological disease. As suggested in Kalman [24], such HCI-related variables can be identified and associated with important health-related conditions. Furthermore, HCI markers can be used for purposes such as unobtrusive detection, diagnosis, and monitoring of various conditions [e.g. 25, 31], as well as for dynamically personalizing the user interface to the needs of users with impairments [15].

1.1 HCI Markers

Our online activity reveals much about who we are, our interests, and our relationships [3]. It is suggested that our online activities and the way we interact with user interfaces also reveals important information about our health, and that the signals created during human-computer interaction (HCI) can be used to detect health-related changes [24]. In the same way biomarkers such as cholesterol and blood sugar levels are used to detect, diagnose and monitor physiological processes such as cardiovascular disease and diabetes, Kalman suggests identifying HCI markers to detect diagnose and monitor HCI-related variables that are affected by conditions such as neurological damage.

One of the chief candidates for HCI marker analysis is online language. An abundance of research links variables such as personality, emotion and neurological health to language use [e.g. 16], but we are still early in the process of understanding the impact of such conditions on online language [e.g. 9, 13]. The goal of the current study is to further our understanding of the link between online language and neurological damage. We attempt to determine whether language patterns associated with brain damage can be detected in online writing. This is a required first step before making use of this information in beneficial ways in existing and new technologies.

1.2 Aphasia

Aphasia is an acquired language disorder, resulting from brain trauma or injury to the language areas of the brain, which may affect all modes of receptive and expressive communication, including speech, language, writing, comprehension, and gesture [18]. Although there are many shared characteristics of aphasic language, people with aphasia present with varying language deficit profiles within and across language domains. A person's language capacities may remain stable in some types of aphasia, or progressively decline, as is the case in Primary Progressive Aphasia (PPA) [29, 30]. Aphasia is often noted for being a frustrating and often debilitating communicative disorder. Because of the increased probability of stroke and neurological disease in older populations, diagnosis and treatment of aphasia and other degenerative language conditions is important for increasingly aging populations, such as the Baby Boomer generation.

While there are different types of aphasia, people with aphasia generally present with problems in both production and comprehension of language. In language production, errors may include the omission of key linguistic features used by neurologically intact speakers, and/or disordered use of these features. In addition, they often present with mild to severe problems with language comprehension [2]. In measurable terms, production problems often lead to overall decreases in sentence length (MLU – mean length utterance), omission of word classes (e.g. prepositions), and a range of semantic, syntactic and phonological errors [33-35].

Users with language disabilities experience unique challenges when they interact via user interfaces. In the case of people with aphasia, the challenges include reading from the screen, using voice commands, and writing, and extensive efforts are focused on developing assistive technologies to overcome these challenges [e.g. 1, 11, 36], and even to use computers to increase empathy towards people with aphasia by developing software that emulates the language distortion they experience [19, 20]. However, since little is known about the manifestation of aphasia during computer-mediated communication, the individual attributes of the online communication of people with aphasia are not being used to diagnose and to monitor the condition.

2. RESEARCH QUESTIONS AND HYPOTHESES

This study asks whether the well-documented language deficits associated with aphasia can be detected in online writing. While research on aphasia *per se* is extensive, there is surprisingly sparse research analysis of online interactions of people with aphasia. Although there are many reasons why we might predict patterns similar to spoken language, there are other reasons why online language may reveal distinctive characteristics [7]. Based on the known characteristics of aphasia in traditional (mainly spoken) communication, we chose seven linguistic variables that are typically measured in spoken aphasic language [See 33 for a detailed analysis of linguistic deficits found in individuals with primary progressive aphasia]. We hypothesized that the online writing of people with aphasia would differ significantly when compared to the online writing of people without aphasia ("controls"). We predict that online writing of people with aphasia will exhibit similar language deficits. If this prediction is confirmed, then these patterns are HCI marker candidates.

Specific hypotheses were formulated for each measurable language variable. For variables measuring linguistic complexity, we hypothesized that people with aphasia would rank lower than controls. For variables measuring linguistic errors, we hypothesized that errors would be significantly higher for people with aphasia than controls. The hypotheses and variables were thus:

Linguistic complexity, as measured by (1), (2), and (3) below will be decreased for people with aphasia as compared to controls.

(1) MLU: the mean number of words produced per utterance.

(2) Open/closed class ratio: the ratio of all open class words (i.e., nouns, verbs, adjectives, and adverbs) to all closed class words produced.

(3) Noun/verb ratio: the ratio of all nouns to all verbs produced.

Linguistic errors, (4), (5), (6), and (7) below, will be produced at higher rates for people with aphasia as compared to controls.

(4) Proportion of ungrammatical utterances: the number of utterances with grammatical errors, divided by total number of utterances.

(5) Proportion of morpheme inflection errors: the number of errors in morpheme inflection, divided by total number of inflected morphemes.

(6) Proportion of open class errors: the number of errors in open class words, divided by the number of all open class words.

(7) Proportion of closed class errors: the number of errors in closed class words, divided by the number of all closed class words.

3. METHOD

3.1 Participants

A public online support group for people with aphasia was the source for the messages analyzed in this study. We first read the online posts of the participants in the support group. We selected six participants with aphasia, and four control participants who did not have aphasia, based on self-descriptions from their posts. For analysis, we selected only participants who posted at least 15 messages, and clearly identified their medical status: (1) a person with aphasia, (2) or a person who does not have aphasia. It was not possible for us to ascertain the official medical diagnosis or standardized participant demographics, since their online posts included only self-reported information. However, based on self-report, the age of the youngest person with aphasia was mid-30's and the oldest about 70. Five of the six people with aphasia mentioned that the cause of their aphasia was a stroke. Most reported living in North America, and English as their native language. Some mentioned command of additional languages such as French and Chinese. For controls, three of the four were relatives of a person with aphasia: a spouse, a child and a parent, and one was the spouse of a speech-language pathologist. No further personally identifying details or direct quotes from the support forum are provided, to protect the anonymity of the participants in the support group.

3.2 Language Coding

We developed a protocol for hand-coding online written language based on existing aphasia research protocols, with necessary adaptations [see 33-35]. The protocol included three phases. First, each posted message was segmented into utterances, based on punctuation, other visual demarcations (e.g. new line) and verb use. Second, the part of speech (POS) of each word was determined, based on the Penn Treebank POS parsing framework [28]. Last, each utterance was coded for errors: written convention errors such as spelling and capitalization errors, and grammatical errors: syntactic and morphological. The results of the coding were used for the analysis described below.

3.3 Analysis

The results of the coding were used to calculate: MLU, total word count, utterance count, count of grammatical and ungrammatical sentences, count of nouns and verbs, count of inflected morphemes and count of morpheme inflexion errors, count of each POS (part of speech), count of open class words and errors in open class words, count of closed class words and count of errors in closed class words. These were used to calculate the variables of interest. Because of the small number of participants, we used a conservative nonparametric Wilcoxon signed-rank test to analyze differences between the two participant groups.

4. RESULTS

Table 1 summarizes the results of coding for each of the ten participants. As expected and as is typical with analyses of spoken language in aphasia research, we see high variability within both the people with aphasia, and control groups (e.g. the number of words and utterances in each post). In Table 2, each participant's score for each variable is presented in detail. Again, we see variability between participants, although the controls clearly show lower rates of linguistic errors. Table 3 presents the statistical analysis: results of the Wilcoxon signed-rank test comparing people with aphasia to controls. Our hypotheses were confirmed for five of the seven variables that showed a significant difference ($p \leq .01$) between people with aphasia and controls. MLU was significantly shorter for people with aphasia, and the rates of the four linguistic error types were higher for people with aphasia. There was no significant difference between the open/closed class and the noun/verb ratios.

Table 1. Results by participant

Participant[a]	101	102	103	104	105	106	901	902	903	904
Mean length of utterance	7.68	8.44	9.25	10.77	10.07	6.08	13.77	13.50	16.49	15.26
Words	1928	996	668	1228	3047	260	1526	1070	2011	2020
Utterances	242	123	72	113	317	33	110	82	126	127
Correct utterances	158	87	44	82	214	25	101	77	116	124
Incorrect utterances	84	36	28	31	103	8	9	5	10	3
Inflected morphemes	350	22	93	220	79	50	175	137	185	275
Morpheme inflection errors	20	2	4	15	13	1	3	1	5	1
POS (parts of speech) tags	2057	1065	646	1297	3199	279	1494	1118	2108	2049
Open class words	1355	582	363	748	1775	145	871	689	1143	1209
Open class errors	65	23	20	12	86	5	4	3	5	6
Closed class words	702	483	283	549	1424	134	623	429	965	840
Closed class errors	27	22	12	10	43	9	4	4	8	1
Nouns	404	189	149	196	551	47	259	228	375	465
Verbs	459	193	121	272	666	62	293	246	414	363

[a] People with aphasia: Participants 101-106. Controls: Participants 901-904.

Table 2. Language Variables for All Participants

Participant[a]	101	102	103	104	105	106	901	902	903	904
Mean length of utterance	7.68	8.44	9.25	10.77	10.07	6.08	13.77	13.50	16.49	15.26
Ungrammatical sentences	34.71%	29.27%	38.89%	27.43%	32.49%	24.24%	8.18%	6.10%	7.94%	2.36%
Morpheme inflection errors	5.71%	9.09%	4.30%	6.82%	16.46%	2.00%	1.71%	.73%	2.70%	.36%
Open class errors	4.80%	3.95%	5.51%	1.60%	4.85%	3.45%	.46%	.44%	.44%	.50%
Closed class errors	3.85%	4.55%	4.24%	1.82%	3.02%	6.72%	.64%	.93%	.83%	.12%
Ratio, open/closed class	.88	.98	1.23	.72	.83	.76	.88	.93	.91	1.28
Ratio, noun/verb	1.93	1.21	1.28	1.36	1.25	1.08	1.40	1.61	1.18	1.44

[a] People with aphasia: Participants 101-106. Controls: Participants 901-904.

Table 3. Comparison of Language Variables: People with Aphasia vs. Controls, and Significance Test Using Wilcoxon Signed-Rank Test

	People with aphasia		Controls		Hypothesis (H_1)	p-value
	Average	SD	Average	SD		
Mean length of utterance	8.72	1.70	14.75	1.39	People with aphasia < Controls	.005
Ungrammatical sentences	31.17%	5.28%	6.14%	2.69%	People with aphasia > Controls	.005
Morpheme inflection errors	7.40%	5.04%	1.38%	1.05%	People with aphasia > Controls	.01
Open class errors	4.03%	1.39%	.46%	.03%	People with aphasia > Controls	.005
Closed class errors	4.03%	1.64%	.63%	.36%	People with aphasia > Controls	.005
Ratio, open/closed class	.90	.19	1.00	.19	People with aphasia > Controls	n.s.
Ratio, noun/verb	1.35	.30	1.41	.17	People with aphasia > Controls	n.s.

5. DISCUSSION

As predicted, people with aphasia showed reduced linguistic complexity and increased presence of errors in their online writing. This demonstrates that some of the major language deficits of aphasia can be detected in online writing of people with aphasia. We discuss the implications of these findings on the study of HCI markers, the implications for practice and for theory, and the limitations of the study.

5.1 Implications for Practice

To the best of our knowledge, this is the first time HCI markers for aphasia are being proposed in the literature. The five variables that differed significantly between people with aphasia and controls unequivocally distinguish between these two groups, and are thus candidate aphasia HCI markers. Extensive additional work needs to be done in order to establish these markers, to evaluate their specificity and sensitivity, and to determine guidelines for their use. A better understanding of these markers has practical as well as theoretical implications, as discussed below.

At present, clinical assessment of aphasia is based on face-to-face interviews, followed by manual interview transcription, and analysis of the transcript by an expert clinician. The establishment of HCI markers for aphasia could augment this practice in several ways. First, additional linguistic samples could now be collected unobtrusively from online language in e-mail correspondence, online posts to social networking sites such as Facebook, blogs, or online groups (health oriented support groups, as well as other special interest groups). The resulting text is already transcribed in digital format making it immediately available for analysis, and it is produced under conditions that are often more naturalistic than the traditional face-to-face clinical evaluation. It is also possible to capture instant messaging sessions, though it is expected that the nature of synchronous communication HCI markers will differ from those described here.

Because clinicians would now be able to collect more extensive and representative language samples from patients with less effort, this could both augment their diagnostic and therapeutic toolset, as well as their ability to monitor longitudinal changes in aphasic language symptoms over periods of months and years. HCI markers could augment current test batteries, as well as allowing clinicians to explore the progression of language decline prior to arrival at the clinic, especially in the case of ongoing deterioration (e.g. in the case of PPA). Thus, an analysis of online language created and archived pre-diagnosis (e.g. old e-mails, blogs, or old Facebook posts) could help evaluate the rate of linguistic decline as well as its trajectory. As online writing becomes more prevalent in the general population as well as with older adults [26, 27], access to such longitudinal repositories of language samples will improve. In regards to monitoring the progression of aphasia, the same principles apply, and the clinicians would be able to better evaluate either recovery (e.g. from stroke-induced aphasia), or decline (e.g. from PPA), and how these are influenced by various interventions.

One of the more exciting possibilities suggested by our findings is that linguistic HCI markers will be useful in earlier detection of progressive aphasia as well as of other progressive neurodegenerative diseases which influence language use, such as Alzheimer's disease [16]. The realization of this vision requires the development of automated or semi-automated parsing and analysis tools [23] that would be able to monitor, on an ongoing basis, language produced by the users. Despite the challenges of automated language analysis, it should be possible to adapt parsing tools to perform automated or semi-automated identification and quantification of HCI markers.

Another intriguing possibility is applying these findings to linguistic HCI markers to improve assistive technologies offered to people with language disorders [e.g. 1, 11, 36]. Lastly, there is the question of whether participation in online discussion forums is also a worthwhile remedial effort and supplemental to face-to-face therapy sessions. These technologies could ostensibly monitor the putative positive impact of ongoing participation in online conversations and interactions.

5.2 Implications for Theory

In a recent paper by Gajos et al. [15], the authors point to the paucity of data on actual behavior of users with disabilities in real world situations. Data on clients' use of technology in clinical settings may be gathered as a part of diagnostic evaluation, at the discretion of the clinician. These data are necessary in order to realize the concept of personalized dynamic accessibility. HCI markers are ideal candidates for data that will allow measuring and modeling users' abilities. The same unobtrusively collected HCI markers that can assist in the detection, diagnosis and longitudinal monitoring of specific conditions, are also critical measures of users' abilities to interact with various digital devices. HCI markers for aphasia are especially interesting, since, as Gajos et al. emphasize, modeling cognitive abilities is one of the toughest challenges. The markers identified in this paper are a small step in the direction of developing such modeling capabilities.

One of the main sources for information about human behavior and health is a result of the study of disorders and illness. Just as metabolic disorders provide clues on the structure of metabolic pathways and anxiety disorders shed light on the processing of fear and anxiety, aphasia and other language disorders teach us about language structure and production. A better understanding of the expression of aphasia in naturally occurring online communication can also strengthen efforts to effectively emulate aphasia in online communication [19, 20], and a similar approach can be applied towards the emulation of other communication disorders. Very little attention has so far been paid to the convergence of CMC and communication disorders, with the exception of work on assistive technologies [e.g. 22, 32]. We suggest that these early findings on the impact of aphasia on CMC could lead to a better understanding of CMC, as well as of aphasia.

Spoken and written communication are quite distinct from each other. One of the earliest questions raised in regards to computer-mediated communication (CMC) is how it relates to these two traditional forms of communication [6, 7, 10, 37]. Is e-mail simply a conversation in written form, or is it an expedited letter? An analysis of the impact of language disorders on CMC provides a new lens through which to explore this question. Which of the spoken manifestations of aphasia are preserved in the online medium, and which ones diminish or disappear altogether? Here we can see that despite the effectively unlimited time to compose an asynchronous CMC message, MLU decreased in asynchronous CMC produced by people with aphasia. On the other hand, the noun/verb ratio and open class closed class ratios were not affected.

The findings reported here inform both our understanding of language production, and our understanding of CMC as utilized by populations with language disorders. The use of CMC by these populations has not been studied in the past, and the preliminary findings reported here suggest new questions: Are these populations empowered by CMC [4, 5]? How does CMC influence the way these populations are perceived by others? And, how can these findings inform the design of CMC artifacts and of assistive technologies [8]?

5.3 Limitations
In this paper we report, for the first time, the results of research that links the study of communication disorders with the study of CMC. As can be expected from early stage research, our findings are limited in many ways, which should be addressed by future research. First, only a fraction of people with aphasia have the technical and language skills to use CMC; Also, as already mentioned, the specificity and sensitivity of the proposed HCI markers still need to be established. In addition, the results reported here are based on a small cohort of participants; the medical information we have about them is based on self-report, and is fragmentary and unverified. Thus, for example, it is not possible to determine whether HCI

markers can be used to distinguish between different types of aphasia. Even this fragmentary information points to the extensive heterogeneity of the participant pool. Moreover, it is still impossible to determine the value of markers such as noun/verb ratio and open/closed class ratio as HCI markers. Future research efforts should be devoted to studying a larger cohort of participants and/or studying subjects whose aphasia has been studied and classified, as well as to compare their language to carefully matched controls.

6. ACKNOWLEDGMENT
Our thanks to Kristina Rodriguez for her assistance with language coding. Funding was provided, in part, by National Science Foundation grant #0953943.

7. REFERENCES
[1] Allen, M., McGrenere, J. and Purves, B. The Field Evaluation of a Mobile Digital Image Communication Application Designed for People with Aphasia. *ACM Trans. Access. Comput.* Article 5 (May 2008). DOI= http://dx.doi.org/10.1145/1361203.1361208

[2] American Speech-Language-Hearing Association *Aphasia*, 2011.

[3] Amichai-Hamburger, Y. *The social net: understanding human behavior in cyberspace.* Oxford University Press, USA, 2005.

[4] Amichai-Hamburger, Y., McKenna, K. Y. A. and Tal, S. A. E-empowerment: Empowerment by the Internet. *Computers in Human Behavior*, 24, 5 (2008), 1776-1789. DOI= http://dx.doi.org/10.1016%2Fj.chb.2008.02.002

[5] Barak, A. and Sadovsky, Y. Internet use and personal empowerment of hearing-impaired adolescents. *Computers in Human Behavior*, 24, 5 (2008), 1802-1815. DOI= http://dx.doi.org/10.1016/j.chb.2008.02.007

[6] Baron, N. S. *Always on: Language in an online and mobile world.* Oxford Univ Press, 2008.

[7] Baron, N. S. Letters by phone or speech by other means: The linguistics of email. *Language and communication*, 18 (1998), 133-170. DOI= http://dx.doi.org/10.1016%2FS0271-5309%2898%2900005-6

[8] Bowker, N. I. Understanding barriers to online experience for people with physical and sensory disabilities using discursive social psychology. *Universal Access in the Information Society*, 9, 2 (2010), 121-136. DOI= http://dx.doi.org/10.1007%2Fs10209-009-0162-3

[9] Cohn, M. A., Mehl, M. R. and Pennebaker, J. W. Linguistic markers of psychological change surrounding September 11, 2001. *Psychological Science*, 15, 10 (2004), 687. DOI= http://dx.doi.org/10.1111%2Fj.0956-7976.2004.00741.x

[10] Collot, M. and Belmore, N. *Electronic language.* John Benjamins, City, 1996.

[11] Daemen, E., Dadlani, P., Du, J., Li, Y., Erik-Paker, P., Martens, J.-B., de Ruyter, B. Designing a free style, indirect, and interactive storytelling application for people with aphasia. In *Proceedings of the 11th IFIP TC 13 international conference on Human-computer interaction* (INTERACT'07). Springer-Verlag, Berlin, Heidelberg, 221-234.

[12] Diamandis, E. P. Cancer Biomarkers: Can we turn recent failures into success? *Journal of the National Cancer*

Institute, 102, 19, 1462-1467.DOI=
http://dx.doi.org/10.1093%2Fjnci%2Fdjq306

[13] Epp, C., Lippold, M. and Mandryk, R. L. Identifying emotional states using keystroke dynamics. In *Proceedings of the CHI 2011* (Vancouver, BC, Canada, (2011), New York. DOI= http://dx.doi.org/10.1145%2F1978942.1979046

[14] Foundation for the National Institutes of Health *The Biomarkers Consortium*. Foundation for the National Institutes of Health, 2011.

[15] Gajos, K. Z., Hurst, A. and Findlater, L. Personalized dynamic accessibility. *interactions*, 19, 2 (2012), 69-73. DOI= http://dx.doi.org/10.1145%2F2090150.2090167

[16] Garrard, P. Cognitive archaeology: Uses, methods, and results. *Journal of Neurolinguistics*, 22, 3 (2009), 250-265. DOI= http://dx.doi.org/10.1016%2Fj.jneuroling.2008.07.006

[17] Gerszten, R. E. and Wang, T. J. The search for new cardiovascular biomarkers. *Nature*, 451, 7181 (2008), 949-952.

[18] Goodglass, H. *Understanding aphasia*. Academic Press, San Diego, CA, 1993.

[19] Hailpern, J., Danilevsky, M., Harris, A., Karahalios, K., Dell, G. and Hengst, J. ACES: Promoting empathy towards aphasia through language distortion emulation software. In *Proceedings of the 2011 annual conference on Human factors in computing systems* (CHI '11). ACM, New York, NY, 609-618. DOI= http://doi.acm.org/10.1145/1978942.1979029

[20] Hailpern, J., Danilevsky, M. and Karahalios, K. *ACES: aphasia emulation, realism, and the Turing test*.In *The proceedings of the 13ᵗʰ international ACM SIGACCESS conference on computers and accessibility (ASSETS '11)*. ACM, New York, NY, 83-90. DOI= http://dx.doi.org/10.1145/2049536.2049553

[21] Hellhammer, D. H., Wüst, S. and Kudielka, B. M. Salivary cortisol as a biomarker in stress research. *Psychoneuroendocrinology*, 34, 2 (2009), 163-171.DOI= http://dx.doi.org/10.1038%2Fnature06802

[22] Jeon, M., Gupta, S., Davison, B. K. and Walker, B. N. Auditory menus are not just spoken visual menus: a case study of unavailable menu items. In *Proceedings of the 28th of the international conference extended abstracts on Human factors in computing systems* (CHI EA '10). ACM, New York, NY, 3319-3324. DOI=http://doi.acm.org/10.1145/1753846.1753978

[23] Jurafsky, D. and Martin, J. H. *Speech and language processing: An introduction to natural language processing, computational linguistics and speech recognition*. Prentice Hall, 2008.

[24] Kalman, Y. M. *HCI markers: A conceptual framework for using human-computer interaction data to detect disease processes*. The 6ᵗʰ Mediterranean Conference on Information Systems (MCIS), Limassol, Cyprus, 2011.

[25] Madan, A., Cebrian, M., Moturu, S., Farrahi, K. and Pentland, S. Sensing the 'health state' of a community.

Pervasive Computing, (2011).DOI= http://dx.doi.org/10.1109%2FMPRV.2011.79

[26] Madden, M. *Older Adults and Social Media*. Pew Research Center, 2010.

[27] Madden, M. and Zickuhr, K. *65% of online adults use social networking sites*. Pew Research Center, 2011.

[28] Marcus, M. P., Marcinkiewicz, M. A. and Santorini, B. Building a large annotated corpus of English: The Penn Treebank. *Computational linguistics*, 19, 2 (1993), 313-330.

[29] Mesulam, M. M. Primary progressive aphasia: a language-based dementia. *New England Journal of Medicine*, 349, 16 (2003), 1535-1542. DOI= http://dx.doi.org/10.1056%2FNEJMra022435

[30] Mesulam, M. M., Wieneke, C., Rogalski, E., Cobia, D., Thompson, C. K. and Weintraub, S. Quantitative template for subtyping primary progressive aphasia. *Archives of neurology*, 66, 12 (2009), 1545. DOI= http://dx.doi.org/10.1001%2Farchneurol.2009.288

[31] Moreno, M. A., Jelenchick, L. A., Egan, K. G., Cox, E., Young, H., Gannon, K. E. and Becker, T. Feeling bad on Facebook: depression disclosures by college students on a social networking site. *Depression and anxiety*, 28, 6 (2011), 447-455.DOI= http://dx.doi.org/10.1002%2Fda.20805

[32] Smyth, K. and Kwon, S. Computer-mediated communication and its use in support groups for family caregivers. *Gerotechnology: Research and practice in technology and aging* (2004), 97-116.

[33] Thompson, C. K., Ballard, K. J., Tait, M. E., Weintraub, S. and Mesulam, M. M. Patterns of language decline in non-fluent primary progressive aphasia. *Aphasiology*, 11, 4/5 (1997), 297-321. DOI= http://dx.doi.org/10.1080%2F02687039708248473

[34] Thompson, C. K., Cho, S., Wieneke, C., Weintraub, S. and Mesulam, M. M. Dissociation between fluency and agrammatism in Primary Progressive Aphasia. *Aphasiology* (January, 2012). DOI= http://dx.doi.org/10.1080%2F02687038.2011.584691

[35] Thompson, C. K., Shapiro, L. P., Tait, M. E., Jacobs, B., Schneider, S. and Ballard, K. A system for the linguistic analysis of agrammatic language production. *Brain and Language*, 51, 1 (1995), 124-129.

[36] Woudstra, M., Al Mahmud, A. and Martens, J.-B. A snapshot diary to support conversational storytelling for persons with aphasia. In *Proceedings of the 13th International Conference on Human Computer Interaction with Mobile Devices and Services* (MobileHCI '11). ACM, New York, NY, 641-646. DOI= http://doi.acm.org/10.1145/2037373.2037474

[37] Yates, S. J. Oral and written linguistic aspects of computer conferencing. *Computer-mediated communication: Linguistic, social and cross-cultural perspectives* (1996), 29-46.

A Readability Evaluation of Real-Time Crowd Captions in the Classroom

Raja S. Kushalnagar, Walter S. Lasecki†, Jeffrey P. Bigham†

Department of Information and Computing Studies
Rochester Institute of Technology
1 Lomb Memorial Dr, Rochester, NY 14623
rskics@rit.edu

†Department of Computer Science
University of Rochester
160 Trustee Rd, Rochester, NY 14627
{wlasecki, jbigham}@cs.rochester.edu

ABSTRACT

Deaf and hard of hearing individuals need accommodations that transform aural to visual information, such as captions that are generated in real-time to enhance their access to spoken information in lectures and other live events. The captions produced by professional captionists work well in general events such as community or legal meetings, but is often unsatisfactory in specialized content events such as higher education classrooms. In addition, it is hard to hire professional captionists, especially those that have experience in specialized content areas, as they are scarce and expensive. The captions produced by commercial automatic speech recognition (ASR) software are far cheaper, but is often perceived as unreadable due to ASR's sensitivity to accents, background noise and slow response time. We ran a study to evaluate the readability of captions generated by a new crowd captioning approach versus professional captionists and ASR. In this approach, captions are typed by classmates into a system that aligns and merges the multiple incomplete caption streams into a single, comprehensive real-time transcript. Our study asked 48 deaf and hearing readers to evaluate transcripts produced by a professional captionist, ASR and crowd captioning software respectively and found the readers preferred crowd captions over professional captions and ASR.

Categories and Subject Descriptors

H.5.1 [**Information Interfaces and Presentation**]: Multimedia Information Systems; K.4.2 [**Social Issues**]: Assistive technologies for persons with disabilities

General Terms

Human Factors, Design, Experimentation

Keywords

Accessible Technology, Educational Technology, Deaf and Hard of Hearing Users

1. INTRODUCTION

Deaf and hard of hearing (DHH) individuals typically cannot understand speech alone. Instead they depend on visual accommodations that transform the spoken auditory information to visual information. Most DHH individuals request accommodations through real-time captions or sign language translation of the audio. But it is difficult to obtain qualified accommodation providers for DHH individuals who are thinly spread as deafness is a low incidence disability [18]. As a result, many DHH individuals find it hard to obtain accommodation providers, especially those who can handle speeches and dialog that involve specialized content knowledge. Accommodation providers prefer to live in close to areas where they can obtain enough demand to provide services. If there is not enough demand for providers in the area, there will be a long term mismatch between DHH students' accommodation needs and availability of accommodation providers. Therefore, for most institutions in terms of obtaining accommodation providers who have the necessary content knowledge, are availabile and not too expensive, it is best to use accommodation services centered on the student such as classmates or on-demand remote providers.

This paper analyzes the readability of a new student-centered approach to real-time captioning in which multiple classmates simultaneously listen to the lecture speech and type in what they hear (caption) in real-time. Although classmates cannot type as quickly as the natural speaking rate of most speakers, we have found that they can provide accurate partial captions. We align and merge the multiple incomplete caption streams into a single, comprehensive real-time transcript. We compare deaf and hearing students' evaluation of the effectiveness and usability of this crowd-sourced real-time transcript against transcripts produced by professional captionists and automatic speech recognition software respectively.

2. BACKGROUND

Equal access to communication is fundamental to students' academic success, but is often taken for granted. In mainstream environments where deaf, hard-of-hearing, and hearing students study and attend classes together, people tend to assume that captioners or interpreters enable full communication between deaf and hearing people in the class. This assumption is especially detrimental as it does not address other information accessibility issues such as translation delays that impact interaction and readability that impacts comprehension.

(a) A stenograph keyboard that shows its phonetic-based keys.

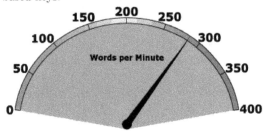

(b) A stenographer's typical Words Per Minute (WPM) limit and range.

Figure 1: Professional Real-Time Captioning using a stenograph

Currently, there are two popular approaches to generating real-time captions that attempt to convey lecture audio in the classroom: professional captioning and automatic speech recognition (ASR). Both professional captioning and ASR aim to provide a real-time word-for-word display of what is said in class, as well as options for saving the text after class for study. We discuss the readability of these approaches and a new approach, which utilizes crowd sourcing to generate real-time captions.

2.1 Professional Captioning

The most widely used approach, Communications Access Real Time (CART), is generated by professional captionists who type in shorthand, and use software to generate captions that can keep up with natural speaking rates. Although popular, professional captioners are not widely available as they have to undergo years of training, which also results in professional captioning services being expensive. Furthermore, captionists usually have inadequate content knowledge and dictionaries to handle higher education lectures in specific fields. is the most reliable transcription service, but is also the most expensive one. Trained stenographers type in shorthand on a stenographic (shorthand writing system) keyboard as shown in Figure 1a. This keyboard maps multiple key presses to phonemes that are expanded to verbatim full text. The stenographists normally need at least 2 to 3 years of training to achieve at least 225 words per minute (WPM) [1], and to type in bursts of up to 300 WPM to be able to consistently transcribe all real-time speech as shown in Figure 1b. The 2-3 year intensive training period and scarcity of qualified captionists partly explains their high costs of over $100 an hour. CART stenographers need only to recognize and type in the phonemes to create the transcript, which enables them to type fast enough to keep up with the natural speaking rate. They also need to build up their personalized dictionary with the words used in the lecture. The dictionary is needed to translate the phonemes to words; if the captioner has to type in new words into the captions and dictionary, their transcription speed slows down considerably. The stenographer can transcribe speech even if the words or phonemes do not make sense to them, e.g., if the speech words appear to violate rules of grammar, pronunciation, or logic. The captioned word shows up as a phonetically spelled word, which the reader can try to guess.

In response to the high cost of CART, computer-based macro expansion services like C-Print were developed and introduced. C-Print is a kind of summarization transcription that is real-time, that was developed at the National Technical Institute for the Deaf. The C-Print captionist balances the tradeoff between typing speed and summarization, by including as much information as possible, generally providing a meaning-for-meaning but not verbatim translation of the spoken English content. C-Print enables operators who are trained in academic situations to consolidate and better organize the text with the goal of creating an end result more like class notes that may be more conducive to for learning. The advantage is that the C-Print captionists need less training, and generally charge about half the rate of CART. Another advantage is that the C-Print caption meaning-for-meaning accuracy and its readability is high [21]. The disadvantage is that the captionist normally cannot type as fast as the natural speaking rate, and cannot produce a verbatim real-time transcript. Also, the captionist can only effectively convey classroom content if they understand that content themselves. A final disadvantage C-Print captions is that the transcript shows the summary that is based on the captionist's understanding of the material, which may be different from the speaker or reader's understanding of the material.

There are several procaptioning issues in higher education. The first issue is content knowledge - higher education lecture information tends to be dense and contain specialized vocabulary. This makes it hard to identify and schedule captionists who are both skilled in typing and have the appropriate content knowledge. Another issue is transcription delay, which occurs when captionists have to understand the phonemes or words and then type in what they have recognized. As a result, captionists tend to type the material to students with a delay of several seconds. This prevents students from effectively participating in an interactive classroom. Another issue is speaker identification, in which captionist are unfamiliar with participants and are challenged to properly identify the current speaker. They can simplify this by recognizing the speaker by name, or asking the speaker to pause before beginning until the captionist has caught up and had an opportunity to identify the new speaker. In terms of availability, captionists typically are not available to transcribe live speech or dialogue for short periods or on-demand. Professional captionists usually need at least a few hours advance notice, and prefer to work in 1-hour increments so as to account for their commute times. As a result, students cannot easily decide at the last minute to attend a lecture or after class interactions with peers and teacher. Captionists used to need to be physically present at the event they were transcribing, but captioning services are increasingly being offered remotely [12, 1]. Captionists often are simply not available for many technical fields [21, 8].

Remote captioning offers the potential to recruit captionists familiar with a particular subject (e.g., organic chemistry) even if the captionist is located far away from an event. Selecting for expertise further reduces the pool of captionists. A final issue is their cost - professional captionists take years to develop an extensive personalized dictionary. They also combine their personalized dictionary with extensive training to keep up with speech with low errors rates, and so are highly compensated.

2.2 Automatic Speech Recognition

ASR platforms typically use probabilistic approaches to translate speech to text. These platforms face challenges in accurately capturing modern classroom lectures that can have one or more of the following challenges: extensive technical vocabulary, poor acoustic quality, multiple information sources, speaker accents, or other problems. They also impose a processing delay of several seconds and the delay lengthens as the amount of data to be analyzed gets bigger. In other words, ASR works well under ideal situations, but degrades quickly in many real settings. Kheir et al. [12] found that untrained ASR software had 75% accuracy rate, but with training, could go to 90% under ideal single speaker, but this accuracy rate was still too low for use by deaf students. In the best possible case, in which the speaker has trained the ASR and wears a high-quality, noise-canceling microphone, the accuracy can be above 90%. When recording a speaker using a standard microphone on ASR not trained for the speaker, accuracy rates plummet to far below 50%. Additionally, the errors made by ASR often change the meaning of the text, whereas we have found non-expert captionists are much more likely to simply omit words or make spelling errors. In Figure 2 for instance, the ASR changes 'two fold axis' to 'twenty four lexus', whereas the c typists typically omit words they do not understand or make spelling errors. Current ASR is speaker-dependent, has difficulty recognizing domain-specific jargon, and adapts poorly to vocal changes, such as when the speaker is sick [6, 7]. ASR systems generally need substantial computing power and high-quality audio to work well, which means systems can be difficult to transport. They are also ill-equipped to recognize and convey tone, attitudes, interest and emphasis, and to refer to visual information such as slides or demonstrations. An advantage is that these systems can be integrated with other online functionality such as multimedia indexing. ASR services charge about $15-20 an hour.

2.3 Crowd Captions in the Classroom

Deaf and hard of hearing students have had a long history of enhancing their classroom accessibility by collaborating with classmates. For example, they often arrange to copy notes from a classmate and share it with their study group. Crowdsourcing has been applied to offline transcription with great success [2], but has just recently been used for real-time transcription [15]. Applying a collaborative captioning approach among classmates enables real-time transcription from multiple non-experts, and crowd agreement mechanisms can be utilized to vet transcript quality [14].

We imagine a deaf or hard of hearing person eventually being able to capture aural speech with her cellphone anywhere and have captions returned to her with a few seconds latency. She may use this to follow along in a lecture for which a professional captionist was not requested, to par-

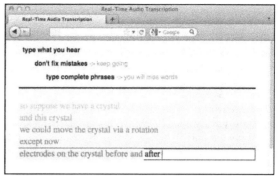

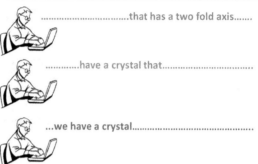

Figure 2: The crowd captioning interface. The interface provides a text input box at the bottom, and shifts text up as users type (either when the text hits the end of the box, or when the user presses the enter key). To encourage users to continue typing even when making mistakes, editing of text is disabled word by word. Partial captions are forwarded to the server in real-time, which uses overlapping segments and the order in segments are received to align and merge them.

ticipate in informal conversation with peers after class, or enjoy a movie or other live event that lacks closed captioning. These use cases currently beyond the scope of ASR, and their serendipitous nature precludes pre-arranging a professional captionist. In previous work, we developed a crowd captioning system that accepts realtime transcription from multiple non-experts as shown in Figure 2. Lasecki et al. have demonstrated that a modest number of people can provide reasonably high coverage over the caption stream, and introduces an algorithm that uses overlapping portions of the sequences to align and merge them using the Legion:Scribe system [15].

Scribe is based on the Legion [13] framework, which uses crowds of workers to accomplish tasks in real-time. Unlike Legion, Scribe merges responses to create a single, better, response instead of selecting from inputs to select the best sequence. This merger is done using an online multiple sequence alignment algorithm that aligns worker input to both reconstruct the final stream and correct errors (such as spelling mistakes) made by individual workers.

Crowd captioning offers several potential benefits over existing approaches. First, it is potentially much cheaper than hiring a professional captionist because non-expert captionists do not need extensive training to acquire a specific skill set, and thus may be drawn from a variety of sources, e.g. classmates, audience members, microtask marketplaces, volunteers, or affordable and readily available employees. Our workforce can be very large because, for people who can hear, speech recognition is relatively easy and most people can type accurately. The problem is that individually they cannot type quickly enough to keep up with natural speaking rates, we have found that they can provide accurate partial captions, which can be combined in real-time to nicely remedy this problem. Recent work has demonstrated that small crowds can be recruited quickly on-demand (in less than 2 seconds) from such sources[4, 3]. Scribe4Me enabled DHH users to receive a transcript of a short sound sequence in a few minutes, but is not able to produce verbatim captions over long periods of time [17].

2.4 Real-time text reading versus listening

Most people only see real-time text on TV at the bar or gym in the form of closed captions, which tend to have noticeable errors. However, those programs are captioned by live captionists or stenographers. To reduce errors, these real-time transcripts are often corrected and made into a permanent part of the video file by off-line captionists who prepare captions from pre-recorded videotapes and thoroughly review the work for errors before airing.

The translation of speech to text is not direct, but rather is interpreted and changed in the course of each utterance. Markers like accent, tone, and timbre are stripped out and represented by standardized written words and symbols. Then the reader interprets these words and flow to make meanings for themselves. Captionists tend not to include all spoken information so that readers can keep up with the transcript. Captionists are encouraged to alter the original transcription to provide time for the readers to completely read the caption and to synchronize with the audio. This is needed because, for a non-orthographic language like English, the length of a spoken utterance is not necessarily proportional to the length of a spelled word. In other words, reading speed is not the same as listening speed, especially for real-time scrolling text, as opposed to static pre-prepared text. For static text, reading speed has been measured at 291 wpm [19]. By contrast the average caption rate for TV programs is 141 wpm [11], while the most comfortable reading rate for hearing, hard-of-hearing, and deaf adults is around 145 wpm [10]. The reason is that the task of viewing real-time captions involved different processing demands in visual location and tracking of moving text on a dynamic background. English literacy rates among deaf and hard of hearing people who is low compared to hearing peers. Captioning research has shown that both rate and text reduction and viewer reading ability are important factors, and that captions need to be provided within 5 seconds so that the reader can participate [20].

The number of spoken words and their complexity can also influence the captioning decision on the amount of words to transcribe and degree of summarization to include so as to reduce the reader's total cognitive load. Jensema et al. [10] analyzed a large sample of captioned TV programs and found that the total set had around 800K words consisting of 16,000 unique words. Furthermore, over two-thirds of the transcript words consisted of 250 words. Higher education

lecture transcripts have a very different profile. For comparison purposes, we selected a 50 minute long clip from the MIT Open CourseWare (OCW) website[1]. The audio sample was picked from a lecture segment in which the speech was relatively clear.We chose this lecture because it combined both technical and non-technical vocabulary. We found that the lecture had 9137 words, of which 1428 were unique, at 182.7 wpm. Furthermore, over two thirds of the transcript consisted of around 500 words, which is double the size of the captioned TV word set. Professional captionists have to familiarize themselves with these extra words and include them in their dictionary in order to be accurate and keep up with the lecture audio.

3. EVALUATION

To evaluate the efficacy of real-time transcripts generated by crowds, we compared deaf and hearing user evaluations on their perceptions of the usability of crowd-sourced real-time transcripts against Computer Aided Real-Time transcripts (CART) and Automatic Speech Recognition transcripts (ASR).

3.1 Design Criteria

Based on prior work as well our own observations and experiences, we have developed the following design criteria for effective real-time transcript presentation for deaf and hard of hearing students:

1. The transcript must have enough information to be understood by the viewer.

2. The transcript must not be too fast or too slow so that it can be comfortably read.

3. Reading must not require substantial backtracking.

3.2 Transcript Generation

We recorded three transcriptions of an OCW lecture in real-time, using professional captioning, non-expert crowd captioning, and automatic speech recognition software.

For the first approach, professional captioning, we hired an expert, professional real-time stenographer captionist who charged $200 an hour to create a professional real-time transcript of the lecture. The captioner listened to the audio and transcribed in real-time. The mean typing speed was about 180 wpm with a latency of 4.2 seconds. We calculated latency by averaging the latency of all matched words.

For our second approach, non-expert crowd captioning, we recruited 20 undergraduate students to act as non-expert captionists for our crowd captioning system. These students had no special training or previous formal experience transcribing audio. Participants then provided partial captions for the lecture audio. The final transcript speed was about 130 WPM, with a latency of 3.87 seconds.

For our third approach, automatic speech recognition (ASR), we used an high end consumer automatic speech recognition *ASR* program, called Nuance Dragon Naturally Speaking 11. We used an untrained profile to simulate our target context of students transcribing speech from new or multiple speakers. To conduct this test, the audio files were played, and redirected to Dragon. We used a software loop

---

[1]http://ocw.mit.edu/

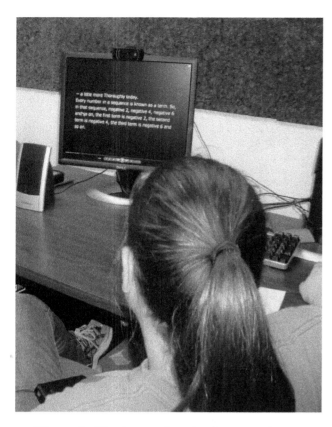

Figure 3: The transcript viewing experience.

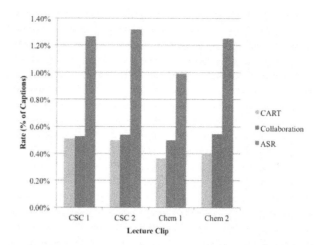

Figure 4: A comparison of the flow for each transcript. Both CART and crowd captions exhibit a relatively smooth real-time text flow. Students prefer this flow over the more choppy ASR transcript flow.

to redirect the audio signal without resampling using Sound-Flower[2], and a custom program to record the time when each word was generated by the ASR. The final transcript speed was 71.0 wpm (SD=23.7) with a latency of 7.9 seconds.

3.3 Transcript Evaluation

We recruited 48 students for the study over two weeks to participate in the study and evenly recruited both deaf and hearing students, male amd female. Twenty-one of the of them were deaf, four of them were hard of hearing and the remainder, twenty-four, were hearing. There were 21 females and 27 males, which reflects the gender balance on campus. Their ages ranged from 18 to 29 and all were students at RIT, ranging from first year undergraduates to graduate students. We recruited through flyers and word of mouth on the campus. We asked students to contact and schedule through email appointment. All students were reimbursed for their participation. All deaf participants were asked if they used visual accommodations for their classes, and all of them answered affirmatively.

Testing was conducted in a quiet room with a 22 inch flat-screen monitor as shown in Figure 3. Each person was directed to an online web page that explained the purpose of the study. Next, the students were asked to complete a short demographic questionnaire in order to determine eligibility for the test and asked for informed consent. Then they were asked to view a short 30 second introductory video to familiarize themselves with the process of viewing transcripts. Then the students were asked to watch a series of transcripts on the same lecture, each lasting two minutes. Each clip was labeled Transcript 1, 2 and 3, and were presented in a ran-

domized order without any accompanying audio. The total time for the study was about 15 minutes.

After the participant completed watching all three video clips of the real-time transcripts, they were asked to complete a questionnaire with three questions. The first question asked "How easy was it to follow transcript 1?". In response to the question, the participants were presented with a a Likert scale that ranged from 1 through 5, with 1 being "Very hard" to 5 being "very easy". The second question asked "How easy was it to follow transcript 2?". In response to this question, participants were prompted to answer using a similar Likert scale response as in question 1. The third question was "How easy was it to follow transcript 3?". In response to this question, participants were promoted with a similar, corresponding Likert scale response to question 1 and 2. Then participants were asked to answer in their own words in response to the questions that asked participants for their thoughts about following the lecture through the transcripts; the first video transcript contained the captions created by the stenographer. The answers were open ended and many participants gave great feedback. The second video transcript contained the captions created by the automatic speech recognition software, in this case, Dragon Naturally Speaking v. 11. The third and final video transcript contained the captions created by the crowd captioning process.

4. DISCUSSION

For the user preference questions, there was a significant difference between the Likert score distribution between Transcripts 1 and 2 or 2 and 3. In general, participants found it hard to follow Transcript 2 (automatic speech recognition); the median rating for it was a 1, i.e.,"Very hard". The qualitative comments indicated that many of them thought the transcript was too choppy and had too much latency. In contrast, participants found it easier to follow either Transcript 1 (professional captions) or 3 (crowd captions). Overall both deaf and hearing students had similar preference ratings for both crowd captions and professional captions (CART),

²http://code.google.com/p/soundflower/

in the absence of audio. While the overall responses for crowd captions was slightly higher at 3.15 (SD=1.06) than for professional captions (CART) at 3.08 (SD=1.24), the differences were not statistically significant ($\chi^2 = 32.52$, $p < 0.001$). There was a greater variation in preference ratings for professional captions than for crowd captions. When we divided the students into deaf and hearing subgroups and looked at their Likert preference ratings, there was no significant difference between crowd captions and professional captions for deaf students ($\chi^2 = 25.44$, $p < 0.001$). Hearing students as a whole showed significant difference between crowd captions and professional captions ($\chi^2 = 19.56$, $p = 0.07$).

The qualitative comments from hearing students revealed that transcript flow as shown in Figure 4, latency as shown in Figure 5 and speed were significant factors in their preference ratings. For example, one hearing student had the following comment for professional captioned real-time transcript: *"The words did not always seem to form coherent sentences and the topics seemed to change suddenly as if there was no transition from one topic to the next. This made it hard to understand so I had to try and reread it quickly"*. In contrast, for crowd captioning, the same student commented : *"I feel this was simpler to read mainly because the words even though some not spelled correctly or grammatically correct in English were fairly simple to follow. I was able to read the sentences about there being two sub-trees, the left and the right and that there are two halves of the algorithm attempted to be explained. The word order was more logical to me so I didn't need to try and reread it"*. On the other hand for the professional captions, a deaf student commented: *"It was typing slowly so I get distracted and I looked repeatedly from the beginning"*; and for crowd captions, the deaf student commented: *"It can be confusing so slow respsone on typing, so i get distracted on other paragraphs just to keep myself focused"*.

Overall, hearing participants appeared to like the slower and more smooth flowing crowd transcript rather than the faster and less smooth captions. Deaf participants appear to accept all transcripts. It may be that the deaf students are more used to bad and distorted inpurt and more easily skip or tolerate errors by picking out key words, but this or any other explanation requires further research. These considerations would seem to be particularly important in educational contexts where material may be captioned with the intention of making curriculum-based information available to learners.

A review of the literature on captioning comprehension and readability shows this result is consistent with findings from Burnham et al. [5], who found that there was no reduction in comprehension of text reduction for deaf adults, whether good or poor at reading. The same study also found that slower caption rates tended to assist comprehension of more proficient readers, but this was not the case for less proficient readers. This may explain why hearing students significantly preferred crowd captions over professional captions, whereas deaf students did not show any significant preference for crowd captions over professional captions. Since deaf students on average have a wider range of reading skills [10], it appears slower captions for the less proficient readers in this group does not help. Based on the qualitative comments, it appears that these students preferred to have a smoother word flow and to keep latency low rather than to slow down the real-time text. In fact,

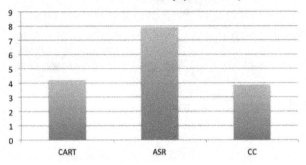

Figure 5: A graph of the latencies for each transcript (professional, automatic speech recognition and crowd). CART and Crowd Captions have reasonable latencies of less than 5 seconds, which allows students to keep up with class lectures, but not consistently participate in class questions and answers, or other interactive class discussion.

many of the less proficient readers as judged by the quality of their typed comments, commented that the captions were too slow. We hypothesize that these students are focusing on key-words and ignore the rest of the text.

5. CONCLUSIONS

Likert ratings showed that hearing students rated crowd captions at or higher than professional captions, while deaf students rated both equally. A summary of qualitative comments on crowd captions suggests that these transcripts are presented at a readable pace, phrasing and vocabulary made more sense and that captioning flow is better than professional captioning or Automatic Speech Recognition.

We hypothesize that this finding is attributable to two factors. The first factor is that the speaking rate typically varies from 175-275 wpm [19], which is faster than the reading rate for captions of around 100-150 wpm [10], especially for dense lectures material. The second factor is that the timing for listening to spoken language is different from the timing for reading written text. Speakers often pause, change rhythm or repeat themselves. The end-result is that the captioning flow is as important as traditional captioning metrics such as coverage, accuracy and speed, if not more. The averaging of multiple caption streams into an aggregate stream appears to smooth the flow of text as perceived by the reader, as compared with the flow of text in professional captioning or ASR captions.

We think the crowd captionists are are typing the most important information to them, in other words, dropping the unimportant bits and this happens to better match the reading rate. As the captionists are working simultaneously, it can be regarded as a group vote for the most important information. A group of non-expert captionists appear to better able to collectively catch, understand and summarize as well as a single expert captioner. The constraint of the maximum average reading real-time transcript word flow reduces the need for making a trade off between coverage and speed; beyond a speed of about 140 words per minute [10], coverage and flow becomes more important. In other words, assuming a limiting reading rate (especially for dense lecture information), the comments show that students prefer to condensed material so that they can maintain reading speed/flow to keep up with the instructor.

One of the key advantages to using human captionists instead of ASR is the types of errors which are generated system when it fails to correctly identify a word. Instead of random text, humans are capable of inferring meaning, and selecting from possible words which make sense in the context of the speech. We anticipate this will make quick-Caption more usable than automated systems even in cases where there may be minimal difference in measures such as accuracy and coverage.

We propose a new crowd captioning approach that recruits classmates and others to transcribe and share classroom lectures. Classmates are likely to be more familiar with the topic being discussed, and to be used to the speaker's style. We show that readers prefer this approach. This approach is less expensive and is more inclusive, scalable, flexible and easier to deploy than traditional captioning, especially when used with mobile devices. This approach can scale in terms of classmates and vocabulary, and can enable efficient retrieval and viewing on a wide range of devices. The crowd captioning transcript, as an average of multiple streams from all captionists, is likely to be more consistent and have less surprise than any single captionist. As each captionist has to type less, the captions are also more likely have less delay, all of which reduce the likelihood of information loss by the reader. This approach can be viewed as a parallel note-taking that benefits all students who get an high coverage, high quality reviewable transcript that none of them could normally type on their own.

We have introduced the idea of real-time non-expert captioning, and demonstrated through coverage experiments that this is a promising direction for future research. We have shown that groups of non-experts can achieve more timely captions than a professional captionist, that we can encourage them to focus on specific portions of the speech to improve global coverage, and that it is possible to recombine partial captions and effectively tradeoff coverage and precision [15]. We show that deaf and hearing students alike prefer crowd captions over ASR because the students find the errors easier to backtrack on and correct in real-time. Most people cannot tolerate an error rate of 10% or more as errors can completely change the meaning of the text. Human operators who correct the errors on-the-fly make these systems more viable, opening the field to operators with far less expertise and the ability to format, add punctuation, and indicate speaker changes. Until the time ASR becomes a mature technology that can handle all kinds of speech and environments, human assistance in captioning will continue to be an essential ingredient in speech transcription.

We also notice that crowd captions appear to have more accurate technical vocabulary than either ASR or professional captions. Crowd captioning outperforms ASR in many real settings. Non-expert real-time captioning has not yet, and might not ever, replace professional captionists or ASR, but it shows lot of promise. The reason is that a single captioner cannot optimize their dictionary fully, as they have to to adapt to various teachers, lecture content and their context. Classmates are much better positioned to adapt to all of these, and fully optimize their typing, spelling, and flow. Crowd captioning enables the software and users to effectively adapt to a variety of environments that a single captionist and dictionary cannot handle.

6. FUTURE WORK

The process of reading real-time captions shows that not all errors are equally important, and human perceptual errors of the dialog is much easier for users to understand and adapt to than ASR errors. Also unlike ASR, crowd captioning can handle poor dialog audio or untrained speech, e.g. multiple speakers, meetings, panels, audience questions. Using this knowledge, we hope to be able to encourage crowd captioning workers to leverage their understanding of the context that content is spoken in to capture the segments with the highest information content.

Non-expert captionists and ASR make different types of errors. Specifically, humans generally type words that actually appear in the audio, but miss many words. Automatic speech recognition often misunderstands which word was spoken, but generally gets then number of words spoken nearly correct. One approach may be to use ASR as a stable underlying signal for real-time transcription, and use non-expert transcription to replace incorrect words. This may be particularly useful when transcribing speech that contains jargon terms. A non-expert captionist could type as many of these terms as possible, and could fit them into the transcription provided by ASR where appropriate.

ASR usually cannot provide a reliable confidence level of their own accuracy. On the other hand, the crowd usually has a better sense of their own accuracy. One approach to leverage this would be to provide an indication of the confidence the system has in recognition accuracy. This could be done in many ways, for example through colors. This would enable the users to pick their own confidence threshold.

It would be useful to add automatic speech recognition as a complementary source of captions because its errors are generally independent of non-expert captionists. This difference means that matching captions input by captionists and ASR can likely be used with high confidence, even in the absence of many layers of redundant captionists or ASR systems. Future work also seeks to integrate multiple sources of evidence, such as N-gram frequency data, into a probabilistic framework for transcription and ordering. Estimates of worker latency or quality can also be used to weight the input of multiple contributors in order to reduce the amount of erroneous input from lazy or malicious contributors, while not penalizing good ones. This is especially important if crowd services such as Amazon's Mechanical Turk are to be used to support these systems in the future. The models currently used to align and merge sets of partial captions from contributors are in their infancy, and will improve as more work is done in this area. As crowd captioning improves, students can begin to rely more on readable captions being made available at any time for any speaker.

The benefits of captioning by local or remote workers presented in this paper aims to further motivate the use of crowd captioning. We imagine a deaf or hard of hearing person eventually being able to capture speech with her cellphone anywhere and have captions returned to her within a few seconds latency. She may use this to follow along in a lecture for which a professional captionist was not requested, to participate in informal conversation with peers after class, or enjoy a movie or other live event that lacks closed captioning. These use cases currently beyond the scope of ASR, and their serendipitous nature precludes pre-arranging a professional captionist. Moreover, ASR and professional captioning systems do not have a consistent way of adding appropriate punctuation from lecture speech in real-time, resulting in captions that are very difficult to read and understand [9, 16].

A challenge in developing new methods for real-time captioning is that it can be difficult to quantify whether the captions have been successful. As demonstrated here, usability and readability of real-time captioning is dependent on much more than just Word Error Rate, involving at a minimum naturalness of errors, regularity, latency and flow. These concepts are difficult to capture automatically, which makes it difficult to make reliable comparisons across different approaches. Designing metrics that can be universally applied will improve our ability to make progress in systems for real-time captioning.

7. ACKNOWLEDGMENTS

We thank our participants for their time and comments in evaluating the captions, and to both the expert and non-expert captionists for transforming the lecture audio to visually accessible captions. This work was supported in part by a NTID Innovation Grant.

8. REFERENCES

[1] Ncra certifications (real-time captioning), 2012. http://www.ncra.org/.

[2] Y. C. Beatrice Liem, Haoqi Zhang. An iterative dual pathway structure for speech-to-text transcription. In *Proceedings of the 3rd Workshop on Human Computation (HCOMP '11)*, HCOMP '11, 2011.

[3] M. S. Bernstein, J. R. Brandt, R. C. Miller, and D. R. Karger. Crowds in two seconds: Enabling realtime crowd-powered interfaces. In *Proceedings of the 24th annual ACM symposium on User interface software and technology*, UIST '11, page to appear, New York, NY, USA, 2011. ACM.

[4] J. P. Bigham, C. Jayant, H. Ji, G. Little, A. Miller, R. C. Miller, R. Miller, A. Tatarowicz, B. White, S. White, and T. Yeh. Vizwiz: nearly real-time answers to visual questions. In *Proceedings of the 23nd annual ACM symposium on User interface software and technology*, UIST '10, pages 333–342, New York, NY, USA, 2010. ACM.

[5] D. Burnham, G. Leigh, W. Noble, C. Jones, M. Tyler, L. Grebennikov, and A. Varley. Parameters in television captioning for deaf and hard-of-hearing adults: Effects of caption rate versus text reduction on comprehension. *Journal of Deaf Studies and Deaf Education*, 13(3):391–404, 2008.

[6] X. Cui, L. Gu, B. Xiang, W. Zhang, and Y. Gao. Developing high performance asr in the ibm multilingual speech-to-speech translation system. In *Acoustics, Speech and Signal Processing, 2008. ICASSP 2008. IEEE International Conference on*, pages 5121 –5124, 31 2008-april 4 2008.

[7] L. B. Elliot, M. S. Stinson, D. Easton, and J. Bourgeois. College Students Learning With C-Print's Education Software and Automatic Speech Recognition. In *American Educational Research Association Annual Meeting*, New York, NY, 2008.

[8] M. B. Fifield. Realtime remote online captioning: An effective accommodation for rural schools and colleges.

In *Instructional Technology And Education of the Deaf Symposium*, 2001.

[9] A. Gravano, M. Jansche, and M. Bacchiani. Restoring punctuation and capitalization in transcribed speech. In *Acoustics, Speech and Signal Processing, 2009. ICASSP 2009. IEEE International Conference on*, pages 4741 –4744, april 2009.

[10] C. Jensema. Closed-captioned television presentation speed and vocabulary. *American Annals of the Deaf*, 141(4):284 – 292, 1996.

[11] C. J. Jensema, R. Danturthi, and R. Burch. Time spent viewing captions on television programs. *American Annals of the Deaf*, 145(5):464–468, 2000.

[12] R. Kheir and T. Way. Inclusion of deaf students in computer science classes using real-time speech transcription. In *Proceedings of the 12th annual SIGCSE conference on Innovation and technology in computer science education*, ITiCSE '07, pages 261–265, New York, NY, USA, 2007. ACM.

[13] W. Lasecki, K. Murray, S. White, R. C. Miller, and J. P. Bigham. Real-time crowd control of existing interfaces. In *Proceedings of the 24th annual ACM symposium on User interface software and technology*, UIST '11, page To Appear, New York, NY, USA, 2011. ACM.

[14] W. S. Lasecki and J. P. Bigham. Online quality control for real-time captioning. In *Proceedings of the 14th International ACM SIGACCESS Conference on Computers and Accessibility*, ASSETS '12, 2012.

[15] W. S. Lasecki, C. Miller, A. Sadilek, A. Abumoussa, D. Borrello, R. Kushalnagar, and J. P. Bigham. Realtime captioning by groups of non experts. In *Proceedings of the 25th ACM UIST Symposium*, UIST '12, 2012.

[16] Y. Liu, E. Shriberg, A. Stolcke, D. Hillard, M. Ostendorf, and M. Harper. Enriching speech recognition with automatic detection of sentence boundaries and disfluencies. *Audio, Speech, and Language Processing, IEEE Transactions on*, 14(5):1526 –1540, sept. 2006.

[17] T. Matthews, S. Carter, C. Pai, J. Fong, and J. Mankoff. In *Proceeding of the 8th International Conference on Ubiquitous Computing*, pages 159–176, Berlin, 2006. Springer-Verlag.

[18] R. E. Mitchell. How many deaf people are there in the United States? Estimates from the Survey of Income and Program Participation. *Journal of deaf studies and deaf education*, 11(1):112–9, Jan. 2006.

[19] S. J. Samuels and P. R. Dahl. Establishing appropriate purpose for reading and its effect on flexibility of reading rate. *Journal of Educational Psychology*, 67(1):38 – 43, 1975.

[20] M. Wald. Using automatic speech recognition to enhance education for all students: Turning a vision into reality. In *Frontiers in Education, 2005. FIE '05. Proceedings 35th Annual Conference*, page S3G, oct. 2005.

[21] M. Wald. Creating accessible educational multimedia through editing automatic speech recognition captioning in real time. *Interactive Technology and Smart Education*, 3(2):131–141, 2006.

Web Accessibility as a Side Effect

John T. Richards
IBM T. J. Watson Research Center
Hawthorne, NY 10532
and University of Dundee, Scotland

ajtr@us.ibm.com

Kyle Montague, Vicki L. Hanson
School of Computing
University of Dundee
Dundee, Scotland

{kylemontague,vlh}@computing.dundee.ac.uk

ABSTRACT

This paper explores evidence for the conjecture that improvements in Web accessibility have arisen, in part, as side effects of changes in Web technology and associated shifts in the way Web pages are designed and coded. Drawing on an earlier study of Web accessibility trends over the past 14 years, it discusses several possible indirect contributors to improving accessibility including the use of new browser capabilities to create more sophisticated page layouts, a growing concern with improved page rank in search results, and a shift toward cross-device content design. Understanding these examples may inspire the creation of additional technologies with incidental accessibility benefits.

Categories and Subject Descriptors

H.5.2 **Information Interfaces and Presentation**: User Interfaces – *Input devices and strategies.* K.4.2 **Computers and Society**: Social Issues – *Assistive technologies for persons with disabilities.* K.4.2 **Computers and Society**: Social Issues – *Handicapped persons / special needs.* K.5.2 **Legal Aspects of Computing:** Governmental Issues – *Regulation*

General Terms

Experimentation, Human Factors, Measurement, Standardization.

Keywords

Web accessibility.

1. INTRODUCTION

The W3C's Web Accessibility Initiative (WAI) and various government regulations highlight the importance of Web accessibility [23]. Web authoring tools now include accessibility support and computer science curricula contain information about accessibility. It might be expected that these changes would have improved, and would continue to improve, Web accessibility.

But such accessibility improvements have not been readily apparent. Studies covering different time periods from many countries and across many types of sites have repeatedly found low levels of compliance.

In recent work [13] we examined progress on Web accessibility over the 14 years from 1999 to 2012, the longest period studied to date. Our analysis of 1,174 high-traffic and government webpages

uncovered growing adherence to some, but not all, accessibility criteria. We suggested that some improvements in accessibility conformance might be due to changes in design and coding practices that improved accessibility as a side effect.

The current paper explores new evidence in support of this possibility examining three trends over the past 14 years that might have indirectly contributed to these improvements. These include: (1) the exploitation of new browser capabilities to create more sophisticated page layouts; (2) a growing concern with improved page rank in search results; and (3) and a shift toward cross-device content design.

2. BACKGROUND

The WAI has developed three sets of guidelines to address the needs of website developers, the creators of software that renders content, and the creators of Web authoring tools. For the present research, the focus is on the Web Content Accessibility Guidelines (WCAG) and the development of accessible Web content [24]. Intended to be used by website developers, these guidelines specify techniques for creating content that will be accessible for disabled individuals either directly or through the use of assistive devices.

The WCAG 1.0 guidelines were published in May 1999. For these guidelines, severity levels were assigned, with checkpoints being classified as priority 1, 2, or 3. Failure to comply with priority 1 checkpoints would be the most critical since this would mean that some groups of disabled users would be completely unable to use that portion of the website.

Soon after the publication of these guidelines, reports began emerging of low compliance, even for priority 1 checkpoints. These studies reported accessibility problems in countries worldwide [7] [15] [17] [21] and across sites as varied as commercial, government, healthcare, culture, and higher education [3] [6] [20] [22] [28]. Furthermore, little evidence of improvement over time could be found, at least over the six years from 1997 to 2002 studied in [10], and the years from 2000 to 2005 studied in [20]. [18] found an actual *decrease* in accessibility across a variety of site types when comparing 2002 and 2003.

Such findings of low compliance with accessibility guidelines were present even following the introduction of government regulations specifying accessibility requirements for government websites. Lack of awareness about accessibility issues by those responsible for websites and a lack of clear guidance for developers are among the reasons cited for low conformance [16] [20].

The WCAG 2.0 guidelines were published in December 2008. The underlying rationale for priority 1, 2, and 3 checkpoints was reconsidered as all criteria (even those in priority 3 checkpoints) can be critical for some disabled users. WCAG 2.0, moved somewhat away from the notion of priority and focused, instead, on overall compliance levels. Level A is always required for a site to be accessible, while level AA and AAA are higher (more stringent) criteria.

WCAG 2.0 guidelines were also created with the explicit goal of all Success Criteria (SCs) being testable, either automatically and with complete reliability ("machine testable") or by knowledgeable humans ("human testable"). A number of automated accessibility checkers exist. Full compliance testing, however, also requires human checking. Human testable criteria have a goal of 80% reliability, with 80% of knowledgeable human evaluators agreeing on conformance. Recent studies, however, have shown that this goal may be elusive. Studies with both novice and experienced evaluators have found agreement far below the target [2] [4].

As with the previous guidelines, indications of low compliance with WCAG 2.0 have emerged [19]. It remains difficult, however, to develop a clear view of accessibility compliance over the entire time period covered by WCAG 1.0 and WCAG 2.0. Studies have used different evaluation techniques, examined different sites and success criteria, and studied relatively short time intervals (as short as two years).

3. PREVIOUS RESEARCH

To address these limitations, Hanson and Richards [13] examined compliance with WCAG guidelines over the 14 years since the introduction of WCAG 1.0 for both high traffic and government websites from two countries that have regulations related to Web accessibility. Their experimental home page corpus was assembled from the top 60 sites in the UK and the US, based on the Alexa [1] traffic ratings as of April 19, 2011. Sites included in *both* the UK and US top 60 (e.g., www.wikipedia.org) were only included once. This yielded a set of 88 top sites. Another 20 government sites, 10 each from the UK and US, were added to this list, balanced between the two countries in terms of website focus (e.g. the departments of education for the two countries, the departments of justice for the two countries, and so on). The Wayback Machine Internet Archive [27] was used to retrieve the home page of each of the resulting 108 sites for the years 1999 through 2010. For each site, the first available instance of the home page for each year (beginning with the January 1 calendar date) was used for the corpus. Home pages for 2011 and 2012 were captured directly from the sites on May 4, 2011, and January 1, 2012. Of course, not all sites existed or had a page archived for all 14 years. The final corpus consisted of a total of 943 home pages for top sites and 231 pages for government sites. Additional details, including a list of sites in the corpus and any missing years in the archive, are given in [13].

In general, Hanson and Richards expected high traffic "top sites", which tend to adopt new standards and recommendations more rapidly than small, less highly frequented sites [5] [14], and government websites (especially government websites from two countries with well established accessibility policies), would provide the best evidence for improvements in accessibility compliance if such improvements existed.

Improvements were, in fact found. Looking, for example, at alternative text descriptions for images – a very well known criterion that is both easily implemented and readily tested – they found a moderate linear trend for improved compliance. By 2012, 44% of content images (defined for these purposes as having both a width and height greater than 32 pixels) on top sites, and 62% of content images on government sites, had compliant alt text. This is still lower than one might hope for, especially for the government sites.

Examining the nature of alt tag errors on the non-compliant images suggested an *intention* on the part of developers to comply with the criterion but an incomplete understanding of *how* to comply. For content images, missing alt attributes declined over the years. However, alt attributes set to an empty string became proportionally greater. For decorative images (defined as those having either a width or height less than 8 pixels), errors over the years were increasingly of the form of *non*-empty alt attribute text (which would be needlessly read aloud by a screen reader). While a more subtle error than an empty alt text string on a content image, this again suggests a failure to understand the intent of the guideline.

Especially intriguing findings emerged in the course of this research with respect to the possible relationship between accessibility compliance and other factors. Nearly all the sites, for example, complied with the accessibility guideline to include a page title. A title allows the page to be identified in a collection of browser tabs or a set of browser windows, may contribute to page rank in search results, and, importantly, is the title given to the description of the page in a search result set (a well-crafted title making it more likely that users will click through to the site itself). Given these non-accessibility reasons for having a title, Hanson and Richards wondered whether the nearly universal accessibility compliance for this criterion was merely a side effect.

Another potential example of incidental reasons for improved compliance was found in the increasing use of headings to structure page content. Screen readers support rapid skipping between headings to find content of interest. This is in addition to the rapid skipping to the main content provided by skip navigation links. Skip navigation was present in around 70% of the government websites in the corpus starting in 2007 but significantly less prevalent in top sites with only about 20% having this in 2012. Headings, on the other hand, were much more common with government sites having them on 90% of home pages in 2012 and top sites having them on 87% of home pages. Headings, of course, provide a powerful technique for *visually* structuring content, especially when combined with CSS. It seemed reasonable to suppose that *this* has driven their widespread use with increased accessibility being a side effect.

Additional clues to the accessibility benefits of changes in coding practices came from the analysis of decorative images (used as spacers), tables, and style sheets as methods of controlling page layout. It was noted that the use of decorative images and tables decreased over the years, while the use of CSS increased dramatically. This is shown in Figure 1 for top sites (government sites showing a similar pattern). In this figure, pages with "clean" layout used *only* CSS.

Decorative image alt tag errors will, of course, decrease as the use of decorative images decreases. And the accessibility benefits of using style sheets, especially as an alternative to tables for layout, will generally accrue whether the use of style sheets is motivated by accessibility concerns or, as is more likely, a desire to have more control over page layout.

These findings suggested that at least some accessibility improvements might, in fact, be side effects of changes in coding practices and the desire to improve webpage design and website prominence. In the work reported here, we investigate this further.

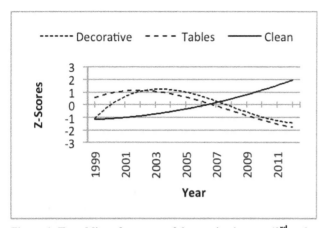

Figure 1. Trend lines for usage of decorative images (3rd order polynomial), tables (2nd order polynomial), and clean CSS layout (2nd order polynomial) for top sites (from [13]).

4. BENEFICIAL WEB TRENDS

We began the research reported in this paper by reviewing multiple Web technology changes since 1999 that might yield beneficial accessibility side effects. Several promising changes surfaced including: (1) the use of new browser features allowing increasingly sophisticated designs while also contributing to the creation of increasingly semantic markup; (2) greater attention to improved page rank in search results generating more indexable and, hence, more navigable structure; and (3) a shift from fixed to relative encodings better supporting multi-device content delivery.

To better understand these potential contributors, our current research supplemented the earlier machine analyses in [13] with detailed manual inspection of pages drawn from four representative websites within the corpus; two government, one popular news media, and one large scale e-commerce website. All but one of these sites had home pages sampled in each of the 14 years with the e-commerce site only missing 1999. In what follows, we report on key observations from this manual inspection, and present additional machine analyses of the full corpus not reported in [13].

4.1 New Browser Features

Web browsers play a pivotal role in mediating between *Web standards bodies* and *Web content developers*, determining, in large measure, what *end users* experience. The interplay between Web standards and Web browsers has been a recurring struggle to reach temporary equilibrium between standards conformance and browser differentiation as browsers compete against one another for market share [11]. In the early years of the Web it was a common occurrence to navigate to a website only to be told that the page was best viewed using a browser other than the one being used. This behavior continued until 2001, which saw the launch of Internet Explorer (IE) 6. By then, IE had captured the majority share of the Web browser market [25] and constituted a defacto standard.

4.1.1 CSS Replacing Layout Tables

With little threat from other browsers, IE had less incentive to improve compliance with emerging Web standards. In particular CSS support, first proposed as a W3C recommendation in 1996 (level 1) and again in 1998 (level 2), was not rapidly incorporated. As a result, developers were forced to find alternative means of creating the complex layouts desired. Nested tables were often

used for this. An example of the nested table approach from one of our manually inspected websites is shown here:

```
<table border=0 cellpadding=0
cellspacing=0 width=100><tbody>
<tr valign=top><td colspan=2>
    <table border=0 cellpadding=0
    cellspacing=0 width=100>
    <tr valign=top><td colspan=2>
    <b><font size="2" face="Arial,
    Helvetica, sans-serif" color="#666666">
    Text to display</font></b>
</td></tr>…
```

This way of controlling page layout started to lose traction in late 2003, coinciding with the release of Safari in 2003, and Firefox in 2004, which better supported Web standards for CSS. While our manually inspected websites continued to use tables for layout for several years beyond this, the use of deeply nested tables decreased. The above markup was used in one of the government sites from 2002-2007, using a table to create a visual list of text and links. Then, with the redesign of the website in 2007, the markup was changed to make use of `div` containers holding unordered lists. This technique helped to ensure that the content would render similarly across browsers, regardless of their level or support for standards. An example of this from the same website is shown here:

```
<table border=0 cellpadding=0 cellspacing=0
width=100><tbody>
<tr valign=top><td colspan=2>
    <div id="leftbox">
    <ul>
        <li>Text to display</li>
        …
    </ul>
    </div>…
```

With the growing adoption of additional browsers, developers were increasingly required to test their pages against several underlying rendering engines (gecko, webkit, mshtml). The separation of HTML content from CSS style was a useful technique for managing these different concerns and this clearly increased over the 14 years of our investigation. In particular, we found an increase in the logical grouping of elements and the reuse of `class` styles, and a decrease in the instances of individual text elements wrapped with `font` and other appearance-determining tags. The cleaner factoring of presentation styles also supported developers in more easily embedding conditional statements within the markup to cause each browser to select the most appropriate CSS, making page rendering more consistent across browsers. Our manual inspection revealed that a number of pages were constructed using HTML and CSS hacks to target presentational attributes to specific rendering engines, browsers, and even browser versions e.g. IE 5, 6, 7, 8, and 9. Our news website, for example, made use of IE specific HTML conditional comments to import specific style sheets for each version of IE using the markup shown here:

```
<!--[if GTE IE 5]>
<style type="text/css" media="screen">
@import'/home/style/ie5_up.2.5.css';
</style><![endif]-->
```

```
<!--[if IE 5]>
<style type="text/css" media="screen">
@import'/home/style/ie5.2.2.css';
</style><![endif]-->
```

The first conditional would cause IE browsers that are greater than or equal to version 5 to import the named CSS, and the second conditional would import another CSS file with specific properties for IE 5 alone. Additional CSS hacks were used to include styles for Firefox, Chrome, Safari, and Opera.

The primary objective of these hacks was to create consistent cross-browser visual appearance. But by encouraging the factoring of styles into separate style sheets, the trend helped improve overall accessibility, first, by making pages easier to parse and re-render with assistive technology, and, second, by making it easier for *user* style sheets to control page layout and presentation (e.g., for those with partial vision or dyslexia).

4.1.2 CSS Replacing Image Splicing and Image Replacement

Web *content* developers share the same desire for differentiation as that noted above for Web *browser* developers. For many, it is not enough to simply provide well-crafted information. The *presentation* must also be appealing to users. One recurring approach to enhancing presentation over the 14 years of our study has been through the use of non-default typography and rich print design techniques such as *kerning* or *tracking* in which the spacing between the characters within a text string is adjusted to achieve greater visual appeal. The goal is straightforward but the method used to adjust the spacing can yield content that is indecipherable for screen reader users. The correct method to produce such typography effects is to use the *letter-spacing* attribute, available to developers since the release of CSS version 1. One *incorrect* method from an accessibility perspective, taken from our news website, is to increase letter spacing by adding non-breaking spaces into words, e.g. S E R V I C E S for which the corresponding markup is:

```
S E R V I C E S
```

While this achieves the desired visual effect, it would result in the word being read aloud by a screen reader as a series of individual characters.

Another variant on this style of visual markup is likely related to the use of visual development tools such as Photoshop. Our manual inspection yielded clues suggesting that such visual tools were often used. Several of our sites appeared to be using a technique known as image splicing where interfaces are first created as static images, then dissected into individual interface components, and finally, composed using tables. This typically manifests as markup such as that shown here (note the image names such as 'home_off_r1_c1.jpg' referring to row 1 and column 1 of the image splice):

```
<table border="0" cellpadding="0" cellspacing="0"
width="751">
    <tr valign="top">
        <td colspan=2>
            <A href="#content"><img name="a1"
src="images/header3/home_off_r1_c1.jpg"
border="0" alt="Skip to Content"
width="41" height="2"></a>
            <a href=" text/index.html"><img
name="a2" alt="Text Only"
```

```
src="images/header3/home_off_r1_c2.jpg"
border="0" width="43" height="2"></a>
            <A href="#quicksearch"><img
src="images/header3/home_off_r1_c3.jpg"
name="a3" alt="Go to Search" border="0"
width="40" height="2"></a>
<img src="images/header3/home_off_r1_c4.jpg"
alt="" width="627" height="2">
        </td>
    </tr>
…</table>
```

This method allowed developers to create designs that cannot be easily achieved with markup alone. Other techniques included scalable Inman Flash Replacement (sIFR), and server side fonts, these two methods becoming available in 2004 and 2008.

Image replacement, a related technique, is when developers use an image-editing package to create the (typically highly-stylized) text and save it as an image. This text image can then be added to an HTML page as an image element or image link, giving the visual appearance of text with rich and otherwise unavailable fonts. Unfortunately, screen readers are unable to read the text from these images, and require developers to provide alt text to describe the image. As noted in Hanson and Richards [13], images continue to lack alt text to a surprising degree. So relying on content authors to create alt text for text embodied as images is not a surefire bet. Other drawbacks of this technique include the lack of clean scalability (since the image is rendered at a particular resolution and clarity suffers from pixelization when its containing page is zoomed or magnified) and the burdensome requirement to create new images (and the associated alt text) every time the text is changed – a more time consuming process then simply replacing one text string with another.

Our manual inspection showed that all of the websites made use of image replacement during the first few years. This was abandoned by 2004 for all but the e-commerce site. During these periods we also noticed missing, or poorly described alt text for many text images, but this gradually improved up to 2008 when all the sites finally began using CSS to produce stylized text. Interestingly, our inspection also found that one of the government websites started using CSS background images to add image buttons to the page, still retaining the text version within the `div` container but using CSS to hide the text from visual presentation.

4.1.3 XHTML Replacing HTML

Our manually inspected pages suggested the presence of another browser feature associated with potentially improved accessibility; over time, more pages specified their `doctype` as XHTML, a trend strongly confirmed within our larger corpus. Looking over all sites, XHTML documents first started appearing in 2002, and grew for top sites to 47.7% of pages by 2012. For government sites, the growth appeared to be more pronounced, attaining 70% coverage by 2012. While the difference between site types did not reach significance (t(26)=.67, p>.05, two-tailed), the increase over time for both types of sites was quite strong (for top sites R^2=.872, for government sites R^2=.903).

Our more detailed manual inspection found, however, that while sites increasingly declared an XHTML `doctype`, they continued to produce markup in the HTML format and used the MIME-type "text/html" (a common failure, as discovered by Goer in a study of 119 XHTML websites, in which only one site was fully compliant with the XHTML specification [8]). This serves as a useful reminder that standards conformance is generally complex and the proper implementation is often misunderstood, even when an intention to conform exists.

4.1.4 Link Title Attributes

Another common misunderstanding surfaced in our analysis of `title` attributes on links. Browsers have come to make use `title` attributes, popping up a tooltip under the mouse pointer to provide (in the ideal case) more information about where a link will go. They are also useful to screen reader users in that this additional information is read aloud. Overall, we see evidence of increased use of `title` attributes over time by both top sites (R^2=.915) and government sites (R^2=.628) with top sites increasing from almost no link titles in 1999 to 9.5% in 2012, and government sites increasing from no link titles in 1999 to 15.2% in 2012 (the difference between top sites and government sites fails to reach statistical significance, $t(26)$=1.86, p>.05, two-tailed).

The accessibility implications of the use of `title` attributes can be highlighted by considering the likely *need* for additional descriptive material based on the nature of the links themselves. Short links, for example, ones with only a single word as the link text such as "here" in the following markup:

```
<a href="www.sitename.com" title="site
description">here</a>
```

and links that are images, especially images without alt tags such as:

```
<a href="www.sitename.com" title="site
description"><img src="image.gif" /></a>
```

are more in need of a useful title, all else being equal, than links having multiple words. This is particularly true if the images are actually of *text* with fancy typography (as discussed above).

Analysis of textual links in our full corpus, split into short (one word) and long (two or more words), shows that short links were more likely to have titles than long links, although this appears limited to top sites (the interaction being significant with $F(1,26)$=8.2, p<.01).

Our manual inspection suggests, however, that while the use of `title` attributes has been increasing, the text provided by them remains somewhat less than ideal. For example, in 2008 one government site provided the following titles for its links:

```
<a href="[link url removed to preserve
anonymity]" title="News">NEWS</a>
```

and

```
<a href="[link url removed to preserve
anonymity]" title="Kids">KIDS</a>
```

The same site goes on to use non-descriptive titles for four embedded media elements, resulting in a screen reader user hearing the title "Click to play video" repeated for each link:

```
<a href="javascript:void(0)" title="Click to
Play Video"
onclick="javascript:popup('/news/.../01/20080107-
7.wm.v.html','394','292')"
onmouseout="window.status=' ';return true"
onmouseover="window.status='Click to Play
Video';return true" target=""><b>
<img src="/news/.../20080107-7_vidbtn68h.jpg"
name="vidbtn" class="homepage-thumb" alt="Play
Video" border="0" align="left">
</b></a>
```

Thus, while our automatic analysis suggests that the increased use of `title` attributes might be improving accessibility, closer inspection reveals that these attributes are being populated with largely redundant information.

For image links, both top sites and government sites show a trend of increasing use of `title` attributes (from 0% to 13.9% for top sites and 0% to 15.8% for government sites). For top sites, the benefit is diminished somewhat by a *reduction* over time in the use of `alt` attributes to describe these images. Government sites show an increased use of `alt` attributes for these images in addition to an increased use of `title` attributes for the links themselves. Government sites also show a reduction in the number of image links possessing neither a `title` nor an `alt` attribute (decreasing from 19.2% to 7.3%). Top sites show no such reduction on this potentially severe accessibility error, one that would force a screen reader user to rely on surrounding context to determine whether an image link should be clicked on.

Our manual inspection again revealed confusion as to how image links should be marked up to support non-visual browsing. Image links should provide a descriptive title attribute for the link itself, and the image should have an alt attribute describing the contents of the image itself (or an empty alt tag for decorative images). We found a common mistake to be using the same text for both `title` and `alt` attributes.

4.2 Search Engine Optimization

A possible accessibility impact of a growing attention to search engine optimization (SEO) was discussed in Section 3 in relation to page titles. Other factors related to SEO are the information richness of alternative text descriptions for non-textual content, the use of title attributes providing a description of link targets, and the use (but not *over* use which can lead to page rank penalization) of appropriate keywords to describe the page.

The Google SEO starter guide [9] describes the importance of providing more descriptive text for links and image alt text to ensure that they can be indexed by the search engine in addition to helping users navigate the content more easily. While we observed a modest improvement over time in the inclusion of alternative text for image links, our manual inspection revealed new issues relating to developers' understanding of the purpose of this attribute. The `alt` tag is meant to provide a textual representation of the image content. However the news, e-commerce, and one of the government websites simply repeated the article titles, or other already provided text. In some cases the text would span two paragraphs, which, in the case of a screen reader user, would be needlessly repetitive. This may reflect a desire to influence page rank by providing more indexable content, or it might be the result of poorly constructed content management systems reusing article variables to automatically populate the `alt` attributes. In either case, the result is less well-structured content that is harder to understand and navigate by screen reader users.

Document keywords such as:

```
<meta name="Keywords" content="radio, tv,
television, internet">
```

have no particular accessibility impact, but they are one of the most obvious ways to influence search engines beyond the number and diversity of inbound links to a page and the page content itself. We examined keyword use over the 14 years of our corpus and found that top sites exhibited a clear trend to more keywords over time (from a mean of 8.9 per page in 1999 to 12.7 by 2012). Government sites, however, showed a trend toward fewer keywords (with a mean of 12.5 per page in 1999 to 4.7 in 2012).

Another area to show changes over the observed years was the increased use of semantic markup. Screen reader software takes advantage of markup semantics to describe page content to visually impaired users in a richer and more meaningful way. When developers neglect to provide the appropriate tags for elements such as headings, lists, and quotations – intermixing content with presentation directives – they not only dilute the clear meaning of the content (possibly impacting search) but also increase the complexity of navigating the page for screen reader users. This can be particularly troublesome when the page contains a large amount of information as found in both our representative news and e-commerce websites.

In our manual inspection we noted many pages that failed to use appropriately semantic markup. From 1999 to 2005, the news website structured its navigation as three separate lists, each with a visible heading and four or more associated list items. The visual headings were given a weightier, larger font to distinguish the three groups, with the list items being stacked beneath them using breaks. This visual appearance was produced using the following (slightly excerpted) markup:

```
<p><font…>World News</font><br />
United Kingdom<br />
Europe<br />
USA<br />
Rest of the world<br/></p>
```

This markup is perfectly valid HTML and produced the desired appearance on all browsers. However, a screen reader's ability to convey the same rich meaning present in the visual rendering of the page is reduced to simply a string of terms: *"World News United Kingdom Europe USA Rest of the world"* with no emphasis on the list heading, and no pauses between the items as they are read aloud. Contrast this with the same content marked up to indicate semantic structure using headings and lists:

```
<h3>World News</h3>
<ul><li>United Kindgom</li>
<li>Europe</li>
<li>USA</li>
<li>Rest of the world</li></ul>
```

A browser is able to present the same visual rendering as the previous version, but when a screen reader is presented with this markup it will output: *"[Heading level 3] World News, [List four items], United Kingdom, Europe, USA, Rest of the world"*, providing overall context, adding pauses between elements to aid comprehension, and giving the user the ability to move quickly between the lists by way of their headings.

In order to maximize the benefit of the header tags from a screen reader perspective, the headings should be logically structured with H1 used for top-level headings, H2 used for sub headings, H3 used for sub-sub headings etc. This structure makes it easier for the screen reader user to skip between the headings when navigating the page, and supports a clearer sense of the content to be expected under a particular heading. These headings are also useful from an SEO perspective, providing the search engine with structural markers for the content found within a page that can be used as keywords for indexing. But while search engines make use of heading tags, the improper ordering of headings poses little to no impact on their indexing of a page.

Our e-commerce site exhibited a lack of sematic markup in its creation of visual headings. From 2000 to 2008 its pages were marked up using combinations of span, font and b tags, to create presentational, but not semantic, structure. We also observed that from 2004 to 2012, key headings were wrapped with

```
<b class='h1'>
```

in a kind of hybrid scheme that allowed the developers to style the visual appearance while still not clearly articulating the semantic structure. This goal could have been achieved more directly using the provided heading tags within HTML along with CSS (with the attendant benefits for screen reader users noted above). The e-commerce site only started using heading tags in 2008 but, curiously, used only H2 and H4, rather than a well-formed hierarchy, and was still using <b class='h1'> for top-level headings. This may have been due to a lack of understanding or a less than full commitment to improving accessibility for all users. Interestingly, the links that made use of the H2 and H4 tags were for products being sold within the e-commerce website suggesting an attempt to improve the indexing of these goods within search engines.

As shown in Table 1 (from [13]), the pages in the full corpus did show a dramatic increase in their use of heading tags over the 14 years studied. Headings also exhibited a fairly deep structure. For top sites, on average, 8.5% of the headings were at level 1, 40.9% were at level 2, and 50.6% were at level 3. Government sites were similar with 9.8% of the headings at level 1, 42.0% at level 2, and 48.2% at level 3.

Table 1. Growth in the use of headings between 1999 and 2012, (from [13]).

Year	Top Sites	Gov Sites
1999	7.5%	18.2%
2000	9.8%	25.0%
2001	7.7%	23.1%
2002	7.8%	13.3%
2003	12.1%	14.3%
2004	23.4%	25.0%
2005	33.3%	47.1%
2006	46.6%	64.7%
2007	61.8%	68.4%
2008	71.4%	84.2%
2009	73.4%	83.3%
2010	77.9%	90.0%
2011	86.4%	90.0%
2012	86.4%	90.0%

Table 2, based on further analysis not reported in [13], shows the distribution of H1, H2, and H3 headings over time (collapsed across top sites and government sites) in the corpus. The shift from a broad but shallow structure to a narrower but deeper structure, and the shift to better balance between H2 and H3 headings, suggests that the hierarchical structure they encode has become more meaningful – and hence, more incidentally useful to screen reader users – over time.

Table 2. Distribution of headings by level over time.

Year	H1	H2	H3
1999	25.0%	6.3%	68.8%
2000	20.8%	8.3%	70.8%
2001	16.7%	8.3%	75.0%
2002	50.0%	12.5%	37.5%
2003	35.3%	38.2%	26.5%
2004	18.7%	30.9%	50.4%
2005	11.5%	34.6%	53.8%
2006	10.1%	37.0%	52.8%
2007	12.7%	41.7%	45.6%
2008	11.5%	45.2%	43.4%
2009	10.0%	43.6%	46.4%
2010	7.5%	40.2%	52.3%
2011	5.4%	39.2%	55.4%
2012	6.6%	41.9%	51.4%
Mean	8.6%	40.7%	50.7%

It is hard to claim increased attention to SEO based on just these results without a much more extensive and detailed analysis of the keywords and header markup. But we know from personal experience as Web content creators, and from the presence of a growing set of SEO consultancies, that SEO concerns loom large for website developers. We suspect, moreover, that a heightened emphasis on factoring accessibility features into page rank – coupled with a clear enunciation of such a policy by major search engine providers – might well have beneficial effects.

4.3 Cross-Device Content Design

Our manual inspection revealed a few techniques and trends that appear to result from attention to cross-*device* in addition to cross-*browser* compatibility. These changes, fueled most recently by the growing use of mobile devices, have the useful side effect of making websites more inherently accessible by making them more automatically adaptable to the characteristics of the rendering device.

One trend we noted in the early years of our sample was that developers were explicitly accommodating growing screen sizes by redesigning pages such that the primary content remained 'above the fold' (i.e., visible without vertical scrolling) while still being consistently rendered across devices. Early designs often adopted the simplest solution to layout consistency through the use of fixed width and height in terms of pixels. By selecting a base resolution to match the average user's screen size, developers could sculpt pages with precision. For displays with higher resolutions, pages would generally center within the screen, maintaining their fixed width and height but at the cost of wasted screen real estate.

Typical screen resolutions [26] for the years 2000 to 2003, 2004 to 2008, and 2009 to 2012 increased from 800x600, to 1024x768, and, then, to larger to larger sizes (most commonly 1280x1024, 1280x800, and 1440x900), with wide screen monitors becoming more popular in recent years.

Our manually inspected websites tracked these changes over time. We also found a trend to move away from fixed pixel values to more fluid sizing using Ems or percentages. This would also improve the ability of some types of adaptation software to adjust textual content to better suit those with limited vision.

For the *smaller* screen sizes commonly found on mobile devices, fixed content sizing has more serious consequences. These include the possible cropping of content and the imposition of a need for either horizontal scrolling or excessive zooming out (to see the larger context) and zooming in to make individual elements legible.

Besides smaller screens, mobile devices tend to have both slower (and more expensive data connections) and slower processors than laptop and desktop machines. This tends to favor the creation of smaller, dynamically loadable content chunks that, in turn, allow for more radical content restructuring (useful for individuals with visual or cognitive disabilities). Page linearization (see [12]) – a very useful technique for people distracted by complex two-dimensional layouts or requiring screen magnifications so large that horizontal scrolling is otherwise needed – is made easier and more flexible by this sort of content modularization.

Although our sample of manually inspected websites is small, our analysis suggests that designers are increasingly considering the range of possible devices that will be used to access their content. This applies to both screen dimensions and interaction modalities. As an example of the latter, we observed support for the scaling of links and other interactive targets for touch-screen devices in our news website in 2012. Such scaling would potentially aid both those with low vision and those with impaired fine motor control.

5. CONCLUSIONS

Earlier research found little evidence for accessibility improvements following the publication of Web accessibility guidelines, the introduction of tool support for accessibility, and the introduction of government accessibility regulations. Hanson and Richards [13], examining website accessibility over the 14 years from 1999 to the present, found that some aspects of accessibility compliance *have* improved. In particular, page titles, image alt text, link titles, and the use of headings and other semantic markup, have shown clear improvements. However, evidence from new manual inspections and new automatic analyses of our full page corpus, raise questions about how much these advances can be attributed to a focus on accessibility per se. The evidence suggests that at least some accessibility improvements have resulted from an exploitation of new browser features to enhance page layout and design, an increased concern for page rank in search results, and changes in coding styles to attain both better cross-browser consistency and cross-device compatibility.

While further research is clearly needed, these results have led us to wonder if future Web technologies could be designed with explicit attention to incidental accessibility benefits. Further enhancements to CSS and the ongoing evolution of the Semantic Web are two areas with clear potential. In addition, changes to search engines to factor accessibility either into the results returned to all users, or the results returned to users with declared accessibility needs, might also productively influence developer behavior. Such side effects may accelerate the creation of a Web that is truly accessible to all.

6. ACKNOWLEDGMENTS

This work was supported by RCUK EP/G066091/1 "RCUK Hub: Inclusion in the Digital Economy" and by Royal Society Wolfson Research Merit Award WM080040 to the third author. We thank Sebastian Stein for comments on ideas in the paper.

7. REFERENCES

[1] Alexa. 2011. http://www.alexa.com/topsites/countries Accessed April 19, 2011.

[2] Alonso, F., Fuertes, J. L., González, and Martínez. L. 2010. On the testability of WCAG 2.0 for beginners. In

Proceedings of the 2010 International Cross Disciplinary Conference on Web Accessibility (W4A '10). ACM, New York, NY, USA, Article 9, 9 pages.

[3] Bigham, J. P., Kaminsky, R. S., Ladner, R. E. Danielsson, O. M., and Hempton, G. L. 2006. WebInSight: making web images accessible. In *Proceedings of ACM SIGACCESS conference on Computers and accessibility* (Assets '06). ACM, New York, NY, USA, 181-188.

[4] Brajnik, G., Yesilada, Y., and Harper, S. 2012. Is accessibility conformance an elusive property? A study of validity and reliability of WCAG 2.0. *ACM Transactions on Accessible Computing (TACCESS), 4, 1*, Article 5.

[5] Chen, A. Q. 2009. Web evolution. *SIGWEB Newsletter Summer*, Article 4 (June 2009), 2 pages.

[6] Davis, J. J. 2002. Disenfranchising the disabled: The inaccessibility of internet-based health information. *Journal of Health Communication, 7(4)*, 355-367.

[7] Disability Rights Commission. 2004. *The Web: Access and inclusion for disabled people.* London: The Stationery Office.

[8] Goer, E. 2003. The XHTML 100. Available at http://www.goer.org/Journal/2003/04/the_xhtml_100.html Accessed May 2, 2012.

[9] Google. 2010. Google search engine optimization starter guide. Retrieved May 3, 2012 from http://static.googleusercontent.com/external_content/untrusted_dlcp/www.google.com/en//webmasters/docs/search-engine-optimization-starter-guide.pdf

[10] Hackett, S., Parmanto, G., and Zeng. X. 2003. Accessibility of Internet websites through time. In *Proceedings of the 6th international ACM SIGACCESS conference on Computers and accessibility (Assets '04).* ACM, New York, NY, USA, 32-39.

[11] Haigh, T. 2008. Protocols for Profit. Web and email technologies as product and infrastructure. In W. Aspray and P. Ceruzzi (eds), *The Internet and American business*, MIT Press, Cambridge, MA.

[12] Hanson, V. L., & Richards, J. T. 2004. A web accessibility service: Update and findings. *Proceedings of the Sixth International ACM Conference on Assistive Technologies, ASSETS 2004.* ACM, New York, NY, USA, 169-176.

[13] Hanson, V. L. and Richards, J. T. Submitted. Progress in website accessibility?

[14] Harper, S. 2008. Web evolution and its importance for support research arguments in Web accessibility. In *Proceedings of Web Science Workshop (WWW2008),* April 21-25, 2008, Beijing, China. ACM.

[15] Hong, S., Katerattanakul, P., Choi, H. R., Kang, Y. S., and Cho, J. 2007. Evaluating government website accessibility: A comparative study. International DSI / Asia and Pacific DSI 2007.

[16] Kelly, B., Sloan, D., Phipps, L., Petrie, H., and Hamilton, F. 2005. Forcing standardization or accommodating diversity? A framework for applying the WCAG in the real world. *In Proceedings of the 2005 International Cross-Disciplinary Workshop on Web Accessibility (W4A) (W4A '05).* ACM, New York, NY, USA, 46-54.

[17] Lazar, J., Beere, P., Greenidge, K., and Nagappa, Y. 2003. Web accessibility in the Mid-Atlantic United States: A study of 50 homepages, *Universal Access in the Information Society*, 331-341.

[18] Lazar, J., and Greenidge, K. 2006. One year older, but not necessarily wiser: Web accessibility trends over time. *Universal Access in the Information Society, 4(4)*, 285-291.

[19] Lazar, J., Wentz, B., Bogdan, M., Clowney, E., Davis, M., Guiffo, J., Gunnarsson, D., Hanks, D., Harris, J., Holt, B., Kitchin, M., Motayne, M., Nzokou, R, Sedaghat, L., and Stern, K. 2011. Potential pricing discrimination due to inaccessible web sites. In P. Campos et al. (Eds.): INTERACT 2011, Part I, LNCS 6946, pp. 108–114.

[20] Loiacono, E. T., Romano, N. C., Jr., and McCoy, S. 2009. The state of corporate website accessibility. *Communications of ACM 52*, 9 (September 2009), 128-132.

[21] Marincu, C., and McMullin, B. 2004. A comparative assessment of Web accessibility and technical standards conformance in four EU states. *First Monday 9(7)* 5 July 2004. Retrieved October 23, 2011 from http://firstmonday.org/htbin/cgiwrap/bin/ojs/index.php/fm/article/view/1160/1080

[22] Petrie, H., King, N., Hamilton, F., and Weisen, M. 2005. The accessibility of museum websites: Results from an English investigation and international comparison. *Proceedings of HCI International. Volume 8 - Universal Access in HCI: Exploring New Dimensions of Diversity.* Las Vegas, NV. July 22 – 27, 2005. Mira Digital Publishing.

[23] W3C. 2011. Web accessibility initiative (WAI). http://www.w3.org/WAI/ Accessed March 1, 2012.

[24] W3C. 2011. Web content accessibility guidelines (WCAG) overview. http://www.w3.org/WAI/intro/wcag.php Accessed February 19, 2012.

[25] W3Schools. 2012. Browser statistics. Retrieved Aril 27, 2012 from http://www.w3schools.com/browsers/browsers_stats.asp

[26] W3Schools. 2012. High screen resolutions. Retrieved April 30, 2012 from http://www.w3schools.com/browsers/browsers_resolution_higher.asp

[27] Wayback Machine. 2012. http://www.archive.org/web/web.php Accessed February 19, 2012.

[28] Zeng, X., and Parmanto, B. 2004. Web Content Accessibility of Consumer Health Information Web Sites for People with Disabilities: A Cross Sectional Evaluation. Journal of *Medical Internet Research, 6 (2)*, e1

How Do Professionals Who Create Computing Technologies Consider Accessibility?

Cynthia Putnam, Kathryn Wozniak*, Mary Jo Zefeldt, Jinghui Cheng†,
Morgan Caputo, Carl Duffield

College of Computing and Digital Media, DePaul University
243 S. Wabash, Chicago, IL, 60604

{cputnam, mzefeldt, mcaputo, cduffield } @cdm.depaul.edu;
*kwoznia1@depaul.edu; †jcheng13@mail.depaul.edu

ABSTRACT

In this paper, we present survey findings about how user experience (UX) and human-computer interaction (HCI) professionals, who create information and communication technologies (ICTs), reported considering accessibility in their work. Participants ($N = 199$) represented a wide range of job titles and nationalities. We found that most respondents (87%, $N = 173$) reported that accessibility was important or very important in their work; however, when considerations for accessibility were discussed in an open-ended question ($N = 185$) the scope was limited. Additionally, we found that aspects of empathy and professional experience were associated with how accessibility considerations were reported. We also found that many respondents indicated that decisions about accessibility were not in their control. We argue that a better understanding about how accessibility is considered by professionals has implications for academic programs in HCI and UX as to how well programs are preparing students to consider and advocate for inclusive design.

Categories and Subject Descriptors

K.7.4 [**The computing profession**]: *Codes of good practice*.
K.7.1 [**The computing profession**]: *Occupations*.

Keywords

Accessibility, professions, inclusive design, diverse users

1. INTRODUCTION

In this paper, we present survey findings about how user experience (UX) and human-computer interaction (HCI) professionals, who are responsible for creating information and communication technologies (ICTs), reported considering accessibility in their work. While we acknowledge that working individuals may not have agency to pursue accessibility in cases where companies or clients do not regard inclusive design as an important consideration, we are interested in understanding how well the message of accessibility has been communicated to those individuals who are on the front lines of creating ICTs and how the message has (or has not) translated to action. This work therefore contributes to discussion about who makes accessibility decisions within the HCI/UX professions. This work also has

implication for academic programs in HCI and UX as to how well programs are preparing students to consider and advocate for inclusive design. In other words, if we can identify if and how UX/HCI professionals consider accessibility in their work and their specific actions, we can better identify gaps in accessibility design knowledge. Specifically, we hope to contribute insights for educators and industry leaders about the importance of accessibility design education for students and employees. We argue that indicators about which disabilities and accommodations UX/HCI professionals consider and their overall level of consideration in conjunction with their level of experience and job title may indicate opportunities for targeted instruction.

1.1 Background

The inclusion of diverse users (e.g., people with disabilities, elderly and young) when designing ICTs is more than just an altruistic ideal; it also makes good financial sense for companies who create ICTs. The World Health Organization (WHO) estimates that about 10% of the world's population lives with a disability (about 680 million) comprising the world's largest minority. It has been estimated that people with disabilities in the US control a large amount of discretionary income ($220 billion annually according to the U.S. Census Bureau) [1]; as such, companies who do not consider inclusive design are losing potential customers. Further, this is a growing population, particularly in western societies, because people are living longer, i.e., the population is aging. Steve Ballmer, CEO of Microsoft reflected this sentiment succinctly in 2001: "As the Baby Boom generation ages, more and more people will face the challenges of reduced dexterity, vision and hearing. So enabling accessible technology is a growth opportunity" [2].

Moreover, many laws support design for inclusion; e.g., [3, 4, 5]. In the US, for example, under Section 508 of the Rehabilitation Act of 1973 (modified in 1998), Congress decreed that all information technology funded by federal agencies must be accessible for people with disabilities [3]. Additionally, the Americans with Disabilities Act (ADA), which explicitly extended civil rights to people with disabilities in 1990, requires that a "place of public accommodation" must be accessible for people with disabilities. In 1996 the US Department of Justice ruled that the Internet is such a public place [4]. Many other countries have also passed similar legislation [6].

Further, companies that do not adhere to current laws of accessibility run the risk of legal action; lawsuits have the potential to add costs associated with making websites accessible for people with disabilities. For example, the National Federation of the Blind (NFB) sued several companies, including Target and

AOL, because their Internet presence was not accessible. Both cases were settled out of court, with the companies agreeing to make their websites accessible [7, 8].

There are also many resources to help companies and professionals learn how to make their ICTs accessible. In the US, for example, the W3C created the Web Accessibility Initiative (WAI), which provides guidelines and resources to help developers and designers create and evaluate websites that are accessible (e.g., section 508 compliant) for all users [6].

In summation, considering accessibility and diverse users in ICT design is: (1) a good decision on moral, financial and legal grounds; and (2) well supported by organizations like the W3C. However, previous work has established that many ICTs are not accessible for people with disabilities [8,9].

1.2 Related Literature

Several researchers have established that website accessibility standards are often unmet. For example, Kane et al. (2007) analyzed the accessibility of 100 college websites and found that many of the top universities' sites were not compliant with current standards [9]. Similarly, Loiacono et al. (2009) reported how well Fortune 100 websites adhered to WAI guidelines between the years 2000 and 2005. Though adherence to guidelines increased over the five-year period, of the 64 companies that remained in the Fortune 100, only 27% were free of any Priority 1 barriers at the end of the study [10]. While previous work (of which the above is just a small sample) has established that accessibility has been inconsistently addressed, we are concerned with factors that contribute to this inconsistency; i.e., with how HCI/UX professionals consider accessibility and diverse users in their work.

Multiple authors cite the rapidly changing nature of ICT professions as a critical reason for identifying (and re-identifying) knowledge and skills required in the industry [11, 12]. The primary focus of researchers is varied: some have specifically focused on differentiating among professional roles in ICT, e.g. [13] while others have sought to understand required knowledge and skills associated with specific roles, e.g. [11, 14].

More closely related to our research question are studies that have asked professionals about how they practiced user-centered design (UCD). Vredenburg et al. (2002) investigated the perception of the impact that UCD practice had on industry, with the goal to shape planning, adoption and training of UCD principles [15]. In an early exploration of how professionals considered users in their work, Gould and Lewis (1985) asked participants at a human factors conference to *"describe approximately three to five major steps you consider good practice for designing, developing and evaluating a new computer system for users"*[16]. Answers were coded for adherence to three UCD principles: (1) early focus on the user; (2) empirical measurement, e.g. usability; and (3) iteration informed by data from users. Gould and Lewis found that that only 2% of their participants mentioned all three principles and 26% did not mention any of the principles[1].

Our investigation is most directly related to studies focused on professionals who share or may share responsibility for making

ICTs accessible. For example, Nahon et al. (2012) reported on the obstacles, challenges and incentives for non-professionals (e.g. blog writers and/or creators of personal websites) to consider accessibility in their work. The authors presented a theoretical framework that described variables they hypothesized would contribute to designer intention; they found that intrinsic motivation was the strongest predictor of a positive attitude that affected the intention to make technology accessible [17]. In similar work, Trewin et al. (2010) surveyed 49 IBM web developers to explore (a) how accessibility was addressed, (b) barriers to creating assessable web sites, and (c) how evaluation tools were used and met user needs [18]. The authors found that evaluation tools were difficult to use; difficulty contributed to barriers for developers when considering accessibility. Other barriers to creating accessible sites included lack of time and lack of knowledge. Similarly, Lazar et al. (2004) reported on the perceptions of webmasters about website accessibility. They found that, while most of their respondents personally expressed support for accessibility, many reported impediments to realizing accessible sites, including lack of time and lack of managerial support [19]. Our work builds on this discussion by expanding the range of job titles considered.

2. Methods

Our research question, "how do HCI/UX professionals report considerations of accessibility in their work" was part of a larger study concerned with how HCI/UX professionals (a) define their work, (b) consider users, and (c) discuss differences in job roles and titles. The larger study involved four surveys: (1) a screening survey; (2) an empathy and accessibility survey; (3) a temperament survey and (4) a survey focused on personas. The first two surveys were piloted in earlier work [21]. We are focused on results from the second survey in this paper; however, background data and the recruitment pool came from screening survey responders.

Screening survey respondents were recruited through 'snowball' sampling from multiple sources that cater to UX and HCI professionals in the US, including: (a) IxDA LinkedIn message boards, (b) Puget Sound SIGCHI website, and (c) UPA message boards. Additionally, responders were encouraged to forward the screening survey link to other working HCI and UX professionals.

The original screening survey link was available between July 2011 and April 2012. We received 1079 responses to the screening survey; however, we kept only responses in which respondents (a) answered at least one of three open-ended responses and (b) responded to open-ended questions in a way we could understand. As such, the screening survey provided a filter for high quality (believable) responders. After filtering for high quality responders, we sent a link for the empathy/accessibility survey to 314 participants. In the next sections we describe (1) the empathy/accessibility survey participants, (2) the survey instrument and (3) data analysis procedures.

2.1 Participants (and screening)

Participants that were deemed as high-quality responders ($N = 314$) from the screener were sent a link to the empathy/accessibility survey through email to an address they had provided. Participants were offered an $8.00 Amazon gift for completing the survey and were sent up to two follow-up reminders. We confirmed that respondents were from our screener

---

[1] In the 2009 pilot study for this project, we found that professionals reporting user-centric job titles (e.g. usability engineer) were very likely to mention at least two principles (65% included two principles), but only 37% of those with designer-centric job titles (e.g., information architect) mentioned at least two of the principles [20].

database by a comparison of email addresses[2]. In total we had 199 responses to the empathy/accessibility survey from respondents that we could match from the screener. Of the 199 respondents, 105 were male, 88 were female (missing information about gender $N = 6$); mean age was 35.3 years ($SD = 7.68$). While most ($N = 139$) reported that they were from the US, many ($N = 60$) were from outside the US, including the United Kingdom ($N = 4$), Brazil ($N = 4$), Germany ($N = 4$) and China ($N = 4$). Of the 139 respondents from the US, locations spanned 26 states with most respondents reporting from Seattle ($N = 30$), Chicago ($N = 27$), San Francisco ($N = 13$), and New York ($N = 10$).

2.2 Instrument

The survey explored two areas: (1) empathy profiles and (2) accessibility considerations of UX /HCI professionals.

2.2.1 Empathy profiles

Empathy, defined as "the projection of one's own personality into the personality of another in order to understand him better" [21], is a key concept to 'walking in user's shoes'. As such, we hypothesized that it would be related to how professionals consider accessibility. In the field of psychology, empathy has been characterized by two broad categories of responses: (1) an intellectual response, i.e., the ability to understand the perspective of another; (2) a visceral response, i.e., the ability to feel the perspective of another at an emotional level [22]. This dual aspect of empathy has led to multidimensional approaches to measure empathetic capacity. For this study, we used the 'Interpersonal Reactivity Index' (IRI) to assign an empathy profile to survey respondents.

The IRI is a 28-item self-report survey created by Mark Davis that uses a multidimensional approach to explore empathy [23]. The IRI has been validated in other studies and it correlates with other measures for empathy [21]. The IRI measures four separate aspects of empathy from most intellectual to emotional: (1) perspective-taking (PT), which measures the tendency to adopt the psychological viewpoint of another; (2) fantasy (FS), which measures the propensity to transport oneself imaginatively into the feelings of fictitious characters from books, movies and plays; (3) empathetic concern (EC), which measures levels of sympathy and concern for another in an unfortunate situation; and (4) personal distress (PD), considered the most emotional response, which appraises feelings of personal anxiety and unease in response to a tense situation involving other people.

2.2.2 Accessibility considerations

After respondents completed the IRI, they were presented with two questions related to accessibility. The first question asked respondents to rate on a five-point Likert scale how important they felt it was to make technology accessible. The second question was an open-ended question that asked: "How do you consider accessibility in your work? In other words, what types of efforts/research is performed to help make the products/services you are involved in creating accessible to diverse users including people with disabilities?" Of the total 199 respondents, 185 answered the open-ended question.

2.3 Data analysis

We used an inductive approach to analyzing the open-ended responses ($N = 185$) on how accessibility was considered. First,

each member of our six-person research group independently separated answers into three segments:

Consideration. Coded if there was any indication of some sort of consideration given to accessibility.

Should. Coded if a respondent indicated that there was no consideration for accessibility but expressed regret or was apologetic.

No Consideration or Did Not Understand (DNU). Coded if the responder indicated that there was no consideration given to accessibility or if we did not understand the response in the context of the question.

Next, we met as a group to resolve any differences about the segment assignment of the responses; there were very few initial disagreements, which were resolved in discussion. We then focused on the 'Consideration' segment and individually identified themes among the responses that were in the 'Consideration' segments.

The first author then built a codebook based on the group's themes; we used the codebook to create a scorecard for each response and rated responses on a five-point ordinal ranking of highest to lowest consideration. Next, each member independently coded the answers using the rules established in the initial codebook. To clarify some ambiguity, group members met once to refine the codebook and coded the answers independently again using the new codebook. We then assessed inter-rater reliability using an intraclass correlation coefficient (ICC). Once responses in the 'Consideration' segment were classified, each member of the team independently identified major themes in the 'Should' segment.

We also investigated associations among how the question of accessibility was answered and other respondent data, including: (1) ranking of the importance of accessibility; (2) empathy profile; (3) reported job title (from the screener); (4) professional experience (from the screener); and (5) geographic location.

3. Findings

Respondents who answered the open-ended question on accessibility (93%, $N = 185$ of 199 responses) were initially segmented into three groups: (1) Consideration (70%, $N = 129$ of 185); (2) Should (19%, $N = 35$ of 185); and (3) No Consideration (11%, $N = 21$ of 185). In the next sections we describe themes we identified in the 'Consideration' and 'Should' segments. We also report on associations we explored among the segmented groups and other respondent data, e.g., empathy profile and job titles.

3.1 'Consideration' Segment ($N = 129$ of 185)

Most (70%, $N = 129$ of 185) of respondents were classified as part of the 'consideration' segment. We identified seven themes that formed the basis for our scoring codebook: (1) Making or creating a special accommodation (applying a solution); (2) Research/inquiry (scoping the problem); (3) Consultation with experts; (4) Laws/guidelines; (5) Consideration for non-disability related changes (e.g. low bandwidth); (6) Personal initiative/advocacy; and (7) Organizational support. We then compiled a scorecard using our seven categories to rate each respondent in the 'Consideration' segment.

3.1.1 Special Accommodation

Special accommodation was scored when respondents mentioned some action(s) or solution(s) taken by the respondent or his/her company to support accessibility. For example, if they added something (e.g. alt text, subtitles) and/or changed something (e.g.

---

[2] If the email address in the second survey did not match, the respondent was sent a request to help us match the email. If we were unable to match the email, the data was thrown out.

coded differently, made text larger) in design/development to support accessibility; Respondent 145 submitted:

> *"We tend to take colorblindness into account a lot in video games, and even if we can't test with colorblind subjects..."*

About one third (36%, $N = 46$ of 129) of 'Consideration' segment responses included some sort of special accommodation[3]. We further classified accommodations into five group types:

Type (A) *Vision impairments*: e.g., mention alt tags, use of headers or semantic web elements, addressing colorblind issues;

Type (B) *Cognitive disabilities*: e.g., plain language, clear text;

Type (C) *Hearing impairments*: e.g., tagging audio with search words, subtitles;

Type (D) *Physical impairments*: e.g., making targets larger, making interfaces tab-able (minimal mouse interaction);

Type (E) *Elderly*: e.g., making text larger.

The response was scored higher if accommodations were mentioned for multiple types of disabilities. For example, Respondent 034 discussed addressing visual, age-related and physical impairments:

> *"Awareness of color blindness and making text larger for older viewers - Larger click areas when possible for motor impairments."*

Of the 46 responses coded with for 'special accommodation, about a quarter (24%, $N = 11/46$) discussed multiple types of accommodations. Accommodations for vision impairments (type A) were mentioned the most (52%, $N = 24$ of 46), followed by physical impairments (type D, 22%, $N = 10$ of 46), elderly (type E, 13%, $N = 6$ of 46), hearing impairments (type C, 7%, $N = 3$ of 46) and cognitive disabilities (type B, 2%, $N = 1$ of 46 responses).

3.1.2 Research/inquiry

We classified a response as research/inquiry if the respondent included some type of user testing, assessment or research to make their product/service more accessible. The submission was scored higher if the respondent discussed: (a) the inquiry in relationship to disability; (b) multiple types of inquiry in relationship to disability; and/or (c) direct interaction with users with disabilities. For example, Respondent 84 discussed using automated tools and usability studies, people with disabilities and direct interaction with users:

> *"I use some automated tools to help look for accessibility issues. I also am aware of the heuristics involved with designing accessible sites for the web. In the past, I had the opportunity to involve users with disabilities and those using assistive technology in assessment and usability studies..."*

About half (53%, $N = 69$ of 129 responses) of 'Consideration' segment responses were coded to include some discussion of research or inquiry. About a third of these responses (35%, $N = 24$ of 69) discussed inquiry directly related to a disability. Only a few responses (9%, $N = 6$ of 69) included multiple methods. Mention of direct interaction with end users in the context of disabilities was also uncommon (10%, $N = 7$ of 69).

---

[3] Numbers (i.e. percentages) are based on agreement among at least four of the six research group members.

3.1.3 Consultation with experts

Consultation was scored if the respondent mentioned any type of consultation with accessibility experts that were external to their company. This was relatively rare; we identified four (3%, $N = 4$ of 129) respondents who included consultation with experts. For example, Respondent 179 included experts as one source for information:

> *"...we have done a lot of research before we really begin our design by search online resources, obtaining information from the experts, getting feedbacks from targeted group of people by phone interview..."*

3.1.4 Laws and guidelines

For the laws and guidelines category, we identified responses that included references to guidelines and best practices; however, this did not include references to internal policies. The submission was scored higher if the respondent mentioned a specific law or guideline, e.g., Section 508, WAI, ADA. Respondent 168 included guidelines and specifics in her submission:

> *"My team is currently very focused on learning more about how to translate the WCAG 2.0 standards into detailed requirements to assist development and evaluation of web applications."*

About a quarter of responses were identified (26%, $N = 34$ of 129) as including reference to a laws and/or guidelines.

3.1.5 Non-disability related considerations

Two respondents (2%, $N = 2$ of 129) expanded the definition of accessibility to address other concerns of inclusion, including low bandwidth, machine CPU and smaller screen sizes, and novice/experts. For example, Respondent 076 submitted:

> *"We take into account different bandwidth restrictions particularly for places where bandwidth is a premium (i.e. India). We take into account different machine (CPU, storage, screen size, etc) restrictions."*

3.1.6 Personal initiative/advocacy

This was coded on a scale from one to three. The response was scored as level one if the participant indicated that they 'tried' to consider accessibility in some way (i.e. they had to write "I try"). Responses were scored as level two if the respondent suggested accessibility was personally *important* to them and/or they raised accessibility concerns to their clients/company. High advocacy (a score of three) was identified if the respondent also included specific details about how they realized their advocacy. For example, Respondent 164 suggested a high level of personal advocacy with this submission:

> *"As a former product owner for a number of web sites, I made accessibility compliance (section 508) a requirement in all projects. I also put together presentations to education other product managers as well as my IT development team to help them understand the basics of accessibility and why it was important to our business."*

We agreed that about a quarter (26%, $N = 33$ of 129) of the submissions classified as 'Consideration' indicated some sort of personal advocacy in their response. Most were coded for level one or two advocacy: (a) level three (high) advocacy (27%, $N = 9$ of 33); (b) level two (medium) advocacy (36%, $N = 12$ of 33); (c) level one (low) advocacy = (36%, $N = 12$ of 33 responses coded for advocacy.)

3.1.7 Organizational support

We scored organizational support on a scale from one to two; one was scored if there was an indication that the organization applied resources to accessibility, even if the respondents themselves are not involved. We scored two for this category if the respondent indicated that there was a specific group or individual in the organization dedicated to accessibility, for example, Respondent 154 submitted:

> "At my company, (a very large software company) accessibility is a baked into the design review process. Although I may not factor accessibility into my every day design work, I know that before any design is fully implemented, it will be reviewed by an accessibility specialist and changes will be made."

About a quarter (26%, N = 34 of 129) were identified as 'Consideration' segment responses that included organizational support; we scored nine of those at level two organizational support.

3.1.8 Consideration scorecard

In summation, special accommodation and research/inquiry were the most commonly identified themes, followed equally by identification of laws and guidelines, initiative/advocacy and organizational support, see Figure 1 for common themes.

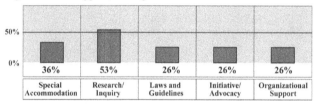

Figure 1: Common themes identified in the 'Consideration' segment

After coding for themes, we created a scorecard for each participant. We also subtracted a point if only one theme was identified; we reasoned that this indicated a narrow level of consideration. We reduced scores down to five groups[4] and assessed inter-rater reliability using an intraclass correlation coefficient (ICC). We had a high level of reliability: ICC = .785, Cronbach's alpha = .956; reliability was significant, $F_{(129,645)}$ = 22.84, p < .001, indicating that we interpreted the codebook similarly.

3.2 'Should' Segment (N = 35 of 185)

About a fifth of the responses (19%, N = 35 of 185 responses) were classified as 'Should'. While we did not create a scoring codebook for this segment, we identified several themes including: (1) shame/guilt/regret; (2) balance; (3) conflict; and (4) signs of hope and progress.

3.2.1 Shame/guilt/regret

We identified this theme when the respondent indicated (46%, N = 16 of 35) that s/he was embarrassed/guilty that his/her current job doesn't consider accessibility or make it a higher priority. For example, Respondent 103 submitted:

> "Unfortunately my job is more concerned with the "gold-plating" than the accessibility of our products."

---

[4] Scores (0-1) = group 1, scores (2) = group 2, scores (3,4) = group 3, scores (5,6) = group 4, scores 7 or over = group 5.

3.2.2 Balance

We identified balance when the respondent blamed external factors or limited resources (31%, N= 11 of 35) for why accessibility was not considered. External forces included time, budget, and/or clients. For example, respondent 046 wrote:

> "Although we consider universal design important and something we would like to consider on all projects, the reality is that most of our clients, don't have the budget to include redundancy to ensure accessibility at all levels."

3.2.3 Conflict

Conflict was coded when the respondent (20%, N = 7 of 35) expressed disagreement with the organization's current practice of ignoring or minimizing accessibility. We identified two levels: (1) the respondent disagreed but didn't express willingness to make effort to change the situation; and (2) the respondent disagreed but reported and effort to change the current practice. For example, respondent 089 submitted:

> "Oddly, when I bring up accessibility as it pertains to people with disabilities, my predominantly young co-workers barely care.....We do usability tests with 50-year-old women, and everyone just acts like the results from those tests don't count because they are only a small segment of our target users. Actually, I think they are the majority of our users and I kind of resent my coworkers at this moment for making so many assumptions."

3.2.4 Signs of hope and progress

Some participants (9%, N = 3 of 35) in this segment also conveyed signs of hope and progress towards accessibility. For example, Respondent 105 submitted:

> "I work with front end developers to ensure that we meet basic accessibility guidelines. We're working towards offering accessibility testing in-house, but this hasn't happened yet unfortunately."

3.3 Associations with other data

We created five (somewhat equal) response groups from our initial segmentation model of the 185 open-ended responses:

1. No consideration (11%, N = 21 of 185 responses)
2. Low consideration, group 1 (25%, N= 46 of 185)
3. Med consideration, groups 2-3 (22%, N = 40 of 185)
4. High consideration, groups 4-5 (23%, N = 43 of 185)
5. Should consideration (19%, N = 35 of 185).

Using univariate tests, we investigated associations among the groups and other respondent data, including (1) ranking of the importance of accessibility; (2) empathy profile; (3) reported job title (from the screener); (4) professional experience (from the screener); and (5) geographic location. For each construct we used an adjusted Bonferroni alpha when conducting multiple comparisons.

3.3.1 Ranking of importance

Consideration groups were highly associated with how respondents rated the importance of accessibility, χ^2 (12, N = 185) = 42.33, p < .001, see Figure 2. While most respondents rated accessibility as either important (50%, N = 93) or very important (32%, N = 60), the distribution of importance roughly followed consideration groups; the Medium and High Consideration groups were the most likely to identify consideration as very important. The 'Should' consideration group rated accessibility as being much less important in their work when compared to other groups.

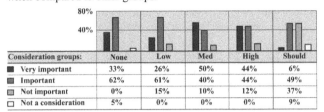

Consideration groups:	None	Low	Med	High	Should
■ Very important	33%	26%	50%	44%	6%
■ Important	62%	61%	40%	44%	49%
▨ Not important	0%	15%	10%	12%	37%
□ Not a consideration	5%	0%	0%	0%	9%

Figure 2: Rating of importance by Consideration groups

3.3.2 Empathy profile

We hypothesized that empathy would be related to how accessibility was considered by ICT professionals. We conducted ANOVA tests to investigate comparisons among the five consideration groups; we used a Bonferonni adjusted alpha for the four tests (.05/4 = .0125). Personal Distress (PD), the most emotional dimension of empathy, was significantly associated with the consideration groups, $F_{(4,177)} = 4.15$, $p < .0125$, see Figure 3. While not statistically significant, there was a pattern where the highest levels of empathy were associated with higher levels of consideration in the EC and PT dimensions.

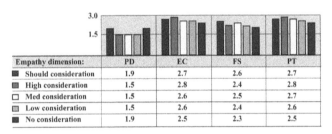

Empathy dimension:	PD	EC	FS	PT
■ Should consideration	1.9	2.7	2.6	2.7
■ High consideration	1.5	2.8	2.4	2.8
□ Med consideration	1.5	2.6	2.5	2.7
▨ Low consideration	1.5	2.6	2.4	2.6
■ No consideration	1.9	2.5	2.3	2.5

Figure 3: Mean empathy score by Consideration groups

3.3.3 Job title

We investigated if job title type was associated with the Consideration groups[5]. While not statistically significant, there were some notable findings, see Figure 4. Forty-seven percent of interaction designers fell into the 'medium' or 'high' consideration groups, and more than half of both usability specialists and user researchers fell into these groups. User experience architects were the most likely to be categorized in the 'Should' group and developers were most likely to be in the low or no consideration groups.

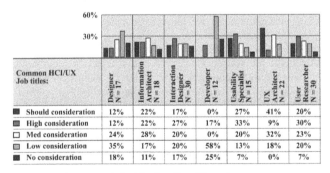

Common HCI/UX Job titles:	Designer N = 17	Information Architect N = 18	Interaction Designer N = 30	Developer N = 12	Usability Specialist N = 15	UX Architect N = 22	User Researcher N = 30
■ Should consideration	12%	22%	17%	0%	27%	41%	20%
■ High consideration	12%	22%	27%	17%	33%	9%	30%
□ Med consideration	24%	28%	20%	0%	20%	32%	23%
▨ Low consideration	35%	17%	20%	58%	13%	18%	20%
■ No consideration	18%	11%	17%	25%	7%	0%	7%

Figure 4: Common job titles by Consideration groups

---

[5] We are reporting only on job titles in which $N > 10$.

3.3.4 Professional experience

We conducted three univariate tests associated with professional experience; as such, we used an adjusted alpha (.05/3 = .016). We first investigated if the number of years of experience and the number of years at the current job were associated with the Consideration groups. While not significant, there were consistent patterns, see Figure 5. The pattern indicated that the more years at a current position, the less consideration was given to accessibility. Conversely, the greater total years of experience, the more consideration was given to accessibility.

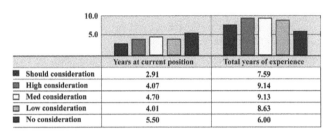

	Years at current position	Total years of experience
■ Should consideration	2.91	7.59
■ High consideration	4.07	9.14
□ Med consideration	4.70	9.13
▨ Low consideration	4.01	8.63
■ No consideration	5.50	6.00

Figure 5: Number of years of professional experience by Consideration groups

We also investigated if the Consideration groups were associated with whether the respondent reported their current job as their first job. We found a significant association, $\chi^2 (4, N = 185) = 20.01$, $p < .001$, see Figure 6.

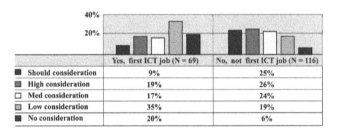

	Yes, first ICT job (N = 69)	No, not first ICT job (N = 116)
■ Should consideration	9%	25%
■ High consideration	19%	26%
□ Med consideration	17%	24%
▨ Low consideration	35%	19%
■ No consideration	20%	6%

Figure 6: First job by Consideration groups

There was also a notable pattern; if the respondent reported the current job as their first they were likely to consider accessibility less but express more regret (i.e., 'Should'). Conversely, if the current job was not their first, respondents were more likely to report a higher level of consideration.

3.3.5 Geographic location

We also investigated if there were any associations among Consideration groups and whether the respondent was from the US; we found no significant associations, see Figure 7. This indicated that there was no evidence of different levels of concern about accessibility worldwide. However, we note that although respondents outside of the US were represented, this representation was not equally dispersed across world regions.

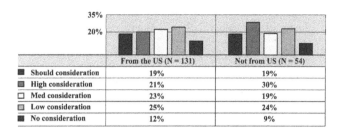

	From the US (N = 131)	Not from US (N = 54)
■ Should consideration	19%	19%
■ High consideration	21%	30%
□ Med consideration	23%	19%
▨ Low consideration	25%	24%
■ No consideration	12%	9%

Figure 7: US v. Other location by Consideration group

4. Discussion

We found that most respondents (83%, N = 153 of the 185 respondents who answered the open-ended question) reported that accessibility was important or very important in their work; however, even when considerations for accessibility were discussed, scope and actions were somewhat limited. We found that the Personal Distress dimension of empathy and professional experience were significantly associated with how accessibility considerations were reported. We found that job titles and location were not significantly associated with how considerations were reported. Additionally, many respondents indicated that decisions about accessibility were out of their control.

4.1 Limited scope and limited action

We identified that 129 of the 185 open-ended responses (70%) included some level of consideration for accessibility. However, only about a fourth (23%, 43 of 185) of the total responses were rated as 'high consideration'; all high scoring responses were those that included two or more of the most common themes. Themes included: (a) making or creating a special accommodation (applying a solution); (b) conducting an inquiry (scoping the problem); (c) demonstrating knowledge of laws and/or guidelines; and/or (d) describing personal initiative and/or advocacy.

Additionally, the type of disabilities considered was largely focused on visual impairments. While obviously this is a very important emphasis, respondents' limited discussion of considerations for other types of disabilities and a narrow consideration of accessibility indicated potential gaps in current education about the wide range of inclusionary concerns.

4.2 Empathy

We hypothesized that individual empathy would be related to how consideration for accessibility was considered. While we saw a possible pattern in EC (empathetic concern), and PT (perspective taking), where higher consideration followed higher empathy, it was only in the PD (personal distress) dimension that the differences among groups were statistically significant. (We hope in future work to investigate this further with a larger sample for more statistical power.) Within the PD dimension, respondents in the 'Should' segment scored higher than those in the 'Consideration' segment. We hypothesized that their high level of personal distress was in part responsible for their expression of guilt or regret about not considering accessibility. (We were somewhat flummoxed about why the 'No Consideration' segment also scored high in PD.) While these findings do not directly affect pedagogical decisions, it does suggest that some students may be more naturally receptive to accessibility concerns.

4.3 Experience

The patterns we saw with level of experience were consistent but not always statistically significant. Professionals who had greater number of total years of experience reported higher levels of accessibility consideration; however, this was not a statistically significant finding. Professionals reporting that they were in their first job in ICT reported lower levels of consideration; 75% (N = 52 of 69) of respondents who reported that this was their first ICT job were classified in lower consideration groups (this was a statistically significant finding). We hypothesized that these related patterns were present because people with greater experience had more control; i.e., a greater agency to actualize inclusive design and therefore reported higher rates of consideration. This may have indicated people new to the workforce are powerless to consider accessibility and therefore, do not. This finding may be related to the 'lack of control' theme.

4.4 Lack of control

Respondents expressed a lack of power/control about how accessibility was considered with both positive and negative ramifications. Many respondents (26%, N = 34 of 185) indicated that their considerations for accessibility were a requirement because of laws, guidelines, or organizational practices; we considered these positive ramifications of exterior forces. On the other hand, some respondents while aware of accessibility concerns, reported little or no control over how accessibility was considered at a higher level in their workplace and discussed trading/sacrificing accessibility for time, budget, and client/company needs. This was expressed in two themes among respondents we categorized in the 'Should' segment (N = 35): (1) the theme of balance when the respondent blamed external factors or limited resources (31%, N= 11 of 35) for why accessibility was not considered and (2) the theme of conflict when the respondent (20%, N= 7 of 35) expressed disagreement with the organization's current practice of ignoring or minimizing accessibility. Lack of control is also a theme established in other related work [19, 20]. This may be an opportunity for educators who prepare future UX/HCI professionals to coach students in developing cost-based arguments for promoting consideration of accessibility issues.

4.5 Conclusions

We argued that considering accessibility and diverse users in HCI/UX professions is (1) a good decision on moral, financial and legal grounds and (2) well supported by organizations like the W3C. Previous work has established that many ICTs are not accessible for people with disabilities. We were interested in exploring how HCI/UX professionals consider accessibility in their work to identify gaps in accessibility design knowledge and contribute to the discussion about who is responsible for creating and advocating for accessible ICTs. We feel that this understanding has implications for academic programs in HCI and UX as to how well programs prepare students to consider and advocate for inclusive design. The absence of an association with geographic location and job titles indicates that these implications may generalize to a wide range of education and training programs.

4.5.1 Limitations of the current study

While our respondents were from a variety of locations and companies, they did not represent a random sample. Additionally, we assessed the levels of consideration primarily from the quality of an open-ended response. While the quality was significantly associated with an independent rating of importance, we acknowledge that low levels of consideration could be in part due to busy professionals lacking time to write a thorough answer. Our findings are also somewhat limited to web-based technologies; most respondents discussed accessibility in the context of the Internet. Moreover, only a few respondents indicated that they considered accessibility in other types of computing technologies, e.g., videogames (2%, $N = 3$) and touch screens (1%, $N = 1$).

4.5.2 Future work

Since this work did not specifically address why considerations for accessibility were often limited in scope, we would like to explore reasons in more depth, this includes an analysis of how accessibility is addressed in current HCI/UX academic programs. A better understanding about how academic programs handle teaching accessibility concerns has the potential to expose barriers that currently prevent academic organizations from implementing accessibility in their programs.

Additionally, we plan to expand our sample to include a greater number of professionals who work in non-web-based ICTs. While the Internet is a vital consideration, applications for touch screens and mobile computing devices will be increasingly important.

5. ACKNOWLEDGMENTS

Thank you to our thoughtful respondents. Also thanks to the DePaul University Research Council for funding this research.

6. REFERENCES

[1] Brown, L. 2008. Enabling Disabled Shoppers. Interent Retailer. Retrieved April 30, 2012 from http://disability-marketing.com/facts/.

[2] Chisholm, W. and May, M. 2009.*Universal Design for Web Applications*. O'Reilly Media, Inc., Sebastopol, CA, USA.

[3] *The Rehabilitation Act Amendments.* Retrieved April 30, 2012 from http://www.access-board.gov/508.htm.

[4] Disabled Persons' Telecommunications Access: Section 255. Retrieved June 18, 2012 from http://www.fcc.gov/guides/disabled-persons-telecommunications-access-section-255.

[5] Burks, M. and Waddell, C. 2001. *Universal Design for the Internet.* The Internet Society Retrieved April 30, 2012 http://www.isoc.org/briefings/002/.

[6] W3C. *Web Accessibility Initiative (WAI).* Retrieved April 30, 2012 from http://www.w3.org/WAI/.

[7] *National Federation for the Blind v. Target.* Disability Rights Advocates, Retrieved April 28, 2012, from http://www.dralegal.org/cases/private_business/nfb_v_target

[8] Cisneros, O. S. 2002. *AOL Settles Accessibility Suit.* WIRED Magazine. Retrieved April 28, 2012, from http://www.wired.com/techbiz/media/news/2000/07/37845.

[9] Kane, S. K., Shulman, J. A. and Shockley, T. J. 2007. A Web Accessibility Report Card for Top International University Web Sites. *In Proceedings of The International Cross-Disciplinary Workshop on Web Accessibility, W4A* (Baniff, Canada, May 7-8, 2007).

[10] Loiacono, E. T., Nicholas C. Romano, J. and McCoy, S. 2009. The State of Corporate Website Accessibility. *Communications of the ACM,* 52, 9, 128 - 132.

[11] Huang, H., Kvasny, L., Joshi, K. D., Trauth, E. M. and Mahar, J. 2009. Synthesizing IT job skills identified in academic studies, practitioner publications and job ads. In *Proceedings of the special interest group on management information system's 47th annual conference on Computer personnel research, SIGMIS-CPR'09* (Limerick, Ireland, May 28–30, 2009).

[12] Nelson, H. J., Ahmad, A., Martin, N. L. and Litecky, C. R. 2007. A comparative study of IT/IS job skills and job definitions. In *Proceedings of the 2007 ACM SIGMIS CPR conference on Computer personnel research: The global information technology workforce* (St.Louis, Missouri, USA, April 19-21, 2007).

[13] Downey, J. 2006. Systems architect and systems analyst: are these comparable roles? In *Proceedings of the 2006 ACM SIGMIS CPR conference on computer personnel research: Forty four years of computer personnel research: achievements, challenges & the future* (Claremont, California, USA, April 13-15, 2006).

[14] Anthony, E. 2003. Computing education in academia: toward differentiating the disciplines. In *Proceedings of the 4th conference on Information technology curriculum* (Lafayette, Indiana, USA, October 16-18. 2003).

[15] Vredenburg, K., Mao, J.-Y., Smith, P. W. and Carey, T. 2002. A Survey of User-Centered Design Practice. *Paper presented at the CHI 2002.* (Minneapolis, Minnesota, USA, April 20-25, 2002)

[16] Gould, J. D. and Lewis, C. 1985. Designing for Usability: Key Principles and What Designers Think. *Communications of the ACM* 28, 3, 300 - 311.

[17] Nahon, K., Benbasat, I. and Grange, C. 2012. The Missing Link: Intention to Produce Online Content Accessible to People with Disabilities by Non-Professionals. In *Proceedings of the 45th Hawaii International Conference on System Sciences* (Maui, HI, USA, January 4-7, 2012).

[18] Trewin. S., Cragun, B., Swart, C., Brezin, J., and Richards, C., 2010. Accessibility challenges and tool features. *Proceedings W4A2010* (Raleigh, NC, USA, April 26-27, 2010).

[19] Lazar, J., Dudley-Sponaugle, A. and Greenidge, K.-D. 2004. Improving web accessibility: a study of webmaster perceptions. *Computers in Human Behavior*, 20, 269–288.

[20] Putnam, C., and Kolko, B. (2012). HCI Professions: Differences and definitions. In *Proceedings of the 2012 annual conference extended abstracts on Human factors in computing systems* (Austin, TX, USA, May 5-10)

[21] Guralinik, D. B. 1976. *Webster's New World Dictionary of the American Language.* William Collins and World Publishing, Cleveland, OH, USA.

[22] Davis, M. H. 1980.A multidimensional approach to individual differences in empathy. *JSAS Catalog of Selected Documents in Psychology*, 10, 85.

[23] Davis M.H. 1983. Measuring Individual Differences in Empathy: Evidence for a Multidimensional Approach. *Journal of Personality and Social Psychology.* 44, 1,114-26.

Helping Visually Impaired Users Properly Aim a Camera

Marynel Vázquez
Carnegie Mellon University
5000 Forbes Avenue
Pittsburgh, PA
marynel@cmu.edu

Aaron Steinfeld
Carnegie Mellon University
5000 Forbes Avenue
Pittsburgh, PA
steinfeld@cmu.edu

ABSTRACT

We evaluate three interaction modes to assist visually impaired users during the camera aiming process: speech, tone, and silent feedback. Our main assumption is that users are able to spatially localize what they want to photograph, and roughly aim the camera in the appropriate direction. Thus, small camera motions are sufficient for obtaining a good composition. Results in the context of documenting accessibility barriers related to public transportation show that audio feedback is valuable. Visually impaired users were not affected by audio feedback in terms of social comfort. Furthermore, we observed trends in favor of speech over tone, including higher ratings for ease of use. This study reinforces earlier work that suggests users who are blind or low vision find assisted photography appealing and useful.

Categories and Subject Descriptors

H.5.2 [**Information Interfaces and Presentation**]: User interfaces – Input devices and strategies, Interaction styles

General Terms

Design, Experimentation, Human Factors

Keywords

Photography, Visually Impaired, Accessibility, Transit

1. INTRODUCTION

The goal of this work is to enable assisted photography for people who would normally have trouble taking a picture due to a visual impairment. There is evidence that people who are blind and low vision desire the ability to photograph people, events and objects, just like sighted users [11]. Furthermore, there is a desire to use cameras to obtain visual information, like the denomination of currency [14]. However, there is a basic barrier in the first step of the photography process. It is difficult to take a picture when one cannot see what is shown in the viewfinder.

Properly aiming the camera is crucial when taking a picture. Besides aesthetics, aiming is important because poor image compositions can make pictures hard to understand, thereby reducing their value. For example, cropped faces are a common result of improper camera aiming, and strongly discourage people with visual impairments from photographing other people. Likewise, a badly aimed picture of an accessibility barrier may not capture adequate information to properly document the barrier.

To the best of our knowledge, little research has explored different interaction modes to help visually impaired users properly aim a camera. Survey data suggests that spoken directions are the preferred type of guidance cue, with respect to audio tones, and vibrations [11]. Systems that rely on spoken information to help users aim the camera include the native iOS5 camera application for the iPhone platform with VoiceOver activated, VizWiz::LocateIt [3], and EasySnap [11]. The former uses face recognition to inform about faces in the view of the camera. The middle uses voice to inform about proximity to an object. The latter provides spoken information about the position of the camera with respect to an initial view. However, each of these systems is limited and has characteristics which can bias results. The iOS5 implementation only works for faces and provides limited feedback on where to aim the camera. VizWiz::LocateIt requires human assistance and may impose a delay of at least 10 seconds per round of feedback. EasySnap in *people mode* is similar to the iOS camera application, and in *object mode* requires users to first take a picture of the object up close. This can be problematic and hard to attain for larger objects, where close proximity could be dangerous.

In this work, we implemented and evaluated three interaction modes to assist visually impaired users during the camera aiming process: speech, tone, and silent feedback. We assume users are able to spatially localize what they want to photograph, and roughly aim the camera in the appropriate direction. Therefore, small camera motions are sufficient for obtaining a good composition.

We are particularly interested in the following research questions:

1. Is audio feedback valuable when users roughly know the direction in which to aim the camera?

2. Is speech-based feedback preferred over methods with more abstract guidance?

3. How do subjective factors (e.g., overall preference, perceived social comfort, and ease of use, etc) change for these interaction modes?

The first question is important because the proposed interaction modes rely on users roughly aiming the camera in the direction of what they want to capture. Therefore, users may feel audio feedback is unnecessary and prefer the silent mode, which has reduced sound contamination on environmental awareness. The other questions seek to identify how the different modes impact preference and acceptance.

We present findings in the context of documenting accessibility barriers related to public transportation. This scenario is motivating because pictures serve as persuasive evidence for promoting changes in transit accessibility [18]. In this context, good composition means a centering model: image subjects, or the main area of interest in an photo, should be framed in the middle. Centering naturally highlights visual evidence for documentation purposes, and increases the chances of including relevant context in images. Alternative composition models, such as the rule of thirds, might be preferred in other cases.

2. RELATED WORK

The process of pointing the camera in the right direction, also known as *focalization* [10], is important when designing camera-based assistive technologies for the visually impaired community. In general, the key to assisting low vision and blind users aim the camera is to transform visual information into another useful representation. Computational approaches to reach this goal can be grouped in two categories: human-driven, and fully automated methods.

Human-driven approaches to help aim the camera rely on human-based knowledge, more than on computing to understand image content. The tele-assistance system for shopping by Kutiyanawala et al. [13] is an example. It was designed to establish communication between a sighted guide and a visually impaired user who carries a camera. The user transmits images of a shelf in a store to the sighted guide through this system, and then the guide uses this data to help pick out target products. The guide further assists in aligning the camera towards targets, and reads nutritional facts from the image to the user. Verbal communication between the sighted guide and the user is key in this process.

To the best of our knowledge, VizWiz was the first crowd-based assisted photography system for blind people [3]. The system was designed to answer visual questions about pictures using Amazon's Mechanical Turk, like "Do you see the picnic tables across the parking lot?". Questions were answered in about 30 seconds, with best times reached with the help of warnings on dark and blurry images. Mitigating poor images was important since they reduced the number of good answers provided by MTurk workers.

VizWiz::LocateIt, a subsystem of VizWiz, was further designed to help blind people locate arbitrary items in their environment [2]. This subsystem provided audible feedback to the user about how much he or she needs to turn the camera in the direction of a target object. Feedback modes included tone and clicking sounds, as well as a voice that announced a number between one and four to indicate how far the user is from the target. Researchers answered requests from users in about 10 seconds for the purpose of evaluating the subsystem, instead of using Mechanical Turk workers. Participants liked the clicking sound to aid in finding a cereal box, and some suggested vibration, verbal instructions, and other familiar sounds as alternatives. No detailed comparison on the perception of feedback modes was provided.

Richardson also explored the use of Mechanical Turk workers to collect information about images [15]. His Descriptive Camera works like a normal camera, in the sense that users aim at what they want to capture. But, instead of producing an image, it outputs a text description of the scene, as provided by a Mechanical Turk worker. In about 6 minutes, the system provides descriptions such as, "This is a faded picture of a dilapidated building. It seems to be run down and in the need of repairs."

Computer vision enables automated approaches for helping aim cameras. The EasySnap framing application [11] relies on image processing to help users aim the camera towards people or particular objects. In the first case, it detects faces, and announces their size and position within the screen. In the second case, it describes how much and which part of the current view of the camera is occupied by an initial, close-up view of an object. Results from a study about the effectiveness of EasySnap to help visually impaired users revealed that most participants thought that the system helped their photography and found it easy to use. Third party observers agreed that 58.5% percent of the pictures taken with EasySnap feedback were better framed than those without, while 12% obtained neutral ratings between the two conditions. The remaining 29.5% were better without feedback.

The PortraitFramer application by the same authors [11] further informs about how many faces are in the camera's sight. Visually impaired users can explore the touchscreen panel of the phone to feel the position of faces through vibration and pitch cues. This information information can then be used to position people in photographs as desired.

Apple's camera application for the iPhone works in a similar manner to PortraitFramer. The release of the iOS5 mobile operating system updated the camera application with face recognition capabilities natively integrated with Apple's built-in speech-access technology. The camera application announces the number of faces in the current view of the camera, as well as a simple descriptor of face position for some scenarios. Common phrases that the system speaks up include "no faces", "one face" and "face centered". Moreover, the system plays a failure tone when users touch the screen outside of a region containing a face, thus providing a physical reference on how well a face is centered.

Other automated, camera-based applications outside of the photography domain also try to provide cues with respect to camera aiming. For example, Liu's currency reader [14] does not actively encourage a particular camera motion, but does provide real time response on whether a bill is readable within the image. This binary feedback is useful for identifying and learning good aiming positions.

Likewise, the mobile application by Tekin and Coughlan [19] tries to automatically direct users towards centering product barcodes in images. Users hold the camera about 10 to 15cm from a product, and then slowly scan likely barcode locations. The system is silent until it finds sufficient evidence for a barcode, and then provides audio feedback for centering. Guidance is provided through four distinct tone or verbal sounds that indicate left, right, up or down camera motions. Initial results published by the authors do not provide insight on particular audio feedback preferences.

Work on camera-based navigation for visually impaired users is also relevant when studying camera aiming. The indoor navigation system with object identification by Hub,

Diepstraten and Ertl [8] answers inquiries concerning object features in front of the camera. The authors use a text-to-speech engine to identify objects, and provide additional spatial information. The system by Deville et al. [5] guides the focus of attention of blind people as they navigate. Rather than speech, these authors use spatial sounds generated from color features to indicate noteworthy parts of the scene.

3. METHOD

We conducted an experiment to study different interaction modes to steer users towards proper camera aiming positions. We framed this study in the context of documenting accessibility barriers related to public transportation. Our motivation in this scenario is twofold: rich multimedia documentation of problems serves as persuasive evidence for promoting changes in transit accessibility [18]; and previous research suggests photos are an attractive reporting method for riders [17]. Besides supporting assisted photography, we hope our findings encourage problem documentation through pictures between the visually impaired community. Empowering these riders to collect visual evidence of problems can lead to better communication between riders and transit authorities. Thus, there is a higher chance issues will get solved faster and more appropriately.

3.1 Assisted Photography Application

We created an interactive application for the iPhone platform to assist visually impaired users during photographic documentation of transit accessibility. We chose this mobile platform because of its versatility, screen reader capabilities, and high levels of adoption between our main target users.

The problem of taking a "good" picture in this context is difficult, but dramatically simplified by the task characteristics. First, aesthetics are not an issue for problem documentation, thereby mitigating a significant challenge. Second, we do not need to know what the barrier is – we only need to know where it is. While being able to automatically annotate barriers might be useful for documentation, it is not essential. This mitigates the need for object recognition. Third, we can assume the rider is able to localize the barrier in space and roughly aim a camera at the target. This means only small camera motions are needed to balance photo composition and correct unwanted camera orientation.

Consider Figure 1a as an example. We can deduce from the initial view of the scene that the area of interest in the picture is related to the stop sign. Thus, one way of improving the image would be to aim the camera towards the upper-right region of the initial view, bringing the sign to the center of the picture. A centering image composition model helps in this context because it naturally highlights evidence, and increases the chances of including relevant context in pictures. Figure 1b shows the suggested view, as automatically proposed by our system in a simulation.

3.1.1 Region of interest selection

Our system automatically selects a region of interest (ROI) in pictures, and suggests it as the main subject of the composition for documentation purposes. Our technique can be described as a method to avoid leaving out information that is expected to be most relevant. This strategy was designed for the transit domain without explicit knowledge of object models, and leverages the fact that this domain is

(a) Initial camera view (b) Suggested final view

Figure 1: Automatically proposed view on simulation test

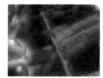

(a) Saliency map (b) Potential ROI (c) Selected region

(d) Original image and suggested center

Figure 2: Automatic ROI selection process, and suggested image center (rectangle)

strongly composed by conspicuous elements. Complete rationale, algorithm details, and evaluation of this approach can be found in [20].

Our system constructs a model of visual attention in an image employing a modified version of saliency maps, as defined by Itti and Koch [9]. These maps highlight visual stimuli that are intrinsically salient in their context, which tends to be the case for transit elements in street pictures.

Possible regions of interest are generated by thresholding the saliency map of an image. These regions are later ranked based on their size and saliency, and the one with highest score is selected as the ROI. Figures 2a, 2b and 2c depict this process.

3.1.2 Image composition assessment

Our system suggests the weighted center of the ROI as the new center for an image, using saliency for the weights. The suggested center is biased towards the most salient point in the ROI, as shown in Figure 2d, which may not be the most salient point in the image. If we chose the most salient point in the image directly, then our proposed center would be driven towards small salient regions that are less likely to be a good composition subject. The point of maximum saliency in Figure 2d is a tiny portion of green grass, for example, which is located in the top-right corner of the picture.

Our system considers the image to have a good composition when the weighted mean of the ROI is near the geometric center of the picture. If this is not the case, then the system enters in an interactive mode to try to help users frame the ROI during problem documentation.

3.1.3 Interaction Modes

After an initial aiming direction is set, users slowly move the phone to improve image composition, based on the location of the center suggested by the system. Every frame received from the camera is processed as fast as possible to track the position of the region of interest, and provide real-time feedback during this phase.[1] Tracking is accomplished through a standard Lucas-Kanade template matching algorithm [1].

Our mobile application operates in one of three feedback modes while the user tries to frame the ROI:

Speech-based feedback: Spoken words provide information about the relative orientation of the suggested center with respect to the middle, as well as the distance between the two. The system repeatedly speaks "up", "down", "left" or "right" to indicate orientation, depending on whether the suggested center is located in the upper part of the image, the lower part, etc. Words are spoken with different pitch as a cue on how close the suggested center is to the middle. Higher pitch means closer.

Tone-based feedback: The pitch of a looping tone indicates distance from the suggested center to the middle of the image. Higher pitch means closer as before. No orientation information is provided.

Silent feedback: The system lets the user capture the scene continuously, without providing any audible guidance.

In all three modes, the collected image is one where the ROI is closest to the center. For this reason, we have nicknamed the silent mode as *paparazzi* mode. A user can simply wave the phone in slow motion and the most centered frame will be selected. This mode is still interesting because it does not reduce surrounding awareness through noise pollution, and allows users to take pictures without attracting others' attention. Similar to the other modes, it requires real-time operation to track the ROI as the camera moves, and does alert when enough data has been collected.

We also tried vowel-like sounds proposed by Harada, Takagi and Asakawa [7] to represent radial directions during the pilot phase of our study. We soon realized that the limited time users had for familiarization with the system was not enough to learn the mapping of these sounds. However, we believe these sounds are promising for providing orientation information when users have the opportunity for longer practice times.

3.1.4 User Interface

The user interface of our application is very simple. When the application starts, the camera view is shown on the full screen. Once roughly aimed, users hold still and tap the touchscreen anywhere. The system quickly suggests a new image center based on the estimated ROI in the initial image, and draws a circle over this point to indicate its location. An "X" mark also appears on the middle of the image as a reference for those who can see the screen. The system plays a short tone afterwards to let users know they can begin moving the camera slowly to center the ROI. One of the feedback modes described previously guides (or not) the user towards the ROI.

A trial finishes in several ways. Ideally, the user will steer the ROI into the center of the image, given a small margin for error. In this case, it saves the last frame as the best image captured. The system fails and stops early, when the ROI exits the image, or camera motion induces extreme blur and tracking fails. Upon finishing, the system plays a sound and shows the best image captured during the aiming process.

3.1.5 Other implementation details

Many final images taken with our system were blurry during preliminary testing. These images showed low spatial detail and had reduced edge sharpness, in comparison to the initial image users tried to capture. This was discouraging for documenting accessibility barriers, so we decided to add blur estimation capabilities to our system. Our hope was that this would help reduce the number of times significantly blurred images were selected as the best captured.

We chose the no-reference blur metric by Crete et al. [4] for our system. The metric is not computationally intensive, and had better agreement with human ratings of blur than other methods found in the literature [12, 6, 16]. The evaluation was performed on 100 images depicting Pittsburgh's public transportation system, which were captured in the wild by team members using our assisted photography application. Figure 3 shows objective blur ratings obtained with [4] versus subjective opinions. More detailed results on blur estimation are out of the scope of this paper.

We altered the frame evaluation criteria of the application when we incorporated blur detection. The final implementation examines the final set of frames and tries to pick the best combination of close proximity to the center and low blur. Note that if the initial image is very blurry, subsequent best frames may be blurry as well. The system does not deal with focus or exposure, though this would be a nice addition.

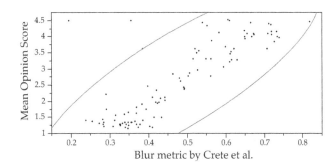

Figure 3: Strongly correlated subjective and objective [4] blur scores ($r = 0.8258$, $p = 0.0001$) on public transportation images. Mean Opinion Scores are in a 5-point scale

---

[1]An average of 16 frames per second are processed with added background logging processes for future data analysis.

3.2 Participants

During recruitment, the participants were informed they would be completing surveys and documenting items in our laboratory. All participants were paid volunteers and fully consented. There were three groups of six participants each: full vision or corrected to full vision (F), low vision (L), and blind (B). While the first group may seem unnecessary, universal design practices recommend testing systems for broad appeal. The second group included participants with a wide range of visual impairments, none of whom could easily read the screen of an iPhone. The third group was limited to participants who could only perceive light or were totally blind.

Participants were recruited from local universities and the general public using contacts in local organizations, and community email lists. Participants were required to be 18 years of age or older, fluent in English, and not affiliated with the project.

3.3 Experimental Setup

We used a real-size, simulated bus shelter inside our laboratory for the study (Figure 4). This included a bench, a tempered glass panel on the upstream side of the shelter, a place to mount route information signs, and a bus stop sign. This shelter is comparable in dimensions and layout to real shelters in the Pittsburgh area. We opted for a simulated shelter in order to limit bias from lighting conditions, bystanders, and inclement weather.

We used a within–subject design, and counterbalanced the three interaction modes (Speech, Tone and Silent) using a 3-level Latin Square. Conditions were tested with two documentation tasks: a damaged and non-accessible schedule sign (shoulder height on side wall near glass), and ground obstacles inside the shelter (back left corner). Participants

Figure 4: Simulated bus shelter used during the experiment. The schedule sign and the obstacles documented by participants are inside the shelter

were asked to take 3 practice pictures during the beginning of each condition to get familiarized with the feedback modes. These pictures were taken at a table in the laboratory, and their content included common objects (e.g., plastic container, magazines, etc.). After practice, participants were asked to take 6 trial pictures per condition, alternating between the schedule and the obstacles. Half of the participants per group started with the schedule as initial documentation task, while the rest started with the ground clutter. The duration of the experiment varied depending on the speed in which participants completed the tasks.

The application started recording data when users tapped the screen, up until they were done taking a picture. The following information was collected per trial image:

- Time since the participant tapped the screen and the system presented the best image (Trial Time)

- Distance from the suggested center to the middle of the first processed image (Initial Distance)

- Distance from the suggested center to the middle of the best image presented to the user (Best Image Distance)

- Whether the user brought the suggested center to the middle, or the application stopped because tracking failed (Reached Middle)

- Percentage of the time that users increased the distance from the suggested center to the middle (Moving Away)

- Average device acceleration (Acceleration)

Participants were asked to imagine they were waiting for a bus and document the aforementioned issues using our assisted photography application. They were free to take pictures from where they thought was best for documentation. We did not guide participants towards the schedule or the obstacles, since we did not want to induce bias for particular camera angles.

While the shelter closely mimicked a real shelter, we worried that participants with visual impairments would not be able to find the schedule or the obstacles quickly during the first trial. This initial learning phase could bias the results, so we gave participants a tour of the shelter at the beginning of the study. We removed the ground clutter to allow participants to navigate freely, and familiarize as they would in a real situation. There was also concern that visually impaired participants would get a sense of where the schedule and the obstacles where, and would try to take pictures from afar without having confirmed the location of the targets. To make the experiment more realistic, we asked these participants to physically find the problems before documenting.

Participants completed a pre-test survey covering demographics, disability, and technology attitudes and a post-test survey covering experiences and preferences. The latter included questions on transit complaint filing, technology use, and 7-point scale ratings for feedback mode preference.

Within the study, each participant completed an identical post-condition survey (Table 1) after each condition. This survey was developed by Steinfeld et al. [17] to study modality preference for rider reports on transit accessibility problems, and was previously validated with wheeled mobility device users. Participants were not shown the index labels.

Table 1: Post-condition survey (7-point scale from strongly disagree to strongly agree; R means reversed for analysis)

#	Question	Ease of Use	Usefulness	Social Comfort
1	Learning to use this method was easy.	×		
2	Becoming skillful with this method was easy.	×		
3	I had no problem physically using this method.	×		
4	Using this method would improve my performance in reporting observations.		×	
5	Using this method for reporting observations would increase my productivity.		×	
6	I feel this method is too slow for everyday use. R		×	
7	I felt uncomfortable using this method when people were around in public. R			×
8	When I use this method, I feel like other people are looking at me. R			×
9	Using this method in front of strangers embarrasses me. R			×
10	I like the idea of using this method.		×	
11	I would have done as good a job without using this method. R		×	
12	Carrying items to do this method on daily trip is such a hassle to me. R		×	
	Cronbach's α:	0.849	0.833	0.828

4. RESULTS

As implied by the research questions in the Introduction, this paper is mostly focused on survey results. Complete analysis of the actual content of the data collected by the participants is deferred to future publications.

4.1 Demographics

A total of 18 participants were recruited for the study. The average age per group was 24, 56, and 55 for (F), (L), and (B), with standard deviations of 6.7, 11.8 and 12.1. The percentage of women that completed the experiment was 50%, 50%, and 83%, respectively. One blind participant indicated wearing hearing aids.

Visually impaired participants reported using white canes (58%), guide dogs (25%), magnifiers on glasses (25%), tinted glasses (25%), and hand-held telescopes (17%), between other devices to get around. All these participants had a cellphone, and 66.7% of these devices had a camera.

All participants in the full vision or corrected to full vision group take photos, while 3 and 1 in the low vision and blind groups do. Three totally blind participants said that they had never taken a picture before the experiment. In terms of device usage, 25% of the participants in the (L) and (B) groups said they take pictures with a phone, and only 33% of the low vision participants use a regular camera.

Only one participant in the fully sighted group said that he had filed a complaint about a transit problem, while 5 people in the low vision and 6 in the blind group indicated having filed complaints. Phone was the common way of reporting problems between visually impaired participants.

4.2 Camera Aiming Statistics

A repeated measures ANOVA on Group and Mode was used to analyze log data recorded by the application. Participants took significantly longer to take pictures in Silent mode than in Speech mode, $F(3) = 5.07$ (p = 0.0068). The interaction between effects showed that there was a significant difference between the two modes for low vision participants.

The difference in Initial Distance between groups and modes was significant, with $F(3) = 8.42$ (p = 0.0035) and $F(3) = 3.56$ (p = 0.0297), respectively. The Tukey post-hoc showed that blind participants started off target significantly more than others. Interestingly, Initial Distance with the tone-based feedback was significantly greater than with speech,

even though audio feedback was only provided after initial distances were logged.

There were significant differences in Group on Best Image Distance, $F(3) = 6.26$ (p = 0.0106), and Reached Middle, $F(3) = 13.86$ (p = 0.0004). Fully sighted participants were able to bring the suggested center significantly closer to the middle with respect to blind participants. Moreover, participants in (F) and (L) reached the middle significantly more times than those in (B).

Differences in Mode on Best Image Distance and Reached Middle were significant as well, with $F(3) = 4.99$ (p = 0.0074) and $F(3) = 10.42$ (p < 0.0001), respectively. Post-hoc analyses showed that when users used Speech, their distances from the suggested center to the middle of the best image were significantly smaller than those obtained in with the other modes. Likewise, participants reached more the middle with Speech.

The interaction between Group and Mode was also significant for Distance and Reached Middle, $F(3) = 2.80$ (p = 0.0261) and $F(3) = 3.45$ (p = 0.009). The post-hoc analysis revealed that Speech gets (B) participants into the final distance and success range of the (L) group. Furthermore, Speech gets (L) participants into the success range of the (F) group for reaching the middle (Figure 5).

The analysis also indicated significant differences in Group and Mode on Moving Away, with $F(3) = 12.37$ (p = 0.0007) and $F(3) = 9.78$ (p < 0.0001). Participants in the full vision group moved away from the target less time than the rest, which is not surprising since they can see the view finder of the camera and will notice when they are not making

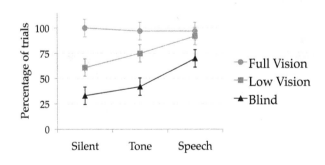

Figure 5: Percentage of trials the target was centered

progress towards centering the target. Trials with Speech feedback had significantly lower percentages of time moving away with respect to other modes.

The average magnitude of device acceleration was significantly different only between groups, $F(3) = 4.65$ (p = 0.0268). Participants in (F) moved the camera significantly slower than those in (B), which was expected because full-vision participants can easily take advantage of the visual information provided through the screen.

4.3 Post-condition ratings

Unless otherwise noted, comparisons were analyzed using a full factorial ANOVA with participant Group and feedback Mode as main effects, followed by a Tukey HSD post-hoc where appropriate. For the purposes of analysis, responses to each question within each post-condition survey category (Ease of Use, Usefulness, and Social Comfort) were flipped to align positive/negative direction, with higher as better, and averaged as a group. Index groups all surpassed the 0.7 reliability acceptance threshold used in the literature (Table 1). ANOVA analyses did not reveal any Ordering effects.

Ease of Use ratings for our application were positive in general (first column of Table 2). There was a significant difference on Ease of Use between participant groups, $F(3) = 6.61$ (p = 0.0030). Full vision or corrected to full vision participants gave statistically significant higher ratings for Ease of Use, with respect to the rest. No other effects or interactions were significant for Group and Mode, but a slight upward trend was observed for Speech.

We realized after running the experiment that there is potential for a small bias in the Ease of Use metric, because the success sound feedback only told participants that a trial had ended, and not whether it had ended successfully. We averaged log statistics per Mode, and checked if there were inconsistencies or unexpected results with respect to Ease of Use. We found that there were significant negative correlations between Ease of Use and Trial Time ($r = -0.4673$, $p = 0.0004$), and between Ease of Use and Moving Away ($r = -0.5381$, $p < 0.0001$). There was also reasonable, significant positive correlation between Ease of Use and Reached Middle ($r = 0.5591$, $p < 0.0001$).

There was a significant difference in Group on Usefulness, $F(3) = 3.57$ (p = 0.0363), and Social Comfort, $F(3) = 5.67$ (p = 0.0064). A post hoc analysis on the former revealed that full vision participants reported significantly reduced Usefulness as compared to low vision participants (second column of Table 2). A post-hoc on the latter result showed that full vision participants gave significantly reduced Social Comfort ratings than low vision participants (third column of Table 2). Even though the interaction between Group and Mode was not significant, we noticed a trend that suggests that Social Comfort is not affected by audio feedback in the case of people with visual impairments.

Table 2: Average ratings on Ease of Use, Usefulness and Social Comfort per group. Standard deviation is shown between parenthesis

	Ease of Use	Usefulness	Social Comfort
Full Vision	6.76 (0.42)	4.69 (0.88)	4.07 (1.62)
Low Vision	5.83 (1.53)	5.69 (1.39)	5.69 (1.59)
Blind	5.46 (1.13)	5.01 (1.12)	4.61 (1.33)

4.4 Post-test ratings

A full factorial ANOVA showed significant differences in Mode on post-test preference ratings, $F(3) = 3.32$ (p = 0.0453). Speech mode ratings where significantly higher at the end of the experiment, than those collected for Silent mode. Even though differences in preference per Group were not significant, there were differences in the interaction between Group and Mode, $F(5) = 13.85$ (p < .0001). Visually impaired participants ended up preferring audio feedback over Silent mode, while participants in the full vision group did the contrary (Figure 6).

4.5 Other Findings

Even though the Speech mode was preferred in many cases, we were able to notice some difficulty with the spoken sounds when the phone was held in an orientation other than straight up. For illustrative purposes, consider the case when the system says "up" to indicate that the suggested center is in the upper part of the image. If the user is holding the phone straight up vertically and is aiming the camera to the front, then it is natural to translate the device upwards to bring the center to the middle of the picture. Nonetheless, if the phone is aimed downwards, e.g., towards the ground, then the user should move the phone forward to frame the suggested center in the middle. This dichotomy was a problem for several blind participants, who ended up translating the phone upwards and not forward when aiming downwards. It was hard for them to understand why it was taking so long to center the target in these cases.

Qualitative data, mostly in the form of interviews and comments, were captured during this study. Only one blind participant expressed no interest at all in photography. She was totally blind, and said that she would only do it if there was a way she could feel images, e.g., feel the shape of buildings and big spaces captured in pictures. All other visually impaired users indicated they like (or would like) to take pictures of events, people, and objects.

A low vision participant was a photographer who has been losing his sight progressively. He cleaned the iPhone camera prior to use, and was very concerned about taking the "best" picture for documentation purposes. *"What do you think tells the best story?"* – he kept repeating to himself. Throughout the experiment he got very excited with the system because it was suggesting centers close to the middle. In other words, the application tended to agree that his aiming was appropriate for documentation.

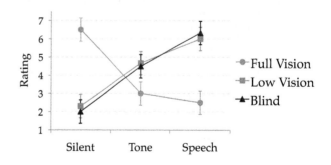

Figure 6: Post-test preference ratings by Mode and User

Multiple visually impaired participants used the application to take a picture of their guide dog, and requested a copy for their personal use. Other participants with visual impairments suggested using the system for documenting potholes, which they considered extremely dangerous.

5. DISCUSSION

Is audio feedback valuable when users roughly know the direction in which to aim the camera?
Yes. Audio feedback helped steering users towards centering targets in pictures, and visually impaired users indicated preference for both Speech and Tone modes, versus Silent mode. Objective data showed that when they interacted with the system in Speech mode, their performance tended to be better (e.g., faster aiming time, more centering, etc).

Is speech-based feedback preferred? How do subjective factors change for these interaction modes?
Speech was preferred over Silent mode, but preferences were not significantly different between Speech and Tone mode. We noticed that visually impaired users were not affected by audio feedback in terms of Social Comfort, though this was not the case for the full vision group.

We observed trends in favor of Speech between the visually impaired community, including slightly higher ratings for Ease of Use. Subjective opinions on Ease of Use and Usefulness were supported by objective data that showed that orientation information (provided only by the Speech mode) seemed to help users center the target more easily.

6. FINAL REMARKS

This study reinforces earlier work that suggests that users who are blind or low vision find assisted photography appealing and useful. Furthermore, it appears there is overall acceptance of assisted photography, including users with full vision, due to the positive ratings of usefulness. The collected results suggest the participants with full vision do find value in the silent *paparazzi* mode, thereby suggesting assisted photography has universal appeal. However, it is clear that the interface may need to change when systems know the user is blind or low vision. The iOS5 camera application's altered behavior when VoiceOver is turned on is a good example of how this can be achieved.

7. ACKNOWLEDGMENTS

The Rehabilitation Engineering Research Center on Accessible Public Transportation (RERC-APT) is funded by grant number H133E080019 from the United States Department of Education through the National Institute on Disability and Rehabilitation Research.

8. REFERENCES

[1] S. Baker and I. Matthews. Lucas-kanade 20 years on: A unifying framework. *Int'l J. Comput. Vision*, 56(3):221 – 255, March 2004.

[2] J. Bigham, C. Jayant, A. Miller, B. White, and T. Yeh. Vizwiz::locateit - enabling blind people to locate objects in their environment. In *Proc. CVPRW'10*, 2010.

[3] J. P. Bigham, C. Jayant, H. Ji, G. Little, A. Miller, R. C. Miller, R. Miller, A. Tatarowicz, B. White, S. White, and T. Yeh. Vizwiz: nearly real-time answers to visual questions. In *Proc. UIST'10*, 2010.

[4] F. Crete, T. Dolmiere, P. Ladret, and M. Nicolas. The blur effect: perception and estimation with a new no-reference perceptual blur metric. In *SPIE Conf. Series*, volume 6492, 2007.

[5] B. Deville, G. Bologna, M. Vinckenbosch, and T. Pun. Guiding the focus of attention of blind people with visual saliency. In *Proc. CVAVI'08*, 2008.

[6] R. Ferzli and L. Karam. A No-Reference Objective Image Sharpness Metric Based on the Notion of Just Noticeable Blur (JNB). *IEEE Trans. Image Process.*, 18(4):717 –728, april 2009.

[7] S. Harada, H. Takagi, and C. Asakawa. On the audio representation of radial direction. In *Proc. CHI'11*, 2011.

[8] A. Hub, J. Diepstraten, and T. Ertl. Design and development of an indoor navigation and object identification system for the blind. In *Proc. ASSETS'04*, 2004.

[9] L. Itti and C. Koch. Computational modelling of visual attention. *Nature Reviews Neuroscience*, 2(3):194–203, 2001.

[10] C. Jayant. Mobileaccessibility: camera focalization for blind and low-vision users on the go. *SIGACCESS Access. Comput.*, (96):37–40, 2010.

[11] C. Jayant, H. Ji, S. White, and J. P. Bigham. Supporting blind photography. In *Proc. ASSETS'11*, 2011.

[12] J. Ko and C. Kim. Low cost blur image detection and estimation for mobile devices. In *Proc. ICACT*, 2009.

[13] A. Kutiyanawala, V. Kulyukin, and J. Nicholson. Teleassistance in accessible shopping for the blind. In *Proc. ICOMP'11*, 2011.

[14] X. Liu. A camera phone based currency reader for the visually impaired. In *Proc. ASSETS'08*, 2008.

[15] Matt Richardson. Descriptive Camera Project. http://mattrichardson.com/Descriptive-Camera/. Last accessed May 2012.

[16] N. Narvekar and L. Karam. A No-Reference Image Blur Metric Based on the Cumulative Probability of Blur Detection (CPBD). *IEEE Trans. Image Process.*, 20(9):2678 –2683, Sept. 2011.

[17] A. Steinfeld, R. Aziz, L. Von Dehsen, S. Y. Park, J. Maisel, and E. Steinfeld. Modality preference for rider reports on transit accessibility problems. TRB 2010 Annual Meeting. Transportation Research Board, 2010.

[18] A. Steinfeld, J. Maisel, and E. Steinfeld. The value of citizen science to promote transit accessibility. In *First Intl. Symposium on Quality of Life Technology*, 2009.

[19] E. Tekin and J. M. Coughlan. A mobile phone application enabling visually impaired users to find and read product barcodes. In *Proc. ICCHP'10*, 2010.

[20] M. Vázquez and A. Steinfeld. An assisted photography method for street scenes. In *Proc. WACV'11*, 2011.

Learning Non-Visual Graphical Information using a Touch-Based Vibro-Audio Interface

Nicholas A. Giudice[1], HariPrasath Palani[1]

[1]Spatial Informatics Program:
School of Computing and Information Science,
University of Maine, 5711 Boardman Hall,
Orono, Maine, USA 04469

giudice@spatial.maine.edu,
hariprasath.palani@maine.edu

Eric Brenner[2], Kevin M. Kramer[2]

[2]Advanced Medical Electronics,
6901 East Fish Lake Road,
Suite 190, Maple Grove,
MN 55368

brenneraeric@gmail.com,
kkramer@ame-corp.com

ABSTRACT

This paper evaluates an inexpensive and intuitive approach for providing non-visual access to graphic material, called a vibro-audio interface. The system works by allowing users to freely explore graphical information on the touchscreen of a commercially available tablet and synchronously triggering vibration patterns and auditory information whenever an on-screen visual element is touched. Three studies were conducted that assessed legibility and comprehension of the relative relations and global structure of a bar graph (Exp 1), Pattern recognition via a letter identification task (Exp 2), and orientation discrimination of geometric shapes (Exp 3). Performance with the touch-based device was compared to the same tasks performed using standard hardcopy tactile graphics. Results showed similar error performance between modes for all measures, indicating that the vibro-audio interface is a viable multimodal solution for providing access to dynamic visual information and supporting accurate spatial learning and the development of mental representations of graphical material.

Categories and Subject Descriptors

H.5.2 [User Interfaces]: Auditory (non-speech) feedback, Evaluation/methodology; K.4.2 [Social Issues]: Assistive technologies for persons with disabilities

General Terms

Design, Experimentation, Human Factors

Keywords

Accessibility (blind and visually-impaired), assistive technology, information graphics, haptic cues, audio cues, android programming, graphs and diagrams.

1. INTRODUCTION

Gaining access to graphical information such as graphs, figures, maps, and images represents a major challenge for blind and

visually impaired people. Access to printed material has largely been solved via screen reading software using text-to-speech, for example, programs such as JAWS for Windows (www.freedomscientific.com) or VoiceOver for the Mac and iOS-based portable devices (www.apple.com/accessibility/voiceover/). However, these programs do not have the ability to convey meaningful information about graphic and non-text-based material. Given the vast amount of information which is conveyed through visually-based representations, whether it is in the classroom, the boardroom, or the living room, blind people will continue to miss out on a major component of our information-driven culture unless new non-visual solutions providing access to graphical information are developed. Although this problem has been widely studied (see Section 3, Current Research), approaches for improving the accessibility of graphical information have not made much progress in reaching blind and low-vision users. As this demographic is estimated to number around 12 million people in the U.S. and 285 million people worldwide [21], the need for developing devices that are both usable and likely to be adopted is of growing societal importance. The path forward requires addressing the following limitations which have plagued progress in this domain: research and development projects all too often languish in research labs; the design of new hardware/software is frequently driven by engineering principles without solid theoretical knowledge of relevant perceptual and cognitive characteristics of the human end-user; the systems developed generally have a steep learning curve and rely on unintuitive sensory translation rules; many solutions necessitate purchase of expensive single-purpose hardware; assistive technology often is built-around non-portable devices; and there is an emphasis in the literature on describing technical design features and algorithms, rather than conducting empirical experiments and behavioral evaluations.

Our goal is to provide access to visually-based graphic material using an intuitive interface that provides dynamic information on a device which is inexpensive (i.e. is based on off-the-shelf commercial hardware vs. highly specialized adaptive equipment), is portable enough to be used in many contexts and environments, is multi-purposed (meaning that the underlying hardware can be used for other applications), and supports universal design principles (i.e., is highly customizable and includes many accessibility features in the native interface). To this end, this paper describes what we call a vibro-audio interface, used for conveying visual information via a commercial tablet, which satisfies these design criteria. We believe that the conjunction of considering these design factors from the onset, along with conducting principled empirical investigations to evaluate and refine the perceptibility, usability, and acceptability of the interface, will not only ensure its efficacy in significantly improving the graphical information gap between blind persons and their sighted peers, but does so via a solution which is likely to be readily adopted. This approach avoids the engineering trap, which we argue is the reason that most assistive technology fails, i.e. development is driven by computational efficiency and often naïve assumptions of the designer without feedback of the functional utility of the technology or its ability to address the most critical needs of actual end-users.

2. SYSTEM OVERVIEW

The vibro-audio interface was based on a Samsung Galaxy Tablet with a 7.0 inch touchscreen running Android OS version 3.2, Target version 13. Vibro-tactile information was generated from the tablet's embedded electromagnetic actuator, i.e., an off-balance motor, which was controlled by Immersion Corporation's embedded haptic player. The haptic effects, i.e., vibro-tactile stimuli, for the experimental application were based on the Universal Haptic Layer (UHL) developed by Immersion Corporation (www.immersion.com/products/motiv/index.html). The UHL is a JAR file containing all the classes, interfaces, and algorithms necessary to create dynamic haptic effects on Android devices. The UHL was installed as a plugin for the JAVA development platform (Eclipse) used to create the experimental code. This provided a set of pre-defined haptic effects which were incorporated into the android source code of the application. Auditory output was delivered from the device's onboard speakers. Users also received kinesthetic feedback as they moved their hand over the tablet's touchscreen. Any object, visual or non-visual, that was displayed on the tablet's screen was referenced to a fixed coordinate system and whenever an on-screen visual element was touched, pre-defined vibration patterns and auditory information could be synchronously triggered at that coordinate [see 17 for technical details on the interface]. Although there is only one vibration motor embedded in the device, the use of one finger provides a strong focal stimulus to the digit touching the screen, which is perceived as a tactile point or line as the finger is moved over the stimulus. It should be noted that other studies using touch-enabled devices have found that use of only one finger was sufficient for vibro-tactile line tracing [7, 16], and previous studies on exploration of haptic maps has shown little improvement in learning between conditions using one or multiple fingers [26]. Many stimulus variables could be manipulated and tested in this interface but in this paper, we used a fixed set of parameters established from earlier psychophysical studies in the lab that identified the vibro-tactile line width which is most conducive to line tracing and contour following and the vibratory patterns which best differentiate edges from vertices [17]. Thus, based on these findings, all lines were rendered with a width of 8.9 mm (0.35 inch), which corresponded to 60 pixels on the tablet's screen. This was also used as the minimum inter-line distance for all stimuli. Lines rendered in the vibro-audio mode were given a constant vibration, based on the UHL effect "Engine_100," which uses an infinite repeating loop at 250Hz with 100 percent power. The vertices, either at the end of a single line or at the intersection of two or more lines, were indicated by a pulsing vibration, as our previous research indicated that this cue was helpful for identifying changes in direction during line tracing and for finding the end of individual lines (e.g., the tops of the bars in our bar graphs). Pulses were given in a 60 x 60 pixel (0.35 x 0.35 inch) region encompassing the entire node at the vertex. As

nodes at non-orthogonal vertices were not symmetric, the width of the pulsing region varied depending on the intersecting angle of the lines. The pulse signal was based on the UHL effect "Weapon_1," which uses a strong infinitely repeating wide pulse at a frequency of 10-20 milliseconds.

We believe that this interface provides a natural mapping of stimulus information to what is being perceived, while also employing a relatively large (7.0 inch) haptic workspace which can be quickly and easily updated in real-time. Another advantage of the touchscreen is that experimental scripts can be used to log the user's movement behavior and actions, which helps in identifying learning and exploration strategies (although this was not the principle goal of this paper). Assuming the experimental software was made available, this interface could be readily implemented on any off-the-shelf smart touch-based device with at least one embedded vibration motor, the UHL installed, and an audio output facility.

3. CURRENT RESEARCH

Much of the empirical research on accessible graphical displays, auditory or haptic, has focused on design guidelines and user preferences of the interface [12, 13], psychophysical factors characterizing optimal display properties to be implemented or the nature of the perceptual mapping employed [19], or interpretation and legibility of specific information being displayed [8]. These are all important aspects to consider when designing and evaluating a new display but the focus of the current paper addresses a different issue; namely, how accurately graphical information from our vibro-audio interface can be learned and represented in memory as a global spatial image. Earlier research in our lab has demonstrated that users have a favorable opinion of the vibro-audio interface we are using and we have already identified the core vibro-tactile parameters for presenting lines and vertices [17]. Thus, our interest here relates to evaluating whether use of this interface leads to development of an accurate spatial representation of the graphical information being conveyed. The logic is that if the vibro-audio interface is to be truly useful, learning must lead to an accurate representation in memory, similar to that derived from visual access, which supports subsequent mental transformations, computations, and behaviors. Our focus here is on spatial properties of the stimuli. Of note, most graphical information is based on spatial information, and a growing body of literature supports the notion that spatial information encoded from different input modalities can lead to common (amodal) representations in memory which function equivalently in supporting spatial behaviors [see 11 for review].

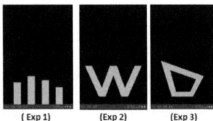

(Exp 1) (Exp 2) (Exp 3)

Figure 1. Example stimuli displayed on the touch-based device with the vibro-audio mode for the three experiments. Analog hardcopy tactile stimuli (not depicted) were used as a comparison in each experiment.

To address this issue, three experiments were conducted that assess comprehension of the relative relations and global structure between elements on a bar graph (Exp 1), pattern recognition via a letter identification task (Exp 2), and orientation recognition of complex geometric shapes on a shape discrimination task (Exp 3). Each experiment represents a different set of behaviors that rely on accessing an accurate spatial representation built up from learning common graphic material. They all compare two display mode conditions, one that employs the vibro-audio tablet interface at learning and another that employs hardcopy tactile stimuli produced by a graphics embosser (the gold standard for tactile output). In this paper, we are concentrating our discussion on these tasks. Thus, other applications using similar auditory, vibro-tactile, or multimodal displays, such as for navigation are not discussed [but see 6].

4. EXPERIMENT 1: GRAPH LEARNING

The ability to access visual representations of numeric data is critical in many educational and vocational contexts. Indeed, the lack of widely available non-visual rendering techniques has had detrimental effects for blind students on learning and conceptualizing graphs and interpreting patterns and trends of graphical data [20]. Over the years, there have been many research projects investigating the use of dynamic information displays providing access to various types of graphs and charts. These non-visual interfaces can be broadly classified into audio-based [20], haptic-based [24], language-based [4], or multimodal interfaces [25]. The greatest amount of work has been done with auditory graph displays utilizing different sonification techniques where changes in the visual data are mapped onto auditory parameters such as pitch, loudness, timbre, or tempo [19]. Various studies have demonstrated the efficacy of this approach for conveying meaningful information in sonified graphs to blind people [2, 20].

As discussed earlier, we believe that some form of tactual output is the best analog to visually rendered graphics and that a haptic-based display is the best choice for conveying visually oriented spatial data. Most of the research addressing haptic graphs beyond static hardcopy renderings has used force-feedback devices, such as the PHANToM from Sensable Technologies, or the Logitech WingMan force feedback mouse [24], or devices that use piezo-electric pins that dynamically move up and down [15]. The pros and cons of different haptic technologies goes beyond the scope of this paper [for review, see 12] but the main limitations of these displays relate to the earlier mentioned shortcomings of cost, portability, usability, and lack of multi-purpose application.

The advent and proliferation of smooth surfaced touchscreen based devices (e.g., smartphones and tablets) has opened the door to a new era of multimodal interfaces incorporating combinations of auditory, vibro-tactile, and kinesthetic cues. With these devices, hand and finger movements over the display provide position and orientation cues through kinesthesis and the presence of visual elements, such as lines and points, are delivered by an external synchronized cue (such as audio or vibration) when the user touches that element on the touchscreen. We differentiate these devices into two categories based on the perceptual cues provided: audio-kinesthetic interfaces, which couple text and sound cues with hand movement; and haptic-audio interfaces, which add vibro-tactile feedback. Examples of audio-kinesthetic interfaces include Timbremap, which uses sonification for representing complex indoor layouts on a touchscreen equipped smartphone [18] and the PLUMB project, which uses sonification to describe auditory graphs on a touch tablet [3]. Research with

both projects supported efficacy of the devices, as users showed clear evidence for accurate perception of the experimental stimuli. Haptic-audio touchscreen-based interfaces differ from traditional hardcopy tactile stimuli and other electronic haptic devices as the cutaneous information being conveyed is purely through vibration on a smooth display surface, rather than the traditional method of feeling embossed lines or moving or vibrating pin arrays. Here, the vibration is generated by rotating electro-magneto vibration actuators which are either fixed internally in the device or fixed to the fingers of the users. An example of the former approach is TouchOver map, which showed that blindfolded-sighted participants could understand a road network through vibration and auditory labels when feeling a smartphone touchscreen, and then were able to accurately reproduce the map using vision while simultaneously exploring the now occluded display [16]. Similarly, the GraVVITAS project demonstrated that graphs, shapes, and maps could be understood by blind users when learned from a touch tablet with external vibrators affixed to the user's fingers [7]. Results from a similar project has shown promising results for apprehending tactile graphs and charts using a touchscreen and multiple piezo-electric motors to stimulate the finger [14]. From a technical standpoint, TouchOver map is most similar to the current research, although we are using a tablet which has twice the screen real estate as the smartphone employed in that project. The GraVVITAS project investigated similar stimuli as we do here, but it used external vibration motors and multiple fingers during exploration. By contrast, we are simply using the internal tablet vibration motor and one point of contact (the dominant finger) on the touchscreen. Importantly, none of these studies required development of an accurate spatial representation to perform the tasks, as is our goal here, and most did not use formal statistical procedures to analyze their data. Despite these differences and the preliminary nature of the research, we interpret the above findings, as well as those from earlier research in our lab with the vibro-audio interface implemented on a smartphone [17], as lending support for the utility of this interface in the current experiments.

4.1 Method

Twelve sighted participants (six males and six females, ages 18-35) were recruited for the study. Three additional blind participants (2 males and 1 female, ages 22-38) also participated. All three were congenitally blind and had no more than light perception. The etiology of blindness was Retinopathy of Prematurity for one participant and Leber's Congenital Amaurosis for the other two. All gave informed consent and were paid for their participation. The study took between 1.5 and 2 hours. Note that it is important to carefully consider whether blindfolded-sighted participants are a reasonable sample when generalizing to blind participants. We believe inclusion is justified here as we are testing the ability to learn and represent non-visual material which is equally accessible to both groups. In support, previous studies with auditory graphs [20] and tactile maps [5] found no differences between blind and blindfolded-sighted groups. Indeed, inclusion of non-representative users (e.g., blindfolded-sighted participants) is generally accepted in the preliminary efficacy testing of assistive technology [see 27 for discussion]. If anything, the performance of the blindfolded-sighted participants in the current experiments represents a conservative estimate of interface efficacy, as this group is likely to be less accustomed to using haptic cues as a primary mode of information gathering. Although our participant samples are too small to make valid statistical comparisons between groups, the similarity of performance observed between blindfolded-sighted and blind participants (as seen in the data figures corresponding to each experiment) provides support for the validity of our inclusion decision.

During the experiment, participants sat on an adjustable chair and adjusted the seat height such that they could comfortably interact with the experimental devices which rested on a 76.2 cm (30 inch) height table in front of them. During the learning phase of each experimental trial, participants wore a blindfold (Mindfold Inc., Tucson, AZ.). In the vibro-audio condition, they used a Samsung Galaxy Tab 7.0 Plus tablet, with a 17.78 cm (7.0 inch) touchscreen as the information display. Vibro-tactile feedback was generated when the user's finger touched the stimulus on the screen and auditory information was provided by tapping the vibrating region (see section 2). In the hardcopy braille conditions, tactile analogs of the same stimuli were produced on paper by a graphics embosser (ViewPlus Technologies, Emprint SpotDot). The paper was then mounted on a second Galaxy tablet such that auditory information could be given in real-time and the user's movement behavior could be tracked via its touchscreen as they felt the hardcopy stimuli (note that no vibro-tactile output was delivered in this condition). Exploration with both displays was done using only one finger (dominant) for all conditions.

4.2 Procedure

A within subjects design was used in the experiment, with participants learning and testing on three bar graphs in each of the two display mode conditions: hardcopy braille and vibro-audio (graph trials were randomized within display mode block, with block order counterbalanced between participants). Each display mode condition included a graph with *3, 4,* and *5* bars (presentation order was randomized within graph set, with set order alternating between participants). Each bar was assigned a name, with set 1 based on food: *pizza, burger, salad, chocolate and ice cream*; and set 2 on fields of study: *biology, physics, chemistry, mathematics, and computer science*. The name was spoken as an audio message when the user tapped on the bar.

The experiment consisted of a practice, learning, and testing phase for each display mode condition, for a total of 10 trials. The first practice trial in each display mode was a demo trial where the experimenter explained the task, goal, and search strategies and the participant explored the stimuli with corrective feedback. In the second practice trial, participants were blindfolded and asked to perform the complete experimental learning and testing sequence. The experimenter evaluated their answers immediately to ensure that they understood the task correctly before continuing. During the learning phase, blindfolded participants were asked to explore the graph and to indicate when they believed that they had learned all of the material represented. They were instructed to learn as quickly and accurately as possible. They were told that the height of each bar represented *how many people liked the specific food category* (Set 1) or *how many people were enrolled in the class* (Set 2). After learning, the experimenter removed the device and the participant was allowed to lift their blindfold. The testing phase consisted of two tasks. In the spatial relation task, participants answered four questions about the graph they just learned. Two of the questions assessed spatial relations between bars. For instance, *"What is the relation between biology and physics?"* The answer required a directional response (e.g., biology *is left/right of physics*), and a height judgment (e.g., biology *is taller/shorter than physics*). The other two questions assessed participant's ability to comprehend the

individual bar position in a global context. For instance, *"Which is the second highest bar?" "What is the middle bar?"* To reduce recall errors, the names of the bars were given in a list.

In the re-creation task, participants were asked to draw the graph on a template canvas of the same size as the display and to label each bar. Five equidistant textbox place holders were provided to indicate the possible bar positions. The only procedural differences for blind participants were that the questions were read aloud by the experimenter and the reproduction task was done with Lego™ pieces on a board (which provided the same position indicators). They labeled each bar by verbally indicating its name. All re-created graphs were analyzed in terms of whether individual bars had the correct label, position, and relative height in relation to the graph's global structure. From this design, we can evaluate several measures as a function of display mode condition. These include learning time from the learning phase, relative height accuracy, relative directional accuracy, relative position accuracy (i.e., individual bar position in relation to the global context), re-creation accuracy, and bar labeling accuracy.

4.3 Results

The most important outcome of this experiment, as shown in Figure 2, is the similarity of performance across all measures for both display modes (braille or tablet) and participant groups (blindfolded-sighted and blind).

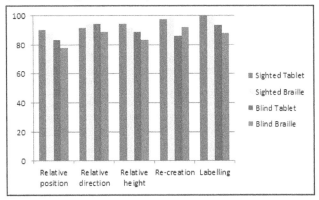

Figure 2. Accuracies on test measures as a function of display mode and subject group.

Corroborating what can be seen in the figure, results of paired-sample t-Tests between the two display modes(tablet and braille) were highly in-significant for all measures ($\alpha = 0.05$ was used for all statistical tests): relative height accuracy ($t(35) = -0.329$, $p = 0.744$); relative directional accuracy ($t(35) = -0.329$, $p = 0.744$); relative positional accuracy ($t(35) = -0.828$, $p = 0.413$); and re-creation accuracy, ($t(35) = -1.000$, $p = 0.324$).

Repeated measures ANOVAs were also conducted on each variable to assess if there were effects of the number of bars (e.g., 3, 4, or 5) between the two display modes; no statistically significant differences were found (all ps >0.05).

What is evident from these data is that use of a vibro-audio interface on a touch-enabled device supports accurate learning of relative relations and global structure of a bar graph. Importantly, the similarity of performance with this interface compared to that observed after learning with traditional hardcopy tactile output suggests the building up and accessing of functionally equivalent spatial representations between display modes. Superior performance for the hardcopy tactile mode was observed in learning time, ($t(35) = -4.924$, $p < 0.001$). This makes sense, as it is easier to find and track the line using the embossed brailled stimuli. Despite these differences, the more important findings of this experiment are the striking similarity in output performance between display modes for both participant groups. We interpret these results as providing compelling evidence that once learned, the representations built up from use of the vibro-audio display supported the same level of spatial behaviors as those built up from hardcopy tactile stimuli.

From these results, it can be seen that in general, both blindfolded-sighted and blind subjects yielded higher accuracy values with the re-creation task than with the spatial relations task. This result may be due to re-creation being done sequentially, whereas performance on the spatial relation questions required making judgments about bars that often required non-contiguous and non-sequential judgments. Also, as seen in Figure 2, participants average accuracy with the tablet mode for measures of positional accuracy, relative direction, relative height, and labeling were numerically higher than in the braille mode. Although not statistically different, this trend suggests that the interface leads to development of a spatial representation of the graph which is at least as good, if not better than from hardcopy stimuli.

5. EXPERIMENT 2: LETTER RECOGNITION

This experiment used the same vibro-audio tablet interface and hardcopy tactile stimuli as Exp 1 but now for recognizing patterns based on capital letters from the English alphabet. Letters represent complex but well known shapes and require participants to trace the contour of the stimuli and build up a global representation of its shape in order to correctly name the letter. This task has been used effectively in the past with different vibro-tactile stimuli [9] as well as visual apprehension with a limited field of view [22, Exp 3]. To our knowledge, non-visual letter recognition has not been studied with vibro-tactile touchscreen devices but early research with systems that converted visual information from camera input into vibro-tactile output were shown to support letter recognition via a 20 x 20 array of vibro-tactile stimulators on the back [10]. A device called the Optacon, which used an array of 144 electro-tactile stimulators felt by the finger, even proved useful for real-time letter recognition and limited reading [1].

Figure 3. Subject tracing stimuli displayed on the touch-based device with the vibro-audio mode.

Although we are using letters as the stimuli in this experiment, our goal here is to compare pattern recognition performance between the vibro-audio interface and hardcopy braille and not to test the efficacy of this interface for reading printed letters, although it could in theory be used in this capacity.

5.1 Method

The same participants, apparatus, and two display modes were used here as in Exp 1. The within subjects design also followed the same procedure of two practice trials and three experimental trials per display mode (counterbalanced). The task in this experiment was for blindfolded participants to explore the stimuli (one of six randomly presented letters) and to name the letter as soon as it was recognized. The six letters used during the experimental trials included: *D, F, M, P, T,* and *W* (with *N* and *C* used in the practice conditions). The letters were selected such that each display mode condition included three unique patterns including a letter with straight lines (*F* or *T*), a letter with curves (*D* or *P*), and a letter with slanted lines (*W* or *M*). A pulsing vibration was provided at each vertex in the vibro-tactile condition. No audio cues were used in this experiment. If the letter was mis-identified, a second learning period was allowed following the same procedure. Incorrect identification on the second learning phase was considered a miss.

Total learning time, number of learning iterations, and pattern recognition accuracy were evaluated as a function of display mode condition.

5.2 Results

As shown in Figure 3, the letter recognition performance for blind participants was done without error in both display modes. However, for sighted subjects, the ~89% letter recognition accuracy performance with the vibro-tactile interface was significantly worse than the 100% accuracy observed in the hardcopy braille mode, as assessed by a paired samples t-Test, $(t(35) = 2.092, p = 0.044)$. This difference is likely due to the impoverished orientation cues available in the tablet mode, which made it harder to detect line orientation, especially if the line was slanted or curved. Although the pulsing vibration at the vertices helped in determining an intersection or end node, there were no orientation cues to assist with non-rectilinear stimuli, which is apparently particularly challenging in the vibro-audio interface. In the braille condition, the embossed lines make it easier to detect line orientation and to follow the lines when they change direction (something that pilot studies in the lab have indicated is challenging with the vibro-audio interface).

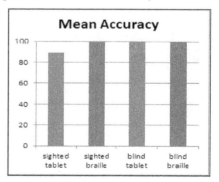

Figure 4. Letter recognition accuracy as a function of display mode and subject group.

The mean exploration iterations (sighted tablet: 1.2, sighted braille: 1.0, blind tablet: 1.2, blind braille: 1.1) for both the modes are greater than 1 iteration, which suggests that even in the braille modes participants made errors in their first recognition attempt. Also, the letters with symmetric patterns contributed to the wrong interpretation. For example, the W was often interpreted as V, U, or M. This occurred because subjects often traced only half (or part) of the object and then guessed that it was U or V. However, when traced fully, subjects tended to count the number of lines and to use this as a strategy to narrow the possible letter alternatives. Finally, as in the previous experiment, a significant difference was observed in learning time, (t(35) = -6.137, p < 0.01). As expected, this manifested with tablet conditions being slower than braille conditions, as discussed earlier.

6. EXPERIMENT 3: ORIENTATION DISCRIMINATION

This experiment investigated the ability to learn and represent the orientation of irregular shapes, consisting of four-sided polygons which were misaligned with the display's intrinsic frame of reference. After learning, participants had to match the learning stimulus with four alternatives based on the same shape presented at four different orientations. Other research has shown that touchscreen devices with external vibration actuators are beneficial in supporting recognition of shapes and patterns [7, 23]. The importance of this experiment is that it not only requires learning a complex shape, as has been previously investigated, but that the representation built up from learning was sufficiently robust to recall and discriminate the target shape in the presence of geometrically identical alternatives.

6.1 Method

The same participants, apparatus, and two display modes were used here as in the previous experiments. The within subjects design also followed the same procedure of two practice trials and three experimental trials per display mode (counterbalanced). The task in this experiment was for the blindfolded participant to explore the shape during a learning phase and to stop once they felt that they were familiar with its global geometry and orientation. Three distinct shapes were used in each display condition (counterbalanced). Only the bounding contour of the shape was rendered and none were readily namable polygons (see figure 1). No audio cues were used in this experiment and the pulsing vibration was provided at each vertex in the vibro-tactile condition. During learning, participants were asked to imagine the vertices, length of the sides, and the orientation of the shape on the display. Once participants indicated that the shape was learned, the experimenter removed the device and placed an A4 size paper containing the same shape in four different orientations. The shapes were numbered from 1 to 4 in a column.

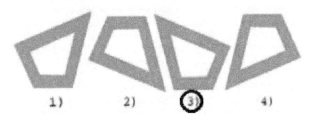

Figure 5. Alternatives for the example shape displayed in Figure 1.

Participants removed their blindfold and marked the alternative which matched the orientation of the shape previously learned. Blind participants performed the same task but made their comparison based on a sheet with 3D cut-outs of the four alternative shapes (all stimuli were size-matched). Measures analyzed included time to learn and orientation accuracy.

6.2 Results

No reliable differences were observed in the paired sample t-Tests conducted between the two display modes for orientation accuracy (t(35) = 0.298, p = 0.768). These results suggest that learning with the tablet mode was functionally equivalent to learning with the braille mode for apprehending shapes and for identifying the reference shape from geometrically identical alternatives.

However, as is shown in Figure 6, the orientation performance with the tablet mode yielded lower numeric means,~83% and ~77% mean accuracy, contrasting with ~86% and ~88% accuracy for the braille mode for sighted and blind subjects respectively.

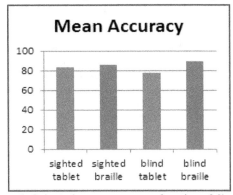

Figure 6. Orientation accuracy as a function of display mode and subject group.

Similar to Exp 2, subjects self-reported difficulty in identifying the slanting lines as they felt that the perceptual cues from the vibro-audio interface were not as "sharp" as with the hardcopy braille stimuli and that it was hard to monitor their hand trajectory when it was not moving in register with one of the intrinsic axes of the device. As with the previous experiments, learning time with the braille stimuli was significantly faster than with the vibro-audio interface, (t(35) = -7.170, p < 0.001).

7. GENERAL DISCUSSION

Three experiments were conducted that assessed the ability to learn and represent three types of graphical information using a newly developed vibro-audio interface [17] and compared performance with traditional hardcopy tactile representations of the same graphics. Overall, our results provided strong support for the efficacy of the vibro-audio interface for accurately perceiving and learning the experimental stimuli and in building up accurate mental representations supporting various spatial operations for both blindfolded-sighted and blind participants. Importantly, error performance did not reliably differ between display modes on any of the measures tested, demonstrating that the vibro-audio interface provides a comparable level of access to graphical material as is possible from a traditional hardcopy medium. These findings are important as this interface provides dynamic and readily implemented information, whereas hardcopy material is static and requires expensive, highly specialized equipment to produce. In addition, as the vibro-audio interface is based on inexpensive, multi-purpose, and commercially-available hardware, it represents a viable alternative to the expense and complexity of existing auditory and haptic solutions which have various shortcomings, as described earlier. Although all participants reported familiarity with touchscreen devices, they had never experienced vibro-audio graphical stimuli as were evaluated here. Indeed, the highly similar results between modes observed across experiments are quite remarkable given the absence of significant training with the vibro-audio interface. This performance occurred with a combined practice period of around 30 minutes, compared to shape and letter recognition proficiency with other assistive technology, (e.g., the optacon) which took well over 100 hours [6]. We interpret this robust finding across all of the experimental conditions and between both blindfolded-sighted and blind participant groups as showing the intuitiveness of the interface. In support, post-experiment debriefing revealed that all participants liked the vibro-audio interface and that the blind participants expressed interest in adopting it as a primary graphics display if it were further developed. Providing increased familiarity and some small modifications to the interface may well improve learning time and some of the behavioral ambiguities we observed, as discussed below.

Although all subjects performed quite well in the Exp 1 graph conditions, their strategy of moving perpendicularly between the tops of the bars (i.e., to gauge their relative heights) was sometimes challenging in the tablet condition as they had trouble moving laterally, often deviating upward during their trace. This behavior was not observed in the hardcopy braille condition, as the lines provided a better fixed reference on the paper. These results, along with the challenges observed in the tablet condition for following slanted and curved lines in the letter and shape recognition experiments, suggest the need for developing a secondary cue to assist with contour tracing and for staying oriented when exploring non-rectilinear stimuli. A related phenomenon is that slight orientations in the stimuli (10 to 20 degrees) were perceived as a straight line in the tablet conditions. This problem could be resolved in the future by using auditory information to indicate deviation from a given line orientation.

In Exp 2, letter recognition performance was influenced by the similarity of the pattern in the tablet condition. That is, letters such as "D" and "P" were interpreted as the same since they have a line and a curve in common. Since these pattern errors were only observed in the first learning attempt, and correct recognition was near perfect after the second learning iteration, this problem is likely due to lack of familiarity with the tablet interface than to actual challenges interpreting the information conveyed. Thus, with the addition of new auditory cues to complement the vibro-tactile information, and more training with the interface, it is likely that many of these challenges would be ameliorated. Even so, it is remarkable how well the tablet device faired compared to the tried and true hardcopy tactile output. Not only was performance with the vibro-audio interface nearly equivalent on most conditions, it was actually better on some, even though this interface was completely new to our participants.

The time taken to learn was significantly different between the braille and tablet modes for all conditions. Although the learning time with the tablet was approximately four times greater than the time taken in the braille conditions, this was not unexpected owing to differences in the way information is conveyed and extracted between modes. As discussed earlier, adding additional complementing cues and allowing greater experience with the vibro-audio interface is predicted to narrow this gap. Future experiments need to investigate which cues might aid in this process. We believe that with additional technical advancements and usability evaluations, the tablet could be improved to support even better performance and provide access to a far broader range of graphics than were tested here with the initial prototype interface.

Future studies will focus on enhancing the ability of the interface such that it can automatically convert existing visual graphics into an accessible form suitable for presentation as vibro-audio graphics. Research will also include identifying the optimal vibrating pattern for different spatial objects and the use of piezo-electric actuators instead of mechanical vibrators. Piezo-electric actuators will enable high definition haptic effects. For instance, Immersion's high definition embedded player is touted to deliver powerful and crisp effects with: (1) a wide haptic band-with (50 - 350 Hz) affording increased range, strength, and precision, (2) superior effects isolation, as the actuator can be mounted to vibrate only the touchscreen, (3) instantaneous, low latency touch feedback which reduces haptic lag time below human perception, and (4) quiet piezo haptics, that reduce noise below the audible range(http://ir.immersion.com/releasedetail.cfm?ReleaseID=4447 61)]. We also plan to further evaluate the usability of this interface for other tasks, such as for non-visual map learning and for assisting spatial learning, navigation, and cognitive map development.

8. ACKNOWLEDGMENTS

We thank Advanced Medical Electronics Corporation for providing the required software and Tablet devices in these experiments, and Bill Whalen for assistance with the manuscript. We acknowledge support from NIDRR grant H133S100049 and NSF grant CDI-0835689 on this project.

9. REFERENCES

[1]   BLISS, J.C., KATCHER, M.H., ROGERS, C.H., and SHEPARD, R.P., 1970. Optical-to-tactile image conversion for the blind. *IEEE Transactions on Man-Machine Systems 11*, 58-65.

[2]   BREWSTER, S.A., 2002. Visualization tool for blind people using multiple modalities. *Disability and Rehabilitation Technology 24*, 11-12, 613-621.

[3]   COHEN, R.F., YU, R., MEACHAM, A., and SKAFF, J., 2005. Plumb: displaying graphs to the blind using an active auditory interface. In *Proceedings of the 7th international ACM SIGACCESS conference on Computers and accessibility (ASSETS05)* ACM Press, New York, NY, 182-183.

[4]   FERRES, L., LINDGAARD, G., and SUMEGI, L., 2010. Evaluating a tool for improving accessibility to charts and graphs. In *Proceedings of the 12th international ACM SIGACCESS conference on Computers and accessibility* ACM, New York, NY, Orlando, Fl, 83-90.

[5]   GIUDICE, N.A., BETTY, M.R., and LOOMIS, J.M., 2011. Functional equivalence of spatial images from touch and vision: Evidence from spatial updating in blind and sighted individuals. *Journal of Experimental Psychology: Learning, Memory and Cognition 37*, 3, 621-634.

[6]   GIUDICE, N.A. and LEGGE, G.E., 2008. Blind navigation and the role of technology. In The *Engineering Handbook of Smart Technology for Aging, Disability, and Independence*, A. HELAL, M. MOKHTARI and B. ABDULRAZAK (Eds). John Wiley & Sons, 479-500.

[7]   GONCU, C. and MARRIOTT, K., 2011. GraVVITAS: Generic Multi-touch Presentation of Accessible

Graphics. In *Proceedings of INTERACT2011* Springer, Berlin / Heidelberg 30-48.

[8]   HOGGAN, E., BREWSTER, S.A., and JOHNSTON, J., 2008. Investigating the Effectiveness of Tactile Feedback for Mobile Touchscreens. In *Proceedings of ACM CHI2008* ACM Press, Addison Wesley, Florence, Italy, 1573-1582.

[9]   LOOMIS, J.M., 1974. Tactile letter recognition under different modes of stimulus presentation. *Attention, perception, & psychophysics 16*, 2, 401-408.

[10]   LOOMIS, J.M. and APKARIAN-STIELAU, P., 1976. A lateral masking effect in tactile and blurred visual letter recognition. *Attention, Perception & Psychophysics 20*, 221-226.

[11]   LOOMIS, J.M., KLATZKY, R.L., and GIUDICE, N.A., in press. Representing 3D space in working memory: Spatial images from vision, touch, hearing, and language. In *Multisensory Imagery:Theory & Applications*, S. LACEY and R. LAWSON (Eds). Springer, New York.

[12]   MACLEAN, K.E., 2008. Haptic Interaction Design for Everyday Interfaces. In *Reviews of Human Factors and Ergonomics*, M. CARSWELL (Ed). Human Factors and Ergonomics Society, Santa Monica, CA, 149-194.

[13]   NEES, M.A. and WALKER, B.N., 2009. Auditory Interfaces and Sonification. In *The Universal Access Handbook*, C. STEPHANIDIS (Ed). CRC Press, New York, 507-521.

[14]   PETIT, G., DUFRESNE, A., LEVESQUE, V., HAYWARD, V., and TRUDEAU, N., 2008. Refreshable tactile graphics applied to schoolbook illustrations for students with visual impairment. In *Proceedings of the 10th international ACM SIGACCESS conference on Computers and accessibility (Assets08)*, 89-96.

[15]   PIETRZAK, T., CROSSAN, A., BREWSTER, S.A., MARTIN, B., and ISABELLE, P., 2009. Exploring Geometric Shapes with Touch. In *Proceedings of INTERACT2009*, 145-148.

[16]   POPPINGA, B., MAGNUSSON, C., PIELOT, M., and RASSMUS-GRÖHN, K., 2011. TouchOver map: audio-tactile exploration of interactive maps. In *Proceedings of the 12th international conference on Human computer interaction with mobile devices* ACM, Stockholm, Sweden, 545–550.

[17]   RAJA, M.K., 2011. The development and validation of a new smartphone based non-visual spatial interface for learning indoor layouts. Unpublished Masters thesis: *Spatial Information Science and Engineering,* University of Maine, Orono (advisor: N.A. Giudice).

[18]   SU, J., ROSENZWEIG, A., GOEL, A., DE LARA, D., and TRUONG, K.N., 2010. Timbremap: enabling the visually-impaired to use maps on touch-enabled devices. In *Proceedings of the 12th international conference on Human computer interaction with mobile devices* ACM, 17-26.

[19]   WALKER, B.N., 2002. Magnitude estimation of conceptual data dimensions for use in sonification. *Journal of Experimental Psychology: Applied 8*, 211-221.

[20]   WALKER, B.N. and MAUNEY, L., 2010. Universal Design of Auditory Graphs: A Comparison of Sonification Mappings for Visually Impaired and Sighted Listeners. *ACM Transactions on Accessible Computing 2*, 3, Article 12, 16 pages.

[21]   WORLD HEALTH ORGANIZATION, 2011. Visual impairment and blindness Fact Sheet, Retrieved 2012 from: http://www.who.int/mediacentre/factsheets/fs282/en/

[22]   WU, B., KLATZKY, R.L., and STETTEN, G.D., 2012. Mental visualization of objects from cross-sectional images. *Cognition 123*, 1, 33-49.

[23]   YATANI, K. and TRUONG, K.N., 2009. SemFeel: a user interface with semantic tactile feedback for mobile touch-screen devices. In *Proceedings of the 22nd annual ACM symposium on User interface software and technology*, 111-120.

[24]   YU, W. and BREWSTER, S.A., 2002. Comparing Two Haptic Interfaces for Multimodal Graph Rendering. In *proceedings of IEEE VR2002, 10th Symposium on Haptic Interfaces for Virtual Environment and Teleoperator Systems*, Florida.

[25]   YU, W. and BREWSTER, S.A., 2002. Evaluation of multimodal graphs for blind people. *Universal Access in the Information Society 2*, 2, 105-124,.

[26]   GIUDICE, N.A., MASON, S.J., & LEGGE, G.E., 2002. The relation of vision and touch: Spatial learning of small-scale layouts. Journal of Vision, 2(7), 522A.

[27]   SEARS, A. AND HANSON, V., 2011. Representing users in accessibility research. Proceedings of the 2011 annual conference on Human factors in computing systems.

Exploration and Avoidance of Surrounding Obstacles for the Visually Impaired

Limin Zeng, Denise Prescher and Gerhard Weber

Technische Universität Dresden

Human-Computer Interaction Research Group

Nöthnitzer Str. 46, 01187, Dresden, Germany

{limin.zeng, denise.prescher, gerhard.weber}@tu-dresden.de

ABSTRACT

Proximity-based interaction through a long cane is essential for the blind and the visually impaired. We designed and implemented an obstacle detector consisting of a 3D Time-of-Flight (TOF) camera and a planar tactile display to extend the interaction range and provide rich non-visual information about the environment. Users choose a better path after acquiring the spatial layout of obstacles than with a white cane alone. A user study with 6 blind people was analyzed and showed extra time is needed to ensure safe walking while reading the layout. Both hanging and ground-based obstacles were circumvented. Tactile mapping information has been designed for representation of precise spatial information around a blind user.

Categories and Subject Descriptors

H 5.2 [**User Interfaces**]: Haptic I/O

K.4.2 [**Social Issues**]: Assistive technology for people with disabilities

Keywords

Haptic user interface, obstacle avoidance, 3D TOF camera, tactile symbol.

INTRODUCTION

Persons who are blind or visually impaired may benefit from GPS-based navigation systems and follow calculated routes while traveling, but most of them are still suffering from various obstacles and hazards on their way. Mobility-related accidents are often painful and sometimes harmful as various hazards like holes, poles, doors and overhead mounted signs are perilous for the body but specifically for the head [20]. White canes detect floor-based obstacles, however, dangerous head-level obstacles are missed and often holes remain undetected. Through training visually impaired people learn to handle more types of obstacles and apply different strategies for circumventing them.

The white cane is an ingenious tool as both haptic and auditory feedback is generated, whilst detecting the surrounding space within a 1 m distance (one step ahead). The detected range is neither sufficient to obtain an overview layout around the whole body nor to decide about a route. In addition to a cane, it is of

advantage to let the visually impaired pedestrian learn about the environment in a larger range, and to decide about a route actively in advance. Electronic travel aids (ETAs) have integrated different digital sensors to detect the environments beyond the end of the cane. But most of them are unable to notify about comprehensive cues with multiple obstacles at the same time, to locate precisely and to explore the properties of nearby obstacles. It's still unclear about their strategies to avoid obstacles if they can access a larger area of the surrounding environments than the range of a white cane.

In this paper, previous work is extended while ensuring possible integration with other ETAs. We designed and implemented a new system by integrating an off-the-shelf 3D Time-of-Flight (TOF) camera to detect surrounding objects up to 7 meters in both indoor/outdoor environments, and a novel multi-line refreshable Braille display (an array of 30x32 pins) to render obstacles precisely. Evaluations have been performed to investigate the performance of our system. In the following, we describe the system and discuss the results of the evaluation.

RELATED WORK

In recent years a number of different approaches have been implemented to detect and represent surrounding obstacles for the visually impaired. Out of scope in this paper are beacons or other types of announcement methods requiring changes to the infrastructure beforehand such as RFID and barcode readers.

Detection of Obstacles

The white cane is one of the most popular assistive tools for the blind due to its low-cost and convenience. However, it is unable to sense the space above knee level, and its available range is limited by its length. Thus, as a first step to prevent obstacles, various electronic sensors have been employed to overcome the disadvantages of white canes.

Ultrasonic Sensor

Since about 1960s a number of systems have adopted the ultrasonic echolocation to detect obstacles within different height levels. Ultrasonic probe [15] was a hand-held torch, and Sonicguide [16] consisted of a transmitter and two receivers which mounted on the frame of glasses. As one pair of ultrasonic sensors has only a narrow field, thus Navbelt [4] and GuideCane [26] used multiple pairs of ultrasonic sensors. However, ultrasonic sensors have a couple of fundamental limitations owing to the wide wavelength of ultrasound at a centimeter level. Thus it fails to detect smooth surfaces and small apertures are not detected, and distance of obstacles is not identified precisely.

Infrared & Laser Sensor

Optical systems (e.g. infrared sensors, laser sensors, and cameras) based on micrometer wavelength overcome the above disadvantages and have the ability of accurate range discrimination, including shape detection. Varied optical devices have been applied to detect surroundings and avoid hindrances [1]. In order to explore a larger field of view, robot systems make use of laser scanners to detect obstacles autonomously [6]. Whereas, it is time-consuming to scan the entire environment point by point through them.

Digital camera & Stereo camera

In order to reduce the time spent to capture a large field of view, digital cameras are employed, such as EYECane [14], See ColOr [3], and vOICe [19]. Nevertheless, it is challengeable that the digital cameras locate obstacles with precise distance and orientation. Stereo cameras not only inherit the advantages from digital cameras including object identification, but also calculate the distance and direction of obstacles [2,12]. One of the biggest drawbacks occurs in a dark or twilight environment as those camera-based systems are unable to work or perform badly. Caution in storing those data is also mandatory in order to respect privacy requirements of other pedestrians.

3D TOF Camera

Recently, affordable and portable time-of-flight (TOF) cameras have been developed and are available on the market. By comparison to stereo cameras and structured light-based depth sensors (e.g. Kinect device[1]), the TOF cameras solve most of problems [23]. A number of stationary applications mostly focus on real-time gesture/body movement interaction, body tracking, interactive games, or 3D scene reconstruction [11, 25]. Furthermore, objects are identified by processing the 3D point clouds in urban environments [10].

Some prototypical systems implemented mobility aids for the visually impaired [5]. The NAVI [30] project uses a Kinect which hardly detects holes and down-step obstacles on the floor while it is worn at the level of the head. Additionally, both of them [5, 30] are lack of evaluations with end users. A recently finished European project, CASBliP, implemented a 3D TOF sensor in an array of 64x1 pixels, which is not enough to detect a large space [7]. Those systems can't classify obstacles precisely one by one.

Representation of obstacles

Rendering information has been attempted manifold through non-visual interfaces, from the early GUI design [21] to daily navigation systems (e.g. [18, 22]), and desktop-based mapping services (e.g. [24]). Most of them depend upon the audio channel, the haptic channel, or audio-haptic interaction to represent graphic/spatial information. As one typical kind of spatial information, the distribution of surrounding obstacles is significant for people who are blind and visually impaired to make correct decisions while finding out a clear path and avoiding potential hindrances.

The acoustic representation of obstacles is a low-cost method, which has been employed widely [4, 7, 16]. In particular, [19] described a novel image-to-sound conversion, which generated corresponding frequency and amplitude of audio signals from images which are captured by digital cameras. Frequency and amplitude variations inform about obstacle cues. However, it appears to be too difficult to obtain the accurate distance and direction, even after a long-time of training. More importantly, the persistent audio output will interfere with hearing to sense the physical world, that might lead to be in dangerous situations.

By comparison to acoustic output, haptic presentation allows users to hear environmental sound and obtain information about obstacles simultaneously. Vibrotactile displays supply non-visual information against human's skin through wearable vibrators. [9] investigated successfully the methodologies how to use a vibrotactile waist belt, to encode the spatial direction through activation of corresponding vibrators, and the distance through different vibration rhythms. Similarly, the NAVI project [30] made use of a waist belt with 3 vibrators. It appears that it is not enough to indicate precise orientation of obstacles. Therefore, a matrix of vibrators integrated in a complex display might enable to render more information. For example, in [8] a vibration array language was proposed to represent the spatial location of obstacles via a vest, equipped 4 by 4 tactors. However, due to insufficient vibrators those systems fail to render multiple obstacles in a complex situation at the same time.

Aiming at representation of obstacles, a tactile display consisting of an array of 8 by 8 actuators against finger-tips was utilized to demonstrate a simple edge-like style of obstacles' locations in the scene [27]. In the same way as above, because of a lack of pins, the system is unable to render detailed distribution of obstacles.

The emerging refreshable multi-line Braille displays have capabilities to equip a number of pins like the commercial HyperBraille display with a matrix of 120 by 60 pins [28], and commercial Dot View series[2], that offer capabilities to render complex spatial content, like street maps [29].

THE 3DOD SYSTEM

System Overview

In our 3D Obstacle Detector (3DOD), we combined an off-the-shelf 3D TOF camera and a novel portable Braille display, towards building up an ETA. A density-based spatial clustering algorithm calculates not only precise distance and orientation of obstacles, but also much more detailed properties (e.g. hanging or floor-based obstacle, width, height), via real-time processing of raw cloud points from the 3D TOF camera. Afterwards the obstacles are represented through abstract tactile symbols on the Braille display. Aiming at avoiding interference from acoustic ETAs, two kind of haptic devices are employed to notify users about obstacles. In addition to the tactile display, a hand-held Wii remote controller[3] equipped with a vibrator indicates whether there is an obstacle close-by immediately.

To detect many more obstacles like holes and descending stairs, we set up the camera around a user's waist. Due to its limited field of view there will be a dark area (see Figure 1), that is not inspected by the system. If the speed of information gathered matches or is lower than the walking speed, this dark area may be neglected.

Equation 1 describes the horizontal length of dark area.

$$D = \frac{H}{\tan(\alpha/2)} - L \qquad (1)$$

---

[1] http://www.xbox.com/en-US/kinect/

[2] http://www.kgs-jpn.co.jp
[3] http://www.nintendo.com

112

Where D indicates the horizontal length of dark area in the front, L is the length of a cane, and H means the height of the amounted camera, while α is the vertical field of view which is completely dependent on the specification of the camera. Obviously, to reduce the value of D on the ground a lower fixed height of the camera is desirable, like moving to the waist. In consequence, we set up the camera around a user's waist to detect many more obstacles like holes and descending stairs.

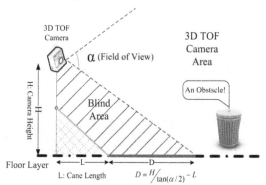

Figure 1. The area detected by a 3D TOF camera

The 3D TOF enables pedestrian to detect a large area in real-time, and the planar, refreshable tactile display conveys the spatial distribution of obstacles through touching against finger-tips or the palm. Besides a portable computer, an enhanced white cane has been employed by integrating a Wii remote controller (see Figure 2).

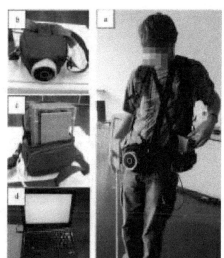

Figure 2. Components of the 3DOD system (a) A subject wears the 3DOD system; (b) 3D TOF camera (weight 1kg); (c) a portable multiple line Braille display (weight 600g); (d) a portable computer;

System Components

- 3D TOF Camera (See Figure 2(b)): gathers direct distances pixel by pixel (160x120) and can detect a range from 0.1m to 7m. Specifically, its optical filter and electronic suppression of background illumination ensure performance in an outdoor environment.

- Mobile multi-line Braille display (see Figure 2(c)): has an array of 30x32 pins and a capability of 5Hz to refresh the screen.

- Wiimote cane: is an enhanced white cane by integrating a Wii remote controller. In addition to its multiple buttons as a basic input channel, its built-in vibrator and speaker are an easy method to represent information via a non-visual interface [13].

- Others: a mobile power unit for the 3D TOF camera; a portable computer (with 2.1G Hz CPU and 4GB RAM) runs the 3DOD system as a host machine to control other components. The computer is connected with the camera and Braille display via USB-cable, while the cane is connected via wireless Bluetooth.

System Description

Work Mode

In the current system we implemented two work modes, the first one is inspection mode, and triggered by users (press button "A" on Wiimote) to obtain and present the latest scene when users are at rest, and the other one is walking mode (press button "B" on Wiimote) to automatically monitor the environment for obstacles while walking. The users can change conveniently between both of them at any time.

Differently to the inspection mode to process the current static frame while at rest, in the walking mode the system will update over time. The walking mode will be interrupted and the Wiimote will be vibrating while some obstacles are closer than 2 meters, and then warn users by the Wiimote and the Braille display (see Figure 3). At this moment, users have to stop walking to check the obstacles appeared on tactile display. Otherwise, the system will continue to monitor automatically. In walking mode the display re-draws its rendering while some obstacles are closer than 2 meters on the move, and this will lead to reduce users' cognitive load and extend the service lifetime of the Braille display.

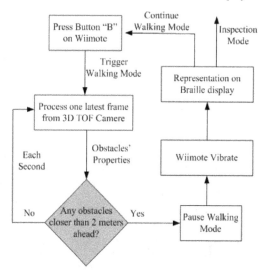

Figure 3. The flow chart of walking mode

Obstacles Detecting

Due to the 3D TOF camera, the system is able to detect a large portion of the environment. The camera can obtain raw 3D point clouds with precise pixel by pixel distance to objects. Pre-processing of raw point clouds is mandatory before classifying clusters and gathering more detailed information about obstacles. Based on [17] we developed an enhanced density-based spatial clustering algorithm which is suitable for a two-dimensional array captured by a 3D TOF camera in one shot. In brief, the algorithm tries to merge nearest neighboring points to shape objects through two pre-defined parameters, the clustering radius γ and the minimum number of points in one real cluster Min. Pts (minimum number of points) to filter possible noise clusters. The modified clustering algorithm is programmed in Microsoft VC++, using the ANN library[4] to search nearest neighboring points.

Representation of 3D obstacles

The strategy of representation
It's challengeable to inform the visually impaired users about the detailed distribution of surrounding obstacles, though a great variety of previous systems have tried to render in different manners, like acoustic output and vibrotactile output. It is not clear how to indicate the size of obstacles (e.g., length, width, and height) and the distribution simultaneously to users, as well as types of 3D obstacles such as ground-based obstacles, and dangerous hindrances over the waist or at head level. Unlike having a guide dog to detect the route and to circumvent, those details are important to blind walkers to find out a clear path, rather than only noticing presence or absence of obstacles.

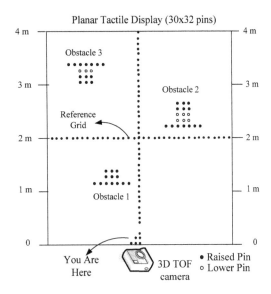

Figure 4. The layout of representation 3D obstacles on a 2D Braille display

In order to render the 3D spatial environment as detailed as possible, we designed a specific layout on the tactile display and a set of tactile obstacle symbols to encode 3D obstacles into a 2D representation. As illustrated in Figure 4, 3DOD renders obstacles in up to 4 meters distance, although the camera can detect up to 7 meters. The resolution of each pin is about 13.3 cm/pin. The symbol "You Are Here" indicates the position of users, while a central reference grid helps users quickly point out the location of obstacles, e.g. in 2 meters or beyond, and left, right or central. In particular, when rendering multiple obstacles on the surface at the same time, users not only find out about the distance and location of them, but they also can estimate the space between obstacles that reveals a possible path.

Tactile Obstacle Symbols
In order to represent obstacle properties as detailed as possible, we pre-defined a set of tactile symbols to inform users through tactile

---

[4] http://www.cs.umd.edu/~mount/ANN/

perception. Currently there are three basic elements of those symbols according to their properties: type, width and height, as shown in Figure 5. It is possible to extend the number of symbols by combining the 3 features to generate new symbols. The symbols allow users to identify not only grounded obstacles but also non-grounded ones. Users will know a rough description of obstacles in width and height, which may help them to find their clear path as well. Additionally, we tested the layout and symbols with several blind users during the design period.

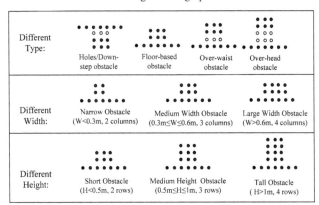

Figure 5. A set of tactile obstacle symbols (black points mean raised pins and hollow circles mean lower pins on a Braille display)

EVALUATION

Participants
We recruited 6 legally blind subjects (3 female and 3 male) to evaluate our system. They have no experiences on ETAs, but all are experienced with white canes or guide dogs. Their occupations are teacher, students, software tester and lawyer. Their mean age is 33.7 years-old. There are two low vision subjects who can only perceive bright light and large colored surfaces, but can't sense anything more than 2 meters. One of them has become factually blind only recently, who is learning Braille and is always going out with her guide dog. Others depend on the normal white canes and are more experienced with Braille. All subjects were told they could leave the evaluation at any time without any consequences.

Procedure
In order to evaluate the whole system systematically, we defined a series of tasks in sequence for the participants, consisting of a training period, a pre-test, a real trial within 2 scenarios in a large emptied lecture hall, and a post-questionnaire. Within the evaluation, the threshold γ is 10cm and Min. Pts is 100 in the clustering algorithm as described above.

Training
This section was divided into two phases, one focused on learning the legend of tactile obstacle symbols while the other was about how to make use of the whole system like the walking mode and the inspection mode. For phase 1, we produced the symbols by a Braille printer on paper and taught them one by one in detail.

On the other hand, in phase 2 another training task was to teach how to use the whole system. At first, we explained on the Wiimote cane that the button "A" starts the inspection mode and the button "B" triggers the walking mode. Secondly, they were trained to feel the active feedback from the Wiimote cane e.g. when there is an obstacle in 2 meters ahead, via the vibrator. Finally, subjects were able to learn a real representation of obstacles on the Braille display. Several symbols were rendered, in order to learn the layout of obstacles on the display, as well as skills to locate obstacles.

Pre-test

Similarly, we prepared two separate pre-tests after the training. At first we launched a test on a new set of samples embossed on paper with 6 new symbols (see Figure 6), to investigate how subects understand and remember those symbols in a short amount of time. Finally subjects were asked to point out the types, width and height of the obstacles.

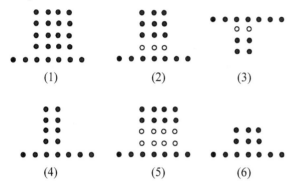

(1) (2) (3)

(4) (5) (6)

Figure 6. The 6 new tactile symbols in the pre-test

Secondly, another pre-test had been conducted in which a box (42x40x52cm) was erected on the ground at the direction of about eleven o'clock in the depth of 2.1 meters. The main purpose of the pre-test was to evaluate how the subjects can locate the box on the Braille display precisely by the inspection mode. As the blind are familiar with the clock system to understand exact orientations, our subjects need to report the precise direction of the box in the way of clock system, like ten o'clock, in addition to the distance. Then the subjects were asked to move towards the box and tried to avoid it by using the walking mode.

Real-trial

After the above preparations, participants would continue to take part in the real trail, which we had prepared in a big enough lecture hall (about 10x16 m) after removing chairs and tables. The subjects were asked to go through the pre-set obstacle zones with white canes and our 3DOD system. The trail consisted of two unique scenarios. Each scenario was built up in the same way and consisted of 12 objects typically encountered in a university context, but placed at pre-defined locations (3 chairs, 1 long table, 4 hanging boards, 1 hanging balloon, 1 thin pole, and 2 boxes), as shown in Figure 7 (note the markings on the floor). Users were not aware of this setup in this phase of the evaluation. Due to insufficient reflection points against black color, the 3 chairs were covered by something else in another color, this improved accuracy of the 3D TOF camera.

The difference between the two scenarios was the arrangements of the 12 obstacles including their starting point and end point (see Figure 9 and Figure 10). Most of the prepared obstacles were located around a diagonal line. At the end point, we set up a speaker to play light music, which indicated the destination for the visually impaired subjects, who had to point out the correct direction of the end point at the starting point. We randomly assigned subjects to start with scenario 1 or 2 using either their white cane alone or our 3DOD system alone. Each individual's behavior was recorded on video and notes were taken such as the

number of obstacles hit and how many obstacles were avoided in each of the scenarios.

Figure 7. The real test environment in a classroom

Post-questionnaire

At the end of our evaluation, we conducted a post-questionnaire with each subject to gather their feedback on our system. We asked eight 5-scale questions (scale of 1 low to 5 high) and 3 open questions as following (in German).

Q1: *How easy was it to remember the symbols?*
Q2: *How easy were symbols discriminated?*
Q3: *How helpful was it to locate obstacles by the central reference grid?*
Q4: *How easy was it to understand the distance on Braille display?*
Q5: *How easy was it to understand the direction?*
Q6: *How helpful was it to know the distribution of obstacles on Braille display?*
Q7: *How do you like the warning messages in walking mode when some obstacle occurs in 2 meters distance?*
Q8: *How do you rate the whole system?*
Q9: *What are your exact strategies to use the system?*
Q10: *Which features didn't you like in the system?*
Q11: *What are your suggestions to improve the system?*

Results

Each participant spent about 2 hours to complete all of the tasks. During the training period, they learned the legends of symbols in a short time (3 minutes in average) and finished the test to identify the properties of 6 pre-selected symbols quickly (2.4 minutes in mean), and with a high mean accuracy of 87.8% (see Figure 8). Errors mainly occurred when pointing out the width and height of symbols. Specifically, 3 users finished without any mistakes, while P2 made a few errors as she is still learning Braille.

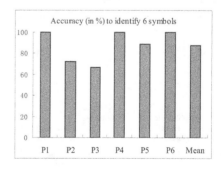

Figure 8. The accuracy of identification of obstacle symbols

In another pre-test, we found all of them would find the box on the floor by using the Braille display, as well as utilized more detailed spatial information (see Table 1). Obviously, most of them pointed out the box at the direction of "10:30 clock" or "11:00 clock" in 2 meters. In fact the box was placed at about 11 clock and 2.1 meters in depth. Moreover, all of them successfully avoided it via the walking mode.

Table 1. Participants' feedback about the location of a targeted box in the pre-test

Participant #	Distance (meter)	Orientation (clock)
P1	2.0	11:00
P2	1.5	11:00
P3	2.5	12:00
P4	2.0	10:30
P5	2.0	11:00
P6	2.0	10:30
Mean	2.0	11:00

In the real trail section, the Figure 9 and Figure 10 indicated the subjects' paths through the area with varied obstacles in scenario 1 and scenario 2 respectively. The decision points are defined as points where the subjects detect an obstacle by their white canes, bodies or our 3DOD system, and at each decision point the subjects paused to decide on the next direction. The subjects using 3DOD had a larger view to choose a route than by using white canes. These subjects performed a detour instead of an approximating diagonal path to the end point.

Additionally, their performances are illustrated in Table 2 and Table 3 respectively. They described several items such as how many decision points to help them choose a route, the number of obstacles hit by bodies and the spending time. The subjects had larger moving areas and needed fewer decision points with 3DOD system (mean 2.50 points/route) than with their white canes (mean 4.83 points/route), furthermore, the T-test found the two mean variables had a significant difference (P=0.017<0.05 while t=3.50).

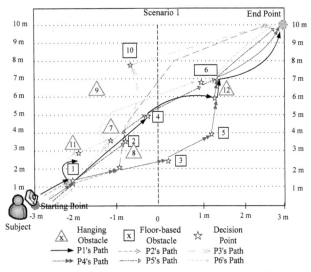

Figure 9. The participants' route plans in Scenario 1 (P2 and P3 used 3DOD, and others used white canes)

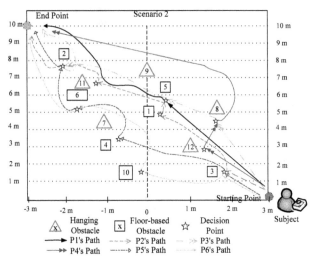

Figure 10. The participants' route plans in Scenario 2 (P2 and P3 used white canes, and others used 3DOD)

Table 2. Subjects' performance in the Scenario 1 [5]

#	Tool	Decision Point*	Hits** (Hanging***)	Time
P1	Cane	5	2(2)	27s
P2	3DOD	2	0(0)	1min32s
P3	3DOD	3	1(1)	2min19s
P4	Cane	6	3(2)	26s
P5	Cane	6	3(2)	25s
P6	Cane	4	2(2)	35s

Table 3. Subjects' performance in the Scenario 2

#	Tool	Decision Point*	Hits** (Hanging***)	Time
P1	3DOD	1	0(0)	1min2s
P2	Cane	5	1(1)	19s
P3	Cane	3	1(1)	43s
P4	3DOD	2	0(0)	1min42s
P5	3DOD	4	0(0)	2min41s
P6	3DOD	3	0(0)	1min35s

All of the subjects with white canes walked fast, and hit (by bodies) all of the hanging obstacles on their way, and parts of floor-based obstacles were circumvented after detecting by white canes. Only P3 and P5 touched the display while walking even if they had planned routes around the obstacles, but the others just walked along the routes until a new warming appears. Besides, P3 hit one hanging paper box which was rotating during the test, since the 3D TOF camera sometimes failed to detect spinning obstacles from too few reflection points.

---

5 Decision Point*: total number of obstacles on the way; Hits**: the number of hitting obstacles by bodies; Hanging***: the number of hanging obstacles;

The results of the post-questionnaire are indicated in Figure 11. Subjects provided their ratings for Q1-Q8 (scale of 1 low to 5 high), and commented on how to make use of the system while in the inspection mode and in the walking mode, as well as their suggestions to improve the system from their points of view.

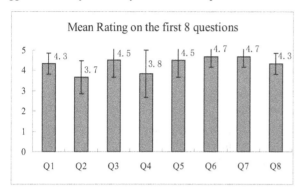

Figure 11. The mean ratings in the post-questionnaire

All of the subjects reported their strategies to use the proposed system as following: walked until were warned by the Wiimote cane, and stopped to touch the whole Braille display to find an open space. While touching the screen, they at first located the referenced grid to seek obstacles in 2 meters, and then explored the remaining space of the display. Besides the multiple and heavy equipments, they mentioned they were unable to walk fast due to the long updating period in one second, and suggested to improve the performance.

Discussion

In general, the blind individuals with white canes and most of ETAs can't access the surrounding environments, to find out an optimal path to avoid obstacles in advance. By contrast to white canes, the 3DOD system provides a better overview to choose an effective and safe route independently before bumping against them. Even if most of the existing ETAs would detect a larger range than white canes, they still failed to present precise spatial layout to users, which the 3DOD system can.

It's obvious that in the real test the proposed 3DOD system requires much more time than users' with the white canes. However, more attention should be paid to the criterion of safety. In the real world, the visually impaired need recovering time from a painless or severely hitting, even a cure leaded to stay at home after an injury.

Besides, the subjects had a basic training in a short amount of time. We observed P3 and P5 touched the display even without any warning messages which wasted time, despite both of them knew the correct operations. As some of our subjects pointed out, to increase the walking speed in the future advanced skills should be taught. For instance, we noted P1 who walked fast with the 3DOD system, only took into account the obstacles around the central reference grid below 2 meters firstly, and touched the whole display to find an open space.

The 3D TOF camera should provide more and precise data for reliable processing in time. Some materials absorb near infrared beams (like objects in dark black). Besides, in our test, the 3D TOF camera sometimes failed to detect spinning obstacles from too few reflection points, such as a rotating paper box. Since the camera was mounted over the cane, the false alarms introduced by the cane were rare, and only one time happened in all of the tests. At present, due to the huge challenges to develop a robust computer vision aid to recognize various objects for the visually

impaired, we rendered the 3D obstacles on 2D Braille display through abstract tactile symbols by encoding type and size of obstacles and their spatial location together. Certainly, the current set of the abstract symbols may be extended in the future.

The subjects were highly satisfied to obtain the distribution of multiple obstacles (averaged rating at 4.7 of 5 in Q6). Even if it needs time and causes extra cognitive load to explore the tactile symbols. Braille displays enable subjects to precisely obtain the distance and direction of any obstacles, even when considering the medium resolution of each pin (about 13 cm per pin). Despite the advantages of our system blind users should continue to use the long cane in conjunction with 3DOD. Combined use appears to be feasible when users are totally unaware of obstacles which occur more sudden as in our scenarios.

Additionally, several limitations were stated as following. The lab evaluation was completed in an indoor environment with pre-placed objects, which was not a realistic environment consisting of various complex scenarios, e.g. drop-off stairs and holes. The available range of the employed 3D TOF camera is too short to detect fast moving obstacle, like a car and a fast bicycle.

CONCLUSION & FUTURE WORK

In the paper, we designed and implemented an interactive system to detect and represent obstacles for the visually impaired, and we also ensured their safety and independent journey. Compared to previous work, the system firstly integrated an off-the-shelf 3D TOF camera to detect the environment beyond the end of the white canes, and a portable multi-line Braille display to represent surrounding obstacles through tactile abstract symbols. The overview layout of nearby obstacles within a larger range supports the users to decide an optimal route in advance.

Differently to attempt to recognize various objects, we applied a real-time clustering algorithm to acquire the locations, directions, types and sizes of surrounding obstacles. With the purpose of representation of obstacles precisely through a non-visual channel, we implemented an interactive haptic-based user interface, consisting of a hand-held vibrating controller and a portable multi-line Braille display. The hand-held vibrating control is not only used to switch between inspection mode and walking mode, but also used to generate vibrotactile perception against hands when there are obstacles closely. In addition to rendering precise spatial distribution of obstacles on the tactile display, we designed a set of tactile symbols to reveal the properties of obstacle through raised and lowered pins, like type and size.

Furthermore, the wearable system has been evaluated with 6 blind users during several prepared experiments. In the tests, the subjects with our proposed system not only would locate obstacles pretty accurately, but also had different strategies to avoid floor-based and over head obstacles by choosing more effective routes than only using the common white canes. Meanwhile, they rated the full system with high grades in the post-questionnaire phase, and their feedback in several ways to help improve the system.

In addition to future work, we need to enhance the performance of the current clustering algorithm. We want to study further on how to reduce users' cognitive loads by tactile displays and improve their walking speed. It's possible to make the system more comfortable by integrating into an embedded system and employ a new model of 3D camera with smaller size. Tracking and presenting with moving obstacles might be investigated as well. Future evaluation work will be planned in real outdoor environments with different conditions (e.g. holes, in a crowd), and will be compared with other off-the-shelf ETAs, but ethical and legal constraints will not allow taking away the long cane.

ACKNOWLEDGMENTS

We thank all of the subjects for taking part in the evaluations, and sharing their feedback to improve our system. The authors also acknowledge financial support from China Scholarship Council.

REFERENCES

[1] Benjamin, J.M., Ali, N. A. and Schepis, A. F. A laser cane for the blind. In *Proc. San Diego Biomedical Symposium*, 12 (1973), 53-57.

[2] Bertozzi, M., Broggi, A. GOLD: A parallel real-time stereo vision system for generic obstacle and lane detection. *IEEE Trans. on Image Processing*, 7 (1998), 62-81.

[3] Bologna, G., Deville, B., Pun, T. On the use of the auditory pathway to represent image scenes in real-time. *Neurocomputing*, 72 (2009), 839-849.

[4] Borenstein, J. The NavBelt - a computerized multi-sensor travel aid for active guidance of the blind. In *Proc. CSUN 1990*, 107-116.

[5] Bostelman, R., Russo, P., Albus, J., Hong, T. and Madhavan, R. Applications of a 3D range camera towards healthcare mobility aids. In *Proc. 2006 IEEE Networking, Sensing, and Control*, IEEE, 416-421.

[6] Burgard, W., Cremers, A.B., Fox, D., Hähnel, D. The interactive museum tour-guide robot. In *Proc. AAAI '98/IAAI '98*, AAAI (1998), 11-18.

[7] CASBliP Project final activity report. http://casblipdif.webs.upv.es, last accessed April 2012.

[8] Dakopoulos, D., Bourbakis, N. Towards a 2D tactile vocabulary for navigation of blind and visually impaired. In Proc. *IEEE SMC*, 2009, 45-51.

[9] Erp, J.B.F.V., Veen, H.A.C.V., Jansen, C. and Dobbins, T. Waypoint navigation with a vibrotactile waist belt. *ACM Trans. Applied Perception*, 2 (2005), 106-117.

[10] Golovinskiy, A., Kim, V.G. and Funkhouser, T.A. Shape-based recognition of 3D point clouds in urban environments. In *Proc. IEEE ICCV 2009*, 2154-2161.

[11] Guímundsson, S., Pardís, M., Casas, J., Sveinsson, J., Aanæs, H. Improved 3D reconstruction in smart-room environments using ToF imaging. *Computer Vision and Image Understanding*, 114 (2010), 1376-1384.

[12] Hub, A., Diepstraten, J. and Ertl, T. Design and development of an indoor navigation and object identification system for the blind. In *Proc. ASSETS 2004*, 147-152.

[13] Hub, A. Making complex environments accessible on the basis of TANIA's augmented navigation support. In *Proc. CSUN 2010*.

[14] Ju, J.S., Ko, E., Kim, E.Y. EYECane: navigating with camera embedded white cane for visually impaired person. In *Proc. ASSETS 2009, ACM Press, 237-238.*

[15] Kay, L. An ultrasonic sensing probe as a mobility aid for the blind. *Ultrasonics*, 2 (1964), 53-59.

[16] Kay, L. A sonar aid to enhance spatial perception of the blind: engineering design and evaluation. *Radio and Electronic Engineer*, 44 (1974), 605-627.

[17] Klasing, K., Wollherr, D., Buss, M. A clustering method for efficient segmentation of 3D laser data. In *Proc. IEEE ICRA 2008*, 4043-4048.

[18] Loomis, J.M., Golledge, R.G. and Klatzky, R. Navigation system for the blind: auditory display modes and guidance. *Presence*, 7 (1998), 193-203.

[19] Meijer, P.B.L. An experimental system for auditory image representations. *IEEE Trans. on Biomedical Engineering*, 39 (1992), 112-121.

[20] Manduchi, R., Kurniawan, S. Mobility-related accidents experienced by people with visual impairment. *Research and Practice in Visual Impairment and Blindness*, 4(2), 2011, 44-54.

[21] Mynatt, E.D., Weber, G. Nonvisual presentation of graphical user interfaces: contrasting two approaches. In *Proc. CHI'94*, ACM Press (1994), 166-172.

[22] Petrie, H., Johnson, V., Strothotte, T., Raab, A., Fritz, S. MoBIC: designing a travel aid for blind and elderly people. *Journal of Navigation*, 49 (1996), 45-52.

[23] Sergi, F., Alenya, G., Torras, C. Lock-in Time-of-Flight (ToF) cameras: a survey. *IEEE Sensors Journal*, Vol. 11, No. 3, 2011, 1917-1926.

[24] Schneider, J., Strothotte, T. Constructive exploration of spatial information by blind users. In *Proc. ASSETS 2000*, ACM Press (2000), 188-192.

[25] Shotton, J., Fitzgibbon, A., Cook, M., Sharp, T., Finocchio, M., Moore, R., Kipman, A., Blake, A. Real-time human pose recognition in parts from single depth images. In *Proc. CVPR 2011*, IEEE (2011).

[26] Ulrich, I., Borenstein, J. The GuideCane-applying mobile robot technologies to assist the visually impaired. *IEEE Trans. on SMC*, 31 (2001), 131-136.

[27] Velazquez, R., Fontaine, E., Pissaloux, E. Coding the environment in tactile maps for real-time guidance of the visually impaired. In *Proc. IEEE Int. Symp. on MHS 2006*, 1-6.

[28] Völkel, T., Weber, G., Baumann, U. Tactile Graphics Revised: The novel BrailleDis 9000 Pin-Matrix device with multitouch input, In *Proc. ICCHP 2008*, 835-842.

[29] Zeng, L., Weber, G. Audio-haptic browser for a geographical information system. In *Proc. ICCHP 2010*, 466-473.

[30] Zöllner, M., Huber, S., Jetter, HC and Reiterer, H. NAVI - A proof-of-concept of a mobile navigational aid for visually impaired based on the Microsoft Kinect. In *Proc. INTERACT 2011*, 584-587.

Understanding the Role of Age and Fluid Intelligence in Information Search

Shari Trewin, John T. Richards[†]
IBM T. J. Watson Research Center
P.O. Box 704
Yorktown, NY 10598, USA
+1 914 784 7616

{trewin,ajtr}@us.ibm.com

[†]Also at University of Dundee

Vicki L. Hanson, David Sloan
University of Dundee
School of Computing
Dundee, UK DD1 4HB
+44 1382 386510

{vlh,dsloan}@
computing.dundee.ac.uk

Bonnie E. John, Cal Swart,
John C. Thomas
IBM T. J. Watson Research Center
P.O. Box 704
Yorktown, NY 10598, USA
+1 914 784 6247

bejohn@us.ibm.com
{cals,jcthomas}@us.ibm.com

ABSTRACT

In this study, we explore the role of age and fluid intelligence on the behavior of people looking for information in a real-world search space. Analyses of mouse moves, clicks, and eye movements provide a window into possible differences in both task strategy and performance, and allow us to begin to separate the influence of age from the correlated but isolable influence of cognitive ability. We found little evidence of differences in strategy between younger and older participants matched on fluid intelligence. Both performance and strategy differences were found between older participants having higher versus lower fluid intelligence, however, suggesting that cognitive factors, rather than age per se, exert the dominant influence. This underscores the importance of measuring and controlling for cognitive abilities in studies involving older adults.

Categories and Subject Descriptors

H.1.2 [**Models and Principles**]: User/Machine Systems – *human information processing*; H.5.2. [**Information interfaces and presentation**]: User interfaces –*evaluation/methodology*;

General Terms

Design, Experimentation, Human Factors.

Keywords

Cognition, age, eye-gaze, fluid intelligence, information search.

1. INTRODUCTION

Older adults are a significant, and growing, group of technology users that are often under-represented in both research and design. The present research seeks to address this under-representation with respect to interface designers, taking into account needs of individual older users.

How can designers make informed judgments about interface structure and design? Traditional usability testing, though effective, can become intractable when many different populations are to be supported. One approach is suggested by Card, Moran and Newell [2], whose seminal work introduced the concept of user models that describe interaction as a series of discrete component steps that are combined to achieve a goal. Embedding age-sensitive models into design tools might be a particularly effective technique for alerting designers early on to problems likely to be experienced by older users. Creating such models requires a deep understanding of the task strategies adopted by different user populations, in addition to variations in cognitive, sensory and motor abilities.

Fluid intelligence represents the ability to reason abstractly and solve novel problems [12]. This research seeks to understand whether age and fluid intelligence are associated with measurable differences in the approach to and performance of an information-search task. If so, then models of goal-directed exploratory behavior could be augmented to include these differences. In this study, we present findings from an information search task in a real-world search space, monitoring mouse moves, clicks, and eye movements, to explore the following questions:

1. How similar is the information search behavior of older and younger adults, controlling for fluid intelligence?

2. How similar is the information search behavior of older adults with different levels of fluid intelligence?

While there are numerous prior studies enumerating strategy differences in information search in older and younger groups, the separation of age and fluid intelligence in this study allows for a more nuanced understanding. We emphasize that older adults are a diverse population and statements about population needs do not necessarily explain the behavior of individual users.

2. LITERATURE REVIEW

While technology experience is an important factor in search ability [11,23], an emphasis in the literature on novice older users has obscured the fact that many older adults are skilled users of the Web. Indeed, when effects of skill are factored out, findings suggest that older adults are no less able (and sometimes seemingly more able) Web searchers than younger adults [4,9,10]. This perhaps surprising finding is reflective of the fact that while older adults may find answers, they seemingly employ very different strategies than younger users [4,9,19]. The phrase "slow but sure" has been used to describe the performance of older users [14], highlighting general findings that older users may be slower and more methodical at each decision point, but employ strategies that may involve fewer clicks to solution.

Effects of cognitive ability have been found related to a variety of task behaviors for older users. For example, eye movements of older adults are slower, with fixation durations 1.2 times that of younger people, and more fixations are required to extract information from a target. Mouse movements are also slower in older adults, with lower peak velocity, longer pauses and more sub movements [17,20,24].

Cognitively, those with stronger fluid intelligence are more able in searching than are those with weaker fluid intelligence abilities [7]. Fluid intelligence is defined by Horn and Cattell as "processes of reasoning in the immediate situation in tasks requiring abstracting, concept formation and attainment, and the perception and eduction of relations." [12] Fluid intelligence is strongly related to working memory [28]. The Letter Sets test [8] is one of several well-established measures of fluid intelligence. It presents 30 items, each consisting of five sets of four letters each. The task is to find the rule that connects four of the sets, and identify the set that does not fit. Prior work has reported mean Letter Sets scores in the region of 21-22 (out of a maximum score of 30) for younger adults and 15-16 for older adults [4,6].

Chin et al [4] studied well-formed and ill-formed information search tasks in a medical information hierarchy for younger and older people. They observed differences in strategy and hypothesized that younger people adopted a broader, more exploratory search strategy, because the cost of clicking was low and the memory demands manageable. In their study, younger people more frequently performed consecutive clicks within the same category, taken as an index of search breadth.

Czaja et al. [7] examined the role of reasoning skills and Internet knowledge in a study of older and younger adults performing health-related Internet search tasks. They compared older adults with high and low performance on the task, finding that the high performers had higher reasoning skills and Internet knowledge. They also found that predictors of performance varied between the younger-old (60-70) and the older-old (70+). Internet knowledge was the strongest predictor of performance for the younger-old group, while cognitive abilities were the strongest predictors for the older-old group.

In Web search, researchers have identified several eye and mouse movement strategies [21]: keeping the mouse still, following the eye with the cursor, and using the cursor to mark an interesting search result. Fluid intelligence may have a role to play in who uses these strategies, and when, but to our knowledge no study has examined this.

Human performance models have been successfully used to explore age-related differences in skilled performance. Jastrzembski and Charness [15] used modeling parameters derived from multiple cognitive aging studies, to successfully predict younger and older performance in mobile phone dialing and texting tasks. In further work, John and Jastrzembski [16] explored a series of models. The most successful model for the older adult group revisited the written instructions in the dialing task more frequently to extract the next set of digits to dial. The best models reflected statistically significant differences between the age groups. Factoring in the impact of working memory

differences on task performance proved instrumental in bringing models of skilled performance into line with observations.

The present study represents a step towards a deeper understanding of older peoples' behavior and the possibly separable role of fluid intelligence in an information search task.

3. STUDY OF INFORMATION SEARCH
3.1 Participants

This paper presents data from two groups of older participants and one group of younger participants. Older participants were recruited from the Social Inclusion in the Digital Economy (SiDE) User Pool, based in Dundee, Scotland. The two older groups differed in their level of fluid intelligence, as measured by their performance on the Letter Sets test [8], administered prior to study recruitment as part of the CREATE battery of cognitive tests [6]. A higher fluid intelligence group (OH), with nineteen people, was selected from those who scored in the top third of the user pool (a score of at least 18 out of 30) on the Letter Sets test, while a lower fluid intelligence group (OL), with twenty-two people, was selected from the lower third of the pool (a score of 12 or less). Thus, this designation of OH and OL was *relative to the overall performance of this participant pool*. Additional recruitment criteria included being comfortable using a mouse, and having no severe disability. Participants self-reported a high level of confidence using the Internet to search for information, and most did so several times a week. Seventeen OH participants, and fifteen OL participants wore glasses.[1]

Younger participants were recruited in Dundee via email and personal contact, and took the Letter Sets test as a part of participating in the study. Of the seventeen younger participants tested, fourteen fell into the high performing range (YH). All were regular Internet users. None reported any disability. One wore glasses.

Three younger participants with Letter Sets scores of 12 or less (YL) are not included in this paper due to the small size of this group. One OL participant is also excluded due to a cognitive impairment acquired after the earlier administration of the Letter Sets task. Table 1 summarizes the included participant groups' age, gender and Letter Sets scores.

Table 1. Summary of the participant groups' gender, age and fluid intelligence.

	N	Women	Age			Letter Sets	
			Mean	Std dev.	Range	Mean score	Std dev.
YH	14	6	22	2.8	18-25	22.6	3.1
OH	19	14	68	4.4	64-78	21.1	2.4
OL	22	11	74	5.6	64-82	4.1	4.1

The YH and OH groups had mean Letter Sets scores of 22.6 and 21.1, a small and not statistically significant difference (t(24)=-1.598, p=0.123, two-tailed). For both groups, these scores are in line with previously reported Letter Sets scores of 21-22 for younger individuals [4,6]. Therefore, the 'YH' group should be interpreted as representing normally functioning younger adults. The mean Letter Sets score of 4.1 in the OL group is well below

---

[1] Information not available for 1 OH and 4 OL participants.

previously reported mean scores of 15-16 for typical older adult groups.

Despite our best efforts at matching for age, the OH and OL groups had mean ages of 68 and 74, a statistically significant difference (t(38.75)=-3.892, p<0.001, two-tailed).

3.2 Materials

The experimental design was adapted from that used by Blackmon et al [1] where participants were asked to find specific items of information in a specially constructed stimulus website representing an online encyclopaedia. Ours was a hierarchical, three level tree-structure of 3938 categories, drawn from the UK version of eBay as of November 2010, and converted to a relational database from which stimulus screens were dynamically constructed.

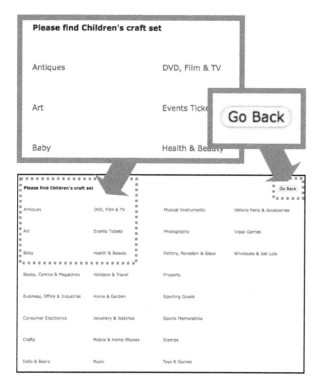

Figure 1. The top-level category page, with magnified sections.

Figure 1 illustrates the top-level category selection page from the study website. Each page was displayed in Internet Explorer's kiosk mode, eliminating all browser paraphernalia, and was served by a web stack running locally on the test machine to eliminate network delays. All navigation required use of the mouse to click on links or buttons within each page. The top-level contained 27 categories such as "Antiques", "Art", "Baby", "Jewellery & Watches", "Musical Instruments", and "Photography". The target to be searched for is shown at the upper left of this page, in this case "Please find Children's craft set." Upon clicking one of the top-level categories, e.g., "Crafts", the page would be replaced by a second-level page containing all subcategories of the selected top-level category, the target string would be changed to "Looking for Children's craft set", and a string would be displayed to the right of that, e.g. "In Crafts", to help the participant keep track of where they were in the hierarchy. On both the second- and third-level pages, the "Go

Back" button would also be enabled making it easy to navigate back up to a higher level. Each page contained between 1 and 4 columns of up to 32 total sub-categories, arranged in column order, and widely spaced for ease of eye fixation analysis.

Items were listed in the same order used by eBay. In most cases that order is alphabetical, but within some categories (e.g. "Art Prints") a date-based order is used. In many categories, a catch-all "Other" category is included as the last option of the set. To eliminate scrolling, 15 large categories were pruned to 32 items each by removing randomly chosen items that were not on the solution path for any task. Visited link color changes were not used, giving no indication of which links had previously been clicked. This allows link revisitation differences to be observed independent of reliance on user interface feedback.

Upon clicking a third-level category – where eBay would present a page with a set of specific auction items – the participant would see either a failure page with the message "This is not the correct location", with the "Go Back" button allowing them to navigate back up, or a success page with "You found the right location for X". The success page also provided a button to start the next task. If the correct third-level category had not been found within 150 seconds, a popup dialog informed them that the task was done and presented a button to start the next task.

The experiment was run with a Tobii X120 eye tracker, a PC running Windows and the Internet Explorer 8 Web browser. The display was a 17" LCD monitor, and the mouse a 2-button scroll wheel Microsoft mouse. The eye tracker data capture rate was 60Hz. The PC was changed due to technical hardware issues midway through the study, from a PC running Microsoft Windows XP, Service Pack 2 to a PC running Microsoft Windows 7. At this time, the eye tracking setup was recalibrated by a Tobii representative.

Eye fixation data and screen capture of task performance were recorded using Tobii Studio v2.2. Mouse move, button press, and button release events were recorded by our own event logger, capturing event timestamps as reported to the operating system event handler function. Link and button clicks were also recorded by the local web server.

Thirty-two tasks were developed. Each task is a request to find an appropriate category for a given goal term, within a 150 second time limit. The goal term is a real world object, such as "Tennis shoes" or "Shampoo". Tasks covered a broad set of the available top-level categories.

We defined easy tasks as those in which the correct category is clearly related to the goal and there are no competing categories at any level, for example "Modern Art Prints", which requires selection of "Art", then "Prints", then "Modern (1900-79)". Intermediate tasks involve competing categories that could serve as distractors for at least one decision point. For example, to find an "Autographed photo of Katherine Hepburn", it is necessary to choose between "Autographs" and "Photographs" at the third level. Hard tasks use terms that do not match the names of the correct links and require selection of a category that may not seem strongly related to the task. For example, to find "Postal scales", it is necessary to choose "Business, Office and Industrial" at the top level, and not "Stamps". The tasks were selected from a pool of 37 candidates in pre-pilot tests so as to balance the number of tasks at each level of difficulty.

3.3 Procedure

The study took place in a quiet office. Participants were first shown a paper-based walkthrough of an example task, which involved viewing printed screenshots of each category page along the solution path, plus the success page, failure page, task timeout message, and the location and function of the Go Back button. Participants were told that there was one correct category for every goal term, and that there was a time limit for each task. They were not explicitly told to complete the task as quickly as possible.

After the task walkthrough, participants were then seated at the PC and eyetracker. Before beginning the study, they completed the on-screen Tobii Studio calibration process (a few-second procedure in most cases), and the facilitator checked that participants could comfortably read 12pt text on the screen, wearing their usual eyeglasses or lenses.

Participants were informed that the first two tasks were treated as practice tasks – that is, data were captured but not used in analysis. Following the practice tasks, participants were presented with the 32 tasks, in randomized order.

After the two practice tasks, and after every third study task, our own additional calibration screen was presented. This consisted of a single button, labelled with a plus symbol (+), appearing in one of 15 different locations with the particular location chosen at random. Participants were instructed to look at the center of the plus symbol and click on the button; on doing so, the button would be redisplayed at a different position. The purpose of this calibration process was to measure the quality of eye tracking calibration over the course of the study, and allow for the correction of any systematic errors by providing fixations on known targets. Further details of these interspersed calibration tasks can be found in [27],

On completion of the study, participants completed a post-study semi-structured interview, administered orally by the facilitator. This included identification of any goal terms that were unfamiliar to participants. Younger participants additionally completed a subset of the cognitive measures carried out with the older participants, including the Letter Sets test.

3.4 Task- and Page-Level Analysis

Analysis of task success and other task-level measures was performed on the full task-level data set. Page-level analysis of mouse movements and fixations is limited to a subset of 25 participants (YH=12, OH=7, OL=6) because technical issues with the earlier PC rendered the eye tracking data for the earliest participants unusable. Page-level analysis includes only those participants who used the second setup, and within that set, only those for whom eye-gaze capture rates greater than 60% were achieved. Fixation data capture rates on search pages were 96.4% for YH, 90.7% for OH, and 82.6% for OL participants.

Fixation data was exported using the standard Tobii fixation filter [26] with default settings (velocity=35, duration=35). For many participants, and especially older participants, this raw fixation data exhibited systematic calibration errors large enough to place recorded fixations entirely off screen. Errors varied systematically over the screen, being more severe at the edges, and larger in the vertical dimension. Bifocal, trifocal, and varifocal eyeglasses, worn by many older participants, posed a challenge to the eye tracking software. However, calibration error was not confined to those wearing eyeglasses. Prior to data analysis, these systematic errors were corrected by using the fixation data from the interspersed calibration tasks in a variant of Hornoff and Halverson's correction algorithm [13].

Because group sizes were uneven, in the following analyses, where Levene's test indicated a significant difference in variance between groups, the more robust non-parametric Kruskal-Wallis test (H statistic, df=2) was used in place of an ANOVA, and the Mann-Whitney U test (2-tailed) was used in place of a t-test. Power values [18] are reported for important non-significant results.

4. RESULTS

The task-level data set includes 1699 tasks (YH=448, OH=599, OL=652). 5 participants did not complete all 32 tasks. Four ran out of time and one stopped after 9 tasks because they became ill. We examine differences between YH and OH to test for potential aging effects, and differences between OH and OL to test for potential effects related to fluid intelligence. YH and OL are not explicitly compared.

4.1 Task Success and Times

Table 2 shows the percentage of attempted tasks that were completed successfully for each group (% success), and the percentage that succeeded without erroneous selections and backtracking (% error free success). Younger participants were faster and more successful than older participants, and those with higher fluid intelligence were faster and more successful than those with lower fluid intelligence. The younger group selected, on average, 0.8 more links to reach a solution, and 5.3 more links in tasks where they failed to find the correct third-level category.

All of the measures in Table 2 show a significant effect of group (Success: H=158.8; Error free success: H=33.9; Task time: H=296.8; Link clicks to success: H=14.1; Link clicks to failure: H=34.5, p=<0.001). As indicated in the table, post-hoc pairwise comparisons (Mann-Whitney U test) indicate significant differences between YH and OH (all p<=0.001) for all measures except error free success (U=130022, p=0.322). The test had power to detect a difference in means greater than 8.7%. Significant differences between OH and OL (all p<0.001) are found for measures of time and success, but not for number of link clicks to success (U=86727, p=0.335, power to detect mean difference of 0.4) or failure (U=17561, p=0.810, power to detect mean difference of 1.1).

Table 2: Mean values for younger (YH) and older (OH and OL) groups on task success and click metrics. '*' between groups indicates a significant difference (p < 0.001).

Measure	YH		OH		OL
% success	92.4 SD=26.51	*	77.6 SD=41.71	*	59.2 SD=49.18
% error free success	52.7 SD=49.98		49.6 SD=50.04	*	36.7 SD=48.22
Time on task (sec)	40.9 SD=43.92	*	66.4 SD=53.85	*	89.9 SD=56.96
Link clicks to success	4.94 SD=3.33	*	4.06 SD=2.00		4.15 SD=2.12
Link clicks to failure	14.18 SD=4.86	*	8.82 SD=3.42		9.18 SD=4.26

4.2 Link Choices

Although initial link choices on correct pages are very highly correlated (between 0.890 and 0.996 at all levels), a deeper analysis reveals interesting differences between the groups.

Overall, there is a significant effect of group on first click correctness (H=15.5, df 2, p<0.001). 73% of YH's first clicks in each task were on the correct top-level category. OH, at 71%, was not significantly different (Mann-Whitney U=130632, df 2, p=0.378, the test had power to detect a difference of means of 8%). OL, at 63%, was significantly lower (U=179640, p=0.003) than OH. OL is more often making choices that do not lead to the solution.

Among tasks that include at least one wrong click, there is a significant overall effect of group on the number of times a participant returned to the top-level page during a task (H=29.714, p<0.001). Mean values are YH=1.5, OH=1.0, and OL=0.8. Among unsuccessful tasks the effect is even stronger. YH participants returned to the top a mean of 4.0 times during the task, OH participants 1.4 times, and OL participants 0.9 times, suggesting a narrower exploration strategy for the older groups with a possibly greater commitment to the top-level category chosen. The effect is significant (H=83.232, p<0.001), with post hoc Mann-Whitney tests showing a significant difference between YH and OH (U=525, p< 0.001), and between OH and OL (U=13611, p< 0.001).

Participants sometimes clicked more than once on the same link within a task. Overall, YH had 0.36 re-clicks per task, OH had 0.38, and OL had 0.64. There is a significant effect of group on the number of re-clicked links per task (H=30.39, p<0.001), with post hoc Mann-Whitney tests showing a significant difference between OH and OL (U=170358, p< 0.001). The very similar observed values for YH and OH do not suggest any meaningful difference between these groups, and there is also no statistical significance (U=129798, p=0.296).

There were some tasks where the groups made different first choices at the top level. For the 'Matchbox car' task, YH participants started in 'Toys and Games' 79% of the time, while OH and OL chose this category 100% and 88% of the time. Some younger participants reported being unfamiliar with this term, and were distracted by the 'Vehicle Parts and Accessories' category. Three tasks related to electronic devices, for example 'Nintendo Wii Controller', were the most commonly reported as unfamiliar to older participants. Older participants favored the 'Consumer Electronics' category for their first click, while younger participants were more likely to select the more specific categories of 'Mobile & Home Phones' or 'Video Games'.

Re-analysis of the task success metrics without the seven tasks having the greatest difference in performance between the older and younger groups resulted in less than 1.5 percentage points difference in the overall results, suggesting that this set of tasks did not overly disadvantage either the younger or older groups.

4.3 Page Level Analysis

The following analyses focus on behavior within a single page of links, as the participant searches for links related to the current goal, and either clicks on a link, clicks on the 'Go Back' button, or continues to visually search until the task times out. These analyses use the page-level data set, which consists of 5634 link page visits across 25 participants (YH=12, OH=7, OL=6).

Table 3 provides median and mean values for the time taken to click on a link, for the subset of 4257 pages in which a link was selected. Both older groups take several seconds longer to make their link selection. Relatively large differences between the median and mean values indicate the skewed nature of the data, with long selection times for some trials. The YH group spent less time than OH moving the mouse prior to clicking on a link, while OH spent less time than OL. Raw numbers of mouse movements were higher for the older groups. Kruskal-Wallis tests indicate a significant effect of group on time to click a link, mouse movement time before clicking, number of mouse movements before clicking, and distance moved by the mouse before clicking (p < 0.001). All pairwise group comparisons are also significant (Mann-Whitney U test, p < 0.001) with the exception of distance moved by the mouse, which was not significantly different between YH and OH (p=0.267), and showed only a 9 pixel difference in mean values – not suggestive of an important difference in mouse usage between groups.

Mouse movement was observed in all groups even on pages where no item was clicked. The number of such pages was small (YH=31, OH=90, OL=76), and no significant group differences in the distance moved by the mouse could be detected.

Finally, OH participants had significantly fewer click errors per page, where a click error is a click that was not on any target. There is a significant effect of group on click errors per page (H=26.6, p<0.001), with pairwise comparisons showing significant differences between YH and OH (U=1953606, p<0.001), and also OH and OL (U=952384, p<0.001).

Table 3. Between group comparison of time taken and mouse actions. '*' between groups indicates a significant difference (p <= 0.01).

		YH	Sig	OH	Sig	OL
Time to a link click (sec)	Median	3.8	*	6.9	*	9.1
	Mean	5.5		9.5		12.3
Time moving the mouse before a link click (sec)	Median	1.1	*	1.7	*	2.4
	Mean	1.7		2.1		3.7
>5 pixel mouse movements before a link click	Median	4	*	5	*	7
	Mean	4.9		7.2		10.2
Distance moved before a link click (pixels)	Median	627		654	*	819
	Mean	769		778		935
Distance moved before a page timeout (pixels)	Median	543		405		307
	Mean	673		546		732
Missed clicks/page	Mean	0.06	*	0.03	*	0.07

As described in the literature review, age-related differences in fixation counts and durations are well established. We focus, instead, on the number of different items fixated, which may shed light on strategy differences. To provide a fair comparison between groups, analysis is limited to those pages for which less than 5% of the fixation data is missing.

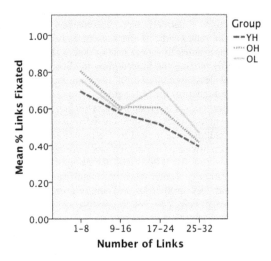

Figure 2. Mean percentage of links fixated on level 2 and 3 pages of different sizes.

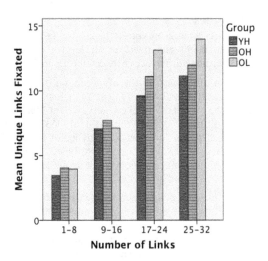

Figure 3. Number of different links fixated on level 2 and 3 pages of different sizes.

Over the 2913 such pages where a link was clicked, a Kruskal-Wallis test indicates a significant effect of group on the number of different links fixated (H=39.6, p< 0.001, mean values YH=8.35, OH=10.0, OL=10.3), and the percentage of the links on the page that were fixated (H=85.1, p<0.001, mean values YH=53%, OH=63%, OL=65%). Pairwise Mann-Whitney U tests indicate a statistically significant difference in fixated links between YH and OH (U=528785, p<0.001), but not between OH and OL (U=142968, p=0.941).

For the top-level page of the hierarchy, the mean number of different links fixated on prior to selecting a link is 7.6 for YH, 12.4 for OH and 18.1 for OL, and these differences are statistically significant (H=49.5, p<0.001).

As the top-level page is viewed in every task, learning effects may be present in these results. This was clarified by exploring the number and percentage of links fixated on lower-level pages, which are less frequently visited. There is a significant effect of group on the percentage of page links fixated on these 2194 pages (p<0.001), and also on the number of different links fixated (p=0.001). Figures 2 and 3 show that as the number of links on the page increases, all groups look at more links, but a lower proportion of the overall links. Between YH and OH the differences of means were 0.9 for number of links fixated and 6% for percent of links fixated, both statistically significant (p<0.001). Between OH and OL the measured differences of means were 0.1 links per page and 1.1% of links viewed. These differences were too small to be statistically significant (p>=0.614). The tests had power to detect differences over 1.1 for number of links per page and 6% for percent of links fixated.

The 27-link top-level page would fall into the 25-32 link page category shown in Figure 3 for lower level pages. The number of different links fixated for OH on the top-level page is in line with the number for lower level pages of similar size (12.4 links vs 12). For YH participants, 7.6 different top-level links are fixated in comparison to 11 on lower level pages of similar size, potential evidence of learning on the top-level page. For OL, fewer links are fixated on lower level pages than the top-level page, perhaps indicating additional attention to the initial choice.

Another potentially interesting difference between the groups is the number of fixations on the goal string situated at the top left of the search page. This was calculated over all pages with 95%

fixation data in which a link was eventually clicked. There was a significant effect of group on the number of goal fixations for these pages (H=231, df 2, p<0.001). The median number of goal fixations was 2 for OH and OL, and 1 for YH. Mean values for OH and OL were 2.7 and 4.1 respectively, while the mean for YH was 1.7. All groups are significantly different (Mann-Whitney U, p<0.001).

5. DISCUSSION

5.1 Comparing the Younger and Older Groups

YH and OH are not significantly different on first time success, decisions made on correct pages, re-clicks on previously visited links, or the distance moved by the mouse. Differences in the overall success rate are probably a result of the tasks being limited in time, since the OH group spent longer on each page and tried fewer links in the same amount of time. Finding the solutions to the more difficult tasks requires exploration of multiple plausible options. The more rapidly these options are explored, all else being equal, the better the chance of success.

Although there are significant differences between the groups on the time from page load to clicking a link, time spent moving the mouse, and number of mouse movements, these are to be expected, given the established differences in mouse movement between older and younger adults [15,17]. In [27], we report movement times for the actions of clicking on the targets in the calibration tasks, for YH and OH. The YH/OH ratio of movement times is 0.689 (1123/1628 msec). In the task data, the ratio of time spent moving the mouse between page load and clicking a link is 0.647. These observed mouse movement differences are in line with normal age-related values, and not necessarily indicative of any difference in information search strategy or way of using the mouse during search.

The older group looked at the goal more frequently (one more fixation per page), which may suggest a difference in the frequency of re-checking the goal before selecting a link. However, older adults are known to use more fixations to extract information, so this does not necessarily suggest any difference in strategy. Forgetting what has already been clicked is not a major factor, given the lack of significant difference in re-clicks.

Older adults typically considered one or two more links than younger participants, before making a selection. The difference in number of links considered on the top-level page is one factor of potential import to design, and should be further investigated. In this study, the YH group considered fewer options when making decisions on the top-level page. This is consistent with Chin et al's work [4,5], in which younger people adopted a more exploratory, interactive search strategy – clicking on more categories until they found the correct one. It may also indicate faster learning of the top-level page by the younger group. Our data do not follow the pattern described by Chin et al in which younger people made more consecutive clicks within a category. In our data, YH participants backed up to the top level more frequently than OH participants in unsuccessful tasks, while there was no difference in the number of back ups from pages at the third level of the hierarchy.

The higher rate of click errors in the younger group is consistent with findings from simple 'point-and-click' tasks [17]. The calibration sessions included in this study, described in more detail in [27], are simple clicking tasks similar to those reported in [17]. Younger participants made three times more errors than older adults in these simple tasks [27]. In the information search tasks, this difference is reduced to two times. This may reflect the larger size of the link targets compared to the calibration targets (which were only 28 pixels high and 34 pixels wide). Less precise positioning is required in the information search tasks, especially along the horizontal extent of the category string.

Overall, there was little evidence of major differences in strategy between YH and OH. This means that existing cognitive models of information search [1,3,25], derived from studies involving younger participants, may be appropriate for modeling older adults with similar levels of fluid intelligence. The observed differences in task success, then, serve to illustrate the cumulative impact of slower perceptual, cognitive and motor operations, over the course of a task.

5.2 Comparing the Groups With Higher and Lower Fluid Intelligence

In comparing the OH and OL groups, note that the statistically significant difference in age, with the OL group older than OH, may have confounded the results.

OH and OL explored the space at about the same rate, trying the same number of links before succeeding or failing. OL also re-selected previously selected links twice as often as OH. This may indicate difficulty remembering whether a link had been clicked (there was no indication in the user interface), or what items lay within a link category. OL participants were also less willing to return to the top level, instead trying more low-level options.

The additional fixations on the goal for OL for some pages (indicated by the higher mean value) may indicate more fixations during initial reading of the goal or more frequent re-checking of the goal before clicking. The ability to keep track of goals may well be related to fluid intelligence, which correlates with working memory.

OL had longer mouse movement distances prior to clicking a link than OH. Longer mouse paths may indicate use of the cursor as a marker, or the pattern of moving the mouse along with the eyes, both described by Rodden et al [21]. Both of these strategies could serve to reduce memory load. However, there are plausible alternative explanations, such as moving the mouse in order to relocate a lost cursor. These potential differences in approach between OH and OL require additional investigation.

OL participants fixated on and presumably considered more links than OH prior to clicking at the top level of the hierarchy, but no significant difference was found at lower levels.

The differences reported here in link reselection, goal and link fixations, mouse movement, and willingness to return to the top level page, are all of relevance to the development of computational cognitive models of information-seeking that can represent specific user populations.

OL participants' higher rate of erroneously clicking in areas with no link was unexpected. This finding warrants further study to confirm whether this effect is reproducible, and if so, to explore the possible relationship of fluid intelligence to motor skill.

5.3 Generalizing to Natural Browsing Tasks

The focus of this study is the selection of links within each page, and the pages in this study represent a real-world search space, taken from the UK eBay hierarchy of items. Consequently, our data provides insight into decision making on well-defined tasks in a naturally occurring, large information hierarchy. Our findings are independent of complexities such as browser controls, overall page design, link formatting and grouping, all of which may affect real-world behavior.

6. CONCLUSIONS

Information search is a complex task that draws on many cognitive abilities, and this paper focuses on fluid intelligence. This study set out to explore differences due to fluid intelligence and age in an information search task based on making selections from lists of options within a larger hierarchy of categories. At a task level, the study results are typical of many studies that compare older and younger individuals – both groups made similar choices, but the younger people were quicker to click on a link, and backed up more readily from paths that were not promising. The time limit on the task lead to lower task success for the older group. By comparing mouse and eye-gaze data between groups of younger and older people, we find little evidence that the younger and older groups approached the task in a different way, or applied different strategies. This is in contrast to some prior studies. Although older adults had lower overall task success, we argue that this was largely due to the nature of the task itself, when combined with normal age-related differences in basic perceptual, cognitive, and motor operations. Indeed, this is a demonstration of the impact that a design, in this case a task design, can have on older adult performance. A different task design with no time limit could have produced quite different task success results.

A second contribution of this study is to present differences in strategy between older adults with higher and lower fluid intelligence. The lower fluid intelligence group made more use of the mouse prior to clicking, which may indicate use of the mouse as a marker to support their search process. We also find that those with low fluid intelligence performed narrower searches, spent more time looking at the goal, spent more time at lower levels in the hierarchy, and had less ability to recover from wrong initial selections. Some studies of older and younger groups have reported similar findings. We hypothesize that these findings may have been more strongly related to fluid intelligence than to age, given the lack of such differences between our older and younger groups matched on fluid intelligence. This underscores the importance of measuring and controlling for cognitive abilities in studies involving older adults.

7. ACKNOWLEDGMENTS

We thank our study participants; Marianne Dee for participant recruitment; and Chris Martin for technical support. This research was supported by an Open Collaborative Research grant from the IBM Research Division, and by RCUK EP/G066019/1 "RCUK Hub: Inclusion in the Digital Economy".

8. REFERENCES

[1] Blackmon, M., Kitajama, M., Polson, P. 2005. Tool for accurately predicting website navigation problems, non-problems, problem severity, and effectiveness of repairs. In *Proceedings of the SIGCHI Conference on Human Factors in Computing Systems (CHI 2005),*. ACM, New York, NY, 31-40.

[2] Card, S. K., Moran, T. P., Newell, A. 1983. *The Psychology of Human-Computer Interaction.* Lawrence Erlbaum Associates, Hillsdale, NJ, USA,.

[3] Chi, E., Rosien, A., Supattanasiri, G., Williams, A., Royer, C., Chow, C., Robles, E., Dalal, B., Chen, J., Cousins, S. 2003. The Bloodhound project: Automating discovery of web usability issues using the InfoScent™ Simulator. In: *Proc. CHI 2003*, ACM, New York, NY, 505–512.

[4] Chin, J., Fu, W., and Kannampallil, T. 2009. Adaptive information search: Age-dependent interactions between cognitive profiles and strategies. In *Proc. CHI 2009*, ACM, New York, NY, 1683-1692.

[5] Chin, J., and Fu, W. 2010. Interactive effects of age and interface differences on search strategies and performance. In *Proc. CHI 2010*, ACM, New York, NY, 403-412.

[6] Czaja, S. J., Charness, N., Fisk, A. D., Hertzog, C., Nair, S. N., and Rogers, W. A., et al. 2006. Factors predicting the use of technology: findings from the Center for Research and Education on Aging and Technology Enhancement (CREATE). *Psychology and Aging, 21*(2), 333-352.

[7] Czaja, S. J., Sharit, J., Hernandez, M. A., Nair, S. N., and Loewenstein, D. 2010. Variability among older adults in Internet health information-seeking performance. *Gerontechnology 9(1)*, 46-55.

[8] Ekstrom, R. B., French, J. W., Harman, H. H., and Dermen, D. 1976. *Manual for kit of factor-referenced cognitive tests.* Educational Testing Services, Princeton, NJ.

[9] Fairweather, P. 2008. How older and younger adults differ in their approach to problem solving on a complex website. In *Proc. 10th International ACM SIGACCESS Conference on Computers and Accessibility* (Assets '08). ACM, New York, NY, 67-72.

[10] Hanson, V. 2010. Influencing technology adoption by older adults. *Interacting with Computers 22*, 6, 502-509.

[11] Hill, R., Dickinson, A., Arnott, J., Gregor, P., and McIver, L. 2011. Older web users' eye movements: experience counts. In *Proc. CHI 2011*, ACM Press, 1151-1160. DOI=http://doi.acm.org/10.1145/1978942.1979115

[12] Horn, J. and Cattell, R. 1966. Refinement and test of the theory of fluid and crystallized general intelligences, Journal of Educational Psychology 57(5), 253-270.

[13] Hornof, A., and Halverson, T. 2002. Cleaning up systematic error in eye tracking data by using required fixation locations. *Behavior Research Methods, Instruments and Computers 2002, 34 (4), 592-604.*

[14] Hines, T. M. and Posner, M. I. 1976. Slow but sure: A chronometic analysis of the process of aging. Paper presented at the *Annual Convention of the American Psychological Association* (September 3 – 7, 1976, Washington, DC).

[15] Jastrzembski, T., and Charness, N. 2007. The model human processor and the older adult: Parameter estimation and validation within a mobile phone task. *Journal of Experimental Psychology: Applied* 13, 4 (2007), 224-248.

[16] John, B. E., Jastrzembski, T. S. 2010. Exploration of costs and benefits of predictive human performance modeling for design. In: Salvucci, D. D., Gunzelmann, G. (eds.) *Proceedings of the 10th International Conference on Cognitive Modeling*, Philadelphia, PA, 115–120.

[17] Keates, S. and Trewin, S. 2005. Effect of age and Parkinson's disease on cursor positioning using a mouse, *Proceedings of the 7th international ACM SIGACCESS Conference on Computers and Accessibility*, ACM, New York, NY, 68-75.

[18] Lenth, R. V. 2006-9. Java Applets for Power and Sample Size [Computer software]. Accessed *July 9, 2012,* from http://www.stat.uiowa.edu/~rlenth/Power.

[19] Paxton, J., Barch, D., Racine, C., Braver, T. 2008. Cognitive Control, Goal Maintenance, and Prefrontal Function in Healthy Aging. *Cerebral Cortex* 18(5), 1010–1028.

[20] Riviere, C. N., Thakor, N. V. 1996. Effects of age and disability on tracking tasks with a computer mouse: accuracy and linearity. *J Rehabil Res Dev.* 1996 Feb;33(1):6-15. PubMed PMID: 8868412.

[21] Rodden, K., Fu, X., Aula, A., and Spiro, I. 2008. Eye-mouse coordination patterns on web search results pages. In *Extended Abstracts of CHI 2008*. ACM, New York, NY, 2997-3002.

[22] Salthouse, T. A. 1995. Differential age-related influences on memory for verbal-symbolic information and visual-spatial information. *Journal of Gerontology* 50B, 193–201.

[23] Sharit, J., Hernàndez, M., Czaja, S., and Pirolli, P. 2008. Investigating the roles of knowledge and cognitive abilities in older adult information seeking on the Web. *ACM Trans. Computer-Human Interaction 15*, 1 (2008), 1-15.

[24] Smith, M. W., Sharit, J., and Czaja, S. J. 1999. Aging, motor control and the performance of computer mouse tasks. *Human Factors*, Vol. 41(3), 389-396.

[25] Teo, L., John, B. E. John, and Blackmon, M. H. 2012. CogTool-Explorer: A model of goal-directed user exploration that considers information layout. *Proc. CHI 2012 (Austin, TX, May 5-10, 2012)*. ACM, New York, NY.

[26] Tobii Technology. 2010. *Tobii Studio 2.x Manual 1.0.* Tobii Technology.

[27] Trewin, S., John, B. E., Richards, J. T., Sloan, D., Hanson, V., Bellamy, R. K., Thomas, J., and Swart, C. 2012. Age-specific predictive models of human performance. In *Extended Abstracts of CHI 2012*, ACM, New York, NY.

[28] Yuan, K., Steedle, J., Shavelson, R., Alonzo, A. and Oppezzo, M. 2006. Working memory, fluid intelligence, and science learning. *Educational Research Review* 1, 83-98.

Elderly Text-Entry Performance on Touchscreens

Hugo Nicolau   Joaquim Jorge
IST / Technical University of Lisbon / INESC-ID
{hman, jaj}@vimmi.inesc-id.pt

ABSTRACT

Touchscreen devices have become increasingly popular. Yet they lack of tactile feedback and motor stability, making it difficult effectively typing on virtual keyboards. This is even worse for elderly users and their declining motor abilities, particularly hand tremor. In this paper we examine text-entry performance and typing patterns of elderly users on touch-based devices. Moreover, we analyze users' hand tremor profile and its relationship to typing behavior. Our main goal is to inform future designs of touchscreen keyboards for elderly people. To this end, we asked 15 users to enter text under two device conditions (mobile and tablet) and measured their performance, both speed- and accuracy-wise. Additionally, we thoroughly analyze different types of errors (insertions, substitutions, and omissions) looking at touch input features and their main causes. Results show that omissions are the most common error type, mainly due to cognitive errors, followed by substitutions and insertions. While tablet devices can compensate for about 9% of typing errors, omissions are similar across conditions. Measured hand tremor largely correlates with text-entry errors, suggesting that it should be approached to improve input accuracy. Finally, we assess the effect of simple touch models and provide implications to design.

Categories and Subject Descriptors

H.5.2 [**Information Interfaces and Presentation**]: User Interfaces – Input devices and strategies

General Terms

Design, Experimentation, Human Factors.

Keywords

Elderly, Touchscreen, Text-Entry, Tremor, Mobile, Tablet.

1. INTRODUCTION

There was a time where touchscreen technology was affordable to a few. Nowadays, this technology is widely spread among different devices, applications and environments, such as ATM machines, information kiosks, ticket machines, health control devices, etc. Most of us use touchscreens on a daily basis due to its enormous success in mobile devices. Indeed, these are increasingly replacing keypad-based applications.

The ability to directly touch and manipulate data on the screen without intermediate devices has a strong appeal, since it provides for a more natural and engaging experience. Moreover,

Figure 1. Participant typing on a touchscreen device.

touchscreens offer high flexibility, making it possible to display different interfaces on the same surface or to adapt to the users' needs and/or preferences [5]. For all their advantages, touch interfaces present similar challenges: they lack both the physical stability and tactile feedback ensured by keypads, making it harder for people to accurately select targets. This becomes especially pertinent to elderly people who suffer from increased hand tremor [16]. This effect becomes worse for interfaces that feature small targets and spacing [9], such as virtual keyboards.

Indeed, mobile text-input is a major challenge for elderly users. Since text-entry is a task transversal to many applications, such as basic communications, managing contacts, editing documents, web browsing, etc., these users are excluded from the innumerous opportunities brought by touch devices to different domains: social, professional, leisure, entertainment, shopping, communication, or healthcare. Still, touch interfaces have the potential to reduce this "technology gap", due to their high customizability, which makes them appropriate to custom-tailored or adaptive solutions that can fit the needs of different users. This highlights the need to understand how elderly people input text on current touchscreen devices. Because there is little or no quantified knowledge on the problems that these users experience with standard virtual keyboards, it is difficult to improve them. Furthermore, since touch interfaces are highly customizable, empirical data can be used to automate and provide user-dependent solutions.

Our goal with this work was to provide the knowledge needed to design both effective and efficient text-entry solutions for elderly people. We performed evaluations with 15 users (Figure 1) and two touch-based devices (mobile and tablet), analyzing the effect of hand tremor on text-entry performance. Also, we thoroughly analyze the users' typing behaviors and performance errors, as well as their comments. We were interested in answering questions such as: What will be the most common input errors and their causes? Will hand tremor be correlated with input performance? Will tablet devices compensate mobile difficulties? How can we enhance text-entry accuracy?

Our main contribution is a thorough understanding of text-entry performance in touch-based devices by elderly users. We provide an empirical body of knowledge to leverage future development of virtual keyboards and a better understanding on how text-input performance correlates to hand tremor. We also demonstrate the potential and virtues of simple touch models and provide design implications that should motivate researchers to develop more effective solutions.

2. RELATED WORK

We discuss related work in two areas: first, we look into previous research that attempts to better understand tremor and how it affects elderly users. Second, we discuss HCI research aimed at creating new touch-based solutions for older adults.

2.1 Elderly and Tremor

Generally, tremor is defined as any involuntary, approximately rhythmic, and roughly sinusoidal motion around a joint. Tremor is present in all individuals and is the most common form of movement disorder with an increased prevalence among elderly individuals [16]. There are two classification systems used in evaluating tremor: type of movement and cause. The first distinguishes whether tremor occurs at rest (resting tremor) or is caused by action. Tremors associated to movement (action) include postural tremor, which occurs with maintained posture; kinetic or intention tremor, which occurs with movement from point to point; and task-specific tremor, occurring only when doing highly skilled activity. Postural tremor is usually detected by having a patient holding the arms stretched out in front, while kinetic or intention tremor can be tested by using the finger-to-nose maneuver. The second tremor classification is by cause. Tremor can be due to a variety of conditions both physiologic and pathologic. Physiological tremor in healthy individuals is characterized as a low amplitude postural tremor with a modal frequency of 8–12 Hz [4] in the hands. Pathological tremor is the most extensive movement disorder and can be observed in several pathologies, such as: Essential Tremor, Parkinson's disease, dystonic disorders, cerebellar disease or head trauma. Most of these pathologies are more prevalent among elderly individuals.

Currently accepted standards for evaluating motor performance include subjective measures such as self-reporting and clinical rating scales. The Unified Parkinson's Disease Rating Scale (UPDRS) rates motor manifestations from 0 to 4, where higher scores denote greater severity [7]. However, there are certain limitations in the utility of this rating instrument, because scores are subjective and imprecise. On the other hand, objective motor assessment is an open challenge for movement disorder specialists. Handwriting and drawing samples have long been used to quantify tremor during movement due to their simplicity [1]; however, these tests are not suitable for measuring resting or postural tremor. Accelerometers are currently one of the most commonly used instrument in tremor studies, since they are capable of providing reliable and objective indices by measuring linear acceleration. Many tremor quantification algorithms use power spectral analysis in the frequency domain [14] and define tremor amplitude as the amplitude of a peak in the power spectrum between 3 and 7 Hz. Analyzing the peak amplitude in the 7-12 Hz spectrum may also prove worthwhile to measure physiological tremor. Overall, objective measures of tremor disorders motivated much research by clinicians in the last decades and it will be of significant relevance to the HCI community as well. With the global increase of the senior population, understanding, modeling and dealing with tremor will be a significant concern in designing future assistive technologies.

2.2 Elderly, Touch, and Text-Entry

There is a large body of work that tries to understand and maximize performance of users when interacting with touch interfaces. Past research has investigated optimal target size, spacing and position [9] to derive recommendations and general guidelines for older adults when these interfaces. Still, most approaches do not consider the particular challenges of text-entry: large number of targets, small key size and spacing. Solutions for able-bodied users have been proposed in order to deal with incorrect characters. Gunawardana et al. [8] presented a method to expand or contract key areas for each press using language models, while others have proposed using touch models to adapt to individual typing patterns [5] and improve overall input accuracy. While text-prediction features have also been explored, older adults usually dislike them [11]. Nonetheless, few researchers have explored the specific needs of elderly users in touch typing tasks.

Chung et al. [3] showed that both younger and older users preferred a touchscreen keypad for numeric entry tasks, since it did not force them to divide their attention between the input device and screen content. Wobbrock et al. [18] proposed a stylus-based approach that uses edges and corners of a reduced touch screen to enable text-entry tasks, showing an increase of accuracy and motion stability for users with motor impairments. Similarly, Barrier Pointing [6] uses screen edges and corners to improve pointing accuracy. By stroking towards the screen barriers and allowing the stylus to press against them, users can select targets with greater physical stability. Wacharamanotham [17] takes a similar approach by proposing a technique that uses swipe gestures towards the screen edges in order to select targets. Although these works insightfully explore the device physical properties to aid people interacting with touchscreens, there is little empirical knowledge about elderly users performing text-entry tasks with traditional virtual keyboards. Previous research does not take into consideration elder challenges (such as tremor) that might affect their use of virtual keyboards. The study reported in this paper bridges this gap by analyzing their performance when typing with touchscreen devices, enabling designers to take advantage of this knowledge to build future solutions.

3. USER STUDY

Touch screen devices are increasingly replacing their button-based counterparts. The physical stability and haptic feedback once provided by buttons are being lost, which makes it harder to accurately select targets. This is especially relevant in text-entry tasks due to both small target size and spacing. In this user study we evaluate two different types of touch devices – mobile phone and tablet – and thoroughly analyze how elderly users enter text.

3.1 Research Questions

This user study aims to answer four main research questions:

1. *How do elderly users perform speed and accuracy wise in touch-based devices?*

2. *What are the most common types of errors and causes?*

3. *Do tablet devices compensate the difficulties of elderly users when using mobile phones?*

4. *Does tremor affect text-entry performance? If yes, how does user performance correlate with hand tremor?*

3.2 Participants

Fifteen participants, eleven females and four males, took part in our user study. Their age ranged from 67 to 89 with a mean of 79 (*sd*=7.3) years old. All participants were right-handed. They were recruited from a local social institution and no pre-screening to recruit participants with or at risk of developing tremor disorders was performed. None of the participants had severe visual impairments and all were able to see screen content. Twelve of the participants owned a mobile phone, however they were only able to receive and make calls. Only one participant had used touchscreen technology before, but had never entered text. Regarding QWERTY familiarity, six participants had used this type of keyboard whether in typing machines (four participants) or personal computers (two participants).

3.3 Procedure

This user study had two main phases: familiarization and evaluation. At the beginning of the first phase, participants were told that the overall purpose of the study was to investigate how text-entry performance is affected by the type of device. Following this, participants filled in a pre-questionnaire about demographics and mobile phone usage. We then explained and exemplified to them how to use a virtual keyboard. Although most participants were reluctant to interact with the devices at the beginning, they seamlessly coped with the "touch-to-select" metaphor and easily understood how to write. Nevertheless, because most of them were not familiar with touch devices and QWERTY keyboards, we asked participants to perform two familiarization tasks using each device. The first consisted in entering single letters. They had to copy a letter, displayed at the top of the screen, to a text box. Participants performed this task for 10 minutes (to guarantee an equal amount of training across individuals). The second task consisted in copying sentences. Error correction (delete) was not available. The sentences had a maximum of five words, similar to those presented on the evaluation phase. Participants performed this task for 20 minutes.

In the evaluation phase, we started by assessing the users capabilities regarding tremor (postural and action tremor) applying two different methods. We first asked participants to draw an Archimedes spiral with each hand without leaning hand or arm on table [1]; we then asked participants to hold the mobile device at the arm's length for 30 seconds with each hand and remain still, while we captured data from the accelerometer sensor [15]. Subjects were then informed about the experiment and how to use our evaluation application. We evaluated the participants' performance with two devices: mobile phone and tablet.

Before each condition participants had a five minute practice trial to get used to the virtual keyboard. We did not force participants to interact with a specific finger, thus they were allowed to choose the most comfortable typing strategy, as long as it was consistent during that condition. For the mobile phone condition, participants had to hold it in their hand, since it is a handheld device (Figure 1); for the tablet device condition, it was placed on the table in front of them. For each evaluation condition, participants copied five different sentences (first sentence was a practice trial), displayed one at a time, at the top of the screen (Figure 2). Copy typing was used to reduce the opportunity for spelling and language errors, and to make error identification easier. Participants were instructed to type phrases as quickly and accurately as possible. Both required and transcribed sentences were always visible. Error correction (delete key) was not

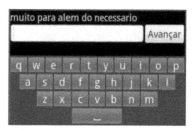

Figure 2. Screen shot of evaluation application. Participants were not able to correct errors. The button 'Avançar' allowed them to continue to the next

available, since we wanted to capture typing performance regardless of correction strategies. Participants were told that they could not correct errors and were instructed to continue typing if an error occurred. Once participants had finished entering each sentence, they pressed the 'next' button. After the five sentences were entered, we asked them to perform the same tasks with a different device. The order of conditions was counter balanced to avoid bias associated with experience. The evaluation procedure took approximately 40 minutes per participant. Each subject entered a total of 10 different sentences. These sentences were extracted from a written language *corpus*, and each one had five words with an average size of 4.48 characters and a minimum correlation with the language of 0.97. Sentences were chosen randomly such that no sentence was written twice per participant.

3.4 Apparatus

An HTC Desire and ASUS Transformer TF101 Tablet were used during the user study. A QWERTY virtual keyboard, similar to android's SDK keyboard, was used in both devices (Figure 2); for the HTC Desire each key was 10x10mm on landscape mode, while for the ASUS tablet each key was 20x10mm. Letters were entered when the user lift his finger from keys. Neither word prediction nor correction was used. All participants' actions were logged through our evaluation application and the user study was filmed to observe the participants' behaviors.

3.5 Dependent Measures

The performance during the text-entry task was measured using different quantitative variables [12]: *words per minute* (*WPM*), *minimum string distance* (*MSD*) error rate, and character-level errors (*substitutions* – incorrect characters, *insertions* – added characters, and omissions – omitted characters). Qualitative measures were also gathered at the end of the experiment by debriefing each participant. We also gathered tremor-related measures of each participant before text-entry tasks in order to characterize their level of impairment.

3.6 Design and Analysis

We used a within subjects design where each participant tested all conditions. For each device condition each participant entered 5 sentences (1 practice + 4 test), resulting in a total of 20 sentences per participant. In summary the study design was: 15 participants x 5 sentences x 2 devices. We performed Shapiro-Wilkinson tests of the observed values for *WPM, KSPC, MSD error rate,* types of errors and tremor measures. If dependent variables were normally distributed we applied parametric statistical tests, such as repeated measures ANOVA, t-test, and Pearson correlations. On the other hand, if measures were not normally distributed, we used non-parametric tests: Friedman, Wilcoxon, and Spearman correlations. Bonferroni corrections were used for post-hoc tests.

4. RESULTS

Our goal was to understand how elderly people input text with traditional touchscreen devices. We describe and characterize each user's tremor profile and relate it with text-entry performance. Moreover, we analyze input speed and accuracy for both device conditions, focusing on type of errors.

4.1 Tremor Profile

Task-specific tremor, which is a type of action tremor, was measured in both hands, using the Archimedes spiral test. The drawings were classified by a clinical professional as Absent, Slight, Moderate, Severe or Marked. For the dominant-hand drawings, 7 participants (46.7%) showed no tremor, 4 (26.7%) showed slight tremor, 1 participants (6.7%) demonstrated moderate tremor, 2 (13.3%) showed severe tremor, and 1 participant (6.7%) demonstrated marked tremor. Regarding the non-dominant hand drawings, 5 participants (33.3%) showed absence of tremor, 6 participants (40%) showed slight tremor, 1 participant (6.7%) demonstrated moderate tremor, 1 (6.7%) showed severe tremor, and 2 participants (13.3%) demonstrated marked tremor. Figure 3 illustrates some examples of drawings.

Table 1. Postural hand oscillation for all axes (m/s^2).

mean (sd)	X	Y	Z	XYZ
Dominant	0.19 (.07)	0.15 (.06)	0.3 (0.13)	0.14 (.04)
Non-Dominant	0.17 (.07)	0.12 (.02)	0.3 (.15)	0.1 (.03)

In addition to subjective measures, we also measured tremor through the device's accelerometer. Particularly, we measured the postural – a type of action – tremor. From the captured data we analyzed three main values: acceleration standard deviations, which correspond to hand oscillations [2]; the peak amplitude in the power spectrum of 3 to 7 Hz, and 7 to 12 Hz. We report the peak amplitude in different frequency ranges since physiological and pathologic tremors are usually distinguishable and may affect users' performance differently. Results for hand oscillation (Table 1) showed a mean magnitude of 0.186 m/s^2 (sd=.074), 0.15 m/s^2 (sd=.06), 0.3 m/s^2 (sd=.13), and 0.137 m/s^2 (sd=.044) for X, Y, Z, and XYZ axis, respectively. Regarding the non-dominant hand, due to a logging issue we were only able to record 9 of the 15 participants' accelerometer data. Mean oscillation was 0.174 m/s^2 (sd=.07), 0.115 m/s^2 (sd=.024), 0.3 m/s^2 (sd=.149), and 0.101 m/s^2 (sd=.03), for X, Y, Z, XYZ axis, respectively. Regarding the frequency analysis, results showed a mean peak magnitude of 0.362 m/s^2 (sd=0.429), and 0.17 m/s^2 (sd=0.17), for the 3 to 7 Hz, and 7 to 12 Hz, respectively. Concerning the non-dominant hand, results showed a mean peak magnitude of 0.17 m/s^2 (sd=0.162), and 0.105 m/s^2 (sd=0.175) for the 3 to 7 Hz, and 7 to 12 Hz, respectively. It is worth noticing that the results for each of the frequency ranges show high standard deviation, suggesting that tremor severity varies widely among participants.

Figure 3. Archimedes spiral drawings. From left to right: absent, slight, severe, marked.

4.2 Text-Entry Performance

In this section we thoroughly analyze input performance regarding speed and accuracy for both device conditions. During text-entry tasks, all participants consistently used their non-dominant hand to hold the mobile device and dominant index finger to select intended keys. However, one of the participants was unable to use the mobile device, due to visual impairments. Although text font was large (Figure 2), participant #9 was not able to read keyboard characters, and therefore did not complete the *Mobile* condition.

4.2.1 Input Speed

To assess speed, we used the words per minute (WPM) text input measure calculated as *(transcribed text – 1) * (60 seconds / time in seconds) / (5 characters per word)*.

Tablets allow higher input rates. Participants typed an average of 4.73 *WPM* (sd=3.06) in *Mobile* and 5.07 *WPM* (sd=2.93) in *Tablet* conditions. A paired-samples t-test was conducted to evaluate the effect of device on text-entry speed. A statistically significant increase in *WPM* [t(13) = -2.752, *p*<.05] was found, suggesting that participants can achieve higher input rates with tablet devices.

Experience makes the difference. Overall, input rate was strongly correlated with QWERTY keyboard experience, which explains 46% [Spearman rho=.648, n=14, *p*<.05] and 29% [Spearman rho=.534, n=15, *p*<.05] of shared variance for *Mobile* and *Tablet* conditions, respectively; that is, participants that used a (non touch-based) QWERTY keyboard in the past inputted text faster.

4.2.2 Input Accuracy

We measured the quality of the transcribed sentences using the *Minimum String Distance* (MSD) *Error Rate*, calculated as MSD(*required sentence, transcribed sentence*) / *mean size of alignments* x 100. Figure 4 illustrates participants' *MSD Error Rate* for both *Mobile* and *Tablet* conditions.

Experience is not enough. As opposed to the results obtained in input speed, there was a weak correlation between quality of transcribed sentences and QWERTY experience for *Mobile* [Pearson r=.145, n=14, *p*=.621] and *Tablet* [Pearson r=.155, n=15, *p*=.58] conditions. This result suggests that previous experience is not enough to compensate for typing errors.

Tablets compensate difficulties. Participants achieved an average *MSD error rate* of 25.97% (sd=19.72%) and 16.55% (sd=11.9%) in *Mobile* and *Tablet* conditions, respectively. Results show a statistically significant decrease of 9.42%, which suggests that elderly users indeed benefit from tablet devices, either due to key size or its static position (on the table).

Hand tremor explains (mobile) error rates. In *Mobile* condition, *Hand Oscillation* of the non-dominant hand in the *Y* [Pearson

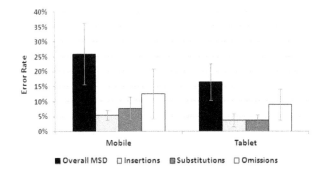

Figure 4. Overall MSD, Insertion, Substitution, and Omission error rate for each device condition. Error bars denote 95% confidence intervals

r=.751, n=9, p<.05] and Z [Pearson r=.613, n=9, p=.079] *axis* were strongly correlated with *MSD error rate*. Since the mobile device was held in the non-dominant hand during text-entry tasks, these results suggest that hand oscillations can explain as far as 56.4% of shared variance. As for *Tablet* condition, we found no strong correlations between tremor measures and *MSD error rate*.

4.2.3 Typing Errors

This section presents a fine grained analysis by categorizing types of input errors: *insertions*, *substitutions*, and *omissions* [12]. Figure 4 shows the type of errors in *Mobile* and *Tablet* conditions.

Omissions are the most common error type. Results show that, on average, omission errors are the most common type in both *Mobile* (*m*=12.65%, *sd*=16%) and *Tablet* (*m*=9%, *sd*=10%) conditions. *Omissions* are often described as cognitive errors, since they do not depend on motor abilities [10]. Instead, users usually forget to type the intended characters or misunderstand the required sentence. Since we did not account for cognitive differences, we cannot confirm this hypothesis. Nevertheless, it would be expected that cognitive errors across device conditions remained unchanged. In fact, no statistical significant differences on *omission error rate* were found between *Mobile* and *Tablet* conditions [Z=-.722, p>.4], suggesting that cognitive demand is constant and may be playing an important role. Further discussion on this topic is available in Section 4.2.6.

Hand tremor can be used to reduce substitutions. *Substitutions* were the second most common error type. Participants obtained a mean 7.8% (*sd*=7%) error rate in *Mobile* and 3.75% (*sd*=3.61%) in *Tablet* condition. For both conditions, we found large positive correlations between *substitution* error rate and *task-specific tremor*; that is, participants with higher hand tremor had higher *substitution* error rates. In *Mobile* both *dominant* [Spearman rho=.624, n=15, p<.05] and *non-dominant hand* [Spearman rho=.541, n=9, p<.05] *task-specific tremor* accounted for 39% and 29% of shared variance, respectively. In *Tablet* condition, *dominant hand task-specific tremor* [Spearman rho=.539, n=15, p=.038] explained 29% of shared variance.

Insertions are not predicted by tremor. Overall, *Insertions* were the least common error type (although no significant differences were found) in both conditions. Moreover, we did not find strong correlations with tremor measures, suggesting that there is a weak relationship between *insertion error rate* and *hand tremor*.

Overall, magnitude of errors is lower in Tablet condition, with one exception. We found significant differences between device conditions for *insertion* [Z=-2.103, p<0.05] and *substitution* [Z=-2.731, p<.01] error rates. On the other hand, no significant differences were found for *omission errors*, suggesting that these errors do not depend on participants' physical abilities.

4.2.4 Insertion Errors

Insertion errors had two main causes: 1) *accidental* touches, for instance when users were scanning the keyboard for the intended key and accidental touched other key; and 2) *bounce* errors, which occurred when a key was unintentionally pressed more than once, producing unwanted characters. In this section we analyze in detail these two types of errors for both device conditions. Knowing how to identify these errors whilst users type can be of great value to prevent incorrect characters from being entered. Error classification was done through visual inspection of both transcribed sentences and video recordings in order to guarantee a

Figure 5. Accidental touch (left) and bouncing errors (right). Time in seconds is represented in *x*-axis.

high level of accuracy. Error rates were calculated as *number of errors / number of keystrokes*.

Accidental touches are less common in Tablet condition. Overall, *bouncing* errors and *accidental* touches account for the majority of insertion errors. Concerning *bounce error rate*, participants obtained a mean of 1.55% (*sd*=1.7%) in *Mobile* and 2.25% (*sd*=3.5%) in *Tablet* condition. Regarding *accidental touches*, participants achieved error rates of 3.28% (*sd*=3.9%) and 1.05% (*sd*=1.22%), respectively, in *Mobile* and *Tablet* conditions. We found a significant decrease of *accidental* touches in the *Tablet* condition [Z=-2.292, p<0.05]. Conversely, *bouncing* errors were not statistically different between device conditions [Z=-.314, p=0.754], although there was an increase of *bounce* errors with the tablet device.

Mobile bounces and accidental touches are related with hand tremor. We found strong positive correlations between mobile *bounce error rate* and tremor measures: *dominant hand Oscillation on the X axis* [Spearman rho=.596, n=14, p=.025] and *non-dominant hand peak magnitude acceleration between 7 and 12 Hz* [Spearman rho=.532, n=9, p=.14]. Regarding *accidental touches*, large correlations were also found, particularly with non-dominant hand tremor: *Oscillation Y axis* [Spearman rho=.762, n=9, p=.017], *Oscillation Z axis* [Spearman rho=.536, n=9, p=.162], and *peak magnitude acceleration between 3 and 7 Hz* [Spearman rho=.508, n=9, p=.162].

Classifying insertions through key press duration and inter-key interval. From illustrations in Figure 5, both *bouncing errors* and *accidental touches* are easily identified due to reduced press duration and inter-key interval. We believe that a significant percentage of these errors can be automatically classified and filtered by analyzing these typing features. Hand tremor features should also be used to improve filtering solutions. Our data show that individuals are consistent in their input behaviors; however, typing patterns may be both user- and device-dependent.

4.2.5 Substitution Errors

In this section we will analyze common substitution patterns and keyboard layouts that emerged from participants' key presses.

Similar difficulties across all keys. In general, participants had similar difficulties across all keys. No row, column or side patterns emerge from the data for both device conditions.

Right-bottom substitution pattern. To analyze the most common substitutions, we created confusion matrices. Some of the most frequent errors in *Mobile* condition were: C→SPACE (6.83%), C→V (3.17%), O→P (4%), T→Y (3.96%), S→Z (4.34%). As we can see there is a clear predominance of right and bottom key substitutions in the data, which suggests that participants found it easier to hit keys in the right-bottom (southeast) direction. These findings may be related to hand dominance, but further investigation is needed to confirm this hypothesis. Additionally, errors are at a distance of one key. Indeed, this pattern can be seen in Figure 6, which illustrates all lift points of *Mobile* condition. The pattern remains unaltered in the *Tablet* condition, with

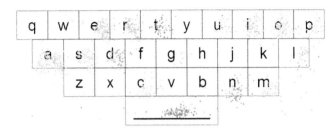

Figure 6. Touch (lift) points for all participants in *Mobile* condition.

common *substitutions* being: C→SPACE (6.8%), R→T (4.2%), S→Z (4.3%), S→D (3%), U→J (1.9%).

Similar and symmetrical letters result in cognitive errors. A common error that cannot be explained by previous substitution pattern is P→Q. We believe this to be a cognitive error, instead of motor error, since it commonly occurred in both conditions. Participants had an improper model of the letter and have confused it with a very similar one (symmetrical: p→q). Indeed, similar problems occurred with the letter 'i', which was frequently replaced by the letter 'l' (3.1%). Participant #11 consistently confused symmetrical letters: m→w (66.7%), n→u (52.85%). These results suggest that some *substitutions* are not due to motor errors alone; cognitive errors play an important role in text input for elderly users.

Most errors are due to poor aiming. In this user study, we were also interested in finding why substitution error occurred; was it due to poor aiming or finger slips? We classified a finger slip as a correct land-on (i.e. land on the correct key) and incorrect lift (i.e. lift on nearby key – substitution). Poor aiming errors consist in landing on and lifting of an incorrect key. Most *substitution* errors were due to incorrect land-on (i.e. *poor aiming*), with an average of 6.71% in *Mobile* and 3.5% in *Tablet* condition. On the other hand, *slips* accounted for an average of 1.1% and 0.24% of typing errors in *Mobile* and *Tablet* conditions, respectively. In fact, slip errors were significantly lower than poor aiming errors in both device conditions: *Mobile* [Z=-3.107, p<.01], *Tablet* [Z=-2.944, p<.01]. Similar results have been reported in [13] for situationally impaired users.

Slip errors are related with hand oscillation, while poor aiming errors are related with task-specific tremor. Different features of hand tremor correlated with *poor aiming* and *slip* errors. While *poor aiming* was strongly correlated with *task-specific tremor* in both device conditions: *Mobile* - [Spearman rho=.541, n=14, p=.046], and *Tablet* - [Spearman rho=.563, n=14, p=.029]; *slip errors* were strongly correlated with non-dominant hand oscillation on XYZ axis only in *Mobile* condition [Spearman rho=.714, n=9, p=.031].

Novel layouts should give more emphasis to key width. Last, we were interested in the overall virtual keyboard layout that would emerge from elderly users touch points. For this analysis, we calculated key centroids for each key across all participants. We removed outlying points that were more than one key distance away from the center of each key in either *x* or *y* direction, to account for transposition or cognitive errors. Additionally, we calculated the standard deviation of finger-lift points for each key in *x* and *y* directions. We then grouped the 26 keys by row and side. Right keyboard side contained the keys P, O, I, U, Y, L, K, J, H, M, N, B, and the left side contained the remaining letters. The keyboards that emerged from this analysis were shifted to the bottom-right in comparison to the traditional QWERTY keyboard,

which was expected from previous findings. Also, we found no significant effect of *row* on deviations for both *x*- and *y*-directions in either *Mobile* or *Tablet* conditions; that is precision is equal across all rows. However, we found a significant decrease of *x*-direction deviations from left to right side of *Mobile* keyboard [t(13)=-3.043, p<.01]. This result suggests that keys on the left side of the *Mobile* keyboards should be slightly wider, when possible. In the *Tablet* condition, we also found a statistically significant increase of *x*-axis *dispersion* relatively to *y*-direction [t(14)=4.039, p<.001]. Again, these findings may be related with hand dominance and demonstrate that elderly users are more susceptible to *x*-direction deviations from their touch centroids.

4.2.6 Omission Errors

Omissions were the most common error type in this user study and are usually associated to cognitive errors. Understanding omission errors is particularly difficult since it is hard to understand the reason why participants failed to enter the intended character/word. Was it because of they forgot it or because the device was unable to recognize the users' touch? In order to answer these questions we resorted to video recordings.

Blank space was the most problematic key. During our user study with elderly participants, we found that forgetting to enter a blank space between words was a common issue. Although participants were instructed before the evaluation session, the concept of a blank character was sometimes difficult to understand. In fact, this key achieved the highest error rate across all keys (25-30%) and *omissions* were the main cause.

Forgetfulness and coordination are real issues. Some participants forgot to transcribe some letters or words during text-entry tasks. For instance, participant #13 usually forgot to transcribe words at the middle and end of sentences. Still, her performance was consistent across device conditions, which suggest that this was a cognitive error. For participant #8, the copy task seemed to be overwhelming as she could not manage and coordinate what she has transcribed and what was yet to be transcribed. She frequently asked things like: "where was I?", "have a written this?", thus resulting in omitted letters and words. These results illustrate some of the challenges in evaluating text-entry performance with elderly people.

Unintentional touches prevented key presses. While *omission* errors may be related with cognitive errors, there were also some issues (although less severe) regarding touch interaction. Particularly, unintentional touches occurred when participants were holding or resting their non-dominant hand on the device. These behaviors resulted in unrecognized key presses since the keyboard only handled a single input point.

4.3 Participants' Comments and Preference

At the end of the user study participants were debriefed and asked about their preferred device. Additionally, we also gathered general comments about their input performance.

When asked about each device ease of use (using a 5-point Likert scale), the median [IQR (Interquartile Range)] attributed by participants was 4.5 [1.75] and 5 [0.5] for *Mobile* and *Tablet* devices, respectively, showing a preference for the tablet device. Participants' classifications were generally high, which may be misleading when considering their difficulties. Still, when directly asked about their preferred device results are clear: thirteen (86.7%) participants chose the *Tablet*: with a 95% adjusted-Wald binomial confidence interval ranging from 60.9% to 97.5%, a lower limited well above the two-choice change expectation of 50%. The main reasons for their choice were the larger key size and spacing. Moreover, some participants also stated that letters (i.e. visual feedback) were easier to see. When asked about their main difficulties, participants referred diverse issues about: 1) key acquisition, particularly in the *Mobile* condition (*"I am always hitting neighbor keys"*; *"The hardest thing is trying not to tremble while texting"*), and 2) keyboard layout, mainly for those with no QWERTY experience (*"The main difficult for me is in knowing where the letters are. I am not used to it"*).

5. TOWARDS INCLUSIVE KEYBOARDS

The analysis presented above provide insight about elderly users' typing patterns and how keyboard features may be improved to better support text input on touch-based devices. In this section, we access the reliability of simple touch models and perform a user-dependent and user-independent analysis. The goal is to demonstrate the potential of such solutions, acknowledging that more efficient models can be found resorting to more sophisticated measures (e.g. tremor features) and algorithms.

5.1 Deal with Insertions

To deal with *insertion* errors, we calculated the optimal inter-key threshold; that is, the value that allowed reducing *insertions* without negatively affecting *MSD error rate*. In this analysis we used 40 values: the number of 25ms intervals from 0ms to 1000ms. Key presses that had an inter-key interval lower than the threshold being tested were considered insertions and were therefore discarded. We then computed *MSD error rate* from all resulting sentences and compared it against the baseline condition.

For the user-dependent analysis, we calculated the optimal inter-key threshold for each participant, based on their typing behavior. Results show that *MSD error rate* dropped, on average, 6.8% in *Mobile*, and 1.8% in the *Tablet* condition. Optimal threshold values varied from 25ms to 1000ms in the *Mobile* condition and from 50ms to 675ms in the *Tablet* condition. For the user-independent analysis, we calculated the mean *insertion* and *MSD error rate* of all participants and choose the inter-key threshold that would allow a higher performance gain (on average). In the *Mobile* condition the threshold was 100 ms and resulted in a reduction of 0.8% of *MSD error rate*. In the *Tablet* condition, the threshold was slight higher, 150ms and resulted in a decrease of 1.1% of *MSD error rate*. It is noteworthy the decrease in performance of the user-independent classifier, especially in the *Mobile* condition. This result suggests that filtering solutions should take into account each user typing behaviors. Moreover, this simple approach removed nearly 30% and 50% of *insertion* errors in the *Mobile* and *Tablet* conditions, respectively.

5.2 Deal with Substitutions

To deal with *substitution* errors, we performed a simple key classification based on the Euclidean distance between two points. Key centroids were calculated for each key and all key presses were re-classified according to the closest centroid. Regarding the user-dependent classification, we used a 10-fold cross-validation to calculate the mean centroid of each key for each training subset of data, and classified the remaining key presses. *MSD error rate* dropped, on average, 11.5%, and 1.2% in the *Mobile* and *Tablet* conditions, respectively. Overall, participants were consistent within themselves, repeatedly hitting the same places for the same keys. For the user-independent classification, we calculated the average of all key centroids for all participants and classified each participant's key presses based on the closest centroid. This approach also reduced *MSD error rates*, on average, by 9.8% for the *Mobile* condition, and 0.6% for the *Tablet* condition. Results show that the *Mobile* gain is higher in both classification approaches. However, the user-independent classification performed worst, suggesting that personalization should be taken into account when designing touch-based solutions for the elderly.

6. DISCUSSION

After analyzing all data, we are now able to answer the research questions proposed at the beginning of this user study.

1. How do elderly users perform speed and accuracy wise in touch-based devices? Elderly users achieved a maximum of 11.5 WPM using the tablet device (mean of 4.7 and 5 WPM for *Mobile* and *Tablet* conditions, respectively). Also, input speed was not correlated with tremor, instead it was strongly correlated with previous QWERTY experience. On the other hand, accuracy was mainly explained by *task-specific tremor* and *hand oscillation*, especially in *Mobile* conditions. Users obtained a minimum *MSD error rate* of 2.5% (mean of 26% and 17% for *Mobile* and *Tablet* conditions, respectively). Curiously, *Error Rate* was not correlated with previous QWERTY experience, suggesting that having some practice with keyboards is not sufficient to compensate the challenges that are imposed by touch interfaces.

2. What are the most common types of errors and causes? The most common error type among elderly people was *omission* errors (9-12.6%). This pattern occurred across device conditions, suggesting that it was due to cognitive errors. Nonetheless, the novelty of the task can also be playing an important role, thus it would be interesting to observe users' performance on a longitudinal study. Following *omission* errors were *substitution* (3.75-7.8%) and *insertion* (3.8-5.5%) errors. *Insertions* were mainly due to bounces and accidental touches; while *substitutions* were mostly due to poor aiming.

3. Do tablet devices compensate the difficulties of elderly users when using mobile phones? Overall, we found a decrease of 9% in MSD *error rate* from *Mobile* to *Tablet* devices. This finding suggests that tablet devices compensate some of the challenges imposed by mobile devices, either due to larger key sizes and/or static positioning. Indeed, users' comments and preference reinforced this result. Regarding types of error, there was a significant decrease of both *insertions* (1.7%) and *substitutions* (4%). No significant differences were found on *omission* errors, suggesting that they are device-independent.

4. Does tremor affect text-entry performance? If yes, how does user performance correlate with hand tremor? Although input speed was mainly related with QWERTY experience, errors were strongly correlated with participants' tremor profile. However, each error type was correlated with different measures of tremor. *Substitutions* were largely explained by a subjective measure - *task-specific tremor*, while *insertion* errors, particularly bounces and accidental touches were strongly correlated with *Oscillation in the X axis* (dominant hand). The non-dominant hand also played an important role in *Mobile* errors: *Hand Oscillation* was strongly correlated with overall *MSD error rate*, *accidental touches*, and *slips*. These findings suggest that future mobile interfaces should take into account users' tremor profile in order to provide more suitable text-entry designs. Still, designers should consider different features of tremor.

7. IMPLICATIONS FOR DESIGN

We derive the following implications from our results:

Shift keyboard layout. Elderly participants theoretically benefit from a layout shift in the bottom-right direction as most substitution errors occur in this direction. This finding may be related to hand dominance, thus further research should explore this hypothesis. Future work should also explore whether this change should be visible to the user, similarly to [5].

Width rather than height. Whenever possible keys should be wider instead of taller. For both devices we found higher x-axis touch dispersion, suggesting that users are more favorable to wider keys. In fact, even though most 12-key physical keyboards respect this layout, it was lost in touch interfaces.

Narrower spacebar. Results of touch deviations suggest that spacebar should be narrower. Reducing its size has the potential to diminish substitution errors. We recommend a spacebar extending from middle of C to middle of B for both devices.

Avoid errors by understanding typing behaviors. Future designs should focus on model users typing patterns by analyzing touch features (e.g. x and y touch position, distance traveled during touch, key press duration, between keys duration etc.) and therefore increase typing accuracy.

Allow personalization. We observed several individual differences regarding typing behaviors, particularly hit point locations, and inter-key interval. Future research should tackle these issues by providing user-dependent solutions.

Deal with poor aiming rather than finger slips. Keyboard designers should deal with poor aiming errors. Although finger slips may occur they only account for a minority of substitution errors, particularly when typing on tablet devices.

Use language-based correctors. Cognitive errors were quite common among elderly users. Simple language-based solutions can provide a suitable answer to these types of errors. For example, to deal with blank space omissions or substitution of similar letters (e.g. p$\rightarrow$q, m$\rightarrow$w).

Compensate hand tremor. Future keyboards should adapt to users' hand tremor characteristics. Results showed large correlations between tremor measures and input accuracy, namely when considering substitution errors. Taking advantage of current mobile sensing capabilities, future solutions should trace users' tremor profile to compensate typing errors.

8. CONCLUSION

We have investigated text-entry performance of 15 elderly users on touch-based devices. Results showed that error rates are still relatively high compared to younger users' performance [13]. Hand tremor was strongly correlated with input errors, indicating that this information can be used to enhance text-entry accuracy. Most common types of error were *omissions* (10.8%), followed by *substitutions* (5.8%), and *insertions* (4.6%). From results emerged error patterns and design implications that should improve typing accuracy and persuade researchers to create more effective solutions for the elderly. Future work should improve proposed solutions and focus in coping with each user's abilities, enabling them to effectively input text on touchscreen devices.

9. ACKNOWLEDGMENTS

We thank all participants and people from *Centro de Dia e Lar de Algueirão Mem Martins*, particularly Luisa Ambrósio and Ana Rodrigues for their insights. This work was supported by FCT: individual grant SFRH/BD/46748/2008; project PEst-OE/EEI/LA0021/201; and project PAELife AAL/0014/2009.

10. REFERENCES

[1] Bain et al. Assessing the impact of essential tremor on upper limb function. *Journal of neurology*, 241(1):54–61, 1993.

[2] Bergstrom-Lehtovirta et al. The effects of walking speed on target acquisition on a touchscreen interface. *In Proc. of MHCI'11*, 143–146, 2011.

[3] Chung et al. Usability evaluation of numeric entry tasks on keypad type and age. *International Journal of Industrial Ergonomics*, 40(1):97–105, 2010.

[4] Elble and Koller. *Tremor*. Johns Hopkins University Press Baltimore, 1990.

[5] Findlater and Wobbrock. Personalized input: Improving ten-finger touchscreen typing through automatic adaptation. *In Proc. of CHI'12*, 815-824, 2012.

[6] Froehlich et al. Barrier pointing: using physical edges to assist target acquisition on mobile device touch screens. *In Proc. of ASSETS'07*, 19–26, 2007.

[7] Goetz et al. Movement disorder society-sponsored revision of the unified parkinson's disease rating scale (mds-updrs): Scale presentation and clinimetric testing results. *Movement disorders*, 23(15):2129–2170, 2008.

[8] Gunawardana et al. Usability guided key-target resizing for soft keyboards. In *Proc. of IUI'10*, 111–118, 2010.

[9] Jin et al. Touch screen user interfaces for older adults: button size and spacing. *Universal Access in Human Computer Interaction. Coping with Diversity*, 933–941, 2007.

[10] Kristensson. Five challenges for intelligent text entry methods. *AI Magazine*, 30(4):85, 2009.

[11] Kurniawan. Older people and mobile phones: A multi-method investigation. *International Journal of Human-Computer Studies*, 66(12):889–901, 2008.

[12] MacKenzie and Soukoreff. Text entry for mobile computing: Models and methods, theory and practice. *Human–Computer Interaction*, 17(2):147–198, 2002.

[13] Nicolau and Jorge. Touch typing using thumbs: understanding the effect of mobility and hand posture. *In Proc. of CHI '12*, 2683–2686, 2012.

[14] Salarian et al. Quantification of tremor and bradykinesia in parkinson's disease using a novel ambulatory monitoring system. *Biomedical Engineering, IEEE Transactions on*, 54(2):313–322, 2007.

[15] Selker et al. Psychosocial indicators via hand tremor. *In Proc. of INTERACT'11*, 596–599, 2011.

[16] Strickland and Bertoni. Parkinson's prevalence estimated by a state registry. *Movement disorders*, 19(3):318–323, 2004.

[17] Wacharamanotham et al. Evaluating swabbing: a touchscreen input method for elderly users with tremor. *In Proc. of CHI'11*, 623–626, 2011.

[18] Wobbrock et al. EdgeWrite: a stylus-based text entry method designed for high accuracy and stability of motion. *In Proc. of UIST'03*, 70, 2003.

Crowdsourcing Subjective Fashion Advice Using VizWiz: Challenges and Opportunities

Michele A. Burton[1], Erin Brady[2], Robin Brewer[1], Callie Neylan[1], Jeffrey P. Bigham[2], Amy Hurst[1]

[1]UMBC
Baltimore, MD 21250 USA

{mburton1, brewer3, neylan, amyhurst}
@umbc.edu

[2]University of Rochester
Rochester, NY 14627 USA

{brady, jbigham}
@cs.rochester.edu

ABSTRACT

Fashion is a language. How we dress signals to others who we are and how we want to be perceived. However, this language is primarily visual, making it inaccessible to people with vision impairments. Someone who is low-vision or completely blind cannot see what others are wearing or readily know what constitutes the norms and extremes of fashion, but most everyone they encounter can see (and judge) their fashion choices. We describe our findings of a diary study with people with vision impairments that revealed the many accessibility barriers fashion presents, and how an online survey revealed that clothing decisions are often made collaboratively, regardless of visual ability. Based on these findings, we identified a need for a collaborative and real-time environment for fashion advice. We have tested the feasibility of providing this advice through crowdsourcing using VizWiz, a mobile phone application where participants receive nearly real-time answers to visual questions. Our pilot study results show that this application has the potential to address a great need within the blind community, but remaining challenges include improving photo capture and assembling a set of crowd workers with the requisite expertise. More broadly our research highlights the feasibility of using crowdsourcing for subjective, opinion-based advice.

Categories and Subject Descriptors

K.4.2. Social Issues: Assistive technologies for persons with disabilities

Keywords

Crowdsourcing, Blind Users, Fashion

1. INTRODUCTION

The language of fashion has been studied for decades and has philosophical and historical roots. *The Psychology of Fashion* states "Fashion is nothing more and nothing less than the systematic encryption, transmission, and interpretation of social meaning. A fashion item itself is only a vehicle that transports cultural information to its destination – the consumer" [17]. Other books present a more practical self-help view such as the seminal book *Dress for Success* where readers are told the book's information will "make you look like a million so you can make a million" [11]. Though one may not believe they can become rich simply by dressing a certain way, the book's title is now engrained in American culture and a generally accepted idiom.

Our clothes can communicate details about ourselves to others. A punk rocker communicates rebellion, pink ruffles communicate feminine youth, and hats or scarfs worn a certain way can communicate gang affiliation. But impressions from clothing are made by visual evaluations, thus making it greatly inaccessible to many people with vision impairments. This means basic information is not available such as uniforms distinguishing police officers and doctors, and more subtle nuances may be missed such as not adhering to a restaurant's dress code and being subjected to social embarrassment.

Because most people they encounter will see and evaluate what they have on, people with vision impairments must find ways of learning about fashion nuances even if the information is not something they readily comprehend. For instance, as one writer for the National Federation of the Blind tells parents in her article, "Then your child ought to be learning that stripes and plaids--whatever those are--don't go together..." [15]. People with vision impairments must also find ways of overcoming the obstacles clothing and fashion present. This includes a heavy reliance on the assistance of sighted companions and low-tech solutions such as tagging clothes with safety pins [10]. Though there are means of coping with limited clothing information, technology can play a large role in addressing and alleviating many challenges.

In this paper we describe a 10-day diary study exploring fashion perception among those with vision impairments which identifies many clothing-related accessibility barriers [4], as well as discuss an online survey we conducted to learn how individuals with and without vision impairments get fashion advice. We present related work on accessible fashion and crowdsourcing [7] (the technique we propose for addressing some of the accessibility issues). We then present a pilot study using VizWiz [2], a mobile phone application for people with vision impairments, to test the feasibility of having sighted people answer subjective fashion questions. We conclude with a discussion of our results, and how our findings can be used for other applications of crowdsourcing subjective information.

2. PRELIMINARY INVESTIGATIONS

2.1 Diary Study on Fashion Perceptions

Our research began with a diary study that explored the question "How is fashion perceived when one is blind or low-vision?" [4] Our focus was on understanding how those with vision impairments make and communicate fashion choices, how the fashion choices of others are communicated to them, and how other senses influence aesthetic perception.

2.1.1 Study Methodology

We recruited eight female participants (no males responded to the study announcement) who were all legally blind (visual acuity 20/400 or less). The participants were diverse in age (21 to 73 years, average 37.25), vision impairment (ranging from low vision to total blindness), and in clothing style (in terms of how they dressed and approached clothing decisions).

We first conducted one-on-one interviews with our participants for one hour (primarily conducted in their homes, two were conducted in their workplace). After the interview we asked them to type diary entries for the next 10 days. To help them get started we told them to begin with what they wore that day and how and why they chose it, but then explained we wanted them to write about anything else they felt was relevant to the study. After completing their diary, we did short phone or email follow-ups. (Two participants did not complete the diary and one completed only seven days.)

2.1.2 Results: Fashion Concerns and Challenges

From this study we found that there are numerous areas of assistance needed by those with vision impairments. We organized our findings from the diary study into two categories - *objective* information such as color, size, and washing instructions, and *subjective* information such as whether items coordinate and whether an outfit is age appropriate. We are exploring technologies to address both the objective and subjective areas but the main focus of this paper is the many subjective aspects of clothing that are inaccessible. Because understanding these nuances requires seeing what others are wearing and having a visual understanding of which clothes fit into certain categories, these areas of fashion presented numerous, even stressful, challenges for our participants.

All of the participants mentioned they simply desired to "fit in" but they could not see what others were wearing to know the latest fashion trends. They mentioned that having white canes and guide dogs made them stand out in an undesirable way and they did not want any other undue attention. This desire to fit in is similar to the analysis of body image and stigma among people with physical disabilities such as in the work found in [19].

Participants also mentioned not readily having access to "flaws" in their attire such as fading, wrinkles, or stains. They recounted how people who saw these flaws in their clothing in turn often looked upon them with pity (a scenario four participants dubbed "poor blind girl"). They felt the person was making a judgment of their inability to be an independent person simply because they could not see this aspect of their clothing.

When asked how they overcome clothing obstacles, participants explained that they rely on the assistance of sighted companions (and even strangers), which was limiting in many ways. One participant, for instance, lived in a remote area where only her sighted husband was available to help her shop, which she knew was not ideal because he did not shop like a female would. Because of this she limited her shopping to stores where they sold outfits that are already coordinated or are only black and white. She also limited her wardrobe to the same clothing combinations (outfits) and did not mix and match her clothing. Another participant had recently moved across country and had not yet made enough friends to have a corpus of people to assist her, thus forcing her to rely mostly on the salespeople who didn't know her and could be motivated simply to make a sale. Yet another participant shopped at yard sales and consignment shops for bargains but was then left without a salesperson to ask and only had a few family members with whom she shopped.

When asked if there were technologies that could assist with clothing decisions, the only device our participants mentioned was

a color identifier. The participants who used the device (only two out of the eight) realized it was limited in its function such as not identifying patterns and misrecognizing certain colors, and mostly used it simply to distinguish clothes that did not have tactually discernible features and were easily confused. No other technologies were mentioned yet participants welcomed the idea of using any technology that could help.

The numerous accessibility challenges expressed by our participants led us to further explore how technology could be used to solve these issues. Intrigued by the idea of using crowdsourcing as one solution we conducted a follow-up online survey to understand how people currently make clothing decisions and to specifically ask how they confer with others.

2.2 Online Survey on Clothing Decisions

We conducted an online survey to understand how people make clothing-related decisions and identify where technology could better assist where there are challenges. The questions did not ask about specific technology solutions; rather we used the results to shape and confirm our ideas and identify potential requirements. Because of the benefits of universally accessible design and deploying technology to widely used devices [14,16], the survey was open to anyone, that is, people with and without disabilities.

Twenty-two adults (11 female) completed the survey, with a majority (16 of 22) between ages 25 and 54. Seven men and two women reported they had some form of vision impairment but we did not record details about their visual ability.

Our participants reported that shopping is a collaborative event regardless of vision ability. For instance, when asked about shopping in a retail store, only two participants (both without a visual impairment) said they shop alone. The remaining participants all shop with companions (family and friends) and most ask those companions for opinions and help finding an outfit. Less than half the participants said they would ask these same opinion questions of the salesperson; however, the percentage of participants with vision impairments that would ask the salesperson's opinion (66%) was higher than those without vision impairments (33%), as was indicated by our diary study participants when describing retail shopping experiences.

We asked participants if they confer with others for special occasion outfits such as an interview or date. We assumed people did not confer with others everyday but would more likely do so for a special event. For the 13 participants who stated "yes" we then asked how they felt about those people – did they have a good core set, want more people, and/or want different people? Participants without vision impairments indicated they had a good core set (6 out of 7) with only one person desiring to have different people to ask. But those with vision impairments wanted more people (5 out of 6) and different people (3 out of 6) with whom they could confer about clothing decisions.

We asked participants to rate their interest in having certain clothing information on a scale of 1 (very interested) to 4 (don't need). Figure 1 shows the total of "Very Interested" and "Somewhat Interested" ratings for all participants for the items listed in the question. The most desired information need was how items in one's wardrobe coordinate, with participants with vision impairments unanimously interested. The only item that was not popular among participants with vision impairments was "knowing when and where I wore something" (only 2 participants indicated they were "Somewhat Interested"). Other responses participants wrote in included knowing if there were stains or imperfections on their clothes, if something was appropriate for the occasion, the type of image/impression being projected by an outfit, and advice on how to dress for a certain body type.

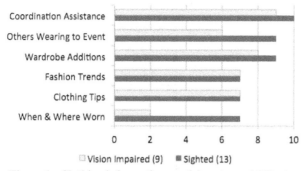

Figure 1 - Clothing information participants would like to have available

From this work we explored the current landscape of accessible fashion for people with vision impairments as well as current collaboration technology for clothing. As we describe in the following related work section, current research and available technologies do not fully address our participants' requirements.

3. RELATED WORK

3.1 Fashion and Assistive Technology

Many new assistive technologies for those with vision impairments are being embedded in clothes such as jackets, shoes, and glasses to assist with object detection [1,3,18]. But these devices are simply using clothes as the shell for the technology, not addressing fashion needs or being designed as fashion targeted for those with vision impairments.

Color identifiers are often used to help identify clothing color -- a fundamental accessibility barrier described by our study participants. Unfortunately, color identifiers (both hardware and software) are reported to have low accuracy rates and are not able to identify patterns [9]. Also, these technologies focus solely on color identification and do not address related clothing nuances such as what other colors will coordinate with the one identified.

There are limited resources to learn fashion nuances, and the current solutions are either impersonal or expensive. Television shows such as *What Not to Wear* help contestants purchase entire new wardrobes based on the advice of stylists (a show two of our diary study participants mentioned watching) [22]. But since the show's medium is television, important visual cues may be missed. There are also many personal stylists that one can hire, including those from a company co-owned by a *What Not to Wear* co-host, but this can be very expensive [23]. There existed a free iPhone application where a person could send a clothing photo and question to a stylist, very similar to our approach using VizWiz [5]. However, our focus is answers from non-experts, a larger and more available population pool. Also, this application is no longer available as the company has been acquired.

As mentioned by our first study's participants and confirmed in our research, there do not appear to be any products that serve as assistive technologies to aid with making clothing decisions and learning about fashion. Though there is promising computer vision-based research to improve automated color and pattern identification and matching as in [21], this technology is not yet commercially available and does not fully address the subjectivity of deciding what it means for items to match. Currently there is a heavy reliance on those who are sighted to assist with these topics,

which can be very problematic since a sighted person may not always be available or be a reliable source. Thus our goal is to develop technology that can help connect people to answer complex fashion questions.

3.2 Gathering the Opinions of Others

When desiring a second opinion, many individuals turn online. Websites such as fashism.com let people give opinions on others' fashion choices, but may be difficult to use for those with vision impairments [24]. For instance, fashism.com requires a picture be uploaded and vision-impaired users generally cannot ensure the photo is clear and focuses on the correct items [8]. On fashism.com they will not receive feedback on their photo; it will simply be posted and analyzed as-is. The responses on fashism.com are limited, as they only support thumbs up/down voting with the option of writing in content (but the majority of responses do not include comments). With so many users and new posts each day (adding up to hundreds of photos to view) there is no guarantee of a response. Lastly, the system is open to the public, which presents the potential issue that people who cannot see their outfits and are not confident in how they will be perceived may be reluctant to share them with thousands of strangers for approval.

There may be an inclination to simply use a social networking site such as Facebook. But depending on the user's settings this also may not be a private venue and if the person is not sure of how they look in an outfit they may be hesitant to post this to a site of acquaintances and colleagues for feedback. Users may also feel they can only ask a certain set of questions or a limited number to avoid the impression that they are helpless because of their disability or the feeling they are bombarding (and annoying) their network. There is also the issue of Web accessibility as many people with vision impairments surveyed about website accessibility listed Facebook in their top ten sites to avoid [20].

There is a need for accessible technology that brings people together in a private, closed setting to address clothing questions that are difficult for a machine to interpret. For instance, detecting stains on clothing would require very sophisticated computer vision techniques, but can be detected easily by a human (though it would be potentially embarrassing to bring up in an open environment). Also, as noted in our online survey, there is a desire to have multiple opinions to answer clothing questions.

Past work has demonstrated that people are willing to use a social network for recommendations and opinions. In an investigation of what questions are asked on social networking sites, Morris, et al found that 29% of their participants' questions asked for recommendations and 22% for opinions [12]. Also, there is work that demonstrates people responding to inquiries when using crowdsourcing [7] do not have to be subject matter experts. In [13], Morris and Picard used remote workers to give participants responses equating to that of a therapeutic treatment for helping relieve stress. This past work on non-experts successfully helping remote people sets a positive precedent for our desired system which aims to send questions to people who are not fashion experts and have them answer subjective, opinion questions. Taking the best of social networking and crowdsourcing and concentrating it on this area seems to have great potential and promise. In the next section we describe how we used the iPhone application VizWiz to test the feasibility of crowdsourcing subjective fashion questions.

4. CROWDSOURCING FASHION ADVICE

4.1 Study Methodology

We conducted a two-week pilot study to test the feasibility of crowdsourcing clothing-related questions, users' trust of the volunteers ("trusted strangers" [6]), and the overall usefulness of the system.

4.1.1 VizWiz Prototype

VizWiz is an iPhone application that provides users with nearly real-time answers to visual questions [2]. Users can take a photo of an object in their environment (such as a thermostat or bottled water); record a question about the object (such as "What is the temperature reading?" or "What brand is this?"); and send the question to a bank of volunteers, Web workers, members of their social network, or to IQ Engines (computer vision program) [25]. Answers are returned almost immediately to the users as a written message that can be displayed with the phone's screen settings for low vision users or read aloud using the built-in screen reader.

If the user selects the "Web workers" source, their question will be answered either by a designated volunteer associated with the VizWiz project (if one is online and available at the time) or by "turkers". "Turkers" refers to people from around the world who have signed up for Amazon's Mechanical Turk ("MTurk") service and are available to complete short tasks on their computer for a small amount of money practically 24 hours a day, seven days a week [26]. Because these workers are always available and a vast majority are sighted, the visual questions asked by VizWiz users can be answered with great accuracy and with an average turnaround time of 90 seconds.

Building upon the success of VizWiz, we hypothesized that this system could be useful in giving users advice on clothing and fashion-related questions. Our goal with this pilot study was to capture data on the feasibility and usefulness of this application in addressing primarily subjective questions about the visual medium of fashion.

For the pilot, users downloaded the VizWiz application currently available in the Apple App Store. Questions were sent to designated volunteer workers for responses. Since we are attempting to address subjective information that would be outside of the realm of computer vision, IQ Engines wouldn't serve our needs. And though we do not entirely discount using a service such as MTurk, we recognized that the responses needed to be appropriate culturally and Web workers live around the world where widely varying fashions exist (for instance, the public fashion of Al Qassim, Saudi Arabia and Miami Beach, Florida are vastly different). Also, we needed to ensure the answers were tactful and constructive and not insulting or insensitive. Lastly, we believe the interactions need to occur in a private and more secure setting since the questions may be sensitive. Future studies should incrementally test for these aspects, however this pilot focused on the feasibility of designated remote workers who are not fashion experts dispensing subjective fashion advice.

4.1.2 Study Participants

Through convenience and snowball sampling (including posts for the study on relevant email lists), we recruited three men and four women ages 27 to 59 (average 44 years). Participants were required to be over 18 years of age, have an Apple device compatible with the VizWiz app (iPhone, iPad, or iTouch), and be legally blind (visual acuity 20/400 or less). Most participants indicated they were "totally blind" (presumed to be complete vision loss) with one participant having a degenerative vision

impairment. Table 1 shows the details of each participant. All of the participants lived in the United States except Participant 2 who lived in the United Kingdom. Given our sensitivity to culture playing a role in fashion we informed him that we were in the United States and he confirmed he was comfortable receiving advice from people in the United States.

#	Gender	Age	Description of Vision Impairment
1	Female	27	Blind
2	Male	34	Blind
3	Male	38	Blind
4	Female	46	Blind
5	Female	48	Retinitis pigmentosa
6	Male	57	Blind
7	Female	59	Blind

Table 1– Description of participants in study to evaluate feasibility of crowdsourcing fashion advice through VizWiz

4.1.3 Trusted Strangers

In prior research on designing a social network to support the independence of young adults with Autism, researchers explored the concept of "trusted strangers" [6]. They were investigating how social media could extend the person's network from family, friends, and close professionals to "people who are willing to commit their time to help the individual…and give the individual trustworthy feedback". These goals are very similar to ours in wanting to extend the network of people asked for fashion advice.

In an effort to study the feasibility of "trusted strangers", we initially only told participants that there were volunteers available to answer their clothing-related questions (not indicating the number of volunteers). At the start of the second week they were emailed descriptions of each volunteer that included their gender, age, and clothing style (see Table 2).

Volunteer Worker Descriptions
Volunteer 1 is a female recent college graduate who has a youthful, casual style that includes the latest fashion trends.
Volunteer 2 is a female young adult with a classic sense of style who loves to dress up even though she's allowed to dress down for what she does.
Volunteer 3 is a female recent government retiree whose style is professional, sophisticated and conservative.

Table 2 – Description of the volunteer workers sent to participants in Week 2

The three volunteer workers included two researchers and a family friend. They were available to answer questions from 8am to 9pm Eastern Standard Time. Participants received at least one answer to every question, but if multiple volunteers were online at once then they would receive responses from everyone online at the time.

4.1.4 Data Gathering: Daily and Weekly feedback

Participants were asked to use the system as they saw fit throughout the two-week period. They were not given a minimum or maximum number of questions to ask, in an attempt to simulate real world usage. Participants were asked to provide daily feedback in the form of either an email or voicemail where they gave a general synopsis of their experience using the application that day, or the reason for not using it. This was used to capture fresh impressions of the interactions and build a richer set of data.

At the end of each week the participants were asked to fill out a survey giving feedback about their use of the system. For each survey we collected demographics including age, gender, and nature of their vision impairment. All questions, including demographics, were free-form text area responses.

For the first week, survey questions focused on the following:

- Timeliness of responses and desired wait time
- Alternate sources of gathering clothing information
- Ways in which the responses were confirmed
- Levels of trust of the workers
- Overall usefulness
- Questions they would not ask in the application

Since participants were given more information about the volunteer workers during the second week, the second survey focused on how their knowledge of the volunteers affected their satisfaction of the system as well as their final feedback.

For the second week the questions included the following:

- Effects of having volunteer descriptions
- Other desired volunteer information
- Preferences for volunteers with same demographics
- Desire for volunteer information if app made public
- Comparison of volunteer responses to peers
- Time for picture preparation
- Overall usefulness
- Suggested improvements and final comments

4.2 Findings

4.2.1 Types of Questions Asked

During the study we received 93 questions total, 77 of which were fashion-related. The excluded questions were primarily about non-clothing items (e.g., identifying a bottle of medicine), tests made to confirm the participant was in the study, or questions submitted either to report an issue or test equipment (e.g., testing the camera because it was not previously working).

Among the valid fashion questions, Figure 2 summarizes their categories. Questions labeled "Visual (Objective)" include questions such as "Can you please describe the shirt?" and "What does this shirt say?" Questions labeled "Fashion (Subjective)" include questions such as "Can I wear these two pieces together?" and "Can this sweater work with business attire, as well as more casual outfits?" Questions labeled "Both" include "Could you please tell me the color of this pair of pants and shirt, and whether they coordinate well for a business casual occasion tomorrow?" One fashion question was excluded from this analysis because the clothing photo came through but no audio.

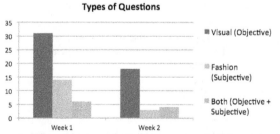

Types of Questions

- Visual (Objective)
- Fashion (Subjective)
- Both (Objective + Subjective)

Figure 2 - Most questions during the study asked for objective information such as identifying color

Overall we noticed a certain strategy and progression among the majority of participants. As a first step, participants wanted to get a feel for taking photos and the necessary lighting as well as what answers they would receive from the volunteer workers. They

asked questions to which they already knew the answer (as they stated in their daily feedback) to test whether the volunteer workers would respond as expected. These validation questions were very basic, such as "What color is this?" (Figure 3A)

By the middle of the first week the questions became more frequent and complex and included more queries about matching, the appropriateness for certain occasions, and even creating entire outfits, such as one participant asking what shoes should be worn with the clothes shown (Figure 3B). Participants commented in their feedback that they began to feel more comfortable with what they were willing to ask and even gained ideas on what to ask based on the responses. For instance, after just the first week Participant 4 wrote in her survey "It grew and stretched my thinking about clothing."

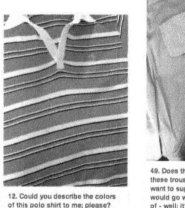

12. Could you describe the colors of this polo shirt to me; please?

49. Does this polo shirt go with these trousers? And; if you also want to suggest what color shoes would go with this particular shade of - well; it's olive.

A.   B.

Figure 3 – Example of basic question asked early in the study (A) and advanced question asked later in the week (B).

One unexpected question we received asked about the appropriateness of a companion's outfit (Figure 4). The fashion choices of those with whom you associate can be almost as much a reflection on you as your own wardrobe. This is especially true for parents and guardians who need to be cautious of what their children are wearing (similar to Figure 4).

30. What is the color of my grandson's shirt? He is turning 10 today and I want to make sure I can take him out in public

Figure 4 - A grandfather asks the volunteers about the appropriateness of his grandson's shirt

Only seven of the photos were taken while the person was wearing the clothes in question. Of those, two specifically asked how they looked in the garments. In these instances the volunteers were able to not only advise the person on the color and style but also about fit and body type. For instance, one user asked how she looked in a pair of pants and was given advice from two volunteer workers that they were not visually flattering because the tapered leg on the pants did not suit her figure.

4.2.2 Building Trust with Helpful Responses

As mentioned, we wanted to gather data on how participants felt with people they did not know (strangers) answering questions the participants could not confirm for themselves. In the second week's survey we asked how participants felt about receiving descriptions of the volunteer workers. Participants 2 and 7 said it was helpful, Participant 1 said it was "interesting but it did not change my use of the system," and the other participants stated it had no effect. (Note: Participant 6 did not complete the final survey.) When asked if they would like to know more about the volunteers, Participant 7 was the only to write a detailed response:

> "Yes, I would like to know if the volunteer preferred 'big city' or 'small town' style of dress. Also, I would be interested to know if the volunteer had exposure or experience with various other cultures. Like color preferences and accent pieces for a complete look." [Participant 7]

Participants 5 and 7 also had preference about the volunteer having the same demographics as theirs. Participant 5 said it would be nice if the person were in the same age range and possibly also be a fashion expert. Participant 7 said they would like someone of the same culture, though not exclusively.

Though it seems the descriptions of the volunteers was helpful and useful, overall it was not what helped the users get more comfortable with using the system. Participant 5 expressed a sentiment in the survey that seemed to be a theme of the other survey and daily feedback:

> "What truly changed how I used the application was the confidence I had using it. I became much more confident with the answers the more I used it." [Participant 5]

Throughout the study the daily feedback was often praise for the responses received from the volunteers with sentiments such as "impressed" and "good as usual". Each volunteer worker made sure they responded with as much detail as possible and even gave advice beyond what was asked. For instance, if someone asked if two garments "matched" they might have also received feedback about other general items that would coordinate with the garments (or coordinate better). One participant asked if a certain tie and pant combination would work well with a white shirt and was given advice that, yes, it would coordinate but look even better if he also wore a black blazer. The continual cycle of helpful feedback seemed to be what made users trust the system, not necessarily knowing who was sending the feedback.

In the first week's survey participants were explicitly asked if they trusted the volunteer workers upon first using the system and then if their trust increased, remained, or decreased if they used the system frequently. While others simply trusted the volunteer workers outright from the start (either from prior VizWiz experience or general trusting of sighted volunteers), Participants 5 and 7 (among the most active when giving feedback about knowing the volunteers) admitted they were hesitant but the responses increased their trust.

> "I was hesitant at first. The more I used the application the more I trusted the workers. Also having sighted confirmation of the results helped." [Participant 5]

Participant 6 did comment in this first survey that they might be more hesitant with a publicly available service, however, confirming our hesitation to open the service to Mechanical Turk.

> "I assumed that anyone entrusted to be a volunteer was trustworthy. If we move to a community of unscreened volunteers, this could be an interesting problem." [Participant 6]

Interestingly, after receiving the first survey one participant emailed one researcher with a question. She explained that the question about trusting the volunteers seemed odd to her because she had always assumed that people without a color blindness condition agreed on clothing and there was no subjectivity. She wanted to know if she should be clarifying in her questions whether she wanted to know "facts" versus "opinions". We reserved answering her question until after the study to prevent influencing how she used the system but later explained that clothing is very subjective and that some colors are difficult to distinguish even without color blindness. We believe this feedback reveals an important perspective in trusting strangers.

Also in the first week's survey participants were asked if they received external confirmation of their answers. We asked this because answers to subjective fashion questions carry more weight when they are externally validated, and we believed this would impact whether or not they trusted the volunteer workers. One participant did not answer this question (mentioning instead a technical issue) but the other six indicated "yes" with one giving the following anecdote:

> "Yes, I did get confirmation of the answers I received. I attended a Professional Workshop [...] and several of the attendees commented on my attire. I also got an affirmative from my sister who I just happened to run into. And without, my even asking, she commented on how nicely I was dressed." [Participant 7] (Portions removed for privacy)

4.3 Challenges

4.3.1 Taking Photos

As with the current instance of the VizWiz application [2], many of the responses and exchanges with users involved assisting them with taking better photos, an obvious caveat of the application. Understandably, users can get frustrated if they have to make multiple adjustments for a question to which they need quick access (or worse if they can never receive an accurate response). For now, however, photos are the most efficient means of remotely sending visual questions to a crowd of respondents so we will continue to monitor outcomes of other blind photography research such as [8] to improve these capabilities.

There were many obvious instances of participants needing to adjust their photos (such as if the photo was all black), and times when the need for modifications was not so easy to detect (Figure 5). The photo on the left (Figure 5A) was given a response of "gray" but the participant stated in their daily feedback they were anticipating "blue" and that let them know they needed to change where they took photos. In the photo on the right (Figure 5B), two volunteer workers gave conflicting responses on color (identifying brown, tan, and *red* vs. brown, tan, and *dark orange*) causing confusion for the participant who actually sent the same question again but received the same responses.

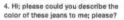
4. Hi; please could you describe the color of these jeans to me; please?

7. What colors are in this material?

A.   B.

Figure 5 – Color questions misidentified by volunteers due to lighting, answering gray when blue was expected (A) and conflicting responses of red and dark orange (B)

4.3.2 Volunteer Coordination

There were a few instances where participants experienced a very long wait for their response because there was no volunteer available to answer their question. Aside from constantly calling or emailing one another, there was no mechanism to ensure that at least one volunteer was online during the 8am to 9pm window. Thus, there were periods where each volunteer went offline, but the other volunteers did not know. This greatly effected how the participants perceived the system. In the first survey we asked participants what they felt would be an acceptable wait time and the responses ranged from 59 seconds to 30 minutes. Four of the seven participants said five minutes and the average of their responses was just over eight minutes.

5. DISCUSSION

Through the feedback we received from our participants we have shown that users are comfortable asking subjective questions to strangers and trusting those responses. There are some questions participants reported not feeling comfortable asking including questions related to undergarments and weight. Nonetheless, many participants said they were comfortable asking anything.

When photos were taken while wearing the clothes in question, the volunteer workers' responses were sometimes different than they would have been if the clothes were only laid out. Realizing it takes more time and effort to take this type of photo and that some users may not be comfortable doing this, we do not think future fashion systems should require users to submit these photos but it may be worth emphasizing to users that their responses may be different when a garment is on their person.

There are certain instances where misidentifying color may always be an issue. Computer screens may render color differently and even in-person in bright daylight people often mistake certain colors such as navy blue for black. It may therefore be helpful to keep a repository of colors that are likely to be confused so that people with vision impairments are aware that even sighted people without any form of color blindness can misidentify colors.

It may also be helpful for actual VizWiz users to contribute to a guide on taking photos. The volunteer workers attempted to guide participants with directions such as "move six inches backward from the garment" or "move towards a window" but this information is given after the fact when users may have moved from their original photo spot and the directions may not translate well for a non-sighted person. It may be more helpful for others with vision impairments to give direction from that point-of-view

and explain that the photo needed depends on the question asked (that is, a few inches away is good for identifying patterns within a garment but a few feet away is needed to understand if multiple pieces match).

Overall it is desirable to expedite the picture taking process. Though users commented they were able to get faster as they used the system more, one participant commented that she needed to set aside 30 minutes to submit questions and she, along with other participants, often commented that they did not have time to use the system on certain days. Though some users may be motivated enough to use the system regardless of the time it takes, others may become too wary of this amount of effort over time and lose interest in the application.

An additional feature to ensure someone is always online is necessary, such as a list similar to instant messaging systems of who is logged in as well as an "away" status if they temporarily step away. There is also a need for a mobile version of this application so a person can easily answer questions while away from home. Typing responses on a mobile Web browser is difficult due to the small screen size; thus, a PC is the best way to type responses but having the volunteer website in front of you all the time is not feasible and could limit volunteer recruitment in the future.

Our participants expressed that they built trust with the volunteers through the accurate and detailed responses they gave, despite not being "experts". Our volunteer workers were ladies who indicated they were comfortable answering fashion questions but did not have a formal expertise. Though one participant mentioned the desire to have an expert answer questions, all of the participants indicated they were satisfied with the responses including the level of detail and honesty when they were told items did not coordinate. All of our volunteers were from the same culture but most participants said that did not matter.

We observed that our participants built trust with the workers through asking questions they already knew the answer to, or asking their sighted friends or family to validate the worker's feedback. We believe that other systems that employ crowdsourcing alternatives to answering subjective questions should employ similar techniques to build similar trust between participants and workers.

Our initial pilot deployment was only two weeks long and had a small participant pool. We believe this may have affected the number of subjective questions we received as users commented they were more comfortable over time, thus a longer study may have yielded more subjective questions. Also some users experienced technical issues with their devices, which impacted their ability to submit questions during the second week. Aside from the reported technical issues, we cannot fully explain the drop-off in questions in the second week. This further motivates the need for a longitudinal study to ensure this application is beneficial long-term.

Overall we feel that there is ample evidence from our participants that it is possible to crowdsource subjective fashion advice and this solution met a need. One of our participants provided the following reply when we asked if they found the application useful at the end of the study:

> "Yes I did, and certainly would use it for this purpose. It is a much needed level of input, and I wil miss the oppotunity to get this valueable feedback." *[Participant 2]* (Comments copied verbatim)

6. CONCLUSION & FUTURE WORK

Fashion is a visual language that is greatly inaccessible to many people with vision impairments. There are currently no technologies that adequately provide assistance for the subjective nuances of fashion such as coordination and appropriateness. We have conducted a feasibility study to evaluate using the VizWiz application to crowdsource visual and subjective fashion questions from people with vision impairments to sighted volunteers willing to answer. Our pilot study successfully demonstrated that this is a viable solution. Our participants trusted the volunteers even though they did not know them and could not confirm the responses themselves. They generally found the system very useful and one they would like to use on a regular basis. We believe this system could be supported by a core set of volunteers by recruiting from volunteer organizations, sororities and fraternities, stay-at-home parents, and retirees.

This study revealed several research challenges including supporting blind photography and customizing the VizWiz interface for these questions. As future work, we will explore an instruction guide for improving the photo capture. Since the workers sometimes provided differing information, we feel that it would be useful to allow users to select their desired number of responses. We also found that the volunteers talked offline about their responses and would like the ability to talk to each other before responding, or see each other's responses.

Additionally, we will investigate how non-experts might be able to answer questions that require fashion expertise. The 24/7 availability of workers from services such as Amazon's Mechanical Turk allows questions to be answered quickly, but there is no way to guarantee the quality of those answers for subjective questions. We hope to build a tool that would allow non-fashion experts to input the visual knowledge available from users' photographs and then aggregate and interpret that information into usable fashion advice, as a supplement to responses from volunteers.

Based on the success of this pilot study, we will continue to study the interaction between workers and users. From what we have gathered, crowdsourcing subjective fashion information can alleviate a great barrier for the blind community and provide valuable knowledge of this visual medium of fashion.

7. ACKNOWLEDGMENTS

We thank our participants for their valuable time, Sharon Johnson who helped answer questions, and Shaun Kane for his advice in analyzing the data. This work was funded by Google and National Science Foundation Award #IIS-1116051.

8. REFERENCES

1. Ambutech. iGlasses. 2011. http://ambutech.com/iglasses.

2. Bigham, J.P., Jayant, C., Ji, H., et al. VizWiz : Nearly Real-time Answers to Visual Questions. *UIST*, (2010), 333-342.

3. Bruning, L. Bats Have Feelings Too. http://www.instructables.com/id/Bats-Have-Feelings-Too/.

4. Burton, M.A. Fashion for the Blind: A Study of Perspectives. *The proceedings of the 13th International ACM SIGACCESS Conference on Computers and Accessibility (ASSETS '11)*, ACM (2011).

5. Glamour. Need Help Figuring Out What to Wear? There's a (Glamour) App for That: Introducing "Ask a Stylist." *Glamour*, 2010. http://www.glamour.com/fashion/blogs/slaves-to-fashion/2010/04/introducing-the-glamour-ask-a.html.

6. Hong, H., Kim, J.G., Abowd, G.D., and Arriaga, R.I. Designing a Social Network to Support the Independence of Young Adults with Autism. *CSCW*, (2012), 627-636.

7. Howe, J. The Rise of Crowdsourcing. *Wired*, 2006. http://www.wired.com/wired/archive/14.06/crowds.html.

8. Jayant, C., Ji, H., White, S., and Bigham, J.P. Supporting Blind Photography. *ASSETS: ACM Conference on Assistive Technologies*, (2011), 203-210.

9. Kendrick, D. (AccessWorld). What Color Is Your Pair of Shoes? A Review of Two Color Identifiers. *AFB AccessWorld*. http://www.afb.org/afbpress/pub.asp?DocID=aw050308.

10. Kornowski, L. How the Blind Are Reinventing the iPhone. *The Atlantic*. http://www.theatlantic.com/technology/archive/2012/05/how-the-blind-are-reinventing-the-iphone/256589/.

11. Molloy, J.T. *Dress for Success*. Warner Books, New York, New York, USA, 1975.

12. Morris, M.R., Teevan, J., and Panovich, K. What Do People Ask Their Social Networks, and Why? A Survey Study of Status Message Q & A Behavior. *CHI 2010*, (2010).

13. Morris, R. and Picard, R. Crowdsourcing Collective Emotional Intelligence. *Collective Intelligence 2012*, (2012).

14. Newell, A.F. Inclusive Design or Assistive Technology. In J. Clarkson, R. Coleman, S. Keates and C. Lebbon, eds., *Inclusive Design – Design for the whole population*. Springer-Verlag, 2003, 172-181.

15. Pierce, B. What is a Spitball? *National Federation of the Blind*. http://nfb.org/images/nfb/publications/books/kernel1/kern0513.htm.

16. Shinohara, K. and Wobbrock, J.O. In the Shadow of Misperception : Assistive Technology Use and Social Interactions. *Design*, (2011), 705-714.

17. Solomon, M.R. *The Psychology of Fashion*. Lexington Books, Lexington, MA, 1985.

18. Strange, A. Haptic feedback shoes let the blind see with every step. *DVICE*. http://dvice.com/archives/2011/12/haptic-feedback.php.

19. Taleporos, G. and McCabe, M.P. Body image and physical disability--personal perspectives. *Social science & medicine (1982) 54*, 6 (2002), 971-80.

20. WebAIM. Survey of Preferences of Screen Readers Users. http://webaim.org/projects/screenreadersurvey/#websites.

21. Yuan, S., Tian, Y., and Arditi, A. Clothing Matching for Visually Impaired Persons. *Technology and disability 23*, 2 (2011), 75-85.

22. What Not to Wear: TLC. http://tlc.howstuffworks.com/tv/what-not-to-wear.

23. Style For Hire. http://www.styleforhire.com/.

24. Fashism - Where the best dressed people rule! http://fashism.com/.

25. IQ Engines. http://www.iqengines.com.

26. Amazon Mechanical Turk. https://www.mturk.com/.

Online Quality Control for Real-Time Crowd Captioning

Walter S. Lasecki and Jeffrey P. Bigham
ROC HCI, Department of Computer Science
University of Rochester
Rochester, NY 14618 USA
{wlasecki, jbigham}@cs.rochester.edu

ABSTRACT

Approaches for real-time captioning of speech are either expensive (professional stenographers) or error-prone (automatic speech recognition). As an alternative approach, we have been exploring whether groups of non-experts can collectively caption speech in real-time. In this approach, each worker types as much as they can and the partial captions are merged together in real-time automatically. This approach works best when partial captions are correct and received within a few seconds of when they were spoken, but these assumptions break down when engaging workers on-demand from existing sources of crowd work like Amazon's Mechanical Turk. In this paper, we present methods for quickly identifying workers who are producing good partial captions and estimating the quality of their input. We evaluate these methods in experiments run on Mechanical Turk in which a total of 42 workers captioned 20 minutes of audio. The methods introduced in this paper were able to raise overall accuracy from 57.8% to 81.22% while keeping coverage of the ground truth signal nearly unchanged.

Categories and Subject Descriptors

H.5.2 [**Information Interfaces and Presentation**]: User Interfaces; K.4.2 [**Social Issues**]: Assistive technologies for persons with disabilities

General Terms

Human Factors, Experimentation

Keywords

captioning, human computation, deaf, hard of hearing

1. INTRODUCTION

Real-time captioning converts aural speech to visual text to provide access to speech content for deaf and hard of hearing (DHH) people in classrooms, meetings, casual conversation, and other live events. These systems need to operate

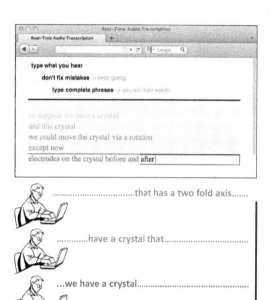

Figure 1: The idea behind Legion:Scribe is that multiple non-expert workers type as much as they can of speech that they hear in real-time, and the system merges it together into a final output stream. This paper considers how to use agreement between the input of different workers to filter this input before attempting to merge it together.

with low latency (generally under 5 seconds) so that DHH users can appropriately place the captions in context [19]. Current options are severely limited because they either require highly-skilled professional captionists whose services are expensive and not available on demand, or use automatic speech recognition (ASR) which produces unacceptable error rates in many real situations [19]. To address this problem, we previously introduced Legion:Scribe [13], a system that allows groups of non-experts to collaboratively caption audio in real time.

The main idea of Legion:Scribe is that while each non-expert worker will not be able to keep up with natural speaking rates (like a professional captionist could), they can type part of what they hear. Legion:Scribe uses new natural language processing techniques inspired by Multiple Sequence

Original	we	have	a	crystal	that	has	a	two	fold	axis
ASR		we	have	a	crystalline	as	a	twenty four	lexus	
Worker 1		you	have	a	crystal	with	a	two	fold	axis
Worker 2	tring tring tring			tring tring tring			tring tring tring			
Worker 3	we	have	a	crystal	tahat	has	a	two	fold	axis
Worker 4	we	have		crystal						
Worker 5	we	have	a	crystal	that	has	a	two	fold	axis
Optimal	we	have	a	crystal		that	has	a	two fold	axis

9 sec. 10 11 12 13 14 15 16 17 18 19 20 21 22 23 24 25 26

Figure 2: Example transcriptions provided by workers from Amazon's Mechanical Turk, illustrating some of the errors that we observe. Worker 2 misunderstood the task directives and typed a description of aural alerts given by the interface. Workers 1 and 3 provide mostly good input that contains some errors. The rest of the work input is accurate.

Alignment (MSA) to then stitch the partial captions back together into a single stream. Its worker interface encourages different workers to cover different portions of the input speech by systematically adjusting their saliency. Because non-expert workers form the base of Legion:Scribe, it has the potential to be cheaper and more readily available than a professional captionist, while maintaining the advantages of human captionists.

The current approach is not sufficiently robust to errant input from the crowd, whether it be accidental, malicious, or simply a typo. In prior experiments, locally-recruited workers of known quality were shown to be able to enter partial captions with high enough accuracy that Legion:Scribe could merge them back together without errors substantially impacting the final stream. However, to fully leverage the elastic, on-demand nature of the crowd, we would like to be able to recruit workers and volunteers without the need to vet them prior to their participation. This paper considers how to deal with the errors that will inevitably arise when using unvetted workers.

In this paper, we present techniques to dynamically rate workers and the input they produce in an online fashion. The key insight is that workers whose input matches that of other workers is more likely to be correct. By estimating quality in an online (real-time) way, our methods may be able to run seamlessly within Legion:Scribe to provide real-time captions more reliably.

The contributions of this paper are the following:

- We introduce the problem of online quality estimation in real-time crowd captioning.

- We introduce methods for both worker quality estimation and word quality estimation that use overlap between workers.

- We demonstrate the efficacy of these methods in an experiment with 42 Amazon Mechanical Turk workers.

1.1 Quality Metrics

The most common method for determining the quality of a caption is the word error rate (WER), which performs a best-fit alignment between the test captions and the ground truth captions. The WER is then calculated as the sum of the number of substitutions (S), deletions (D), and insertions (I) divided by the total number of words in the ground truth caption (N), or $\frac{S+D+I}{N}$. However, determining the quality of captioning is difficult [20]. A key advantage of human captionists over ASR is that humans tend to make more reasonable errors. Humans infer meaning from context, influencing their prior probability toward those words

that make sense in context. We anticipate this will make Legion:Scribe more usable than automated systems even when traditional metrics are similar. Figure 2 shows an example of the errors often made by ASR - in that case substituting, "twenty four lexus" for, "two-fold axis". Such problems with relying solely on WER have been noted before [20].

We define two additional metrics that can be automatically calculated to help characterize the performance of real-time captioning. The first is *coverage*, which represents how many of the words in the true speech signal appear in the union of the partial captions that are received. While similar to recall in information retrieval, we use coverage in this work because we alter the definition of recall slightly in calculating it by requiring that a word in the test signal appear no later than 10 seconds after the word in the ground truth signal to count. We define *precision* similarly, as the fraction of words in the test caption stream that appear in the ground truth within a 10 second time window. Compared to WER, coverage and precision are looser measures of alignment, but we believe they are particularly useful in understanding the potential of our approaches.

In terms of latency, in order for DHH individuals to participate in a conversation or in a lecture, it is important that captions are provided quickly (within about 5 seconds [19]). Calculating latency is not straightforward because captions being tested are not the same as the ground truth. In this paper, we measure latency by first aligning the test captions to the ground truth, and then averaging the latency of all matched words. We also investigate the causes of latency due to the worker (as opposed to network connection or processing delay).

2. RELATED WORK

Crowd captioning builds from work in (i) real-time captioning, and (ii) real-time human computation.

2.1 Real-Time Captioning Systems

Automated speech recognition (ASR) attempts to provide text-to-speech services without human intervention. Currently, ASR is capable of working well in ideal situations with high-quality audio signal and equipment, but degrades quickly in many real settings since it is speaker-dependent, has difficulty recognizing domain-specific jargon, and adapts poorly to vocal changes, such as when the speaker has is sick [10, 9]. ASR systems require substantial computing power and special audio equipment to work well, which lowers availability. To account for these causes of error *respeaking* was created. In this approach, a person located in a

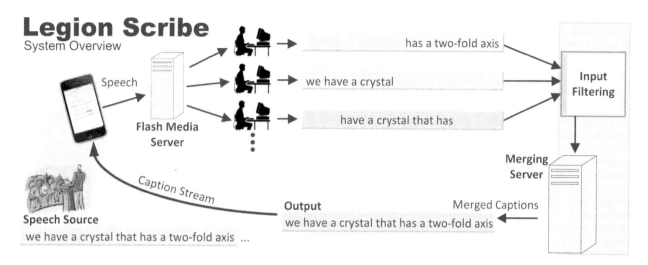

Figure 3: Legion:Scribe allows users to caption audio on their mobile device. The audio is sent to multiple non-expert captionists in realtime who use our web-based interface to caption as much of the audio as they can. These partial captions are sent to the merging server to be merged into a final output caption stream, which is then forwarded back to the user's mobile device. This paper considers the "Input Filtering" stage above, which uses agreement between workers to estimate the quality of both workers and their inputs.

controlled environment is connected to a live audio feed and repeats what they hear to an ASR that has been extensively trained for their voice [11]. Respeaking works well for offline transcription, but simultaneously speaking and listening requires professional training. Crowd captioning aims to allow people without special training to help generate transcripts.

Communications Access Real-Time Translation (CART) is the most reliable captioning service, but is also the most expensive. Professional stenographers type in shorthand on a "steno" keyboard that maps multiple key presses to phonemes that are then automatically expanded to verbatim text. Stenography typically requires 2-3 years of training to achieve the 225 words per minute (WPM) needed to consistently caption speech at natural speaking rates.

Non-verbatim systems attempt to reduce the cost of professional captioning systems such as CART by using macro expansion of customizable abbreviations. For example, C-Print captionists need less training, and generally charge around $60 an hour [19]. However, they normally cannot type as fast as the average speaker's pace of 150 WPM, and thus cannot produce a verbatim transcript. Crowd captioning employs captionists with no training and compensates for slower typing speeds and lower accuracy by combining the efforts of multiple individuals.

2.2 Real-Time Human Computation

People with disabilities have long solved accessibility problems with the support of people in their community [6]. Increasing connectivity has made remote services possible that once required human supporters to be co-located. Real-time captioning by non-experts leverages human computation [17], which has been shown to be useful in many areas, including writing and editing [4], image description and interpretation [5, 18], and protein folding [8]. Existing abstractions obtain quality work by introducing redundancy and layering into tasks so that multiple workers contribute and verify results at each stage [15, 12]. For in-

stance, the ESP Game uses answer agreement [18] and Soylent uses the multiple-step find-fix-verify pattern [4]. Because these approaches take time, they are well suited for real-time support. Crowd captioning enables real-time transcriptions from multiple non-experts to be used to find crowd agreement as a means of ensuring quality.

Human computation has been applied to offline transcription with great success [2]. Scribe4Me allowed deaf and hard of hearing people to receive a transcript of a short sound sequence in a few minutes, but was not able to produce verbatim captions over long periods [16].

Real-time human computation has recently started to be explored by systems such as VizWiz [5], which was one of the first to target nearly real-time responses from the crowd. It introduced a queuing model to help ensure that workers were available quickly on-demand. For Crowd captioning to be available on-demand requires multiple users to be available at the same time so that multiple workers can collectively contribute. Prior systems have shown that multiple workers can be recruited for collaboration by having workers wait until enough workers have arrived [18, 7]. Adrenaline combines the concepts of queuing and waiting to recruit crowds (groups) in less than 2 seconds from existing sources of crowd workers [3]. Real-time captioning by non-experts similarly uses the input of multiple workers, but differs because it engages workers for longer continuous tasks.

Legion enables real-time control of an existing user interface by allowing the crowd to collectively act as a single operator [14]. Each crowd workers submits input independently of other workers, then the system uses an *input mediator* to combine the input into a single control stream. Our input combination approach can be viewed as an instance of an input mediator. A primary difference is that while Legion was shown effective using a mediator in which the crowd's input was used to elect a representative leader to be given direct control for small periods of time, we use a synthesis of the crowd's input to create the final stream.

3. LEGION SCRIBE

Legion:Scribe is a system that provides users with on-demand access to real-time captions from groups of non-experts from their laptop or mobile devices (Figure 3). When the Legion:Scribe app is started, it immediately begins recruiting workers from a set of volunteer workers using quik-Turkit [5]. Previous experiments have shown that Mechanical Turk workers can provide useful input in terms of coverage, but the signal was too noisy to use reliably, do to the high number of low-quality workers [13]. When users are ready to begin captioning they press the start button, which then begins forwarding audio to Flash Media Server (FMS) and signals the Legion:Scribe server to begin captioning. We use FFMPEG to stream audio from the user to FMS using the RTMP protocol for real-time audio streaming.

Once connected, workers are presented with a text input interface designed to encourage real-time answers and designed to encourage global coverage (shown in Figure 4). Legion:Scribe rewards workers with points that can optionally correspond to money depending on the crowd. In our experiments, we paid workers $0.005 for every word the system thought was correct. This interface is discussed further in the next section.

As workers type, their input is forwarded to an input combiner running on the Legion:Scribe server. The input combiner is discussed in the next section and is modular to accommodate different implementations without needing to modify the rest of the Legion:Scribe system. Once the inputs have been merged, we present users with the current transcrtip on a dynamically updating web page.

Merging partial captions allows for either an emphasis on coverage or accuracy. However, these two properties are at odds: using more of the worker input will increase coverage, but maintain more of the individual worker error, while requiring more agreement on individual words will increase accuracy, but reduce the coverage since not all workers will agree on all words. Legion:Scribe allows users to either let the system choose a default balance between the two, or select their own balance using a slider bar in the that allows them to select from values that range from 'Most Accurate' to 'Most Complete'.

When users are done captioning, they can stop or pause the application to terminate the audio stream. This will let workers complete their current transcription task and ask them to continue captioning other audio for a time in case the users needs to resume captioning quickly.

Legion:Scribe is also able to forward the live output to a second group of workers who are asked to use an editing interface to correct the final stream. While this is optional, it can help correct many of the easily identifiable small errors made by workers and the input combiner. Additionally, users themselves have the option of making corrections to the final stream for errors such as out-of-order words, or a term known to them that remote workers may have missed. The user interface allows users to edit, add or delete words within the transcription, in realtime. As the transcription is generated, the meta information is visually presented to assist the user with the edits. Legion:Scribe returns information such as the confidence of each spelling, possible alternative words and arrangements.

The interface can be shared by other people on different computers, affording for a collaborative environment where interested groups are able to curate a transcript, fixing any

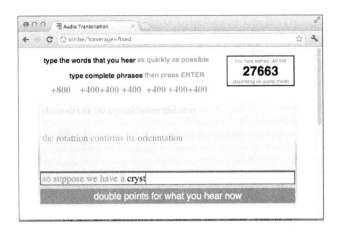

Figure 4: The captioning interface shown to workers by Legion:Scribe. It encourages workers to cover specific portions of the audio using both audio and visual cues during 'bonus rounds', (periods in which workers are incentivized to participation).

collisions within the graph. Many of the common edits are abstracted by the interface to allow for interactions such as a two click replacement for typos or word replacement by alternatives, visual contrast to draw attention to low confidence outputs and transitions to confirm a change made by other collaborators.

4. ONLINE QUALITY ESTIMATION

To estimate the quality of workers and the captions they produce in real-time, we primarily consider agreement between the captions that different workers produce. The idea is that workers whose captions overlap the most with other workers are likely to be the best, whereas workers who rarely overlap with other workers are likely to be the worst. This matches both our intuition that it should be difficult to guess the input that another worker will provide, and follows from prior work in achieving quality work from the crowd, e.g. the ESP Game [18].

In our case, input that is provided by more than one worker is likely to be correct. In practice, estimating words that are contributed by more than one worker is not as simple as it first appears due to alignment. How do we know that a worker's mention of word w is really a match of another worker's mention of w? Legion:Scribe aligns the partial phrases contributed by each worker to form a final output stream, but is often strict resulting in low coverage. For the filtering step described in this paper, we use a relaxed notion of agreement that says two workers agree on a word if each says it within t seconds of one another, where t is a parameter that can be tuned that we set to be 10 seconds.

4.1 Per Worker Quality

Our first approach is to use word-level agreement to dynamically determine if a particular worker is producing high-quality input. The idea is to again look at word-level agreement over the sliding time window, but to use agreement to assign a quality score to the worker, instead of using it to select whether a word is passed on. The per worker quality score is simply the fraction of words produced by a worker within the time window that have also be contributed by another worker during the time window. Using agreement to

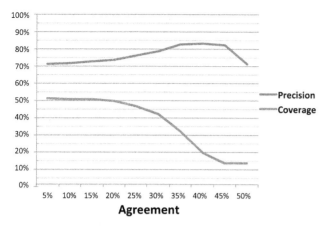

Figure 5: Graph showing an example in which workers captioning a clip actually did worse overall as our per-worker agreement threshold was increased beyond the optimal point.

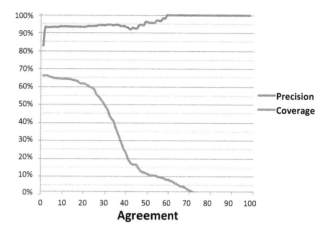

Figure 6: The tradeoff in terms of coverage and precision that we experience when requiring increasing required worker agreement. Even minimal overlap with other workers (0.1) improves precision. Requiring too much agreement negatively affects coverage, which eventually goes to zero.

judge the quality of workers and then forwarding the input of "good" workers on immediately has been used before in real-time crowdsourcing systems [14], but not for real-time captioning or other natural language tasks.

One of the main drawbacks of this system is that there is minimal fine-grained control over what input is accepted. Instead, we rely on trusted workers to continue providing valid input. This reliance results in two problems: first, if a previously reliable worker begins to input poor quality captions, we will still accept the input immediately, even if it's clear they are now an outlier. Second, increasing the threshold for reliability does not result in a completely monotonic change in accuracy because invalid input from users who have not yet been rated, or good workers who make mistakes are included into a smaller set of correct answers, and their contributors then down-weighted, preventing possible good input from being added by the worker.

Figure 5 shows an example of such a situation, in which fewer number of bad inputs are forwarded to the system, but those included represent an increasing proportion of the inputs as even good workers are barred from contributing due to such low tolerances for bad workers by the system. One way to avoid this is to start workers below the minimal thresholding value, requiring them to "prove" themselves before accepting their input. However, this potentially reduces coverage too much at the beginning of a session or at any point of particularly high turnover in the crowd.

4.2 Word-by-Word Quality

Our second approach seeks to filter out words that are unlikely to appear in the true signal because too few workers agree on the word. This filtering step receives each word in real-time and looks back to see if it appears at least k times in the past t seconds. The effect is that at least k workers need to contribute the word before it will be passed through this filtering stage. Many crowd algorithms are based on redundancy like this; however, in a real-time system like Legion:Scribe, the benefit of the added confidence achieved through redundancy comes at the cost of both latency and coverage. Since words will not be passed through to the user until they are input by at least k workers, latency is increase by the time provided for this agreement to occur. Further-

more, correct words that are contributed may not be passed through at all if they are covered by too few workers within the timespan t, even if they are eventually said by enough other workers. This creates a tradeoff in the selection of t that balances response time, with giving workers sufficient chance to implicitly agree on content.

5. EXPERIMENTS

In order to test our quality estimation methods, we conducted experiments with workers recruited through the Amazon Mechanical Turk microtask marketplace [1]. For Legion:Scribe to scale, we believe it will be beneficial to be able to recruit workers online from elastic marketplaces like this one. Mechanical Turk provides a valuable testbed for this paper because workers vary substantially in their reliability and in the quality of work that they provide. A number of other research projects have used it as a way to quickly and easily recruit crowd workers to test various crowd algorithms intended to improve worker reliability [12, 4, 5].

5.1 Data Collection

We collected a data set of speech selected from freely available lectures on MIT OpenCourseWare[1]. These lectures were chosen because a primary goal of Legion:Scribe is to provide captions for classroom activities, and because the recording of the lectures roughly matches our target as well – the clips generally consist of continuous speech captured by a microphone in the room. There are often multiple speakers, e.g. students asking questions. We chose four 5-minute segments that contained speech from courses in electrical engineering and chemistry, and had them professionally transcribed at a cost of $1.75 per minute. Despite the high cost, we found a number of errors and omissions, which we manually fixed to ensure no errors were observed. This data set is described in more detail in [13].

To collect data on Mechanical Turk, we modified the base captioning interface (Figure 4) in two ways. First, we introduced a 45 second video that turkers were required to

[1]http://ocw.mit.edu/courses/

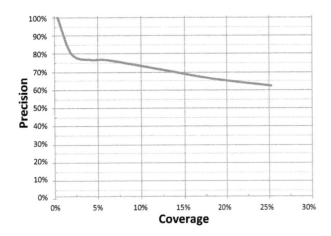

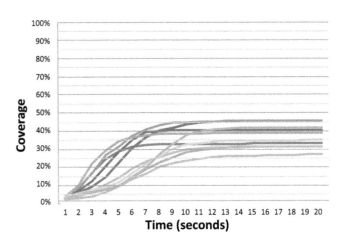

Figure 7: The tradeoff between coverage and precision encountered when increasing the required redundancy. Although dependent on the number of workers, results showed that requiring redundancy increased precision at the cost of coverage.

Figure 8: Graph showing the varying coverage rates of workers as acceptable latency is increased. The plots of each worker's coverage level off prior to 10 seconds, with very little additional coverage gained after that point. Thus, we choose 10 seconds as our window time for comparing answers.

play (and presumably watch) that described the captioning process before they were allowed to caption. Workers were paid $0.02 for watching this video, but could not collect any payment until they had captioned at least $0.05 of work. Second, we modified the interface so that in addition to showing points achieved, it also showed an amount of money that these points would be worth when redeemed. Our exchange rate for points was approximately 500 points per cent USD. This works out to an achievable pay rate of approximately $20.00 per hour depending on the skill of the worker and the speech content of what they are captioning, which is a very good rate for the Mechanical Turk marketplace. We expect that workers will initially receive less, then over time will be able to achieve this rate.

Workers were recruited using the quikTurkit real-time recruitment tool [5]. Throughout the experiment, the number of workers actively engaged varied, but never dropped below four. A total of 42 workers contributed to the task over a 20-minute time period, which cost a total of $9.55 USD (a rate of just under $30.00 per hour). We maintained a fairly constant worker pool with 14, 16, 19, 17 workers potentially contributing to each of the four clips, respectively.

Workers seemed to enjoy the task. Four of the workers wrote to us after the task remarking positively about the work[2]. For instance, one worker wrote "I was curious if you had any plans to schedule these HITs in the future. I find them fascinating and fun and would like to look out for them." We have not yet tried to optimize cost, but the positive reaction to the task suggests that either a paid or volunteer model may be appropriate for attracting workers for Legion:Scribe.

We manually looked over the results from each worker to understand the types of errors made. Most workers gave what appeared to be reasonable captions, although we noticeably more spelling errors than in the tests with local workers presented in [13]. Approximately a quarter of the workers gave clearly bad input, most often because they did

not understand the instructions or because they were unable to hear the sound for some reason. One of the audio clues given to workers by the interface is a beeping sound before the "bonus period" starts. Two workers typed these beeps, one as "beep" and the other as "tring." Another worker typed 65 words of the form, "I cannot hear the sound I don't know what I'm supposed to do." Although these examples are relatively easy for people to spot manually, Legion:Scribe previously had no way to filter them out automatically and would have likely included them in the final caption stream.

5.2 Quality Estimation Results

We analyzed both per worker and word-by-word quality estimation methods on the data collected to explore how they affect the three evaluation metrics that we introduced previously (Section 1.1). We focused on precision and coverage because WER is highly dependent on the method used to merge inputs together. Estimating worker quality focuses on improving the input to the merge step, thus our goal is to improve precision without substantially lowering coverage.

5.2.1 Per Worker Quality Estimation

We also considered worker-level quality estimation. Figure 6 shows the effect of increasing the level of agreement required between workers to include a given word. Requiring even modest agreement (of just 10%) can result in substantially higher precision (82.9% to 93.2%) with no change in overall coverage. This is due to the fact that input with no agreement whatsoever is almost always errant (typically from workers who misunderstood the task and were, for example, captioning non-speech sounds instead).

5.2.2 Word-by-Word Quality Estimation

Figure 7 shows the tradeoff seen when applying our word-by-word quality estimation. As expected, requiring increased redundancy amongst worker input before accepting a word improved precision, but also decreased coverage. With no redundancy requirement, precision was 57.9%, but rose to 81.2% when requiring redundancy of just 2 workers. Requir-

---

[2]It is not particularly common to receive feedback from workers, and even less common to receive positive feedback

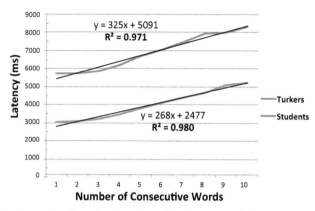

Figure 9: Graph showing the latency plots for student volunteers and Mechanical Turk workers.

ing redundancy at levels of more than a small proportion of workers caused coverage to drop severely. Although this is heavily dependent on the number of actively participating workers, it seems that substantial benefit can be achieved by only requiring low levels of redundancy. This eliminates only very rare input, which is often indicative of a worker-specific erroneous input. Otherwise, workers must consistently caption highly overlapping segments, hurting the overall transcript generated and requiring greater numbers of workers (which increases costs).

5.2.3 Latency

Although we did not explicitly consider latency in our measures of error or in our metrics for estimating quality, it was clearly a factor because the latency with which words are receives directly impacts whether they will be in the time window or not used for agreement. How latency changes as additional workers are added plays a significant role in the ability to use crowds of captionists. Unsurprisingly, the trend is that with more workers, average latency goes down, from a single worker average of 4.4 seconds, to a group average of 2.6 seconds. We expect this because each new worker may type a particular word faster than the rest either by chance or because that word appeared nearer to the beginning of the partial caption they contributed. Figure 8 shows the coverage over time of individual workers. Importantly, the latency graph helps to justify the 10 second window use for the rest of the tests because it shows that by 10 seconds most words that will be received have been received.

We also investigated the types and causes of latency seen in workers. There are 2 main types: initial delay and progressive delay. We compared a group of 20 student workers, to a group of 21 turkers and found that the initial delay was significantly different between the two groups - 2477ms on average for student workers, and 5091ms for turkers. Interestingly, this shift was the only major difference between the groups. We measure the delay based on the position in the current chain of words being typed. The additional latency incurred by each word was lower for students, but closely mirrored turkers, both showing a linear trend with $R^2 = 0.98$ and $R^2 = 0.97$ respectively. There was an average of a 268ms additional latency per word for students, and 397ms for turkers (as shown in Figure 9). Based on this, we want to encourage workers to type shorter segments when possible in order to decrease latency.

6. DISCUSSION

This paper has demonstrated that the quality of captions and their providers can be determined in an online fashion as they are received. It is clear that even crowd workers drawn from Amazon's Mechanical Turk can caption real-time audio, which helps to validate the approach used by Legion:Scribe. Not only were workers able to collectively cover the input speech, but they also seemed to enjoy the task based on the feedback we received. The challenge going forward is to remove the noise from the captions they provide and merge it into a usable output stream.

The methods introduced for quality estimation successfully allowed precision and coverage to be tuned, although both had tradeoffs. The word-by-word method improved accuracy, but at the cost of both latency and coverage. The per-worker quality metric had a more interesting response. At lower levels of agreement (10%-30%), it caused precision to rise but at the cost of coverage, which is what we expected. However, at higher levels of agreement, precision actually went down due to instability caused by very few workers being selected at any given time. This effect would likely be mitigated by larger numbers of workers, but for crowd captioning to be effective the number of workers needed should be small. Each method currently requires parameters to be tuned, although it seems likely that both receive the most benefit when using relatively low agreement (2 word agreement for per-word, and 10% agreement for per-worker), as coverage decreases at a higher rate than the accuracy increases after low levels of agreement.

We saw no instances in our data set of workers who changed dramatically in quality over the course of the study. Workers started with low or high quality and seemed to stay consistent. If this trend holds over longer trials, then it would be possible to block bad workers entirely, or to give good workers more leeway when they disagree with the others.

Finally, we observed few examples of crowd workers be outright malicious. Instead, workers identified as being low quality via this method generally experienced an error with the caption input page (e.g., no sound played), or misunderstood the task they were to do (e.g., described background noise in the sound clip instead of typing words). Therefore, estimating the quality of workers may allow us to identify usability problems with future systems that may not be detected as quickly or reliably using other means.

7. FUTURE WORK

Real-time crowdsourcing has the potential to dramatically lower the cost of real-time captioning and dramatically increase its availability. By using crowd workers available from many existing sources (such as Amazon's Mechanical Turk), instead of relying solely on volunteers, crowd captioning can be made scalable enough for real-world deployment.

An important step for engaging the crowd in real-time captioning is determining what input is good and what is not. Classifying input in this way enables systems to pay workers appropriately for their input, encouraging workers to provide high-quality input. This paper has introduced methods for doing so at the level of workers and individual words, and suggests a number of opportunities for future work. Future work may explore building reputation over time in order to avoid bootstrapping models of workers dynamically during each session, perhaps allowing workers who have demonstrated they consistently contribute high-quality inputs to override the crowd decision.

The final goal of this system is to provide high-quality real-time captions for deaf and hard of hearing people using less reliable sources of labor such as general crowds. Legion:Scribe is a complex system with many components, and research thus far has primarily gone to demonstrating the feasibility of the approach. In this paper in particular, we have worked with the assumption that removing errant input early will make later merging stages easier, but it may be that later approaches may benefit from considering all of the input at once even if some of it is incorrect. We also assume that filtering this bad input will improve the usability of the captions for deaf and hard of hearing people; investigating the tradeoff between removing errant words and readability is a promising area for future work.

Our current approach only uses agreement with other human workers to estimate quality, meaning we require more workers than is necessary to cover the input speech because some are providing redundant inputs. Future work therefore may look at other signals of quality - for instance, spelling, grammar, or agreement with ASR - that may be more robust. More robust models may be possible by using these signals in conjunction with crowd agreement.

8. CONCLUSIONS

In this paper we have explored real-time quality control in real-time captioning in order to improve the quality of transcripts generated from crowd workers of initially unknown quality. We do this by introducing methods that can estimate the quality of workers and each word they contribute. We demonstrated the utility of these methods, through our experiments using workers from Mechanical Turk, by showing they can increase the resulting accuracy of captions while keeping the coverage of the speech signal nearly constant.

9. ACKNOWLEDGEMENTS

This work has been supported by Google and NSF Awards IIS-1149709 and IIS-1116051.

10. REFERENCES

[1] Amazon's mechanical turk. http://www.mturk.com.

[2] Y. C. Beatrice Liem, H. Zhang. An iterative dual pathway structure for speech-to-text transcription. In *Proceedings of the 3rd Workshop on Human Computation (HCOMP '11)*, HCOMP '11, 2011.

[3] M. S. Bernstein, J. R. Brandt, R. C. Miller, and D. R. Karger. Crowds in two seconds: Enabling realtime crowd-powered interfaces. In *Proceedings of the 24th annual ACM symposium on User interface software and technology*, UIST '11, p 33–42, 2011. ACM.

[4] M. S. Bernstein, G. Little, R. C. Miller, B. Hartmann, M. S. Ackerman, D. R. Karger, D. Crowell, and K. Panovich. Soylent: a word processor with a crowd inside. In *Proceedings of the 23nd annual ACM symposium on User interface software and technology*, UIST '10, p 313–322, 2010. ACM.

[5] J. P. Bigham, C. Jayant, H. Ji, G. Little, A. Miller, R. C. Miller, R. Miller, A. Tatarowicz, B. White, S. White, and T. Yeh. Vizwiz: nearly real-time answers to visual questions. In *Proceedings of the 23nd annual ACM symposium on User interface software and technology*, UIST '10, p 333–342, 2010. ACM.

[6] J. P. Bigham, R. E. Ladner, and Y. Borodin. The design of human-powered access technology. In *Proceedings of the 2011 SIGACCESS Conference on Computers and Accessibility (ASSETS 2011)*, ASSETS 2011, p 3–10, 2011. ACM.

[7] L. Chilton. Seaweed: A web application for designing economic games. Master's thesis, MIT, 2009.

[8] S. Cooper, F. Khatib, A. Treuille, J. Barbero, J. Lee, M. Beenen, A. Leaver-Fay, D. Baker, Z. Popovic, and F. Players. Predicting protein structures with a multiplayer online game. *Nature*, 466(7307):756–760, 2010.

[9] X. Cui, L. Gu, B. Xiang, W. Zhang, and Y. Gao. Developing high performance asr in the ibm multilingual speech-to-speech translation system. In *Acoustics, Speech and Signal Processing, 2008. ICASSP 2008. IEEE International Conference on*, p 5121–5124, 2008.

[10] L. B. Elliot, M. S. Stinson, D. Easton, and J. Bourgeois. College Students Learning With C-Print's Education Software and Automatic Speech Recognition. In *American Educational Research Association Annual Meeting*, New York, NY, 2008.

[11] T. Imai, A. Matsui, S. Homma, T. Kobayakawa, K. Onoe, S. Sato, and A. Ando. Speech recognition with a re-speak method for subtitling live broadcasts. In *ICSLP-2002*, p 1757–1760, 2002.

[12] A. Kittur, B. Smus, and R. Kraut. Crowdforge: Crowdsourcing complex work. Technical Report CMUHCII-11-100, Carnegie Mellon University, 2011.

[13] W. S. Lasecki, C. D. Miller, A. Sadilek, A. AbuMoussa, and J. P. Bigham. Real-time captioning by groups of non-experts. In *Proceedings of the 25rd annual ACM symposium on User interface software and technology*, UIST '12. *To Appear*, 2012.

[14] W. S. Lasecki, K. I. Murray, S. White, R. C. Miller, and J. P. Bigham. Real-time crowd control of existing interfaces. In *Proceedings of the 24th annual ACM symposium on User interface software and technology*, UIST '11, page 23–32, 2011. ACM.

[15] G. Little, L. B. Chilton, M. Goldman, and R. C. Miller. Turkit: human computation algorithms on mechanical turk. In *Proceedings of the 23rd annual ACM symposium on User interface software and technology*, UIST '10, p 57–66, 2010. ACM.

[16] T. Matthews, S. Carter, C. Pai, J. Fong, and J. Mankoff. Scribe4me: evaluating a mobile sound transcription tool for the deaf. In *Proceedings of the 8th international conference on Ubiquitous Computing*, UbiComp'06, p 159–176, 2006. Springer-Verlag.

[17] L. von Ahn. *Human Computation*. PhD thesis, Carnegie Mellon University, Pittsburgh, PA, 2005.

[18] L. von Ahn and L. Dabbish. Labeling images with a computer game. In *Proceedings of the SIGCHI conference on Human factors in computing systems*, CHI '04, p 319–326, 2004. ACM.

[19] M. Wald. Creating accessible educational multimedia through editing automatic speech recognition captioning in real time. *Interactive Technology and Smart Education*, 3(2):131–141, 2006.

[20] A. A. Ye-Yi Wang and C. Chelba. Is word error rate a good indicator for spoken language understanding accuracy. In *IEEE Workshop on Automatic Speech Recognition and Understanding*, 2003.

Designing for Individuals: Usable Touch-Screen Interaction through Shared User Models

Kyle Montague, Vicki L. Hanson, Andy Cobley
School of Computing
University of Dundee
Dundee, Scotland

{kylemontague,vlh,acobley}@computing.dundee.ac.uk

ABSTRACT

Mobile touch-screen devices are becoming increasingly popular across a diverse range of users. Whilst there is a wealth of information and utilities available via downloadable apps, there is still a large proportion of users with visual and motor impairments who are unable to use the technology fully due to their interaction needs. In this paper we present an evaluation of the use of shared user modelling and adaptive interfaces to improve the accessibility of mobile touch-screen technologies. By using abilities based information collected through application use and continually updating the user model and interface adaptations, it is easy for users to make applications aware of their needs and preferences. Three smart phone apps were created for this study and tested with 12 adults who had diverse visual and motor impairments. Results indicated significant benefits from the shared user models that can automatically adapt interfaces, across applications, to address usability needs.

Categories and Subject Descriptors

H.5.2 **Information Interfaces and Presentation**: User Interfaces – *Input devices and strategies*. K.4.2 **Computers and Society**: Social Issues – *Assistive technologies for persons with disabilities.* K.4.2 **Computers and Society**: Social Issues – *Handicapped persons / special needs.*

General Terms

Design, Experimentation, Human Factors.

Keywords

Shared user modelling, adaptive interfaces, mobile touch screens.

1. INTRODUCTION

Touch-screen devices offer software designers greater flexibility and freedom with their application interfaces. Interactions need not be limited by physical buttons and keypads, but instead can be built using on-screen targets of variable sizes and touch interactions, able to respond to a large array of interaction methods far beyond a simple button click. These features make touch-screen devices ideal candidates for adaptive user applications. These adaptive applications rely on detailed representations of a user's characteristics and abilities in order to

make predictions and suggestions about a suitable interface for that person. The contribution of the current research is in the development and testing of a new method for providing cross-device, cross-application adaptations. Introduced in this paper is the Shared User Modelling (SUM) Framework. Through the use of this framework, there is the potential to allow otherwise independent applications the ability to learn from each other, thus minimizing the collection process from one application to another.

This paper describes the framework and presents a user study with disabled participants and highlights potential benefits of the framework. The long-term goal of this research is to improve usability across a range of applications and devices. As an initial test of the framework, the current study focuses on the dynamic collection and utilization of touch information in smartphone applications.

We focus on the use of SUM as a case of designing for individuals. To this end, the work investigates interfaces adapted to specific individual needs. The participants in the study present a cross section of visual and motor impairments. The touch adaptations studied in this work are applied without regard to the stated user impairment, based, instead, on input gathered from each individual.

2. BACKGROUND

2.1 Adaptive Interfaces

It is common for users to be able to set preferences for single applications they use on a device. Google Chrome, Microsoft Outlook, and Adobe Reader on computers all allow users to specify individual preferences for display and behaviours. On mobile devices, BBC News, iBooks, and Mail, for example, similarly allow for such individual settings. There are two obvious problems with application preferences. The first is that users must know that there is the ability to set these preferences and must understand their own needs well enough to specify these preferences. In short, they must be relatively sophisticated users [14]. The second problem with this approach is that preferences set in one application must then be set again for other applications. This setting of preferences is a tedious problem, particularly for users who, due to disability, have difficulty with the application interface.

More broadly useful than this individual application setting of preferences is the ability to set preferences on a device. All PC and mobile device operating systems provide means for setting display and input properties that will affect applications on the device. This has the advantage that preferences do not need to be set separately for each application. This option still requires users to be able to set their preferences, however. To overcome such limitation, various means of adapting interfaces to user needs have been proposed.

For example, Trewin [14] developed the Dynamic Keyboard which had the ability to learn about users' keyboarding abilities and automatically adapt PC settings to adjust for user abilities. In that work, Trewin examined system keyboard accessibility features that could be monitored (such as key repeat delay, key repeat rate, debounce time, and sticky keys), automatically adjusting operating system parameters of these features based on user needs. The novel aspect of this work was that the Dynamic Keyboard constantly monitored typing ability, continually changing settings throughout a session based on changing user abilties. Such continual updating of user needs is critically important for disabled users, many of whom have fluctuating accessibility needs not only from session to session, but even within a computing session.

Gajos et al. [4] examined adaptive interface mechanisms based on users stated preferences vs. their abilities. These authors compared their SUPPLE and SUPPLE++ adaptive interface systems. SUPPLE generated desktop application interfaces in real-time based on users' preferences inputs. SUPPLE++ generated this interface based on ability information collected in a motor performance task. Their results showed that while users favoured inputting their preferences, adaptive interfaces generated from abilities assessments produced more substantial performance improvement.

Like the Dynamic Keyboard and SUPPLE++, our SUM Framework generates adapted user interfaces based on user abilities collected during application use. Critically, the SUM Framework takes these adapted interfaces one step further than these device-specific applications by adapting across individual devices. By relying on web services, our shared user model has the ability to share information about user needs and preferences across not only applications, but also across devices. Thus, ability information obtained from, for example, Tweeting on a mobile device can be uploaded to provide information to adjust, for example, the Facebook interface on the user's PC.

2.2 Shared User Modelling

User models (UM) provide software applications with context such as user abilities, the domain knowledge of the user, user goals and interests, and their background outside this domain [2]. UM contain a structured collection of information about an individual user, to be utilised by adaptive systems in order to provide a tailored experience within an application.

With each session a user's knowledge, experience and goals develop and change. To ensure that adaptive systems are always working from the most up-to-date UM, there is a need for applications to share UM data across applications, as well as across devices. The SUM Framework takes as it starting point the idea of user models, but provides the web services needed to be able to adapt not only across applications, but also across multiple devices [11].

We describe here the technical underpinnings of the framework followed by a first evaluation of components of the framework.

3. SUM FRAMEWORK

This SUM Framework allows interaction data to be collected and stored locally within the app, while also communicating with the SUM web services to synchronise model data from other interaction instances.

To allow applications and devices to share a working user model it is essential that the model exists as an entity outside of any one application or device. In this case the user model is stored on the

web and accessed via a series of web services. Since it is not always possible to have Internet connectivity the framework keeps a local copy of the model and intermittently performs synchronisations with the web-based model. The SUM framework provides an application programming interface (API) wrapper for developers to access Web Services via HTTP requests conforming with the representational state transfer (RESTful) architecture. Before accessing the SUM framework, applications must be registered and receive user authentication to access an individual's user model. Once authorised, applications can request and update user model data through the API.

Currently the SUM Framework does not automatically generate interfaces as seen in the SUPPLE++ system [3], instead SUM provides developers with the optimal properties for objects e.g. font sizes, target sizes, modalities etc. based on their user model. As such there is still a need for designers to consider task workflows and interface controls.

3.1 Mobile Touch-Screen Accessibility

The capacitive touch-screens commonly found in mobile devices are able to track from one to eleven simultaneous touch inputs. As such there is a great variety of potential interaction methods each with a multitude of variations. The most popular techniques are tapping, swiping and pinching. Studies involving users with severe motor disabilities have achieved promising results, using tapping [5], while other work with participants with tremors identified tapping alone to be unsuccessful, and favoured the combination of a single touch with swiping [15] for this user group.

Mobile touch-screen devices are commonly equipped with a range of input sensors: microphone, ambient light sensor, accelerometer and in some cases 3-axis gyroscope. Combined with the highly sensitive capacitive touch-screen, it is possible to infer information on the user, surrounding environment and current activity e.g. walking. All of these can have an effect on user performance within applications [8, 16].

The SUM Framework uses time-codes and application IDs to group interaction data from all of these sensors, which is passed to the gesture recognisers to identify the intended interaction and call the appropriate action. The raw interaction data and inferred gestures are also stored locally within the database to be intermittently synchronised with the collective shared model on the web. The capacitive touch-screen sensor is capable of tracking up to eleven (usually five) simultaneous touch inputs, each touch consists of an id, x,y coordinate, timestamp, and action e.g. *Begin, Moving, Ended*.

Single touch instances can be clustered together using their ID, timestamp and action states to create more complex gesture movements. Using this same clustering we can get timings, accelerations of movement and even oscillation around a fixed target, as observed in users with tremors. The SUM Framework couples this touch data with the x,y location and dimensions of the object the user interacted with. This allows information to be derived on the user's accuracy and precision levels to be calculated for objects of varying sizes and screen locations. SUM records touch interactions in a similar method to Henze et al. [6] study. From our collected touch-screen data, optimal target sizes, minimum and maximum touch durations can be calculated on a per user basis across various screen locations within the device. Interaction data is clustered into *sessions,* to help process and analyse the changes in ability over time, and throughout different real world environments.

4. EVALUATION OF FRAMEWORK

Our research examines the ability of shared user models and adaptive interfaces to facilitate the use of smart phone apps for individuals with disabilities. This initial research evaluates the touch interaction component of the SUM Framework, examining the framework's ability to improve the user experience across varying applications on a mobile device.

This research was conducted with adults who have a variety of disabilities that limit their ability to interact with touch screen displays. Early testing indicated that the physical characteristics of our participants cause them to experience difficulties in two areas: interacting with the on-screen controls, and retrieving information from the device display. Therefore, we focussed on these two areas, seeking to determine whether shared user modelling can provide for easier interactions and an improved user experience.

In order to evaluate the potential accessibility benefits of our approach, three loosely related applications were created for an Apple iPod touch. Using these apps we are able to make comparisons between the Static (non-adaptive) interfaces and Adaptive interfaces sharing user model data. Each participant used all three apps over the course of two experimental sessions.

4.1 Experimental Apps

The three iPod Touch apps specifically developed for this study were: *Target Practice*, *Indoor Navigation* and a *TV Guide*, shown in Figures 1 – 3. Each application required the participant to interact with on-screen controls using a single touch. Within the *Target Practice* and *Indoor Navigation* applications the device responded only to a tap interaction. However whilst the primary input for the TV Guide was a single tap, it also required the users to swipe vertically to scroll through the TV listings. The interface adaptations created in the apps for visually impaired users also provided for scaling of text sizes and provided a text-to-speech option. Those adaptations, however, were largely based on user preferences as input, rather than abilities input. For the purpose of the current SUM Framework investigation, these adaptations will not be analysed in detail, although the user satisfaction ratings (to be described later) will be reflective of the fact that adaptations

Figure 1. Target Practice app showing both interface versions of the gameplay interface: static (left) and adaptive (right).

Figure 2. Indoor Navigation app showing both interface versions of the way-finding instruction page: static (left) and adaptive (right) with low vision user (20/50)

Figure 3. TV Guide app showing both interface versions of the all programmes page: static (left) and adaptive (right) with low vision user (20/50).

were made for the visually impaired participants.

The Apple iPod Touches used for the study were 2nd Generation. The devices are shipped with no accessibility support. Each of the three experimental apps was designed and built to conform with the iOS interface guidelines [7]. For all three, interface elements were given minimum bounds of 10mm (60px on this device) identified in previous research to be the optimal target size for daily users of these devices [9, 12]. The apps were all embedded with the SUM Framework for device monitoring and shared user model communication. All sensor data was logged within each app.

The apps shared user models by synchronising with the web services after each session was complete. Likewise at the beginning of each session the app would request the latest user model from the web services. Adaptations were applied specifically to users receiving the adaptive interface; default values were employed for the static interfaces.

User	Age	Gender	Method	Impairment	Current Accommodations
P1	67	Female	Static	VM – tremors in hands, short-sighted	Medication to suppress symptoms
P2	58	Male	Static	VM - spinal injury, muscle spasms, Sensitive to light	Medication to suppress symptoms, powered wheel-chair.
P3	57	Female	Static	M – Dopa-responsive dystonia, muscle cramps, tremors in hands	Reduced sensitivity of keyboard and mouse to minimise errors.
P4	66	Male	Static	M – spinal injury, muscle cramps, hand and wrist pains	Medication to relieve pain,
P5	66	Female	Adaptive	V – Retinal detachment, Macular Degeneration, diplopia	Guide Dog, magnifying glasses, screen reader software on PC
P6	65	Female	Adaptive	VM – Macular Degeneration in left eye, tremors in hands	Powered wheel-chair, full-time carers, mobile with large buttons
P7	67	Female	Adaptive	V – no binocular vision, reduced vision in left eye.	Magnifying glasses
P8	21	Female	Adaptive	M – hypermobility syndrome, locking joints and tremors in hands	Powered wheel-chair, medication to suppress symptoms
P9	71	Female	Adaptive	M – Myalgic Encephalomyelitis. muscle twitches and spasms in arms and hands.	Medication to suppress mobility symptoms not cognitive.
P10	64	Female	Static	V – reduced vision in left eye	Larger print, Screen Magnification on PC
P11	23	Male	Adaptive	V – registered blind, issues adjusting to changes in light levels	Monocular, Screen Magnification on PC, mobile with large buttons.
P12	22	Female	Static	VM – Ataxia with Oculomotor Apraxia reduced levels of vision, muscle twitches in hands and difficulty with fine motor control	Powered wheel-chair, full-time carers, mobile with large buttons

Table 1. Participant profile, impairment classification (Visual =V, Motor = M, VM = both) and interface evaluation method

4.1.1 Target Practice

The Target Practice app, shown in Figure 1, was designed to get baseline data about participants' abilities at the time of test. As users with disabilities can often experience fluctuations in ability, this baseline data was essential. The app generated 200 pairs of targets within the screen. Users were asked to tap the 'green targets only' (none of the participants indicated that they were colour blind). The target positions were pseudo-random as constraints were applied to the position generator to ensure good distribution of the targets. Specifically, the screen was divided into three sections vertically and horizontally, with the centre section twice the size of the other two for the vertical divisions (1:2:1) and three times the size of the other two for the horizontal divisions (1:3:1).

4.1.2 Indoor Navigation App

The *Indoor Navigation* app (Figure 2) was designed to provide users with individually tailored way-finding instructions. The system made adaptations to the interface delivered to the user. Way-finding routes were kept consistent for each participant.

Participants were asked to complete two indoor way-finding tasks within the University's School of Computing building (an unfamiliar environment for them), using only the instructions provided by the *Indoor Navigation* app. This navigation was accomplished via stored location information and the user's ability to match descriptions or images to their current location [10]. The navigation tasks required that the participant physically navigate from one location to another. Each participant performed both routes, however the order in which the participants carried out the tasks was counterbalanced.

Instructions were provided as text way-finding directions and accompanying images, with the option to have text read aloud using the audio button.

4.1.3 TV Guide App

The TV Guide app, shown in Figure 3, provided users with fixed TV listings for seven channels and 28 programmes. Users were asked to find specific TV programmes. To do this, they needed to browse through lists and grids of channels and programmes. Upon finding the programme they were asked to name the TV channel it airs on, date and time, read aloud the description text and state available access formats (such as Audio Description being available).

4.2 Participants

We were interested in examining the utility of shared user modelling for individuals with disability. We were not interested in specific adaptions. Thus, for example, we were not interested in what adaptations would be needed for people with low vision vs. what adaptations would be used by people with impaired hand use. Rather, we wished to test whether a model could be created that would dynamically change application features. For this reason, we recruited users with a variety of disabilities to give our model a test across a diverse range of users.

A total of three male and nine female adults were recruited. They ranged in age from 21-71 (M=54, SD=20). All possessed characteristics that would qualify them as low vision and/or mobility impaired. Table 1 provides information about the participating individuals and their characteristics.

In addition, all participants were required to own and use a mobile phone (although not necessarily a smart phone) and have a computer.

All participants were able to travel to the university for the purposes of experimental testing. Some were able to travel alone, while others needed to be accompanied by their carer or guide dog.

4.3 Procedure

An experimental session consisted of testing with two of the experimental apps, administration of a paper and pencil questionnaire and semi-structured with the researcher. They were given vouchers (worth £10) for their participation in each session. The tasks were structured as two sessions, as follows:

4.3.1 Session 1

Experimental sessions were conducted in a university environment and began with participants being given an overview of the research and completing the Informed Consent form. All participants then completed the following steps, in order:

- *Interview*: This background interview collected data about participants' mobile phone use, computer experience, handedness, and experience with touch screen devices. Of the 12 participants, all used a mobile phone on a daily basis. Only three owned touch-enabled smart phones and they were the only participants to have previously used a touch-screen mobile device. The researcher also discussed participants' abilities, asking questions about the use of glasses and assistive technology devices.

- *Target practice tasks*: Each participant did the target practice task twice – once with the Adaptive interface and once with the Static interface. Participants' touches were analysed throughout the target practice task to produce the interaction changes for the Adaptive condition. These changes were uniform *scaling of target sizes* and adjustments to *touch duration* bounds. Target scaling factors were calculated based on a participant's *precision* (distance from target centroid) when tapping targets. This *scaling factor* was the mean *precision*/2. To eliminate outlier values, minimum (10th percentile for individual user) and maximum (90th percentile per individual users) were calculated.

- Static interfaces had consistent target bounds of 60x60 pixels and no *minimum* or *maximum* touch duration. The order of these two conditions was counterbalanced between participants such that half received the Static interface first. While using the target practice app, participants were asked to relax in an armchair (or their own wheelchair). Each test with the target practice task lasted about four to five minutes (Static, M = 291 seconds, SD = 278.2 and Adaptive, M = 213 seconds, SD = 111.5).

- *Preferences set*: Following the target practice task, the user inputs were synchronised with the SUM server and individual preferences with respect to tapping were stored. In addition, participants were asked about their preferences in terms of audio and text presentation and set their preferred volume level. These preferences were entered into the user model.

- *Indoor Navigation app*: Participants were then given the Indoor Navigation app with the interface version matching their allocated group. The group assignment for these two apps is shown in Table 1.

  For the Adaptive condition, two types of changes were made. The first applied the scaling factor and touch duration bounds from the target practice task to the Indoor Navigation interface elements. Then the individual's preferences for text, audio and images were applied, thus altering the modalities present in the interface. For the Static condition, the interface

was shown with no accessibility adaptations, as with the target practice app.

Participants averaged about four minutes to complete each of the two *Indoor Navigation* tasks. Participants were able to complete all of the tasks with one exception in the *Indoor Navigation* study. This inability to complete one task was due to a technical disruption caused by a loss of Wi-Fi connectivity.

- *SUS questionnaire for Indoor Navigation app*: The Simple Usability Scale (SUS) questionnaire [1] was administered. This questionnaire consists of 10 questions about usability, with participants being asked to respond on a 5 point Likert scale. Although this questionnaire was initially designed to be a paper and pencil test, it became clear with the first few participants that it was difficult for them to read even the 14-point text and/or mark their answers. The researcher, therefore, adopted the procedure of reading the statements aloud to participants and asking them to verbally indicate their responses ("Strongly agree" "Agree" "Neutral" "Disagree" or "Strongly disagree").

- *Informal interviews:* Each session ended with the experimenter asking the participant for feedback on her/his experience. This was augmented with the researchers recorded observations.

The total session time for this first session was between 45 and 70 minutes, with most participants completing in one hour.

4.3.2 Session 2

The structure of this second session was similar to that of the first:

- *Interview*: The experimenter began by asking participants about any known changes in their abilities since the previous session. This was useful, particularly in one case, in which the participant had had a change of medication and was more comfortable with the touch-screen than in the first session.

  The experimenter asked questions about their TV viewing habits, whether they used subtitles (captioning), on-screen TV guides, on-demand services, recording systems, and how they planned their TV viewing.

- *Target practice tasks*: Participants again did both target practice tasks, using the Static and Adaptive interfaces in the same order they had used them in Session 1.

- *Vision test*: Participants were given a Snellen eye test for both distance and reading. The results of this reading test were added to the individual's user model to identify a font size for optimal viewing. iOS uses a variation of Helvetica by default, and its pixel size is 16px for normal text. The assumption was that this text would be the minimum size anyone should be given. Thus, 20/20 vision was allocated 16px, the rest of the font sizes were calculated based on this value; for example, for 20/50 vision, 50/20*16px (our default size for this font) therefore the size was set at 40px.

- *TV Guide app*: Each participant then performed the tasks for the TV Guide app. Participants were tested with either the Static or Adaptive interface per their group assignment shown in Table 1. For the Adaptive interface, elements were adjusted consistent with the methods used in the *Indoor Navigation* version, with the addition of the Snellen results being used to scale text. The static interface again had no adaptations and participants received the device default text sizes and touch properties. The tasks for the TV Guide app took, on average, 20 minutes to complete.

- *SUS questionnaire*: Participants were verbally asked the questions from the SUS questionnaire, with respect to their experience with this session's experimental app.

- *Discussion*: Participants were given the opportunity to comment on any features of the apps they wished. The experimenter also followed up on observations during the session.

The total duration of this second session was about one hour, ranging between 50 and 90 minutes for the 12 participants. The time between the two sessions varied, depending on availability. In one case, the two sessions occurred on the same day. For the other participants, the second session took place from one week to three months after the first session.

5. RESULTS

Our data analysis examined whether the adaptive interfaces would result in a better user experience than the static interfaces. These analyses examined touch errors and patterns as well analysis of usability ratings. These quantitative analyses are augmented by experimenter observations.

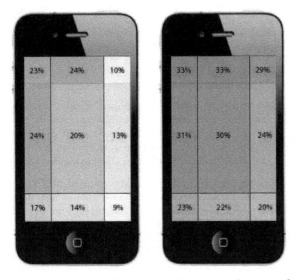

Figure 4. Target practice app touch error rate heat map for both Adaptive (left) and Static (right) interface conditions.

5.1 Touch Errors and Patterns

In terms of touch errors, we hypothesised that the SUM adaptive interfaces would result in fewer errors than the static interface. To test this, we examined touches in the target practice task. For this task, it was clear whether or not an error was made. If the participant hit the wrong target or touched outside of the target this was counted as an error.

Overall, there were 3997 touches (3603 within target practice app) with the Static interface for the three apps, and 3259 (2989 within target practice app) for the adaptive interfaces.

In the target practice task, participants were asked to touch all green targets. Even though there was a green target in each pair of target stimuli, in some instances participants made no attempt to tap the target. This was due to the fact that some believed the dark green target to be a shade of brown or black, not green. Therefore, touch error rate was based only on the attempted (not actual) targets within this task.

As hypothesised, the SUM Adaptive interfaces produced fewer touch error than did the Static interface t(11) = 1.977, p < .05, one tailed (d = .632). The mean number of touch errors per target practice interface was 18.83 (SD=19.41) and 27.67 (SD=26.36) for the Adaptive and Static interfaces.

The touch data for target practice taps was segmented into the 1:2:1, 1:3:1 sections used to distribute the touch targets to investigate the spread of the errors. Shown in Figure 4 are the error rate heat maps for the Adaptive and Static interface conditions. Whilst the Adaptive interface has lower error rates, both interfaces have a similar pattern with lower error rates in the bottom vertically and right-hand side horizontally. We had expected to see smaller numbers of errors in the bottom of the screen as the distance from the arm support increases [5]. In that study, higher error rates were reported as the distance from the arm support increased. Although our participants were not asked to hold the device in a particular manner, the researcher observed similarities between their hold and touch configurations. For example, participants grasped the device in the left hand and used one finger or a combination of thumb, index and middle fingers from their right hand. As the device is thus positioned closer to the origin of the participant's right hand (used for interactions), the distance to the target is lower in these areas. This could explain the lower error rates along the right-hand side.

Screen Location	Touch Location		
	Above	*Origin*	*Below*
Top	45.6%	3.0%	51.5%
Centre	39.4%	2.7%	57.9%
Bottom	46.3%	2.0%	51.7%

Table 2. Summary of vertical touch locations relative to target origins within vertical screen locations.

Screen Location	Touch Location		
	Left	*Origin*	*Right*
Left	30.2%	1.5%	68.3%
Centre	29.5%	2.2%	68.3%
Right	31.9%	1.3%	66.8%

Table 3. Summary of horizontal touch locations relative to target origins within horizontal screen locations.

As well as identifying error rates within specific screen locations, our data also revealed the touch locations relative to the centre of the targets. Tables 2 and 3 summarise the finger locations relative to all targets hit or missed during the target practice exercise. The term *origin* refers to hitting the target's centroid x or y coordinate exactly (dependent on the screen locations, vertical or horizontal). Of these, statistical analyses showed significant differences in the error locations for the vertical-vertical errors (Table 2), $X^2(4)$ (N=6232) = 29.84, p<.001. Specifically, within the vertical locations there was a relatively even distribution between participant touches above and below the origin, but for the horizontal touch locations the participants selected the right of targets the majority of the time.

The capacitive touch-screens found in the iPod devices are highly sensitive and able to detect touch input with next to zero finger pressure, often seen as one of the advantages of the technology. For some individuals, however, this highly sensitive screen is challenging. Three of our participants experience intermittent hand tremors. As a consequence, they found themselves making unintentional taps. P1 and P9 both own iOS devices. P9 chooses not to use her iPod touch, however, because of these issues. Instead she uses an LG touch-screen phone because *"it has a much lower sensitivity than the iPod"*.

Figure 5 details the touch durations the individual users collected from interactions within the mobile apps. There are noticeable differences between each of the participant's touch durations, so much so that there does not appear to be a minimum and maximum duration that would be optimal for everyone. The SUM Framework uses this data and adjusts the level of sensitivity by applying more restrictions to the tap gesture recogniser. By default a tap is recognised when an input does not match any other gesture. In an attempt to reduce the number of involuntary inputs, the tap recogniser was given minimum and maximum durations for the Adaptive interfaces. P9 was able to notice the benefits to this change during the second session when she intentionally tried to test it with a double tap the screen, only to find that it would identify the one input and disregard the other.

5.1.1 Scrolling
Both the Target Practice and TV Guide apps required only a single tap input to interact with the interface elements. The TV Guide app makes use of scrollable panels to present more content within a single page, such as a list of all programmes. These scrollable panels caused a great deal of confusion for P12 when trying to locate TV programmes positioned further down the grid off-screen. Since she had never used a smart phone until taking part in this study, her working knowledge of grids and lists came from her computer experience. To look for content not on-screen, P12 looked for scroll bars as well as *previous* and *next* page buttons. When asked by the researcher if she was able to find the *Inbetweeners* TV programme within the page, P12 stated that it wasn't on the page. The researcher then prompted the participant that there was more content below, and she was then able to perform the required scroll gesture to complete the tasks.

The iPod touch is capable of two types of scrolling. One, free scroll with acceleration, will move faster or slower depending on the swipe input speed and will keep scrolling until it decelerates and stops. The second type of scrolling uses a paging effect so that regardless of the swipe input speed, the panel will only scroll one page. Both types of scrolling were incorporated in the TV Guide app: free scroll for the 'all programmes grid' and page scroll for the 'all channels' grid and 'programme detail' pages. P5, P6 and P12 shared similar problems when using the free scroll. Their comments included *"When you do it [scroll], it just keeps going and I can't read it," "I can't see it quick enough,"* and *"I don't like it moving past"*.

The researcher also observed changes in grip style when participants were required to scroll rather than tap. When scrolling, the device was repositioned and given a firmer grip to ensure that it wasn't dropped when performing the necessary swipe gesture. For some participants this resulted in unusual behaviour of the device caused by their unintentional touches when tightening their grip. While the iPods have a bezel edge on all four sides of the screen, this was much too small for a number of our participants to hold without creating involuntary touch input. A small bezel appears to be a design trend for touch-screen

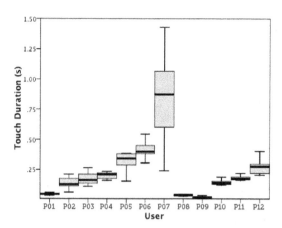

Figure 5. Boxplots of participant touch durations.

technologies as it maximises screen size but minimises device dimensions. This trend may make the devices more challenging for users with diverse needs.

5.2 Usability Ratings
The SUS questionnaire is designed to produce measures of usability. We hypothesised more positive usability ratings for the Adaptive interfaces than for the static interface. Recall that in the Adaptive condition the interfaces were designed for meeting individual needs for touch, visual display and text-to-speech preferences.

In total, there were 12 SUS scores for the Adaptive interfaces (6 for both the *Indoor Navigation* and *TV Guide* app), and 12 SUS scores for the Static interfaces, although each participated rated different apps in the adaptive and static conditions. There was only a small and statistically nonsignificant (p>.05) difference in the SUS scores in these two conditions (the mean usability rating for the Adaptive interfaces was 3.33 [SD=0.27], compared with the mean usability rating of 3.10 [SD=0.71] for Static interfaces). We suspect that there were various reasons contributing to the small difference and the fact that users, overall, did not give high ratings to the adaptive interfaces. Primarily, participants' use of the apps was limited. Not only did participants have limited time with the apps tested, it is important to note that they only viewed the apps in one condition. Thus, they did directly compare the apps under both the Adaptive and Static conditions. The apps were new to the participants and, regardless of condition, they had to learn the new app. Thus, their comfort with the apps, regardless of interface, was likely limited. More extended testing with the apps and in multiple conditions should help to better understand the extent to which the SUM Framework adaptations are perceived.

6. CONCLUSIONS
This study provides initial support for the feasibility of a shared user modelling approach to adaptive interfaces in designing interfaces for individuals. Using the SUM Framework outlined here, user performance improved. In terms of performance, touch errors in this study were reduced by adjusting on-screen elements to match the required target size, touch duration, and font size for individual users. Unlike previous work in this area [5], our participants were not constrained to researcher defined seating or holding positions, but asked to use the device as they would their own mobile. This freedom provided information about the range

of problems users might experience in real world situations. In particular, touch patterns related to the bezel were identified.

Our studies span three unique applications, placing the participants in both laboratory and real world environments. Notably, our user models for the adaptations were not based on one-time data collection about user abilities [4] but rather were taken from continuously updated ability data [14]. Further evaluations with longer collection periods are required to provide more detailed representations of the users' characteristics and interaction abilities. We acknowledge that studies such as this cannot fully cover the of diversity of disabled populations [13]. The research has sought, however, to identify types of touch-screen requirements and provide an initial framework for automatically providing needed adaptations.

This research has focused on a device similar to a smart phone (the iPod touch), although this will also work with multi-touch tablet devices. The device monitoring and shared user model data is software platform and device independent. Each device is profiled within the database, which allows data collected from one device to be applied to another using adjustment factors. The researchers already have an Android version in development, and future studies aim to include multiple devices and software platforms.

It should be remembered that the SUM Framework approach does not automatically generate interface components as does SUPPLE++ [4]. Rather, this user modelling approach provides information to application models about optimal settings for individual users. The SUM Framework seeks to provide a means whereby users do not need to set their preferences app by app on each device. Rather, the goal is to provide a means whereby these can be set across apps and across devices using, in many cases, ability information that captures the current and changing needs of disabled users.

Our results were obtained from individuals with substantial visual and/ or motor impairments. While adaptive interfaces may be particularly useful for people with this severity of disability, more minor adaptations can also be very useful for those with less severe impairments, such as people exhibiting age-related vision loss. The SUM Framework provides a potentially powerful way to improve usability for a large number of people with diverse needs.

7. ACKNOWLEDGMENTS

Support for this project was provided by RCUK Digital Economy Research Hub EP/G066019/1 – SIDE: Social Inclusion through the Digital Economy, and by a Royal Society Wolfson Award to the second author. We thank our participants who provided so many insights, Marianne Dee who helped us locate participants for the research, as well as John Richards who provided comments on early versions.

8. REFERENCES

[1] Brooke, J. 1996. SUS – A quick and dirty usability scale. *Usability evaluation in industry.* 189, (1996), 194.

[2] Brusilovsky, P. and Millan, E. 2007. User Models for Adaptive Hypermedia and Adaptive Educational Systems. 4321/2007, (2007), 3 – 53.

[3] Gajos, K.Z., Wobbrock, J.O. and Weld, D.S. 2007. Automatically generating user interfaces adapted to users' motor and vision capabilities. *Proceedings of the 20th annual ACM symposium on user interface software and technology.* (2007), 231–240.

[4] Gajos, K.Z., Wobbrock, J.O. and Weld, D.S. 2008. Improving the performance of motor-impaired users with automatically-generated, ability-based interfaces. *Proceeding of the 26th annual SIGCHI conference on Human factors in computing systems.* (2008), 1257–1266.

[5] Guerreiro, T., Nicolau, H., Jorge, J. and Gonçalves, D. 2010. Assessing mobile touch interfaces for tetraplegics. *Proceedings of the 12th international conference on Human computer interaction with mobile devices and services.* (2010), 31–34.

[6] Henze, N., Rukzio, E. and Boll, S. 2011. 100,000,000 taps: analysis and improvement of touch performance in the large. *Proceedings of the 13th International Conference on Human Computer Interaction with Mobile Devices and Services.* (2011), 133–142.

[7] iOS Human Interface Guidelines: https://developer.apple.com/library/ios/#documentation/User Experience/Conceptual/MobileHIG/Introduction/Introductio n.html. Accessed: 2012-02-28.

[8] Kane, S.K., Wobbrock, J.O. and Smith, I.E. 2008. Getting off the treadmill: evaluating walking user interfaces for mobile devices in public spaces. *Proceedings of the 10th international conference on human computer interaction with mobile devices and services.* (2008), 109–118.

[9] Lee, S. and Zhai, S. 2009. The performance of touch screen soft buttons. *Proceedings of the 27th international conference on Human factors in computing systems.* (2009), 309–318.

[10] Kyle Montague. 2010. Accessible indoor navigation. In *Proceedings of the 12th international ACM SIGACCESS conference on Computers and accessibility* (2010), 305-306.

[11] Montague, K., Hanson, V. and Cobley, A. 2011. Adaptive interfaces: a little learning is a dangerous thing... *Universal Access in Human-Computer Interaction. Design for All and eInclusion.* (2011), 391–399.

[12] Perry, K.B. and Hourcade, J.P. 2008. Evaluating one handed thumb tapping on mobile touchscreen devices. *Proceedings of graphics interface 2008.* (2008), 57–64.

[13] Sears, A. and Hanson, V. 2011. Representing users in accessibility research. *CHI '11: Proceedings of the 2011 annual conference on Human factors in computing systems.* (2011).

[14] Trewin, S. 2004. Automating accessibility: the dynamic keyboard. *ASSETS'04: Proceedings of the ACM SIGACCESS conference on Computers and Accessibility* (2004).

[15] Wacharamanotham, C., Hurtmanns, J., Mertens, A., Kronenbuerger, M., Schlick, C. and Borchers, J. 2011. Evaluating swabbing: a touchscreen input method for elderly users with tremor. *CHI '11: Proceedings of the 2011 annual conference on Human factors in computing systems.* (2011).

[16] Wilson, G., Brewster, S. and Halvey, M. 2011. The effects of walking, feedback and control method on pressure-based interaction. *MobileHCI '11: Proceedings of the 13th International Conference on Human Computer Interaction with Mobile Devices and Services.* (2011).

PassChords: Secure Multi-Touch Authentication for Blind People

Shiri Azenkot*, Kyle Rector*, Richard E. Ladner*, and Jacob O. Wobbrock†
Computer Science & Engineering*, The Information School†
DUB Group
University of Washington
Seattle, WA USA 98195
{shiri,rectorky,ladner}@cs.washington.edu, wobbrock@uw.edu

ABSTRACT

Blind mobile device users face security risks such as inaccessible authentication methods, and aural and visual eavesdropping. We interviewed 13 blind smartphone users and found that most participants were unaware of or not concerned about potential security threats. Not a single participant used optional authentication methods such as a password-protected screen lock. We addressed the high risk of unauthorized user access by developing *PassChords*, a non-visual authentication method for touch surfaces that is robust to aural and visual eavesdropping. A user enters a PassChord by tapping several times on a touch surface with one or more fingers. The set of fingers used in each tap defines the password. We give preliminary evidence that a four-tap PassChord has about the same entropy, a measure of password strength, as a four-digit personal identification number (PIN) used in the iPhone's Passcode Lock. We conducted a study with 16 blind participants that showed that PassChords were nearly three times as fast as iPhone's Passcode Lock with VoiceOver, suggesting that PassChords are a viable accessible authentication method for touch screens.

Categories and Subject Descriptors

H.5.2 [**Information Interfaces and Presentation**]: User Interfaces – *Input devices and strategies, Voice I/O.*; K.4.2 [**Computers and society**]: Social issues – *assistive technologies for persons with disabilities.*

Keywords

Blind, mobile devices, touch screens, security, privacy.

1. INTRODUCTION

Mobile devices pose different security risks than traditional computers and require alternative security measures [1, 4, 13, 18]. For example, the small size and mobile nature of handheld devices increase the risk of loss or theft. Yet

Figure 1: When entering passwords with an iPhone and VoiceOver, a user's input is spoken as she touches the screen, posing a severe security risk.

people routinely access email communications, contacts' information, online banking, and other private data without adequate user authentication mechanisms. Password entry on small touch keyboards is a common frustration for people [13], resulting in the use of shorter passwords, or avoidance of password protection entirely. Much recent work in the security literature has discussed such challenges, as well as the importance of mobile device security in general.

To the best of our knowledge, there are no published explorations of mobile device security for people with disabilities. Use of access technology on-the-go poses unique security risks for blind people that do not arise when sighted people use mobile devices, or when blind people use traditional computers. Blind people commonly interact with mobile devices via screen readers, such as Apple's VoiceOver for iOS devices, which read the contents of the screen and the user's input. Moreover, mobile computing with screen readers is often performed in public places, raising the risk of bystanders eavesdropping on one's private information. Suppose a blind person checks her email at a bus stop. A bystander may hear the blind person's device speaking the contents of an email, or information about the blind user's travel destination.

Another security issue that differs for blind and sighted users is accessibility of password entry. User authentication is an effective and common way to protect private data [15]. A recent study found that when smartphones were left unattended in public places, 89% of people who found the phones attempted to access the phone owner's private information[1]. Use of a password to unlock the device screen protects against unauthorized user access. Yet password entry is likely to be an obstacle for blind users, since even sighted users find password entry on small touch screens to be a major frustration [14]. Moreover, screen readers introduce a severe vulnerability by speaking touched keys during password entry (see Figure 1). Over the past decade, the security community has explored the use of graphical authentication techniques as an alternative to alphanumeric passwords [16, 21, 25, 26]. These techniques do not require text entry but are inaccessible to blind people.

In this paper, we explore security issues that arise for blind people when using mobile devices. We focus on smartphone use, because of the wealth of private information that is accessed on these devices. We interviewed 13 blind smartphone users to discover their attitudes and specific behavior patterns that affect security risks. Most participants were not concerned with security issues, and none used optional authentication mechanisms to protect their information.

We sought to improve mobile device security by presenting a new accessible and secure authentication method called *PassChords*. PassChords are based on Input Finger Detection [3] and consist of several multi-point touches, defined by the set of fingers touching the screen. The PassChords algorithm determines which fingers touch the screen in each tap based on an initial set of reference points which the user inputs anywhere on the screen. Reference points indicate the approximate position of the user's fingers. PassChords have no audio feedback, so they are robust to aural eavesdropping. In a study with 16 blind people, we found that PassChord entry was nearly three times as fast as entry of accessible personal identification numbers (PINs) and had about the same authentication failure rate.

In summary, we present two contributions: (1) a study of security risks for blind mobile device users, and (2) Pass-Chords, a new authentication technique for touch screens that is accessible, fast, and robust to aural eavesdropping.

2. RELATED WORK

Related work falls into two categories: security issues for blind people and mobile authentication techniques for the general population. Our work is the first, to our knowledge, to focus on security issues for blind mobile device users and develop and evaluate an accessible touch screen authentication method.

Kane et al. [17] discussed patterns and challenges of mobile device use for people with visual impairments and briefly mentioned users' privacy concerns. The authors did not delve into potential security problems. The study was conducted in 2009, before the iPhone introduced VoiceOver[2], the built-in screen reader on iOS devices. Since blind people now use touch screen devices, new security challenges have arisen, which we focus on in this paper.

Some work has been done in the area of accessible security, but, to our knowledge, none has focused on mo-

[1]StreetWise Security Zone. 2012. The Honey Stick Project. http://www.streetwise-security-zone.com/members/streetwise/adminpages/honeystickproject
[2]Apple, Inc. iPhone Accessibility. http://www.apple.com/accessibility/iphone/vision.html

bile devices. Kuber and Sharma proposed accessible authentication methods for desktop computers using a tactile mouse [19]. Several papers discussed the accessibility of CAPTCHA's [6, 12, 24], which are used to verify human users, but do not protect against unauthorized access. Our work concerns user authentication with accessible and secure password techniques.

The security community has widely acknowledged the inadequacy of alphanumeric passwords, and alternative authentication methods have been proposed. Graphical passwords [25] have been studied extensively over the past decade, including techniques that require users to select a sequence of photos that are displayed on the screen [10], to select a sequence of points in displayed images [26], or to draw a "secret" shape or design on a grid [16, 21]. These techniques are generally inaccessible to blind people.

One potentially accessible technique is TapSongs [27], a rhythm-based authentication method for devices with a single binary sensor (e.g., button). (TapSongs were later utilized and extended by Nokia researchers in their Rhythm-Link system; they named such rhythm-based passwords "tapwords" [20].) A difference between TapSongs and Pass-Chords is that the duration of a TapSong was about 6-8 seconds, while PassChords tended to be less than 4 seconds long. Also, it is not clear what the entropy of TapSongs is so it is difficult to evaluate their security strength, although the Nokia researchers made some attempt to do so [20].

Biometric authentication offers another potentially accessible alternative to graphical or alphanumeric passwords [29]. Robust biometric techniques (e.g., iris scans, hand and fingerprint recognition) often require special hardware, that has not been adopted on mainstream mobile devices. Our approach is lightweight and requires only a touch surface.

3. THREATS AND DEFENSES

We outline security threats for blind mobile device users and possible defenses against them. Like sighted people, we assume blind people access private data such as email communications, text messages, social networking, online banking, contacts information, and travel directions. We also assume blind people use their devices in public places like buses, street corners, and cafes, where others are present nearby. Unlike for sighted people, however, we believe the following threats pose far greater risks for blind people because of screen reader technology or the lack of security features available in specialized access technologies.

We consider the following threats in this paper:

Aural eavesdropping. Casual or malicious bystanders may overhear private information spoken by screen readers. Additionally, as a user enters input, the screen reader echoes the user's button selections. This occurs when a user enters a password as well, as shown in Figure 1. The threat of aural eavesdropping has been studied in the security literature for more subtle audio feedback such as keystroke sounds [5, 11, 2], highlighting the severity of the threat for screen reader output.

Visual eavesdropping. Casual or malicious bystanders may oversee private information displayed on a mobile device screen. If a person with low-vision is using large fonts or screen magnification, people may see the screen's contents from an extended distance.

Unauthorized user access. Both blind and sighted people face this threat, which occurs when a device is misplaced, lost, or stolen. We are interested in this threat because, as we discuss below, blind people may find it far more challenging to defend against it.

To assess the risk posed by the threats listed above, we enumerate possible defenses. In the following section we discuss how and when these defenses are used through an interview study, and asses threat risk.

Headphones. One can mitigate the risk of aural eavesdropping by using headphones when listening to screen reader output. However, when on-the-go, blind people use their hearing to understand their environment and using headphones may be unsafe or inconvenient. A blind person may not want to use headphones every time she enters a password to unlock her screen.

Screen occlusion. It is possible to physically cover a screen with a hand or use software such as the iPhone's Screen Curtain[3]. Some access technologies such as Braille displays or audio recorders may be used instead of smartphones, as they do not have screens at all. Not displaying visual output would mitigate the risk of visual eavesdropping but may be impractical or difficult to use. Also, people with some functional vision may benefit from visual output.

Password protection. Protecting a device with a password that requires a user to authenticate herself before using a device is an effective defense against unauthorized user access. Many access technologies do not have password locks, however. People using smart devices that do have such features may find the standard password techniques to be too slow and error-prone (in addition to being insecure, because of screen readers speaking the input password).

4. SECURITY-RELATED USAGE PATTERNS

Defenses against security threats have trade-offs and may negatively impact a user's experience with a device. We conducted interviews with blind people to understand how and why possible defenses were practiced. This enabled us to asses the risk of the security threats in our model.

4.1 Method

4.1.1 Participants

We recruited 13 participants (6 male, 7 female). The average participant age was 51 years (age range 26–64). We required that participants (1) were legally blind and (2) used smartphones daily. Two participants had some functional vision, one had light perception, and the remaining 10 were completely blind. Participants were recruited through email lists that catered to blind people.

4.1.2 Procedure

We conducted a semi-structured interview with each participant. All interviews were conducted over the phone and lasted about 20 minutes. We began by asking participants for demographic information such as gender and age. Then, we asked questions in the following categories: (1) context and frequency of mobile device use, (2) types of information accessed on mobile devices, (3) use of passwords on mobile devices, (4) use of headphones, and (5) use of screen occlusion techniques.

---

[3]Apple, Inc. iPhone Accessibility.
http://www.apple.com/accessibility/iphone/vision.html

4.1.3 Analysis

The interviews were transcribed, coded, and then organized based on interview questions.

4.2 Results

All participants owned iPhones that they used with the VoiceOver screen reader. When on the go, 6 participants also carried a Braille notetaker, 2 carried accessible GPS systems, 1 carried a portable CCTV, and 1 carried a laptop. All devices were used on a daily basis in various contexts, including public places such as streets, cafes and restaurants, and also at home and at an office.

As expected, participants stored a wealth of private and personal information on their devices:

> *Gosh, you know [my iPhone] is just a part of me. I can't think of anything I don't do [on it].*

Participants regularly accessed private information, including email communications, social networking sites, and location-tracking applications such as Four Square. Nearly half of the participants used banking applications on their iPhones. One participant expressed a preference for accessing private data on her Braille notetaker, because others could not hear or see what she was reading.

None of the participants used optional authentication features to protect the information on their devices. In fact, the iPhone was the only device mentioned that *had* an authentication feature. All but one of the participants were aware of the iPhone's password protection feature, the Passcode Lock, and had decided not to use it. Some participants stated using the Passcode Lock was inconvenient: "No, [Passcode entry] is inconvenient—I don't want to do that"; others thought it was unnecessary: "...because I have my [iPhone] with me all the time."

Passwords were entered only when required by some applications that participants used, such as Facebook and Netflix. These passwords were usually stored by the applications, however, and did not require repeated entry. One participant expressed concern regarding aural eavesdropping, noting that VoiceOver spoke a key label as it was touched during password entry.

All participants used headphones when listening to screen readers in public spaces; 12 participants used headphones regularly (but not exclusively), and the remaining participant used them occasionally. Three participants (partly) attributed headphone use to concerns about aural eavesdropping, but most used headphones to avoid disturbing others around them or simply for better sound quality. There was a trade-off between the advantages of headphones and the need to hear sounds in one's environment.

> *I like to listen on the headphones but I don't like to have my hearing completely blocked out because it's hard to hear a bus stop and if there is something happening on the bus I need to be hearing. You know, like a fight or who knows?*

The iPhone's Screen Curtain feature, which disables visual output, was used by 10 participants; not being able to see the screen may serve as a security advantage for them. Four participants used the Screen Curtain to prevent visual eavesdropping, and most participants cited the desire to save battery power (the advertised purpose of the Screen Curtain).

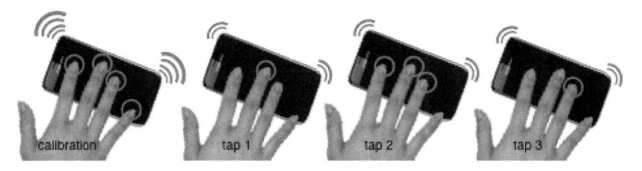

Figure 2: A user calibrates (left) and enters a 3-tap PassChord. The blue circles show which fingers contact the screen in the figure but do not appear as output to the user. Note that the fingers are not striking bounded regions like buttons; rather, the finger locations are interpreted probabilistically, meaning some flexibility in their hit-location is allowed, while the number and identity of the fingers is appropriately strict.

I love that people can't look over my shoulder and see what I'm doing.

No other screen occlusion techniques (e.g., holding the device close to one's chest) were used.

While participants occasionally mentioned security threats, their primary concerns were related to iPhone accessibility. Participants had difficulty inputting text and accessing information from applications that were not compatible with VoiceOver. Several participants noted the physical challenge of interacting with their devices while using a cane. Only three mentioned the security risks associated with online banking, location tracking, and aural and visual eavesdropping. One participant acknowledged the need for better security mechanisms, although, like other participants, he did not use optional authentication methods.

I feel like I should use [security features on [my iPhone] and I'll probably be sorry one day that I didn't.

4.3 Discussion

Our results indicate that a minority of users are aware of security threats, including aural and visual eavesdropping, and unauthorized user access. This is disturbing, but not surprising given that related work found that the general population lacks awareness and understanding of security threats [9, 15, 22]. We concur with this prior work that users should receive better training—whether from Orientation & Mobility instructors or blindness organizations in general— about potential mobile device security risks.

The finding that our participants did not use optional authentication methods like the Passcode Lock to protect their devices from unauthorized user access was most alarming. Clarke and Furnell [9] report that one third of 297 (all sighted) participants locked their phones with PIN-based authentication, noting that this ratio was low. The fact that no participants used a Passcode Lock in our study was egregious, highlighting the severe risk of unauthorized user access. Text entry rates with VoiceOver were only about 4 words per minute (WPM) [3], so it may be infeasible for blind people to enter a PIN every time they unlocked the screen of their phone.

Security threats from aural and visual eavesdropping were mitigated by use of headphones and the Screen Curtain. Although all participants used headphones, they acknowledged

their disadvantages. Security defenses should, therefore, not solely rely on headphone use, especially for highly private information such as passwords. Screen Curtains were not used by all participants, and participants were generally unaware of the need for protect against visual eavesdropping. It would be interesting to interview people who used magnification rather than screen readers, since magnification increases the risk of visual eavesdropping.

5. SECURE AUTHENTICATION WITH PASS-CHORDS

The most severe security problem we identified from our study is the risk of unauthorized user access, which may be attributed to lack of user awareness, and the inaccessibility and insecurity of current password techniques. To address this problem, we developed a new touch screen authentication method that is entirely non-visual, faster than PIN techniques, and robust to aural eavesdropping.

5.1 Design Principles

When developing an authentication method, we considered several design principles based on our interview study, our threat model, and standard authentication guidelines [1, 23]. These principles emphasize both security and usability.

1. Speed. Users should be able to enter a password quickly.

2. Robust to aural eavesdropping. Users should be able to input a password without audio feedback that broadcasts their input.

3. Robust to visual eavesdropping. There should be little or no visual indication of the user's input.

4. High password strength. Password strength should not be sacrificed and the technique should be robust to guessing or brute-force attacks.

5. High recall. Passwords should be easy to remember.

5.2 The PassChords Technique

PassChords are a new authentication technique based on Input Finger Detection [3], where a user taps a touch surface several times with 1 to 4 fingers (see Figure 2). The PassChord is defined by the set of fingers used in each tap. At the beginning of a PassChord entry, the user calibrates the touch surface by entering reference points, which the PassChords algorithm uses to model the true locations of the fingers on the screen.

The PassChords algorithm determines which fingers touched the screen using Maximum Likelihood (ML) detection given the finger reference points. In Input Finger Detection [3], the variance of each finger is tracked and used in the ML detection. Since PassChords are short and we assume that, unlike in text entry, a user will not enter many PassChords in succession, we do not track variance. Instead, we assume equal variance for each fingers. ML thus reduces to finding the set of reference points that have the minimum combined distance from the set of input points.

As the user enters a PassChord, she receives only vibration feedback with no visual or audio output. A short vibration is produced when the user touches the screen. To calibrate, a user presses 4 fingers to the screen until a second vibration is produced less than a second later. No further feedback is needed because, as with any chording technique, people can discern their input through proprioception. Techniques that rely on a fingertip at a certain position require audio feedback because different inputs "feel" the same.

We believe that PassChords would be easy to remember because the chording nature of the technique is evocative of playing a piano or another chording instrument. Also, people may associate numbers with the fingers used, allowing similar recall techniques to numeric passwords.

5.3 Entropy

Information entropy is a commona measure of password strength, indicating how robust a technique is to guessing or brute-force attacks [8]. In this metric, the information entropy of a password of n symbols from a symbol set of size m is $\log_2 m^n$, measured in bits. In other words, the information entropy of a password technique is the minimum number of bits needed to encode the set of all possible passwords, assuming all symbols are equally likely.

In one tap of a PassChord, there are 15 possible finger combinations. Each of 4 fingers is either touching the screen or not, and a tap where all fingers are not touching the screen is invalid. A PassChord with 4 taps therefore has information entropy $\log_2 15^4 \approx 15.6$ bits. By contrast, consider a standard PIN's information entropy. Each digit in the PIN has 10 possible inputs, so a 4-digit PIN has information entropy $\log_2(10^4) \approx 13.3$. Both the 4-tap PassChord and the 4-digit PIN require the same number of symbols as input, but the information entropy of the PassChord technique is higher, indicating it may be more robust to attacks.

The information entropy assumes that all symbol entries are equally likely, which is probably not true for PIN entry and certainly not true for tap entry. As we will see in our study, some finger combinations are more likely than others because of the physiology of the hand. For example, simultaneously tapping the middle and pinky fingers is more difficult than tapping the index finger. A better estimate of the entropy of password strength is the first-order entropy:

$$H = n \sum_{i=1}^{m} p_i \log_2(1/p_i), \qquad (1)$$

where p_i is the probability of symbol i occurring in any position in a password. We will empirically calculate H from user data to estimate the security strength of PassChords.

5.4 Evaluation

To evaluate the PassChords authentication technique, we sought to compare PassChords to a standard password technique. We chose the iPhone's Passcode Lock with VoiceOver as a basis for comparison, which consists of a 4-digit PIN that is entered with an on-screen number pad.

5.4.1 Method

Participants. We recruited 16 blind participants (8 male, 8 female), with an average age of 51 (age range 27–61). While all were legally blind, five participants had some vision and were able to identify numbers on an iPhone's number pad. The remaining 11 had no functional vision. Eight participants had experience with VoiceOver on iOS devices. We recruited participants through mailing lists that communicated with blind people.

Apparatus. We built prototype applications for PassChord and PIN entry. We did not use an iPhone's built-in Passcode so we could instrument the application. The PIN application was visually similar to the iPhone's Passcode Lock, enabling split-tap and double-tap selection of keys. As with the iPhone, the PIN application spoke button labels as they were touched, but did not provide feedback when a number was entered. Both applications logged every user input.

A Samsung Galaxy phone was used for all user studies, with a 4-inch screen.

Procedure. Participants completed two sessions, one with each authentication method. The beginning of each session included a training period, where we taught participants how to use the method for the current session. Participants practiced the method until they were able to authenticate with three different passwords.

After training, participants entered three passwords: the first was prescribed by the experimenter and the other two were created by the user. We sought to simulate a realistic password creation and entry scenario, so we asked participants to create a password, confirm it, and then enter it 20 times. The confirmation of a password allowed participants to practice their new password and ensure they had created it as intended.

The first PIN was a randomly generated sequence of 4 digits. The first PassChord included three touches, each consisting of one randomly selected finger. We anticipated certain multi-finger combinations would be difficult for participants, so we gave them a PassChord where each touch included only one finger. For the next two PassChords, we instructed participants to create a PassChord where at least one of the touches had more than one finger. For both methods, participants were instructed to create passwords that were "realistic."

Participants were able to correct errors during password entry. The VoiceOverPIN number pad included a BACKSPACE key. A PassChord could be "reset" if the user made an error by calibrating and re-entering the PassChord. Such errors and corrections were included in the time measured for a given password entry.

After entering three PassChords repeatedly, we asked participants to create yet another PassChord which they were tasked to memorize. Two days after the study we called each participant and asked them to repeat the memorized PassChord. We instructed participants to behave as though

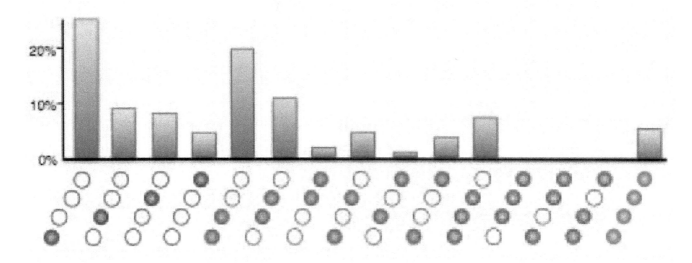

Figure 3: PassChord pattern frequencies. A sequence of circles represents a tap pattern, with the index finger shown on the bottom left and the pinky finger on the top right. Certain patterns were chosen far more often than others.

this was a "real" password, and use whatever memorization technique seemed appropriate.

Design and Analysis. The study was a within-subjects factorial design with two factors, *Method* and *Order*. The levels of *Method* were (PassChords, VoiceOverPIN) and the levels of *Order* were (1, 2). The *Order* factor indicated whether the current *Method* was performed first or second in the study, allowing us to evaluate possible crossover effects.

We analyzed two measures: authentication time and failure rate. The former was measured as the difference between the time of the first and last touch events of a password (including PassChord calibration), and the flatter was the proportion of times the user failed to authenticate. The failure rate included completed passwords that turned out to be incorrect, not counting errors that were corrected by the user with the BACKSPACE key or a re-calibration. Such errors were subsumed by the password entry time. Both measures were analyzed with mixed-effects model analysis of variance, with a fixed effect for *Method* and a random effect for *Participant* to account for correlated measurements for different methods within subjects. Authentication times were averaged for trials in each method. We used a significance level of $\alpha = 0.05$.

Neither authentication time nor failure rate was normally distributed ($W = 0.90$, $p < 0.001$ for time; $Shapiro - WilkW = 0.89$, $p < 0.001$ for failure rate). Therefore, we used the nonparametric *Aligned Rank Transform* procedure [28], which enables the use of ANOVA after alignment and ranking, while maintaining the integrity of interaction effects.

5.4.2 Results

Authentication time. PassChords were nearly three times as fast as VoiceOverPINs. The mean authentication time for PassChords was 2.67 seconds ($SD = 0.722$), while that for VoiceOverPIN was 7.52 seconds ($SD = 2.40$). This difference resulted in a significant effect of *Method* on authentication time ($F_{1,13} = 113.6, p < 0.001$).

The number of taps per PassChord ranged between 3 and 6 taps, and the mean time per tap was 0.62 seconds ($SD = 0.17$). The mean time for a VoiceOverPIN input was 1.89 seconds ($SD = 0.60$). Thus, it is evident that PassChords would have outperformed VoiceOverPINs if we had required an equal number of inputs for each. The large difference was not surprising since participants often had to search for the correct VoiceOverPIN input by moving their finger across the screen while listening to screen reader output.

Strangely, there appeared to be an asymmetric skill transfer between methods. Participants who entered PassChords after they had entered VoiceOverPINs performed better with PassChords than participants who entered PassChords first. This resulted in a significant effect of *Order* ($F_{1,13} = 12.8, p < 0.01$) and a significant interaction of *Method* by *Order* ($F_{1,13} = 10.0, p < 0.01$). As Figure 4 shows, however, the difference between method entry times was incontrovertible, in spite of the effect of order.

Failure rate. There was no speed-accuracy trade-off, as the failure rate was slightly lower for PassChords than for VoiceOverPIN. Participants failed to authenticate 16.3% of the time with PassChords ($SD = 14.5\%$) and 20.2% of the time with VoiceOverPIN ($SD = 17.3\%$). This differences were not significant, however ($F_{1,13} = 1.49, n.s.$).

Recall. Twelve of the 16 participants (75%) remembered their PassChord two days after they were asked to memorize it. Most participants tapped the password several times to memorize its "feel," and associated the fingers in each tap with numbers to memorized their pattern.

Password strength. We assess password strength by observing common patterns in the 32 user-generated PassChords. Our prior discussion of entropy assumed a uniform distribution of possible inputs. This is not the case, however, for user-generated passwords. Prior work shows that the most common digit in alphanumeric passwords is 1, and the most common letters are *a*, *e*, *o*, and *r* [7]. Such patterns reduce the difficulty of guessing or brute-force attacks, so they are important to identify and avoid [8].

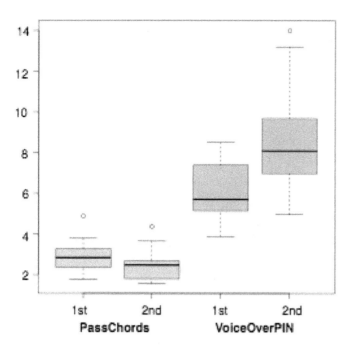

Figure 4: Boxplots of password entry times (in seconds) for the first and second half of the study and for each method. Although there is an asymmetric skill transfer, PassChords were irrefutably faster than VoiceOverPINs.

Figure 3 shows the frequency of each tap pattern in the user-generated PassChords. A striking trend was the frequent use of the index finger, which was present in 66.5% of taps. The pinky finger was used least, in only 14.6% of taps (see Table 5.4.2). Users tended to create passwords with repeating finger combinations and individual taps were often made with adjacent fingers. The most common PassChord length was three taps, although this may be attributed to the length of the initial, prescribed PassChord that served as an example.

Finger	Frequency
Index	66.5%
Middle	51.7%
Ring	36.6%
Pinky	14.6%

Table 1: Frequencies of finger use in PassChord taps. There was a strong preference for using the index finger, which is often used for touch screen input.

5.5 Discussion

We have shown through the design and evaluation of PassChords that our design principles were satisfied. In terms of usability, PassChords are nearly 75% faster to enter than accessible PINs, with comparable authentication failure rates. While merely preliminary, our study of PassChord recall demonstrated that there were no unexpected obstacles with PassChord memorization.

The security of PassChords was considered in their design and evaluation. Unlike accessible PINs, PassChords pro-duce no audio feedback, so they are more resistant to aural eavesdropping. PassChords also display no visual feedback, making visual eavesdropping more challenging. It would be interesting in future work to assess the threat of "shoulder-surfing" attacks that occur when an adversary eavesdrops by looking over a user's shoulder and observing her finger motions.

The data collected in our study, which included 112 Pass-Chord taps and 128 PIN digits, yields preliminary estimates of the security strength in terms of first-order entropy using Equation (1). The first-order entropy of 4-tap PassChords was $H \approx 12.6$, comparable to the first-order entropy of 4-digit PINs of $H \approx 12.7$. Our sample size was too small to produce these estimates with high confidence, but they give a rough idea for the security strength of both methods.

The security strength of PassChords can be improved by ensuring that the distribution of taps is as close to a uniform distribution as possible and using as many taps as possible. This leads us to several guidelines to help users create more secure PassChords:
1. Use each finger at least once in your PassChord.

2. Use taps of one, two, and three fingers.

3. Use four or more taps in your PassChord.

Since knowledge-based passwords are common authentication mechanisms, we believe PassChords will impact the security of mobile devices for blind people. They are an important first step at addressing security challenges for blind mobile device users, as discussed in our threat model. Since entering passwords on small touch keyboards is challenging for sighted users as well, we believe PassChords would benefit people with all visual abilities.

6. FUTURE WORK

There is much potential for future work in the area of security for people with disabilities. It would be interesting to explore security risks for people with other disabilities, such as deaf people or those with motor impairments. Users with low-vision may experience security and privacy threats related to magnification that vary greatly from those for people with little to no functional vision, which we have focused on in this work.

We plan to deploy PassChords and study user password behavior in the field. It would be interesting to see how performance improved with practice, and analyze the guessing entropy with a larger data set of user-generated passwords. We are interested to determine how robust PassChords are to "shoulder-surfing" attacks.

Finally, we plan to address other security risks discussed in this paper. The PassChords technique aims to prevent unauthorized user access and password eavesdropping, but open questions remain regarding the prevention of aural and visual eavesdropping in general.

7. CONCLUSION

We have presented (1) an investigation of security issues related to blind mobile device users and (2) the new Pass-Chords authentication technique that addresses the threat of unauthorized user access. The PassChords technique is unique because it provides no audio or visual feedback, making it robust to eavesdropping attacks yet fully accessible to blind people. We have shown through an evaluation with 16 blind people that PassChords were significantly faster to enter than accessible touch screen PINs. We believe Pass-Chords will be useful for both blind and sighted people, and hope that this work will shed light on security issues for people with various disabilities.

8. ACKNOWLEDGMENTS

The authors thank Alan Borning and Tadayoshi Kohno. This work was supported in part by the National Science Foundation under grant CNS 0905384 and grant IIS-0952786, and by the US Department of Education under grant H327A100014.

9. REFERENCES

[1] N. Asokan and C. Kuo. Usable mobile security. In *ICDCIT*, pages 1–6, 2012.

[2] D. Asonov and R. Agrawal. Keyboard acoustic emanations. In *IEEE Symposium on Security and Privacy*, pages 3–11, 2004.

[3] S. Azenkot, J. O. Wobbrock, S. Prasain, and R. E. Ladner. Input finger detection for nonvisual touch screen text entry in perkinput. In *Proc. GI'12*, New York, NY, USA, 2012. ACM.

[4] N. Ben-Asher, N. Kirschnick, H. Sieger, J. Meyer, A. Ben-Oved, and S. Möller. On the need for different security methods on mobile phones. In *Proc. MobileHCI'11*, pages 465–473, New York, NY, USA, 2011. ACM.

[5] Y. Berger, A. Wool, and A. Yeredor. Dictionary attacks using keyboard acoustic emanations. In *Proc. CCS'06*, pages 245–254, New York, NY, USA, 2006. ACM.

[6] J. P. Bigham and A. C. Cavender. Evaluating existing audio captchas and an interface optimized for non-visual use. In *Proc. CHI'09*, pages 1829–1838, New York, NY, USA, 2009. ACM.

[7] M. Burnett. *Perfect passwords*. Syngress Publishing, Rockland, Massachusetts, 2006.

[8] W. E. Burr, D. F. Dodson, W. T. Polk, and D. L. Evans. Electronic authentication guideline. In *NIST Special Publication*, 2004.

[9] N. Clarke and S. Furnell. Authentication of users on mobile telephones: A survey of attitudes and practices. *Computers Security*, 24(7):519–527, 2005.

[10] R. Dhamija and A. Perrig. Deja vu: A user study using images for authentication. In *Proc. USENIX Security Symposium*, pages 45–58, Berkeley, CA, USA, 2000. USENIX Association.

[11] D. Foo Kune and Y. Kim. Timing attacks on pin input devices. In *Proc. CCS'10*, pages 678–680, New York, NY, USA, 2010. ACM.

[12] J. Holman, J. Lazar, J. H. Feng, and J. D'Arcy. Developing usable captchas for blind users. In *Proc. ASSETS'07*, pages 245–246, New York, NY, USA, 2007. ACM.

[13] M. Jakobsson. Why mobile security is not like traditional security, 2011. http://www.markus-jakobsson.com/wp-content/uploads/fc11jakobsson.pdf.

[14] M. Jakobsson, E. Shi, P. Golle, and R. Chow. Implicit authentication for mobile devices. In *Proc. HotSec'09*, pages 9–9, Berkeley, CA, USA, 2009. USENIX Association.

[15] W. Jansen, K. Scarfone, C. M. Gutierrez, D. Patrick, D. Gallagher, and D. Director. Guidelines on cell phone and pda security recommendations of the national, 2008.

[16] I. Jermyn, A. Mayer, F. Monrose, M. K. Reiter, and A. D. Rubin. The design and analysis of graphical passwords. In *Proc SSYM'99*, pages 1–1, Berkeley, CA, USA, 1999. USENIX Association.

[17] S. K. Kane, C. Jayant, J. O. Wobbrock, and R. E. Ladner. Freedom to roam: a study of mobile device adoption and accessibility for people with visual and motor disabilities. In *Proc. ASSETS'09*, pages 115–122, New York, NY, USA, 2009. ACM.

[18] V. Kostakos. Human-in-the-loop: rethinking security in mobile and pervasive systems. In *CHI EA '08*, pages 3075–3080, New York, NY, USA, 2008. ACM.

[19] R. Kuber and S. Sharma. Toward tactile authentication for blind users. In *Proc. ASSETS'10*, pages 289–290, New York, NY, USA, 2010. ACM.

[20] F. X. Lin, D. Ashbrook, and S. White. Rhythmlink: securely pairing i/o-constrained devices by tapping. In *Proc. UIST'11*, pages 263–272, New York, NY, USA, 2011. ACM.

[21] P. C. v. Oorschot and J. Thorpe. On predictive models and user-drawn graphical passwords. *ACM Trans. Inf. Syst. Secur.*, 10(4):5:1–5:33, Jan. 2008.

[22] K. Poulsen. Mitnick to lawmakers: People, phones and weakest links, 2009. http://www.politechbot.com/p-00969.html.

[23] B. Schneier. The secret question is: why do IT systems use insecure passwords? *The Guardian*, 2009. http://www.guardian.co.uk/technology/2009/feb/19/insecure-passwords-conflickerb-worm.

[24] S. Shirali-Shahreza and M. H. Shirali-Shahreza. Accessibility of captcha methods. In *Proc. AISec'11*, pages 109–110, New York, NY, USA, 2011. ACM.

[25] X. Suo, Y. Zhu, and G. Owen. Graphical passwords: a survey. In *Computer Security Applications Conference, 21st Annual*, page 472, dec. 2005.

[26] S. Wiedenbeck, J. Waters, J. Birget, A. Brodskiy, and N. Memon. Passpoints: Design and longitudinal evaluation of a graphical password system. In *Proc. USENIX Security Symposium*, pages 102–127, Berkeley, CA, USA, 2005. USENIX Association.

[27] J. O. Wobbrock. Tapsongs: tapping rhythm-based passwords on a single binary sensor. In *Proc. UIST'09*, pages 93–96, New York, NY, USA, 2009. ACM.

[28] J. O. Wobbrock, L. Findlater, D. Gergle, and J. J. Higgins. The aligned rank transform for nonparametric factorial analyses using only anova procedures. In *Proc. CHI'11*, pages 143–146, New York, NY, USA, 2011. ACM.

[29] Q. Xiao. Security issues in biometric authentication. In *Information Assurance Workshop, 2005. IAW '05. Proceedings from the Sixth Annual IEEE SMC*, pages 8–13, june 2005.

"So That's What You See!" Building Understanding with Personalized Simulations of Colour Vision Deficiency

David R. Flatla and Carl Gutwin

Department of Computer Science, University of Saskatchewan

110 Science Place, Saskatoon, Canada, S7N 5C9

david.flatla@usask.ca, gutwin@cs.usask.ca

Figure 1. Difference between generic simulation of CVD and personalized simulation. Left: original image; middle: personalized simulation for one of our study participants; right: generic dichromatic deuteranopic simulation (www.vischeck.com).

ABSTRACT

Colour vision deficiencies (CVD) affect the everyday lives of a large number of people, but it is difficult for others – even friends and family members – to understand the experience of having CVD. Simulation tools can help provide this experience; however, current simulations are based on general models that have several limitations, and therefore cannot accurately reflect the perceptual capabilities of most individuals with reduced colour vision. To address this problem, we have developed a new simulation approach that is based on a specific empirical model of the actual colour perception abilities of a person with CVD. The resulting simulation is therefore a more exact representation of what a particular person with CVD actually sees. We tested the new approach in two ways. First, we compared its accuracy with that of the existing models, and found that the personalized simulations were significantly more accurate than the old method. Second, we asked pairs of participants (one with CVD, and one close friend or family member without CVD) to discuss images of everyday scenes that had been simulated with the CVD person's particular model. We found that the personalized simulations provided new insights into the details of the CVD person's experience. The personalized-simulation approach shows great promise for improving understanding of CVD (and potentially other conditions) for people with ordinary perceptual abilities.

Categories and Subject Descriptors: K.4.2 [**Social Issues**]: Assistive technologies

Keywords: Colour vision deficiency, colour vision simulation

1. INTRODUCTION

Colour vision deficiencies (CVD), also called 'colour blindness,' are conditions in which a person perceives fewer colours than other people. CVD can arise from genetic factors (e.g., eight

percent of men have reduced sensitivity to the red-green colour axis), or can be acquired through factors such as age (e.g., cataracts or yellowing of the lens), exposure to chemicals (e.g., solvents such as styrene), or brain injury (e.g., stroke or trauma).

Colour vision deficiencies cause many different problems, ranging from minor annoyances (e.g., being unable to differentiate between visited and unvisited website links) to difficulties that compromise safety (e.g., when alert messages do not stand out from the background). Although CVD has many implications for professional activities, our focus in this paper is on the profound effects that it has on everyday life. Some of these effects are well known, such as the stereotype of a man with red-green CVD who can't match the colour of his socks, but there are many other commonplace activities where reduced colour perception dramatically changes experience and ability. For example, a person with CVD may have difficulty buying or picking fruit (since we use colour to judge ripeness), cooking meat (since the difference between 'rare' and 'well done' is primarily a colour difference), communicating with others about things in the world ("Quick – hand me the green one!"), and sharing the aesthetic experience of rainbows, flowers, fireworks, or paintings.

These problems are not life-threatening, and people with CVD develop coping strategies to successfully get around most of the problems. However, as with many other disabilities and impairments (e.g. low visual acuity, hearing or memory loss, reduced mobility, or chronic medical conditions), there is a non-trivial degree of frustration in dealing with a world that is organized for the ergonomist's '95th percentile'.

Part of this frustration arises from the difficulty that people with CVD have in communicating their perceptual experience to family, friends, and co-workers. Most CVDs are much more complex than the stereotypical 'inability to tell red from green,' and it is difficult for those with ordinary colour vision to imagine what life is like for the person with CVD.

One technique that can help to improve this understanding is simulation – that is, altering images using a model of CVD in order to show a person with ordinary colour vision what the image looks like to someone with a colour vision deficiency. Simulation has been successfully used in other domains, such as aphasia [9], to help convey the experience of a condition to other people.

Digital methods for simulations of CVD also exist (and have existed for many years, e.g., [16][12][3]), but existing techniques suffer from three main shortcomings when used as tools for conveying understanding of a person's colour experience.

First, publically-available systems (e.g., Vischeck [5]) only simulate dichromatic CVD (a severe form where one type of retinal cone cell is missing), but a majority of cases of genetically-caused CVD (75%) involve anomalous trichromacy – a less severe form of the condition in which all three photoreceptors are retained, but one has a shifted colour sensitivity. Dichromatic simulations are therefore too extreme for most cases of CVD. Simulations of anomalous trichromacy do exist, but require information about how much the affected cone is shifted – a value that is not available from existing colour vision tests. Second, current systems need to know the specific type of CVD the user has, but individuals rarely know the type of their condition. Third, existing methods only simulate one type of CVD at a time, but there are cases (especially in older adults) where an individual has a combination of genetic and acquired colour vision deficiencies.

These limitations mean that although current simulations can provide a rough indication of the kinds of problems faced by people with CVD, the specific experience of a particular individual is still difficult to understand. The specificity of the simulation is actually very important, since it is the specific experience of a particular individual that the person without CVD wishes to understand. Approximations can demonstrate general problems, but can never achieve the goal of showing exactly how the world looks to a spouse, a child, a parent, or a close friend.

To address this problem, we have developed a CVD-simulation method that can provide a much more accurate and specific view of how a particular individual sees colour. Instead of using a standard model of CVD as the basis for the simulation, our method builds an individualized model of a person's colour perception from empirical data [8][7]; this model exactly captures the type and severity of the person's colour vision deficiency, including conditions such as anomalous trichromacy and multiple simultaneous deficiencies. Using the exact type and severity of CVD for an individual, we then alter the colours of images to show exactly what a particular person with CVD can see.

We tested our new simulation method in two ways. First, we quantitatively evaluated the approach's accuracy by comparing the existing dichromatic model of CVD to our personalized model. Using each model, we performed CVD simulation of the calibration procedure used in [7] and had people without CVD run the calibration. This essentially induced CVD in people with ordinary colour vision and allowed us to measure their resulting colour differentiation abilities. Our tests showed that the personalized simulation measurements were significantly closer to CVD participants' colour differentiation ability measurements than the existing dichromatic simulation measurements – calibration measurements were only two 'just-noticeable steps' away in a perceptually uniform colour space [11].

Second, we investigated our method's ability to help people share understanding of CVD conditions. We asked pairs of people (each pair having one CVD person and one non-CVD spouse, family member, or close friend) to view and discuss pictures of everyday scenes that had been simulated using the CVD participant's individualized model. We found that even for pairs that had known each other for years, the simulations provided the non-CVD participants with a variety of new insights into the other person's experience with colour.

Our work makes four main contributions: first, we propose the use of personalized simulations of CVD to increase understanding of CVD for people without CVD; second, we develop a personalized CVD simulation method that is based on empirical measurements of an individual's colour differentiation abilities; third, we show that personalized CVD simulations produce substantially more accurate representations of CVD colour perception than existing models of CVD; and fourth, we show that personalized simulations can help improve understanding of CVD for people without CVD. Personalized simulation works well in the CVD domain, and shows promise for helping to share the experiences of other types of extraordinary users as well.

2. BACKGROUND
Here we summarize different types of CVD, existing simulation systems, and the standard method for dichromatic simulation.

2.1 Types of CVD
CVD can be caused by a number of internal and external factors. Internal factors are intrinsic to the user (e.g., genetic causes or acquired conditions). External factors are environmental or situational issues outside the user (e.g., lighting levels, or wearing tinted glasses). Due to the transient nature of externally-induced CVDs, we will only focus on internal causes of CVD here.

Genetic CVD. The human X chromosome contains the genetic information that determines the presence and sensitivity of the long and medium wavelength sensitive cones in the retina [1]. Due to variations in this chromosome, some individuals do not have one of these cone types (*dichromacy* - more specifically, *protanopia* for missing long-wavelength cones and *deuteranopia* for missing medium-wavelength cones), or have a variant form of one of these cone types that exhibits a shifted peak wavelength sensitivity (*anomalous trichromacy* – *protanomalous* for long-wavelength, and *deuteranomalous* for medium-wavelength) [2][25]. Men have only a single X chromosome, so their rate of genetic CVD is much higher (8% in Caucasians) than in women (~0.5%), who have two X chromosomes [4]. Short-wavelength cone genetic CVD (*tritanopia* and *tritanomalous*) is much rarer because this cone type is encoded on a non-sex-linked chromosome. Other rare types of genetic CVD occur in individuals who are missing two cones (*cone monochromacy*) or three cones (*rod monochromacy*) [1].

Acquired CVD involves damage to the vision system from events such as accident, disease, or exposure to harmful chemicals. These often result in colour perception that is similar to tritanomaly and tritanopia, because the number of short-wavelength cones is relatively small compared to the number of long and medium sensitive cones, and these are therefore more susceptible to retinal damage [13]. Exposure to ultraviolet light has been linked to yellowing of the lens with age as well as to the development of cataracts. Both conditions result in yellow-tinged colour vision; in one study almost 64% of British participants over the age of 65 showed some signs of this yellowing [6]. Many other acquired CVDs (such as those caused by retinopathy) exist, and can even be caused by depression or by antidepressants or Viagra [27].

All types of CVD cause similar problems for our purposes – they make it difficult for people to differentiate among colours that can be distinguished by most other people. This leads to difficulties in any situation that requires colour differentiation to accomplish some task, such as buying fruit, cooking meat, identifying children's toys, getting dressed, navigating, enjoying the visual arts, and decorating [4][20][21].

2.2 Types of CVD Simulations

The earliest digital simulation of CVD, by Meyer and Greenburg in 1988 [16], describes an approach for translating colours within a colour space in order to model dichromatic colour vision. This work was extended by colour science researchers to provide an algorithm for simulating dichromacy [3][23][24]. These simulations show non-CVD individuals what images look like for people with any of the three types of dichromatic vision (protanopia, deuteranopia, or tritanopia).

More recently, simulations of anomalous trichromacy have been developed [12][14]. These simulations require both the type of anomalous trichromacy and additional information about the severity of the condition. This is typically expressed in the amount of peak sensitivity shift of the anomalous cone (expressed in nanometres). However, this type of information is not readily available from existing colour-vision tests.

2.3 Dichromatic CVD Simulation Details

To simulate the appearance of an image for someone with CVD, the colour of each pixel in the image is replaced by the colour perceived by the person with CVD. As people with CVD perceive fewer colours than people without CVD, this process of mapping original colours to replacement colours is typically compressive – different original colours will map to the same replacement colours, e.g., people with protanopia perceive particular shades of pink, grey, and turquoise all as a single grey. To identify a replacement colour, both the set of colours that are perceived identically, and the colour this set maps to need to be identified.

To find the set of colours that are perceived identically for people with dichromacy, CVD color *confusion lines* are utilized. In the 1976 CIE L*u*v* perceptually-uniform colour space [26], every colour has a sphere around it that defines a discrimination boundary for that colour for people without CVD – colours inside the sphere are not differentiable from the original colour and colours outside the sphere are differentiable [22]. When measuring the discrimination spheres for people with dichromacy, it was found that the sphere had been elongated in one dimension to form an ellipsoid [15] that exceeds the L*u*v* gamut, and the direction of elongation was unique to the type of dichromacy. The line defined by the elongation (the major axis of the ellipsoid) is a color confusion line – the line or set of colours that are perceived identically by someone with dichromacy [22]. Confusion lines for each type of dichromacy are shown in Figure 2.

Confusion lines allow the identification of original image colours that are indistinguishable for someone with dichromacy, but what colour does someone with dichromacy actually perceive? This is akin to knowing that a man with inherited CVD confuses red and green, but not knowing what he actually sees. To answer this question, a special set of colours that are perceived identically by people with and without dichromacy has been identified using measurements from people with unilateral dichromacy – a condition in which a person has dichromacy in one eye but ordinary colour vision in the other eye. People with unilateral dichromacy have identified that spectral colours of 475nm (blue) and 575nm (yellow) are identically perceived by people without CVD and those with protanopia and deuteranopia. People with tritanopia perceive spectral colours of 485 nm (blue-green) and 660nm (red) the same as people without CVD [3]. Each pair of identically-perceived spectral colours define two half-planes in L*u*v* colour space. Each half-plane is defined by the spectral colour and the achromatic axis (grey scale colours from black to white) [16][3]. These half-planes are shown in Figure 3

(protanopic and deuteranopic on the left, tritanopic on the right), and are represented by the white line in each image in Figure 2.

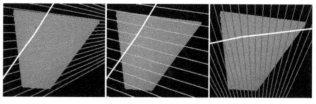

Figure 2. Confusion lines for protanopia (left), deuteranopia (middle), and tritanopia (right). White lines represent colours perceived identically by people with and without CVD.

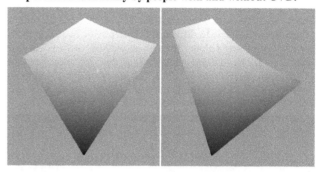

Figure 3. Colours perceived identically by people with dichromacy and people with normal colour vision – protanopia and deuteranopia (left) and tritanopia (right).

To simulate how an image appears to someone with dichromacy, the colour of each pixel in an image is converted into L*u*v* colour space, shifted along its respective colour confusion line to the half-plane for the dichromacy being simulated, and then converted back to RGB. The resulting RGB colour is used to paint the corresponding output pixel in the simulation image.

3. PERSONALIZED CVD SIMULATION

Three shortcomings of existing dichromatic simulations were identified above:

1. Dichromatic simulations are too extreme for most types of CVD.

2. People with CVD usually do not know the type and severity of their CVD.

3. People can have multiple CVDs.

To address these three shortcomings, our method utilizes empirical measurements of each user's colour differentiation abilities to determine the types and severities of the individual's CVDs. Once the types and severities are known, a two-stage reduced-severity dichromatic simulation is employed to simulate the individual's colour vision. By measuring the types and severities of CVDs, the second shortcoming is addressed; a reduced-severity simulation helps address the first shortcoming; a two-stage simulation allows red-green and blue-yellow discrimination difficulties to be incorporated into the simulation.

We also identified that the dichromatic simulation technique described above assumes that everyone without CVD has identical colour perception abilities, but recent research has identified variations in colour perception abilities among the non-CVD population [18]. To address this, we consider both the CVD and non-CVD individual during simulation. To accomplish this, our method measures the colour vision abilities of the person with CVD and the colour vision abilities of the non-CVD person who will be viewing the simulation. To gather this information, we use the ICD calibration procedure [7][1].

The calibration procedure presents a gapped circle of a particular colour on a grey background (Figure 4). If the user can see the colour, they respond by indicating the orientation of the gap in the circle. If they cannot see the circle, they press the space bar. The sequence of colours is carefully chosen from the three confusion lines that intersect the neutral (grey) point in the isoluminant plane (L*=50.0) shown in Figure 2. Three confusion lines intersecting the neutral grey point give six lines of colours to present to the user, one in each direction out from the neutral grey. By presenting colours that progressively move away from the neutral point (similarly to the colour vision test presented in [17]), we are able to identify the *discrimination limit* for each line – the point at which the user is able to differentiate between the neutral grey and the confusion line colour. Because individuals with CVD have difficulty differentiating colours along the confusion line that aligns with their type of CVD, the discrimination points for people with CVD are generally farther away from the neutral grey point than the discrimination points for people without CVD.

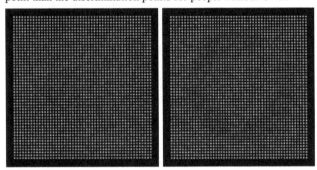

Figure 4. Calibration task presented to user. User indicates orientation of circle gap to indicate they can see the colour.

The six discrimination limits for the CVD and non-CVD individuals are then used to generate a best-fit ellipse roughly centered on the neutral grey point (Figure 5). As we use a perceptually uniform colour space (CIE L*u*v*) for this calibration task, the best-fit ellipse for someone without CVD is roughly circular. For individuals with CVD, the best-fit ellipse is stretched along the confusion line for their type of CVD. This best-fit ellipse is called a discrimination ellipse [19][26], and is a cross-section of the discrimination ellipsoids described above.

To perform a simulation, the discrimination ellipses are used to inform a 'partial' dichromatic simulation – meaning that instead of shifting colours all the way along a confusion line to its corresponding point on the dichromatic half-plane (as in dichromatic simulation), we only shift colours a fixed distance toward these half-planes along the confusion line. This results in a partial dichromatic simulation, which aligns well with the colour vision experience of anomalous trichromacy; a small shift represents a minor degree of anomalous trichromacy, and a larger shift represents severe anomalous trichromacy.

To perform the partial dichromatic simulation, we must determine the amount to shift along each confusion line. This information is derived from comparing the two discrimination ellipses described above. First, the angle of the major axis of the discrimination ellipse for the individual with CVD is compared to the angle of

[1] Calibration and modeling mechanisms are unchanged from previous research; the novel contribution here is in the simulation process, which is new work that has not been discussed in any earlier publication.

the confusion lines for the neutral grey point. The confusion line angle that is closest to the major-axis angle is chosen as the 'primary' CVD. The confusion line angle that is closest to the minor-axis angle is then chosen as the 'secondary' CVD. Due to the nearly parallel nature of protan and deutan confusion lines, the primary and secondary CVD can never be protan and deutan (or vice versa), resulting in the configurations shown in Table 1.

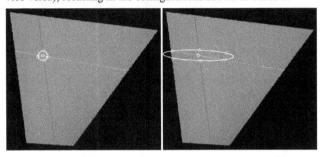

Figure 5. Typical discrimination ellipses for people without CVD (left) and people with red-green CVD (right).

Table 1. Possible configurations of primary and secondary CVDs. Protan and deutan never co-occur.

Primary	protan	deutan	tritan	tritan
Secondary	tritan	tritan	protan	deutan

Once the primary and secondary CVDs are identified, the amount of shift along each confusion line is determined. Due to the impossibility of protan and deutan co-occurring, we simplify this step to identifying a 'red-green' shift amount (either protan or deutan), and a 'blue-yellow' shift amount (tritan). To find the primary CVD shift amount, the absolute difference between the major axis half-length and the average of the major and minor axes' half-lengths for the non-CVD ellipse is calculated. Similarly, the secondary CVD shift amount is the absolute difference between the CVD minor-axis half-length and the same non-CVD average. The non-CVD average axis half-length is used because the discrimination ellipses for people with ordinary colour vision are generally circular, resulting in arbitrary major axis angles. To compare axis lengths, they must be rotationally aligned, so averaging the half-lengths represents the non-CVD discrimination ellipse as a circle, thereby making it rotationally invariant and simplifying the shift amount calculations.

For each pixel in an input image, the simulation colour for that pixel is determined using existing dichromatic simulation techniques for the primary CVD. The length of the L*u*v* colour space vector from the original colour to the dichromatic colour is found and compared to the primary CVD shift amount. If the primary shift amount is greater than the vector length, then the dichromatic simulation colour is used. If the primary shift amount is less than the vector length, however, the colour along this vector that is the 'primary shift' distance from the original colour is used. We call the colour that results from this primary CVD simulation step the 'primary replacement colour'.

To simulate the secondary CVD effects on colour vision, the secondary CVD dichromatic simulation colour for the primary replacement colour is found using existing dichromatic simulation techniques. The length of the L*u*v* vector from the primary replacement colour to this dichromatic colour is found and compared to the secondary CVD shift amount. If the secondary shift amount is greater than this vector length, then the pixel in the output simulation is painted the primary replacement colour. If the secondary shift amount is less than this vector length, then the colour that is 'secondary shift amount' distance along this vector from the primary replacement colour is used to paint the output simulation pixel.

4. EVALUATION

We assessed the personalized simulation approach in a user study with five pairs of participants, where each pair consisted of one person with CVD (4 males – 2 mild deutan, 1 medium deutan, 1 strong protan; 1 female – unclassified red-green) and one without (3 males, 2 females). Each participant performed the HRR colour vision plate test [10], then performed calibration tests to build a personalized model. The non-CVD participant then carried out another calibration, but this time the colours were altered using their partner's CVD simulation. The results from this calibration were used to evaluate the accuracy of the simulation. After calibration was finished, both participants engaged in a qualitative exploration of original and simulated versions of 16 images.

4.1 Simulation Accuracy

To see whether our personalized simulation more accurately simulates the CVD user's colour vision than the existing dichromatic simulation, we compared the discrimination limits generated by each simulation to the CVD participant's limits. We calculated the average absolute difference for each comparison. As shown in Figure 6, the personalized simulation had a significantly lower average absolute difference (paired, two-tailed t-test, p<.01). We illustrate this difference in Figure 7 by showing the discrimination ellipses for the three models: the CVD person's model, the personalized simulation with the non-CVD user, and dichromatic simulation with the non-CVD user.

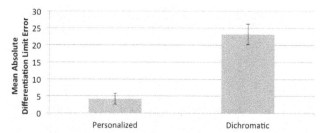

Figure 6. Mean absolute difference between simulated model (non-CVD user) and actual model (CVD participant).

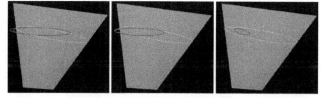

Figure 7. Original CVD discrimination ellipses (red) for three deutan participants, their non-CVD simulation discrimination ellipses (blue), dichromatic simulation ellipses (green).

4.2 Qualitative Evaluation

To evaluate whether personalized simulations of CVD aid the understanding of CVD for people with ordinary colour vision, we selected 16 images from the internet depicting situations that often pose difficulties for individuals with CVD (Figure 8). Specific difficulties are described below. Once the calibrations were completed, we simulated the appearance of each image with the CVD user's model, and presented the images (original and simulated side by side). The participants explored the sixteen image-pairs together, discussing differences and similarities. In some cases, the experimenter would pose questions about some aspect of the image in order to follow up on comments made by

the participants. This part of the study was videotaped for later analysis. The study was complete when participants were finished exploring the sixteen image pairs.

To present the qualitative results from the exploration, we grouped the images into four categories (Outdoors, Food, Safety, Play), and discuss each category below. Images and categories were based on personal experience with CVD (the first author has medium-severity protanopic CVD), as well as surveys reported in previous literature [4][21].

Figure 8. Images used in the exploration phase of the study.

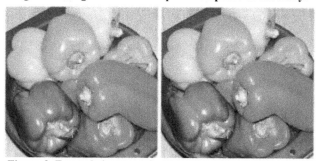

Figure 9. Example image and personalized simulation (right).

4.2.1 Outdoors

The colour differences contained within natural scenes often present a challenge to individuals with CVD. This challenge can range from purely aesthetic differences (e.g., the colours of a rainbow), to more practical implications (e.g., picking apples).

Participants responded strongly to the image of outdoor scenes. When examining the apple-tree image, one CVD participant remarked "Those are apples on the ground?! I thought they were just rocks"; most CVD participants commented on the difficulty of picking apples in real life. Participants without CVD noticed that the foliage appeared much less vibrant in the CVD simulation, and also commented on the severe reduction in contrast between the red apples and green leaves. One non-CVD person commented "Those look the same to you, but they are substantially different to me."

The rainbow and Christmas tree images also provided dramatic revelations about CVD colour perception. The simulation of the rainbow was often reduced to a band of blue and a band of yellow; when a non-CVD person remarked on this, the CVD participant exclaimed "That's how they have always looked to me!" Similarly, non-CVD participants regularly remarked on how the Christmas tree (and foliage in general) looked under-watered and unhealthy in the CVD-simulated images. One non-CVD participant said to her partner "Now I understand why you think evergreen trees are ugly!" and another remarked "All foliage is rotten in your world?!"

4.2.2 Food

Colour is an important indicator for many types of food: the ripeness of fruit (e.g., bananas become more yellow as they ripen), how cooked meat is (e.g., rare versus medium steak), and whether something is spoiled or about to spoil (e.g., tomatoes going bad).

When presented with this set of images, CVD participants immediately recalled their own difficulties with colour-dependent foods, and several remarked that the two images looked the same. This prompted several responses from the non-CVD participants. The 'greenness' of unripe bananas often disappeared in the simulated image, prompting one non-CVD participant to observe "I wouldn't eat these (pointing at two bananas), but in this one (pointing to the simulation), they are the same!" When discussing the tomatoes, one non-CVD participant remarked "It's a wonder you can find any tomatoes at all – they're all green!" Difficulties with tomato colour were also discussed by a CVD participant who said that one tomato was a "strange colour," to which his non-CVD partner replied, "No, it's an almost-ripe tomato." Another non-CVD participant remarked that some of the simulated image tomatoes looked either "not yet ripe – or spoiling." Regarding the peppers, several non-CVD participants remarked on the "strange" colour of the orange peppers in the simulated image, with one commenting that "[they] now look completely unappetizing!"

The most powerful responses in this set of images were to the steak image. Many non-CVD participant responses expressed shock and disbelief that their CVD partner could not see the pink in the meat or the blood in the juices. This elicited responses such as "I'm not letting you barbecue anymore!" and "No wonder you don't ever want to cook meat!"

4.2.3 Safety

In addition to food characteristics, colour helps us when detecting illness (e.g., rashes), as well when we navigate the world around us (e.g., traffic signs). Trouble differentiating colours in these circumstances can have clear implications for personal safety.

Participants who viewed these images responded differently to the traffic images (stop sign and traffic light) than to the skin images (rash and sunburn). Traffic images elicited anecdotal evidence of how individuals with CVD successfully navigate the driving world by relying on redundant encodings (e.g., the position of traffic lights and the shape of stop signs) or other drivers (e.g., watching other cars or asking for help from a passenger), and by driving more defensively. The traffic images elicited several comments from non-CVD participants (e.g., "That's why you call the green light white!"), even though none of the non-CVD participants remarked on feeling unsafe when driving with their CVD partners. This suggests that the discussion around the traffic images helped non-CVD participants gain understanding of the coping strategies used by people with CVD.

When examining the rash and sunburn image, individuals with CVD would closely examine the original image, stating that they could see something discoloured on the skin, but were unsure of what it was. One CVD participant remarked that neither image (rash or sunburn) would "indicate any cause for concern." This prompted recollections from non-CVD participants regarding their CVD partner getting severe sunburns in the past ("...and now I know why!" one said). Similarly, a non-CVD participant said that the sunburned girl "just looks embarrassed to you" (referring to his CVD friend).

4.2.4 Play

One participant with CVD commented that his mother figured out he had CVD when he "kept bringing home elephants coloured pink." This highlights the difficulty people with CVD have with children's activities and toys, because of their reliance on colour. This series of images helped non-CVD participants get a clearer understanding of their CVD partner's difficulties. The crayon image was examined closely by all participants. Many commented on the overall muted state of the crayons in the CVD simulation, but noticed that yellows and blues were often retained (an important realization, as people with protan and deutan CVD largely retain their ability to distinguish yellows and blues). Many non-CVD participants also commented on how the clear colour differences in the original image were reduced to subtle variations in brightness in the simulated image; one CVD participant agreed, stating "I have to worry about specific shades and tones, because that's all that is different." The coloured candy image had non-CVD participants playing the 'can I sort them?' game with their CVD partners. These discussions again brought up comments about large colour differences being reduced to subtle variations in similar shades, and one non-CVD participant commented on her partner's ability to pick out tiny variations in brightness or intensity to identify different colours. She further commented that she would likely miss these subtleties because to her the colours are "just different." When presented with the image of the blocks, one non-CVD participant exclaimed "Now I understand why you hate yellow," to which her partner replied "It's too bright!"

4.2.5 Other observations and survey responses

Most participants greatly enjoyed the exploration sessions, and discussed a wide range of colour-related topics. We observed that most of the CVD participants remarked at least once on the similarity of the original and simulated images, providing additional evidence of the personalized simulations' accuracy. In addition, the CVD users seemed to find value in the simulations, even though they were designed primarily for the non-CVD users; in several cases CVD participants learned new things about how their partner saw the world, information that could help future communication with people who have ordinary colour vision.

Finally, both before and after the exploration session, we asked non-CVD participants to complete a short questionnaire asking how well they felt they understood the CVD participant's condition. The responses after the session were almost universally higher (mean of 0.9 higher on a seven-point scale), indicating that the personalized simulations did help provide new understanding of the everyday experience of CVD. (We note that this increase may be partially due to the effects of simulation more generally, since some pairs may not have used other simulation tools).

5. DISCUSSION

Our study showed three main findings:
- Personalized colour-perception models (that were originally designed for recolouring tools) can be used as the basis for simulations of a particular person's CVD;
- These personalized simulations accurately simulate a person's colour vision deficiency for another (non-CVD) person, and are substantially more accurate than the standard dichromatic model;
- Using the personalized simulation to explore images of everyday scenes led to new insights and understanding for CVD/non-CVD pairs of participants;

In the next sections we provide explanations for these results, and then discuss three main issues that arise from our experience with personalized simulations: improvements to the current technique, further applications of the approach within the CVD domain, and applications to other domains of assistive technology.

5.1 Explanations of Study Results

We measured accuracy by comparing each CVD users' colour-perception model with the simulation-induced model for their partner. As shown above (Figure 7), the discrimination ellipses for the two models were very similar for all pairs of participants – and much more similar than for the standard dichromatic model.

The reason for this improvement follows directly from the basic premise of this work – that an empirical model of an individual's actual colour perception provides a much better foundation for a simulation tool than a generic model of CVD. The standard dichromatic models do not work well for most people with CVD because the dichromatic discrimination ellipses are much larger than those corresponding to anomalous trichromacy (which is much more prevalent, but much harder to model [14]). As a result, the standard models produce incorrect simulations that do not accurately convey a particular person's CVD experience.

The success of the personalized simulations in the exploration part of the study is more difficult to assess, since we did not ask people to use the standard CVD simulations during the exploration phase. However, our observations highlight two points that argue for the value of our approach. First, the fact that long-time couples and friends found new insights in the exploration phase suggests that the personalized simulation provided information that they had not found through other means (including available tools such as Vischeck [5]). Second, it was clear from our observations that participants appreciated the specificity of the simulation, and the close match to the experience of the person with CVD. CVD participants made several remarks about how the two images (e.g., Figures 1 and 9) looked the same to them, and much of the discussion between the two people involved specific details of the simulation (e.g., small differences in the colour of a tomato). These detailed explorations would not have been possible with the generic dichromatic simulation, due to its inaccuracy for most types of CVD.

5.2 Improvements to the Current Technique

There are two main possibilities for improving our current technique: extension to monochromatism and handling variations in luminance perception.

As described above in Section 2.1, individuals who have zero or one cone types have monochromatic vision. Our simulation currently handles this case by setting very large R-G and B-Y shift amounts (essentially removing all red-green and blue-yellow contrasts). However, the dominant perceived hues of the secondary CVD (blue and yellow for protan and deutan; red and blue-green for tritan) remain in the simulated image, because the primary and secondary simulation steps occur independently (except that the second step takes input from the first). To address this, we can perform the secondary CVD simulation step within a constrained colour set – the set of colours that are perceptible to the user according to the primary CVD simulation. This would allow the secondary CVD simulation step to incorporate the effects of the primary CVD, thereby reducing or eliminating the dominant perceived hues of the secondary CVD in the simulation.

A second way to improve the technique is to incorporate simulation of perceived brightness for different types of CVD. For example, in cone monochromatism, colours that maximally stimulate the single cone type appear much brighter than for non-CVD individuals. To incorporate these further personal variations, additional calibration steps that measure perceived brightness could be added to the calibration procedure, and used to inform the L*u*v* coordinates of the original input colour.

5.3 Further Application to the CVD Domain

The simplicity of the personalized approach and its success in helping participants share the experience of CVD suggest that the method could be used more broadly; here we consider four directions for wider deployment.

- *Web-based deployment.* The modeling and simulation mechanisms used in the tool and study can be repackaged for a platform such as the WWW, and can be used in an unsupervised fashion (like existing tools, but with a modeling stage added to the process). In addition, a Web deployment can allow server-side performance optimizations (such as parallelization) for large or complex images.

- *A community of simulations.* A web-based approach would also provide an opportunity for people to share their models more widely. A broad set of models and associated simulations would be a valuable resource for visual designers – essentially as an extended version of existing tools such as Vischeck [5]. A community of models would allow designers to test a proposed design under simulations from several different CVD participants in order to ensure visibility and usability for a wider range of real-world users.

- *Images from people's real lives.* The images used in the study initiated considerable discussion for our participants, but there would likely be more opportunity for shared understanding if participants could produce simulations of images from their own daily lives; this would couple the specificity of the personalized approach with objects and scenes from people's local context. The main issue in simulating arbitrary images is the number of colours in the image (computation time is proportional to this number), but quantization or resizing can be used to reduce processing time (or to provide an initial simulation while a finer-grained version is produced).

- *Real-time mobile simulation.* An extension to simulating people's real-life images is the idea of moving the simulator to a mobile device such as a smartphone, and allowing CVD and non-CVD users to create simulations on demand in everyday use. A mobile version of the tool can be used to improve understanding, but also extends the approach to become an accommodation aid for a non-CVD person – that is, as they go through daily life, they can immediately answer the question "Will my friend with CVD be able to see that?"

5.4 Application to Other Assistive Domains

The overall approach of personalized models and simulation can also be applied more widely than just in the domain of CVD. First, the idea of simulation from modeling is itself a generalizable concept – the personalized models of CVD were not originally conceived as a tool for improving understanding, but rather as a tool for improving accessibility (e.g., [8][7]). As a result, models that capture perceptual or other capabilities can be used in many ways, and the example of personalized simulation shows that they can provide other benefits.

Second, the basic mechanisms for modeling and simulation described here can be applied to other areas of assistive technology. In general, the approach is applicable to any condition where people's perceptual capabilities can be empirically tested, and where those capabilities are based in underlying psychometric functions (so that they can be modeled accurately). Two areas where the approach could work well are hearing loss and low visual acuity. As with CVD, these conditions have many variants, and personalized models could be used both for new assistive technologies as well as for simulations that help to improve understanding of living with these conditions.

In addition, it may also be possible to extend the approach to some muscular conditions that affect motor control (e.g., Parkinsonian tremors). For example, it may be possible to empirically record and model the characteristic movements of these conditions for a particular person, and then simulate them for people without the condition (e.g., by adding movements to a mouse cursor in order to demonstrate the difficulties experienced in carrying out targeting actions). These kinds of applications would complement work already done to simulate conditions such as aphasia [9], but would add the value of providing an experience that is specific to a particular person.

6. CONCLUSIONS AND FUTURE WORK

Simulation tools can provide an understanding of what a person with CVD experiences, but current simulation methods do not provide accurate reflections of most CVD users' perceptual abilities. We developed a new simulation approach that uses a personalized model to provide a much more accurate simulation of a particular person's experience with CVD. The new approach was shown to be much more accurate than the standard model, and proved to be a valuable aid in helping non-CVD people to understand a CVD person's view of the everyday world. The personalized-simulation approach provides a valuable new tool for people with CVD and those who live and work with them.

In future work, we plan to explore all three directions outlined in the discussion above. First, we will continue to refine and improve upon the current tools by extending it to cone monochromatism and variations in perception of brightness. Second, we will deploy the model much more widely, by developing a public website where people can build personalized models and view simulations of images from their own lives, and by developing a mobile application that allows non-CVD people to dynamically check any scene to see how it appears to someone with CVD. Third, we plan to extend the personalized-simulation approach to other assistive-technology domains such as hearing loss and low visual acuity.

7. REFERENCES

[1] Birch, J. *Diagnosis of Defective Colour Vision*, 2nd ed. Oxford University Press, 2001.

[2] Birch, J. Extreme Anomalous Trichromatism. In Mollon, Pokorny, Knoblauch, eds., *Normal and Defective Colour Vision*, Oxford Press, 2003, 364-369.

[3] Brettel, H., Vienot, F., Mollon, J. Computerized Simulation of Color Appearance for Dichromats. *Journal of the Optical Society of America A.*, 14(10), 1997, 2647-2655.

[4] Cole, B. The Handicap of Abnormal Colour Vision. *Clinical and Experimental Optometry*, 87(4-5), 2004, 258-275.

[5] Dougherty, R., Wade, A. *Vischeck*. www.vischeck.com

[6] Davies, I.R.L, Laws, G., Corbett, G.G., Jerret, D.J Cross-Cultural Differences in Colour Vision: Acquired "Colour-Blindness" in Africa, *Personality and Individual Differences*, 25, 1988, 1153-1162.

[7] Flatla, D.R., Gutwin, C. Improving Calibration Time and Accuracy for Situation-Specific Models of Color Differentiation. *Proc. ASSETS 2011*, 195-202.

[8] Flatla, D.R., Gutwin, C. Individual Models of Color Differentiation to Improve Interpretability of Information Visualization. *Proc. CHI 2010*, 2563-2572.

[9] Hailpern, J., Danilevsky, M., Harris, A., Karahalios, K., Dell, G., Hengst, J. ACES: Promoting Empathy Towards Aphasia Through Language Distortion Emulation Software. *Proc. CHI 2011*, 609-618.

[10] Hardy, L.H., Rand, G., Rittler, M.C. H-R-R Polychromatic Plates. *J. Optical Society America*, 44, 1954, 509-521.

[11] Heer, J., Stone, M. Color Naming Models for Color Selection, Image Editing and Palette Design. *Proc. CHI 2012*, 1007-1016.

[12] Kondo, S. A Computer Simulation of Anomalous Color Vision. In Ohta, ed., *Color Vision Deficiencies IX*, Kugler & Ghedini, 1990, 145-159.

[13] Lomax, R., Ridgway, P. Meldrum, M. Does Occupational Exposure to Organic Solvents Affect Colour Discrimination? *Toxicological Reviews*, 23(2), 2004, 92-121.

[14] Machado, G., Oliveira, M., Fernandes, L. A Physiologically-based Model for Simulation of Color Vision Deficiency. *IEEE TVCG*, 15(6), 2009, 1291-1298.

[15] MacAdam, D. Visual Sensitivities to Color Differences in Daylight. *J. Optical Soc. of America*, 32(5), 1942, 247-274.

[16] Meyer, G., Greenburg, D. Color-Defective Vision and Computer Graphics Displays. *IEEE CGA*, 8(5), 1988, 28-40.

[17] Mollon, J.D., Astell, S., Reffin, J.P. A Minimalist Test of Colour Vision. In Drum, Moreland, Serra, eds., *Colour Vision Deficiencies X*, Kluwer Academic Publ., 1991, 59-67.

[18] Neitz J., Jacobs, G. Polymorphism of the Long-Wavelength Cone in Normal Human Colour Vision. *Nature*, 323, 1986, 623-625.

[19] Poirson, A.B., Wandell, B.A. The Ellipsoidal Representation of Spectral Sensitivity. *Vision Res.*, 30(4), 1990, 647-652.

[20] Spalding, J.A.B. Colour Blind Artists: Do the Vischeck Transformations Work? *Clinical and Experimental Optometry*, May, 2010, 188.

[21] Steward, J.M., Cole, B.L. What Do Color Vision Defectives Say About Everyday Tasks? *Optometry and Vision Science*, 66(5), 1989, 288-295.

[22] Stone, M. *A Field Guide to Digital Color*. A.K. Peters, 2003.

[23] Vienot, F., Brettel, H., Mollon, J. Digital Video Colourmaps for Checking the Legibility of Displays by Dichromats. *Color Research and Application*, 24(4), 1999, 243-252.

[24] Vienot, F., Brettel, H., Ott, L., Ben M'Barek, A., Mollon, J. *What Do Colour-Blind People See? Nature*, 376, 1995, 127-128.

[25] Wandell, B. *Foundations of Vision*. Sinauer, 1995.

[26] Wyszecki, G., Stiles, W. *Color Science: Concepts, Methods, Quantitative Data and Formulas*, 2nd ed. Wiley, 2000.

[27] Yates, J.T., Diamantopoulos, I., Daumann, F.J. Acquired (Transient and Permanent) Colour Vision Disorders. In *Operational Colour Vision in the Modern Aviation Environment*, NATO Technical Report 16, 2001, 43-51.

Evaluation of Dynamic Image Pre-Compensation for Computer Users with Severe Refractive Error

Jian Huang, Armando Barreto and Malek Adjouadi
Department of Electrical and Computer Engineering
Florida International University
Miami, FL 33174
jhuan004, barretoa, malek.adjouadi@fiu.edu

ABSTRACT

Visual distortion and blurring impede the efficient interaction between computers and their users. Visual problems can be caused by eye diseases, severe refractive errors or combinations of both. Several image enhancement methods based on contrast sensitivity have been used to help people with eye diseases (e.g., age-related macular degeneration and cataracts), whereas few methods have been designed for people with severe refractive errors. This paper describes a new pre-compensation method to counter the visual blurring caused by the severe refractive errors of a specific computer user. It preprocesses the pictorial information through dynamic pre-compensation in advance, aiming to present customized images on the basis of the ocular aberrations of the specific computer user. The new method improves the previous static pre-compensation method by updating the aberration data according to pupil size variations, in real-time. The real-time aberration data enable us to generate better suited pre-compensated images, as the pre-compensation model is updated dynamically. An empirical study was conducted to evaluate the efficiency of the new pre-compensation method, through an icon recognition test. From the results of statistical analysis, we found that participants achieved significantly higher accuracy levels in recognizing the icons with dynamic pre-compensation, than when viewing the original icons. The accuracy is also significantly boosted when the icons were processed with dynamic pre-compensation method, in comparison with the previous static pre-compensation method.

Categories and Subject Descriptors

H.1.2 [**User/Machine Systems**]: Human information processing; K.4.2 [**Social Issues**]: Assistive technologies for persons with disabilities

General Terms

Performance, Design, Experimentation, Human Factors

Keywords

Refractive error, image pre-compensation, image enhancement, ocular aberration, icon recognition.

1. INTRODUCTION

Refractive error (e.g., myopia, hyperopia and astigmatism) is a common cause of visual impairments in humans, leading to blurred vision in higher or lower degree depending on its severity. Myopia affects more than 30.5 million Americans age 40 or older and approximately 25% of American adults require some form of correction to see clearly beyond an arm's length [18]. Although refractive error seldom causes blindness, it does produce substantial visual loss that impacts the learning and working efficiency as well as other daily life activities [6, 27].

With respect to its impact on computer accessibility, the blurring caused by refractive error impedes the efficient interaction between the computer and its users. The refractive error can be corrected by spectacles, contact lenses or refractive surgery (e.g., LASIK) in most cases. However, some visual impairments can not be relieved through these methods. For those people with eye diseases (e.g., cataracts, glaucoma, macular degeneration), the benefit acquired from spectacles or contact lenses is limited. The prevalence of these diseases usually increases with aging, combined with refractive errors [14, 18, 20]. Besides, general spectacles and contact lenses are not able to correct high order aberrations, causing the correction of high order ocular aberrations to be one of the most active areas in the adaptive optics community [9, 11, 19, 24]. Therefore, it is still meaningful to seek new approaches to facilitate computer access for individuals with different visually impairments.

Although the studies in this area are still few to date, several image enhancement techniques have been developed and published. In the early studies, heuristic and empirical filters were used to improve the text reading ability of individuals with visual impairments [15, 16, 10]. Similar techniques were also used to facilitate face recognition on monitors for people with central visual field loss [22]. Other approaches include thresholding and edge highlighting of the images for display [17, 21]. Most of these studies primarily focus on the contrast enhancement of the pictorial information presented. Thus, the enhancements applied are based on the contrast

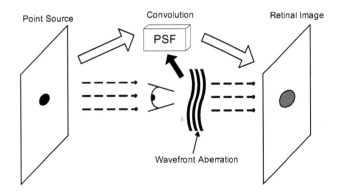

Figure 1: Image formation as a convolution process.

sensitivity function (CSF), which reflects the contrast differentiation ability in different spatial frequencies but not the optical characteristics of the eyes. Generally, these methods are not generic since the amount of enhancement needs to be tailored on the basis of the preferences of the users.

Alonso, et al. [1, 2] proposed a new method to neutralize the visual degradation, by which all the images displayed on the screen were pre-compensated in advance based on the ocular aberration of specific computer user. Although this method yielded improvements of visual performance, the effect was not as large as expected. This was most likely due to the mismatch between the measured ocular aberration that is used to generate the pre-compensation and the ocular aberration at the time of actual viewing. The optical properties of the human eye are not static even in a steady viewing environment, but fluctuate over time. These fluctuations are not large under normal circumstances and hence produce little impact on vision. However, the variations of pupil size , primarily caused by the changes of the illumination conditions, produce considerable impacts on the aberration of the eye. In order to minimize pupil variations, the pupils of participants in previous studies were pharmacologically dilated before the tests, by using a combination of tropicamide and phenylephrine [3]. While this approach lessened the pupil size mismatch problem, it is not an essential solution that could be used in practical applications.

To address this limitation, we improve the static pre-compensation method dynamically adjusting the ocular aberration model used for pre-compensation on the basis of real-time updates of the pupil size. In this study, the pupil data were collected through an eye tracking system, for resizing the ocular aberration from the one measured through a Hartmann-Shack sensor to the current one, dynamically. To validate the efficiency of our method, participants were recruited to perform an icon recognition task on the computer screen with or without applying dynamic pre-compensation respectively. For comparison, the same task was also performed when the static pre-compensation was applied.

2. BACKGROUND

2.1 Human Visual System

Image formation on the retina is the first step in the human's visual process. The optical properties of the the human eye are mainly determined by the cornea, iris, pupil and lens. Various eye diseases or problems are caused once

dysfunctions exist in these components. Even though the human eye is quite complex, if we consider these components as a whole, the imaging process of the human eye can be simply described as mapping of the intensity distribution of the object viewed on the retina according to the optics of the eye.

2.2 Ocular Aberration

Based on the wave theory, the manner in which the intensities of an external object are distributed on the retina is determined by the wavefront characteristics of the eye. The wavefront aberration function of the human eye (ocular aberration) is defined as the difference between the actual aberrated wavefront and the ideal spherical wavefront when light comes into the eye, from a distant point source. The ocular aberrations of the entire eye are combinations of the aberrations primarily from the cornea and lens. All human eyes have some degree of aberrations and any ocular aberration will degrade the resulting retinal image. Refractive error is mainly caused by low order aberrations, including spherical error (e.g., myopia, hyperopia) and cylindrical error (e.g., astigmatism, presbyopia). The low order aberrations contribute most of the degradation to the vision quality [8].

Benefiting from the development of the Shack-Hartmann sensor, measurement of ocular aberration has become readily available. It is usually reported as a set of Zernike polynomials and coefficients, through which the corresponding ocular aberration $W(r, \theta)$ can be reconstructed by:

$$W(r,\theta) = \sum_{i=0}^{\infty} z_i P_i(r,\theta). \tag{1}$$

where z_i represent the measured Zernike coefficients and $P_i(r,\theta)$ represent the corresponding Zernike polynomials in polar form. Note that the Zernike polynomials are a function of the pupil radius (r).

2.3 Formation of Retinal Image

The process of image formation on the retina can be further simplified by introducing the point spread function (P-SF), which is defined as the image formed by a single point source on the retina. Considering the object viewed by the eye as a two-dimensional array of point sources with variable intensities, the formation of an image on the retina can be described as the convolution of the intensity array and the PSF of the eye (Figure 1). This process is expressed mathematically as [26]:

$$i(x,y) = o(x,y) * PSF(x,y). \tag{2}$$

where $o(x,y)$ is the ideal image of the viewed object and $i(x,y)$ is the retinal image attained by convolution. In our study, $i(x,y)$ is the original image for display, in the form of an intensity matrix. For computation simplicity, Fourier transform is always performed on the PSF to generate the optical transfer funciton (OTF):

$$OTF(u,v) = \mathcal{F}\{PSF(x,y)\}. \tag{3}$$

and the modulation transfer function (MTF) that is the magnitude of the complex-valued OTF:

$$MTF(u,v) = |OTF(u,v)|. \tag{4}$$

3. METHODS

All the elements (e.g., pictures, text, icons) displayed by modern computers can be represented in the form of digital images. Thus, the computer, as one side of interaction with its user, is capable of preprocessing the images before display. Most assistive techniques based on image preprocessing, including our image pre-compensation method, are built on this premise. Due to the visual degradation caused by the ocular aberrations, most computer users with severe refractive errors encounter difficulties to view images without processing, presented on the screen. This triggers the intuitive idea to present images that are particularly designed or modified instead. The idea of image pre-compensation is similar with image restoration in some degree. As a priori knowledge of the degradation (or part of it) needs to be available in the process of image restoration, the ocular aberration of the specific computer user is also required at first to produce customized pre-compensation. In practice, ocular aberration can be readily measured by an aberrometer. Even so, the image pre-compensation discussed here has a substantial difference with image restoration. Instead of post-processing the degraded image to recover it from degradation, the image pre-compensation method alters the images to be viewed in a particular manner, aiming to neutralize the blurring caused by the ocular aberration of the specific computer user.

3.1 Static Image Pre-Compensation

Unfortunately, most algorithms successfully used in image restoration are not appropriate for use in image precompensation, as the images processed will be "blurred" again at viewing. One effective method is Inverse Wiener Filtering (IWF), as described in detail in [1, 2]. Applying the basic form of Inverse Wiener Filtering, the pre-compensated image c(x,y) can be generated in the spectral domain by:

$$c(x, y) = \mathcal{F}^{-1}\{\frac{O(u,v)}{OTF(u,v)} \frac{MTF(u,v)^2}{MTF(u,v)^2 + K}\}. \quad (5)$$

In the equation above, $O(u,v)$ is the Fourier transform of the original image for display. K is the regularization parameter, which is used to suppress the undue amplification of ocular aberration errors especially when the value of $OTF(u,v)$ is close to zero at some frequencies. The generated pre-compensated image $c(x,y)$ is the one actually presented to be viewed, with particular modifications designed to be "blurred" by the user's eye.

Figure 2(b) shows an example of what a computer user would perceive when viewing the icon shown in Figure 2(a) by simulation. It is generated based on an ocular aberration with -6D spherical error. Figure 2(c) is the image produced after applying pre-compensation. The simulation result in Figure 2(d) shows what the same user would perceive when viewing the pre-compensated image (Figure 2(c)). From it, we find that the perceived shape and edges of the pre-compensated icon, as perceived, are much sharper than Figure 2(b), although its overall contrast is reduced. The simulation results show the feasibility of the image pre-compensation as a potential way to relieve the visual blurring caused by refractive error.

3.2 Variation of Ocular Aberration

The validity of the above static pre-compensation is contingent on the assumption that the measured ocular aber-

Figure 2: (a) One icon (Save) for display; (b) What a user with -6D spherical aberration perceives when viewing (a); (c) Icon after pre-compensation; (d) What a user with -6D spherical aberration perceives when viewing (c).

ration is the same with the ocular aberration at the time of viewing the compensated image. However, in practice, this assumption is not always met as the ocular aberration may vary with changes of illumination, accommodation and other psychophysical factors. Even under steady viewing conditions, the optics of the human eye is not constant, exhibiting temporal instability in the form of fluctuations [23]. The magnitude of these fluctuations are approximately 0.03-0.5 diopters and with frequencies up to 5 Hz [5]. Recent studies have shown that fluctuations exist not only in the defocus error but also in other high order aberrations [12, 13, 23]. However, since our pre-compensation method is for the benefit of the population with severe refractive error, it is reasonable to disregard the ocular aberration variations caused by these small fluctuations.

On the other hand, the change of ocular aberration caused by pupil variation cannot be ignored. It is well known that the pupil size varies with the illumination conditions. Thus, the pupil size of a user sitting in front of the computer is likely to be different from the size at the time of wavefront measurement. Specifically, considering that we always measure the aberration under relatively dark conditions, the pupil size difference under these two cases can be quite large. As mentioned in the last section, the ocular aberrations measured by aberrometers are reported as a set of Zernike coefficients. In practice, these coefficients are associated to a specific pupil radius. This means that once the pupil size changes, the aberration will also be changed correspondingly and needs to be recalculated. Thus, if we perform pre-compensation based on the measured aberration directly, the pre-compensated image may not be suitable as

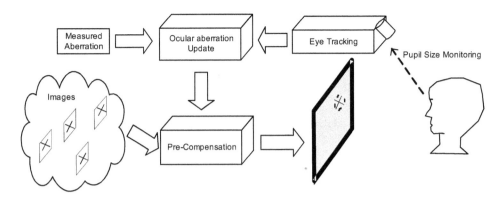

Figure 3: Schematic of the dynamic image pre-compensation system.

the aberration data used to generate the compensation may have changed considerably. This fact requires us to update the ocular aberration of a specific computer user along with the pupil size variations. Fortunately, if the aberration data for a large pupil is available, methods have been developed to derive the new aberration according to a new pupil size, typically a smaller one [4, 7, 25].

3.3 Dynamic Image Pre-Compensation

In order to resolve the aberration mismatch problem, we improved the pre-compensation method, which was originally static, to make it dynamic by monitoring the pupil data and updating the aberration in real-time. The conversion method used in our study is proposed by Campbell [4]. Its basic idea is that the same area of a surface will be described by different sets of Zernike coefficients if a different aperture radius is used to find the coefficients. Through a conversion matrix C, this approach is able to convert one Zernike coefficient vector c associated with an original pupil radius to another vector z' associated with a new pupil radius by:

$$z' = C z. \tag{6}$$

The conversion matrix C is dependent on the ratio of original pupil size to the new pupil size. The details of the conversion algorithm are given in [4].

To implement our dynamic pre-compensation method, each specific computer user was required to undergo the aberration measurement through an aberrometer only once. The measurements were conducted under dark conditions to ensure that the pupils of the participants were dilated. This is necessary since the ocular aberration is only expected to be resized from a large pupil size to a small pupil size. If aberration data was collected with a relatively small pupil size (under bright illumination conditions), then deriving the aberration corresponding to another large pupil size was not reliable, as it would require aberration data which would not be available in the measurement. In practice, the measured aberration data, including the "base" pupil diameter, would be stored in a file with identity codes. Thus, computer users assisted by our system would need to log in first for retrieval of their individual data. During the use of computer, the real-time pupil data needed for updating the aberration can be collected by an eye tracking system. Detailed information of this process will be provided in the next section. Figure 3 illustrates the schematic of our dynamic image pre-compensation system.

3.4 Side Effects of Pre-Compensation

Although the IWF achieved good performance in recovering the shape of the image, it has two major side effects, which can be observed in Figure 2(d).

The first one is the ringing artifacts, most pronounced around the regions with abrupt intensity transitions. Regularization is always required by the process of Wiener Filtering in order to suppress high frequency errors. As a trade-off, the regularization error is distributed across the whole frequency spectrum, as shown in equation (6), leading to the ringing artifacts in the image. In practical implementation, beyond the simulation stage, there are always small discrepancies between the model used to generate the pre-compensation and the actual optical system. This will make the ring artifacts more problematic.

The second one is the noticeable contrast decrease of the perceived image after pre-compensation. In general, the IWF behaves like a high pass filter. Thus, the pre-compensated image usually has a wider range than the original image, even involving negative values. Nevertheless, regular display devices (e.g., LCD) only have limited intensity scales. Thus, the intensity values computed need to be shifted and scaled before the pre-compensated image can be displayed. The downscaling in this process will narrow the range of intensities, causing part of the contrast loss.

4. EVALUATION

The objective of this research is to relieve the blurred vision of those computer users with severe refractive errors, hence facilitating their daily computer access. The evaluation of our dynamic image pre-compensation method was conducted through an empirical study. Our evaluation has two major hypotheses. The first one is that the dynamic pre-compensation method will improve the visual performance of the participants, comparing with the circumstance in which the images are presented without any processing. The second one is that the dynamic pre-compensation is superior to the static pre-compensation in removing the visual blurring. If the hypotheses are confirmed, the evaluation will also assess how much improvement was achieved.

Our study was designed on the basis of an icon recognition task. As one of the most popular elements for computer display, icons are widely used in graphic user interfaces to facilitate the interaction between human and computers. Correct and efficient icon recognition is required for many computer-based tasks. Thus, it is appropriate that the vi-

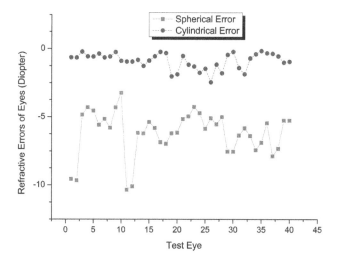

Figure 4: Refractive errors of 20 participants (40 eyes) in the study.

Figure 5: Eight icons used in the icon recognition test (Copy, Document, Folder, Email, Picture, Printer, Save and Delete).

sual performance was evaluated through the accuracy of icon recognition on the computer screen.

As the pre-compensation is generated based on the specific ocular aberration, the pre-compensation for two eyes (even though they belong to the same user) should also be different. Thus, the icon recognition test in our study was based on the monocular vision of participants.

4.1 Participants

Twenty participants were recruited to take part in our icon recognition study. The ages of participants ranged from 20 to 33 years old (26.7±3.4). Thirteen of them were male and seven of them were female. Most of them are undergraduate or graduate students, with high degree spherical or cylindrical errors, or with both. The spherical aberrations of participants ranged between -3.24 and -10.34D (-6.17±1.63D) and the cylindrical aberrations of participants ranged between -0.22D and -2.44D (-0.88±0.58D). Detailed information of the participants' refractive errors is shown in Figure 4. All the participants performed the same icon recognition test with both the left eye and the right eye. Thus, 40 eyes in total were tested in the study. Written informed consent was given by all the participants before the test.

4.2 Instruments and Environment

Before the icon recognition test, initial ocular aberrations of participants were measured through an aberrometer (CO-AS-HD, Wavefront Sciences). The reported Zernike coefficients included up to the 6th order, stored with a specific base pupil diameter. Participants were not allowed to wear glasses or contacts during the tests.

The icon recognition tests were performed on an interface developed using Visual C#, upon which the icons were presented. The test data of participants was categorized and recorded in a database for post analysis.

In order to monitor the pupil variations of participants, an eye tracking system (T60, Tobii) was used to collect the real-time pupil data of the participants. The Tobii T60 eye tracker is able to provide pupil size measurements and other eye data at a rate of 60 Hz. In our study, only the pupil diameter data were considered. The eye tracker is integrated

in a 17-inch TFT computer monitor, which is also used as the display device in our study.

4.3 Design and Procedures

During the icon recognition tests, the participants were instructed to sit in front of the computer monitor. The distance between the participant and the computer screen was fixed to be 25 inches. Once the participants were sitting in a comfortable position, they were not permitted to move forward or backward to change the distance. As the test was based on the monocular vision, one eye was covered by an eye patch while the other eye was being tested. The tests were conducted under office light conditions ensuring that the pupil size was smaller than the base pupil size. After completing the test of one eye, the participant was allowed to take a 5 minutes break before testing the other eye.

The icons selected for the test were 8 common icons, including Copy, Document, Folder, Email, Picture, Print, Save and Delete (Figure 5). We created two versions of the icons, at two different sizes. The small version icons were 48 pixels (side) and the large ones were 72 pixels (side). All icons were black and white, without any color information. The participants were required to memorize the names of these eight icons before the test. Reviewing the icons was not permitted once the test started.

For comparison, icons would be presented with three different processing methods, that is: original icons (Original), static pre-compensated (SPC) icons and dynamic pre-compensated (DPC) icons. In the case of dynamic pre-compensation, each icon was processed in real-time on the basis of the monitored pupil size at the time when the icon was displayed. The icon would not be updated anymore until the next icon was requested. Every icon was presented only once. Thus, there were 8(icons)×2(sizes)×3(methods)=48 trials for each eye's test session. The order of the trials was as follows: all icons processed by the same method (Original, SPC, DPC) were presented as a block of 16 trials, with 8 small icons shown first, followed by 8 large icons, both in randomized orders. The order in which the three methods were applied and presented was also randomized. For each trial the participant was required to state, verbally, the identity of the icon displayed, so we could record the recognition as correct or incorrect. During the test, the participant was not told if the recognitions were correct or incorrect. Aside from this, the participants did not need to perform any other actions. In preliminary tests we found that participants got tired easily after prolonged monocular viewing. Therefore, to reduce the overall test duration, we presented each icon for only 3 seconds in this study. After that, the icon would

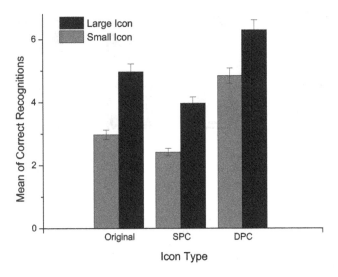

Figure 6: Average correct recognitions for three different types of icons (Original, SPC and DPC). The error bars are based on 95% CI.

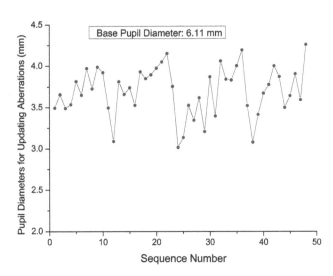

Figure 7: Typical pupil variations during the icon recognition test, comparing with the base pupil diameter. The pupil diameters plotted were recorded at the time that icons were presented.

disappear from the screen. Participants were made aware of this 3 second time limitation before they started the test session.

Our statistical evaluation used a repeated measures factorial design with two factors: the icon type, with three levels (original, SPC and DPC) and the icon size, with two levels (small and large). The dependent variable was the number of correct recognitions made by the participants, which could range from 0 to 8.

A two way ANOVA analysis with repeated measures was conducted to evaluate the effects of different processing methods and icon sizes on the recognition accuracy. We also investigated the interactions between pre-compensation method and icon size in the evaluation.

After the icon recognition trials were completed, the participants were asked which characteristic of the compensated images (distinguishable to the partcipants by their darker backgrounds) hindered their recognition of the icons most. We planned on using this feedback from the participants to seek further improvements of the pre-compensation method.

4.4 Results

We found that the main effect of icon type on the recognition accuracy was significant, $F(1.66, 64.8) = 48.52$, $p<0.01$. This shows that applying pre-compensation did impact the recognition accuracy of participants in the tests. As shown in Figure 6, the means of correct recognitions are 3.98, 3.20 and 5.58, corresponding to the three different types of icon (orignial, SPC and DPC) respectively. By applying dynamic pre-compensation to the original icons, the mean of correct recognition number increased from 3.98 to 5.58 with the average accuracy ratio increasing from 49.8% to 69.8%. Not surprisingly, the Tukey comparison showed that the difference between dynamically pre-compensated icons and original icons was significant, $p<0.01$.

Comparing with SPC icons, DPC icons had an increase on the average correct recognitions, from 3.20 to 5.58 (the accuracy ratio increased from 40% to 69.8%). The difference between SPC icons and DPC icons was also significant, $p<0.01$. It was noted that the average correct recognition

number with static pre-compensation was lower than the average for original icons. This observation seems to imply that a pre-compensation performed based on a mismatched pupil size could make the icon recognition process even more difficult.

As we expected, there was a significant effect of the icon size on the accuracy, $F(1,39) = 153.54$, $p<0.01$. The mean of correct recognitions increased from 3.42 (small size) to 5.08 (large size). The interaction between the icon type and icon size was not significant, $F(2,78) = 2.21$, $p = 0.116$.

4.5 Interpretation of Results

The significant difference between DPC icons and original icons indicates that the dynamic image pre-compensation method indeed improved the visual performance of the participants, confirming our first hypothesis. The enhanced recognition accuracy ratio achieved with DPC icons, in comparison with SPC icons, supports our hypothesis that the dynamic method provides better visual performance than the static method, as the pre-compensation generated dynamically is better suited to the real aberration data for each trial while the SPC icons were generated based on the initially measured ocular aberrations only.

The average correct recognition of SPC icons was lower than the average recognition of original icons. This could be explained by the fact that, for most participants, the pupil diameters recorded to update the aberrations were markedly smaller than the base pupil size. From this, we infer that the real aberrations while viewing the SPC icons were also markedly different from the measured ones. If the mismatch of pupil size was large enough, the degradation caused by inadequate compensation was, perhaps, more challenging than the natural distortions of the original images. One typical record of pupil variations is shown in Figure 7, in which the pupil diameters of one participant, used to update the aberration data during the test, are plotted and the base pupil diameter associated with the originally measured aberration data is also shown.

The reason for the increased accuracy ratio from small size

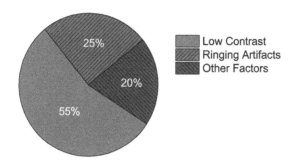

Low Contrast
Ringing Artifacts
Other Factors

Figure 8: The results from surveying to which factor hindered the recognition of icons most. 11 participants reported low contrast. 5 participants reported ringing artifacts and other 4 participants reported other factors.

icons to large size icons is quite intuitive, as icons with large size are less vulnerable to the distortion of their features by ocular aberrations and, therefore, more easily recognized. The analysis shows that there is no significant interaction between icon type and icon size, which indicates that the pre-compensation method achieved positive effects on small icons and large icons. For the DPC icons, this implies that the dynamic pre-compensation method enhanced the recognition accuracy of small icons and large icons similarly.

4.6 Improving the Method

Even though DPC icons provided the best recognition accuracy in our study, the vision quality after applying the dynamic pre-compensation was still far from fully satisfactory. Regarding the factor that most hindered the participants' recognition of pre-compensated icons, the reduction of contrast seems to have been predominant. As shown in Figure 8, 55% of the participants believed that the key shortcoming was the low contrast of pre-compensated icons; 25% of answers pointed to ringing artifacts and 20% of answers pointed to other factors (e.g., abnormal blurs and edge overlapping). These answers indicate that the benefits of the pre-compensation method were mainly limited by the problems of low contrast and ringing artifacts.

Both the low contrast and the ringing artifact problems are introduced by the process of Inverse Wiener Filtering. The contrast reduction is primarily caused by the wide range of intensity values after pre-compensation, while the ringing artifacts are due to the spreading of regularization and modeling errors. Even though the interplay between these two negative effects requires further investigation, we believe, at this point, that they are associated or coupled to some degree. Based on the answers from the participants, it is likely that a considerable improvement can be achieved by finding a way to increase the contrast after pre-compensation. One possible way is restricting the pre-compensation within a particular range of the frequency spectrum, even if this also will cause the loss of some details, as trade off.

5. CONCLUSION

Computer users with severe refractive errors frequently encounter difficulties to view the pictorial information displayed on a computer monitor without vision correction. Traditional means to resolve this problem include spectacles, contact lenses and refractive surgery. This paper de-

scribed a new approach to preprocess the images through dynamic and customized pre-compensation, aiming to relieve the visual blurring or distortion caused by the ocular aberrations of each specific computer user. The dynamic pre-compensation method improves previous work, in which the pre-compensation was generated based on a fixed model, by taking into account the dynamic characteristics of the human eye. As the ocular aberration changes with pupil size variations, we updated the aberration model used to calculate the pre-compensation according to the real-time pupil size measurements obtained through an eye tracking system. In order to evaluate the performance of our method, an empirical study was conducted with 20 participants in the form of an icon recognition test. We found that the participants achieved improved recognition accuracy when the icons with dynamic pre-compensation were presented. The average accuracy for dynamically pre-compensated icons was significantly higher than the accuracy for icons with static pre-compensation as well as the the accuracy for original icons without any processing.

Even though the benefits attained by our method were achieved under laboratory conditions, the encouraging results from our study strengthen our belief that the dynamic image pre-compensation is a promising way to improve the visual performance of computer users with severe ocular aberrations. Based on the simulation results and answers from the participants in our evaluation, the performance of our method is mostly limited by two major problems (low contrast and ringing artifacts). Overcoming these two challenges may require exploration of new pre-compensation algorithms, as alternatives to the Inverse Wiener Filtering.

6. ACKNOWLEDGMENTS

Our thanks to the participants for their patience and contribution to this study. This research was supported in part by the U.S. National Science Foundation under grants CNS-0959985 and CNS-0940575. Jian Huang is supported by a Presidential Fellowship from Florida International University.

7. REFERENCES

[1] M. Alonso, A. Barreto, and J. G. Cremades. Image pre-compensation to facilitate computer access for users with refractive errors. In *Proc. ACM SIGACCESS conf. Comp. Access.*, pages 126–132, 2004.

[2] M. Alonso, A. Barreto, J. A. Jacko, and M. Adjouadi. A multi-domain approach for enhancing text display for users with visual aberrations. In *Proc. ACM SIGACCESS conf. Comp. Access.*, pages 34–39, 2006.

[3] M. Alonso, A. Barreto, J. A. Jacko, and M. Adjouadi. Evaluation of onscreen precompensation algorithms for computer users with visual aberrations. In *Proc. ACM SIGACCESS conf. Comp. Access.*, pages 219–220, 2007.

[4] C. E. Campbell. Matrix method to find a new set of zernike coefficients from an original set when the aperture radius is changed. *J. Opt. Soc. Am. A.*, 20(2):209–217, 2003.

[5] W. N. Charman and G. Heron. Fluctuations in accommo-dation: a review. *phthalmic Physiol. Opt.*, 8:153–163, 1998.

[6] N. Congdon, B. O'Colmain, C. C. Klaver, and et al. Causes and prevalence of visual impairment among adults in the united states. *Arch. Ophthalmol.*, 122(3):477–485, 2004.

[7] G. Dai. Scaling zernike expansion coefficients to smaller pupil sizes: a simpler formula. *J. Opt. Soc. Am. A.*, 23(3):539–547, 2006.

[8] G. Dai. *Wavefront Optics for Vision Correction.* SPIE, Washington, 2008.

[9] E. Dalimier, C. Dainty, and J. Barbur. Effects of higher-order aberrations on contrast acuity as a function of light level. *Journal of Modern Optics*, 55(4):791–803, 2008.

[10] E. Fine and E. Peli. Enhancement of text for the visually impaired. *J. Opt. Soc. Am. A.*, 12(7):1439–1447, 1995.

[11] A. Guirao, J. Porter, D. Williams, and I. G. Cox. Calculated impact of higher-order monochromatic aberrations on retinal image quality in a population of human eyes. *J. Opt. Soc. Am. A.*, 19(1):1–9, 2002.

[12] H. Hofer, P. Artal, B. Singer, J. L. Aragon, and D. R. Williams. Dynamics of the eye's wave aberration. *J. Opt. Soc. Am. A.*, 18(3):497–506, 2001.

[13] D. R. Iskander, M. J. Collins, M. R. Morelande, and M. Zhu. Analyzing the dynamic wavefront aberrations in the human eye. *IEEE Trans. Biomed. Eng.*, 51(11):1969–1980, 2004.

[14] J. H. Kempen, P. Mitchell, K. E. Lee, and et al. The prevalence of refractive errors among adults in the united states, western europe, and australia. *Arch. Ophthalmol.*, 122(4):495–505, 2004.

[15] T. Lawton. Image enhancement filters significantly improve reading performance for low vision observers. *Ophthalmic Physiol. Opt.*, 12(2):193–200, 1992.

[16] T. Lawton, J. Sebag, A. A. Sadun, and K. R. Castleman. Image enhancement improves reading performance in age-related macular degeneration patients. *Vision Res.*, 38(1):153–162, 1998.

[17] S. J. Leat, G. Omoruyi, A. Kennedy, and E. Jernigan. Generic and customized digital image enhancement filters for the visually impaired. *Vision Res.*, 45(15):1991–2007, 2005.

[18] R. Leonard. *Statistics on vision impairment: A resource manual.* Arlene R. Gordon Research Institute of Lighthouse International, New York, 2002.

[19] J. Liang, D. R. Williams, and D. T. Miller. Supernormal vision and high resolution retinal imaging through adaptive optics. *J. Opt. Soc. Am. A.*, 14(11):2884–2892, 1997.

[20] B. Munoz, S. K. West, and G. S. Rubin. Causes of blindness and visual impairment in a population of older americans: the salisbury eye evaluation study. *Arch. Ophthalmol.*, 118(6):819–825, 2000.

[21] E. Peli, J. Kim, Y. Yitzhaky, R. B. Goldstein, and R. L. Woods. Wideband enhancement of television images for people with visual impairment. *J. Opt. Soc. Am. A.*, 21(6):937–950, 2004.

[22] E. Peli, E. Lee, C. L. Trempe, and S. Buzney. Image enhancement for the visually impaired: the effects of enhancement on face recognition. *J. Opt. Soc. Am. A.*, 11(7):1929–1939, 1994.

[23] S. Plainis, H. S. Ginis, and A. Pallikaris. The effect of ocular aberrations on steady-state errors of accommodative response. *J. Opt. Soc. Am. A.*, 5(5):466–477, 2005.

[24] L. Sawides, E. Gambra, D. Pascual, C. Dorronsoro, and S. Marcos. Visual performance with real-life tasks under adaptive-optics ocular aberration correction. *Journal of Vision*, 10(5):1–12, 2010.

[25] J. Schwiegerling. Scaling zernike expansion coefficients to different pupil sizes. *J. Opt. Soc. Am. A.*, 19(10):1937–1945, 2002.

[26] L. N. Thibos. *Seeing: Handbook of Perception and Cognition, 2 ed.* Academic Press, San Diego, CA, 2000.

[27] S. Vitale, R. D. Sperduto, and F. L. Ferris. Increased prevalence of myopia in the united states between 1971-1972 and 1999-2004. *Arch. Ophthalmol.*, 127(12):1632–1639, 2004.

Effect of Presenting Video as a Baseline During an American Sign Language Animation User Study

Pengfei Lu

The Graduate Center, CUNY
City University of New York
Doctoral Program in Computer Science
365 Fifth Ave, New York, NY 10016
+1-212-817-8190

pengfei.lu@qc.cuny.edu

Hernisa Kacorri

The Graduate Center, CUNY
City University of New York
Doctoral Program in Computer Science
365 Fifth Ave, New York, NY 10016
+1-212-817-8190

hkacorri@gc.cuny.edu

ABSTRACT

Animations of American Sign Language (ASL) have accessibility benefits for many signers with lower levels of written language literacy. Our lab has conducted several prior studies to evaluate synthesized ASL animations by asking native signers to watch different versions of animations and to answer comprehension and subjective questions about them. As an upper baseline, we used an animation of a virtual human carefully created by a human animator who is a native ASL signer. Considering whether to instead use videos of human signers as an upper baseline, we wanted to quantify how including a video upper baseline would affect how participants evaluate the ASL animations presented in a study. In this paper, we replicate a user study we conducted two years ago, with one difference: replacing our original animation upper baseline with a video of a human signer. We found that adding a human video upper baseline depressed the subjective Likert-scale scores that participants assign to the other stimuli (the synthesized animations) in the study when viewed side-by-side. This paper provides methodological guidance for how to design user studies evaluating sign language animations and facilitates comparison of studies that have used different upper baselines.

Categories and Subject Descriptors

H.5.2 [**Information Interfaces and Presentation**] User Interfaces – *evaluation/methodology*; K.4.2 [**Computers and Society**]: Social Issues – *assistive technologies for persons with disabilities*.

General Terms

Design, Experimentation, Human Factors, Measurement.

Keywords

Accessibility Technology for People who are Deaf, American Sign Language, Animation, Baseline, User Study.

1. INTRODUCTION

For various educational and language exposure reasons, a

majority of high school graduates (typically at age 18-21) who are deaf in the U.S. have lower-than-average levels of literacy in written English; specifically, the average is a fourth-grade (age 10) English reading level or below [24]. So, many adults who are deaf have difficulty reading text that may appear on websites, captioning, or other media. More than half a million people in the U.S. use American Sign Language (ASL), a language with a distinct word order, linguistic structure, and vocabulary than English [19]; many adults have more sophisticated fluency in ASL than in English. Thus, presenting information as computer animations of ASL can make information and services accessible to deaf people with lower English literacy, as explained in [7].

While videos of human signing can be used in some applications and websites, there are limitations. If the information is frequently updated, it may be prohibitively expensive to continually re-film a human performing ASL for the new information. Computer synthesized animations allow for frequent updating, automatic production of messages (via natural language generation or machine translation techniques), wiki-style applications in which multiple authors script a message in ASL collaboratively, or scripting of messages by a single human author for presentation in an anonymous fashion (that does not reveal the face of the human author, as would happen in a video of them performing ASL). Assembling video clips of individual signs together to synthesize ASL messages does not allow for sufficient control, blending, and modulation to produce smooth transitions between signs, subtle motion variations in sign performances, or proper combinations of facial expressions with signs. Thus, animated virtual human characters are used by sign language synthesis research systems.

As part of our research on ASL animation, our laboratory has conducted studies to evaluate the understandability and naturalness of ASL animations. Typically, we ask native ASL signers to view our animations and then answer comprehension and subjective Likert-scale questions about the animations. We have developed several novel methodologies for conducting such studies, including: protocols to screen for native ASL signers [9], scripts of ASL stimuli that contain specific linguistic phenomena of interest [10, 11], comprehension questions presented in ASL with answer choices presented with images and photos corresponding to each choice (to enable participation by signers with limited English skills) [8], etc. In this paper, we investigate another important methodological issue; specifically, we examine the question of what type of upper baseline should be presented in an ASL animation evaluation study.

Our evaluation studies drive our research, as we explore alternative mathematical models for specifying the movements of an animated character to produce a clear and understandable animation. For instance, we have conducted studies that focus on the use of space around a signer to represent entities under discussion, the movement of verb signs, etc. [8, 9, 11]. Typically, in a study, we wish to compare whether one version of our animations (based on one mathematical model) out-performs another version of animations (based on a different model). We sometimes use comprehension questions in our evaluation studies; so, the scores that participants achieve depend not only on the animation stimuli shown but also on the difficulty of the comprehension questions. Thus, we often included an upper baseline (a third type of animation for comparison purposes) in our studies to make the results more meaningful. Usually, we have used a computer animation (of a visually identical animated character) whose movements were carefully specified by a native ASL signer with animation software experience. The rationale for this choice was that we believed the movements of the character specified by a human animator were an "ideal" that we sought to achieve with our animation models used for automatic synthesis.

Other researchers at conferences have sometimes asked why we have not included videos of humans performing ASL sentences as the upper baseline in our studies. We had been wary of including videos of humans because we were concerned that this might lead participants to focus on the superficial appearance of the human and the signing character, not on their movements, which were the focus of our research program. For instance, our experimental studies typically include additional time for the participants to provide unstructured feedback comments about the animations they have seen that day, and the comments about aspects of the character movement are most useful for our research. As a lab studying the linguistic movements of the body during ASL (and not the computer graphics issues related to how to display human figures), we were not focusing our research on the photorealism or graphical qualities of the character, but rather on its movements.

This paper explores what type of upper baseline should be used in user-based experimental studies of sign language animations – specifically, whether videos of a human signer would be a better upper baseline than a character animated by a human. Section 2 surveys evaluation methodologies currently used in the research community, and section 3 provides additional motivation for this research. Sections 4 and 5 describe our experimental study in which we replicate a study previously published in 2010 [10] and replaced the upper baseline in that study with a video of a human signer, and the results of the experiment study. Section 6 discusses our conclusions and future work.

2. RELATED WORK

Few researchers have explicitly discussed methodological aspects of sign language animation user-studies. We searched the literature for examples of studies where we can identify the use of particular baselines (the original authors may not have discussed their studies in these terms). Researchers studying animations of *non-signing* virtual humans are also discussed briefly in this survey below. We see that evaluation conducted can be organized into three categories with regard to the upper baseline used.

The first category is where no upper baseline exists. Although evaluation against a baseline usually results in more meaningful scores, many user-studies don't include any baselines. To test the

feasibility of their approach, researchers ask users to evaluate the human animation under development without any baselines for comparison [22], conduct their experiment in multiple steps trying to improve at every step [3], or improve the parameters of their animation models through repeated presentation of an animation with slightly modified parameters values [3].

The second category is research in which videos of a human are used as an upper baseline for comparison to the animation being generated. For example, Kipp et al. compare avatars to human signers [13]. While not used as an upper baseline, an instructional video of a native signer appeared in the interface of the software presenting animations in studies conducted by Schnepp et al. [23, 21]; the video's use may have impacted participants' scores given to animations. Researchers studying non-signing virtual characters have also sometimes used videos of humans as a baseline for comparison, e.g. [1, 4].

The last category is research in which animation was used as an upper baseline in the evaluation; this seems to be the most popular approach in sign language animation (and non-signing virtual human) research. The similarity of appearance between the virtual characters in the "upper baseline" animation and the character in the animation under evaluation seems to vary across the studies. Further, this category can be divided into two subcategories by the way the upper baseline animation is created and manipulated.

The first covers upper baseline animations controlled by a human animator without any motion-capture data. As discussed above, up to now, this is the approach we have favored in our prior studies, in which we asked a human animator to carefully produce an animation of a virtual human to serve as our upper baseline [11, 15, 18]. Researchers studying the animation of non-signing virtual human characters (performing gestures along with speech) have employed a similar methodology, e.g. [2].

Finally, many researchers create their upper baseline animation by combining an animation tool, an animator, and data from a real human (collected via motion capture). Some researchers use a virtual human for the upper baseline that is visually identical to the character used in the animations being evaluated ([5, 6]), and some use a visually different character ([12] and part of the experiment in [5]). Kipp et al. [14] showed participants sign language animations produced by a variety of techniques. Non-sign-language animation researchers have also used virtual humans driven by motion-capture as upper baselines [20].

3. PRIOR RESULTS & HYPOTHESES

Given the diversity of study designs in the sign language animation research community, it is useful to understand the advantages of using human-video or animation upper baselines. In order to quantify the effect of showing videos of human signers in an ASL animation evaluation study, we needed to conduct an identical study in two ways: (1) once *without* using videos of human signers as an upper baseline and (2) once *with* such videos. Since we have up to now (with one exception, discussed below) conducted studies in which an animation produced by a skilled human animator was the upper baseline, we decided to replicate a previously conducted study, replacing the upper baseline with a video of human signer performing identical ASL stories as the animated character. We can examine how the comprehension scores, Likert-scale subjective evaluation responses, and feedback comments in the study may differ. Before discussing the details of this study replication in sections 4 and 5, we first wanted to discuss a pair of prior studies that almost (but not quite) had this same structure. The results of this prior pair of studies formed our hypotheses for the work presented in sections 4 and 5.

An ongoing project at our laboratory is to collect a large sample of sign language sentences using motion-capture equipment worn by native signers. We wanted to evaluate whether we had correctly calibrated our motion-capture equipment to obtain clear movement data from the human signers. So, in [16], we evaluated virtual human animations based on our motion-capture recordings by comparing them to an upper baseline, which consisted of an animation of a virtual human character designed by a human animator. A few years later, in [17], we conducted a similar study to evaluate virtual human animations based on our motion-capture recordings, but we used a different upper baseline: in this new study, we showed a video of the human wearing the motion-capture equipment during the recording session. In both studies, native ASL signers who saw the animations/videos answered comprehension questions and Likert-scale subjective evaluation questions; by comparing how the scores in the two studies change, we gain insight into the effect of using a different upper baseline.

Changing the upper baseline did not produce a difference in the comprehension question scores for the other stimuli in the study (the motion-capture-based animations), which had similar scores in both studies [17]. More interesting was the effect on the Likert-scale subjective scores (1-to-10 for naturalness of movement, perception of understandability, and grammatical correctness of the animations). In the later study (with the human video upper baseline), the motion-capture-based animations received lower subjective scores than they had in the prior study (with the animation upper baseline). We speculated that seeing a video of real human as one of the stimuli being evaluated in a study led participants to assign lower subject ratings to the animations [17]. That is, none of the animations subjectively seemed as good when shown in comparison to videos of real people signing. But this was just speculation: to determine if including videos of humans as a baseline in a study would produce a depressive effect on subjective scores for other stimuli (and what the magnitude of this effect would be), we would need to conduct a carefully controlled pair of studies that were identical in all aspects, except for one of them including videos of real humans as an upper baseline (as we discuss in sections 4 and 5 of this paper). The pair of studies described above [16, 17] was not a sufficient test because the script of the stories in the two studies was not identical; further, the animations evaluated were motion-capture-based animations, not synthesized ASL animations (our lab's primary focus).

While not a perfect test, this prior pair of studies helped us formulate hypotheses of how displaying videos of humans as an upper baseline would affect the results of a study evaluating synthesized ASL animations. We hypothesize the following:

- **H1:** A human video upper baseline will receive higher comprehension question accuracy scores than an animated-character upper baseline produced by a human animator.
- **H2:** The upper baseline used (human video or animated character) would not affect the comprehension questions accuracy scores for the other stimuli shown in the study.
- **H3:** A human video upper baseline will receive higher Likert-scale subjective scores than an animated-character upper baseline.
- **H4:** Using a human video upper baseline will depress the subjective Likert-scale scores that participants assign to the other stimuli (the synthesized animations) in the study.

4. REPLICATING A STUDY FROM 2010

Because the pair of studies discussed above [16, 17] had more differences between them than merely the addition of a human video as an upper baseline, they didn't allow us to isolate how this aspect of the study design affected the collected data. Thus, we selected a study originally presented at ASSETS 2010, and we decided to replicate this study, with the only change being the use of a human video as an upper baseline, instead of an animation.

In [10], we evaluated a model we designed for synthesizing the movements of "inflected" verb signs, whose movements depend on locations in the space around the signer where the verb's subject and object have been previously set up. We wanted to know how understandable ASL animations, in which the verbs were produced using our new model, would be, compared to: (1) a lower baseline consisting of "uninflected" versions of the verb signs (the unvarying/uncustomized dictionary form of each sign whose movement doesn't indicate subject/object) and (2) an upper baseline consisting of animations of inflected versions of each verb produced by a native ASL signer human animator.

We conducted an evaluation study with native ASL signers that consisted of two parts: In part 1, participants viewed animations of a virtual human character telling a short story in ASL. Each story included instances of the inflected verbs. Fig. 1 shows a story transcript; colors indicate locations around the signer where the verb's subject/object are located. After watching each story animation (of one of three types: inflected, uninflected, animator-produced) one time, participants answered multiple-choice comprehension questions. Questions focused on whether they understood and remembered the subject and object of each verb. For each story viewed, participants also responded to three 1-to-10 Likert-scale questions about how grammatically correct, easy to understand, or naturally moving the animation appeared.

In part 2 of the study, participants viewed three versions of an animation of a single ASL sentence side-by-side on one screen, as depicted in Fig. 2(a). The sentences shown side-by-side were identical, except for the version of the verb which appeared in each: version produced by our mathematical model, uninflected version of the verb (lower baseline), or version of the verb carefully created by a native ASL signer using animation software [25] (upper baseline). The participants could re-play each animation as many times as they wished. Participants were asked to focus on the verb and respond to a 1-to-10 Likert-scale question about its grammaticality, understandability, and naturalness in each of the three versions of the sentence. We used the methodology for similar ASL evaluation studies in [8, 9].

HELLO, MY NAME #CHARLIE.
I YOUR NEW BOSS.
MY ASSISTANT #JEFF THERE$_{RED}$
    WILL GIVE$_{RED}$→$_{YOU}$ YOU NEW INFORMATION.
WHEN YOUR OFFICE READY,
    MY MANAGER #BOB THERE$_{BLUE}$ WILL TELL→$_{YOU}$ YOU.
YOUR NEW PHONE HE$_{RED}$ WILL GIVE$_{RED}$→$_{YOU}$ YOU.
I SORRY.
HE$_{RED}$ LOSE YOUR KEY.
HE$_{BLUE}$ SCOLD→$_{RED}$ HIM$_{RED}$.
NOW, HE$_{BLUE}$ FORCE HIM$_{RED}$ PAY NEW KEY.

Fig. 1. Script for a story shown in the study.

To evaluate the four hypotheses listed in section 3, we needed to replicate our 2010 study [10], using the same set of passages, and questions. The only difference in our new 2012 study is that we replace the upper baseline animations from the 2010 study with videos of a human signer. Specifically, we recorded a human performing the 9 stories (with inflected versions of the verbs) for part 1 of the study and the 12 sentences (with inflected versions of the verbs) for part 2 of the study. For example, the top row in Fig. 2 shows what the participants saw in the part 2 (side-by-side comparison) in 2010 and the lower row (Fig. 2(b)) shows what they saw in 2012. All the other animations and their sequencing in this pair of studies were identical. All of the instructions and interactions for the study, in both 2010 and 2012, were conducted in ASL by a native signer, who is professional interpreter.

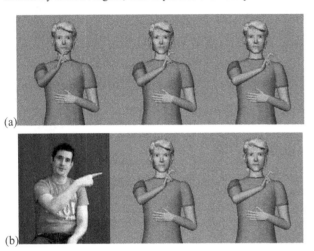

Fig. 2. Screenshots of the side-by-side comparison portion of the studies as shown to participants in (a) 2010 and (b) 2012.

In prior work, we had developed methodologies to ensure that responses given by participants are as ASL-accurate as possible. In [9], we discussed the importance of participants being native ASL signers and the study environment being ASL-focused with little English influence; we developed questions to screen for native ASL signers. For the 2010 study, ads were posted on New York City Deaf community websites asking potential participants if they had grown up using ASL at home or had attended an ASL-based school as a young child. Of the 18 participants recruited for the study, 12 participants learned ASL prior to age 5, and 4 participants attended residential schools using ASL since early childhood. The remaining 2 participants had been using ASL for over 15 years, learned ASL as adolescents, attended a university with classroom instruction in ASL, and used ASL daily to communicate with a significant other or family member. There were 12 men and 6 women of ages 20-56 (average age 30.5).

For our new study in 2012, we also recruited 18 native ASL signers as participants using similar techniques. Of the 18 participants, 16 participants learned ASL prior to age 5, and 10 participants attended residential schools using ASL since early childhood. The remaining 2 participants had been using ASL for over 13 years, learned ASL as adolescents, attended a university with classroom instruction in ASL, and use ASL on a daily basis to communicate with a significant other or family member. There were 12 men and 6 women of ages 22-49 (average age 32.8).

To produce the human video upper baseline, we recorded the videos from a native signer in our studio, where we asked the signer to sit on a stool in front of a blue curtain to match the background color in the animations we presented to the participants. The human signer also wore a green t-shirt on the day of the recording, which was similar to a virtual human character. The camcoder was placed facing the signer at his head height, which matches the perspective of the virtual human in the animations we presented to the participants in the experiment. We used one large monitor in front of the signer to display the story scripts (like the example in Fig. 1) during the recording. The signer had time to memorize and practice each of the scripts prior to the recording session. All of the instructions and interactions for the recording session were conducted in ASL by another native signer (a research assistant in our lab) sitting behind the camcoder – this was important to ensure that the signing being recorded was as fluent as possible. To produce videos which have the same time duration as the upper baseline animations that had been used in 2010, we asked the native signer being recorded to practice several times before the recording, and we used a stopwatch to measure how many seconds he took for each story during the practice and recording. Finally, after making several recordings of each story, we picked the one video recording of the story with the closest time duration to the upper baseline animation from 2010. We cropped and resized the video files to match the height/width of the 2010 upper baseline animations – and to approximate the same placement of a human in a the video frame as how the virtual human character had appeared in the animation in 2010. The framerate and resolution of the video was identical to the animation from 2010.

For this study, it was not only important that the sequence of signs performed in the story should match the animations, but also the locations in the surrounding signing space where the human or character points (to represent entities under discussion) needed to be identical. Fig. 3 illustrates how we set up small colored paper squares around the studio (with colors that matched the script in Fig. 1) to guide the human where to point or where to aim the motion path of inflecting verb signs during the recording session.

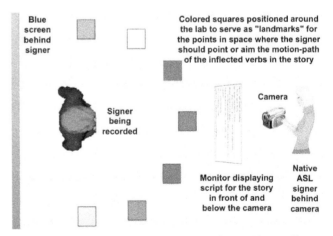

Fig. 3. Diagram of an overhead view of recording studio.

In order to serve as an effective upper baseline for comparison in a study, we would like to "control" as many of the variables of the ASL performance as possible – so that it is mostly the variable we care about which differs between the upper baseline and the animation under primary evaluation scrutiny (which for us, was the synthesized animation using our verb inflection model). Producing a video recording of a human that "matched" the animations being shown as stimuli in the study was very difficult. At a minimum, we needed the signer to perform the same "script" of signs as the other (animation) versions of stimuli shown in the study, and we had to employ the colored squares described above to indicate where the signer should point or how the verbs motion paths should be aimed. Since ASL has no standard written form, we had to explain our notation scheme to the participant being recorded. Because the stories were a bit complicated (an average of 55 signs in length, included 3-5 main characters set up at various locations in the signing space, with 3-5 inflected verbs per story), the signer required a lot of practice in order to perform each story smoothly. Even when we asked the signer to try not to look at the scripts too much during the recording process, the signer still needed to glance at the script occasionally during the performance, which produces a somewhat infelicitous video with the signer's eyes glancing between the monitor displaying the story transcripts and the camcorder.

Further, the script notation does not capture all of the subtleties of performance that are part of ASL; it is merely a loose sketch of what must be signed. We also had to let the signer know how to control the speed of the signing, facial expressions, torso movement, head movement, etc. The signer had to practice before he was able to finish a story in a certain numbers of seconds. We also asked the signer not to add embellishments, e.g., additional emotional facial expressions, which hadn't appeared on our virtual human character's face. This coaching and scripting process is a delicate "balancing act" – on one hand, we want to record a natural, fluent version of the sentences from the human signer, but on the other hand, we want to control as many variables as possible so that they are held constant between our upper-baseline video and our animation being evaluated. Some participants in the study noticed problems in the human video, e.g., commenting "… person signs well but need little [more] facial expression." Other participant comments appear in section 5.

5. RESULTS AND COMPARISON

This section discusses and compares the results obtained in the original 2010 study and the new 2012 study – this includes the comprehension-question and Likert-scale scores collected in part 1 of the studies (after a participant viewed a story one time) and the Likert-scale scores collected in part 2 of the studies (in which participants assigned a score to each of the three sentences which they viewed side-by-side). In Fig. 4, 5, and 6, which display the results, the thin error bars in each graph display the standard error of the mean. Green colors indicate data collected in 2010, and purple, in 2012. Animator10 and Video12 were the upper baselines, Uninflect10 and Uninflect12 were the lower baselines, and Model10 and Model12 were the versions of the animations produced using our verb inflection model. Note that Uninflect10 and Uninflect12 were identical stimuli, the only difference was that the evaluation scores were collected in either the 2010 or 2012 study – likewise for Model10 and Model12.

To check for statistical significance, one-way ANOVAs were used for comprehension-question data, and Kruskal-Wallis tests for Likert-scale scores. The following comparisons were planned and conducted: (1) all three values from 2010, (2) all three values from 2012, (3) Video12 and Animator10, (4) Model12 and Model10, and (5) Uninflect12 and Uninflect10. Any of these planned comparisons that were statistically significant ($p<0.05$) have been marked with a star in Fig. 4, 5, and 6.

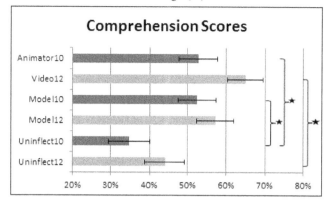

Fig. 4. Results of Comprehension Scores

Fig. 4 displays the comprehension-question accuracy scores from "part 1" of the 2010 and 2012 studies. There was no significant difference between Animator10 and Video12; so, hypothesis H1 was not supported. This was a surprising result: our videos of a human signer did not achieve higher comprehension scores than the animations of a virtual human with the verbs carefully animated by a human. This indicates that our upper baseline used in the 2010 study was a reasonable choice. Another surprising result (though not statistically significant) was that the 2012 scores for Model and Uninflected seemed a little higher. While no story was displayed more than one time during the study, we speculate that seeing a video of a human performing some of the ASL stories (with 3-5 characters set up in space and extensive use of inflected verbs) may have helped participants grasp the idea of the *overall genre* of the stories shown in the study, and perhaps this led to better comprehension scores for Model and Uninflect.

Since the differences between Model10/Model12 and between Uninflect10/Uninflect12 were not significant, then hypothesis H2 was partially supported – changing the upper baseline didn't significantly affect these scores. Of course, the support for H2 isn't clear. In 2010, there was a significant difference between Model10 and Uninflect10, in 2012, this significant difference could no longer be observed. So, H2 is only partially supported.

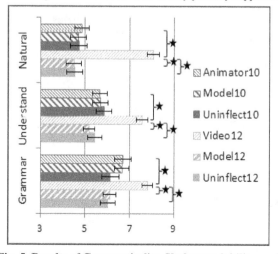

Fig. 5. Results of Grammaticality, Understandability, and Naturalness Likert-Scale Scores in the Two Studies

Fig. 5 displays the 1-to-10 Likert-scale subjective scores for grammaticality, understandability, and naturalness from "part 1" of the studies. Video12 had significantly higher grammaticality, understandability, and naturalness scores than Animator10 – thereby supporting hypothesis H3, that video of a human would get higher subjective Likert-scale scores than a virtual character animated by a human. Given that there was no significant difference in the comprehension scores between these, it was interesting that the subjective scores were significantly different. Participants subjectively preferred the videos, although there was no significant improvement in the comprehension scores.

In a similar vein, we note that Video12 had significantly higher Likert-scale scores than Model12 (Fig. 5) but did not have significantly higher comprehension scores than Model12 (Fig. 4). Videos of human signers seem to get higher subjective scores than do animations of virtual characters, but there isn't always a significant benefit in the comprehension scores. Given this observation, it is reasonable for future ASL evaluation studies to include both comprehension and Likert-scale subjective questions, since they seem to be measuring different aspects of animations.

The results in Fig. 5 did not support hypothesis H4; there was no significant depression in the Likert-scale scores for Model or Uninflect when we used the video upper baseline in 2012. When we examine the Likert-scale scores obtained during side-by-side comparisons in Fig. 6, we will see some contradictory results.

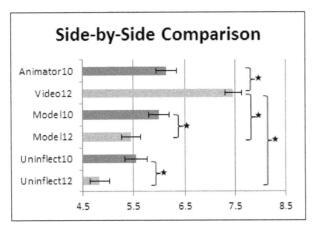

Fig. 6. Results of Side-by-side Comparison Scores

Fig. 6 displays the Likert-scale subjective scores collected from participants in 2010 and 2012 during "part 2" of the studies (the side-by-side comparison of identical sentences, with different versions of the verb in each, which could be replayed many times). Video12 is significantly higher than Animator10, further supporting hypothesis H3 (human videos would get higher Likert-scale subjective scores than animation upper baselines).

In Fig. 6, hypothesis H4 *was* supported: Using a human video upper baseline depressed the subjective Likert-scale scores that participants gave to the animations. Model12 was significantly lower than Model10, and Uninflect12 was significantly lower than Uninflect10. The magnitude of this depression is 10%-20%. This is not a surprising result; when looking at videos of humans in direct comparison to animations of a virtual human character, it is reasonable that participants would feel that the animations are less natural/grammatical. What is surprising is that we had not observed any significant depression in Fig. 5 when looking at the

Likert-scale data from part 1, in which participants assigned a Likert-scale subjective score to a story that they had just watched.

One explanation for this result may be that the depressive effect may depend on whether participants are assigning Likert-scale subjective scores to videos in a side-by-side direct comparison (as in part 2, Fig. 6) or sequentially throughout a study (as in part 1, Fig. 5). Perhaps in the side-by-side setting, the video looks very distinct from the other two stimuli, which are both animations. Another possible explanation for this result may be that during part 1 of the study, when watching a story one time and then answering the comprehension questions, the participants may have been very focused on the task of trying to understand and remember as much information as possible from the stories. Thus, they may have been less focused subjectively on the superficial appearance of the animations/videos.

Based on the feedback comments in 2012, participants indicated they felt comfortable with the experiments and animations/videos presented, writing: "It was overall good," "It is interesting to watch it," "That's a learning experience for me to get used to ASL animation," and "Would love to see the software!" The most frequent comments from participants were on the topic of the signing/appearance of the virtual human when comparing to the real human in the videos; some participants wrote: "The robot needs to look/sign more like a human," "Some pointing names were a little confusing," "When robot fingerspell a person name need little clearer," "The position of the eyes isn't exactly helpful," and "Some signs I could not understand like 'you,' it is easily overlooked. I didn't realize it was referring to "you" the whole experiment." Another theme in the feedback comments was that the facial expression of the virtual human character needs improvement, writing: "Lack of facial expression makes it quite difficult for me to understand the avatar", "I would like to see more facial expression but like eyebrows, mouth movement," etc.

As discussed in section 4, when creating baselines for comparison to animations in a study, a balance must be achieved between matching the content of the stimuli across versions and allowing for natural signing. Some of the comments of participants in the study indicated that in a few cases, we were not successful at this. Specifically, when producing the script for the human to perform in the video recordings, we included every sign that was performed by the virtual human character in the upper baseline animations from 2010. When a signer sets up points in space to represent entities under discussion, the signer may refer to these items later in the conversation by pointing to them. Because the movement path of an inflected ASL verb indicates the location around the signer where the subject and object of the verb are established, it is common (but not required) for signers to omit pointing to the subject/object before/after the verb (because the location in space that represents those entities is already indicated by the motion-path of the verb). The human animator who produced our upper baseline animations in 2010 still included some extra "pointing" to these locations, and so we included them in the script given to the human signer in 2012. In the feedback comments in 2012, some participants said: "Most verbs shouldn't end with the pointing of the finger (or direction) as the action already indicated that much," "too many endings were a pointing, it threw off my attention a lot," etc. What is interesting is that no participants criticized this in 2010, thus, when they saw a human signer performing this extra pointing movement, it felt more unnatural and warranted a comment at the end of the study.

6. CONCLUSIONS AND FUTURE WORK

This paper gives methodological guidance on the use of upper baselines in user-based evaluations of sign language animations. By replicating a past study and replacing the animated-character upper baseline in that study with a video of a human signer, we quantified how the evaluation scores collected were affected by this modification. This research has two key contributions: (1) This paper provides guidance for *future* sign language animation researchers who are designing a user-based evaluation study. They can make a more informed choice of which type of upper baseline to use for comparison in their study. (2) This paper provides guidance for readers of *previously published* studies who are trying to compare the results of studies that had used different upper baselines (animated-character or human-video). Given the results of our paper, it is easier for readers to understand how the scores might have been affected by the different study design.

Specifically, we examined four hypotheses in this study:

- **H1: Not supported.** Videos didn't get higher comprehension scores than our animated-character upper baseline. This indicates that an animated-character with proper movements can be an effective upper baseline for comprehension studies.
- **H2: Partially supported.** Changing to a video upper baseline didn't significantly affect the comprehension scores for the other stimuli, but a statistically significant difference between the "Model" animations and the "Uninflect" lower baseline animations in 2010 was no longer observed in 2012.
- **H3: Supported.** Human videos received higher Likert-scale subjective scores than an animated-character upper baseline.
- **H4: Should be split into two hypotheses** – for sequential collection of Likert-scale subjective evaluation scores during a task also involving answering comprehension questions (H4a) or during simultaneous side-by-side comparison (H4b).
  - **H4a: Not supported.** Using a human video upper baseline did not depress the subjective Likert scale scores that participants assign to the other stimuli during part 1 of our studies. Perhaps this was due to signers being asked to also answer comprehension questions during part 1 (and thus were less attuned to the subjective animation quality) or perhaps the depressive effect on Likert-scale subjective scores doesn't occur during sequential stimuli presentation.
  - **H4b. Supported.** A significant depression was measured in the Likert-scale scores of the "Model" and "Uninflect" animations during the side-by-side comparisons.

In short, the results presented in this paper indicate that either form of upper baseline is potentially valid for use in a user-study to evaluate animations of sign language – there are merely some effects on the scores collected that must be taken into account when comparing the results across studies. Thus, researchers should consider the goals of their research and the specific aspects of sign language animation that they are focusing on when selecting an appropriate upper baseline. Researchers studying computer graphics issues relating to the visual appearance of a virtual human for sign language animations may wish to include videos of humans as an upper baseline – since this would serve as an "ideal" of photorealism. Further, researchers who wish to convey to a lay audience the overall understandability of their sign language animations (i.e., the current state of the art) may prefer using videos of humans as an upper baseline because it makes it easier to communicate to a lay audience the current quality level of their animations. Alternatively, researchers who are studying linguistic issues for sign language animations (e.g., sequencing of signs, the speed/timing of signs, the movement paths of the hands during certain signs, the timing of facial movements that relate to the signs, etc.) may find an animated-character baseline more useful to their research. For researchers who are not studying computer graphics issues related to the character's appearance, more useful data may be obtained from comparing their animations to an upper baseline of an animated character – thereby isolating the movement/timing from the appearance. For researchers who are not adjusting appearance aspects of a character, such a baseline may serve as their "ideal" of the correct movements and timing for a virtual character. The downside is that it is more difficult to convey to non-specialists the current quality level of their animations, because they are not being directly compared to a human video. Of course, researchers with enough time/resources to conduct a study with participants to compare a larger number of groups of animations and videos may wish to include both forms of upper baseline.

Researchers should also consider that while using a video upper baseline may yield evaluations that are easier for a lay audience to understand, it could lead to misconceptions. The human might do things that ASL animation technology will not be able to do in the next decade or two, e.g., automatically planning subtle emotional aspects of facial movement, automatically constructing complex 3D classifier predicate expressions, etc. Researchers using video upper baselines would need to explain these limitations to manage the expectations of a lay audience being presented their results.

Further, producing a human video that is a good upper baseline is harder than researchers may expect (see section 4). Depending on the specific linguistic phenomena that you are trying to keep constant across all of the versions of animations/videos shown in a study, the human performer's task is difficult to impossible. In our study, much work was required to assure that the human had identical sign sequencing, identical subject/object and pointing locations, and approximately similar overall time duration as the animations to which it was being compared. If a researcher needed to produce an upper baseline that also held constant some aspect of signing that is very detailed (e.g. precise millisecond timing of speed/pauses, exact height of the eyebrows, etc.), then asking a human to exactly perform this could be nearly impossible.

In future work, we want to explore the reason why no depressive effect was measured for H4a: Was it because the participants had also been asked to perform a comprehension task or because they were provided Likert-scale subjective ratings sequentially (not side-by-side)? A follow-up study could disambiguate this. When a depression of Likert-scale scores does occur due to a video upper baseline, we are also interested in determining if this could lead to a "compression" of the scores for the "middle" stimuli (animation being evaluated) and the lower baseline (as these two values are compressed downward toward the lower end of the Likert scale). If so, this would be undesirable because it could be more difficult to distinguish differences between the lower baseline and the animation being evaluated. Unfortunately, we could not address this issue in the current paper because the Likert-scale scores for Uninflect10 and Model10 were already indistinguishably close (there was little room for them to get any closer in our 2012 study.) In future work, we would need to use as a starting point a study with lower baseline, our model, and upper baseline animations with a significant difference between all three cases in the Likert-scale scores. By replicating such a study, we could determine if the use of a video upper baseline led to this "compression" effect.

7. ACKNOWLEDGMENTS

This material is based upon work supported in part by the US. National Science Foundation under award number 0746556 and award number 1065009, by the PSC-CUNY Research Award Program, by Siemens A&D UGS PLM Software through a Go PLM Academic Grant, and by Visage Technologies AB through a free academic license. We would like to thank our advisor Matt Huenerfauth for his support and contributions to this paper. Jonathan Lamberton assisted with the recruitment of participants and the conduct of experimental sessions described in this paper.

8. REFERENCES

[1] Ahlberg, J., Pandzic, I.S., You, L. 2002. Evaluating face models animated by MPEG-4. In *I.S. Pandzic, R. Forchheimer (eds.), MPEG-4 facial animation: the standard, implementations and applications*, Wiley & Sons, 291–296.

[2] Bergmann, K. 2012. The production of co-speech iconic gestures: empirical study and computational simulation with virtual agents. Dissertation, Bielefeld University, Germany.

[3] Davidson, M. J., Alkoby, K., Sedgwick, E., Berthiaume, A., Carter, R., Christopher, J., Craft, B., Furst, J., Hinkle, D., Konie, B., Lancaster, G., Luecking, S., Morris, A., McDonald, J., Tomuro, N., Toro, J. and Wolfe, R. 2000. Usability Testing of Computer Animation of Fingerspelling for American Sign Language. *Presented at the 2000 DePaul CTI Research Conference*, Chicago, IL, November 4, 2000.

[4] Garau, M., Slater, M., Bee, S., and Sasse, M. A. 2001. The impact of eye gaze on communication using humanoid avatars. In *SIGCHI'01*, Seattle, USA. ACM, NY, USA.

[5] Gibet, S., Courty, N., Duarte, K., and Le Naour, T. 2011. The SignCom system for data-driven animation of interactive virtual signers: Methodology and evaluation. *ACM Trans. Interact. Intell. Syst.* 1, 1, Article 6 (October 2011), 23 pgs.

[6] Huenerfauth, M. 2006. Generating American Sign Language Classifier Predicates For English-To-ASL Machine Translation. Doctoral Dissertation, Computer and Information Science, University of Pennsylvania.

[7] Huenerfauth, M., Hanson, V. 2009. Sign language in the interface: access for deaf signers. In C. Stephanidis (ed.), *Universal Access Handbook*. NJ: Erlbaum. 38.1-38.18.

[8] Huenerfauth, M., Lu, P. 2012. Effect of spatial reference and verb inflection on the usability of American sign language animation. In *Univ Access Inf Soc*. Berlin: Springer.

[9] Huenerfauth, M., Zhao, L., Gu, E., Allbeck, J. 2008. Evaluation of American sign language generation by native ASL signers. *ACM Trans Access Comput* 1(1):1-27.

[10] Huenerfauth, M., Lu, P. 2010. Modeling and Synthesizing Spatially Inflected Verbs for American Sign Language Animations. In *Proceedings of The 12th International ACM SIGACCESS Conference on Computers and Accessibility (ASSETS 2010)*, Orlando, Florida, USA. New York: ACM Press.

[11] Huenerfauth, M., Lu, P., and Rosenberg, A. 2011. Evaluating Importance of Facial Expression in American Sign Language and Pidgin Signed English Animations. In *Proceedings of The 13th International ACM SIGACCESS Conference on Computers and Accessibility (ASSETS 2011)*, Dundee, Scotland. New York: ACM Press.

[12] Kennaway, J. R., Glauert, J. R. W. and Zwitserlood, I. 2007. Providing signed content on the Internet by synthesized animation. *ACM Trans. Comput.-Hum. Interact.* 14, 3, Article 15 (September 2007).

[13] Kipp, M., Heloir, A., Nguyen, Q. 2011. Sign language avatars: animation and comprehensibility. In *H. Vilhjálmsson, S. Kopp, S. Marsella, K. Thórisson (eds.), Intelligent Virtual Agents* (Vol. 6895). Springer, 113-126.

[14] Kipp, M., Nguyen, Q., Heloir, A., and Matthes, S. 2011. Assessing the deaf user perspective on sign language avatars. In *Proceedings of ASSETS'11*, Dundee, Scotland. ACM, New York, NY, USA, 107-114.

[15] Lu, P., Huenerfauth, M. 2011. Synthesizing American Sign Language Spatially Inflected Verbs from Motion-Capture Data. *Second International Workshop on Sign Language Translation and Avatar Technology (SLTAT)*, in conjunction with *ASSETS 2011*, Dundee, Scotland.

[16] Lu, P., Huenerfauth, M. 2010. Collecting a Motion-Capture Corpus of American Sign Language for Data-Driven Generation Research. *Proceedings of the First Workshop on Speech and Language Processing for Assistive Technologies (SLPAT), The 11th Annual Conference of the North American Chapter of the Association for Computational Linguistics (HLT-NAACL 2010)*, Los Angeles, CA, USA.

[17] Lu, P., Huenerfauth, M. 2012. Collecting and Evaluating the CUNY ASL Corpus for Research on American Sign Language Animation. Manuscript submitted for publication.

[18] Lu, P., Huenerfauth, M. (2012, in press). Learning a Parameterized Lexicon of American Sign Language Inflecting Verbs from Motion-Capture Data. *Proceedings of the Second Workshop on Speech and Language Processing for Assistive Technologies (SLPAT), Human Language Technologies: The 12th Annual Conference of the North American Chapter of the Association for Computational Linguistics (HLT-NAACL 2012)*, Montreal, Canada.

[19] Mitchell, R., Young, T., Bachleda, B., & Karchmer, M. 2006. How many people use ASL in the United States? Why estimates need updating. *Sign Lang Studies*, 6(3):306-335.

[20] Pražák, M., McDonnell, R. and O'Sullivan, C. 2010. Perceptual evaluation of human animation timewarping. In *ACM SIGGRAPH ASIA 2010 Sketches (SA 2010)*. ACM, New York, NY, USA, Article 30, 2 pages.

[21] Schnepp, J. and Shiver, B. 2011. Improving Deaf Accessibility in Remote Usability Testing. In *Proc. of ASSETS'11*, Dundee, Scotland. ACM, New York, 255-256.

[22] Schnepp, J., Wolfe, R. and McDonald, J. 2010. Synthetic Corpora: A Synergy of Linguistics and Computer Animation. *Fourth Workshop on the Representation and Processing of Sign Languages, LREC 2010*. Valetta, Malta.

[23] Schnepp, J., Wolfe, R., Shiver, B., McDonald, J. and Toro, J. 2011. SignQUOTE: A Remote Testing Facility for Eliciting Signed Qualitative Feedback. *2nd Int'l Workshop on Sign Language Translation & Avatar Technology*, Dundee, UK.

[24] Traxler, C. 2000. The Stanford achievement test, 9th edition: national norming and performance standards for deaf & hard-of-hearing students. *J Deaf Stud & Deaf Educ* 5(4):337-348.

[25] VCom3D. 2012. Homepage. http://www.vcom3d.com/

Design and Evaluation of Classifier for Identifying Sign Language Videos in Video Sharing Sites

Caio D.D. Monteiro, Ricardo Gutierrez-Osuna, Frank M. Shipman III
Department of Computer Science and Engineering
Texas A&M University
College Station, Texas, 77843-3112
1-979-862-3216

caioduarte.diniz@gmail.com, rgutier@cse.tamu.edu, shipman@cse.tamu.edu

ABSTRACT

Video sharing sites provide an opportunity for the collection and use of sign language presentations about a wide range of topics. Currently, locating sign language videos (SL videos) in such sharing sites relies on the existence and accuracy of tags, titles or other metadata indicating the content is in sign language. In this paper, we describe the design and evaluation of a classifier for distinguishing between sign language videos and other videos. A test collection of SL videos and videos likely to be incorrectly recognized as SL videos (likely false positives) was created for evaluating alternative classifiers. Five video features thought to be potentially valuable for this task were developed based on common video analysis techniques. A comparison of the relative value of the five video features shows that a measure of the symmetry of movement relative to the face is the best feature for distinguishing sign language videos. Overall, an SVM classifier provided with all five features achieves 82% precision and 90% recall when tested on the challenging test collection. The performance would be considerably higher when applied to the more varied collections of large video sharing sites.

Categories and Subject Descriptors

I.4.9 [**Image Processing and Computer Vision**]: Applications. K.4.2 [**Computers and Society**]: Social Issues – *Assistive technologies for persons with disabilities.*

General Terms

Algorithms, Design, Experimentation, Human Factors.

Keywords

Sign language, ASL, video analysis, video sharing, metadata extraction.

1. INTRODUCTION

Sign languages have developed in many countries and regions. These languages have their own vocabulary, syntax and grammar that is distinct from the spoken/written language of their region [19]. Unlike written communication, however, and more like

spoken communication, signing provides a wealth of non-verbal information. Thus, video sharing websites offer a great opportunity for members of the deaf and hard of hearing community to exchange signed content. Unfortunately, video sharing services do not have the ability to locate untagged or unlabeled sign language (SL) content. As a result, members of this community rely on ad-hoc mechanisms to pass around pointers to internet-based recordings, such as email, blogs, etc.

In what follows, we will use the term "SL video" to denote videos where one person faces the camera and records an expression in a SL; examples of SL video are shown in Figure 1. While other forms of videos can include sign language (e.g. video of a conversation between signers), these deliberate recordings of an individual's message are a form of sign language document meant to be accessed by others.

Figure 1. Examples of SL video from video sharing sites

While early work on recognizing SL in video is underway, most of the efforts focus on translating the sign into English (or another spoken/written language). Because of the complexity of the problem, most of this work emphasizes the recognition of hand shape and orientation but such capabilities, while necessary, are not sufficient to translate sign language. The meaning of American Sign Language (ASL) is determined by a combination of five characteristics: the shape of the hand(s), the position of the hand(s), the palm orientation of the hand(s), the direction and speed of motion of the hand(s), and the facial expression. Without taking into account all five components, true translation of ASL is not possible. For example, a hand shape and orientation recognizer could identify the sign for "help" but without position and motion information would be unable to identify who was helping whom and without the facial expression would not know whether the help was going to happen or not, or whether it was a statement of fact or a question. Even with accurate identification of a sign, the concept of that sign must be translated based on the context and prior content, similar to translating between spoken/written languages.

The work presented here aims at a shorter-term goal: automatically identifying sign language video found in video sharing sites. Such a capability would immediately allow members of the deaf and hard-of-hearing community to limit their searches within the large corpora of videos to those in sign language.

The next section further describes the motivation for this project. This is followed by an overview of related work. We then describe the design of the classifier and its evaluation. Finally, we give directions for future work and conclusions from the project.

2. MOTIVATION

Approximately 0.5% of the US population is functionally deaf using the definition "at best, can hear and understand words shouted in the better ear" [10]. For many that become deaf early in life, sign language is their primary means of communication. As is true with spoken languages, a unique community has formed around ASL with its own cultural norms and expectations [15]. The same is true in many other countries.

Many who grow up deaf learn English as a second language – ASL being their first learned language. Combined with late-identification of hearing loss and the lack of communication during formative periods of the brain's development, this means that the average reading/writing skills among members of the deaf population are well below average. Holt et al. [11] found that the median reading comprehension for deaf and hard-of-hearing 17- and 18-year-olds is at a 4.0 grade level, indicating half the population has a lower reading level than typical hearing students at the beginning of 4th grade. As such, for large portions of the deaf community, much of the information available on the Internet is difficult to locate and understand. For the internet to more fully support this community, information needs to be available in sign language.

Figure 2. Videos returned on the first page of results for query "sign language" that are not in sign language. Two are for songs with "sign language" in the title, one is on sign language recognition research, and one refers to the language in signs.

On-line video sharing sites, such as YouTube, have provided members of the deaf and hard of hearing community a way to publish and access content in sign language. Since these sites are developed for sharing all video, it is difficult to locate SL video on a particular topic unless it is accurately tagged for both topic and language. Studies of community-assigned tags indicate that tags alone are unlikely to provide reliable access to the contents of a collection [7][12]. Even when appropriately applied, tags related to sign language, such as "ASL", are ambiguous since they could be indicating that the video is either in sign language or about sign language. Figure 2 shows examples of such videos returned by YouTube for "sign language". The ability to identify sign language video would help resolve such ambiguities and also would be valuable when used in conjunction with tags to locate sign language videos (when tags exist). When tags are not available, a likely event when videos include sign language interpretation in a region of the video, the results of our work could greatly improve access.

3. RELATED WORK

While a few web sites provide access to SL video, research related to these projects primarily concerns aspects of SL translation – either handshape or sign recognition. These efforts can be classified according to whether they rely on standard unaugmented video, require signers to wear visual markers to help tracking of hands (e.g. colored gloves, infrared tags), or use data gloves and other sensors.

3.1 Locating Sign Language Video

To locate SL video, people either go to Internet video sharing sites, such as YouTube or sites devoted to SL such as http://www.deafvideo.tv/ or http://www.deafread.com/vlogs/. To the best of our knowledge, there is no previous work on automatically discriminating SL from other forms of content in video, neither are we aware of previous work on classifying SLs based on video information. An ASL video directory, http://www.aslvlog.net/, has started to categorize ASL videos according to topic. While covering a wide range of topics, there are relatively few videos found on this site compared to the 51800 videos found on YouTube that are returned from the query "ASL", 61400 for "sign language", 2390 for "British sign language", and 3090 for "'lenguaje de señas". Several academic projects provide SL content, such as SignStream [14], or the European ECHO project [3], but these corpora are designed for researchers engaged in sign language translation efforts rather than for the deaf and hard of hearing or for detecting sign language or identifying the sign language in use.

3.2 Recognizing Sign Language in Unaugmented Video

Recognizing the content of SL from video only, as is available on video sharing sites, is a very difficult problem. In one of the earliest studies, Starner et al. [18] used hidden Markov models (HMMs) to recognize a vocabulary of 40 words for a single signer. The goal was to provide a SL-to-English translator that would allow the deaf to communicate in one-on-one situations. Thus, in addition to testing the approach with a camera facing the signer, the authors also mounted a camera on a hat worn by the signer in order to create a portable system. The resulting recognition rates were 92% for the desktop camera and 98% for the head mounted camera. Limitations for our application are the small size of the vocabulary and the quantity of training data required for each signer.

One component of recognizing a sign is recognizing handshape. Somers and Whyte [17] used a hybrid of 3D models and silhouettes to identify the handshape (called "hand posture" in Irish Sign Language). With a set of eight images (2 for each of four handshapes) and a vocabulary of eight handshapes, their approach achieved a classification rate of 50%.

Instead of using a learned vocabulary or 3D model, other researchers have treated the problem as a lookup problem – with the goal of finding the sign in a database of known signs through image similarity. Dimov et al. [5] used a database of known signs, represented by a series of 2D projections, to do a similarity search to recognize alphabet signs. With a vocabulary of seven letter signs and an average of 49 instances of each in the database, the authors achieved a classification rate of 96%. Potamias and Athitsos [16] also used nearest neighbor search of images for handshape recognition. With a set of 20 common ASL handshapes, the accuracy was 33% on 256x256 images across a number of ASL signers.

Given the five components to each sign – handshape, position, palm orientation, motion, and facial expression – using a variety of video features and techniques is required. Caridakis et al. [2] presented an architecture for providing features for hand trajectory, region, and shape to a combination of self-organizing maps, Markov chains, and HMMs for recognition. To the best of our knowledge, the work was not implemented or evaluated so there are no accuracy results or vocabulary estimates.

3.3 Detecting Sign Language

Detecting sign language is a much simpler problem than translating it. As an example, Cherniavsky et al. [1] developed an activity detection technique for cell-phone cameras that could determine whether a user was signing or not with 91% accuracy, even in the presence of noisy (i.e., moving) backgrounds. The algorithm was used to determine when the video phone user was signing and when they were watching the video of their conversational partner in order to effectively use network bandwidth during a sign language conversation on mobile devices. Thus, it is unlikely this algorithm would be as successful in distinguishing between sign language videos and other videos involving people gesturing.

3.4 Limitations and Challenges

A challenge for the above approaches is that most approaches work only modestly with relatively small vocabularies unless they rely on data gloves or other obtrusive equipment, and are single-signer approaches that require large amounts of training data. Signer-dependent solutions are not practical for video classification. Another difficulty is that only a handful of authors (e.g. [9]; [20]) have attempted to recognize signs in sentences or phrases rather than as isolated expressions. Finally, most of these efforts do not discuss the speed of expression – a fluent signer communicates very rapidly with other fluent signers but will drastically slow down for non-fluent signers. Given these challenges, our approach to supporting the sign language community avoids translating SL in the first place.

4. DESIGN OF SL-VIDEO CLASSIFIER

The SL-Video classifier is composed by two components: the first is responsible for video processing and analysis in order to generate video features and the second is responsible for using the features to classify the videos into those that are SL video as we have defined it and those that are not.

4.1 Video processing

Each video is analyzed frame by frame by a video processing subsystem, developed using openFrameworks [12], an open source toolkit that includes video processing functionality.

The first step in extracting video features is to define the background and foreground of each frame image. The background is meant to contain all non-moving elements in the video, while the foreground is the portion of the image that varies from frame-to-frame. Once the foreground and background for the video frames are determined, the results are combined with face detection to compute the video features that are used to classify the video.

4.1.1 Background Modeling

Since the identification of SL video must work with a wide variety of already existing videos, it cannot assume a pre-defined or static background model. Although plenty of SL videos contain a person signing in front of the camera with no background changes, some videos have changes in the background due to lighting changes or moving background objects. So a dynamic background [5][7] is best suited for this task.

Since the goal is to classify if the video contains sign language or not, it is not important to fully identify the signer as a single foreground object. This is good because an additional difference from some video contexts is that the person signing is often already seated in front of the camera at the beginning of the video. This allows a relatively simple dynamic background model without losing information needed by the classifier.

Our background model is built in real time as a running average of the grayscale frames of the video, with a learning rate value which can be adjusted to alter how fast the background model changes over time. Having a high learning rate results is a highly dynamic background model where just the most abrupt movements are detected, while with a low learning rate any slightly change in the image will be detected. For this task a learning rate of 0.04 has proven to be a suitable choice. Thus the background model for a background pixel BP at time t is:

$$BP_t = .96 * BP_{(t-1)} + .04 \, P$$

where P is the grayscale value of the pixel at time t. Figure 3 (c) shows the background model for the video at the time shown in Figure 3 (a).

The foreground image is obtained through the subtraction of the current video frame from the current background image. Every pixel where the subtraction result is greater than a threshold (our threshold is 45) is considered as a foreground pixel. Figure 3 (d) shows the results of this process for the frame in Figure 3 (a). To avoid noise in the foreground image that can result from objects moving in the background of the signer and the results of normal body movement, a spatial filter is used to remove small regions of foreground pixels in the image, the result of which is shown in Figure 3 (b). As shown in Figure 3, our background model can contain the whole image, including the signer except for his or her hands and arms. Now with the final foreground model, we can start the feature extraction process.

**Figure 3. (a) the incoming frame of the video, (b) the final foreground image,
(c) the actual background model and (d) the intermediate foreground image**

4.1.2 Feature Extraction

Before calculating the features used for classification, we need to identify the position of the signer's head. This is done through face detection based on Haar-like features [20]. Figure 3 (a) shows a white box around the face location.

Combining the foreground model and the results of face detection, we can calculate the amount of movement in regions relative to the face, indicated by the nine regions shown in Figure 3 (b). This provides information regarding the positions and movements of the two hands relative to the head.

Initially, we computed the quantity of movement in each of the nine regions for each frame of the video as the movement of the hands relative to the body is one of the most unique features on sign language, and probably the easiest to recognize. Because of the quantity of data (9 values for every frame of the video), we further condense the data into five single-value features per video that can be provided to a classifier.

The five features were developed with the intuition that the quantity and location of sign language motion is distinct from the motion associated with normal gesturing (as done by a politician at a podium), domain-oriented gesturing (like a weatherperson), and other forms of human motion (dance, mime, charades). These include features concerning the overall quantity of movement, the continuity of movement, and the location of the movement relative to the face.

The type of SL video which we are attempting to identify has a single signer who signs fairly continuously, resulting in a large amount of movement when compared with other videos of people. With regards to the quantity of movement, we compute two features: (VF1) the number of pixels included in the final foreground model for each frame, averaged across frames, and (VF2) the percentage of pixels that are included in the final foreground model for at least one frame. VF1 is a measure of the total amount of activity in the video while VF2 is a measure of how the spatial distribution of that activity changes over multiple frames. With regards to the continuity of motion, we compute one feature: (VF3) the average difference between the final foreground pixels in one frame and in the previous frame. To differentiate SL video from other videos of fairly continuous human motion we included two features associated with the location of motion: (VF4) the symmetry of motion, measured as the average number of final foreground pixels that are in a symmetric position relative to the center of the face, and (VF5) the percentage of frames with non-facial movement, measured as the average percentage of pixels outside of the facial rectangle that are part of the final foreground. As many signs are made with a single hand or using different gestures for each hand and some signs that are symmetric, SL videos are likely to fall within a symmetry band. Similarly, SL videos contain significant hands/arms and torso movements relative to head movement, so the number of frames containing foreground pixels outside the face region is an important feature. Once computed, these five features are used to classify the video as being SL video or not.

4.2 Classifier

Since the goal of the project is to classify the videos between Sign Language and non-Sign Language, a binary classifier is suitable. We explored several classifiers but chose a Support Vector Machine (SVM) classifier [3] due to its performance compared to other classifiers (e.g., Gaussian classifiers, nearest neighbors) at an early stage in the project. The SVM was trained on a dataset containing SL videos and non-SL videos, each video represented by the five feature values described in the previous section. As illustrated in Figure 4, the SVM classifier works by projecting the original feature vector (5-dimensional) into a higher dimensional space by means of a non-linear mapping. By choosing the mapping carefully, computation in the high-dimensional space can be performed implicitly (i.e., through the so-called kernel trick). Operating in this high-dimensional space also improves the probability that classes become linearly separable.

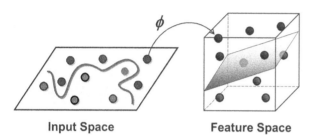

Figure 4. Example of a SVM classifier model, the black line represents the borderland between one class and another

5. EVALUATION OF CLASSIFIER

Evaluation of our approach consisted of developing a corpus of SL videos and non-SL videos, preprocessing this corpus to generate the features described for each video, and using these features to classify the video.

5.1 Developing a Training/Testing Corpus

In order to evaluate the classifier we created a collection of 192 videos, including 98 Sign Language videos (including 78 in American Sign Language and 20 in British Sign Language) and 94 non-Sign Language videos. The videos were selected from video sharing sites like YouTube, Vimeo, etc. Most of these videos were located based on tags or metadata indicating they had some relationship to sign language.

Figure 5. Examples of non-Sign Language videos that are visually similar to sign language videos and thus likely false-positives for the classifier

The majority of the non-Sign Language videos were selected by browsing for likely false-positives based on visual analysis (e.g. the whole video consists of a gesturing presenter, weather forecaster, or other person moving their hands and arms.) A small subset of the non-Sign Language videos were chosen as they included tags or metadata indicating a relationship to sign language (e.g. videos you would likely locate when searching for videos in sign language.) While we found a number of such videos (e.g. Figure 2), we kept the number of videos collected due to tag/metadata confusion low as we found they tend to be visually distinct from the sign language videos and thus not difficult for our classifier. For example, if the video does not include a person for most of the duration, it will be very easy to classify it just based on face detection. Figure 5 shows examples of non-SL videos in the database.

5.2 Processing of Videos

The videos chosen were in the MPEG4 format and were subsampled to 1 minute length each. This time was chosen as it is long enough for feature extraction yet keeps the processing requirements bounded despite the length of the original video. We are currently not looking at cases where a single video includes segments we would consider SL video and other segments of non-SL video.

The subsampled interval for each video was randomly chosen, just assuring that this interval was not on the start of the video or at the end in order to avoid any front or back matter (e.g. credits at the end or titles or other pre-presentation content at the beginning). The video processing and feature extraction routines were then run on each subsample and the results were stored for use by the various classifiers considered.

5.3 Results

The classifier was tested on 1000 executions for each context; in each execution the training and test data were selected randomly, accordingly to the training set size of the experimental unit.

The performance measures considered are the precision (number of correct SL classifications divided by all SL classifications), recall (number of correct SL classifications divided by the total number of SL videos in the testing set), and the F1 score (a combination of precision and recall). Table 1 shows the results for different training set sizes; in all cases, examples not included in the training set were used for testing.

Table 1. Results obtained when varying the size of the training set for the classifier with all five visual features as inputs

# Videos/Class	Precision	Recall	F1 Score
15	81.73%	86.47%	0.84
30	83.62%	88.11%	0.85
45	80.67%	91.00%	0.85
60	82.21%	90.83%	0.86

As the number of videos used to train the classifier is increased, the precision stays relatively stable (irregularly varying within a 3% band) but recall increases by more than 4%. This indicates that while more training data improves the classifier, it works well with only 15 videos per training group.

Given this result, we explored the relative value of the five visual features. As a reminder, the five video features are:

- VF1: the number of pixels included in the final foreground model for each frame, averaged across frames

- VF2: the percentage of pixels which are included in the final foreground model for at least one frame

- VF3: the average difference between the final foreground pixels in one frame and in the previous frame

- VF4: the symmetry of motion, measured as the average number of final foreground pixels that are in a symmetric position relative to the center of the face

- VF5: the percentage of frames with non-facial movement, measured as the average percentage of pixels outside of the facial rectangle that are part of the final foreground

We first explored the performance of the classifier when we remove each of the features. We again use 15 videos per training class and provide all but one of the videos features as input. Table 2 presents the results.

Table 2. Results when one feature is not provided to the classifier with a training set of 15 videos/class

Video Feature Removed	Precision	Recall	F1 Score
VF1	80.36%	86.25%	0.83
VF2	78.34%	85.41%	0.82
VF3	78.90%	83.62%	0.81
VF4	72.80%	74.30%	0.74
VF5	78.86%	85.60%	0.82

The results show that the feature that added the most discriminating power to the classifier when compared to the other features is VF4, a measure of the symmetry of motion relative to the face. Without VF4, the precision dropped almost 9% and recall dropped more than 12% from the performance of the classifier with all five features. There was not a strong effect from dropping any of the other four features, implying they may overlap in the type of information they are providing to the classifier. VF1 was the least valuable feature in this context – its removal resulted in a 1.3% drop in precision and a drop of 0.2% in recall.

Finally, we explored which single visual feature provided the most discriminative power when used as the sole input to the classifier. Again, the classifier was trained on 15 videos from each class. The results are shown in Table 3.

When comparing the ability of a single video feature to classify SL video the results again indicate the best predictor is VF4. The difference between this feature and the other four is significant; Feature 4 alone outperforms the other four features combined.

This result is interesting because it gives direction in the search for additional video features that might be valuable for this task. VF4 is a measure of the symmetry of motion relative to the face of the signer indicating alternative measures comparing movement on the two sides of the body should be explored.

Table 3. Results when only one feature is provided to the classifier with a training set of 15 videos/class

Video Feature	Precision	Recall	F1 Score
VF1	70.48%	60.14%	0.65
VF2	73.57%	53.26%	0.62
VF3	65.65%	64.03%	0.65
VF4	75.95%	83.69%	0.80
VF5	56.31%	49.52%	0.53

As observed from the results, with a good feature selection, the SVM is successful at classifying the majority of videos as being either SL video or not, even with small training sets. Given the non-SL videos were selected to be as similar to sign language video as possible, we expect that such a classifier would perform at a quite high degree of accuracy when applied to the broader collections found on video sharing sites.

5.4 Discussion of Failures

Working with videos collected from video sharing sites results in a variety of issues that impact classification performance. Poor illumination, sudden illumination changes, and poor video resolution resulted in some videos being incorrectly classified.

Examples of videos that are difficult to classify are shown in Figure 6. We already have discussed why videos may be incorrectly classified as being SL video: a presenter facing the camera and gesturing fairly constantly makes correct classification difficult, such as the newscaster in Figure 6 (a). Some SL videos were not detected because the signer was sitting too far from the camera or was not facing the camera resulting in their face not being detected, as in Figure 6 (b). Additionally, signing in front of backgrounds with lots of movement (Figure 6 (c)) is not detected because the hand/arm blobs get combined with the other activity. The background model also causes problems when the background includes colors that match the skin tone or shirt color of the signer, such as the couch in Figure 6 (d).

Figure 6. Examples of videos which are difficult to successfully classify with current approach.

These problems point to the need to improve the current process for modeling the background and to improve on our simple approach of equating face detection in a frame to face location.

6. FUTURE WORK

Our initial success leads to a variety of directions for future work. First, we want to improve our background modeling process to increase the accuracy of the final foreground blobs being the hands and arms of the signer for SL video. Additionally, we hope to develop a more adaptive background model, capable of additional video situations, such as videos with more than one signer, videos with the signer in different positions relative to the camera, etc. Similarly, we want to improve on the use of face detection. In particular, we can use the knowledge that a face was detected in a prior frame and there is no reason to believe the person has moved or the shot has changed to infer the position of the head in subsequent frames.

We also are attempting to identify additional meaningful video features that will increase the SVM performance. While we compared different types of classifiers early on in the project, we plan to examine the performance of other classifiers (e.g. Neural Networks) with the video features we have since developed.

Additionally, we plan to develop a larger collection of SL video and non-SL video to increase the variety of videos being used for training and evaluation. Finally, we plan for the current approach to serve as a starting point to more complex tasks in this area, such as attempting to classify SL videos based on which sign language is found in the video (American Sign Language, British Sign Language, etc.) and to identify videos that have sign language translation within a region of the video.

7. CONCLUSIONS

YouTube, Vimeo and other general purpose video sharing sites are being used to share sign language presentations among the sign language community. Currently, pointers to these videos are emailed or otherwise communicated from person to person. To locate such videos using the search facilities provided by the sites requires the existence and accuracy of tags or other metadata indicating a relationship to sign language.

We have presented an approach to classifying videos as being sign language videos or not without any previous information about them. A SVM classifier was provided with five video features identified as potentially valuable for this process. The extraction of the five features relies on relatively simple background modeling and face detection.

A collection of videos for training and testing the classifier was created by selecting SL videos and non-SL videos that were likely false positives from video sharing sites. Our evaluation showed that training the classifier does not require large quantities of training data – while the classifier improved with more examples, 15 examples for each category were sufficient to have greater than 81% precision and 86% recall.

Comparison of the five video features showed that a measure of the symmetry of motion relative to the center of the face was the most accurate feature when used alone for classification. Alone it was more accurate than using the other four features combined.

The goal of this capability is to increase access to sign language presentations for members of the sign language community. The existing classifier could be applied to video sharing sites so users could filter their search results with accuracy rates much higher than reported here since the non-SL videos in our collection were chosen to be hard to differentiate from sign language videos.

Our future work looks to improve on the current classifier by improving the video processing techniques used for feature extraction and by identifying alternative features. Further, we plan to apply the classifier to new settings, such as identifying sign language translation in a region of a video and for identifying which sign language is being used in an SL video.

8. ACKNOWLEDGMENTS

This material is based upon work supported in part by the National Science Foundation under Grant No. DUE 09-38074, by a gift from Microsoft Corporation, and by NPRP grant # [08-125-2-03] from the Qatar National Research Fund (a member of Qatar Foundation). The statements made herein are solely the responsibility of the authors.

9. REFERENCES

[1] N. Cherniavsky, R.E. Ladner, and E.A. Riskin, "Activity detection in conversational sign language video for mobile telecommunication", *Proceedings of the 8th IEEE International Conference on Automatic Face & Gesture Recognition (FG '08)*, 2008, pp.1-6.

[2] G. Caridakis, O. Diamanti, K. Karpouzis, and P. Maragos, "Automatic Sign Language Recognition: Vision Based Feature Extraction and Probabilistic Recognition Scheme from Multiple Cues", *PETRA '08: Proceedings of the 1st International Conference on PErvasive Technologies Related to Assistive Environments*, 2008.

[3] N. Cristianini and J. Shawe-Taylor, *An Introduction to Support Vector Machines: And Other Kernel-Based Learning Methods, First Edition.* Cambridge University Press, 2000.

[4] O. Crasborn, J. Mesch, D. Waters, A. Nonhebel, E. van der Kooij, B. Woll and B. Bergman, "Sharing sign language data online. Experiences from the ECHO project," *International Journal of Corpus Linguistics 12(4)*, 535–562, 2007.

[5] R. Cucchiara, C. Grana, M. Piccardi, and A. Prati. "Detecting moving objects, ghosts and shadows in video streams". *IEEE Transactions on Pattern Analysis and Machine Intelligence*, 2003, pp. 1337-1342.

[6] D. Dimov, A. Marinov, and N. Zlateva, "CBIR Approach to the Recognition of a Sign Language Alphabet", *CompSysTech '07: Proceedings of the 2007 International Conference on Computer Systems and Technologies*, 2007.

[7] Brian Gloyer. "Video-based freeway-monitoring system using recursive vehicle tracking". *Proceedings of SPIE*, 1995, pp. 173-180.

[8] M. Heckner, T. Neubauer, and C. Wolff, "Tree, funny, to_read, google: What are Tags Supposed to Achieve?", *Proceedings of the 2008 Workshop on Search in Social Media*, 2008, pp. 3-10.

[9] J.L. Hernandez-Rebollar, "Gesture-Driven American Sign Language Phraselator", *ICMI '05: Proceedings of the 7th International Conference on Multimodal Interfaces*, 2005, pp. 288-292.

[10] J. Holt, S. Hotto, and K. Cole, *Demographic Aspects of Hearing Impairment: Questions and Answers, Third Edition*, Center for Assessment and Demographic Studies, Gallaudet University, 1994.

[11] J. Holt, C. Traxler, and T. Allen, *Interpreting the Scores: A User's Guide to the 9th Edition Stanford Achievement Test for Educators of Deaf and Hard-of-Hearing Students.* Gallaudet Research Institute Technical Report 97-1. Washington, DC: Gallaudet University, 1997.

[12] Z. Lieberman and T. Watson. http://www.openframeworks.cc/ Accessed September 2011

[13] C. Marshall, "No Bull, No Spin: A Comparison of Tags with Other Forms of User Metadata", *Proceedings of the ACM/IEEE Joint Conference on Digital Libraries*, 2009, pp. 241-250.

[14] C. Neidle, S. Sclaroff, and V. Athitsos. "SignStream™: A Tool for Linguistic and Computer Vision Research on Visual-Gestural Language Data," *Behavior Research Methods, Instruments, and Computers, 33:3*, pp. 311-320, 2001.

[15] C. Padden, "The Deaf Community and the Culture of Deaf People", *Readings in Diversity and Social Justice*, edited by M. Adams, W. Blumenfeld, H. Hackman, M. Peters, and X. Zuniga, 2000, pp. 343-352.

[16] M. Potamias and V. Athitsos, "Nearest Neighbor Search Methods for Handshape Recognition", *PETRA '08: Proceedings of the 1st International Conference on PErvasive Technologies Related to Assistive Environments*, 2008.

[17] G. Somers and R.N. Whyte, "Hand Posture Matching for Irish Sign Language Interpretation", *ISICT '03: Proceedings of the 1st International Symposium on Information and Communication Technologies*, 2003, pp. 439-444.

[18] T. Starner, J. Weaver, and A. Pentland, "Real-Time American Sign Language Recognition Using Desk and Wearable Computer Based Video", *IEEE Trans. On Pattern Analysis and Machine Intelligence*, 1998, pp. 1371-1375.

[19] C. Valli and C. Lucas, *Linguistics of American Sign Language: An Introduction*, Gallaudet University Press, Washington D.C., 2000.

[20] P. Viola and M. Jones. "Rapid object detection using a boosted cascade of simple features", *CVPR '01: Proceedings of the 2001 IEEE Computer Society Conference*, pp. 511-518, 2001.

[21] C. Vogler and D. Metaxas, "Towards Scalability in ASL Recognition", *Proceedings of Gesture Workshop '99*, 1999.

Turning Off-The-Shelf Games into Biofeedback Games

Regan L. Mandryk, Michael Kalyn, Yichen Dang, Andre Doucette,
Brett Taylor, Shane Dielschneider
University of Saskatchewan, Department of Computer Science
Saskatoon, SK, Canada
firstname.lastname@usask.ca

Figure 1. Columns show levels of texture-based biofeedback. Rows show customizations of an effect for two games (Portal, Nail'd).

ABSTRACT

Biofeedback games help users maintain specific mental or physical states and are useful to help people with cognitive impairments learn to self-regulate their brain function. However, biofeedback games are expensive and difficult to create and are not sufficiently appealing to hold a user's interest over the long term. We present two systems that turn off-the-shelf games into biofeedback games. Our desktop approach uses visual feedback via texture-based graphical overlays that vary in their obfuscation of an underlying game based on the user's physiological state. Our mobile approach presents multi-modal feedback (audio or vibration) of a user's physiological state on an iPhone.

Categories and Subject Descriptors

H5.2 [**Information interfaces and presentation**]: User Interfaces – *Graphical user interfaces*.

Keywords

Biofeedback, neurofeedback, EEG, game, FASD.

1. INTRODUCTION

Fetal alcohol exposure is the most prevalent cause of intellectual impairment in the western world [6]. An accurate account of the incidence of fetal alcohol spectrum disorder (FASD) is unknown but estimates range from 3 per 1000 live births to 10 per 1000 children being affected by prenatal alcohol exposure [4], which translates to thousands of affected infants born each year in Western Canada alone [1]. Kids with FASD are usually co-diagnosed with Attention Deficit Hyperactivity Disorder (ADHD). Using biofeedback (BF) to train brain function self-regulation (called neurofeedback training) using EEG has been effective at reducing the symptoms of ADHD, and at reducing differences of ADHD children from normative EEG databases [3].

Biofeedback training systems encourage a specific mental or physical state in the user through a BF loop. These systems gather a user's physiological state through sensing hardware, and present feedback so the user can adjust their state. BF training systems often use games because playing games is intrinsically motivating for a broad range of users [5]. Although BF games are increasing in popularity with the advent of low-cost physiological-sensing hardware, creating engaging BF games remains difficult because the game's mechanics (i.e., rules and procedures) must be altered to create the BF loop. For example, the doors in an exploration game could be locked if users are not within a physiological threshold. This means that each BF game is a custom creation, which is both expensive and time consuming; choosing to play off-the-shelf games as BF games is simply not possible. As a result, BF games have a number of problems. First, they tend to be toy applications that don't hold a user's interest in the long term, which is a problem because BF training requires repeated exposure to yield results [7]. Second, a user who wants to play a BF game has little choice over the game genre, and may not be motivated to play a game from a limited selection. Third, the physiological system being trained is integrated with the game, leaving no option for a user who may wish to train a different physiological system from that being offered within a game.

We present two systems that turn off-the-shelf games into BF games. In our desktop system, we provide feedback visually by presenting a graphical overlay on top of a running game that obscures the underlying game when the user is not in the desired physiological state (see Figure 1). In our mobile system, we provide multi-modal feedback through audio or vibration cues on an iPhone. Both systems work with off-the-shelf games, so users can train with games that they enjoy, and both systems decouple physiological sensing from gameplay so users can choose what to train (e.g., relaxation, focus) separately from their game choice.

2. RELATED WORK

Biofeedback training has been used to help patients with Asperger's Syndrome [8], to reduce the frequency of seizures in patients with epilepsy [2], and for children with tic disorder, autism, schizophrenia, and learning disabilities (see [2]). In non-disabled individuals, BF has been used to improve working memory and attention [9]. BF training has also been shown to improve the behaviour of children with ADHD [3]. Children with ADHD exhibit higher power in the Theta band of EEG (related to decreases in attention and retention of material) and lower power in the low Beta band of EEG (related to increases in hyperactivity and impulsivity) [7]. Neurofeedback training has helped children with ADHD lower the ratio of Theta/low Beta activity, by lowering Theta activity or increasing low Beta activity [2], [7].

Instead of providing BF through simple feedback, games are used because they are intrinsically motivating for many users and will encourage participation, potentially resulting in improved training compliance [5]. Many BF games (e.g., [8], [9]) might be better described as interactive systems because they lack the uncertain and quantifiable outcome of a game. Pope and Palsson [5] designed a hardware solution that worked with Playstation games by altering the performance of a game controller based on a user's EEG. In a study comparing their game-based system to a traditional BF system with children with ADHD, the authors found that both approaches resulted in improvements, but that children and parents were happier with the game system [5].

3. SYSTEM

Biofeedback systems have two general requirements. First, they must sense a user's physiological state; and second, they must provide this sensed state to the user through a feedback mechanism. Our BF system had additional requirements. First, as we wanted to engage players over the long term, our system had to operate with off-the-shelf games. And second, users should have choice over what aspect of their physiology to train, and this choice should not be decided by their choice of game.

Desktop System. We use texture-based overlays in our desktop system, rendered in real time in a transparent overlay on top of a running game. Traditionally, BF games work by not allowing the user to progress unless they are in the desired physiological state. In our case, the textures obscure the game graphics, making it harder and less enjoyable to play, and potentially impossible to progress if there is enough obfuscation of the game display. Similar to traditional approaches, we vary feedback depending on the user's state; the textures have different obscuring parameters (e.g., transparency, position) that vary continuously along a scale, providing varying levels of obfuscation. Players want to play with no or little obfuscation (see Figure 1), motivating them to maintain the desired physiological state. Our graphical overlays can be chosen from an all-purpose set or be customized to be consistent with the visual style, theme, or genre of the game, so that they appear to be integrated with the underlying game. In addition, the graphical effects are consistent with current abstract in-game visualizations that players are already familiar with using (e.g., tunnel vision representing poor in-game health).

Mobile System. Because of the mobility and flexibility of training-on-the-go provided by a smartphone, we decided to integrate multi-modal feedback into our mobile system. In our vibration cue approach, after passing a certain physiological threshold, we mirror increases in sensed physiological state with increases in vibration. In the audio condition, we increase the volume of a song (although volume of the phone can still be changed with the volume control); in the track condition, we increase the frequency of the ticking sound in a ticking clock. In all cases, the feedback has four levels that are presented in the background to running

applications. Although we intend for the system to be as training-on-the-go, it could also be used in the background to any activity that a user engages in, including playing desktop games.

Physiological Sensors. Although our system can work with any physiological sensor with a software development kit (SDK), we demonstrate the software with Neurosky's Mindset or Windwave, which are single-electrode EEG devices. The Neurosky platform was chosen for its simplicity of deployment, relative robustness of signal, and SDK quality. We modified the use of the Mindset by moving the electrode from the forehead to EEG location Cz, on the top of the head, which produces a better signal for training [7].

4. FUTURE WORK AND CONCLUSIONS

To investigate whether our system can help children with FASD reduce their symptoms related to ADHD, we have conducted a 24-week study in collaboration with experts in brain plasticity. We are also exploring BF beyond gameplay, investigating how our approach can be integrated into a person's day for BF training.

This research presents the first general solution for turning off-the-shelf software into biofeedback systems where the user chooses which physiological trait to train. We focus on games – leveraging the millions of dollars and years of development that go into triple-A titles, and ensuring an engaging play experience.

5. ACKNOWLEDGMENTS

Thanks to NSERC and the GRAND NCE for funding.

6. REFERENCES

[1] Clarren, S., & Lutke, J. (2008). *Building clinical capacity for Fetal Alcohol Spectrum Disorder diagnoses in Western and Northern Canada. Canadian Journal of Clinical Pharmacology, 15*(2), e223-e237.

[2] Heinrich, H., Gevensleben, H., & Strehl, U. Annotation: Neurofeedback — Train your brain to train behaviour. *J. Child Psychology and Psychiatry, 48*, (2007), 3–16.

[3] Lubar, J.F., Swartwood, M.O., et al. Evaluation of the effectiveness of EEG neurofeedback training for ADHD in a clinical setting as measured by changes in T.O.V.A. scores, behavioral ratings, and WISC-R performance. *Biofeedback and Self Regulation, 20*, (1995), 83–99.

[4] May, P., & Gossage, P. (2001). Estimating the prevalence of Fetal Alcohol Syndrome: A summary. *Alcohol Research & Health, 25*(3), 159-167.

[5] Pope, A.T. & Palsson, O.S. Helping video games ''rewire our minds'', NASA TR (2001).

[6] Spohr, H.L., Willms, J., and Steinhausen, H.C. Prenatal alcohol exposure and long- term developmental consequences. *The Lancet, 341*, (1993), 907-910.

[7] Thompson, M. and Thompson L. *The Neurofeedback Book: An Introduction to Basic Concepts in Applied Psychophysiology*. The Association for Applied Psychophysiology and Biofeedback, Colorado, USA, 2003.

[8] Thompson, L., Thompson, M., & Reid, A. Neurofeedback outcomes in clients with Asperger's Syndrome, *App. Psychophysiology Biofeedback, 35*, (2010), 63-81.

[9] Vernon, D., Egner, T., Cooper, N., et al. The effect of training distinct neurofeedback protocols on aspects of cognitive performance. *International Journal of Psychophysiology, 47*, (2003), 75–85.

Smart Phone Application for Indoor Scene Localization

Nabeel khan
Computer Science Department
University of Otago
nabeel@cs.otago.ac.nz

Brendan McCane
Computer Science Department
University of Otago
mccane@cs.otago.ac.nz

ABSTRACT

Blind people are unable to navigate easily in unfamiliar indoor environments without assistance. Knowing the current location is a particularly important aspect of indoor navigation. Scene identification in indoor buildings without any Global Positioning System (GPS) is a challenging problem. We present a smart phone based assistive technology which uses computer vision techniques to localize the indoor location from a scene image. The aim of our work is to guide blind people during navigation inside buildings where GPS is not effective. Our current system uses a client-server model where the user takes a photo from their current location, the image is sent to the server, the location is sent back to the mobile device, and a voice message is used to convey the location information.

Categories and Subject Descriptors

K.4.2 [**Computers and Society**]: Social Issues—*Assistive technologies for persons with disabilities*; I.4.8 [**Image Processing and Computer Vision**]: Scene Analysis

Keywords

Blind people, Indoor Navigation, Features, Voice.

1. INTRODUCTION

The number of blind people in the world is about 39 million with another 246 million with visual impairments. A wide range of products based on GPS are available to assist blind people during outdoor navigation, but GPS is not accurate indoors and it cannot provide details such as which floor the user is on. The emergence of low cost touch-based smart phones with cameras in the last few years have made it possible to develop cheaper navigation solutions based on computer vision techniques. Smart devices are already in use by blind people for reading emails, messages etc. So it is relatively easy for a blind person to use a smart phone application. Our proposed smart phone application can be used by a blind person to take a photo of the current scene and determine their location whenever they want. The proposed vision based solution can be used in any building for which a suitable database of images has been collected.

2. PROPOSED SYSTEM

The proposed system uses a client server paradigm. The client side refers to an Android application currently running on an *HTC*

Wildfire S (2.3 Gingerbread) smart phone. The server uses computer vision techniques to match the query photo sent by the phone [3]. Our system consists of two independent modules:-

1. **Mapping:-** The building intended for navigation needs to be mapped first. A large number of images covering all locations within a building are captured and stored along with the corresponding location information on the server. Images are represented by features which represent the unique parts of an image and are used for image matching. Our server uses a Visual Bag of Word (BoW) approach based on SIFT type of features for image matching [2, 3]. The generated features from the stored mapped images are clustered by approximate k-means to obtain the visual word's frequency for every image. The server stores this information in a data structure referred as an "inverted index" and then waits for the client request. The index is generated off-line and plays a key role in robust image matching.

2. **Scene Localization:-** Upon user request, the application takes a photo of an indoor place from the camera, sends the photo to the server using a wireless Internet connection and waits for a reply. When the server gets the photo, it uses the index to quickly retrieve 100 mapped images most similar to the query photo. These similar images are then ranked in ascending order giving higher ranks to the images closer to the query photo. If the top three ranked images vote for the same indoor location, the server simply returns that corresponding location. Otherwise geometry information is checked between the query and the top ranked images one by one via a fundamental matrix. If a reasonable number of features of the top ranked database image (at least 20%) indicate a relationship against the query photo, then the location of that ranked image is returned followed by a voice message.

3. APPLICATION DESIGN

The interface of our application is shown in Figure 1. Blind people can use a voice powered intelligent virtual assistant to launch the application on the phone. The application starts with a welcome message and waits for user input. The blind person clicks the scene localization button and gets a voice message regarding the current location. The phone can be held either in landscape or portrait position. The simple interface of our application provides high accessibility, although a voice activated button would further improve the interface.

4. EXPERIMENTS

The application takes 2–4 seconds on average for localization and is evaluated on indoor images taken from office buildings where

(A) Send Image to Server   (B) Voice Message

Figure 1: User interface of our application. The localization button captures and sends the photo to the server. The returning location information from the server is communicated to the blind person via a voice message.

scene matching is challenging due to high self-similarity between the images. Sometimes our application fails to find a match for the query photo, the user is then instructed to turn around and take another photo. In our experiments, we consider such cases a wrong match for strict analysis. Moreover mapped images are taken from a different camera for unbiased system evaluation. The used datasets [1] and results are as follows:-

1. **CS Indoor:-** It contains images of our computer science building. 1586 images are captured from three floors of the building representing 25 places such as corridors, labs, halls etc. For testing, we used a smart phone to take pictures during the night, noon and early morning. The system performed poorly at night and gave an overall accuracy of 81%. This can be attributed to the glass structure of our building which results in reflections at night therefore resulting in wrong matches. Nevertheless the overall performance of the system is quite good and can further go up by excluding "no location" as wrong matches in our evaluation.

2. **Commerce Indoor:-** It contains images of another office building covering about 2 floors. 864 images are currently captured representing 14 places like corridors, stairs, atrium etc. For evaluation, we used a smart phone to take 137 photos and the system gives 92.7% accuracy with 10 wrong matches.

5. CONCLUSION

The aim of our current work is to provide a cheap assistive technology for blind people. The proposed application can guide blind people during indoor navigation. The system works very well in buildings displaying high self-similarity between locations and should work even better in heterogeneous buildings where matching is relatively easier. The incorporation of GPS to load the appropriate mapped index on the server can make our application scalable to any number of buildings. Currently, the system works entirely from two-dimensional images and provides localisation at a room-based level. We are investigating three-dimensional matching strategies that will allow for finer scale localisation with a final target being a full indoor navigation system.

6. ACKNOWLEDGMENTS

We will like to thank Disability Information and Support Center at the Otago university for arranging interviews with blind people to capture the requirements analysis.

7. REFERENCES

[1] N. Khan. Indoor images of office buildings (nz). http://www.cs.otago.ac.nz/pgdweb/nabeel/ Downloads/.

[2] N. Khan, B. McCane, and G. Wyvill. Sift and surf performance evaluation against various image deformations on benchmark dataset. In *Proc. of IEEE DICTA*, pages 501–506, 2011.

[3] N. Y. Khan, B. Mccane, and G. Wyvill. Homography based Visual Bag of Word Model for Scene Matching in Indoor Environments. In *Proc. of IVCNZ*, 2011.

Specialized DVD Player to Render Audio Description and its Usability Performance

Claude Chapdelaine
Vision and Imaging, CRIM
405 Ogilvy Avenue, Suite 101
Montreal (Quebec) Canada
(514) 840-1234
Claude.Chapdelaine@crim.ca

ABSTRACT

We intend to demonstrate a DVD Player rendering audio description (AD) that was designed based on the needs of blind and visually impaired individuals. In this paper, we present the three added specialized features of our player and their usability performance. The CRIM DVDPlayer provides 1) context information on the content, 2) basic and an augmented quantity of AD and 3) recall functions on key information (scene identification, actions in the scene and the actors in the scene). The performance of these features was evaluated in a seven months usability testing. Our usability results are summarized.

Categories and Subject Descriptors

H.5.2 [**User Interfaces**]: Evaluation/methodology; K.4.2 [**Social Issues**]: Assistive technologies for persons with disabilities.

Keywords

Multimedia, accessibility, audio description, blind and visual impairment, usability study.

1. INTRODUCTION

Audio description (AD) is added audio to audio-visual content that aims at describing the relevant visual elements to blind and low vision individuals in order for them to fully understand the content. Users' studies [1][2] were conducted to determine the amount and type of information needed by blind and visually impaired (BVI) individuals to listen to an audio-video content without confusion or frustration that would otherwise cause the individuals to quit.

We adapted more specifically our player to DVD in order to provide access to commercial contents often inaccessible to BVI individuals. In Canada, the situation is critical for the French BVI where they have only two to three hours of television with AD per weeks and no DVD with AD in French language are available. The available AD broadcasted by television station is regulated, but there is no incentive or laws to make AD available in theater, cinemas or for DVD. In the DVD market, the only films or televisions series with available AD are English production since the DVD production from France has a European regional indicator that will not play in North American DVD players and with many software players. This situation gave us an opportunity

to give access to cultural contents to French BVI. This paper includes a description of the specialized functions and its usability performance.

2. CRIM DVD PLAYER

As seen in Figure 1, the CRIM DVDPlayer[1] has the same functionalities as existing software players [3][4] that enables users to play, stop, rewind, forward the video and switch the size to full screen. Also, as the existing accessible players, audio feedback is giving on all the interactions made by the user.

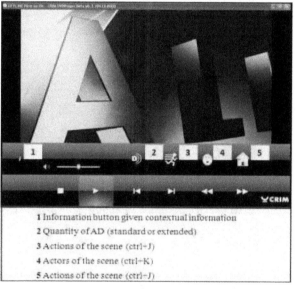

1 Information button given contextual information
2 Quantity of AD (standard or extended)
3 Actions of the scene (ctrl+J)
4 Actors of the scene (ctrl+K)
5 Actions of the scene (ctrl+J)

Figure 1. Screen shot of the CRIM DVDPlayer with specialized functions indicators.

Beside the regular accessible functions found in existing video player, we added three specialized functions to enhance the user experience. The player provides context information on the content, standard and an extended quantity of AD and recall functions on key information such as scene identification, actions in the scene and the actors in the scene. Our DVD player synchronizes AD in real time while playing a commercial DVD for which we also produced the AD. This production includes a process to add AD for the starting images and to time the display of the selection menu to start the video. The player then render audio help to start de DVD. This step allows the user to be completely autonomous. Since commercial DVD (and even the ones with available AD) can only be started by navigating and pressing visual button without audio feedback. Thus, playing a

---

[1] Pattern pending.

DVD requires a sighted person to select the AD option and start the video. In the following sub-sections, we detail the specialized functions and summarize the already published usability performance obtained by users 'test [5].

Giving context

The contextual functions are displayed after clicking on the "I" button for information (see figure 1, indicator 1). The information window offers a first menu indicating the list of keyboard shortcuts for controlling the player. The second menu is a synopsis that can be read by a synthetic voice. If the DVD has more than one content, i.e. a television series, a pull down menu list of all the episodes contained in the DVD with their synopsis. The third menu is the list of actors listed in a pull down list (see figure 2). Each page offers a picture of the actor (for people with residual vision), an audio description of the actor with its role in the video. The page also has a button that enables the user to hear the voice of the actor. This last function is to facilitate voice discrimination which is the principal mean by which individuals who are blind or with low vision with low acuity can more easily recognize the speaking persons in a scene.

Figure 2: Screen shot of contextual information of one actor.

Different Quantity of AD

The quantity of AD changed at anytime by clicking on the AD button (see figure 1, indicator 2). By default, the quantity is set to standard which gives AD in the available gap between dialogues. A second click, extend the quantity of AD and where more information was entered by the scripter, the player automatically stops the DVD, renders the AD and starts de DVD again. The idea to have providing more than one level of AD was recommended in the Web Content Accessibility Guidelines (WCAG), but to our knowledge our player is the first to implement the recommendation.

Recall assistance

The three recalls functions: actions of scene, actors in scene and scene identification (see figure 1, indicator 3, 4, 5) helps the users confirm or obtain specific information at anytime. They were designed to mostly to avoid confusion by viewers. This corresponds to an observation made in a prior study [1] where participants were not completely certain of what they heard, for example they asked "Is this Marc?" without stopping the video and the experimenter would quickly confirm it was Marc.

3. USABILITY PERFORMANCE

As mentioned before the detail results of the usability performance is available in [5] that we briefly summarize here. For seven months, our player was available to 43 French BVI individual. They had access to 104 DVD and they listened to 171 hours and 37 minutes. The evaluation was done after the DVD was returned in 85% of the cases. The usability of the functions was subjectively rated by the participant on their ease of use and their necessity. A total of 70% changed the quantity of AD as they needed. All participants rated this function easy to use and greatly appreciated. The recall functions for the scene, actors or actions were rarely used in the first session (13% of cases). After the first evaluation where these functions were mentioned, we observed a 55% increase of usage in subsequent sessions. There were rated easy to use in 97% of cases. A total of 94% of the participants appreciated having these functions, 6% appreciated having them "more or less" and none deprecated them.

4. CONCLUSION

We presented the CRIM DVDPlayer that offers regular accessible command to play a DVD plus added specialized functions that addressed the needs of BVI individuals. We showed that their usability performance was excellent and we would like the opportunity to demonstrate the capacity of our player.

5. ACKNOWLEDGMENTS

This research was funded by CRIM with the help of the MDEIE (Ministry of development, economic, innovation and exportation) and by the Office des personnes handicapées du Québec (OPHQ). We express our gratitude to the people who gave their time to evaluate our player. And, I extend a special thank you to David Byrns for his original and diligent coding.

6. REFERENCES

[1] Chapdelaine, C. 2010. In-Situ Study of Blind Individuals Listening to Audio-Visual Contents" In 12th International ACM SIGACCESS Conference on Computers and Accessibility (ASSETS'10),Orlando, Florida, October 25-27, pp. 59-66.

[2] Chapdelaine, C., Jarry, A. 2010. Lessons Learned from Blind Individuals on VideoDescription, 3rd Applied Human Factors and Ergonomics (AHFE) International Conference, Miami.

[3] Quick time Player. http://www.apple.com/quicktime/

[4] Microsoft Media Player. http://windows.microsoft.com/en-US/windows/products/windows-media

[5] Chapdelaine, C. 2012. Descriptive Video Services Assistive in *Technology for Blindness and Low Vision*, R. Manduchi, & S. Kurniawan Eds. CRC Press. 367-387. (to be published)

[6] Web Content Accessibility Guidelines (WCAG) 2.0, http://www.w3.org/TR/WCAG/

IDEAL: a Dyslexic-Friendly eBook Reader

Gaurang Kanvinde
Accessible Systems
C/2, MadhavBaug Society
Sir M V Road, Andheri(E),
Mumbai 400 058, India
gaurang@accessiblesystems.co.in

Luz Rello
Web Research Group &
TALN, Centre for Autonomous
Systems and Neuro-Robotics
Universitat Pompeu Fabra
Barcelona, Spain
luzrello@acm.org

Ricardo Baeza-Yates
Yahoo! Research Barcelona
& Web Research Group,
Universitat Pompeu Fabra
Barcelona, Spain
rbaeza@acm.org

ABSTRACT

We present an ebook reader for Android which displays ebooks in a more accessible manner for users with dyslexia. The ebook reader combines features that other related tools already have, such as text-to-speech technology, and new features, such as displaying the text with an adapted text layout based on the results of a user study with participants with dyslexia. Since there is no universal profile of a user with dyslexia, the layout settings are customizable and users can override the special layout setting according to their reading preferences.

Categories and Subject Descriptors

H.5 [**Information Interfaces and Presentation**]: User Interfaces—*Screen design*; K.4 [**Computers and Society**]: Social Issues—*Assistive technologies for persons with disabilities*

General Terms

Design, Experimentation, Human Factors

Keywords

Dyslexia, Assistive Technologies, Readability, Text-to-Speech, eBook Reader, e-book, Android

1. INTRODUCTION

Previous work with people with dyslexia [2, 6] proved that changes in the presentation of the text might alleviate some of the problems that they encounter when reading a text. Since ebooks readers provide the possibility of adapting the layout of the book to the users needs, here we present the first ebook reader application, which has an option for displaying the ebooks for people with dyslexia. The guidelines for developing this option are based on (1) data collected from a set of experiments carried out with a group of 22 participants with dyslexia [6], and (2) the use of the think aloud technique with 14 of those participants using a beta version of the reader. To the best of our knowledge, there are no similar applications which offer an adapted layout to users with dyslexia when reading ebooks in mobile devices.

Moreover, there are three reasons motivating the decision to develop a dyslexic-friendly option in the IDEAL eBook

Reader: (1) the increasing growth of ebook usage in the last years, for instance, in January 2011 the Association of American Publishers reported that ebook sales increased by 115.8 percent [1]; (2) the fact that people with dyslexia represent a relatively large group of people, for example it is estimated that from 10 to 17.5% of the U.S.A. population has some level of dyslexia [3]; and (3) the use of accessibility practices for user with dyslexia is beneficial for all, since dyslexic-accessible practices can alleviate difficulties faced by all users including other users with disabilities [4].

2. RELATED WORK

Among the mobile applications for users with dyslexia there are: spell checkers such as *American Wordspeller & Phonetic Dictionary* which converts phonetic spelling to proper spelling; applications that exploit speech recognition such as *Dragon Search and Dragon Dictate* to search and dictate email or messages; and software that uses text-to-speech for reading texts to people with dyslexia such as *Web Reader* or *CapturaTalk*.

Although people with dyslexia are encouraged to modify the settings of ebook readers to facilitate their reading [2], to the best of our knowledge there is no application which adapts automatically the text layout with dyslexic-friendly parameters. Our application also includes standard features for users with dyslexia such as text-to-speech technology and the spelling of words out loud.

3. IDEAL EBOOK READER

The IDEAL eBook Reader is an ebook reader for Android devices developed by Accessible Systems of India.[1] This application displays ebooks that have been formatted according to ePub, a free and open ebook standard by the International Digital Publishing Forum (IDPF). Epub is a globally adopted set of rules that define how an ebook should be constructed. When ebooks follow this standard, they can be displayed with the same convenience and accessibility on a wide variety of platforms and devices. This way we bring accessibility to mainstream reading environments so users do not have to stay with special DAISY books and devices. We explain below the general features of the IDEAL eBook Reader:

(a) It adjusts the text to maximize the utilization of the screen, without exceeding the screen boundary even with a large font-size (see Figure 1a and 1b).

---

[1]http://www.accessiblesystems.co.in

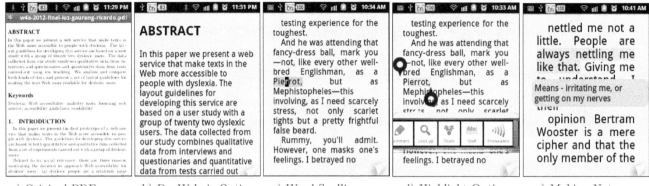

| a) Original PDF | b) DysWebxia Option | c) Word Spelling | d) Highlight Options | e) Making Notes |

Figure 1: Examples of screenshots of the IDEAL eBook Reader (from b to e).

(b) It allows the user to customize and store how the ebook will be displayed. This includes font style and size, colour (background and font), brightness contrast, font size, and the character, line and paragraph spacing. For user with dyslexia there is an option called DysWebxia which sets all the parameters to our dyslexic-friendly guidelines (see Figure 1b).

(c) It displays the table of contents of the ebook allowing the navigation to specific places within the ebook.

(d) It supports text-to-speech technology that enables users to listen to the ebook content as an audio book. The tool is compatible with a wide range of text-to-speech engines, and hence multiple languages are also supported. The text being read out loud is highlighted to make it easier to follow the reading. Control of the speech is gesture based, that is, the user can select the piece of text to be read. It is possible to read even word-by-word or letter-by-letter if the user wishes (see Figure 1c and 1d). In this way, a person with dyslexia can learn how to read new words.

(e) It allows the user to write a comment over a phrase (see Figure 1e).

When the IDEAL eBook Reader starts, you can open an ebook from your phone memory, or you can download one from online sites such as Project Gutenberg or Feedbooks. Once an ebook opens, the user can set the dyslexic-friendly option or customize the text layout. To start and stop speech, we double tap the screen; to move to the next paragraph, we swipe the finger across the screen from right-to-left; and to move to the previous paragraph, we swipe the finger across the screen from left-to-right.

4. USER STUDY

The parameters that the IDEAL eBook Reader uses for displaying the text adapted for people with dyslexia are based on a previous user study [6]. To that previous study we added the results of the application of the think aloud technique.

Twenty two native Spanish speakers with a confirmed diagnosis of dyslexia took part in this study. We used two semi structured interviews, one questionnaire, one reading test recorded by the eye tracker, and the think aloud technique. The recordings of the eye tracker provided the quantitative data regarding the readability of the text layout while through the interviews and questionnaires we gather the data regarding the user preferences [6]. Finally, we presented a beta version of the IDEAL eBook Reader to 14 of the participants, using the think aloud technique. They tried the application and proposed improvements to the interface. The parameters that our study took into consideration were grey scale in the font, grey scale in the background, color pairs (background/font), font size and character, line and paragraph spacing.

5. FUTURE WORK

The use of complicated language has been extensively pointed out as one of the key problems that people with dyslexia encounter. However, all the existing applications at the moment, including ours, only modify its design but not its content. Future work include the enrichment of the ebook reader by adding new reading assistance features, such as graphical schemes [5], addressing the complexity of the language in the text.

6. REFERENCES

[1] Association of American Publishers. AAP reports january 2011 book sales, March 2011. http://es.scribd.com/doc/50948417/AAP-Reports-\\January-2011-Book-Sales.

[2] P. Gregor and A. F. Newell. An empirical investigation of ways in which some of the problems encountered by some dyslexics may be alleviated using computer techniques. In *Proceedings of the fourth international ACM conference on Assistive technologies*, ASSETS 2000, pages 85–91, New York, NY, USA, 2000. ACM.

[3] Interagency Commission on Learning Disabilities. *Learning Disabilities: A Report to the U.S. Congress.* Government Printing Office, Washington DC, U.S., 1987.

[4] S. Kurniawan and G. Conroy. Comparing comprehension speed and accuracy of online information in students with and without dyslexia. *Advances in Universal Web Design and Evaluation: Research, Trends and Opportunities, Idea Group Publishing, Hershey, PA*, pages 257–70, 2006.

[5] L. Rello, R. Baeza-Yates, H. Saggion, and E. Graells. Graphical schemes may improve readability but not understandability for people with dyslexia. In *Proceedings of the NAACL HLT 2012 Workshop Predicting and improving text readability for target reader populations (PITR 2012)*, 2012.

[6] L. Rello, G. Kanvinde, and R. Baeza-Yates. Layout guidelines for web text and a web service to improve accessibility for dyslexics. In *International Cross Disciplinary Conference on Web Accessibility (W4A 2012)*, Lyon, France, April 2012. ACM Press.

FEPS: A Sensory Substitution System for the Blind to Perceive Facial Expressions

Md. Iftekhar Tanveer, A.S.M. Iftekhar Anam, Mohammed Yeasin,
A.K.M. Mahbubur Rahman, Sreya Ghosh
Electrical and Computer Engineering, University of Memphis
Memphis, TN 38152, USA
{mtanveer, aanam, myeasin, arahman, sghosh}@memphis.edu

ABSTRACT

This work demonstrates a visual-to-auditory Sensory Substitution System (SSD) called *Facial Expression Perception through Sound* (FEPS). It is designed to enable the visually impaired people to participate in a more effective social communication by perceiving their interlocutor's facial expressions. The earlier SSDs provided feedback on inferred emotions, where as, this system responds to the facial movements. This is a better method than emotion inference due to complexities in expression-to-emotion mapping, the problem of capturing multitude of possible emotions derived from a limited facial movements and the difficulty to correctly predict emotions due to lack in ground truth data. In this work, the user's ability to understand the facial expressions has been ensured by a usability study.

Categories and Subject Descriptors

H.5.2 [**User Interfaces**]: Auditory (Non-speech) feedback;
K.4.2 [**Social Issues**]: Assistive Technologies for persons with disabilities

General Terms

Algorithms, Design, Human Factors

Keywords

Blind, Facial Expression, Sensory Substitution System

1. INTRODUCTION & RELATED WORKS

The inability to perceive facial expression in social settings is a severe setback for the visually impaired individuals, since over 80% of the information is carried through non-verbal modes of communication [1]. A Sensory Substitution Device (SSD) can compensate human's deficiency in processing one sensory channel (e.g. vision, audition, haptic etc.) by utilizing one or more alternative channels. In this demo, we describe a cellphone based SSD, which is worn around the neck, that can inform its user of the facial expressions of the interlocutor through auditory feedback. To achieve real-time performance, the cell phone transmits the captured video frames to a server over the network. The server performs the analysis of facial expressions and sends the results back to the cell phone. With stable network

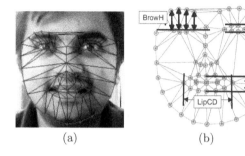

Figure 1: (a) Picture of the landmark points tracked by the face-tracker (b) Four facial features calculated from the tracked landmark points

connectivity and lighting condition, the whole process takes around 500 milliseconds.

The early design of sensory substitution devices was focused on mapping all the visual information to a tactile or auditory channel [6, 2]. However, this kind of SSDs were not properly usable as they were prohibitively "confusing" to the users [4]. On the other hand, SSDs that were focused to extract only a particular information rather than the entire visual field, became more usable and commercially successful [5].

The iFeeling system[8] and the SSD implemented by the "Team F.A.C.E."[3] of University of Maryland are designed to be focused on human face. These systems attempt to infer emotion from the facial movements and produce feedback based on the inferences. However, it is unwise to produce feedback on emotional contents in stead of the detected movements. The reasons are, **Firstly**, the cultural differences in expression-to-emotions mapping may lead a system to be biased by cultural idiosyncrasies. **Secondly**, various combinations of face and head movements can convey a large amount of emotional contents. Selecting only a subset of these emotions for feedback can under-utilize the potential of an SSD. **Finally**, it is hard to implement a robust natural emotion prediction system. Due to these reasons, FEPS is designed to sonify the facial movements directly.

2. DESIGN

FEPS is designed based on the philosophies proposed by Belardinelli et al.[4]. The facial movements associated with eyelids, eyebrows, lips, and mouth are selected for auditory feedback. To extract these movements, it is necessary to track several landmark points on the face. This is done using

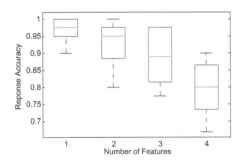

Figure 2: Box plot of the accuracies of identifying the facial features and events

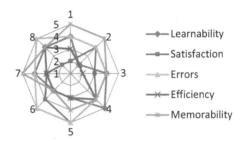

Figure 3: Radar diagram of subjective evaluations. Responses from the eight users are placed in circular arrangement. The response in 5-point Likert scale has been arranged radially.

Table 1: Average Time using a Samsung Galaxy S II, UoM wifi and an Intel Xeon E5630 machine with 6GB RAM

Environment	Time (Millisecs)
In front of Campus Library	500
Campus Coffee Shop	322.5
Building Corridors	312.5
Labs in different building	250
Same Lab where the Server resides	250
Controlled Environment	181.81

Jason Saragih's Constrained Local Model (CLM) algorithm [9]. The facial movements are detected from the distances between several pairs of landmarks as shown in Figure 1. These distances, as a function time (i.e. video frame number), constitute the temporal signal of the facial movements. The signals are filtered and differentiated to detect the sudden peaks and drops – denoted as "up" and "down" events. The users get notified about these events through auditory feedback.

3. EVALUATION

FEPS is evaluated for its speed and usability. Table 1 shows the time required to produce audio feedback. It is observed that, with stable network connection, the time delay is primarily contributed by the face tracker. The speed of the tracker varies under different lighting conditions.

Usability of FEPS is also evaluated on three blind and five sighted students. Before the evaluation process, the participants train themselves by making facial expressions and listening to FEPS feedback. In the test, 16 videos containing mimicry of facial expressions are sonified and the participants are requested to report what "up" or "down" events they could understand from the audio feedback. In the first four videos only one facial feature is sonified for each video. The rest of the videos are more challenging as they contained sonification of two to four facial expressions. Figure 2 shows a box plot of the performances of the subjects for correctly identifying the events and features.

In addition, FEPS is evaluated for subjective evaluation using the method proposed by Nielsen[7]. The users are asked to answer few questions for evaluating Learnability, Efficiency, Memorability, Error and Satisfaction in the use of FEPS. The answers are in a five-point Likert scale where higher values are indicative of positive and satisfactory results. Figure 3 shows the responses of the users in a radar diagram. The mean responses of the participants on Learn-

ability, Satisfaction, Errors, Efficiency, and Memorability are 3.625, 3.375, 4.375, 3, and 4.25 respectively.

4. CONCLUSION AND FUTURE WORK

The design of FEPS integrates knowledge from several related fields such as Neuro-science, Human Factor, and Human-Computer Interaction. It is designed to reduce the cognitive load of the user in perceiving emotions and facial behavioral expressions. The pilot study illustrates the efficacy and utility of the proposed solution. In the future, experiments will be performed to evaluate the user's understanding of emotional contents by listening to the feedback from FEPS.

Acknowledgments We are grateful for suggestions from Prof. Dr. Max H. Garzon at Computer Science in University of Memphis and the anonymous reviewers of the paper. Thanks to Jason Saragih for sharing his code.

5. REFERENCES

[1] M. Argyle et al. The communication of inferior and superior attitudes by verbal and non-verbal signals. *Br. J. Soc. Clin. Psychol.*, 9(3):222–231, 1970.

[2] P. Bach-y Rita et al. Vision substitution by tactile image projection. 1969.

[3] D. Astler et al. Increased accessibility to nonverbal communication through facial and expression recognition technologies for blind/visually impaired subjects. In *13th ACM ASSETS conference*, pages 259–260. ACM, 2011.

[4] O. Belardinelli et al. Sonification of spatial information: audio-tactile exploration strategies by normal and blind subjects. *UAHCI*, pages 557–563, 2009.

[5] J. Linvill and J. Bliss. A direct translation reading aid for the blind. *Proceedings of the IEEE*, 54(1):40–51, 1966.

[6] P. Meijer. An experimental system for auditory image representations. *Biomedical Engineering, IEEE Transactions on*, 39(2):112–121, 1992.

[7] J. Nielsen. The usability engineering life cycle. *Computer*, 25(3):12–22, 1992.

[8] S. Réhman and L. Liu. ifeeling: Vibrotactile rendering of human emotions on mobile phones. *Mobile Multimedia Processing*, pages 1–20, 2010.

[9] J. Saragih, S. Lucey, and J. Cohn. Deformable model fitting by regularized landmark mean-shift. *IJCV*, 91(2):200–215, 2011.

SymbolPath: A Continuous Motion Overlay Module for Icon-Based Assistive Communication

Karl Wiegand
Northeastern University
360 Huntington Ave
Boston, MA 02115, USA
wiegand@ccs.neu.edu

Rupal Patel
Northeastern University
360 Huntington Ave
Boston, MA 02115, USA
r.patel@neu.edu

ABSTRACT

Augmentative and alternative communication (AAC) systems are often used by individuals with severe speech impairments. Icon-based AAC systems typically present users with arrays of icons that are sequentially selected to construct utterances, which are then spoken aloud using text-to-speech (TTS) synthesis. For touch-screen devices, users must lift their finger or hand to select individual icons and avoid selecting multiple icons at once. Because many individuals with severe speech impairments have concomitant limb impairments, repetitive and precise movements can be slow and effortful. The current work aims to enhance message formulation ease and speed by using continuous motion icon selection rather than discrete input. SymbolPath is an overlay module that can be integrated with existing icon-based AAC systems to enable continuous motion icon selection. Message formulation using SymbolPath consists of drawing a continuous path through a set of desired icons. The system then determines the most likely subset of desired icons on that path and rearranges them to form a meaningful and grammatical sentence. In addition to demonstrating the SymbolPath module, we plan to present usability data and discuss iterative modifications to the software.

Categories and Subject Descriptors

H.5.2 [**User Interfaces**]: Graphical User Interfaces; K.4.2 [**Social Issues**]: Assistive Technologies for Persons with Disabilities

Keywords

AAC, Icons, Continuous Motion

1. MOTIVATION

Many individuals with speech impairments severe enough to preclude spoken communication also have accompanying limb impairments that must be considered when designing assistive communication interfaces [4, 3]. Icon-based AAC systems offer the potential for faster and less effortful message formulation compared to letter-based systems [6] and thus are often used by individuals with compromised motor function; however, manual methods of icon selection on current icon-based AAC devices require precise and discrete movements that hinder communication rate and ease.

Additionally, the complex and repetitive nature of discrete movements can further contribute to fatigue. Several letter-based approaches to continuous selection have demonstrated commercial success (e.g. Swype, SlideIT, TouchPal, and ShapeWriter [2]), but no such approaches currently exist for word-based or icon-based formulation. This project aims to enhance message formulation ease and communication rate by combining continuous motion icon selection with a free-order language model.

2. IMPLEMENTATION

SymbolPath is implemented in Python as an overlay module for traditional icon-based AAC systems. A simple single-layer array serves as the interface for the current work. The top row is dedicated to displaying the message being formulated and the remainder of the interface is arranged as a grid of candidate icons (Figure 1). Icons are grouped based on lexical roles: actors, verbs, objects, and modifiers. Icon groups are color coded and arranged from left to right to mirror the subject-verb-object syntax in English. To formulate a message, users create a continuous path through a set of desired icons. To further reduce the physical demands of message formulation, the order of icons on the path is not constrained by syntax: users can select icons in close physical proximity rather than in syntactical order. The only requirement is that a continuous path be drawn through all desired items without breaking contact with the interface. During message formulation, the treaded path is displayed for feedback. Once the user breaks the path or enters the message formulation window, the language module attempts to concatenate a meaningful and syntactically accurate utterance from the set of selected icons. The text-to-speech synthesizer then voices the message. SymbolPath is compatible with any input modality that can provide a continuously varying analog signal such as a stylus, mouse, joystick, or laser pointer.

Two major issues need to be resolved in order to enable continuous motion icon selection: (1) superset pruning, because the user's path may include both target elements and bystander elements, and this superset must be pruned to yield the most likely desired candidates; and (2) syntactic reordering, because the user may have selected icons in an unordered way and the system must reorder those icons in the proper syntax of the target language.

Semantic disambiguation is required for situations in which removing or reordering words could dramatically alter the meaning of the potential message. SymbolPath relies on a combination of semantic frames, semantic grams, and phys-

Figure 1: Sample message formulated using SymbolPath. The user creates a path as she traverses through the target (girl, reading, book, big) and intermediary icons (e.g. clapping, listening, bicycle), which are then pruned and reordered to generate a meaningful and syntactically complete message.

ical characteristics of the path to generate a prioritized list of potential utterances. Although the demonstration version automatically selects the most likely utterance to enhance communication speed, it can also display the list of potential utterances for user verification prior to speech generation.

2.1 Semantic Frames

Fundamental to the design and functionality of SymbolPath is the use of semantic frames [1], in which the predicate or verb of an utterance is the central element of a frame that can be filled by a set of relational items [5]. Thus, SymbolPath generates syntactically complete utterances by relying on the semantic frames of predicates in the selected path. Because each icon group is associated with a set of possible syntactic and semantic roles, the superset of selected icons is pruned by assessing subset probabilities within a given semantic frame. This approach provides a rudimentary solution to the issue of syntactic reordering, but does not address the issue of semantic disambiguation, especially with regard to assigning statistical values to potential utterances.

2.2 Semantic Grams

To prioritize the list of potential utterances, SymbolPath leverages prior work in the areas of subset completion and non-syntactic prediction [8]. Specifically, semantic grams, or sem-grams, are used to assign each potential utterance a value that corresponds to the probability of that combination of words appearing in a sentence together, regardless of order. Semantic ambiguity is not a concern because lexical roles are specified for each icon based on its grouping.

2.3 Path Characteristics

In addition to the probabilities of each potential utterance based on its semantic coherence, the physical characteristics of the path are also considered. Once the list of potential utterances has been prioritized semantically, the rankings are adjusted based on the two-dimensional collision space of the continuous motion path and each icon's surface area. Icons that collided with a larger area of the user's drawn path are assigned a greater likelihood than icons that were only marginally on the drawn path.

3. FUTURE DIRECTIONS

SymbolPath does not currently support complex utterances that contain multiple verbs (e.g. "I like to play baseball"), utterances that contain multiple actors and participants (e.g. "I like to play chess with my brother"), or utterances that make extensive use of modifiers (e.g. "I really drank that huge soda too quickly"). Although many of these situations can be supported through the use of semantic tagging, the current work aims to develop automated solutions to these problems. One potential approach is to supplement sem-gram statistics with corpus-based frame statistics in order to determine probabilities for each semantic frame and its arguments. While large corpora of AAC messages are unavailable, there have been recent efforts to simulate corpora that may be useful for obtaining such frame statistics [7]. Additionally, each user's message formulation history may be used to automatically refine the language model between sessions. Future work on SymbolPath may also include smoothing of the physical path to accommodate users with hand or arm tremors, as well as a calibration mode to detect each user's movement preferences and adjust the path's physical characteristics accordingly.

4. REFERENCES

[1] C. J. Fillmore. Frame semantics and the nature of language. *Annals of the New York Academy of Sciences*, 280(Origins and Evolution of Language and Speech):20–32, Oct. 1976.

[2] P. O. Kristensson and S. Zhai. SHARK2: a large vocabulary shorthand writing system for pen-based computers. In *Proceedings of the 17th annual ACM symposium on User interface software and technology*, UIST '04, pages 43–52, New York, NY, USA, 2004. ACM.

[3] J. Light, D. Beukelman, and J. Reichle. *Communicative competence for individuals who use AAC: From research to effective practice*. Paul H. Brookes Publishing Co., 2003.

[4] J. Matas, P. Mathy-Laikko, D. Beukelman, and K. Legresley. Identifying the nonspeaking population: a demographic study. *Augmentative and Alternative Communication*, 1(1):17–31, Dec. 1985.

[5] R. Patel, S. Pilato, and D. Roy. Beyond linear syntax: An Image-Oriented communication aid. *Journal of Assistive Technology Outcomes and Benefits*, (1):57–66, 2004.

[6] J. Todman, N. Alm, and L. Elder. Computer-aided conversation: A prototype system for nonspeaking people with physical disabilities. *Applied Psycholinguistics*, 15(01):45–73, 1994.

[7] K. Vertanen and P. O. Kristensson. The imagination of crowds: Conversational AAC language modeling using crowdsourcing and large data sources. In *Proceedings of the Conference on Empirical Methods in Natural Language Processing (EMNLP)*, pages 700–711. ACL, 2011.

[8] K. Wiegand and R. Patel. Non-Syntactic word prediction for AAC. In *Proceedings of the Third Workshop on Speech and Language Processing for Assistive Technologies*, pages 28–36, Montréal, Canada, June 2012. Association for Computational Linguistics.

Automated Description Generation for Indoor Floor Maps

Devi Paladugu, Hima Bindu Maguluri*, Qiongjie Tian*, Baoxin Li

Computer Science and Engineering, Arizona State University

{apaladug,hmagulur,qtian5,bli24}@asu.edu

ABSTRACT

People with visual impairment can face numerous challenges navigating a new environment. A practical need is to navigate through unfamiliar indoor environments such as school buildings, hotels, etc., for which commonly-used existing tools like canes, seeing-eye dogs and GPS devices cannot provide adequate support. We demonstrate a prototype system that aims at addressing this practical need. The input to the system is the name of the building/establishment supplied by a user, which is used by a web crawler to determine the availability of a floor map on the corresponding website. If available, the map is downloaded and used by the proposed system to generate a verbal description giving an overview of the locations of key landmarks inside the map with respect to one another. Our preliminary survey and experiments indicate that this is a promising direction to pursue in supporting indoor navigation for the visually impaired.

Categories and Subject Descriptors

H.5.2 [**Information Interfaces and Presentations**]: User-centered design. K.4.2 [**Social issues**]: Assistive technologies for persons with disabilities.

Author Keywords

Visually Impaired, Indoor Floor maps, Navigation, Verbal Description

1. INTRODUCTION

Assistive technologies for the visually impaired have seen tremendous developments. Nevertheless, there still remain many practical barriers for a blind individual who strives to lead an independent and active life [1]. One such problem faced repeatedly in their everyday life is navigation, especially when visiting new places. Indoor navigation in unfamiliar places, in spite of being a big hindrance factor, has not received enough attention from researchers and developers. Sonar, camera, laser based devices and infrared based signage are some devices developed in the last decade to help with indoor navigation via obstacle detection [1]. However, these devices require sensory devices to be strategically placed inside the building, which is a constraint. Further, these devices do not provide an overall sense of the location or help with planning a visit to a new location. People still largely depend on seeking human help around the location to get directions.

A simple and effective solution is to describe a floor map, when available, in terms of a scheme of relative positions. Using a relative scheme eliminates the need for having multiple devices tracking user position in real-time. A system that generates a verbal description combined with a user-friendly interface can be very useful in helping the user to get a sense of relative positions

of locations and thus might reduce the need for totally relying on "asking for directions". Say a student who is visually impaired wants to go to a local library that he has never visited before (or with which he has little familiarity). He could gain knowledge of the key locations before he gets there, if a verbal description of the major landmarks and their geographical relation are readily available. An automatic indoor map description generator that can be easily used by a visually-impaired user may thus greatly benefit the blind population in promoting and supporting a more active life style.

2. SYSTEM AND DESIGN

The first problem towards building a system to provide verbal description of a floor map is to determine the availability of a usable digital map of good resolution. A majority of public buildings have their floor plans published on their website. However, in general, it is very difficult if not impossible for a visually impaired user to go through all the links on a web site to locate and assert that a file/link is indeed a floor plan. Secondly, given an image of the floor plan, the components of the plan need to be determined automatically. Thirdly, assuming all the components of the map can be segregated, finding the right way to describe these components is another challenging task. To the best of our knowledge, there is no fully automatic solution that completely solves the problems in an end-to-end system. This demo will present a prototype system that we have developed for working around the problems presented above. The system provides a simple interface for a user to type in the search keywords for the place he is interested in visiting. The system then uses these keywords to extract the URL/domain of the relevant website. A keyword-based search is employed to parse all the URLs obtained from the website to find the appropriate floor plan, if it indeed exists. Automated image process algorithms are then deployed to extract useful landmarks in the map. Finally, the system generates a verbal description that is presented on the screen as well as read out to the user. The current version of the system has been focused on public libraries, to properly constrain the domain to some degree. The overview of the system is illustrated in Figure 1.

2.1 WebCrawler Interface

We designed an interface that takes in a set of keywords or an URL and downloads the relevant image or pdf files. We used Google's "I am feeling lucky" search URL format to obtain the first link, given the keywords. Given this URL, we use the CURL and DOM features in a simple PHP script combined with keyword search to extract the required URLs containing the floor plan(s).

2.2 Key Landmark Localization

In this step, common landmarks of the domain (e.g., libraries) are located in a map. The processing steps also include text detection and recognition. Below are the major processing steps:

* Indicates equal contribution.

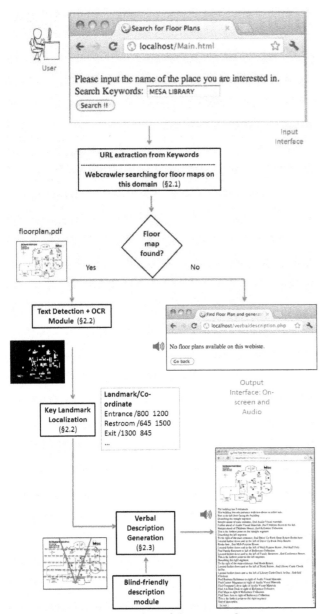

Figure 1. An overview of the proposed system.

Pre-processing: This step includes removing the color information, detection and removal of the legend, line removal.

Text Detection: We use spatial frequency variations along vertical, horizontal and diagonal direction for each pixel to estimate if a pixel contains text [2].

Text Region Post-processing: Text blocks are detected and the orientations of text are estimated and compensated for OCR.

OCR: We integrate Tesseract [3] to process the segmented text regions to obtain the text corresponding to each region.

Auto-correction and OCR: For initial refinement, we use a standard dictionary and spell check on every detected word to correct some bad detection and recognition results.

For words corresponding to key locations, we save the centroid of each detected text box and the corresponding text for the subsequent stages.

2.3 Verbal Description Generation

We performed a small-scale case study and analyzed how blind users verbally describe a building that they are familiar with and also tried to learn how they usually receive layout information from sighted individuals. We asked a small group of blind users to describe a building on campus that they are familiar with, to another blind individual who is new to the building. We analyzed the descriptions and tried to mimic the observations when designing the verbal description, resulting in the "Blind-friendly description model" shown in Figure 1.

The most natural way to describe a building as seen from our case study can be summarized as follows: Describe the rooms or landmarks encountered when walking straight into the main entrance door. Then describe locations to the left and to the right either with respect to the objects described previously or with reference to the entrance. As an attempt to simplify this task, we divide the map into three segments: "straight", "left" and "right". It is intuitive to divide into three regions as shown in Figure 1. Once we have each point categorized into a segment, we further divide the map into grids, to give the user a sense of distance between the relative points. Based on the grid location and segment, we use simple grammatical rules to generate verbal description.

3. SUMMARY

The contribution of this work is three-fold. First, a simple interface that eliminates all the work needed from a user to obtain a map is implemented. Second, automated algorithms were designed to factorize the map into the necessary components needed for description generation. Thirdly, a simple but efficient way to describe a floor plan learnt from the visually impaired users during a case study is proposed. The system will be demonstrated on the conference.

4. ACKNOWLEDGEMENT

This material is based upon work supported in part by the National Science Foundation under Grant No. 0845469. Any opinions, findings, and conclusions or recommendations expressed in this material are those of the authors and do not necessarily reflect the views of the National Science Foundation.

5. KEY REFERENCES

[1] Giudice, N.A., & Legge, G.E. (2008). Blind navigation and the role of technology. In A. Helal, M. Mokhtari & B. Abdulrazak (Eds.), Engineering handbook of smart technology for aging, disability, and independence (pp. 479-500): John Wiley & Sons.

[2] Z. Wang, et al., "Instant tactile-audio map: enabling access to digital maps for people with visual impairment," ACM SIGACCESS conference on Computers and Accessibility, Pittsburgh, Pennsylvania, USA, 2009.

[3] http://code.google.com/p/tesseract-ocr/

Non-visual-cueing-based Sensing and Understanding of Nearby Entities in Aided Navigation.

Juan Diego Gomez
University of Geneva
Computer Science Department
Geneva, Switzerland
+41 (22) 379 0152

juan.gomez@unige.ch

Guido Bologna
University of Geneva
Computer Science Department
Geneva, Switzerland
+41 (22) 379 0152

guido.bologna@unige.ch

Thierry Pun
University of Geneva
Computer Science Department
Geneva, Switzerland
+41 (22) 379 0152

thierry.pun@unige.ch

ABSTRACT

Exploring unfamiliar environments is a challenging task in which additionally, unsighted individuals frequently fail to gain perception of obstacles and make serendipitous discoveries. This is because the mental depiction of the context is drastically lessened due to the absence of visual information. It is still not clear in neuroscience, whether stimuli elicited by visual cueing can be replicated by other senses (cross-model transfer). In the practice, however, everyone recognizes a key, whether it is felt in a pocket or seen on a table. We present a context-aware aid system for the blind that merges three levels of assistance enhancing the intelligibility of the nearby entities: an exploration module to help gain awareness of the surrounding context, an alerting method for warning the user when a stumble is likely, and, finally, a recognition engine that retrieves natural targets previously learned. Practical experiences with our system show that in the absence of visual cueing, the audio and haptic trajectory playback coupled with computer-vision methods is a promising approach to depict dynamic information of the immediate environment.

Categories and Subject Descriptors

K.4.2 [**computers & society**]: Social Issues – *Assistive technologies for persons with disabilities, Handicapped persons/special needs.*

Keywords

Context-aware aid, visually impaired, visual cueing, assistance.

1. INTRODUCTION

According to the World Health Organization, 285 million people are visually impaired worldwide. In this context, the research community is increasingly focusing on the development of assistive technology. In fulfilling such purpose the study of strategies to depict visual information to the blind has attracted

significant interest. Notwithstanding, the representation of dynamic environmental visual cues through assistive systems is lagging behind the growing requirements of the blind community for independent living. This work targets to efficiently convey visual information hardly attainable otherwise. We propose a model for assistive navigation/exploration (fig.1) aimed at fostering awareness of context by increasing the intelligibility of nearby entities and easing the interpretation of spatial relations:

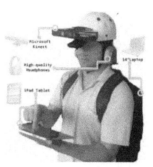

Figure 1. *The assistance system based on context-aware computing presented in this work.*

I. An exploration module that makes it possible for the users to touch with their fingers through an iPad, the whole 3D-image captured by a range camera in real time. The color and position of touched points are encoded in instruments sounds and sonic effects, respectively [2]. This module exploits the audio and haptic trajectory feedback to convey significant visual cues. Particularly, the use of spatialized sound allows understanding of spatial relations as sounds are perceived from 3D locations.

II. An alerting method based on range-imaging processing that prevents the user from stumbling by informing about unexpected entities lying on his way and potentially leading to a fall. At some point, this algorithm can also predict the trajectory of detected obstacles to keep/suspend a warning. This method allows the blind to find a clear path in the interest of safe navigation.

III. A recognition engine that uses state-of-the art object recognition methods to learn natural objects. There is a training phase supported by tracking and bootstrapping methods followed by an online searching process. This latter informs the user about the presence of learned objects in real time during exploration, if any. Unlike I and II, this engine is able to perceive and depict complex visual information in a much higher level of abstraction.

2. EXPLORATION MODULE

Presenting nontextual or dynamic information through no heavily visual methods continues to be a challenge in aided navigation. In our system, pictures of a real-time 3D video stream are made possible to be touched with the fingers over an iPad. We convey the visual information of touched points by encoding its color and actual spatial position respectively, into instruments sounds and sonic effects (i.e. spatialization of sound) [3]. Ideally, our interface (fig. 2) turns the iPad into a door for the user to enter and sense the environment.

In general, when the user wants to explore the nearby space, (s)he will rapidly scan the touchpad with one or more fingers; the principle here is that finger movements will replace eye movements and more information from the image as a whole is made accessible in parallel. This provokes a proactive interaction to selectively explore, to discover points of interest, make comparisons, and, furthermore, enjoy a greater sense of independence.

Figure 2. *Spatialization of sound is meant to create the illusion framed in this figure (leftmost). In our work, this allows to let the user hear the sound of a touched point in the picture (iPad) like it is coming from its counterpart point in the real world. In this example the user is touching (within the image displayed on the iPad he holds) the right-up corner of the chair's back. The others in this figure are random pictures of experimental sessions.*

3. ALERTING METHOD

The alerting method is range-imaging-based algorithm whose purpose is to warn the visually impaired user when a threatening situation is likely to happen as consequence of an unexpected obstacle. Once a warning has been launched, the user is expected to timely stop for a potential stumble be avoided. This also allows the blind to find a safe, clear path to advance through. Our guarding algorithm will run nonstop as long as the user is exploring. This user therefore, will be able to focus on gaining a context insight by means of the haptic-based interface, rather than minding his step.

To test this algorithm, we stuck the camera of our system on top of a rolling chair's back, which in turn carried the rest of the system on its seat. A person leaned on the chair arms so as to roll it down a corridor (with plenty of obstacles) while pushing with his walk. The end result is a video that shows the performance of our method: http://youtu.be/X426HAZaiYQ

4. RECOGNITION ENGINE

Based on the strategy proposed by Kalal et al [1], we have implemented a detecting-and-tracking hybrid method for learning the appearance of natural objects in unconstrained video streams. Thus, we allow visually impaired users gaining awareness of certain objects they otherwise could fail to perceive, or simply need others help to do so. Notice that sometimes looking for an object (e.g. a fallen object) may end up in an embarrassing situation that might lower their feeling of dignity. In general, we look forward to letting an unsighted individual be aware of serendipitously encounters such as a person on his way to the toilet but also, conscious searches such as for a telephone, an exit, a trash can etc. Our recognition engine permits: (1) Learn the object during a tracking phase. (2) When the learning meets an end, a sighted user provides the name of the object. (3) When the navigation/exploration task is being performed (fig. 3), the unsighted user is notified about the presence of the learned object through an earcon, audio icon or simply spelling out the name every time following detection.

Figure 3. *Samples of real time detections of our recognition engine for three objects sequences. The yellow square represents the area were the object is thought to be, when detected. Rows 1 and 2: a trash can. Rows 3 and 4: an exit way. Rows 5 and 6: a telephone. These objects were selected as common targets by legally blind users in a survey.*

5. CONCLUSIONS

We presented a mobility aid system for unsighted individuals to allow them sensing and understanding a great deal of visual information about their immediate environment. The three levels of assistance that our context-aware system provides were described in this paper: an exploration module, an alerting method and a recognition engine. This system assesses the actual feasibility of assistive technologies to efficiently convey compacted visual information hardly attainable otherwise. We have showed that the use of the audio and haptic trajectory feedback is an effective method to encode visual features such as color and depth which in turn, make the environment more intelligible.

6. REFERENCES

[1] Kalal, Z., Matas, J. and Mikolajczyk, K (2010). P-N Learning: Bootstrapping Binary Classifiers by Structural Constraints. In proceedings of CVPR'10, International Conference on Computer Vision and Pattern Recognition. San Francisco CA, US.

[2] Bologna, G., Deville, B., Gomez, J. and Pun, T (2010). Toward local and global perception modules for vision substitution. Neurocomputing, Vol. 74, Issue. 8, Pag. 1182–1190, Pub. date: October 2010.

[3] Ordonez, C., Navarun, G. and Barreto, A (2002). Sound spatialization as a navigational aid in virtual environments. In proceedings of CSI, The 6th Computer Security Institute Conference. Orlando Fl, US.

EZ Ballot with Multimodal Inputs and Outputs

Seunghyun "Tina" Lee[1], Xiao Xiong[2], Liu Elaine Yilin[1,3], Jon Sanford[1,3]

Center for Assistive Technology and Environmental Access[1] Georgia Institute of Technology Atlanta, GA, USA	School of Literature, Media, and Communication[2] Georgia Institute of Technology Atlanta, GA, USA	School of Industrial Design[3] Georgia Institute of Technology Atlanta, GA, USA

{tinalee, xxiong6, yliu451}@gatech.edu, jon.sanford@coa.gatech.edu

ABSTRACT

Current accessible voting machines require many voters with visual, cognitive and dexterity limitations to vote with assistance, if they can vote at all. To address accessibility problems, we developed the EZ Ballot. The linear layout of the EZ ballot structure fundamentally re-conceptualizes ballot design to provide the same simple and intuitive voting experience for all voters, regardless of ability or input/output (I/O) device used. Further, multimodal I/O interfaces were seamlessly integrated with the ballot structure to provide flexibility in accommodating voters with different abilities.

Categories and Subject Descriptors

H.5.2. Information interfaces and presentation: User Interfaces–input devices and strategies.

General Terms

Design, Human Factors.

Keywords

Accessible voting, multimodal input, multimodal output, gestural input

1. INTRODUCTION

Compared to older technological voting systems such as paper ballots, levers, or punch cards, electronic voting machines are capable of being adapted to provide access to voters with a broad range of disabilities through a variety of alternative inputs and outputs [1,7]. These features, which are typically added to existing hardware and/or software architecture, have primarily focused on accommodating voters with the types of impairments (i.e., vision and dexterity) that are most likely to limit access to voting machines. However, despite providing technical accessibility, the accessible input and output features that are added to a conventional ballot not only make the voting experience more complex and difficult for voters with vision and dexterity limitations compared to voters without disabilities, they generally ignore and can exacerbate problems experienced by voters with cognitive limitations.

To address these problems, we developed a prototype of an EZ ballot that integrates a simplified ballot design with a range of I/O interfaces. The linear layout of the ballot structure fundamentally re-conceptualizes ballot design to provide the same simple and intuitive voting experience, regardless of ability or I/O interface used. Further, multimodal input and output interfaces are seamlessly integrated with the ballot structure to provide the

flexibility to accommodate voters who are most likely to have problems with voting machines, including people with cognitive, visual and dexterity limitations. Ultimately, this prototype could be generalized to other applications such as electronic kiosks.

2. RELATED WORK

Voters with vision, cognition and dexterity limitations experience different types of problems using accessible voting machines. For blind and visually-impaired voters, voting takes significantly longer (31 vs. 5 minutes) compared to sighted voters [7] and navigating a ballot often leads to confusion [3, 5, 8]. These difficulties can often be attributed to the accessible features that are added to standard ballots, which are designed to be used visually. For voters with cognitive limitations who can be confused and overwhelmed by the amount of information and visual complexity of a full-face or the lack of overall orientation in page-by-page ballots, there is a need to incorporate more cognitive supports [6]. To provide access to voters with dexterity limitations, a variety of assistive technology inputs (e.g., sip-and-puff, jelly switch devices) have been added to voting machines. In addition to creating set up problems for poll workers who are unfamiliar with these input devices [8], they can negatively affect the voting experience.

A number of efforts have been undertaken to develop alternative ballots, such as the zoomable voting interface which provides an overview of the entire ballot as well as a detailed zoomed view of each race [1], and Prime III, which offers multimodal touch and/or voice and/or A/B switch inputs [4]. However, each of these systems only accommodates voters with specific limitations. To date, there are no voting systems that accommodate all voters across the range of ability.

3. DESIGN OF EZ BALLOT
3.1. EZ Ballot Structure

To provide equal access for voters with cognitive, visual and dexterity limitations, the EZ Ballot was designed with a simple, consistent linear structure. To reduce cognitive demand, EZ Ballot breaks down the voting process (e.g., contests, candidates, review of the ballot and casting the ballot) into simple questions that are easy to understand and answer using either a "yes" or "no" response, which provides consistency and simplicity. Each screen contains only one question that is presented both visually and verbally (see Figures 1). For example, "Do you want to vote for democratic Barack Obama & Joe Biden for president and vice president?" will be displayed visually and through audio (see Figure 1). The question itself serves as a prompt that can remind and orient voters. Responses on the existing prototype are limited to pressing a physical buttons on the left and right sides of the device or by using touch buttons on the iPad touch screen.

ASSETS'12, October 22–24, 2012, Boulder, Colorado, USA.
ACM 978-1-4503-1321-6/12/10.

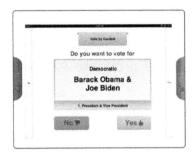

Figure 1. EZ Ballot interface

3.2. Multimodal Inputs of EZ Ballot

EZ ballot is designed with integrated multimodal inputs to provide flexibility for users with different levels of vision and dexterity. Multimodal inputs include physical tactile input, touch screen input, and gestural inputs. The physical tactile input is designed with two conductive buttons on each side of the screen where the iPad is typically grasped (see Figure 2). Though not following the principle of proximity between physical buttons and onscreen ones, button placement will be varied and tested as part of the next phase of the project. The buttons also have embossed letters of "Y" and "N" for the voters with visually impaired. Although red and green are indistinguishable to individuals who are color blind, the colors were chosen as they are internationally recognizable for yes and no buttons. For individuals who are color blind, buttons can be differentiated by contrast, text, and icons.

Gestural interfaces can be 2D touch gestures that use of fingers on touchscreens or 3D air gestures that involve free movement in space [9]. In this project, we will embed 2D multi-finger gestures (e.g., pinching and scrolling) for magnification and navigation that recognizes defined gestures, such as swipe, circle, zoom, or a gestural development kit, which permits user-defined gestures such as a check. For 3D gestures Kinect technology or Apple iSight, which recognizes air gestures using the iPad camera, will be used to record head gestures (e.g., shaking up and down), or hand gestures (e.g., thumbs up and down).

"No" tactile button   "Yes" tactile button

"No" touch screen button   "Yes" touch screen button

Figure 2. Multimodal Inputs of EZ Ballot Prototype

3.3. Multimodal Outputs of EZ Ballot

EZ ballot was also designed with integrated multimodal outputs to provide flexibility for users with different cognitive and visual abilities. Multimodal outputs include visual, speech, and tactile feedback. To provide multi-modal outputs orientation and feedback cues, a progress bar and non-speech sounds will be incorporated in the EZ Ballot. To compensate for the linear structure of the EZ Ballot, which currently provides no cues about the nature of the overall ballot, an overview of the ballot and progress bar will be added in the next phase to orient the voters to the overall voting process. In addition, based on feedback from

visually-impaired users in the pilot testing, non-speech sound will be added to indicate that an action has occurred.

4. INITIAL USER STUDIES

In a pilot study, users reported that the prototype was easy to use and understand. A blind user particularly liked the simplicity of the "yes" and "no" tactile buttons and the ability to use both hands compared to a typical one-handed keypad. A dexterity-impaired user responded that the touch screen buttons were easy to use. Similarly, an English-as-second-language speaker preferred the simple "yes" and "no" questions which make the process easy to understand.

5. ONGOING WORK

Usability studies are currently being conducted to identify and refine issues with the EZ ballot structure and the I/O interfaces. A total of 40 participants, including 10 participants with visual, dexterity, and cognitive impairments and ten without disabilities, will be recruited. Four sample ballots covering a range of contest types (e.g., choose one, choose three, write-in, referendum) will be designed that require no more than 10 minutes each to complete. Quantitative measures of task performance will include task completion, task success (accuracy of voting), number of assists required (asking for help), and the number of errors made (incorrect inputs). Following each trial, participants will be asked to complete a post-trial interview to elicit in-depth, qualitative feedback about the usability of each of feature and their satisfaction with the EZ Ballot.

6. REFERENCES

[1] Bederson, B. 2008. Voting Technology: The Not-So-Simple Act of Casting a Ballot, from http://www.cs.umd.edu/~bederson/voting/USACM-bederson-feb-2008.pdf.

[2] Bederson, B. B., Lee, B., Sherman, R. M., Herrnson, P. S., & Niemi, R. G. 2003. Electronic voting system usability issues. Paper presented at the *Proceedings of the SIGCHI conference on Human factors in computing systems*, Ft. Lauderdale, Florida, USA.

[3] Burton, D., & Uslan, M. 2004. The Ballot Ballet: The Usability of Accessible Voting Machines. AccessWorld, 5(4).

[4] Gilbert, J. 2005. PRIME III: One Machine, One Vote for Everyone, from http://www.juangilbert.com/

[5] Gilbert, J., McMillian, Y., Rouse, K., Williams, P., Rogers, G., McClendon, J., . . . Cross, E. 2010. Universal access in e-voting for the blind. Universal Access in the Information Society, 9(4), 357-365.

[6] Ott, B.R., Heindel, W.C., Papandonatos, G.D. 2003. A survey of voter participation by cognitively impaired elderly patients, Neurology 60(9): 1546-1548.

[7] Piner, G. E., & Byrne, M. D. 2011. The Experience of Accessible Voting. Proceedings of the Human Factors and Ergonomics Society Annual Meeting, 55(1), 1686-1690.

[8] Runyan, N., & Tobias, J. 2007. Accessibility Review Report for California Top-to-Bottom Voting Systems Review.

[9] Saffer, D. 2008. Designing Gestural Interfaces: Touchscreens and Interactive Devices: O'Reilly Media.

Breath Mobile – A Software-Based Hands-free and Voice-free Breathing Controlled Mobile Phone Interface

Jackson Feijó Filho
Nokia Technology Institute
Av. Torquato Tapajós, 7200 - Col.
Terra Nova. Manaus-AM Brasil.
69093-415
+55 92 8134 0134

jackson.feijo@indt.org.br

Thiago Valle
Nokia Technology Institute
Av. Torquato Tapajós, 7200 - Col.
Terra Nova. Manaus-AM Brasil.
69093-415
+55 92 8109 0999

thiago.valle@indt.org.br

Wilson Prata
Nokia Technology Institute
Av. Torquato Tapajós, 7200 - Col.
Terra Nova. Manaus-AM Brasil.
69093-415
+55 92 8805 1071

wilsonprata@gmail.com

ABSTRACT

This work proposes the use of a low-cost software based breathing interface for mobile phones as an alternative interaction technology for people with motor disabilities. It attempts to explore the processing of the audio from the microphone in mobile phones to trigger and launch software events. A proof of concept of this work is demonstrated by the implementation and experimentation of a mobile application prototype that enables users to perform a basic operation on the phone, such as calling through "puffing" interaction.

Categories and Subject Descriptors

H.1.2 [**User/Machine Systems**], K.4.2 [**Social Issues**]: Assistive technologies for persons with disabilities, Handicapped persons/special needs.

General Terms

Algorithms, Performance, Design, Experimentation, Human Factors, Languages.

Keywords

Breathing, Alternative hci, Mobile, Accessibility.

1. INTRODUCTION

Assistive technologies have been researched and developed as an important part of the field of human–computer interaction. Many forms of assistance have been created for technology users with particular disabilities that reduce their capabilities to use some devices. Several alternative user interfaces for users with motor disabilities have been developed and reported. Typically, these solutions include methods that implement speech recognition techniques, eye-trackers and sip-and-puff controllers [4]. Speech recognition software is well documented to be particularly useful for textual input aid, while additional devices are usually employed as pointing devices, allowing the control of e.g. the mouse pointer [3].

This work will initially debate on the problems of these solutions, positioning of prior work, followed by the advocacy of the present solution and explanation of its functioning. In the end, final considerations will state this is a valuable alternate method

ASSETS'12, October 22–24, 2012, Boulder, Colorado, USA.

ACM 978-1-4503-1321-6/12/10.

for hands-free and silent interaction with a mobile phone interface.

2. PROBLEM SPACE AND PRIOR WORK

The interaction of people with motor disabilities and their mobile phones have challenged the academy and industry to develop alternative software and hardware solutions. These solutions will not rely on any manual interaction e.g. keystroking, screen-touching. Interactions through other physiological signals are often considered. Speech recognition is also a solution used by the targeted audience.

2.1 Interaction through Physiological Signals

Common physiological measures already used in previous Human Computer Interaction (HCI) and Accessibility works include: cardiovascular, electrodermal, muscular tension, ocular, skin temperature, brain activity and respiration measures. These solutions typically require extra hardware, which makes these alternatives more expensive to final users. Not to mention they are 'immobile' computer oriented solutions (desktops, laptops, etc) and do not cover mobile phones. The work [2] presents a sip-and-puff remote control that aims mobile devices, but again, it requires extra hardware.

2.2 Voice/Speech Recognition

Speech recognition is able to present itself as a software based solution. But it affects the privacy of the user, as it implies the representation of whatever is being commanded through the form of speech to the periphery auditory. Some hardware work has been developed to minimize peripheral representations of speech and improve privacy, as in [1] but again this requires not only extra and expensive hardware but the burden of wearing cochlear implants.

3. BREATH MOBILE SOLUTION

The proof of concept application of this work was developed using native code in a smartphone running Symbian OS with the S60, Symbian^3 platform. Due to it being: multitasking enabled, having the capability of sending OS software events (e.g. send a key code to the keyboard buffer) and having the capability of processing the audio stream from the microphone to e.g. measure sound levels.

It attempts to detect three distinct event based on 'puffing': a single short puff, a double short puff and a long puff. The single short puff throws a right (forward) arrow key event to the keyboard buffer. The double short puff throws a left (back) arrow key to the keyboard buffer. The long puff throws a selection (enter/ok) key to the keyboard buffer.

3.1 Audio peaks and silences states
Here is a machine state diagram for the functioning of this system (see Figure 1)

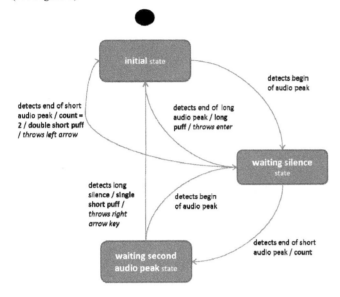

Figure 1. The state diagram shows the management of peaks, long puffs and silence.

The detection of an audio puff from silence starts a time counter that will wait for silence. The machine will remain on this state until the sound level goes below what is set to be the audio puff. When the audio puff ends (sound level goes low), the time counter is checked. If it was a long 'puff' it throws the enter key event. If it was a short 'puff' it will briefly wait for the second short puff. But if a long silence is detected, it means a single short puff was detected and a right arrow key event is thrown. But if another short puff is detected within the time limit, it qualifies a double short puff and a left arrow key event is thrown.

4. EXPERIMENT
The experiment consisted in one trying to perform the task of making a phone call using the present application, which is running in the background. The phone was not to be touched during the experiment. For the phone interface we were using, six steps were needed. See below:

1. Select Contacts from main menu – single short puffs, until cursor reaches the "Contacts" application. *Expected result – Contacts application is highlighted.*

2. Open Contacts application – one long puff. *Expected result – Contacts application open.*

3. Select contact "John" - single short puffs, until cursor reaches the "John" item on the contacts list. *Expected result – Contact John is highlighted.*

4. Open "John" contact – one long puff. *Expected result – John communication options menu opens.*

5. Select option "Call" - single short puffs, until cursor reaches "Call" item on the menu. *Expected result – Call option is highlighted.*

6. Execute "Call" command – one long puff. *Expected result – Call initiates.*

A group of eight mobile phone users, college students, touch screen phone users, between 17 and 25, non-disabled, were selected to perform the process above. Future work will include experiment results from motor disabled users. Each student performed the task list from beginning to end in one single round, with no interaction with the other students, until they were all done.

5. RESULTS
The number of unsuccessful attempts, before performing the tasks correctly, was noted.

1. First single short puffs: 12 attempts

2. First long puff: 20 attempts

3. Second single short puffs: 6 attempts

4. Second long puff: 8 attempts

5. Third single short puffs: 2 attempts

6. Third long puff: 5 attempts

It was clear that there was a learning curve on using the software - particularly, the duration of the long puff was unclear to the users. The distance users took from the phone in order to puff varied. Overall, all the participants were able to complete the task list.

6. REFERENCES
[1] Wilson, Blake S., Finley, Charles C.,Lawson, Dewey T., Wolford, Robert D., Eddington, Donald K., Rabinowitz, William M., Better speech recognition with cochlear implants, Journal Nature, 1991/07/18/print, issue 352, p236-238.

[2] Jones, M., Grogg, K., Anschutz, J., Fierman, R. A Sip-and-Puff Wireless Remote Control for the Apple iPod. Assistive Technology: The Official Journal of RESNA,Volume 20, Issue 2, 2008, 107-110.

[3] Sibert L.E., Jacob R.J.K., Evaluation of eye gaze interaction. Proceedings of CHI 2000 Conference on Human Factorsin Computing Systems. ACM Press (2000), The Hague, pp 281–288.

[4] Kitto, K.L. Development of a low-cost sip and puff mouse. In: Proceedings of 16th Annual Conference of RESNA. RESNA Press (1993), Las Vegas, pp 452–454.

What is Wrong with this Word?
Dyseggxia: a Game for Children with Dyslexia

Luz Rello   Clara Bayarri   Azuki Gorriz

Cookie Cloud
Barcelona, Spain

ABSTRACT

We present *Dyseggxia*, a game application with word exercises for children with dyslexia. We design the content of the game combining linguistic and pedagogical criteria as well as corpus analysis. The main contributions are (i) designing exercises by using the analysis of errors written by people with dyslexia and (i) presenting Spanish reinforcement exercises in the form of a computer game. The game is available for free on iOS and Android.

Categories and Subject Descriptors

K.3 [**Computers in Education**]: Computer Uses in Education—*Computer-assisted instruction*; K.4 [**Computers and Society**]: Social Issues—*Assistive technologies for persons with disabilities*

General Terms

Design, Experimentation, Human Factors

Keywords

Dyslexia, Pedagogical Exercises, Spanish, Game, Android, iOS.

1. INTRODUCTION

More than 10% of the population in Europe has dyslexia. Dyslexia is a neurologically based learning disability which typically results from a deficit in the phonological component of language. It is characterized by difficulties with accurate word recognition and by poor spelling, especially with new words, unfrequent words, very long words, complex words and phonetically and orthographically similar words [2].

To overcome dyslexia children undertake exercises with words, among other activities. Typically, these exercises appear in books with all the limitations of paper-based exercises, such as the added difficulty of writing on paper since dysgraphia[1] is comorbid with dyslexia. Moreover, these exercises are frequently repetitive and homogeneous thus making these tasks tedious.

---

[1]Dysgraphia refers to a writing disorder associated with the motor skills involved in handwriting, among others.

Dyseggxia[2] was designed to integrate pedagogical exercises in a more appealing and up-to-date format: a game for mobile phones and tablets.

2. RELATED WORK

We divide work related to our application in two areas. **(a) Exercises for children with dyslexia.** Apart from the printed books with word exercises [1], we found resources in the Web containing exercises for children with dyslexia such as *El patinete*,[3] with printable exercises and *Espacio Logopédico*,[4] with an exercise book. **(b) Mobile and tablet applications related to dyslexia:** Most existing tools are devoted to text processing, spellchecking and word prediction. The most closely related applications are those that target children with learning disabilities such as: *Dyslexic like me*,[5] with guidance for children with dyslexia, or *Dyslexia Quest*, with short games. We also found applications for improving spelling, such as *Word Magic*. In Spanish, we found only *Dislexia Ejercicios Prácticos*, with games.

To the best of our knowledge, *Dyseggxia* differs from previous work in two aspects. First, none of the existing applications for mobile or tablet in Spanish contains reinforcement word exercises inspired by pedagogical books. Second, *Dyseggxia* is based on different kinds of empirical data, such as the analysis of errors written by people with dyslexia.

3. CONTENT DESIGN

For the creation of the content we distinguish: (1) the selection of the word and the design of the exercice, (2) the choice of the specific word modification, (3) the assignment to the correct level of difficulty, and (4) the text layout.

(1) Exercises: To select the target words of the exercises, we establish linguistic criteria, e.g., we select only lemmas and existing words, and avoid pseudowords or foreign words. We design five types of exercises by taking into consideration existing pedagogical exercises to support dyslexia [1].

  a. **Insertion:** The user is given a word with a missing letter represented by a blank space and is asked to fill it with a letter from a set, e.g. **i_posible {n,s,r,p,m,b}* → *imposible*, '*impossible*'.

---

[2]http://www.dyseggxia.com
[3]http://www.elpatinete.com
[4]http://www.espaciologopedico.com
[5]See http://itunes.apple.com for this and the following examples of mobile applications.

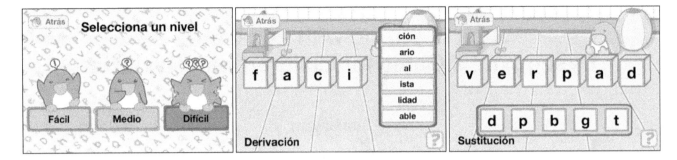

Figure 1: Dyseggxia: difficulty levels (left), derivation exercise (middle) and substitution exercise (right).

b. **Omission:** The user is given a word with an extra letter and is asked to identify and remove it, e.g. *verdazd → verdad, 'truth'.

c. **Substitution:** A word with a wrong letter is displayed and the user is asked to identify and substitute the wrong letter by the correct letter from a set, e.g. *verpad {d,p,b,g,t} → verdad, 'truth' (see Figure 1, right).

d. **Derivation:** The root of a word is displayed together with a set of suffixes, where only the correct one should be identified, e.g. *faci {lidad,al,ista} → facilidad, 'easiness' (see Figure 1, middle).

e. **Separation:** A set of words, normally composed of a lexical word and a small word or/and functional word is shown without spaces, where the user is asked to separate the character chain into different words, e.g. *osopanda → oso panda, 'panda bear'.

(2) Word modification: To determine the modification of the word for each exercise we manually analyzed the errors from a corpus of texts written by dyslexic children [3]. We extracted the most frequent errors and created linguistic patterns [5] to use them in the design of the tasks. For instance, similar letters representing similar sounds, such as occlusive consonants <d,b,p,g,t>, tend to be mistaken more, so we use them as distractors (see Figure 1, right).

(3) Levels: The levels of the exercises were designed by taking into consideration the difficulties of dyslexic people described in cognitive literature [2]. Therefore, we took into account five variables: (a) word frequency, (b) word length, (c) phonetic similarity, (d) orthographic similarity, and (c) the derivational difficulty of the word. There are three levels: easy, medium and hard (see Figure 1, left). As the difficulty level increases the target word is less frequent, longer, has a higher number of neighbors,[6] more frequent neighbors, and has a more complex morphology.

(4) Text Layout: Since the presentation of text has an effect on the reading speed of people with dyslexia, we used recommended text layout parameters to present the exercises. These guidelines are based on the data extracted from a user study with a group of twenty-two participants with dyslexia [4].

---

[6]Neighbors are all the words with the same length as the target word which differ in only one letter.

4. IMPLEMENTATION

The application has been designed by using the Model-View-Controller pattern and a high abstraction of platform-dependent tools in order to make it easily portable from Android to iOS and later to any other platform as needed. The high abstraction allows us to reuse the logics of the application on all platforms and just reimplement platform-dependent layers, mainly data persistence and view controllers.

5. FIRST RESULTS AND FUTURE WORK

Dyseggxia can be downloaded for free from the Apple App Store for iPhone and iPad[7] and the code is open source and freely available.[8] So far, we performed a heuristic evaluation and a preliminary formative evaluation using the think aloud technique with seven children with dyslexia. The results are promising: all participants found the tool helpful and more appealing than performing the exercises on paper, the difference between levels were clearly perceived and we received some suggestions for improving the game. Future work includes an evaluation with a focus group to measure the impact of the game in learning words and the improvement of the application by extending the target words and by adapting it to more languages.

6. REFERENCES

[1] C. Baro Tizón. Conocer la dislexia y corregirla (Understanding and overcoming dyslexia). *Innovación y experiencias educativas*, 14:1–9, 2009.

[2] F. Cuetos and F. Valle. Modelos de lectura y dislexias (Reading models and dyslexias). *Infancia y Aprendizaje*, 44:3–19, 1988.

[3] L. Rello, R. Baeza-Yates, H. Saggion, and J. Pedler. A first approach to the creation of a Spanish corpus of dyslexic texts. In *LREC Workshop Natural Language Processing for Improving Textual Accessibility (NLP4ITA)*, Istanbul, Turkey, May 2012.

[4] L. Rello, G. Kanvinde, and R. Baeza-Yates. Layout guidelines for web text and a web service to improve accessibility for dyslexics. In *International Cross Disciplinary Conference on Web Accessibility (W4A 2012)*, Lyon, France, April 2012. ACM Press.

[5] L. Rello and J. Llisterri. There are phonetic patterns in vowel substitution errors in texts written by persons with dyslexia. In *21st Annual World Congress on Learning Disabilities (LDW 2012)*, Oviedo, Spain, September 2012.

---

[7]http://itunes.apple.com/es/app/dyseggxia/id534986729?mt=8

[8]http://dyseggxia.com/download

Tapulator: A Non-Visual Calculator using Natural Prefix-Free Codes

Vaspol Ruamviboonsuk
Computer Science and Engineering
University of Washington
Seattle, WA 98195
vaspol@cs.washington.edu

Shiri Azenkot
Computer Science and Engineering
University of Washington
Seattle, WA 98195
shiri@cs.washington.edu

Richard E. Ladner
Computer Science and Engineering
University of Washington
Seattle, WA 98195
ladner@cs.washington.edu

ABSTRACT

A new non-visual method of numeric entry into a smartphone is designed, implemented, and tested. Users tap the smartphone screen with one to three fingers or swipe the screen in order to enter numbers. No buttons are used—only simple, easy-to-remember gestures. A preliminary evaluation with sighted users compares the method to a standard accessible numeric keyboard with a VoiceOver-like screen reader interface for non-visual entry. We found that users entered numbers faster and with higher accuracy with our number entry method than with a VoiceOver-like interface, showing there is potential for use among blind people as well. The Tapulator, a complete calculator based on this non-visual numeric entry that uses simple gestures for arithmetic operations and other calculator actions is described.

Categories and Subject Descriptors

K4.2 [Social Issues]: Assistive technologies for persons with disabilities, H.1.2 [User/Machine Systems]: Human factors

General Terms

Design, Human Factors.

Keywords

Number entry, Calculator, Non-visual interface, Blind.

1. INTRODUCTION

Simple math calculation is one of the daily tasks that we usually perform using a calculator. Currently, calculators are easy to use and can be found everywhere. Calculators on smartphones commonly have soft buttons with 20 buttons or more where ten are reserved for the digits 0 through 9. There are additional buttons for the decimal point, five arithmetic operations, *clear current number, clear current calculation, backspace*, and *equals* (calculate). Smartphone calculators can be made non-visually accessible by using a touch screen reader pioneered by Kane *et al.* [3] and found on iPhones (VoiceOver) and Android phones (TalkBack). Blind and low-vision users of smartphones typically use these screen readers that allow a user to explore the screen with a finger without activating any controls, listening to what is under the finger. Activation of a button, for entering a digit or other action, requires a double tap anywhere or split tap while touching the button.

In this demonstration, we present the Tapulator, a new non-visual approach to a multi-touch screen calculator that uses simple gestures instead of buttons. In particular, a natural prefix-free

code for entering digits with up to three fingers is used. Similar to a screen reader, auditory, rather than visual, feedback is used to indicate what digits and operations are entered.

The Tapulator is universally designed and can be used by anyone to make a calculation in a non-visual way, and there is no need to learn how to use a touch screen reader. For blind and low-vision users, the Tapulator can be faster for doing a calculation than a typical accessible button calculator because there is no need to explore the screen to find the right button to enter a digit or other operation.

For this demonstration, we examine in detail number entry without a decimal point. We provide some preliminary results that number entry is faster and more accurate using the Tapulator than using a button calculator with a touch screen reader. We then briefly describe the design of the full Tapulator.

2. RELATED WORK

Text entry, including numeric digits, is a long studied field. The H4-Writer of MacKenzie *et al.* uses Huffman codes [3], which are optimal prefix-free codes to enter text [6]. Such codes are not generally easy to remember, but once they are memorized, good input rates can be achieved. For Tapulator numeric input we also use a prefix-free code, but it is natural and easy to learn. Another key difference between MacKenzie *et al*'s work and ours is that the implementation of H4-Writer uses buttons, while the Tapulator implementation accepts touches anywhere on the screen.

The Perkinput text entry method, introduced by Azenkot *et al.* [1], is a Braille-based text entry system for multi-touch screens. Like the Tapulator, Perkinput does not have buttons, but unlike the Tapulator, Perkinput requires calibration to determine which fingers correspond to which touch points.

A study of gestures for multi-touch screens created by blind users by Kane *et al.* [5] indicates that blind people have different preferences for gestures than do sighted users. In addition, blind users were generally not as precise as sighted users when making gestures that required the production of a specific shape such as a circle or triangle. Following these findings, the Tapulator does not use any gestures other than taps and swipes.

3. TAPULATOR NUMERIC ENTRY

For numeric entry, the Tapulator uses a simple prefix-free code that uses multi-finger taps with one to three fingers and swipes. A prefix-free code requires that no codeword is a prefix of another. This allows a multi-digit number to be entered unambiguously as a sequence of codewords. The code is natural, where 0 is represented by a swipe; the digits 1 and 2 are represented by one and two finger taps, respectively; the digit 3 is represented by a two-finger tap followed by a swipe (i.e., 3 and 0).

The digit 4 is represented by a three-finger tap followed by a one-finger tap (i.e.. 3 and 1). Table 1 describes the complete code.

Table 1. Tapulator numeric codes.

Numbers	Code	Gestures
0	0	swipe
1	1	1-finger tap
2	2	2-finger tap
3	3 + 0	3-finger tap + swipe
4	3 + 1	3-finger tap + 1-finger tap
5	3 + 2	3-finger tap + 2-finger tap
6	3 + 3 + 0	2 × (3-finger tap) + swipe
7	3 + 3 + 1	2 × (3-finger tap) + 1-finger tap
8	3 + 3 + 2	2 × (3-finger tap) + 2-finger tap
9	3 + 3 + 3	3 × (3-fingers tap)

As can be readily seen, this code is easy to remember and this is validated to some extent in our preliminary evaluation. Note that this is not an optimal prefix-free code, assuming that all digits are equally likely. An optimal code that uses four symbols has an average of 1.8 actions per digit, while the Tapulator code has 2.1 actions per digit, where an action is a tap or a swipe. An optimal code would likely require more time to learn, which may inhibit adoption.

During our design process, we considered a five-symbol code where a four-finger tap represents the number 4. We found through formative evaluations that since the fourth finger (the "pinky") is typically much shorter than the other three fingers, four-finger tapping is somewhat awkward to perform on small touch screens.

4. PRELIMINARY EVALUATION

To compare Tapulator numeric entry with standard accessible numeric entry (hereafter, the "standard"), we present (1) a theoretical analysis of the techniques and (2) an empirical comparison with five users.

In the standard calculator there are two components to entering a digit. The first is the seek time to find the digit's button. The effort needed during the seek time is difficult to quantify but it does require listening to the buttons touched until the correct button is found. When the button is found, a double or split tap is needed to enter the digit. At first blush, this appears to be more difficult than an average of 2.1 taps per digit.

Our empirical evaluation included a study with five sighted participants, who entered 10 six-digit numbers on a smartphone using the Tapulator and the standard method. Participants held the smartphone beneath a desk so that they were unable to see the screen. After a brief training period, participants entered numbers at an average rate of 1.99 seconds per digit ($SD = 1.25$) with Tapulator, and 2.77 seconds per digit ($SD = 1.24$) with the standard method. The error rates of the final transcribed numbers were far lower for Tapulator entry: participants averaged a Mean String Distance (MSD) of just 1.0% on the Tapulator and 14.2%

with the standard method. Thus, the Tapulator out-performed the standard calculator in both speed and accuracy. Unsurprisingly, all five participants preferred the Tapulator to the other method.

While these results are only preliminary, they show the Tapulator has potential to out-perform a calculator with buttons for blind and low-vision people. We plan to conduct a more rigorous evaluation with blind users in the future.

5. TAPULATOR GESTURES

We do not have space to describe all the gestures needed for the Tapulator. All the operations, other than numeric entry, will begin with a three-finger swipe so as not to be confused with numeric entry. The gestures are natural corresponding to the operations as printed, making them also easy to learn. For example, "equals" is a two-finger swipe from left to right and plus is two consecutive swipes, up to down, then left to right. This is similar to the technique presented by Findlater *et al.* [2] for entering non-alphanumeric characters.

6. CONCLUSION AND FUTURE WORK

The Tapulator is in an early stage of development. More evaluation has to be conducted with blind participants with a fully implemented Tapulator, comparing it to a button calculator. We also plan to compare various potential codes for their ease of learning and use.

ACKNOWLEDGEMENTS

This work was partially funded by the National Science Foundation Grant No. IIS-1116051 and the Department of Education Grant No. H327A100014.

REFERENCES

[1] S. Azenkot, J.O. Wobbrock, S. Prasain, and R.E. Ladner (2012). Input Finger Detection for nonvisual touch screen text entry in Perkinput. In *Proceedings of Graphics Interface 2012* (GI '12). Toronto, Ontario: Canadian Information Processing Society, 121-129.

[2] Findlater, L., Lee, B.Q. and Wobbrock, J.O. (2012). Beyond Qwerty: Augmenting touch screen keyboards with multi-touch gestures for non-alphanumeric input. Proceedings of the ACM Conference on Human Factors in Computing Systems (CHI '12). New York: ACM Press, pp. 2679-2682.

[3] D.A. Huffman (1952). A method for the construction of minimum-redundancy codes. *Proceedings of the I.R.E.* 1098–1102.

[4] S.K. Kane, J.P. Bigham, J.O. Wobbrock (2008). Slide Rule: making mobile touch screens accessible to blind people using multi-touch interaction techniques. *Proceedings of the 10th International ACM SIGACCESS Conference on Computers and Accessibility* (ASSETS '08). 73-80.

[5] S.K. Kane, J.O. Wobbrock, R.E. Ladner (2011). Usable gestures for blind people: understanding preference and performance. *Proceedings of the 2011 Annual Conference on Human factors in Computing Systems* (CHI '11). 413-422.

[6] I.S. MacKenzie, R.W Soukoreff, J. Helga (2011). 1 thumb, 4 buttons, 20 words per minute: design and evaluation of H4-writer. *Proceedings of the 24th annual ACM symposium on User interface software and technology* (UIST '11). 471-480

Design Goals for a System for Enhancing AAC with Personalized Video

Katie O'Leary[1], Charles Delahunt[2], Patricia Dowden[3], Ivan Darmansya[4], Jiaqi Heng[4],
Eve A. Riskin[2], Richard E. Ladner[4], Jacob O. Wobbrock[1]

[1]Information School
DUB Group
{kathlo, wobbrock}@uw.edu

[2]Electrical Engineering
delahunt@uw.edu
riskin@ee.washington.edu

[3]Speech & Hearing Sciences
dowden@uw.edu

[4]Computer Science
& Engineering
{blinkerz, jiaqih, ladner}
@cs.washington.edu

ABSTRACT

Enabling end-users of Augmentative and Alternative Communication (AAC) systems to add personalized video content at runtime holds promise for improving communication, but the requirements for such systems are as yet unclear. To explore this issue, we present *Vid2Speech*, a prototype AAC system for children with complex communication needs (CCN) that uses personalized video to enhance representations of action words. We describe three design goals that guided the integration of personalized video to enhance AAC in our early-stage prototype: 1) Providing social-temporal navigation; 2) Enhancing comprehension; and 3) Enabling customization in real time. Our system concept represents one approach to realizing these goals, however, we contribute the goals and the system as a starting point for future innovations in personalized video-based AAC.

Categories and Subject Descriptors

H.5.2 **[Information Interfaces and Presentation]:** User Interfaces-*Graphical user interfaces (GUI)*. K.4.2 **[Computers and Society]:** Social Issues-*Assistive technologies for persons with disabilities.*

General Terms

Design, Human Factors.

Keywords

Complex Communication Needs, Video, AAC

1. INTRODUCTION

Since the release of the Apple iPad in 2010, speech-generating Augmentative and Alternative Communication (AAC) applications for children with Complex Communication Needs (CCN) have been a rapidly growing consumer-driven trend [1]. Popular examples of AAC applications include Proloquo2Go, Tap to Talk and Voice4u. Like *Vid2Speech*, these applications target beginning communicators with CCN who are preliterate and preverbal, but they feature only static symbols (Figure 1).

Like written words, static AAC symbols are representations of concepts for communication. But for children with CCN, written words are less recognizable, and therefore more difficult to learn and use, than iconic representations like color photographs or drawings [9]. For example, a photograph of a ball is easier to recognize than the written word "ball." Action words like "want," however, are not well-represented in static iconic form because they are dynamic and ephemeral, rather than concrete and material [7].

Designing AAC systems that overcome the limitations of static symbols for representing action words is crucial because there is evidence that action words are the most substantial part of a young child's vocabulary [3]. Furthermore, with modern smartphones and tablets, we have the ability to capture video in everyday settings relevant to specific users, enabling real-time personalization of AAC content. However, owing to the lack of video-based AAC, the requirements for AAC systems using personalized video content are as yet unclear.

Figure 1: Typical static symbols for the action word "want" found in current AAC applications. Left image courtesy of The Picture Communication Symbols ©1981–2011 by Mayer-Johnson LLC. All Rights Reserved Worldwide. Used with permission. Right image courtesy of SYMBOLSTIX, LLC. Used with permission.

Figure 2. Current *Vid2Speech* interface.

Vid2Speech, our AAC prototype, exploits the potential of personalized video for creating recognizable representations of action words. Vid2Speech is the first prototype tablet-based speech-generating system for children with CCN that enhances AAC with personalized video of action words. By illuminating the design goals for Vid2Speech, we provide a framework for successful integration of personalized video in AAC applications.

2. RELATED WORK

Previous work has explored the value of motion effects in AAC [5]. Findings suggest that cartoon animations of action words are easier to recognize than static icons [10,11]; black-and-white video is easier to recognize than animated line drawings [8]; and animation accelerates learning of static icons [4]. Finally, work by Light & McNaughton [6] suggests that personalization and "just-in-time" capture of language concepts should be key priorities for future AAC systems. Our system is designed to build on these findings by combining motion effects and real-time personalization to increase transparency of action words.

3. VID2SPEECH DESIGN GOALS

The Vid2Speech interface displays photos of the child's scheduled activities across the top of the screen. The user navigates through the schedule to access communication concepts categorized by activity. For example, the park activity contains personalized videos and photos of actions like swing, see saw, and slide (Figure 2). The photos are pressed to play the videos; pressing the photo for swing will play a video of the user swinging.

To develop the early stage prototype of Vid2Speech, we created the following three design goals for video-based AAC:

- Providing social-temporal navigation
- Enhancing comprehension
- Enabling customization in real time

These design goals are described in detail below.

3.1 Providing Social-Temporal Navigation

Young children with CCN may have difficulty understanding and navigating traditional grid displays [2,6]. Research suggests that when asked, children represent language concepts holistically, in context and based on familiar experiences, rather than atomized and hierarchically categorized in discrete parts (i.e. a wagging dog tail categorized under animals) [6]. To facilitate access to videos in Vid2Speech, we have categorized videos according to time of day, place and social situation. For example, the video of "swinging" is categorized under the social activity "park" which is accessed at a particular time of day. This social-temporal navigation provides an accessible and predictable scaffold for adding and using personalized content.

3.2 Enhancing Comprehension

While static representations of action words are less effective than animated or moving representations, there are compelling reasons to retain rather than abandon static symbols. Firstly, displaying multiple moving videos simultaneously on the screen has the potential to maximize the cognitive load for the user and become distracting [5]. Retaining static icons for action words, while correlating them with personalized videos, leverages the advantages of video for illuminating the meanings of static symbols to aid comprehension. The videos help the user learn the correlated static symbols – perhaps even written words – so that the videos can be faded as the user develops into a fluent communicator.

3.3 Enabling Customization in Real Time

Caregivers of children with CCN, such as parents, speech therapists and teachers, do not typically have access to or time for specialized video editing or recording equipment for AAC. Vid2Speech is designed to help caregivers capitalize on serendipitous moments for language learning and growth by capturing personalized videos in real time using a tablet's built-in cameras. While we expect the initial customization of the software to take some time, the software can be customized incrementally as situations and communication opportunities arise.

4. FUTURE WORK

Our next goal is to investigate the ways in which personalized video compares to standardized animated graphics for enhancing AAC for children with CCN. By developing a relationship with caregivers and children, we hope to engage these important stakeholders in a participatory design process before evaluating a final version of the Vid2Speech system.

5. ACKNOWLEDGMENTS

This project has been developed with funding from Intel.

6. REFERENCES

[1] Announcing the AAC-RERC White Paper on Mobile Devices and Communication Apps (2011). *Augmentative and Alternative Communication*, 27, 2, 131-132.

[2] Beukelman, D. R., & Mirenda, P. (1998). Augmentative and alternative communication: Management of severe communication disorders in children and adults. Baltimore: P.H. Brookes Pub.

[3] Bloom, L., & Lahey, M. (1978). Language development and language disorders. New York: Wiley

[4] Fujisawa, K., Inoue, T., Yamana, Y., & Hayashi, H. 2011. The Effect of Animation on Learning Action Icons by Individuals with Intellectual Disabilities. *Augmentative and Alternative Communication*, 27, 1, 53-60.

[5] Jagaroo, V., & Wilkinson, K. 2008. Further Considerations of visual cognitive neuroscience in aided AAC: The potential role of motion perception systems in maximizing design display. *Augmentative and Alternative Communication*, 24, 1, 29-42.

[6] Light J. & McNaughton D. 2012. Supporting the communication, language, and literacy development of children with complex communication needs: State of the science and future research priorities. *Assistive Technology*, 24, 1, 34-44.

[7] Lloyd, L. L., Fuller, D. R., & Arvidson, H. H. (1997). Augmentative and alternative communication : A handbook of principles and practices. Boston: Allyn and Bacon.

[8] Mineo, B., Peischl, D., & Pennington, C. 2008. Moving targets: The effect of animation on identification of action word representations. *Augmentative and Alternative Communication*, 24, 2, 162-173.

[9] Mirenda, P., & Locke, P. A. 1989. A comparison of icon transparency in nonspeaking persons with intellectual disabilities. *Journal of Speech and Hearing Disorders*, 54, 2, 131-40.

[10] Schlosser, R. W., Shane, H., Sorce, J., Koul, R., & Bloomfield, E. 2011. Identifying Performing and Under Performing Graphic Icons for Verbs and Prepositions in Animated and Static Formats: A Research Note. *Augmentative and Alternative Communication*, 27, 3, 205-214.

[11] Schlosser R.W., Bloomfield E., Debrowski L., Deluca T., Miller S., Schneider D., Neff A., Shane H., Sorce J., & Koul R. 2012. Animation of graphic symbols representing verbs and prepositions: Effects on transparency, name agreement, and identification. *Journal of Speech, Language, and Hearing Research*, 55, 2, 342-358.

Liberi and the Racer Bike: Exergaming Technology for Children with Cerebral Palsy

Zi Ye[2], Hamilton A. Hernandez[2], T.C. Nicholas Graham[2], Darcy Fehlings[1,3],
Lauren Switzer[1], Md Ameer Hamza[2], Irina Schumann[2]

[1]Bloorview Research Institute
Holland Bloorview Kids
Rehabilitation Hospital
Toronto, ON, Canada

[2]School of Computing
Queen's University
Kingston, ON, Canada

[3]Department of Paediatrics
University of Toronto
Toronto, ON, Canada

(zi, hamilton, graham, ameer)@cs.queensu.ca, (dfehlings, lswitzer)@hollandbloorview.ca

ABSTRACT

Children with cerebral palsy (CP) often have limited opportunities to engage in physical exercise and to interact with other children. We report on the design of a multiplayer exercise video game and a novel cycling-based exergaming station that allow children with CP to perform vigorous exercise while playing with other children. The game and the station were designed through an iterative and incremental participatory design process involving medical professionals, game designers, computer scientists, kinesiologists, physiotherapists, and eight children with CP. The station combines a physical platform allowing children with CP to provide pedaling input into a game, and a standard PC gamepad. With this station seven of eight children could play a cycling-based game effectively. The game is a virtual world featuring several minigames, group play, and an in-game money-based reward system. Abilities and limitations associated with CP were considered when designing the game. The data collected during the design sessions shows that the games are fun, engaging and allow the children to reach exertion levels recommended by the American College of Sports Medicine.

Categories and Subject Descriptors

H.5.2 [Information Interfaces And Presentation]: User Interfaces – Input devices and strategies;

General Terms

Human Factors, Design.

Keywords

Cerebral palsy, children, exergames, exergaming station

1. INTRODUCTION

Cerebral palsy (CP) is a group of disorders that affect development of motor function [3]. Children with CP find it difficult to participate in traditional exercise and thus it is difficult for them to get the benefits associated with physical activity. As they become adults, multiple factors including a lack of exercise can result in muscular deconditioning, causing a reduction in mobility. This loss of mobility in turn limits the opportunities for social participation.

Exergames, video games whose play requires physical activity, represent a promising way of enabling children with CP to get the physical activity they need while also allowing them to interact with other children in fun ways. Nintendo Wii Sports and Kinect Adventures are examples of exergames for the general population. Some of these games have been used for rehabilitation of motor function. These are almost uniformly focused on extending range of motion and improving balance [1,4], but little has been done in terms of physical fitness [7]. Designing hardware that allows children with CP to play exergames vigorously is challenging due to the muscle weakness, limited mobility and spasticity that are typical of CP. Additionally, the design of the exergames themselves should avoid involving quick, accurate and fine motor movements, because they are difficult for children with CP and therefore prevent continuous vigorous exercise.

We designed a physical station and an exergame that allow children with CP to engage in vigorous exercise while playing and socializing with other children. We conducted seven participatory design sessions involving medical professionals, game designers, computer scientists, kinesiologists, physical therapists, and eight children with CP. In each session we tested and refined the physical station, focusing on safety, comfort and ease of use. We tested the game in terms of playability, exertion, engagement and fun. Results show that the game is fun, engaging and allows the children to reach exertion levels recommended by the American College of Sports Medicine.

2. THE PHYSICAL STATION

We considered three main challenges when designing the station: the physical challenge, the control challenge and the vigour challenge.

To address the physical challenge it is necessary that the station allows the children to move easily from their mobility aid into the station, to be stable and safe while performing the physical activity, and to provide vigorous input to the games in a safe and comfortable way. For the control challenge, it is necessary that the physical activity input be mapped naturally to different game styles, and that the actions in the games be triggered using a simple control scheme that considers limitations such as spasticity and poor fine motor control. For the vigour challenge, it is necessary that the station allow the children to reach levels of energy expenditure leading to improved health, as recommended by the American College of Sports Medicine [6].

Motivated by the proven effectiveness of bicycles for allowing vigorous exercise [5], the stability and comfort provided by recumbent bikes, and the natural mapping of cycling input to the movement of in-game avatars, we designed a recumbent cycling-

Figure 1. The Racer Bike

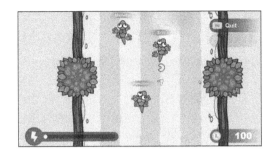

Figure 2. The Gekku Race minigame in Liberi

station that we called the Racer Bike (Figure 1). This station includes safety features such as adjustable pedal frames to secure the children's feet; a non-slip seat, a seat belt and lateral pads to avoid slipping; handles that make it easy for the children to enter and exit the station, and a solid back that allows the children to put more force on the pedals. Only three of eight children could play a cycling-based game effectively with the seating options tested in early sessions, while seven of eight could play effectively using the Racer Bike.

An additional benefit of this station is that it leaves the children's hands free, allowing them to use a gamepad. We tested different gamepad control schemes. To address limitations in the children's fine motor skills, we settled on a simple scheme using only one-button to trigger in-game actions and one joystick to specify direction, removing the difficulty of pressing two buttons consecutively, pressing two buttons at the same time, and pressing unwanted buttons accidentally.

More details on the design of the Racer Bike have been published earlier [2].

3. THE EXERGAME

To allow children with CP to have a fun, vigorous and engaging experience, we developed Liberi, a cycling-based network game suitable for children with CP. The main challenges for the design of Liberi were to provide high playability, short and long term motivation, opportunities for interactions between players, and activities that motivate continuous and vigorous physical activity.

Aiming for long term motivation, we included several minigames in Liberi for variety. These minigames allow a choice of competitive and cooperative group play. Additionally, an in-game scoring system allows the players to earn money and collect resources in the minigames, and spend them in in-game shops to enhance their character's abilities.

We tested the minigames iteratively in each session, and based on the feedback, we modified them to improve playability, fun, and exertion. We found that the difficulty of the minigames, high cognitive load in the mechanics or strategy, and the need for high accuracy in positioning the avatar affected playability. Also, minigames involving frequent stopping and starting of pedaling increased the difficulty of play, and decreased the levels of exertion. These led to simplification of the minigames' designs. This simplification was challenging, as oversimplification can reduce fun, with negative consequences to long term engagement.

Figure 2 shows one of the most successful minigames in Liberi, the Gekku Race, where each player controls a "gekku" racing to the top of a wall. The players can shoot cashews or fire at their competitors to hold them back from winning. Gekku Race led to vigorous gameplay according to heart rate and perceived exertion data. Standard and custom questionnaires and discussions with the children and their parents indicated that the game is fun.

4. THE DEMO PRESENTATION

In our demo presentation ASSETS' attendees will play our Liberi exergame; trying competitive and cooperative minigames using one of our exergaming stations, pedaling the bike and using a gamepad. They will play over a network with members of our team at Queen's University in Canada. Additionally, we will play recordings of our design sessions showing the children using the station and playing the game.

5. ACKNOWLEDGMENTS

This work was carried out within the NEUROGAMe project, supported by the GRAND and NeuroDevNet Networks of Centres of Excellence. The work was further supported by an NSERC Research Tools and Instruments grant.

6. REFERENCES

1. Deutsch, J.E., Borbely, M., Filler, J., Huhn, K., Guarrera, P., and Guarrera-Bowlby, P. Use of a low-cost, commercially available gaming console (Wii) for rehabilitation of an adolescent with cerebral palsy. Physical Therapy 88, 10 (2008), 1196-1207.
2. Hernandez, H.A., Graham, T.C.N., Fehlings, D., Switzer, L., Ye, Z., Bellay, Q., Hamza, M.A., Savery, C., and Stach, T. Design of an exergaming station for children with cerebral palsy. Proceedings of CHI, ACM Press (2012), 2619-2628.
3. Rosenbaum, P., Paneth, N., Leviton, A., Goldstein, M., Bax, M., Damiano, D., Dan, B., and Jacobsson, B. A report: the definition and classification of cerebral palsy April 2006. Developmental Medicine and Child Neurology Supplement, (2007), 8-14.
4. Sandlund, M., Waterworth, E.L., Häger, C., and Lindh Waterworth, E. Using motion interactive games to promote physical activity and enhance motor performance in children with cerebral palsy. Developmental Neurorehabilitation 14, 1 (2010), 15-21.
5. Warburton, D.E.R., Bredin, S.S.D., Horita, L.T.L., Zbogar, D., Scott, J.M., Esch, B.T.A., and Rhodes, R.E. The health benefits of interactive video game exercise. Applied Physiology, Nutrition, and Metabolism 32, 4 (2007), 655-663.
6. Whaley, M.H., Brubaker, P.H., Otto, R.M., and Armstrong, L.E. ACSM's Guidelines for Exercise Testing and Prescription. American College of Sports Medicine, Indianapolis, 2006.
7. Widman, L., McDonald, C., and Abresch, T. Effectiveness of an upper extremity exercise device integrated with computer gaming for aerobic training in adolescents with spinal cord dysfunction. The Journal of Spinal Cord Medicine 29, (2006), 363-370.

Blue Herd: Automated Captioning for Videoconferences

Ira R. Forman, Ben Fletcher, John Hartley, Bill Rippon, Allen Wilson

IBM Research

11501 Burnet Road

Austin, TX 78759

{formani, bfletch, jhartley, bjripp, wilsona}@us.ibm.com

ABSTRACT

Blue Herd is a project in IBM Research to investigate automated captioning for videoconferences. Today videoconferences are held among meeting participants connected with a variety of devices: personal computers, mobile devices, and multi-participant meeting rooms. Blue Herd is charged with studying automated real-time captioning in that context. This poster explains the system that was developed for personal computers and describes our experiments to include mobile devices and multi-participant meeting rooms.

Categories and Subject Descriptors

H.5.2 [Information Interfaces and Presentation]: User Interfaces – input devices and strategies; K.4.2 [Computers and Society] – Assistive technologies for persons with disabilities

Keywords

accessibility, speech recognition, automated captioning, transcriptions.

1. INTRODUCTION

The use of videoconferencing is increasing everywhere: business, education, and even by individual consumers. Although a boon to the general population, this increase will disadvantage people who are deaf or hard of hearing. Video relay systems do provide a remedy, but they are expensive. In addition, the number of translators is limited and scheduling can be problematic. IBM Research started the Blue Herd project to investigate a remedy for this problem; specifically, the project is investigating automated real-time captioning in the context of videoconferences. To be consistent with IBM's goals, the project works to augment Lotus Sametime [2].

Today videoconferences are held among meeting participants connected with a variety of devices: personal computers, mobile devices, and multi-participant meeting rooms. Blue Herd is charged with studying automated real-time captioning in that context. A successful outcome of the investigation would primarily mean videoconference participants could retain flexibility of device choice while including their deaf and hard of hearing colleagues. In addition, everyone would have the benefit of captioning, a technology that helps overcome noise and distraction during videoconferences.

2. DESIGN

IBM Sametime implements videoconferencing; that is the service to which Blue Herd adds captioning. Figure 1 depicts the Windows user interface for a Sametime meeting and the channels of communication among the meeting participants, which from bottom to top are:

- **discussion channel**, which is used for instant messaging among the participants

- **content channel**, which permits one participant to share all or part of the screen with the others

- **audio/video channel**, which allows the participants to see one another

- **caption channel**, where the automated captions appear

The first three channels are standard in Sametime Meetings. The caption channel is added to meeting automatically if the meeting owner has installed the Blue Herd plug-in. The caption channel is implemented as a multiparty chat that is special because the caption channel has two representations on the display. As shown in Figure 1, there is the caption window, which is a black-background window that displays the last lines of the conversation and resembles what we see on broadcast television. In addition there is the transcription window, which displays the full transcript (not shown in Figure 1).

The above describes the meeting context for Blue Herd, Sametime Meetings. The speech recognition context is provided by the Project Jumbo plug-in [1]. To provide natural captioning, the system must have a full duplex connection to the speech engine. That is, while you are speaking, the speech engine should be returning transcribed words to the captioning application. This may seem obvious, but neither Dragon Go! nor Siri work this way; both are half duplex, that is, each sends audio to the server and waits for a response. Currently, the full duplex property is achieved by each user a dedicated speech engine; this aspect of the prototype also obviates problems with speaker identification for single speaker devices.

Our Project Jumbo plug-in provided Blue Herd with a number of design principles (so much so that the software base of Project Jumbo was subsumed into Blue Herd). In order of importance, here are the design principles.

- *Speech focus does not follow keyboard focus:* Keyboard focus refers to the window to which typed input is sent. Typical dictation products (for example, Dragon NaturallySpeaking) have the capability to input recognized text as if it were typed. This capability is unsuitable for automated captioning for videoconferences, because participants in such conferences are on-line and keyboard focus may shift at the whim of the operating system or other applications. For Blue Herd, every meeting window and every chat window has a button to direct speech focus there. Speech focus stays there no matter where keyboard focus goes. This allows one to speak in meeting and be transcribed while taking notes in an independent window.

• *Hands-free operation once focus is set:* Once one has selected speech focus, there should be no additional manual actions required: just speak and be transcribed. Note that when recognized text is directed to the keyboard focus for an application like instant messaging, an additional send action is required of the user. Voice commands are a good solution for instant messaging, but in a videoconference, your colleagues do not want to hear you say "send" each time you need to change the captions on their screen.

• *One push switch of speech focus:* With a captioning button in all meeting and chat windows, pressing that button becomes the natural way to switch speech focus.

• *User choice of speech engines:* A user may have a preferred speech engine, mostly likely the one that provides the greatest accuracy. Where possible, the user should have a choice. Blue Herd currently supports three local speech engines that run on the speaker's machine: Dragon NaturallySpeaking on Windows, Microsoft Speech on Windows, and the speaker independent IBM Attila engine on Linux. Suitable cloud-based speech engines may also be used in the future, when such engines become available.

• *Captioning for videoconferences is not dictation:* Captioning is being done in the context of interactive communication and no editing facility is necessary. The meeting is moving forward on the audio channel and captioning must keep up. Many errors made by the speech engine can be ignored because the meaning is clear (for example, adding or eliding an article). The project team's experience shows speakers generally monitor their captions and are proactive in correcting them. When captioning is off the mark, non-speakers can use instant messaging to ask the speaker for a clarification. This sort of thing happens all of the time with conference calls when some participant has an inadequate cell phone connection. The speaker is obligated to monitor the instant messages; this is what is required to be inclusive. Participation by deaf colleagues does not change the speaker's desire or obligation to communicate clearly, only the mechanisms change.

3. POSTER PROPOSAL

In February 2012, Blue Herd became operational on the Sametime desktop client for all IBMers around the world. In our laboratory, we have prototype software for a multi-participant conference room and also for iPhone and Andriod mobile observers (an observer can see the captions but not be captioned). The poster session will consist of a videoconference with remote colleagues making live, captioned mini-presentations on the design. Thus, the presentation will be the demo of the system. (We will have recorded videos as backup in case connectivity does not adequately support videoconferencing.) The project team does use this system intermittently with deaf colleagues; discussion of that experience will be part of the poster.

4. ACKNOWLEDGMENTS

Blue Herd is indebted to the following for their help, advice, or encouragement: Thomas Brunet, David Byrd, Bill Carter, Peter Fay, Ben Gold, William Holmes, Bill Huber, John Kistler, Fernando Koch, Cathy Laws, Wen Liu, Marlon Machado, Brendan Murray, Mitch Nichols, Yong Qin, Qing Quan, DeclanTarrant, Rich Schwerdtfeger, Andi Snow-Weaver, Jay Somineau, Mike Strack, and Shari Trewin. Finally, we thank Dimitri Kanevsky, Sara Basson, Edward Epstein, and Peter Fairweather for their patent [3], which obviated any intellectual property issues.

5. REFERENCES

[1] Forman, I.R., T. Brunet, P. Luther, and A. Wilson, Using ASR for Transcription of Teleconferences in IM Systems, in Universal Access in Human-Computer Interaction. Applications and Services, C. Stephanidis (ed.) LNCS 5616, Springer-Verlag, 2009, 521–529.

[2] IBM, http://www.ibm.com/software/lotus/sametime

[3] Kanevsky, D. et al., "System and Method for Teleconferencing with Deaf or Hearing Impaired," US Patent 6,618,704, 2003.

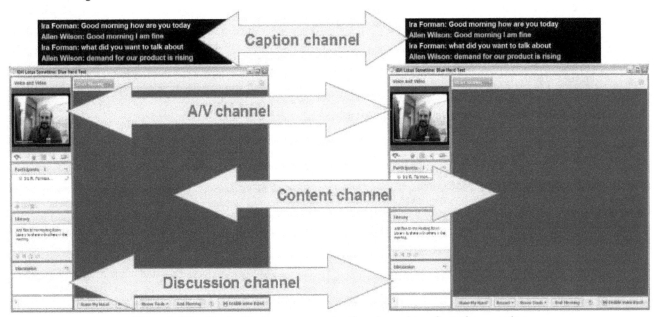

Figure 1. Blue Herd adds a new communication channel to a Sametime meeting.

Toward the Development of a BCI and Gestural Interface to Support Individuals with Physical Disabilities

Kavita Krishnaswamy and Ravi Kuber

UMBC

{ kavi1, rkuber } @umbc.edu

ABSTRACT

In this paper, we describe a first step towards the development of a solution to support the movement and repositioning of an individual's limbs. Limb repositioning is particularly valuable for individuals with physical disabilities who are either bed or chair-bound, to help reduce the occurrence of contractures and pressure ulcers. A data gathering study has been performed examining attitudes towards using BCI and gestural devices to control a robotic aid to assist with the repositioning process. Findings from a preliminary study evaluating a controller interface prototype suggest that while BCI and gestural technologies may play a valuable role in limiting fatigue from interacting with a mouse or other input device, challenges are faced accurately identifying specific facial expressions (e.g. blinks). Future work would aim to refine algorithms to detect gestures, with a view to augmenting the experience when using a BCI and gestural device to control a robotic aid.

Categories and Subject Descriptors

H.5.2 User Interfaces – *Input devices and strategies*

General Terms

Human Factors.

Keywords

BCI, Gestural interfaces, Physical disabilities.

1. INTRODUCTION

Robotic interfaces offer considerable promise to individuals with physical disabilities. Examples include solutions designed to support the retrieval of objects [2] and to assist with household chores [5]. However, research has yet to extensively focus upon the ways in which physically-disabled users can independently control robotic support aids, and the ways in which interaction potential can be maximized during this process. Brain Computer Interfaces (BCI) have been developed to support individuals with neuromuscular disorders, when other methods of interaction (e.g. eye gaze, speech input) may not be feasible for use. In this paper, we describe an exploratory study examining attitudes to the use of non-invasive BCI and gestural technologies to support tasks such as repositioning limbs. A prototype of a controller interface has been evaluated. The long term goal of the research would be to interface a robotic aid with the controller, to assist the process of repositioning limbs, thereby reducing the likelihood of developing stiffness in the muscles and pressure ulcers.

2. RELATED WORK

Assistive robotic interfaces have been developed to aid individuals with physical disabilities to perform tasks which others take for granted. Examples include Robovie R3, a robot designed to behave as a guide in a grocery store, carry shopping items, and locate nearby products [3]. In contrast with other solutions, it is able to assist the user to express emotions or sentiments. For example, the robot is able to grasp the hand and hug others. In terms of BCI-controlled interfaces, the FRIEND robot provides individuals with severe physical disabilities with 90 minutes of temporary independence from caregivers [1]. EEG signals can be used to generate the task sequences necessary to perform robotic operations. To gain a deeper understanding of the ways in which BCI and gestural technologies would benefit physically-disabled users, a data gathering study was performed.

3. DATA GATHERING STUDY

Due to the difficulties identifying individuals with severe physical disabilities, three participants were recruited for the study. Participants were asked to describe the ways in which they currently interact with computing technologies, and their attitudes towards using BCI and gestural interfaces to support limb repositioning. Their case studies are presented below.

Case Study #1: Alex is a 43 year old computer teacher with Limb-Girdle Muscular Dystrophy and Polio. Alex needs help with typing to reduce fatigue because he can only use the keyboard for half-an-hour per day. He has never tried using BCI and gestural technologies, but envisions these technologies could assist him when navigating through a graphical interface or when entering data. As he has the ability to make facial gestures and head movements, he is keen to use BCI and gestural technologies to aid him when interacting with the Web. He suggests that mapping mouse movements to facial gestures (e.g. by turning the head slightly either left or right to move the cursor in the respective direction) would reduce the physical strain on him. Alex limits his sitting time to 2 to 3 hours because he is unable to find a caregiver to help him to reposition himself, or to assist him with his physical therapy. He would be interested in using BCI technologies to gain assistance on demand for repositioning his arms to stretch above the head, and aiding him to perform leg stretches, when a caregiver is not available.

Case Study #2: Betty is 28 years old and has been diagnosed with Spinal Muscular Atrophy. She has full control of facial muscles, but has difficulty turning her head to the left side. She often sits in a reclined position to maximize neck control and reduce the occurrence of pressure ulcers. As her range of movement is limited, she requires assistance for personal care (e.g. bathing, feeding). She is able to interact with a laptop and touchpad mouse, using two fingers from each hand. While Betty is excited that BCI may provide an alternative to the slow process of typing and traversing hierarchical menus, she is eager to use this technology to gain more independence, by controlling a robot to assist with limb repositioning and personal care. She hopes that the same technologies can be used to non-invasively monitor her physiological condition and alert caregivers when a problem is detected. BCI offers her more potential compared to using an eye-gaze system, as she finds it difficult to visually focus for long periods of time. Her poor level of neck control can make the process of keeping her head upright challenging. Breathing issues have caused her difficulty to use speech-input solutions. However, a solution able to monitor the user's EEG activity or facial/lip movements when silently mouthing words is thought to offer considerable potential to improving her communication with caregivers and medical professionals.

Case Study #3: Tim is a 31 year old entrepreneur with Duchenne Muscular Dystrophy. He has full control of facial movements but finds tilting his head difficult. He uses voice-recognition to access his computer. He can move his hands once they are situated in specific locations, but often experiences muscle stiffness. He relies on caregivers to help reposition his limbs, but can only do this during the day, when they are around to assist him. He limits trips to the bathroom because of difficulty with obtaining assistance transferring himself to the patient hoist lift. Tim has not used BCI and gestural technologies before, but hopes these will assist him to control a robotic aid to perform personal care tasks. He suggested that performing a gesture, such as looking up or down, could convey to a robotic aid to help him transfer to the lift, while looking left or right would execute the necessary series of actions to assist him when using the bathroom. Actions could be confirmed by performing a nodding gesture.

Findings from the interviews have revealed that BCI and gestural interfaces could offer considerable potential to support individuals with physical disabilities to achieve greater levels of independence. This would provide an alternative when caregivers are unavailable or when respite is needed.

4. PROTOTYPE DESIGN & EVALUATION

A controller interface prototype was developed for limb repositioning using the Emotiv Epoc headset[1] (Figure 1). The device is able to detect emotional information, facial expressions and conscious thoughts. The user is able to control the on-screen avatar's limbs (Figure 2) by issuing a set of specified facial gestures that are detected using EEG sensors embedded within the device (Expressiv suite). A future robotic aid will be able to reposition the appropriate limb based on these commands. Examples of gestures created include looking left or right to raise the left or right arm, or blinking to lower either arm. The solution is customizable, enabling users with limited physical capabilities, to perform the gestures available to them. Commands are also accessible through keystrokes, for users with some level of movement in one or both arms.

An exploratory study was performed to determine the feasibility of using BCI technologies to control the on-screen avatar's limbs. We aimed to determine the effectiveness of detecting the following facial gestures: smiling, winking, blinking, looking left and looking right. Three participants without disabilities (2 male, 1 female, aged 24-58) were selected to execute ten randomly-

presented arm tasks using the keyboard and performing facial gestures with the headset, to determine the feasibility of the solution.

Preliminary results have suggested that while all participants were able to interact with the avatar using both methods of input, participants spent 90.3s (SD: 123.1s) longer performing tasks using BCI and gestural technologies compared with the keyboard condition. Certain facial gestures were detected within a shorter time period compared with others. Examples including looking to the left or right to raise the avatar's arms (Left Arm: Keystroke: 1.8s (SD: 1.0s), BCI: 9.3s (SD: 6.2s); Right Arm: Keystroke: 3.8s (SD: 1.5s), BCI: 33.5s (SD: 24.8s)). The greatest difficulties were experienced when detecting blinks to lower the arms (M: 136.4s, SD: 188.3s). Findings contrasted with those of Lievesley et al. [4], whose participants found the blink action easiest to perform during their training process. The researchers also suggest the headset itself can be cumbersome to use, and is not recommended for individuals who retain a small amount of head movement. Our future work would examine ways in which these algorithms could be refined to ensure that gestures are more accurately detected.

| **Figure 1: Emotiv Epoc Headset** | **Figure 2: Robot Controller interface accessed using BCI** |

We also aim to develop the system to cater to the needs of individuals who are not able to make fully expressive facial gestures (e.g. small raises of the brow which may not be visually detectable), prior to more extensive evaluations with target users. Further study is also needed to identify ways to maintain levels of comfort, particularly for longer periods of device usage.

5. REFERENCES

[1] Grigorescu, S.M., Lüth, T., Fragkopoulos, C., Cyriacks, M. and Gräser, A., 2012. A BCI-controlled robotic assistant for quadriplegic people in domestic and professional life. *Robotica*, 30 (03), 419–431.

[2] Jain, A. and Kemp, CC., 2010. EL-E: An assistive mobile manipulator that autonomously fetches objects from flat surfaces. *Autonomous Robots*, 28, 45–64.

[3] Hornyak, T., 2012. Robovie R3 robot wants to hold your hand. http://news.cnet.com/8301-17938_105-20002981-1.html

[4] Lievesley, R., Wozencroft, M. and Ewins, D., 2011. The Emotiv Epoc neuroheadset: An inexpensive method of controlling assistive technologies using facial expressions and thoughts? *Journal of Assistive Technologies*, 5 (2), 67–82.

[5] Liu, K., Sakamato, D., Inami, M. and Igarashi, T., 2011. Roboshop: multi-layered sketching interface for robot housework assignment and management. In *Proceedings of CHI '11*, 647–656.

---

[1] Emotiv Epoc - http://www.emotiv.com

An Electronic-Textile Wearable Communication Board for Individuals with Autism Engaged in Horse Therapy

Halley P. Profita
University of Colorado – Boulder
UCB 430
Boulder, Colorado 80309
halley.profita@colorado.edu

ABSTRACT

Horse therapy is becoming an increasingly popular physical therapy activity for individuals with social, communication, or cognitive impairments as a means to help enhance social and interpersonal skills [1]. However, horse therapy and other very physically engaging therapies pose a challenge for those who rely on a communication board to communicate as the highly unstable nature of such activities impedes device operation. In such an instance, users are typically forced to abandon their communication board [2], rendering them unable to convey vital pieces of information throughout the duration of the physical therapy activity. This poster presents the Electronic-Textile (E-Textile) Wearable Communication Board - a device that was developed specifically to fill this void and support the communication needs of individuals with autism during horse therapy.

Categories and Subject Descriptors

H.5.2 [**User Interfaces**]: User-Centered Design

General Terms

Human Factors

Keywords

Electronic Textiles, Communication Board, Autism, Horse Therapy, Wearable Technology, Assistive Technology

1. INTRODUCTION

For many individuals with aphasia, ataxia, autism, or other verbal limitations, an augmentative and alternative communication device is an extremely serviceable item for interacting with those in one's external environment. Such communication devices are advantageous because they can be highly personalized and can even permit for speech output. However, these more advanced electronic devices can often be heavy and cumbersome, making them a nuisance to transport or use in mobile contexts. In the case of physically demanding activities, such as horse therapy or adaptive skiing, many users will abandon their communication board altogether because these activities create usage barriers that threaten irreparable damage. Creating a communication board

that can withstand the rigors of the environment while complementing the physical therapy activity can greatly enhance a user's independence and support their progress in the therapeutic activity.

2. BACKGROUND

2.1 Autism and Horse Therapy

Individuals with autism are characterized as having impaired social and communication skills [3]. Recently, many individuals with autism have been participating in horse therapy as it promotes social bonding and teaches greater self-awareness [1]. However, a fundamental disadvantage of participating in horse therapy is the inability of an individual with autism to use a communication board to verbally communicate during the physical therapy activity. This is typically due to the large dimensions of a communication board as well as the required two-handed interaction: one hand to hold the device and another hand to point at the desired symbol. The lack of a communication board can create emotional and physical barriers during horse therapy as users cannot convey vital pieces of information such as if the user is scared or in pain. Such a boundary can emotionally limit the positive progress that can be made during horse therapy. To address this issue, the E-Textile Wearable Communication Board (Figure 1) was created to be able to support the user during physical therapy activities.

3. THE SYSTEM

3.1 The Electronic-Textile Wearable Communication Board

To support a user during horse therapy, the iconic hard-shelled, cumbersome, hefty electronic communication board was redesigned into a lightweight, textile-based wearable device that still permits for verbal output. The device attaches to the thigh via an adjustable strap and offers 9 large, activity-specific, symbolic buttons for communication. A thin speaker with a slim profile is integrated in the device to permit for audio output. The pictures and programmable sayings are customizable, permitting for easy repurposing of the system.

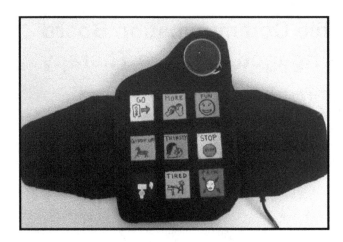

Figure 1. E-Textile Wearable Communication Board.

3.1.1 Hardware & Software

The innovation behind this wearable communication board is the use of conductive and non-conductive textiles, permitting for lightweight integration and wiring of electronics. These e-textiles can then be sewn or glued down to prevent shifting during riding. The exterior of the device uses neoprene as it is a flexible, breathable, and robust material that can get dirty or minimally moist without affecting the functionality of the device. An adjustable canvas strap was used for attaching the device to the user's thigh. The symbols were painted on using waterproof acrylic paint and were color-coded for quick spotting and recognition. A Sparkfun MP3 Trigger and thin speaker were selected for creating the button-operated audio output. Sayings were recorded using a Mini-SD card and a personal computer before being transferred onto the MP3 Trigger. For this prototype, an external power source was used, but ideally the device would have a thin rechargeable battery to maintain a light weight and permit ease of charging.

3.1.2 Design Considerations

Since it is common for users to have different communication boards for different contexts (i.e., a more advanced device for the home, a wallet sized device for grocery shopping, etc.), it was important to design a communication board to fully support the specific activity of horse therapy rather than trying to design for a one-size-fits-all device. Prior to prototyping, AT Specialists at Assistive Technology Partners in Denver, Colorado were consulted for direct input and guidance on the communication board requirements. Due to the inherent challenges of designing an assistive piece of technology to be used during a physical activity, a number of design considerations had to be taken into account to incorporate features into the device that would best support the user during the activity.

1. WEARABILITY: For an individual with autism, a wearable system is ideal as many times the user will drop or run away from objects, leaving them behind. Wearability offers a secure, hands-free solution for ensuring that the board remains securely with the user.

2. COMFORT: Most electronic communication boards are bulky, heavy and hard-cased. Since users will already be participating in a physical activity, making the system as comfortable as possible was a design goal. The fabric-based construction made the system functional and soft for wearability. The system is lightweight so as not to shift or cause the user discomfort.

3. DIGITIZED VERBAL OUTPUT CAPABILITIES: The impetus behind making the device electronic was to give the user verbal abilities so as to minimize the two-handed interaction required by static communication boards. A digitized system also permits for the therapists to be able to hear the audio output from a minimal distance in the event that they cannot always maintain visual attention with the system.

4. ROBUSTNESS: This exterior of the device is constructed out of neoprene so that it can withstand rugged handling, dirt, and light moisture. The acrylic paint used to create the buttons was optimal for withstanding the elements as well. The internal components are sewn in place to prevent shifting.

5. EASE OF USE: This programmable communication board permits a caregiver to easily record nine different sayings for a specific activity. The device is color-coded and uses buttons as the input mechanism, making it very straight forward for the user to operate.

6. LOCATION: The location of the thigh was selected so that the device would not obstruct the actual activity of riding the horse while still remaining on the user and within an arm's reach for operation.

7. COST: Many portable electronic communication boards cost upwards of $500.00. This system was developed for ~$160.00, making it more economically viable as well as making an individual less cautious about taking it out into the field.

8. MODULARITY: This system was designed to be reprogrammable, permitting for the device to be repurposed for another activity or to grow and change with the needs of the user.

4. CONCLUSIONS

This work highlights the ever present need for easily customizable assistive technologies that can support user independence in new or dynamic situations. The Electronic-Textile Wearable Communication Board demonstrates a promising new area for the application of e-textiles to create innovative solutions for assistive technologies.

5. ACKNOWLEDGEMENTS

Special appreciation for help and guidance during this project goes to Dr. Clayton Lewis, Dr. Michael Lightner, and Dr. Katie Siek of the University of Colorado – Boulder, as well as Christina Perkins of Assistive Technology Partners in Denver, CO.

6. REFERENCES

[1] "Complete Guide to Hippotherapy." Cute Home Pets. 1 May 2012. <http://www.cutehomepets.com/complete-guide-to-hippotherapy/>.

[2] Perkins, Christina. Personal Interview. 25 April 2012.

[3] "Autism Fact Sheet." National Institute of Neurological Disorders and Stroke. 27 April 2012.< http://www.ninds. nih.gov/disorders/autism/detail_autism.htm>.

Tongible: A Non-contact Tongue-based Interaction Technique

[1]Li Liu, [2]Shuo Niu, [2]Jingjing Ren, [3]Jingyuan Zhang

[1]HCI&VR Research Center
Shandong University
Jinan, Shandong, 250101, China
lliu@sdu.edu.cn
lliu@sdu.edu.cn

[2]Shandong Province Key Lab of
Software Engineering
Shandong University
Jinan, Shandong, 250101 China
{shoenneil,
jingjingren1992}@gmail.com

[3]Department of Computer Science
The University of Alabama
Tuscaloosa, AL 35487, USA
zhang@cs.ua.edu

ABSTRACT

Using tongue to access computer for people with none or minimal upper limb function has been studied in recent years. These studies mainly focus on utilizing mechanical or electromagnetic devices. These devices, however, must contact to people's oral cavity and cause hygiene problems or accidental ingestion. This work presents an interaction technique named Tongible that employs tongue as input without any mechanical or electromagnetic assistive device. In Tongible, six gestures of tongue are captured by an RGB camera and used as basic controlling gestures. Preliminary usability testing suggests that Tongible is effective in pointing and text entry for people with dexterity impairment.

Categories and Subject Descriptors

H5.2 [**Information interfaces and presentation**]: User Interfaces - *Input devices and strategies*; K.4.2 [**Computer and Society**]: Social Issues – *assistive technologies for persons with disabilities*.

General Terms

Design, Experimentation, Human Factors

Keywords

Tongue-Computer Interface, non-contacted, *tile*, interaction

1. INTRODUCTION

Many people live with dexterity and mobility challenges caused by war, vehicular accidents, electric shock, accidents of birth, etc., which reduce a person's physical functionalities in lifting, reaching and manipulating objects by using arms, hands and/or fingers [1]. Suffering from limitation of movement, people are not able to interact with a conventional computer because its input devices, such as keyboard and mouse are designed for hand-use. To address this problem, we propose Tongible, a hand-free interaction technology using tongue as input device without any equipment contacted to the oral cavity. When using Tongible, people with dexterity impairment reach out their tongue to the up, down, left and right positions, and a pointer on the screen will move to the corresponding place.

2. SYSTEM IMPLEMENTATION

The input of Tongible is real-time video stream captured by an RGB camera connected to a computer. When using the system, the user keeps her/his head straight in front of the camera and

This work is supported by NSFC(U1035004) and IIFSDU

reach out her/his tongue to the up, down, left and right of the mouth cavity. The gestures of the tongue is analyzed and recognized as one of the six tongue positions (Showed in Figure1) through a serious image processing procedures and pattern recognition techniques. Six discrete tongue gestures are mapped to different computer instructions such as moving the pointer to up, down, left or right. Therefore using tongue interface is similar to the operation of joystick.

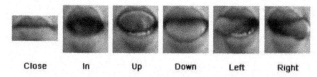

Figure 1. Close and In gestures and four directional gestures to be recognized by the system.

In order to improve the operability of the system, the interaction paradigm related to the tongue interface is studied. Non-pixel based graphical interface and ambiguous input methods are leveraged to improve the operability of component selecting and character entry [2]. The system analyzes the meaning of all pixels and categories them into *tile*s. In each *tile*, the smallest accessible unit, all pixels share the same operation handlers and give the same feedback after the user does the same action on one *tile*. The relative positions of all *tile*s are tracked so that from one *tile* the user can access to the nearby up, down, left and right *tile*s.

The ambiguous n-key texting method is employed to achieve fast text entry through tongue-interface [3]. In Tongible, all 26 English characters are mapped to two keys, characters from 'a' to 'n' are mapped to the left key and the rest characters are mapped to the right key. Users spell the word by manipulating the two keys using the left and right tongue position. The system consults a dictionary and lists all words that match the input character sequence.

3. USER STUDY

In the user study, test programs based on pointing task and text entry task are designed to study the user behavior of using tongue interface and evaluate the performance of the system. Three females and two males aging from 22-28 participated the user study.

In the pointing task study, an array of *tile*s is aligned horizontally without overlaying on the display and a pointer controlled by the tongue gesture slides *tile* by *tile* on the array. In the test program showed in figure 2, the distance between the green start and red end is set to 10 *tile*s. The task includes 9 tasks. In one task, a subject is asked to move the pointer to the red target *tile* using the Left and Right gesture. The sliding speed of the pointer is set to

50mspt (milliseconds per *tile*) in the first task, 100mspt in the second, 150mspt in the third, etc. The speed in the last task is 450mspt.

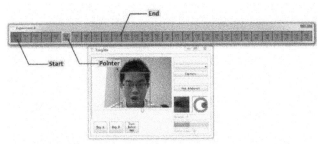

Figure 2. Screen shot of the test program. Every subject moves the pointer from the green start *tile* to the red end *tile* using the tongue-computer interface.

To evaluate the performance of Tongible in the context of practical use, a text entry test is designed as Figure 3 shows, which uses an ambiguous input method. In the user experiment program, the left and right gestures are used to manipulate an ambiguous key. The characters from 'a' to 'n' are mapped to the left key and the rest characters from 'o' to 'z' are mapped to the right key. The up and down gestures are used to select the word which is disambiguated from the key sequence.

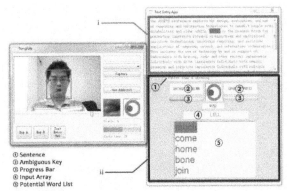

Figure 3. Screenshot of the texting task. Frame I is the texting panel which shows the article. Frame II is the control panel for character entry and word selecting.

4. RESULT ANALYSIS

Figure 4 shows the user study result. The move-time curve in red shows that the time used for covering distance grows linearly. And the time for adjustment (blue) approaches to 0 with the decrease of the pointer speed. As the pointing task equals move time plus adjustment time, the task-time curve showed in black reaches the lowest point at 250mspt. At this speed the user tends to finish the pointing task in the shortest time.

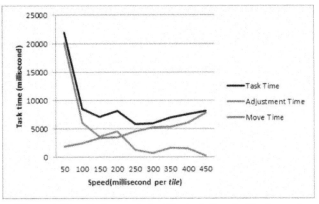

Figure 4. Result of user study. The task time in black equals the adjustment time (blue) plus the move time (red).

In the text entry task, after several times training, two experienced subjects achieved the approximate time of 122 seconds when texting the sentence 'faster than a speeding bullet'.

5. FUTURE WORK

Task modes should be specified to meet the user's demand in controlling computer. In the future, studies on different task modes will be carried out to implement a higher usable interaction paradigm which suits the tongue interface.

6. REFERENCES

[1] Ziegler-Graham, K., MacKenzie, E.J, Ephraim, P.L., Travison, T.G., and Brookmeyer, R. Estimating the Prevalence of Limb Loss in the United States: 2005 to 2050, *Archives of Physical Medicine and Rehabilitation,* Volume 89, Issue 3, March 2008, Pages 422-429, ISSN 0003-9993, 10.1016/j.apmr.2007.11.005.

[2] Chang, T.H., Yeh, T., and Miller, R. 2011. Associating the visual representation of user interfaces with their internal structures and metadata. In *Proceedings of the 24th annual ACM symposium on User interface software and technology* (UIST '11). ACM, New York, NY, USA, 245-256.

[3] MacKenzie, I.S. 2009. The one-key challenge: searching for a fast one-key text entry method. In *Proceedings of the 11th international ACM SIGACCESS conference on Computers and accessibility* (Assets '09). ACM, New York, NY, USA, 91-98.

Effectiveness of the Haptic Chair in Speech Training

Suranga Nanayakkara [1, 2]
suranga@sutd.edu.sg

Lonce Wyse [3]
lonce.wyse@nus.edu.sg

Elizabeth A. Taylor [3]
etaylor@pacific.net.sg

[1] Singapore University of Technology and Design, 20 Dover Drive, Singapore, 138682
[2] MIT Media Lab, 75 Amherst Street, Cambridge, MA, 02142
[3] National University of Singapore, 21 Lower Kent Ridge Road, Singapore, 119077

ABSTRACT

The 'Haptic Chair' [3] delivers vibrotactile stimulation to several parts of the body including the palmar surface of the hand (palm and fingers), and has been shown to have a significant positive effect on the enjoyment of music even by the profoundly deaf. In this paper, we explore the effectiveness of using the Haptic Chair during speech therapy for the deaf. We conducted a 24-week study with 20 profoundly deaf users to validate our initial observations. The improvements in word clarity observed over the duration of this study indicate that the Haptic Chair has the potential to make a significant contribution to speech therapy for the deaf.

Categories and Subject Descriptors

K.4.2 [**Computers and Society**]: Social Issues—Assistive technologies for persons with disabilities; H.5.2 [**Information Interfaces and Presentation**]: User Interfaces—Haptic I/O;

General Terms

Human Factors

Keywords

Haptic feedback, Speech therapy

1. INTRODUCTION

In our previous work, we developed a 'Haptic Chair' to enhance the musical experience of the Deaf using vibrotactile feedback [3]. During the earlier user studies, it became apparent that the Haptic Chair had the potential to be more than just a tool for enhancing the pleasure of 'listening to music'. In this paper, we explore ways to make the speech therapy sessions both more effective and more enjoyable for the students. We focus on the speech therapy sessions conducted at the Dr. Reijntjes School for the Deaf, Sri Lanka (www.shoolforthe deaf.lk). In a typical speech therapy session at the school, a deaf user and a speech therapist sit in front of a mirror. The deaf user watches the speech therapist's lip movement in the mirror and tries to mimic those movements. We observed that the users are often able to mimic the lip movement, but either they generate no sound or they generate sound very different from the example provided by the therapist. This is not surprising given the lack of audible feedback. Furthermore, it was also clear that many profoundly deaf students did not enjoy the speech therapy sessions, which is a common problem worldwide.

Almost a century ago, Gault [2] proposed a method of presenting speech signals *via* a vibrator placed on the skin. This provided a

motivation for exploration of vibrotactile feedback for speech therapy and education. The concept underlying the Haptic Chair [3] is to generate vibrotactile stimulation from audio signals, delivering them to different parts of the body through the chair without adding any additional artificial effects into this communications channel by signal-processing the original audio output. The design of the Haptic Chair was extended so that users would be able to sense amplified vibrations produced by their own voice as well as others such as teachers or therapists. With this modification, we saw immediate effects on the awareness the profoundly deaf users had of whether they were matching the sound production pattern accompanying lip movements they could see. Our results suggest that this kind of display can, to some extent, function as an effective substitute for the traditional 'Tadoma' [5] method of speech instruction wherein students touch the throat or lips of their teachers.

There is a long history of research on the use of electronic speech training aids to improve speech therapy and a comprehensive overview of such devices can be found in [1]. Recently, software applications have been developed to provide alternative forms of speech therapy. Examples include *SpeechViewer III* (www.synapsea daptive.com) and *Tiga Talk* Speech Therapy Games (www. tigatalk.com). These tools provide visual feedback by transforming spoken words and sounds (phonetic sounds) into imaginative graphics or animations of lip-movements. This visual feedback is intended to reduce the need for constant guidance by a therapist. However, based on our previous work, when the speech therapist is present, we believe that, vibrotactile feedback might be a more effective additional sensory input. The mechanism of providing a tactile sensation through the Haptic Chair is quite similar to the common technique used by deaf people, called 'speaker listening'. In speaker listening, deaf people place their hands or feet directly on audio speakers to feel vibrations produced by audio output. However, the Haptic Chair provides a tactile stimulation to most of the body simultaneously in contrast to 'speaker listening' where only one part of the body is stimulated at any particular instant and not necessarily within an optimal frequency range. This is important since feeling sound vibrations through different parts of the body plays an important role [4].

2. METHOD

2.1 Participants

Twenty students (eleven boys and nine girls; median age nine years ranging from six to eleven years) from the Dr. Reijntjes School for the Deaf, Sri Lanka took part in the study. All were profoundly deaf (eight born deaf, 11 were deaf before the age of one year, and one before the age of two years). The speech therapist of the school helped us conduct the study and the participants were told that they could stop taking part at any time.

This study was approved by the Internal Review Board of the National University of Singapore.

2.2 Procedure

All participants were asked to articulate the test cases (20 words) at the beginning of the study (week 0). The speech therapist judged the clarity of each of the spoken words on a continuous scale of 0 to 1. A very clearly spoken word was given a score 1 and a completely unclear word was given a score 0. In addition, we asked an independent listener who was a native speaker of Sinhalese (a professional language instructor), to judge the clarity of each of the words. The speech therapist and the independent listener were in the same room while listening. However they were not allowed to discuss any kind of information regarding the evaluation. This helped mitigate any bias in the speech therapist's judgment. The initial assessment was used to divide the participants into two groups with similar speech abilities: (1) *The Experimental group:* received speech therapy while they were sitting in the Haptic Chair; and, (2) *The Control group:* received speech therapy while they were sitting on the standard chair used by the speech therapist at the deaf school. With a pilot study, we excluded the possible bias (psychological effect) of sitting on a standard chair and on the Haptic Chair. All the participants received voice feedback through headphones and visual feedback from the mirror. Only the experimental group received the additional vibrotactile feedback through the Haptic Chair. Participants from both groups received speech therapy for 1.5 hours per day over a period of 24 weeks. After every four-week block, the speech therapist and the independent listener assessed the clarity of the same test cases. This assessment was done without using the Haptic Chair in order to make a fair comparison. In addition, the independent listener was not aware of which students were in the control and experimental groups.

2.3 Results

Four participants (out of the 20) did not complete the entire study. One from the experimental group (after eight weeks) and three from the control group (two after eight weeks, one after 12 weeks) dropped out from the study. Their scores were included in the calculation of means during the period of their participation. Figures 1 and 2 show the mean score for each of the groups assessed by the speech therapist and the independent listener respectively. Both the speech therapist's and the independent listener's assessments showed a similar trend. However, as might be expected, the independent listener's scores were lower than the speech therapist's scores. This might have been due to the fact that the speech therapist was more familiar with the individual students' accents. All participants showed an increase in performance with time. This is expected due to the familiarity they gain with the test word set as well as the teaching that is part of the therapy.

Based on the speech therapist's assessment (Figure 1), there was no significant difference in performance between the two groups during the first eight weeks. However, from week 12 onwards, the group who used the Haptic Chair performed significantly better than the control group. At the end of the 24th week, the experimental group's performance score was significantly higher, t(14) = 2.55, p <0.05, than that of the control group. From the independent listener's assessment (Figure 2), the two groups showed similar performance during the first 12 weeks. The experimental group performed significantly better from week 16 onwards. At the end of week 24, on average subjects in the group that used the Haptic Chair were able to pronounce 75% percent of the test words clearly. This score is significantly higher, t(14) =

5.39, p <0.001, than the score of the group who went through the standard speech therapy program.

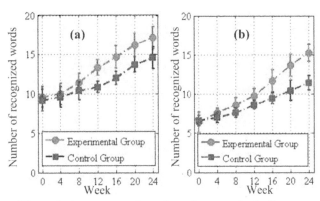

Figure 1: Average number of words recognized after every 4-weeks with 95% confidence interval; (a) by the speech therapist (b) by the independent evaluator

We asked the speech therapist and the independent listener to provide qualitative observations such as general speech ability, voice quality, omission of certain sounds and other general comments. The speech therapist reported that the Haptic Chair was intuitive to include and use in the speech therapy sessions. Both the speech therapist and the independent listener agreed that the participants who used the Haptic Chair were more enthusiastic about attending speech therapy sessions.

3. CONCLUSION AND FUTURE WORK

We conducted a 24-week long study to evaluate the effectiveness of the Haptic Chair in speech therapy sessions for profoundly deaf students. Our results suggest that the additional vibrotactile feedback provided by the Haptic Chair had a positive impact on speech learning in this context. In future work, we will explore the possibility of providing customized (e.g. separated by frequency bands) vibrotactile feedback through different vibration elements to different locations on the body. Moreover, we are focusing on extending the Haptic Chair concept into a wearable device. We hope that these future works will lead to more effective uses of the vibrotactile channel for communication *via* speech for the profoundly deaf.

4. REFERENCES

[1] Braeges, J. L., Houde, R.A. Use of speech training aids. *Deafness and Communication: Assessment and Training*, Ed. Sims, D., Walter, G. and Whitehead, R. Published Baltimore, Williams and Wilkins, 1982.

[2] Gault, R. H. "Touch as a substitute for hearing in the interpretation and control of speech," *Arch. Otolaryngol*, 3, pages 121-135, 1926.

[3] Nanayakkara, S. C., Taylor, E., Wyse, L. and Ong, S. H. An enhanced musical experience for the deaf: Design and evaluation of a music display and a haptic chair. In *Proc. CHI'09*, pp. 337-346, 2009.

[4] Palmer, R. (1997). Feeling Music, Based on the paper presented at the 3rd Nordic Conference of music therapy, Finland.

[5] Reed, C. M., Doherty, M. J., Braida, L. D., and Durlach, N. I. Analytic study of the Tadoma method: Further experiments with inexperienced observers, *Journal of Speech and Hearing Research,* 25, pp 216-223, 1982.

Access to UML Diagrams with the HUTN

Helmut Vieritz
RWTH Aachen
Dennewartstr. 25-27
D-52068 Aachen, Germany
+49 241 80 911 36

Daniel Schilberg
RWTH Aachen
Dennewartstr. 25-27
D-52068 Aachen, Germany
+49 241 80 911 30

Sabina Jeschke
RWTH Aachen
Dennewartstr. 25-27
D-52068 Aachen, Germany
+49 241 80 911 10

{Helmut.Vieritz, Daniel.Schilberg, Sabina.Jeschke}@ima-zlw-ifu.rwth-aachen.de

ABSTRACT

Modern software development includes the usage of UML for (model-driven) analysis and design, customer communication etc. Since UML is a graphical notation, alternative forms of representation are needed to avoid barriers for developers and other users with low vision. Here, Human-usable Textual Notation (HUTN) is tested and evaluated in a user interface modeling concept to provide accessible model-driven software design.

Categories and Subject Descriptors

H.1.2 [**Information Systems**]: Models and Principles – *human information processing*.

Keywords

Unified Modeling Language (UML), Human-usable Textual Notation (HUTN), Accessibility, Modeling.

1. INTRODUCTION

Software development is an interesting work for visually impaired programmers and developers. It is mostly text reading and writing based on programming languages as Java or C# and therefore accessible for Screenreaders, Braille devices and other assistive technology. However, writing and testing source code is only one activity among others in the development process. Especially in professional environments, analysis and modeling gain more and more importance with the growth of the project. Beside programming languages, other formal notations are used for the communication between software architect, developer, customer and user. In the last decade, the Unified Modeling Language (UML) [1] became the Lingua Franka in design and modeling of software artifacts. It facilitates the communication for the involved people with formalized and easy-to-understand diagrams such as the use case diagrams. Within UML, a graphical notation and a generic metamodel are combined for object-oriented software modeling. Behavior description is supported by use case or activity diagrams etc. Component or class diagrams allow the description of software structures. Especially UML class diagrams are widely supported by development tools as the Eclipse Modeling Framework (EMF), Rational Rose, Magic Draw etc. All these reasons help to understand why UML became the new standard for software design.

But on the other side, the UML graphical notation creates new barriers for some visually impaired people. Diagrams mix up text and graphical information and can be very detailed. Essential information such as object relations is only given by graphical layout. Therefore, without the support of alternatives, the use of UML diagrams is very restricted for software developers with low vision. Thus, a requirement exists to provide accessible presentation alternatives for UML diagrams.

In the next chapters, the state of the art is discussed first. Then, a concept for a text-based notation is used as an alternative for UML diagrams. The results of the evaluation are discussed and finally, a conclusion and outlook is given.

2. RELATED RESEARCH

The TeDUB project and Accessible UML [2] provides access to UML based on the XMI format. At first, diagrams are interpreted and then the user can navigate them with a diagram navigator using a joystick or keyboard navigation. Thus, diagrams need an extra transformation for accessible usage. Direct editing of diagrams is not possible.

Different approaches exist to translate visual graphics into haptic presentation. Typically, they are restricted to very simple diagrams. An interesting approach was elaborated by Kurze [3] when haptic presentation was much more powerful if the mental representation by the user is considered.

3. HUTN-BASED UML NOTATION

3.1 Concept

The presented concept of textual notation for graphic models is part of the INAMOSYS approach in user interface (UI) modeling. INAMOSYS uses UML Activity and class diagrams for the task and presentation modeling of accessible Web applications and product automation systems [4]. Activity diagrams describe navigation; user action and workflow (e.g. see fig. 1). Class diagrams describe the abstract structure of the UI.

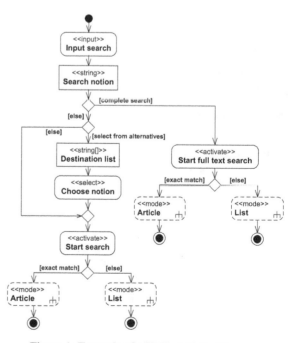

Figure 1: Example of a UML Activity Diagram

The alternative notation of the task and presentation models aims to have direct access to the design process for users with low vision. Direct access means that the model presentation and manipulation does not need additional transformations. Therefore, the Human-Usable Textual Notation (HUTN) [5] was used for UML diagram manipulation. As UML and XML Metadata Interchange (XMI), HUTN is based on the same metamodel Meta Object Facility (MOF) [6] and was developed in 2004 by the OMG. It is intended to provide an easy and quick way for changing details in diagrams by developers. HUTN provides short notations for modeling artifacts as objects, relations, attributes or methods. Until now, tool support such as the Epsilon-plugin [7] is very rare and a UML adaption for HUTN is still missing. Therefore, usage of HUTN needs the translation from UML to HUTN with the MOF metamodel.

For our evaluation, HUTN was adapted for the INAMOSYS task and presentation modeling with activity and class diagrams. The models were generated with the EMF tools for the Eclipse platform including Epsilon for the HUTN access. Listing 1 shows a part of the corresponding HUTN presentation for fig. 1.

```
@Spec {
  metamodel "Task_Model" {
    nsUri: "Task_Model"
  }
}
package {
  Activity "Submode_Search" {
    activity: Activity "Submode_Search"
    Rel1: Workflow "Workflow1" {
      Rel2: input "[Input search]" {
        name: "[Input search]"
      }, Structured Activity Node
"<<Search>>[Search notion]" {
        name: "<<Search>>[Search notion]"
      }, activate "<<activate>>[start full text
search]" {
        name: "<<activate>>[start full text
search]"
      }
      ...
    }
  }
}
```

Listing 1: Part of HUTN-notated Task Model

Model notation is semantic identical in UML and HUTN. The textual notation does not describe graphical layout as the size and position of symbols, boxes, arrows and lines. However, the power of modeling is not affected since layout is a non-semantical aspect of UML modeling.

3.2 Evaluation and Results

Evaluation method was a heuristic test by two modeling experts. The quality and functionality of the diagrams were tested with screen reader (JAWS 10.0) including the following issues:

- User can identify the metadata of the diagram (title, type, author etc.)
- User has orientation and overview during reading the diagram and navigation is possible
- Diagram elements can be identified
- User understands the meaning of the text elements
- User can manipulate the models

Table 1 summarizes some positive and negative results of the evaluation.

Table 1: Evaluation Summary

+ Direct manipulation of UML diagrams
+ Simple and generic principles for notation
+ Short, well-readable notation
+ Avoidance of redundant information
- Complex nesting of elements is hard to read
- Closing of elements may be ambiguous
- Additional data for automatic model transformation as ID attributes cause more workload for human reading

Generally, HUTN provides a good access to UML models. Since it has low redundant information, the user must know the syntax properly.

4. CONCLUSIONS AND OUTLOOK

In the presented concept, HUTN was used for the text-based presentation of UML activity and class diagrams and evaluated with screen readers. The results have shown that HUTN presentation is much shorter and easier to understand than earlier approaches based e.g. on the XML-conform XMI format. An accessible presentation and manipulation of UML models is possible. Nevertheless, HUTN has some weaknesses regarding the orientation in long documents or the deep nesting of elements. HUTN files are presentable with standard assistive technologies as Braille devices or screen readers. Until now, tool support is very rare and does not corresponding with the advantages for people with low vision. Due to the used tools, the model support is restricted to a subset of MOF. Further work is necessary to provide a complete HUTN-support for UML models. Even, the publicity is not accord with the chances for inclusion of people with low vision.

5. ACKNOWLEDGMENTS

We give our thanks to Deutsche Forschungsgemeinschaft (DFG) for funding the INAMOSYS project.

6. REFERENCES

[1] Object Management Group (OMG) 2010: *Unified Modeling Language (Version 2.4.1)*. http://www.omg.org/spec/UML/2.4.1/, last visited:6/21/2012.

[2] Schlieder, C. et. al. 2005: *Technical Drawings Understanding for the Blind (TeBUB)*. http://www.kinf.wiai.uni-bamberg.de/research/projects/TeBUB/, last visited: 06/21/2012, Bamberg.

[3] Kurze, M. 1999: Methoden zur computergenerierten Darstellung räumlicher Gegenstände für Blinde auf taktilen Medien. PhD thesis, FU Berlin.

[4] Vieritz, H. et. al. 2011: *User-Centered Design of Accessible Web and Automation Systems*. USAB 2011: 367-378.

[5] OMG 2004. *Human-usable Textual Notation (HUTN)*. http://www.omg.org/spec/HUTN/, last visited: 6/21/2012.

[6] OMG 2012: Meta Object Facility. http://www.omg.org/mof/, last visited: 06/21/2012.

[7] Epsilon Community: *Eclipse-Epsilon*. http://www.eclipse.org/epsilon/, last visited: 06/21/2012.

An Interactive Play Mat for Deaf-blind Infants

Crystal O'Bryan
Virginia Commonwealth University
401 West Main Street
Richmond, VA
001-804-828-7839
obryancn@vcu.edu

Amina Parvez
Virginia Commonwealth University
401 West Main Street
Richmond, VA
001-804-828-7839
aparvez@vcu.edu

Dianne Pawluk
Virginia Commonwealth University
401 West Main Street
Richmond, VA
001-804-828-9491
dtpawluk@vcu.edu

ABSTRACT

There is a great need for the development of interactive toys for deaf-blind infants (1-3 year olds) to motivate their exploration of their environment, and develop their motor and cognitive skills. We describe relevant design criteria, gleaned from the literature and a discussion with professionals who work with deaf-blind children. We then present a toy consisting of a play mat with three activity areas: one for remembering and repeating vibration patterns and two for matching textures. Vibrators which turn on as the infant moves in the direction of an activity area, measured by pressure sensors, are used to encourage the infant to explore in that direction.

Categories and Subject Descriptors

K.4.2 [**Computing Milieu**]: Social Issues – *Assistive technologies for persons with disabilities, Handicapped persons/special needs.*

General Terms

Design, Human Factors.

Keywords

Deaf-blind; Assistive Technology; Cognitive Development.

1. INTRODUCTION

The combined loss of sight and hearing is significantly greater than either single loss alone (Gleason, 2008). Typically, when one loses vision, compensation methods heavily rely on the use of hearing and vice versa. These options are not available to individuals who are deaf-blind. In addition, vision and hearing are considered the two "distance" senses: objects and people do not have to be within reach to be observed.

The development stage typically spanning infancy is important for the development of motor coordination as well as laying the groundwork for cognitive development. During this period, children learn by actively exploring their environment (Johnson et al., 2000). Self-initiated activity during this time is also an important driving force in a child's growth from less to more mature modes of behavior. The role of *external stimuli* in motivating this development through exploration is *crucial* in this

ASSETS'12, October 22–24, 2012, Boulder, Colorado, USA.
ACM 978-1-4503-1321-6/12/10.

stage (McInnes and Treferry, 1982). An infant with normal vision and hearing naturally explores by responding to sights and sounds in the environment that they may experience at a distance and move toward.

However, in absence of vision and hearing, motivation to explore is minimal. It is for this reason that a deaf-blind infant's communication, social development and cognitive activity are usually delayed and, unfortunately, the infant is typically treated as mentally retarded. Thus, there is a great need to provide a different method of stimulating these potentially intelligent infants (Szeto and Christensen, 1988) to avoid these unnecessary development delays. The purpose of our work is to develop a play toy for a deaf-blind infant to develop their cognitive skills.

2. PREVIOUS WORK

There have been relatively few devices designed for individuals who are deaf-blind, let alone for infants specifically. Several devices, such as the Tactaid II, have been designed to convert speech to vibrations through the use of a microphone and vibrators. These can also be used to pick up environmental noise (e.g., footsteps, doorbells) to make individuals more aware of their surrondings (Szeto and Christensen, 1988). Mechanically created structures, such as Nielson's Little Room, Dunnett's BeActiveBoxes, as well as improvised spaces, have been used to give an infant the opportunity to learn about space and reach for objects. One interesting component, initially designed for the Little Room, is for the child to lie on their back on a resonance board which works like a drum to give auditory and vibratory feedback from the child's movement and interaction with objects (Johnson et al., 2000).

3. DESIGN CONSIDERATIONS

The design considerations for the play toy were determined from reading the literature on deaf-blind infants and discussing the design with Peggy Sinclair-Morris and Julie Durando who work with deaf-blind children. Several ideas that motivated the design were: (1) the need for the toy to move the deaf-blind child from the reactive-passive state to an interactive state, (2) the need to give results of that interaction, so that they can make the connection that they did something (Gleason, 2008), (3) the desire to have tasks that developed the infant cognitively, (4) the need to clearly define the space for the child to play and explore and (5) the need to present objects in the same position to help develop the concept of object permanence (Johnson et al., 2000). Cost and safety were additional concerns.

In addition, very few children are totally deaf and totally blind; most have some usable vision and/or hearing. Vision can be stimulated using bright and/or reflecting toys and hearing by creating sounds.

4. DESIGN

4.1 Overall Design

A play mat design was chosen so as to clearly define the space for the child to play and explore (Figure 1). It also contains three activity areas, which were fixed in position to help establish object permanence.

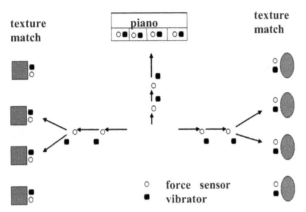

Figure 1: Overall play mat design with three activity areas: one for remembering and repeating a vibration pattern (piano) and two for matching textures. Vibrators which turn on as the infant moves in the direction of an activity area, measured by pressure sensors, are to encourage the infant to explore in that direction.

The idea is that the infant is to be placed in the middle of the mat. As an infant moves in a direction, whether randomly or purposefully, a pressure sensor will sense the movement and will cause a vibrator to vibrate further along in the direction of the closest activity. For this, a force sensing resistor (Interlink Electronics, Figure 2) will be mounted beneath an approximately 2"x4" yellow plate resting on a "button" which focuses the force onto the force sensing resistor. The vibrator (pancake type, Figure 2) will also be mounted beneath a 2"x4" reflective plate which it will vibrate. Analog electronics will be used to sense the force and trigger the subsequent vibrator. However, the sensors and vibrators in the activity areas will be controlled by an Arduino microcontroller.

Figure 2: Force Sensing Resistor and Pancake Motor

4.2 Piano

The piano is to consist of a modified version of a Little Tykes "piano" for which a piezoelectric vibrator (Figure 3) and force sensing resistor are mounted on each key. The first key will be the initial key: when the child touches this key a sequence of different frequencies of vibrations, produced by the piezoelectric buzzer, will occur. The infant will then have to mimic the vibration pattern by pressing the remaining three keys, each of which is associated with one frequency of vibration. If they are

correct, all the keys will produce a smooth vibration (high frequency tone) and otherwise they will produce a harsh vibration. The sequences will start with one note and build over time as the child interacts with the device during a play session.

Figure 3: Little Tykes Baby Tap-a-Tune which is to be modified by placing a piezoelectric vibrator on top of each key. Additionally, a force sensing resistor (Interlink Electronics) will be mounted between the piezoelectric disk and the top of the key

4.3 Texture Match

The texture matching activity areas will each consist of 2 pairs of matching textures mounted, using magnets, to colored geometric shapes raised above the play mat. Magnets are used so that the parent or intervener can change the location of the matching textures, with dipswitches on the microcontroller housing used to reprogram the matches. The matching game will work by the infant making contact with a texture on an initial block for a certain amount of time. At first, when the infant contacts the block with a matching texture, a smooth vibration will be presented on that texture immediately. However, as the game is played an increasing number of times, the infant will be required to contact the match for a certain amount of time before the vibration is presented. This is meant to ensure that the "reward" does not occur by random touching.

5. FUTURE WORK

After completion of the play mat and subject to IRB approval, the playmat will be tested with deaf-blind infants through the Virginia Project for Children and Young Adults with Deaf-Blindness. We expect that from observing their interaction with the play mat, some modifications may be needed before an appropriate design is finalized.

6. ACKNOWLEDGMENTS

Our thanks to Peggy Sinclair-Morris and Julie Durando of the Partnership for People with Disabilities, Virginia Commonwealth University.

7. REFERENCES

[1] Gleason, D. 2008. *Early Interactions with Children who are Deaf-Blind*. The Natonal Information Clearinghouse on Children who are Deaf-Blind.

[2] Johnson, K., Griffin-Shirley, N. and Koeing, A.J. 2000. Active learning for Children with Visual Impairments and Additional Disabilities. Journal of Visual Impairment and Blindness, 94 (9), 584-594.

[3] McInnes, J.M. and Treffry, J.A. 1982. Deaf-blind Infants and Children. A Developmental Guide. University of Toronto Press, Canada.

[4] Szeto, A.Y.J. and Christensen, K.M. (1988). Technological Devices for Deaf-Blind Chiren: Needs and Potential Impact. IEEE Engineering in Medicine and Biology Magazine. September 1988, 25-29.

Investigating Authentication Methods
Used by Individuals with Down Syndrome

Yao Ma[1], Jinjuan Heidi Feng[1,2], Libby Kumin[3], Jonathan Lazar[1,4], Lakshmidevi Sreeramareddy[1]

[1]Department of Computer and Information Sciences
Towson University
8000 York Road
Towson MD, 21252
{yma1, jfeng, jlazar, lsreeramareddy}@towson.edu

[3]Department of Speech-Language Pathology
Loyola University Maryland
4501 North Charles Street
Baltimore, MD 21202
lKumin@loyola.edu

[2]Information Systems Department
UMBC
1000 Hilltop Road
Baltimore, MD 21250

[4]Radcliffe Institute for Advanced Studies
Harvard University
8 Garden Street
Cambridge, MA 02138

ABSTRACT

Although there have been numerous studies investigating password usage by neurotypical users, a paucity of research has been conducted to examine the use of authentication methods used by individuals with cognitive impairment. In this paper, we report a longitudinal study that investigates how individuals with Down syndrome interact with three user authentication mechanisms. It confirms that many individuals with DS are capable of using traditional alphanumeric passwords as well as learning other authentication methods. Contrary to previous belief, the result suggests that mnemonic passwords may not be easier to remember for individuals with DS during initial usage.

Categories and Subject Descriptors

K.4.2 [**Computers and society**]: Social issues: Assistive technologies for persons with disabilities

General Terms

Security, Human Factors

Keywords

Cognitive impairment, Down Syndrome, Authentication

1. INTRODUCTION

People with cognitive impairments such as Down syndrome (DS) use computers to complete a wide variety of workplace and everyday tasks on the Web (e.g., e-commerce, communication tasks such as email and Facebook) [3]. Many of those tasks require user authentication However, most research about authentication methods only focus on working age neurotypical users [e.g., 1, 4]. To date, no study has empirically examined the use of authentication methods by people with cognitive disabilities. If users are unable to effectively use authentication applications, it will be difficult for them to access online resources. This study investigates how users with Down syndrome

interact with different types of authentication mechanisms in the web environment. The result of this study provides insight on the design of effective authentication methods for people with DS.

2. RELATED WORK

The use of most authentication applications heavily depends on an individual's cognitive abilities such as memory. When using the most widely adopted alphanumeric passwords, linguistic skills are also crucial. Alphanumeric passwords have fundamental limitations regarding the actual password space and the difficulty in remembering the passwords [1]. Studies have found that graphical passwords are easier to remember than alphanumeric password [2]. However, graphical passwords tend to have smaller password space, making them more vulnerable to brute force attack. Mnemonic passwords are passwords that are short form of the pass-sentence or pass-phrase used for authentication (e.g., "I8myo2day" for "I ate my oatmeal today"). Compared to alphanumeric passwords, mnemonic passwords are expected to be easier to remember and more secure [5].

Down syndrome is a genetic condition that affects a person's overall development, including the areas of cognitive, linguistic, sensory perception, and motor skills. People with DS often have difficulty using and remembering the alphanumeric passwords [3]. However, no empirical study has examined how people with DS interact with authentication mechanisms. Therefore, our knowledge is quite limited regarding the effectiveness and challenges of existing authentication solutions when used by people with DS or other types of cognitive disabilities.

3. METHOD

We conducted a six week longitudinal study to examine how individuals with DS interact with three authentication methods: traditional alphanumeric passwords, mnemonic passwords, and recognition-based graphical passwords. Alphanumeric passwords were chosen because they are currently the most widely adopted authentication method on the Web. Mnemonic and graphical passwords were chosen because they are believed to be easier to remember than alphanumeric passwords [2, 5]. In addition, both methods can be adopted without any additional equipment or substantial training.

In this study, both the traditional password and mnemonic password were required be at least six digits long and contain uppercase and lowercase letters, and numbers. In addition, the mnemonic password had to be created based on a memorable sentence or phrase. The graphical password was designed with 120 images selected from CD covers. Users first created their passwords by selecting 3 images from all 120 images. Each image could only be used once. In the authentication stage, the user selected the three images from a collection of 30 images. The order of the 30 images on the authentication page was always randomized each time the page was loaded. The three images had to be selected according to the pre-defined order.

Participants

Ten individuals with DS (eight females and two males) were recruited in this study. The age range was from 18 to 39 (average: 27.8). All participants had previous computer experience (average: 14.7 years) and Internet experience (average: 9 years). Participants had an average of three web application accounts that required a password.

Tasks and Procedure

The experiment was conducted in the context of an e-commerce website developed by the research team. The site provided a natural, real-life environment for the authentication task. A within-subject design method was adopted and each participant interacted with all three authentication methods. Each participant completed three sessions during a six week period, two weeks for each session. In each session, participants used one of the three authentication methods to visit the website five times on different days (no more than one visit on a single day). The order of the authentication methods for each participant was randomized to control the learning effect. During the first visit, the participants registered their accounts by creating a user name and a password. Then they logged into their account to select one item that they liked. During the remaining four visits, the participants directly logged into their account to select one item that they liked. If participants forgot a password, they could send request to the researchers to retrieve the password.

4. PRELIMINARY RESULTS

Regarding efficiency, participants spent an average of 187 seconds registering the account with the traditional alphanumeric password, 242.7 seconds with the mnemonic password, and 311 seconds with the graphical password. A Repeated Measures ANOVA test suggests that there is no significant difference in registration time between the three conditions ($F (2, 18) = 0.78$, n.s.). During the first visit, participants spent an average of 42 seconds logging in their accounts using the traditional alphanumeric passwords, 48 seconds using the mnemonic passwords, and 70 seconds using the graphical passwords. During the fifth visit, the average login time was 38 for traditional passwords, 31 seconds for mnemonic passwords, and 40 seconds for graphical passwords. A Repeated Measures ANOVA test suggests that there is no significant in login time between the three conditions ($F (2, 18) = 0.84$, n.s.). However, there is significant difference in login time between the five trials ($F(4, 36) = 3.14$, $p < 0.05$). Participants became faster logging into their account as they gained more experience in the authentication methods.

Regarding accuracy, we counted the number of visits with failed attempts for each condition. The total number of visits with failed attempts is 13 for traditional alphanumeric passwords, 18 for mnemonic passwords, and 8 for graphical passwords. A nonparametric Friedman Two Way Analysis of Variance test found no significant difference between the three conditions ($X^2(2) = 3.36$, n.s.).

To gain insight on memorability, we counted the number of times that participants forgot and requested their passwords. The total number of requests is 0 for traditional alphanumeric passwords, 4 for mnemonic passwords, and 1 for graphical passwords. A nonparametric Friedman Two Way Analysis of Variance test suggests that mnemonic passwords are significantly more likely to be forgotten than the other two methods ($X^2(2) = 8.38$, $p < 0.05$).

5. CONCLUSIONS

This study collected the first set of empirical data on the performance of authentication tasks conducted by individuals with DS. All ten participants successfully completed all visits in the six week period, confirming that many participants with DS are capable of using traditional alphanumeric passwords as well as learning new authentication methods. No significant difference was observed among the three methods regarding efficiency and accuracy. However, the mnemonic passwords are more likely to be forgotten than the alphanumeric passwords and the graphical passwords. This contrasts with previous belief that mnemonic passwords are easier to remember than alphanumeric passwords. Two possible explanations are that users with DS have more experience using alphanumeric passwords, or that the idea of the mnemonic password might be too linguistically abstract for some individuals with DS during initial usage. Currently, we are examining underlying issues including the interaction patterns and strategies, the nature of the passwords created, the causes of failed attempts, as well as workload and user preference.

ACKNOWLEGEMENT

This material is based upon work supported by the U.S. National Science Foundation under Grant IIS-0949963. Any opinions, findings, and conclusions or recommendations expressed in this material are those of the authors and do not necessarily reflect the views of the NSF.

6. REFERENCES

[1] Adams, A. and Sasse, A. (1999). Users are not the enemy: why users compromise computer security mechanisms and how to take remedial measures. Communications of the ACM, 42(12), 40-46.

[2] Brostoff, S. and Sasse, A. (2000). Are Passfaces More Usable Than Passwords? A Field Trial Investigation. *Proceedings of HCI 2000*, 405-424.

[3] Feng, J., Lazar, J., Kumin, L., and Ozok, A. (2010). Computer usage by children with Down syndrome: Challenges and future research. *ACM Transactions on Accessible Computing*. Vol. 2(3). 13-56.

[4] Grawemeyer, B. and Johnson, H. (2011). Using and managing multiple passwords: A week to a view. *Interacting with Computers*. Vol. 23(3). 256-267.

[5] Kuo, C., Romanosky, S., and Cranor, L. (2006). Human selection of mnemonic phrase-based passwords. *Proceedings of SOUPS* 2006. 67-68.

WatchMe: Wrist-worn Interface that Makes Remote Monitoring Seamless

Shanaka Ransiri [1]
shanaka@sutd.edu.sg

Suranga Nanayakkara [1,2]
suranga@sutd.edu.sg

[1] Singapore University of Technology and Design, 20 Dover Drive, Singapore, 138682
[2] MIT Media Lab, 75 Amherst Street, Cambridge, MA, 02142

ABSTRACT

Remote monitoring allows us to understand the regular living behaviors of the elderly and alert their loved ones in emergency situations. In this paper, we describe WatchMe, a software and hardware platform that focuses on making ambient monitoring intuitive and seamless. WatchMe system consists of the WatchMe server application and a WatchMe client application implemented on a regular wristwatch. Thus, it requires minimal effort to monitor and is less disruptive to the user. We hope that the WatchMe system will contribute to improving the lives of the elderly by creating a healthy link between them and their loved ones.

Categories and Subject Descriptors

H.5.2 [Information Interfaces and Presentation]: User Interface.
K.4.2 [Computers and Society]: Social Issues–Assistive technologies for persons with disabilities.

General Terms

Design, Human Factors

Keywords

Assistive interface, ambient display, health monitoring.

1. INTRODUCTION

As people age, incessant monitoring by their children/guardians or caretakers becomes indispensable. With busy schedules, it is immensely difficult for young people in a family to stay close to the older family members [9]. Thus, remote elderly sensing/monitoring systems that help to keep track of the behavior of elderly parents or loved ones has become important. These systems provide an opportunity for the elderly to stay healthy in their homes instead of moving to a strange place like elderly nursing homes where the rate of depression is high [8]. Moreover, social isolation can be eliminated to some extent through reminding them of the care bond they have with their loved ones. Technologies that promote these kinds of interactions have shown to reduce loneliness and depression among the elderly [3, 12]. However, most of the existing non-invasive remote monitoring systems are difficult to use due to the technical complexity required to interact with them [10, 5].

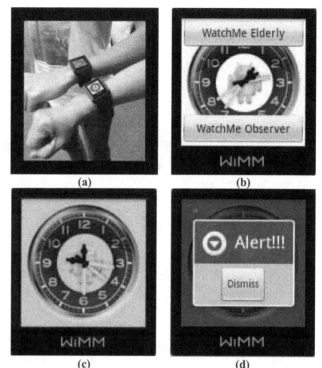

Figure 1. WatchMe client application

This motivated us to design the 'WatchMe' platform. WatchMe is a hardware and software platform that makes ambient monitoring seamless. One of the major benefits of WatchMe is that this monitoring device is as simple as a regular 'wristwatch' and requires no complex technical configurations. Caretaker's WatchMe watch can be paired with the WatchMe watch of the person who needs support, using a simple tap gesture. In addition to the uncomplicatedness of pairing and switching among different caretakers, the wristwatch interface requires minimal effort for ambient monitoring. It is also less disruptive compared to having to take a device, such as a mobile phone, out of the pocket periodically, to check the condition. The suggested platform can also be used to monitor and collect health related data constantly and recognize significant patterns to identify prominent psychological conditions.

2. RELATED WORK

There have been attempts ('Digital Family Portrait' [7], 'CareNet Display' [2]) of monitoring the behavior and health condition of the elderly using a portrait of the elderly that acts as the ambient display. These systems require complicated installations of sensors and cameras in the home where the older family member lives. Shimokakimoto and Suzuki propose an intuitive interface similar to a chair, which is employed to investigate physical and psychological activity of the body while the user is relaxing in a normal environment [10]. The system proposed by Segura et al [11] has mapped the urine output and the movement of a patient to an ambient display of blinking and moving flower-like objects. In addition, smart-phone based applications and other stand-alone devices for remote elderly sensing already exist in the market (e.g. www.medapps.net). Most of those either requires the use of a dedicated extra device or they do not provide an easy-solution for pairing the remote observer and the elderly user [1, 6].

3. WATCHME SYSTEM

The WatchMe system consists of two major modules: WatchMe server and WatchMe client application (Elderly/Observer). The architecture of this system is shown in Figure 2, where the WatchMe server was implemented on Java-SE 1.7 as an http server and the WatchMe client was implemented on a wristwatch running Android 1.6 (http://www.wimm.com). Although several WatchMe devices are connected to the WatchMe Server, only the paired devices communicate with each other.

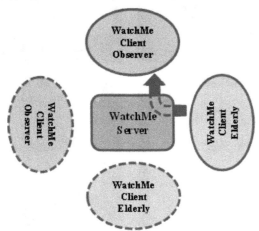

Figure 2. Overview of the WatchMe system

The process of remotely monitoring health condition is initiated with the pairing of two WatchMe clients. For the pairing, two watches running the WatchMe client application need to be in close proximity and the WatchMe wristwatches tapped (Figure 1a). Then, the application displays a window on two screens to select the role—WatchMe Observer for the caretakers, WatchMe Elderly for the elderly person to be monitored (Figure 1b). From this point onwards, remote sensing is enabled and both WatchMe applications show a regular watch face with a green color background to indicate successful pairing (Figure 1c). For the current implementation, we chose to monitor the movements using the inbuilt 3-axis accelerometer of the wristwatch. However, our modular implementation allows the system to be extended with different sensors attached directly to the watch or via bluetooth to monitor conditions such as blood pressure, heart rate, etc.

The WatchMe client (Elderly) application on an elderly person's watch monitors the accelerometer data and pushes the results to the WatchMe server. WatchMe client (Observer) application on the caretaker's watch periodically communicates with the WatchMe server to update itself. The background color of the caretaker's watch face changes from green to red corresponding to small movements (small variations of accelerometer data) to large movements (large variations of accelerometer data) of the elderly person's watch. The current implementation also monitors for emergency situations such as a fall based on the readings of the

accelerometer data [4]. When a fall is detected, the WatchMe Observer's watch face background becomes red and the application alerts the caretaker with a pop up message and vibration (Figure 1d). At the same time, a similar pop-up message with vibration alert is shown on the elderly person's watch, which can be used to disarm a false detection of a fall.

4. CONCLUSION AND FUTUREWORK

WatchMe is still a work in progress. So far, we have developed a modular platform that makes the ambient health monitoring of elderly people intuitive and seamless. We plan to conduct a formal user study to validate our decision of using a wristwatch as an ambient monitoring system. In future, we will explore integrating more sensors (such as blood pressure sensors and temperature sensors) with the WatchMe client. This will be useful for predicting and preventing hazardous health conditions. We also plan to extend this work beyond the assistive interface domain and explore the use of wrist-worn interfaces for social and professional networking.

5. ACKNOWLEDGMENTS

The International Design Center (IDC) of the Singapore University of Technology and Design (SUTD) has supported this work with IDC grants IDG31100104 and IDD41100102.

6. REFERENCE

[1] Chan V., Ray. P., and Parameswaran N. Mobile e-Health monitoring: an agent-based approach. *Communications-IET*. 2, 2, pp. 223-230, 2008.

[2] Consolvo S., Roessler P., and Shelton B.E. 2004. The CareNet Display: Lessons Learned from an In Home Evaluation of an Ambient Display. In *Proc. UbiComp'04*, pp.1-17.

[3] Czaja S.J., Guerrier J., Nair S.N., and Laudauer T. Computer communication as an aid to independence for older adults. *Behavior and Information Technology*. 12, 4, pp.197- 207, 1993.

[4] Dai J., Bai X., Yang Z., Shen Z., and Xuan D. Mobile phone-based pervasive fall detection. *Personal Ubiquitous Comput*. 14, 7, pp. 633-643, 2010.

[5] Holzinger A., Searle G., and Nischelwitzer A. On some aspects of improving mobile applications for the elderly. In *Proc. UAHCI'07*, pp. 923-932, 2007.

[6] Milosevic M., Shrove M.T., and Jovanov E. Applications of Smartphones for Ubiquitous Health Monitoring and Wellbeing Management, *Journal of Information Technology and Application,* 2011 (accepted).

[7] Mynatt E.D., Rowan J., Craighill S., and Jacobs Annie. 2001. Digital family portraits: supporting peace of mind for extended family members. In *Proc.CHI'01*, pp.333-340.

[8] Rovner B.W., German P.S., Brant L.J., Clark R., Burton L., and Folstein M.F. 1991. Depression and mortality in nursing homes. *JAMA*. 265, 8, pp.993-996, 1991.

[9] Ruyter B. and Pelgrim E. 2007. Ambient assisted-living research in carelab. *Interactions*. 14, 4, pp. 30-33, 2007.

[10] Shimokakimoto T. and Suzuki K. 2011 A Chair-type Interface for Long-term and Ambient Vital Sensing. In *Proc. EMBC'11*, pp.1173-1176.

[11] Segura D., Favela J., and Tentori M. Sentient Displays in Support of Hospital Work. *Advances in Soft Computing*. 51, pp. 103-111, 2009.

[12] Tsai T.H. and Chang H.T. 2009. Sharetouch: a multi-touch social platform for the elderly. In *Proc. CAD/Graphics'09*, pp.557-560.

Musica Parlata* : a Methodology to Teach Music to Blind People

A. Capozzi
Liceo Musicale
Alfano I
84132 Salerno, Italy
info@musicaparlata.it

R. De Prisco, M. Nasti, R. Zaccagnino
Dipartimento di Informatica
University of Salerno
84084 Fisciano (SA), Italy
robdep@unisa.it,
michele.nasti@gmail.com,
roccojazz@gmail.com

ABSTRACT

Music education for blind people heavily relies on Braille. The use of Braille for music causes difficulties for the blind student: new meanings for the Braille symbols have to be learned and the reading of the music is not immediate. Moreover, in the majority of the cases, music teachers don't know Braille. Although Braille remains the primary means for music education for blind people, alternative methods can help. We propose a new methodology that helps the reading of music scores by means of a software that *sings* the *name* of the notes. Singing the name of the notes provides to a blind user a direct perception of the score. Moreover the information is directly conveyed to the student through the ear. Although the method has several limitations we believe that it is effective. The methodology is not intended to "replace" Braille, but only to offer a different approach to the study of music.

Categories and Subject Descriptors: L.2.1 [Learning]: Individualised Learning Solution

General Terms: Human Factors, Experimentation

Keywords: Music learning, Accessibility, User interfaces for blind people.

1. INTRODUCTION

The standard approach to music for blind people requires reading Braille music. However reading Braille music is a specialized skill and even if one already knows Braille reading Braille music requires further efforts. Not every blind person is able to read Braille music. This means that if a blind person wants to approach music there is a serious first obstacle.

In order to use Braille for music, it is necessary to give new meanings to symbols already used for letters and numbers and mathematics notation. The "symbols" needed to represent music (i.e., clefs, key signatures, notes, notes duration,

accidentals, fingerings, irregular note-grouping, ties, slurs, musical markings, repetition symbols, etc.) are much more complicated than the symbols used for regular text (letters, numbers, punctuation). Some music symbols require several Braille symbols (even 3 or 4) to be represented. A complete explanations of the Braille music symbols can be found in the Music Braille Code [3], published by the Braille Authority of North America.

In many cases the blind person will just decide to abandon the studies. This is particularly true for people wishing to play music only for fun and thus do not have the time nor the desire to go through a difficult learning process in order to become skilled in reading Braille music. A more direct way for taking the first steps in the study of music would encourage the student in pursuing the goal.

Often, the teacher too is not able to use Braille. In such cases also the teacher has to go through the same difficult learning process and if the teacher is not able to become skilled with Braille music the resulting lessons will be poor. This can be very frustrating both for the teacher and for the student. A tool that allows to teach music to blind people without using Braille can be very useful in such cases.

Hence, methods to study music without using Braille can help blind people to approach the study of music. *Musica Parlata* is a methodology developed to help blind students reading music scores without using Braille. The software provides a direct perception of the notes by singing (with the correct pitches) the names of the notes in melodic lines and by speaking the name of chords.

2. RELATED WORK

The creation of computer assisted tools to help blind people with music has been an active area. However most of the tools available today involve Braille. Due to space limitations, we will not cite Braille oriented work. One project that is somewhat similar to *Musica Parlata* is the *Spoken Music* [1] project. However there is a fundamental difference: while Spoken Music "reads" the score, *Musica Parlata* "sings" the scores. *Musica Parlata* sings the names of the notes and also reads the chords "in time" with the music, that is, in the exact moment in which the notes (or the chords) have to be played. The information that *Musica Parlata* is able to convey is restricted to the notes of melodic lines (and the chords) but it is given on the fly with the music and the blind student gets a precise perception of the temporal

---

*"Musica Parlata" means, in Italian, "Spoken Music". We have decided to keep the Italian name because "Spoken Music" has already been used for another project [1] and thus using the same name could have caused confusion.

position and duration of the notes. This is a fundamental difference with *Spoken Music* and we believe that it is also an innovative idea that can be very effective.

3. MUSICA PARLATA

The idea of *Musica Parlata* has been developed over a long time and it sprung from direct teaching experiences by Alfredo Capozzi. *Musica Parlata* helps the reading of a score sheet by singing the name of the note (using the correct pitch) or speaks the chord. Earlier version of the software were ad-hoc solutions which caused several troubles to the blind user. The current version of the software, that we are presenting in this paper, is a stand-alone program, with a 1-click installer and a easy-to-use interface. The audio engine uses Csound [2].

The *Musica Parlata* player is multi-track, allowing a maximum of 20 tracks. The tracks contain normal audio material but can also contain special audio with the names of the notes. Clearly we can add any other information we like. For example we can add the chords (this is especially useful if we are dealing with pop music), or the click of a metronome. The musical material has to be prepared by the "programmer" of the song. Figure 1 shows the screen-shoot of the graphic interface of the program. Obviously, every functionality can also be used through the keyboard.

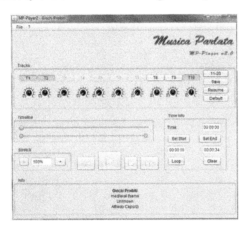

Figure 1: The *Musica Parlata* graphic interface. All the functionalities can be controlled through the keyboard.

As in any multi-track audio software the user can mute or un-mute each track, create loops, adjust the volumes, control the execution speed, etc. All these functionalities are pretty obvious and every software dealing with multi-track songs does provide them. However *Musica Parlata* has special tracks that are used to sing the names of the notes. The visually impaired student will hear the names of notes to play: memorizing the notes will be much easier (compared to memorize them after reading the notes in a Braille score) and the student can try to play immediately while "listening" to the score. The method is immediate in the sense that the student does not need any special study to start using the proposed learning method.

Musica Parlata has two major limitations: it is difficult to "read" simultaneously several melodic lines, although the reading of two melodic lines is quite comprehensible. Notes with a very short duration are also a trouble because it is difficult, if not impossible, to sing the name in the short time of the duration of the note.

Download and demo. The software is freely available for download in the website `music.dia.unisa.it`, in the `Download` page. The current version has been developed for Windows. The site contains also some videos that show the use of the software.

4. USABILITY TEST

We have administered a small-scale usability test involving 30 people, 10 of which were blind. The non blind people have used the software through the graphical interface. In the test we have provided a series of tasks to be performed using the software. For each task the user had to use a specific song and perform several actions ranging from moving within the song, adjusting the volumes, muting or un-muting specific tracks, listening to specific parts of the song, speeding up or slowing down the playing, using either the visual interface (for non-blind) or the keyboard commands (for blind) provided by the software. After performing a task the user has been asked a series of questions regarding the usability of the software. Moreover some user provided also additional specific comments. Both blind and non-blind people have found the software easy to use. Some of the non-blind people that took the test are teachers and they had enthusiastic comments about the software. Some believe that the software can be useful also to non-blind students. The blind people that took the test also found the program easy to use, although in some cases they reported specific difficulties, as, for example, the presence of echoes that in some cases made difficult the "reading" of the score.

5. CONCLUSIONS AND FUTURE WORK

Musica Parlata is a software developed to help blind people to study music. It *sings* the *names* of the notes. It is very effective for monophonic instruments or for two-voice scores. The main and innovative feature of the tool is that it "reads" the score by singing the name of the note (or the chord) to be played so that the students gets both the name and the correct pitch of the note and at the same time has the hands free so that it is possible to immediately play the notes. Although the idea was born a long time ago, the previous versions of the software suffered from several drawbacks which made it not very usable. The current version of the software is a first major step towards an effective tool. Future work includes support of MIDI files so that it will not be necessary to produce ad-hoc music files. A usability test involving a wider audience would be helpful especially for understanding where the software needs to be improved.

6. REFERENCES

[1] D. Crombie, S. Dijkstra, E. Schut, N. Lindsay. Spoken Music: Enhancing Access to Music for the Print Disabled. In *Proceedings of the 8th International Conference on Computers Helping People with Special Needs (ICCHP)*, Springer LNCS 2398, pp. 201–213, 2002.
[2] Csound. http://www.csounds.com/
[3] The Music Braille Code. http://www.brailleauthority.org/music/music.html
[4] Musimathics Laboratory, University of Salerno, Italy. http://music.dia.unisa.it/

Supporting Employment Matching with Mobile Interfaces

Ziyi Zhang, D. Scott McCrickard
Department of Computer Science
Virginia Tech
2202 Kraft Drive
Blacksburg VA USA 24060
zzhang|mccricks@vt.edu

Shea Tanis
Coleman Institute
for Cognitive Disabilities
325 Iris Avenue Suite 200
Boulder CO USA 80301
shea.tanis@cu.edu

Clayton Lewis
Department of Computer Science
University of Colorado, Boulder
430 UCB
Boulder CO USA 80309-0430
clayton.lewis@colorado.edu

ABSTRACT

People with cognitive disabilities need careful matching to find appropriate employment. However, it can be difficult for them to articulate their worries and concerns in a timely and useful manner. This work demonstrates how appropriately-designed technology can assist in accommodating cognitive disabilities, providing avenues to assess their concerns about work environments. A mobile application was developed with targeted repeated multimedia surveying to assess work concerns, with temporal- and geo-tagged answers stored for review by a personal assistant, employer, job coach, or person with a cognitive disability. An expert review provided feedback to ensure an appropriate application.

Categories and Subject Descriptors

H.5.2 [**Information Interfaces and Presentation**]: User Interfaces—*training, help, and documentation*

General Terms

Design, Human Factors.

Keywords

cognitive disabilities, mobile computing

1. INTRODUCTION

Cognitive disabilities—including birth or developmental disabilities, brain injury and stroke, and severe and persistent mental illness—affect tens of millions of people worldwide [3]. Cognitive disabilities can lead to difficulties with memory, attention, problem-solving, and comprehension, and people with cognitive disabilities can become frustrated or overwhelmed in workplace situations. However, appropriate placement in supportive work environments can lead to productive situations, both for the employer and employee.

This paper describes the application development aspects of a joint effort that includes researchers in computer science, cognitive science, and disability advocacy. The community of researchers developing technologies for people with cognitive disabilities has begun to create design guidelines (e.g., limiting

text or choices on a screen, providing multiple navigation paths to information, and increasing size of selectable areas on a screen) and to identify interface techniques (e.g., [2]). In our development effort, researchers investigating cognitive disabilities enlighten technology developers about the skills and limitations strengths and challenges faced by the target user population, and the technology developers lead the exploration of new and emerging mobile platforms, toward identifying a solution of mutual benefit.

The work described here has as its primary focus to develop a mobile questionnaire application for people with moderate to severe cognitive disabilities. These people typically need support in their daily lives, but can become productive members of society through appropriate training of work related tasks with minimal assistance or supervision in an integrative environment. Specifically, this work seeks to create a mobile application that will ask a set of questions about the work environment to the user in a way that will elicit helpful responses in making an appropriate employment match.

As a secondary purpose, our work seeks to provide a flexible platform for tailoring questionnaires for people of various cognitive abilities. Several configuration files allow a personal assistant, support staff or employer with minimal computer skills to control aspects of the questionnaire such as the questions asked, the content of responses, repetition number and style, delay between presenting of chunks of information, and voice type and content in the presentation of the questions and responses. These factors will allow a personal assistant or employer of people with cognitive disabilities to individualize the questionnaire to meet the strengths of the employee and assess the unique attributes of the job. The application is developed on the Google Android platform and will be available on the Android Marketplace.

2. APPLICATION DETAILS

Our mobile application lets people with cognitive disabilities give evaluative feedback via a questionnaire, with results summarized for their personal assistants, job coaches, employers, and themselves. These responses are logged for easy interpretation, so their work environment and situation can be tailored to better fit their needs and abilities.

We targeted an inexpensive solution with sufficient ability to satisfy user goals. As such, we decided to develop a free application for the Android platform—the free development environment and ease of software deployment had great appeal: applications are easily distributable after paying a small one-time fee, and the developer can upload as many applications as desired the Android Marketplace. Any compatible Android device can download and use the application. In addition, Android devices are generally less expensive than other platforms, with a wide range of available devices.

Development of this application was guided by a series of expert evaluations by three evaluators: an interface design expert, a computer scientist with expertise in cognitive science, and an expert in cognitive disabilities. The expert review was helpful in identifying not only appropriate language for the questions, but in making decisions on button size, centering of text, the length of time between the reading of responses, and the use of voice cues. Many of the design decisions that were made differ from those made for other user populations, but they are vital for success when used by people with cognitive disabilities. Key aspects of the design—like the ability to match the demographics of the target users to the faces and voices featured in the application—emerged from the expert review as well. While the use of icons to represent the answers is used in publication, the application is easily customizable to allow any voice or face (from established symbol/voice sets or taken by the assistant of people familiar to the user) to be used. It is our expectation that this level of flexibility will enable the application to be used not only for the targeted population of people with moderate-to-severe cognitive disabilities, but with other populations as well.

While we were designing the application, there were several very important factors that we had to consider. Our target user, people with cognitive disabilities, played a major role in our design decisions. We wanted to keep the application simple and easy to use, both for accommodating cognitive disabilities as well as the physical disabilities that sometimes accompany them [1]; hence the use of very large buttons and fonts. To accommodate literacy limitations, the application reads each answer choice aloud, and both text and images on the buttons reflect choices. These multimedia forms of communication assist the person cognitive disabilities discriminate button meaning. We also decided to ask one question at a time, important so the user does not have to keep track of and worry about multiple questions at once. Clutter and excessive content represented to the user could be detrimental to the accuracy of the responses.

The user is presented with the survey questions as soon as the application is opened. The first question is displayed in large font at the top. The user now has the option of choosing to respond to the question by clicking on one of the response buttons. If the user needs additional help, he or she can click on the speech button. This will initiate a process that reads aloud the question that is being asked and the possible answer choices. For each reading, the text or response button that is being read will be highlighted (see figure 2) to replicate scanning techniques used by augmentative or alternative communication systems. There is also a five-second delay between each reading. This pause aids comprehension and ensures that the users with cognitive disabilities can understand and differentiate the question being asked and the responses that are available. Once the user has selected a response to the question, the application will automatically display the text for the next question, repeating the process until all questions are answered. Survey results can be displayed on screen, with a more detailed log (with full timestamp and geo-tag data) in a file on the device's memory card.

The application is highly configurable to support changes to the questions based on user demographics, spoken responses, delay times between reading of responses, and the images that are displayed. This configurability allows an assistant or employer to tailor the application to the skills and abilities of the target users,

and to create a usage environment that makes the user more comfortable; e.g., the developer can include faces or voices that match the gender or ethnic demographic of the users.

Once the user has selected a response to the question, the application will automatically display the text for the next question, repeating the process until all questions are answered. Survey results can be displayed on screen, with a more detailed log (with full timestamp and geo-tag data) in a file on the device's memory card. After all questions have been asked, the timestamped, geo-tagged results are displayed and saved in plain text format on the device. The logged responses can then be emailed to another computer or examined on the device.

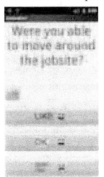

Figure 1. A screenshot from the mobile application (left) and the results page after survey completion (right).

3. CONCLUSIONS AND FUTURE WORK

This paper describes the development process and results of a job questionnaire application for people with cognitive disabilities. The mobile application described here was targeted for young people with moderate to severe cognitive disabilities who need a straightforward way to provide feedback about a workplace environment when exploring different employment options or environments. The feedback will help assistants and employers tailor a job that matches each person's skills.

In the future, our most important next step will be deployment in work settings with people with moderate to severe cognitive disabilities. Improvements to the application will seek to make it more configurable, so people with little computer knowledge can configure the application. Display of survey output will reflect changes in answers as they correlate with time and location. In addition, the application will be deployed via the Google Marketplace, with the expectation of use across many populations

4. ACKNOWLEDGMENTS

Our thanks to the REU students for early development efforts, and the US NSF (IIS-1135149, IIS-0851774) for their support. The opinions in this paper are not necessarily shared by the NSF.

5. REFERENCES

[1] Lewis, C. Simplicity in cognitive assistive technology: A framework and agenda for research. *Universal Access Information Society 5*, 351-361, December 2006.

[2] Lewis, C. Sullivan, J. & Hoehl, J. Mobile technology for people with cognitive disabilities and their caregivers—HCI issues. In *Proc HCII*, July 2009.

[3] Waldrop, J. & Stone, S. Census 2000 Brief: Disability Status 2000. Press release, March 2003.

Combining Emotion and Facial Nonmanual Signals in Synthesized American Sign Language

Jerry Schnepp, Rosalee Wolfe,
John C. McDonald
School of Computing, DePaul University
243 S. Wabash Ave., Chicago, IL 60604 USA
+1 312 362 6248

{jschnepp,rwolfe,jmcdonald}@cs.depaul.edu

Jorge Toro
Department of Computer Science
Worchester Polytechnic Institute
100 Institute Road
Worcester, MA 01609 USA

jatoro@wpi.edu

ABSTRACT

Translating from English to American Sign Language (ASL) requires an avatar to display synthesized ASL. Essential to the language are nonmanual signals that appear on the face. Previous avatars were hampered by an inability to portray emotion and facial nonmanual signals that occur at the same time. A new animation system addresses this challenge. Animations produced by the new system were tested with 40 members of the Deaf community in the United States. For each animation, participants were able to identify both nonmanual signals and emotional states. Co-occurring question nonmanuals and affect information were distinguishable, which is particularly striking because the two processes can move an avatar's brows in opposing directions.

Categories and Subject Descriptors

I.2.7 [**Artificial Intelligence**]: Natural Language Processing – language generation, machine translation; K.4.2 [**Computers and Society**]: Social Issues – assistive technologies for persons with disabilities.

General Terms

Design, Experimentation, Human Factors, Measurement.

Keywords

Accessibility Technology, American Sign Language

1. INTRODUCTION

An automatic English-to-ASL translator would help bridge the communication gap between the Deaf and hearing communities. Text-based translation is incapable of portraying the language of ASL. A video-based solution lacks the flexibility needed to dynamically combine multiple linguistic elements. A better approach is the synthesis of ASL as animation via a computer-generated signing avatar. Several research efforts are underway to portray sign language as 3D animation [1][2][3][4], but none of them have addressed the necessity of portraying affect and facial nonmanual signals simultaneously.

2. FACIAL NONMANUAL SIGNALS

Facial nonmanual signals appear at every linguistic level of ASL [5]. Some nonmanual signals carry adjectival or adverbial information. Figure 1 shows the adjectival nonmanuals OO (small) and CHA (large) demonstrated by our signing avatar.

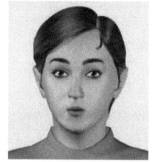 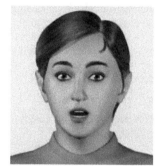

Nonmanual OO – "small size"   Nonmanual CHA – "large size"

Figure 1: Nonmanual signals indicating size

Other nonmanuals operate at the sentence level [6]. For example, raised brows indicate yes/no questions and lowered brows indicate WH-type (who, what, when, where, and how) questions.

Affect is another type of facial expression which conveys emotion and often occurs in conjunction with signing. While not strictly considered part of ASL, Deaf signers use their faces to convey emotions [7]. Figure demonstrates how a face can convey affect and a WH-question simultaneously.

WH-question, happy   WH-question, angry

Figure 2: Co-occurrence

3. SYNTHESIZING CO-OCCURANCE

We characterize linguistic facial nonmanual signals and affect poses as a set of facial muscle transformations which combine to create facial animations. We use a framework that represents syntax, lexical modifiers and affect as separate, but co-occurring influences on the position and timing of subordinate geometric components. This has the flexibility to synthesize novel utterances. See [8] for implementation details.

4. INITIAL EVALUATION

An initial study measured the perceptibility of affect in the presence of co-occurring nonmanual signals that could potentially interfere. For this, we created two pairs of sentences. Each pair consisted of one sentence with happy affect and one sentence with angry affect. The first pair combined the WH-nonmanual with each of these emotions. The second pair combined the CHA nonmanual with the same two emotions.

Twenty people participated in a face-to-face setting at Deaf Nation Expo in Palatine Illinois, and another twenty were recruited through Deaf community websites and tested remotely using SignQUOTE [9]below. All participants self-identified as members of the Deaf community and stated that ASL is their preferred language. In total, 40 people participated. Participants viewed animations of synthesized ASL utterances and were asked to repeat the sentence, rate its clarity, and identify the emotion in the animation using a five-point Likert scale. All testing was conducted in ASL.

5. RESULTS

For each animation, every participant repeated the utterance correctly. This included all of the processes that occurred on the face. Seventy-eight percent rated the WH-Happy animation as clear or very clear while sixty-five percent indicated that the WH-Angry animation was clear or very clear. For both animations combining the CHA nonmanual signal with either happy or angry affect, seventy five percent of participants indicated the animations were clear or very clear.

The majority of participants perceived the intended affect in each animation. Figure 3 displays the perceived affect for the WH-Happy and WH-Angry animations. Data for the perceived affect of the CHA-Happy and CHA-Angry animations are similar.

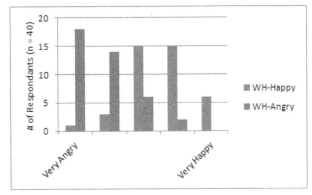

Figure 3: Perception of emotion in the presence of a WH-question nonmanual signal

6. DISCUSSION AND FUTURE WORK

In the case where the WH-nonmanual occurs simultaneously with happy affect, the brows are influenced by both in a competing manner. The WH-nonmanual tends to pull the brows downward, but a happy affect tends to push the brows upward. Despite these opposing influences, seventy-eight percent rated the animation as clear or very clear. This shows that the new technique has promise for portraying both affect and co-occurring nonmanual signals that are recognizable to members of the Deaf community.

Going forward, we plan to develop and evaluate additional nonmanual signals and follow up with more rigorous testing.

7. REFERENCES

[1] VCom3D. n.d. *Sign Smith 3.0 user manual.* http://www.vcom3d.com/docs/Sign_Smith_Studio3.0_Users Guide.pdf.

[2] Huenerfauth, M., Lu, P. and Rosenberg, A. 2011. Evaluating importance of facial expression in American Sign Language and pidgin signed English animations. In *Proceedings of the 13th International ACM SIGACCESS Conference on Computers and Accessibility* (Dundee, UK, October 22 - 24, 2011). ASSETS'11. ACM, New York, NY, 99-106. DOI= http://doi.acm.org/10.1145/2049536.2049556.

[3] S. Gibet, N. Courty, K. Duarte, and Le Naour, T. 2011.The signcom system for data- driven animation of interactive virtual signers: Methodology and evaluation. ACM Transactions on interactive intelligent systems. 1, 1 (Oct. 2011), 1-26. DOI= http://doi.acm.org/10.1145/2030365.2030371.

[4] Elliott, R., Glauert, J. and Kennaway, J. 2004. A framework for non-manual gestures in a synthetic signing system. In *Proceedings of the Second Cambridge Workshop on Universal Access and Assistive Technology* (Cambridge, UK, March 22 - 24, 2004). CWUAAT 04. 127–136. http://www-edc.eng.cam.ac.uk/cwuaat/04/39-pat-elliott_cwuaat-2004.pdf.

[5] Valli, C., Lucas, C. and Mulrooney, K. 2005. *Linguistics of American Sign Language: An Introduction.* 4th ed. Washington, DC: Gallaudet University Press.

[6] Neidle, C., Kegl, J., Maclaughlin, D., Bahan, B., and Lee, R. 2000. *The Syntax of American Sign Language: Functional Categories And Hierarchical Structure.* Cambridge, Massachusetts: MIT Press.

[7] Weast, T. 2008. Questions in American Sign Language: A quantitative analysis of raised and lowered eyebrows. Doctoral dissertation. The University of Texas, Arlington.

[8] Schnepp, J. 2012. A representation of selected nonmanual signals in American Sign Language. Doctoral dissertation. DePaul University, Chicago, Illinois.

[9] Schnepp, J., Wolfe, R., Shiver, B., McDonald, J., and Toro, J. 2011. SignQUOTE: A remote testing facility for eliciting signed qualitative feedback. In *Proceedings of the Second International Workshop on Sign Language Translation and Avatar Technology* (Dundee, UK, October 23, 2011) http://vhg.cmp.uea.ac.uk/demo/SLTAT2011Dundee/4.pdf.

Displaying Braille and Graphics with a "Tactile Mouse"

Victoria E. Hribar
Virginia Commonwealth University
401 West Main Street
Richmond, Virginia 23284
001-804-828-7839
hribarve@vcu.edu

Laura G. Deal
Virginia Commonwealth University
401 West Main Street
Richmond, Virginia 23284
001-804-828-7839
deallg@vcu.edu

Dianne T.V. Pawluk
Virginia Commonwealth University
401 West Main Street
Richmond, Virginia 23284
001-804-828-9491
dtpawluk@vcu.edu

ABSTRACT

Refreshable tactile displays that move with the hand, such as those that resemble computer mice, can be utilized to display tactile graphics faster and more cost effectively to individuals who are blind and visually impaired than traditional paper methods of creating tactile diagrams. However, in tactile diagrams, the word labels can be as important as the diagram itself and so it is important that these displays can present Braille. In this work, we present and discuss findings from a study which used three methods of displaying Braille and tactile graphics simultaneously with a tactile mouse: Braille and graphics at the same amplitude level, Braille and graphics at different amplitude levels, and Braille with a box around it, The simplest method, Braille and graphics at the same amplitude, surprisingly proved to be the most effective.

Categories and Subject Descriptors

K.4.2 [**Computing Milieu**]: Social Issues – *Assistive technologies for persons with disabilities, Handicapped persons/special needs.*

General Terms

Design, Human Factors

Keywords

Haptics, haptic mouse, visually impaired, tactile graphics, Braille

1. INTRODUCTION

Visual graphics are used in a variety of applications at work, school, and in daily living to effectively communicate a wide range of information. Unfortunately, individuals who are blind and visually impaired cannot directly access this information. While word descriptions can be used to summarize graphics, certain advantages of using graphical information, such as the ability to discover patterns and spatial relationships, are lost. Tactile diagrams can be used instead or in addition to word descriptions so as to fully present the information to individuals who are blind and visually impaired. Particularly if many diagrams are needed, refreshable graphics displays can be more cost-effective, faster, and less cumbersome than traditional methods of creating tactile diagrams.

Currently, two types of mechanical refreshable displays exist. One type is a "full page" pin display which consists of a large matrix of pins that can move up and down (e.g., hyperBraille, Metec AG). Rotard and his colleagues (2005) have considered displaying Braille and graphics on these types of displays. However, these

displays are expensive due to the large number of pins needed and can be difficult to maintain, while still covering a relatively small total area. Their pin spacing (i.e., 2.5 mm for the hyperBraille) can also be limiting for presentation of tactile graphics. The other type of display consists of a small tactile display which move with the user's hand over a virtual diagram (e.g., [1-3]). These are less limiting for presentation of graphics since the span of the diagram is limited only by the position tracking system used. These systems are also more cost effective and easier to maintain because they contain less pins. In addition, these devices have the ability to resolve significantly finer position information, through motion of the hand.

The use of Braille is important for tactile graphics as the word labels used can be as important in interpreting a diagram as the graphics themselves. Currently, labels are commonly presented in multimedia systems through audition (e.g. Talking Tactile Tablet, Touch Graphics; [3]). However, there are few limitations to the use of speech: (1) it precludes access to labels for individuals who are deaf-blind, a small but underserved group; and (2) it presents social issues associated with the use or non-use of headphones. Therefore, being able to clearly interpret Braille on graphics displays is an important issue. In addition, for small moveable displays, if Braille is easily read, these devices can be used to access virtual, full pages of Braille at a much lower cost than traditional Braille.

Although small, moveable tactile display systems are beneficial in several ways, two key problems exist for presenting Braille on these smaller tactile displays. One difficulty is that if treated simply as a part of the diagram, the contact with the Braille is too quick to easily be interpreted. In a previous paper [6], we presented a method that modified the presentation method so that users could effectively interpret Braille. Another concern was that, even for paper tactile graphics, it can be difficult to separate the Braille from textures used in the graphic. However, textures are a very effective means of conveying information and so it is not desirable to exclude them from the diagram.

2. DEVICE

In this work we used a haptic display system previously developed in our laboratory that uses relays to select one of four possible amplitudes for each actuated pin [1]. Although displays that can vary continuously in amplitude do exist (e.g., [3]), they require expensive amplifiers to work. This low cost device has four main components: a Braille cell (P15, Metec AG) which houses a 2x4 pin array constituting the tactile interface, the electronics to drive it, an RF transmitter directly underneath the pin array to keep track of absolute position with a graphics tablet, and a mouse casing (Figure 1). The maximum amplitude level and the minimum amplitude level are fixed, but the middle two amplitudes can each be adjusted using a potentiometer.

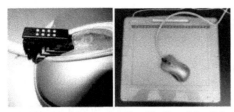

Figure 1. Tactile Mouse for Tactile Graphics Display

3. METHODS

We evaluated three different methods of presenting Braille in combination with graphics that used texture. Each map contained five 3 letter country abbreviations (where the letters were notrepeated between labels of a single diagram), borders between countries, and several textured areas which represented various features of the countries. Method 1 presented both the features and Braille at equal amplitude (the highest possible level). Method 2 also presented both the features and Braille at the highest possible amplitude level but with a box surrounding the 3 letter Braille abbreviation. Finally, method 3 presented the Braille at the highest possible amplitude level and the features at approximately half the amplitude.

Braille was presented using our previously developed method [5], where, within a 100x100 pixel area, a single Braille character would be presented independent of mouse movements. Stringing these boxes together with different Braille characters was used to form words. Textures were presented as either spatial square wave gratings or evenly spaced dot patterns. Borders of countries and states were presented with temporal square wave vibrations of 20 and 71 Hz, respectively.

Participants were asked to find the Braille labels on the diagram and then explore the respective country using the borders to determine which features it contained. Once the participant completed finding the Braille, reading the Braille, finding the features, and determining the features for each of the five countries on each map, the map was completed. The subject then answered a short questionnaire regarding that map and the ease of both finding and identifying the correct Braille letters and the map's features. The total time to complete the map was recorded for each map.

For this study, participants were required to be proficient in reading grade one Braille. For each method, questions were asked about two maps drawn in a counterbalanced manner across subjects from a pool of six. The two maps for each method were presented in blocks, counterbalanced across subjects. A training map was given before each block so the subject was familiar with the method being presented and using the device for that particular method.

Because of the small sample size, non-parametric methods, such as the related-samples Friedman's two-way analysis of variance by ranks, were used for the analysis.

4. RESULTS

There were nine participants, ages 19-59, approximately half of whom were completely blind and half with low vision, with the age of onset being from birth to only a couple of years.

In terms of performance, the number correct for finding and reading Braille, performance was 100% and close to 100% respectively. No statistical difference was found between methods. However, there was a statistical difference between methods for finding and identifying the graphical features ($p=0.048$). Further analysis showed that method 3 did significantly worse than other methods ($p=0.042$ for method 1 and $p=0.017$ for method 2), but there was no significant difference between methods 1 and 2. Finally, in terms of total time taken, there was no difference between the three methods.

In terms of usability, there was no statistically significant difference between the methods in terms of ease of finding the Braille ($p=0.508$) or ease of identifying the Braille ($p=0.368$). The method used did have an effect, however, on the usability of finding features ($p=0.020$) and correctly identifying them ($p=0.006$). It was found that Method 3 was significantly more difficult to find features than Method 1 ($p=0.006$); however, no other differences were significant. Method 3 also did statistically worse than Methods 1 ($p=0.007$) and 2 ($p = 0.041$) in identifying the features, although there was no significant difference between Methods 1 and 2.

5. DISCUSSION

While finding Braille with the tactile mouse was successful with all methods, displaying Braille and graphics alongside one another created difficulty for certain methods of presentation. In contrary to our original expectations, when Braille and graphics were displayed at different amplitudes (Method 3), it performed the poorest and subjects found it difficult to find and identify features. This could be because the lower amplitude level was insufficient stimulation for identifying graphics (however, higher amplitudes were difficult to discriminate from the maximum level). We had expected Method 1 to be the poorest performing and most difficult method as we expected, like for paper graphics, the user could easily confuse the Braille letters for textures. Contrary to what we expected, Methods 1 and 2 were much better in terms of performance and ease of use. This may be because there was already a large difference between the presentation of Braille, which was static over a small area, from that of graphics, which created vibrations as the mouse moved across them.

Thus, it recommended that the simplest method to use, Method 1, be used to present Braille. This is also more cost-effective, as it does not require the additional electronics needed to present the multiple amplitudes.

6. ACKNOWLEDGMENTS

This work is funded by NSF CBET Grant #0754629.

7. REFERENCES

[1] Headley, P., and Pawluk, D. 2010. A Low-Cost, Variable Amplitude Haptic Distributed Display for Persons who are Blind and Visually Impaired. ASSETS'10, October 25–27, Orlando, Florida.

[2] K. Rovira and O. Gapenne. 2009. Tactile Classification of Traditional and Computerized Media in Three Who Are Blind. Journal of Visual Impairment and Blindness. July, 430-435.

[3] Petit, G., Defresne, A., Levesque, V., Hayward, V. and Trudeau, N. 2008. Refreshable Tactile Graphics Applied to Schoolbook Illustrations for Students with Visual Impairment. ASSETS 2008, October 13-15, Halifax, Canada.

[4] Rotard, M., Knodler, S. and Ertl, T. (2005). A Tactile Web Browser For the Visually Disabled Proceedings of the 16th ACM Conference n Hypertext and Hypermedia, 6-9 September, 15-22.

[5] Headley, P., V. Hribar, and D. Pawluk 2011. Displaying Braille and Graphics on a Mouse-like Tactile Display. ASSETS'11, October 24–26, Dundee, Scotland.

A Participatory Design Workshop on Accessible Apps and Games with Students with Learning Differences

Lisa Anthony[1], Sapna Prasad[2], Amy Hurst[1], Ravi Kuber[1]

[1]UMBC Information Systems
1000 Hilltop Circle
Baltimore MD 21250 USA

[2]Landmark College Institute for Research and Training
1 River Road South
Putney VT 05346 USA

lanthony@umbc.edu, SapnaPrasad@landmark.edu, amyhurst@umbc.edu, rkuber@umbc.edu

ABSTRACT

This paper describes a Science-Technology-Engineering-Mathematics (STEM) outreach workshop conducted with post-secondary students diagnosed with learning differences, including Learning Disabilities (LD), Attention Deficit / Hyperactivity Disorders (AD/HD), and/or Autism Spectrum Disorders (ASD). In this workshop, students were actively involved in participatory design exercises such as data gathering, identifying accessible design requirements, and evaluating mobile applications and games targeted for diverse users. This hands-on experience broadened students' understanding of STEM areas, provided them with an opportunity to see themselves as computer scientists, and demonstrated how they might succeed in computing careers, especially in human-centered computing and interface design. Lessons learned from the workshop also offer useful insight on conducting participatory design with this unique population.

Categories and Subject Descriptors

K.4.2 [**Computers and Society**] Social Issues – *assistive technologies for persons with disabilities*.

General Terms

Design, Human Factors.

Keywords

Participatory design, learning differences, cognitive disabilities, accessibility, STEM, education, human-computer interaction.

1. INTRODUCTION

One of the most pervasive obstacles to STEM education for many students is access [1], particularly for students with LD, AD/HD and ASD. Research in STEM education finds it essential for these students to participate in group problem solving and to follow common scientific practices in their courses so they have the practical experience to inform their consideration of a STEM major [1]. These immersion and inquiry-based experiences offer students, regardless of ability, time to test their own understanding and reasoning skills [2], and empower them to create a self-portrait of being successful in STEM [3].

We held a workshop at Landmark College designed to engage post-secondary students, all of whom self-identify with one or more learning difference (LD, AD/HD or ASD), and to stimulate their interest in computing fields. Faculty and graduate students from UMBC facilitated participatory design (PD), a frequently

used design method in computing fields such as human-centered computing (HCC), to equip Landmark students to evaluate accessible mobile applications ("apps") and games. PD focuses on designers collaborating directly with intended users throughout the design and development process [4]; users are empowered to make decisions about the design as a part of the team. Researchers have worked with diverse user groups, including users with visual impairments [5] or memory impairments (e.g., aphasia, amnesia) [6], aiming to understand how to promote their involvement in the design process. Design methods often must be adapted to support the abilities of the target users, sometimes significantly [6]. Attentional and learning disabilities present a somewhat unique challenge in PD, requiring a focus on hands-on activities and frequent breaks, which we incorporated into our workshop.

The main goals of the workshop were (a) to enable UMBC students to better understand the needs of individuals with learning differences, and (b) to help Landmark students to gain an understanding of the interaction design process and to develop skills which they might perform in an HCC-related role.

2. WORKSHOP DESIGN

The one-day workshop was divided into three sessions. In the morning, we introduced the concepts of HCC and PD. We emphasized how HCC takes into account users' individual needs, preferences, and abilities when designing technology. As an ice-breaker and to gauge the interests of the Landmark students, we led a group discussion about their opinions on apps, games, and technology. This discussion also helped empower the Landmark students to feel that they had expertise to contribute in the design activities. In the afternoon, students interacted with the app and game prototypes in small, self-chosen teams (4 Landmark students and 1 or 2 UMBC researchers). After two PD sessions, the UMBC students presented how the designs had evolved that day. The day ended with group reflection, and the Landmark students completed surveys about their experience.

PD teams worked for 60 minutes with each of 2 (out of 4) game prototypes, developed for individuals with learning differences and multiple disabilities in a UMBC graduate-level Assistive Technology class. More information about the prototypes can be found at http://landmarkandumbc.wordpress.com/. The PD teams were introduced to the prototypes and asked to think of ways to strengthen the existing designs, to make them more usable, or to make the interaction experience more engaging. UMBC students facilitated the sessions, demonstrating the apps through both low- and high-fidelity prototypes. For example, working prototypes of the apps were demonstrated, and paper screenshots were also used. Teams captured ideas using both public (whiteboards and easels) and private (sheets of paper) record-keeping materials

Figure 1. Graduate students facilitated the PD sessions, asking questions, showing prototypes and capturing ideas.

(Figure 1). The second design session extended the designs of the group who had evaluated the same prototype in the first session.

A total of 12 Landmark students participated in the workshop (2 females, 7 STEM majors), aged 18-22. All participants self-reported having two or more disabilities (9 students reported AD/HD, 5 students reported LD, and 4 students reported ASD).

3. LESSONS LEARNED

The workshop evaluation surveys revealed that the students felt they had had engaging, inquiry-driven conversations with the UMBC faculty and graduate students. According to all of the Landmark students, the PD sessions were the most interesting portion of the workshop, and for some, this experience either increased or confirmed their consideration of STEM careers. The surveys also revealed that the students enjoyed relating HCC methods to their own lives and interests. Observationally, Landmark students were enthusiastic about being team members, engaging in critical thinking, and giving feedback on how to make the apps and games more accessible for diverse users. The use of the hands-on PD method enabled these students to remain engaged, attentive and responsive throughout the activity. Small groups of 3 to 4 students allowed teamwork while still enabling each student to feel included. Of note is that the students became personally invested in the design process. Follow-up surveys indicated these positive feelings were retained after the workshop.

In designing such educational experiences, we recommend the consideration of (a) **communicative differences**, (b) **visual or verbal thinking**, (c) **personal context**, and (d) **inclusive empowerment**. For example, we developed strategies to encourage discussion between individuals with difficulties **communicating** with one another by focusing on small group interactions. Students were more willing to contribute their ideas during small group sessions compared to the large group session, and were more open to peer-instruction within the small groups. Second, students preferred either **visual or verbal** approaches to design. Some had little difficulty describing their design ideas, whereas others opted to diagrammatically represent ideas which were challenging to verbalize (Figure 2, sketched as the student described his ideas for the app). Third, relating the tasks to the **context** of students' daily lives (e.g., using apps and games) also helped generate student interest. The students were able to contextualize the designs, offering personal insights into how the applications would meet their own needs or the needs of their peers. Fourth, we aimed to be **inclusive**; by using both working prototypes and paper prototypes, every member of the team was hands-on during design activities. We suggest bringing multiples of each prototype: some students strongly identified with the working prototypes, while others preferred paper.

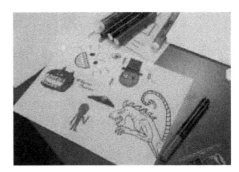

Figure 2. Image of drawings that students created while thinking about the design of a mobile app.

Based on our workshop, to implement a PD approach to teach STEM concepts or to generate STEM interest in students with learning differences, we believe that accessibility, novelty, and student decision-making must be incorporated into the lesson. Structuring the workshop in a hands-on approach allows students to come up with their own questions and gather data, imperative to make these topics accessible to students with learning differences. We hypothesize that students' personal investment resulted from several factors: (1) increased awareness of the methods employed by scientists, (2) recognition of the practical applications of PD, (3) understanding limitations of current technology, and (4) appreciation of the impact that computing fields have on the daily lives of diverse user populations.

Prior work has established the benefits for HCC students to participate in educational activities to increase their awareness of designing for disability [7]. This workshop focuses on the reciprocal relationship of including PD in STEM outreach for students with disabilities. We anticipate building on and refining this model in future PD workshops for students with learning differences to stimulate interest in computing fields and STEM.

4. ACKNOWLEDGEMENTS

Workshop funded by the Alliance for Access to Computing Careers (AccessComputing@UW, National Science Foundation (NSF) CISE BPC awards #CNS-0540615, CNS-0837508, CNS-1042260). The authors thank Geoff Burgess, Michelle Bower, Patrick Carrington, Flynn Wolf, Barbara Linam-Church, and Kirk Norman for support running the workshop.

5. REFERENCES

[1] Burgstahler, S. 2002. Universal design of distance learning. *Information Technology and Disabilities* 8, 1 (2002).

[2] Melber, L., & Brown, K. 2008. "Not like a regular science class": Informal science education for students with disabilities. *The Clearing House* 82, 1 (2008), 35.

[3] Wieman, C. & Perkins, K. 2005. Transforming physics education. *Physics Today* 58, 11 (2005).

[4] Ellis, R. D. & Kurniawan, S. 2000. Increasing the usability of online information for older users: a case study in participatory design. *Intl. J. Hum-Comput Int* 12, 2 (2000), 263-276.

[5] Kuber, R., Yu, W. & McAllister, G. 2007. Towards developing assistive haptic feedback for visually impaired internet users. In *Proc. CHI 2007*, 1525–1534.

[6] Wu, M., Richards, B., & Baecker, R. 2004. Participatory design with individuals who have amnesia. In *Proc. PDC 2004 Vol. 1*, 214-223.

[7] Kurniawan, S.H., Arteaga, S., & Manduchi, R. 2010. A general education course on universal access, disability, technology and society. In *Proc. ASSETS 2010*, 11-18.

Hybrid Auditory Feedback: A New Method for Mobility Assistance of the Visually Impaired

Ibrar Hussain, Ling Chen, Hamid Turab Mirza, Abdul Majid, and Gencai Chen

Zhejiang University
College of Computer Science
Hangzhou, P.R. China, +86-0571-87953052
{ibrar, lingchen, hamid306, majid, chengc}@zju.edu.cn

ABSTRACT

In this paper we present a novel concept of hybrid auditory feedback in mobility assistance for people with visual disabilities in indoor environment. Hybrid auditory feedback is a gradual conversion of sound from speech-only to non-speech (i.e., spearcons) based on the sound repetitiveness and the users' frequency of the travelled route. Using a within-subject design, eight participants carried out a task using a mobility assistant application and followed a same route for few days. Preliminary results suggest that hybrid sounds in auditory feedback are more effective than non-speech and are pleasant compared to speech-only.

Categories and Subject Descriptors

H.5.2 **[Information and Presentation]**: User Interfaces - auditory feedback, K.4.2 **[Computers and Society]**: Social Issues – assistive technologies for persons with disabilities.

General Terms

Design, Experimentation, Human Factors

Keywords

Speech, non-speech, hybrid, auditory feedback, mobility assistance, visually impaired.

1. INTRODUCTION

People with visual disabilities mainly rely on the audio for the delivery of information in mobility assistant applications. For example, a museum guide [2] which helps visually impaired in indoor navigation has a vocal user interface (VUI) for auditory feedback. It exploits an embedded Text-to-Speech engine for the feedback and transmits information about describing artworks/sections and giving direction tips on the fly. Though, speech sound is used as an auditory feedback in mobility assistance and ubiquitous computing applications, however, sometimes repetitive speech-only instructions become annoying and irritating. On the contrary, non-speech audio cues (i.e., spearcons) are short and pleasant. Spearcons are created by speeding up a spoken phrase until it is not recognized as speech [3]. However, they are inadequate in presenting crucial and detailed information.

Our work is primarily based on the assumption that; gradual conversion of sound feedback, from speech to non-speech with respect to sound repetitiveness, route travelled frequency, and users comfort may result in improved mobility experience. By combining the good aspects and eliminating the inadequacies of speech and non-speech sound, we come up with the concept of 'hybrid auditory feedback' in mobility assistant applications for people with visual disabilities. Hence, the diminished or lack of the visual channel as a source of information for users with visual disabilities is compensated for with the information obtained from sense of hearing. It is for this reason that the auditory feedback that a user gets should convey meaningful information along with the minimal irritation caused in the users' ear. Therefore, we are providing user with an auditory feedback in hybrid sound. This may result in better user experience compared to speech and non-speech.

Following is a real life scenario that highlights the significance of our approach in auditory feedback. For instance, Simon is visually impaired and an employee in a company, his office is on 2nd floor. Since, every day when he enters the office building he follows the same path. Thus, over period of time speech instruction becomes very repeating/ irritating. Therefore, gradually our proposed method converts all the speech instructions to non-speech. This makes the experience less irritable. Same goes, from his desk to washroom, his desk to lunch room etc. However, once every month he needs to go to 1st floor to submit his monthly bills. This is obviously not his very frequent/regular path. Auditory feedback on less frequent path may remain as human speech; however, over the time and with the users' familiarity of the environment, our technique will gradually convert the speech-only instructions to non-speech.

2. PROPOSED METHOD

In this work, we propose a new form of sound, i.e., "hybrid audio". Based on the measures such as, (i) sound repetitiveness, and (ii) route travelled frequency. We propose a method to gradually achieve the right mix between speech and non-speech sound for an individual. Our criterion for sound conversion, are:

a) Sound feedback on frequently traveled path of a user can be changed to non-speech sound.

b) Repetitive instructions (e.g., *"...rotate left...", "... carry on in this direction", "Please, stop!"* etc.) can be converted to non-speech.

c) Dynamic/frequent changing information may remain as speech.

Consider a phrase, which is divided into two parts:

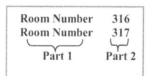

Figure 1 Identifying repetitive part (i.e., part 1) and dynamic part (i.e., part 2) in feedback instruction

Figure 1 shows an example, where 'Part 1' remains constant and there is no change in representation. However, 'Part 2' is dynamic and it keeps on changing (e.g., 316, 317). In hybrid auditory feedback, the repetitive part (i.e., part 1) will be gradually changed to non-speech and less repetitive/dynamic part (i.e., part 2) will remain as speech-only. However, over period of time and with users' familiarity to the environment, our method will also convert (e.g., gradually increasing the frequency of speech) the dynamic part of speech phrase from human speech to non-speech.

3. PRELIMINARY STUDY

We carried out a preliminary study to better understand the user experience with audio listening for indoor mobility assistance. We hypothesized that hybrid auditory feedback in mobility assistant applications are less-irritative than repetitive speech-only and conveys meaningful information compared to non-speech. We recruited eight people (5 male, 3 female, average age=23.38, SD=2.63) for the study. Participants were recruited via local blind organization and via word of mouth. All participants were employed for the period of 10 days for the experiment.

Each participant had given a task, which was that every participant had to walk in a hallway, approximately 230 meters in length on a ground floor of the building, having several doors and turns by the time destination is reached. Every day the task had to be repeated ten times, during 0900 – 1200 hours. Before the commencement of a task, participants were provided with the mobility assistant application, like Navatar [1], deployed on smart phone. They were requested to observe the audio listening during the entire task. There were three listening conditions: speech-only; hybrid and non-speech. At the end of each task, all participants were provided with the questionnaire that had five measures of the impression of the task for each type of audio listening. The numbers in parentheses refer to the scores of a 7-level assessment. Feeling good(7) – Uncomfortable(1), Enjoyed (7) – Painful(1), Love(7) – Hatred(1), Funny(7) – Bored(1), Calm (7) – Annoyed(1). In addition to the questions asked, data regarding their choice of audio listening was also recorded.

3.1 Results and Discussion

The result was analyzed using one-way analysis of variance (ANOVA) and within-subjects design. The independent variable is feedback factor (i.e., non-speech (NF), Speech-only (SF), hybrid (HF). In particular, for "Feeling good–Uncomfortable", a statistical test showed that SF and NF are uncomfortable than HF ($F_{(2,14)}=9.23$, $p<0.01$). For "Love–Hatred", a statistical test demonstrated that SF and NF are more dislikeable than HF ($F_{(2,14)}=8.70$, $p<0.01$). For "Calm–Annoyed", a statistical test illustrated that participants were more annoyed with SF and NF compared to HF ($F_{(2,14)}=15.95$, $p<0.01$). For "Enjoyed–Painful", a statistical test depicted that SF and NF were painful than HF ($F_{(2,14)}=14.29$, $p<0.01$). There was no difference in HF compared with NF and SF for "Funny–Bored" ($F_{(2,14)}=3.27$, $p<0.10$).

From the results and posterior interview held with participants, it is observed that hybrid sound is convenient compared to non-speech and more enjoyable compared to repetitive speech-only. A possible explanation for this might be that non-speech cannot possibly convey meaningful information of the immediate indoor environment. Secondly, human-speech takes longer time and with the repetition, it becomes irritative, compared to hybrid, which at the same time take less time and produces minimal irritation in user ears.

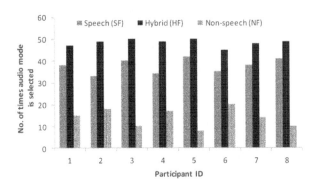

Figure 2 Audio mode selection in the auditory feedback over period of time using same path

The results in Figure 2 show that on the whole, each participant listened to the auditory feedback hundred times in the experiment. It is noted that initially participants preferred listening to speech as an auditory feedback. However, over the period of time and with the users' familiarity to the environment, they changed the listening feedback mode from speech to hybrid. In comparison, participants listened to non-speech audio fewer times than speech and hybrid.

4. CONCLUSIONS AND FUTURE WORK

In this paper, we introduced a new concept of using hybrid sound for feedback purposes in mobility assistance for people with visual disabilities. Though, speech sound seems to be an obvious choice for auditory feedback. However, repeated use of speech sound produces irritation in user ears. On the other hand, relying only on non-speech sound is also not very helpful and can miss to represent critical information. However, with the introduction of hybrid sound, the irritation in users' ear can be lessened and it can also represent dynamic information to the visually impaired. Furthermore, preliminary result from the experiment and interview with the participant's shows that hybrid sound is understandable compared to non-speech; less-irritative and convenient compared to speech-only and effective compared to other auditory cues. Future user studies will include a large number of visually impaired users, and hybrid sound will be evaluated while navigating in more complex indoor environment.

5. ACKNOWLEDGMENTS

This research is funded by the Ministry of Industry and Information Technology of China (No.2010ZX01042-002-003-001), the Natural Science Foundation of China (No. 60703040), the Zhejiang Provincial Natural Science Foundation of China (No.Y107178), Department of Science and Technology Zhejiang Province (Nos. 2007C13019, 2011C13042).

6. REFERENCES

[1] Fallah, N., Apostolopoulos, I., Bekris, K., and Folmer, E.2012. The user as a sensor: navigating users with visual impairments in indoor spaces using tactile landmarks. *In CHI*. ACM, Austin, Texas, USA, 425-432.

[2] Ghiani, G., Leporini, B., and Paternò, F. 2008. Supporting orientation for blind people using museum guides. *Ext.Abstracts CHI*. ACM, New York, USA, 3417-3422.

[3] Walker, B.N., Nance, A., and Lindsay, J. 2006. Spearcons: speech-based earcons improve navigation performance in auditory menus. *In Proceedings of the 12th International Conference on Auditory Display(ICAD)*, London, UK, 63-68.

ClickerAID: A Tool for Efficient Clicking Using Intentional Muscle Contractions

Torsten Felzer
Inst. for Mechatronic Systems
Techn. Universität Darmstadt
Petersenstr. 30, D-64287 Darmstadt, Germany
felzer@ims.tu-darmstadt.de

Stephan Rinderknecht
Inst. for Mechatronic Systems
Techn. Universität Darmstadt
Petersenstr. 30, D-64287 Darmstadt, Germany
rinderknecht@ims.tu-darmstadt.de

ABSTRACT

This is to propose a demo and poster about a tool designed to assist persons who are temporarily or permanently unable to reliably operate the buttons of a physical pointing device, for example because of tenosynovitis (TSV). It monitors a dedicated muscle of the user and emulates a click event at the current position of the mouse pointer in response to a contraction of that muscle (as small as raising the eyebrow). The ClickType (= type of the click) – left, right, single, double, drag – is selected by the user (who is also responsible for moving the mouse pointer) and stays valid until the selection of a new one.

Categories and Subject Descriptors

H.5.2 [**Information Interfaces and Presentation**]: User Interfaces—*Input devices and strategies*; K.4.2 [**Computers and Society**]: Social Issues—*Assistive technologies for persons with disabilities*

General Terms

Human Factors

Keywords

Human-computer interaction, mouse clicks, intentional muscle contractions, eye tracker, tenosynovitis, layered windows

1. INTRODUCTION

Many persons with physical disabilities have problems using the standard keyboard to operate a computer. An idea that is followed in various alternative solutions is to replace the keyboard with some form of pointing device.

A prominent example is an eye tracker, which allows its user to move the mouse pointer across an on-screen keyboard by altering the point of gaze. If the user is unable to press buttons on a physical device, there are several options for selecting the target pointed to. For eye tracking, the most common method is dwelling, meaning that a target is selected if the pointer rests over it for a certain amount of time. However, this dwell time limits the information transfer rate [2]. Alternatives include speech recognition [3], eye blinks [4], and tooth clicks [5].

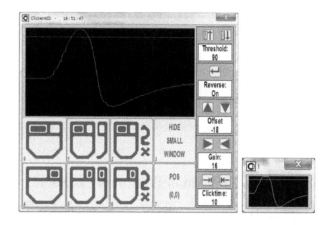

Figure 1: Left: Configuration window offering to select desired ClickType and to adjust muscle activity curve; Right: Small version of activity curve.

ClickerAID is another example in this line of research. It uses intentional muscle contractions, yet not relying on any particular muscle. The user decides what works best for her or him (eyebrow, jaw, cheek, chin, etc.), which makes the system very flexible.

2. SYSTEM DESCRIPTION

2.1 General Behavior

The user first decides for a suitable muscle group that he or she is able to reliably control at will (e.g., the brow muscle). The muscular activity of that muscle group is then acquired with the help of a piezoelectric sensor put in contact with the skin directly over the muscle and, in the brow example, kept in place with a flexible headband. ClickerAID finally compares the intensity of the input signal to an adjustable threshold. Whenever the threshold is exceeded, the software detects a contraction event and executes a corresponding code segment (resulting in the emulation of a mouse click).

If the time interval between two consecutive contraction events is shorter than a certain parameter, the second contraction is regarded as the final part of a 'double contraction' and triggers a different program reaction – to be detailed in the poster.

2.2 Program Configuration

The configuration window (shown in fig. 1) consists of three parts: the curve showing the activity of the dedicated muscle on a black background, several large buttons for selecting the ClickType (as well as hiding and positioning the small window), and a vertical strip on the right for adjusting the muscle activity curve.

The goal of adjusting the activity curve is to ensure that the user is able to intentionally and reliably issue contraction events, which are characterized by the curve exceeding the threshold. The adjustment (which should be done with the assistance of a caregiver) only needs to be done once.

Once the activity curve is properly adjusted, the user chooses the type of clicks she or he wishes to issue. The software supports three types of left clicks (single, drag, and double) and the same types of right clicks. Clicking on the button with the symbol representing the desired ClickType makes the configuration window disappear.

A much smaller window informing the user about the live muscle signal appears, and from that point forward, the program generates the desired click whenever the user issues a contraction. When the user needs a different ClickType, he or she reopens the configuration window by clicking on the small window.

2.3 Choosing the Small Window's Location

The bottom right button opens a semi-transparent window with a grid showing possible locations and crosshairs marking the currently chosen location overlaid over the desktop (see fig. 2).

The crosshairs move with the mouse pointer. After a final click, the small window (as exemplified in the right part of fig. 1) appears at the location in the center of the crosshairs (which simultaneously disappear, of course).

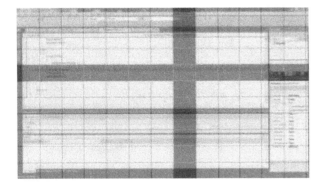

Figure 2: Grid and crosshairs to indicate the desired location of the small window.

The purpose of the small window is to provide the user with some visual feedback about the ongoing muscle signal and about the detected contraction events (it also flashes highlighting these instants). In addition, the small window indicates the currently selected ClickType in its title bar.

3. PARTICIPATORY DESIGN

The tool was inspired by "Ethan", a 30-year-old law student, who has tenosynovitis since age 22. Ethan came to us a few months ago, because he had heard of our eyebrow-operated HaMCoS (= HAnds-free Mouse COntrol System) prototype from 2008 [1]. Ethan uses speech recognition as keyboard replacement, but for pointer manipulation, he is much more efficient using a physical pointing device – unfortunately, clicking is very painful for him after some time.

However, HaMCoS offers clicking in conjunction with pointer movement. When needed for clicking only, it is not really a viable alternative. To help Ethan, we decided to rewrite parts of the code, exclusively concentrating on clicking. Ethan finally reviewed the outcome in a second meeting. One of the first things he said was: "I can't wait to play that video game [...] I had to neglect because of my troubles." He indicated that ClickerAID exactly meets his needs, and that he will gladly adopt it for his future work.

4. CONCLUSION

This paper described ClickerAID, a tool emulating clicks of a two-button mouse device in response to tiny contractions of a dedicated muscle of the user. The system therefore allows its user to 'quickly click without physically clicking' and requires only a minimum amount of physical effort. It is ideal for anyone who has problems with physical clicking, no matter what the cause for that handicap might be.

The user is responsible for moving the mouse pointer to the location where he or she intends to issue a click. For example, the tool could be used in combination with a touchscreen surface, where pointing can be done very easily, but where clicking is particularly challenging for persons with physical disabilities due to a lack of haptic feedback. Or it could be used in combination with a tracking device (e.g., an eye tracker) to eliminate the dwell time needed for selection.

5. ACKNOWLEDGMENTS

This work is part of a larger project concerning an assistive text entry and computer operation solution. It is financially supported by DFG grant FE 936/6-1.

6. REFERENCES

[1] T. Felzer and R. Nordmann. Evaluating the Hands-Free Mouse Control System: An Initial Case Study. In *Proc. ICCHP '08*, pages 1188–1195. Springer, 2008.

[2] P. O. Kristensson and K. Vertanen. The potential of dwell-free eye-typing for fast assistive gaze communication. In *Proc. ETRA '12*, pages 241–244. ACM, 2012.

[3] F. Loewenich and F. Maire. Hands-free mouse-pointer manipulation using motion-tracking and speech recognition. In *Proc. OZCHI '07*, pages 295–302. ACM, 2007.

[4] P. Mistry, K. Ishii, M. Inami, and T. Igarashi. BlinkBot – Look at, Blink and Move. In *Proc. UIST '10*, pages 397–398. ACM, 2010.

[5] X. A. Zhao, E. D. Guestrin, D. Sayenko, T. Simpson, M. Gauthier, and M. R. Popovic. Typing with eye-gaze and tooth-clicks. In *Proc. ETRA '12*, pages 341–344. ACM, 2012.

Assistive System Experiment Designer ASED: A Toolkit for the Quantitative Evaluation of Enhanced Assistive Systems for Impaired Persons in Production

Oliver Korn
University of Applied
Sciences Esslingen,
Kanalstr. 33,
73728 Esslingen, Germany
oliver.korn@
hs-esslingen.de

Albrecht Schmidt
University of Stuttgart, VIS,
Pfaffenwaldring 5a
70569 Stuttgart, Germany
albrecht.schmidt@
vis.uni-stuttgart.de

Thomas Hörz
University of Applied
Sciences Esslingen,
Kanalstr. 33,
73728 Esslingen, Germany
thomas.hoerz@
hs-esslingen.de

Daniel Kaupp
University of Stuttgart,
Keplerstraße 7,
70174 Stuttgart, Germany
kauppdl@
studi.informatik.
uni-stuttgart.de

ABSTRACT

This paper introduces the toolkit ASED: Assistive System Experiment Designer. Combining a specially constructed assembly table and new software it allows measuring the performance of impaired persons when using assistive systems for production environments (ASiPE). The ASiPE design tested using ASED transgresses the state of the art by three enhancements. With the help of ASED we are able to quantify and rank their effects on work quality and performance. The ASED toolkit, however, is not confined to the design tested but can be used for the experimental analysis of every kind of manual process.

Categories and Subject Descriptors

H.5.2 [**User Interfaces**]: Evaluation/methodology, Interaction styles, User-centered design H.1.2 [**User/Machine Systems**]: Human factors, Human information processing, Software Psychology; H.5.1 [**Multimedia Information Systems**] Evaluation/methodology, Artificial, augmented, and virtual realities; H5.m [**Miscellaneous**]: HCI; I.2.10 [**Vision and Scene Understanding**]: Motion; K.4.2 [**Social Issues**]: Assistive technologies for persons with disabilities

Keywords

Assistive technology, Evaluation, User-Centered Design, Human Computer Interaction (HCI), Motion Recognition, Disabled

1. INTRODUCTION

Working in manual production requires the repeated performance of a sequence of tasks with high accuracy at a reasonable speed. The permanent repetition of a single or very few of these assembly sequences makes this kind of work prone to becoming dull, even for cognitively impaired workers who may have to retrain the task at the next morning. This underutilization leads to "boredom and a feeling of lacking appreciation" [1: 29], reduced motivation and increases the likeliness of mistakes.

2. STATE OF THE ART

Current computer-based assistive systems in production environments (ASiPE) focus on the quality control of work results rather than the support of the worker in the process. The few systems offering process support focus on controlling the workers' "picks" from boxes (fig. 1, green) and describing the upcoming steps of the current assembly sequence.

3. REQUIREMENTS

In our research we have studied the requirements for future ASiPE that address the needs of cognitively impaired persons more aptly [2, 3, 4]. Systems being able to take into account both the context and the user in real time would offer better assistance, more security and potentially more fun. To achieve this, the following requirements have to be met:

1. process-orientation (additional to result-orientation)
2. natural interaction (additional to haptic displays)
3. display of relevant information directly at the workplace (in-situ projection)
4. integration of motivating mechanisms (gamification)

In order to test if a new ASiPE meets these requirements in studies with cognitively impaired users, ASED needs to support motion detection (requirements 1 and 2), in-situ projection and gamification. To quantify the effect of each potential enhancement on work performance and work quality, ASED supports both setting-up experiments and logging all relevant user data. The quantification of individual enhancements then allows prioritizing their realization within the development process.

4. ASED: EXPERIMENTAL TABLE

ASED is based on a regular assembly table – however, the complexity has been lowered by reducing it to the core elements: a work space and several boxes for assembly parts (fig. 1, 2).

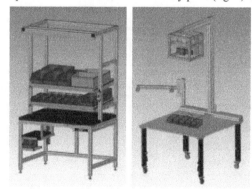

Figure 1. A regular assembly table (left) and the assembly table constructed for ASED (right)

The base to the left holds a monitor with a haptic display required to map state of the art assistive systems which use touch screens. It also displays the gamification elements. The top mount construction holds the sensor used for motion detection (currently a Kinect) and the projector used for the in-situ projection.

Figure 2. A worker in an experiment designed by ASED

The projector is fixed 1.4 meters above the work area to provide sufficient lens coverage for the working area and to ensure that workers with cognitive impairments are not irritated. The table's height is adjustable to provide equal conditions for wheelchair-bound persons. To allow experiments at various sheltered work organizations, the table has to be dismountable for transport.

5. ASED: SOFTWARE

The ASED software component has been developed to allow measuring performance in a wide range of manual work processes. It relies strongly on the benefits of motion recognition: marker-less real-time analysis of human body movement [5]. By using motion recognition, the work processes become transparent and can be analyzed and visualized in real-time – a prerequisite for gamification and context-specific in-situ projection.

ASED provides an easy and effective way for setting-up experiments (figure 2). At first 3-dimensional boxes are defined as "trigger areas". These areas are then observed by the depth-sensor of the Kinect. In the second step "causes and effects" are assigned. A cause can be the passage of a user's hand through a trigger area or just the exceeding of a time limit. ASED also allows events like hand gestures or triggers for the gamification element. Currently the effects 'jump to process step', 'create timestamp' and 'trigger external action' are implemented.

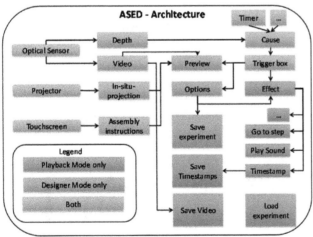

Figure 3. Architecture of the ASED software

For each process step ASED allows configuring what the touchscreen and by the projector show. Multimedia contents (images, sound, and video) can be included easily. Once the design phase of an experiment is completed, it can be saved as an XML-file and run using ASED's playback component. The following sequence illustrates a typical experiment cycle:

- the experiment is initialized by assigning a user ID
- ASED runs a short configuration cycle to adjust projector and Kinect
- the experiment starts with the first assembly instruction
- the touchscreen shows the instruction, while the projector highlights the relevant box to pick from
- motion detection observes the relevant trigger areas
- once the user's hand enters a trigger area, the sum of the z-values measured by the motion detection system changes significantly
- once a trigger is activated , the effects are initiated
- in case of an error timestamps are generated when the hand enters and when it leaves the wrong trigger area

This exemplary scenario shows ASED's potential: it allows designing as wide a range of causes and effects as the experiment requires. However it also is designed to save the data integrity and restrict changes which affect the comparability of the results after the experiment started. As a backup for the analysis, ASED does not only save the timestamps but also the video stream for later analysis. Thus statistical outliers can be cross-checked by comparing the timestamps with the video stream.

6. CONCLUSION

We introduced the ASED toolkit for empirical studies measuring the performance of workers using assistive systems in production environments. The toolkit has been specifically designed to help researchers in the field of assistive technologies for persons with impairments or disabilities. It combines a compact table and new software integrating motion detection to automate the evaluation of human movements. Thus it offers support and standardization potential for research on accessibility and ergonomics.

7. NEXT STEPS

The next steps will be to complete the main study on the enhanced ASiPE until the middle of 2013. During this time the ASED software will be improved to support additional requirements.

8. ACKNOWLEDGMENTS

Our thanks go to the company "Schnaithmann Maschinenbau GmbH" for building the experimental table and to the sheltered work organization in Heilbronn for supporting the tests.

9. REFERENCES

[1] McGonigal, J.: *Reality is Broken: Why Games Make Us Better and How They Can Change the World*, London: Random House, 2011

[2] Korn, O.: Industrial Playgrounds. How Gamification Helps to Enrich Work for Elderly or Impaired Persons in Production, *Proceedings of the ACM EICS 2012*

[3] Brach, M. & Korn, O.: Assistive Technologies at Home and in the Workplace – A Field of Research for Exercise Science and Human Movement Science. *EURAPA (European Review of Aging and Physical Activity)*, vol. 9, 2012

[4] Korn, O.; Schmidt, A.; Hörz, T.: Assistive Systems in Production Environments: Exploring Motion Recognition and Gamification *Proceedings of the ACM PETRA 12*

[5] Shotton, J.; Fitzgibbon, A.; Cook, M.; Sharp, T.; Finocchio, M.; Moore, R.; Kipman, A.; Blake, A.: Real-Time Human Pose Recognition in Parts from Single Depth Images. *Proceedings of the IEEE CVPR* 2011

Optimizing Gaze Typing for People with Severe Motor Disabilities: The iWriter Arabic Interface

Areej Al-Wabil, Arwa Al-Issa, Itisam Hazzaa, May Al-Humaimeedi, Lujain Al-Tamimi,
Bushra Al-Kadhi

Software Engineering Department, College of Computer Science, King Saud University, Saudi Arabia
aalwabil@ksu.edu.sa

ABSTRACT

Communication in the Arabic language with gaze using dwell time has been made possible by the development of eye typing interfaces. This paper describes the design process for developing iWriter, an Arabic gaze communication system. Design considerations for the optimization of the gaze typing interfaces for Arabic script are discussed.

Categories and Subject Descriptors

K.4.2 [**Social Issues**]: Assistive technologies for persons with disabilities; H.5.2. [**Information interfaces and presentation**]: User Interfaces - Evaluation/methodology

Keywords

Augmentative and Alternative Communication; Severe Motor Disability, AAC, Gaze communication, Locked-in syndrome, eye typing, eye tracking.

1. INTRODUCTION

A growing societal recognition for the needs of individuals with severe motor disabilities has primarily driven researchers to use eye tracking technologies in building gaze communication systems that do not depend on muscle movements for input. Gaze communication systems have been demonstrated in assistive technologies generally targeting users with severe motor disabilities such as motor neuron disease (MND), amyotrophic lateral sclerosis (ALS), spinal muscular atrophy, spinal cord injury, cerebral palsy, locked-in syndrome and Guillain-Barrè Syndrome (GBS) [6]. Eye typing systems are becoming increasingly accessible to intended user populations due to advances in eye tracking hardware and software, trend of decreasing costs of such systems, and proliferation of open source programs that use the eyes for selection and target acquisition of elements on the interface. Examples are pEYEwirte, Dasher and GazeTalk [5]. However, AAC support for communication in Arabic is inadequate with eye typing limited to two commercial products, Grid and MyTobii.

In recent years, systems have been developed to facilitate text entry by gaze using dwell time with low-cost hardware components in place of commercial gaze tracking products [2]. Researchers have examined the performance of gaze interaction

extensively with able-bodied users, and less with actual intended user populations. For example [4] evaluated point and selection interfaces, and [3] cited several approaches for gaze text entry evaluations. Comparison of gaze selection with other input modalities has also been reported (e.g. [3]). As gaze typing systems progress from the proof of concept phase, the optimization of interface designs of such systems has emerged as a crucial factor for improving the user experience of people who rely on this single modality of interaction for communication. Studies have examined the optimization of on-screen keyboards for gaze entry in English and other languages. What is less known is whether the optimization of on-screen keyboards in languages such as Arabic can improve the interaction of users with this communication method, especially with users who are prone to experience fatigue from extended use of gaze for target acquisition [6].

The overall aim of our project is to design, develop, and evaluate an Arabic language gaze communication system that we refer to as the iWriter. In the design of iWriter, we considered two different keyboard designs: Standard and Vertical to accommodate the needs of users who have limited horizontal eye movements, such as some cases of people with locked-in syndrome. Image-based communication for predefined phrases is also included in the system. The iWriter system is designed to be used in clinical settings and home environments. A User Centered Design (UCD) approach was adopted in this project from early requirements' gathering phases. A subject matter expert, a consultant neurologist, was involved as a design partner. Initial involvement was in requirements' discovery sessions for our intended user population and to assess the prototypes that are developed in design iterations of iWriter. The neurologist indicated that an optimized layout might be helpful, and highlighted the need for vertical layouts as some users would have limited horizontal eye movement. We are not aware of previous studies of optimizing Arabic interfaces for dwell-based typing and therefore we intend to address this inadequately understood design issue.

2. OPTIMIZING ARABIC GAZE TYPING

Typing with the eyes is quite different from typing with ten fingers mainly because eye typing does not allow for parallel processing. In hand typing, the motor movement of fingers on physical or virtual keypads can be simultaneous; as one finger is often involved in selecting a key while another finger prepares for the next stroke. Consequently, distances between keys and the actual size of the keys become crucial for optimizing the layout of the on-screen keyboard. The distribution of Arabic letters within the layout is equally important to support effective interaction in gaze typing. We conducted the design of prototypes in two phases, namely spatial configuration layouts and assessing gaze selection followed by optimal arrangement of letters in the Arabic on-screen keypad and assessing typing throughput which accounts for error rates and speed of typing.

For the first phase, a diagnostic approach was followed by using a Tobii X120 eye tracker, Tobii Studio software and six able-bodied participants for examining interaction with a selected layout of an on-screen Arabic keyboard. Keypad size was (1.5 cm) and it was selected based on an extensive literature and product review of gaze typing products and Arabic text entry systems. The letters of the Arabic alphabet in the selected keypad were listed in a three row arrangement for on-screen Arabic keyboards. Digits were listed on the first row with the back-space key. This version was used to examine visual layout and selection feasibility with varying dwell times. Success rates, time on typing tasks, visual scan paths of participants (as depicted in Figure 1), intensity of gaze fixations, and the drift of the eyes were measured. Tasks involved simulating the typing of four Arabic phrases comprised of letters with varying distribution across the keyboard and repetition of letters within a word. The results were 10 detected drifts, 3 incorrect selections out of a total of 31 letters. Evidence from the exploratory study suggests that the layout and key size were sufficient to support gaze selection and communication.

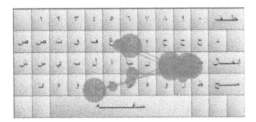

Figure 1. On-screen Arabic keyboard used in experiment.

Existing Arabic keypads have their flaws which have resulted from the transition from typewriters to physical keyboards, to virtual keypads in interfaces for selection with cursors, stylus or fingers. Optimizing Arabic keypads has not been feasible as prior research has shown that alternative layouts that are radically different than the current standard rarely succeed for reasons such as resistance of users to migration, retraining required and market inertia. While the argument for how the current layout became ubiquitous, to a degree that making any changes would mean too much disruption of what people have gotten used to, applies to traditional input modalities, gaze typing interfaces are relatively new and are susceptible to adopting optimized configuration. Users, especially those with disabilities can benefit from keypads that are different from the prevailing layouts as optimized interfaces offer opportunities for reducing fatigue by remedying the problematic characteristics of prevailing Arabic keypads. Further optimization work remains for the second phase; remapping the distribution of Arabic letters on the keypad according to the frequency of letters. The optimized Arabic interfaces have been shown to support faster typing and less fatigue in typing with traditional keypads [1]. However, this has not been examined with gaze-based typing and our understanding of how this translates to eye typing is limited.

For users with limited horizontal eye movement, paper-based communication boards currently used in clinical settings inspired the interface design and are being considered for presenting segments of the Arabic alphabet vertically. Initial prototype design is depicted in Figure 2.

Figure 2. Vertical Keyboard for Arabic Gaze Typing.

Usability evaluations of the developed system are underway with a sample comprised of two patients with Locked-In Syndrome and three patients with Motor Neuron Disease.

3. ACKNOWLEDGMENTS

This work was supported by grant RGP-VPP-157 from the Malaz Research Center of King Saud University (KSU) and the College of Computer and Information Sciences in KSU.

4. REFERENCES

[1] Al-Radaideh, Q. and Masri, K. (2011). Improving mobile multi-tap text entry for Arabic language. *Comput. Stand. Interfaces* 33, 1 (January 2011), 108-113.

[2] San Agustin, J., Hansen, J., Hansen, D., and Skovsgaard, H. (2009). Low-cost gaze pointing and EMG clicking. In *Proceedings of the 27th Conference on Human factors in computing systems* (CHI'09). ACM, NY, USA, 3247-3252.

[3] Räihä, K. and Ovaska S. (2012). An exploratory study of eye typing fundamentals: dwell time, text entry rate, errors, and workload. In *Proceedings of the 2012 ACM annual conference on Human Factors in Computing Systems* (CHI '12). ACM, NY, USA, 3001-3010.

[4] Zhang, X. and MacKenzie, I. S. (2007). Evaluating eye tracking with ISO 9241 -- Part 9. In Proceedings of HCI International 2007, China, 779--788.

[5] Urbina, M.H. and Huckaufy A. (2010). Alternatives to Single Character Entry and Dwell Time Selection on Eye Typing. In *2010 Symposium on Eye-Tracking Research & Application*, (New York, USA, 2010), ACM, 315-322.

[6] Majaranta, P. and Räihä, K.J. (2007). Text entry by gaze: Utilizing eye-tracking. In I. S. MacKenzie and K. Tanaka-Ishii (eds.), Text Entry Systems: Mobility, Accessibility, Universality. Morgan Kaufmann.

Toward a Design of Word Processing Environment for People with Disabilities

Adam Sporka, Ondřej Poláček
Department of Computer Graphics and Interaction
Czech Technical University in Prague, Faculty of Electrical Engineering
Karlovo nám. 13, 12135 Praha 2, Czech Republic
Tel.: +420-22435-7654, +420-603-287-605
{sporkaa, polacond}@fel.cvut.cz

ABSTRACT

The study presented in this paper is aimed at identifying text editing actions that are routinely performed by the users when composing a text document but which are not directly supported by common word processors. The results of this study will help a design of a novel word processing interface controlled by device with a limited number of input signals, operated by people with certain motor disabilities.

Categories and Subject Descriptors

H.5.2 Information Interfaces and Presentation: User Interfaces—Input devices and strategies

General Terms

Performance, Design, Experimentation, Human Factors.

Keywords

Text input, word processing, motor impairments, work in progress

1. INTRODUCTION

People with severely affected dexterity of hands face numerous problems when using computing equipment, especially when typing and editing text.

Numerous research studies have been published in which various alternative methods of typing text are examined, e.g. QANTI [1] or Dasher [2]. Most of these methods offer solution to the problem of typing new text only. Text editing is usually limited to corrections of immediate typos.

Text editing is however a complex task involving operations such as entry of new characters as well as revising previously entered text (rephrasing, changing order of statements, etc.), working with literature and external sources of data, or text/page formatting as described for example in the work by Mo and Witten [3].

Commonly available word processing software tools offer this functionality but the control of this functionality is optimized for standard keyboard and mouse as it heavily relies on the classic WIMP paradigm (windows, icons, menus, pointer).

Various methods exist that emulate keyboard and/or mouse, such

as the eye tracking-controlled mouse cursor [4] or the on-screen keyboard. These methods are meant to mediate the access to the WIMP user interfaces. However, this mediation is typically on the expense of speed of interaction which results in inefficiencies.

We believe that the efficiency of typing by means of alternative techniques may improve by redefinition or augmentation of the standard set of text editing actions.

2. THE STUDY ORGANIZATION

The study presented in this paper is a part of the project TextAble which aims at development of efficient interaction methods for text editing using myoelectric signal detectors for people with motor disabilities. The methods will be based on mapping a limited number of input signals, measured on the user's body, onto elementary text editing actions: character input and text editing operations.

The purpose of this study is to identify relevant text editing actions which are routinely performed by the users when composing a text document. (The frequency and typical sequence of these operations will be determined in a subsequent study.) These actions would include typing a new word, deleting an entire sentence, but also correcting the grammar etc.

7 people (2F, 5M) took part in this study. They all were experienced authors of technical documents as well as experienced typists. They had no medical condition that would require any compensation beyond corrective lenses. The study was performed in the Czech language. OpenOffice.org Writer tool was used as the word processing environment.

Each participant took one session. At the beginning, the purpose of the study was explained to the participant. Then the participant was asked to read an on-line article on a current political issue (the same article was presented to all of the participants) and write a short essay (500 to 1000 characters) in which the gist of the article was to be presented. No constraints were imposed: The participants were allowed to go back to the text of the article, to copy and paste portions from the article to the target document, and to use any formatting they desired.

The participants were observed by the experimenter. (The computer screen of the computer was recorded for subsequent analysis and the keystrokes as well as mouse movement and clicks were logged.) At the end of the session the participant was debriefed (the experimenter asked the participant about some immediate observations) and was presented a small gift as a reward.

3. RESULTS

The following text contains an overview of observations of particular text editing actions. Reordering sentences and paragraphs was not observed in this test.

The participants (each referred to as P<#>) differed in the achieved complexity of sequence of the text editing actions. While some participants created the text linearly, i.e. typing text from the beginning to the end, save for the occasional use of backspace (P4, P5), others took a more complex approach to composing the text: For example, P1 started with a formal outline which he would expand into full sentences later on.

Certain text editing actions were obvious that they would be encountered: **Writing new text** and **navigation** (Go to beginning / end of the document / paragraph / sentence, go to the previous / next word, go to specific location within a sentence).

3.1 Visual presentation

* **Survey of the contents:**
  * P1 was scrolling through the entire article first in order to see how long the article was and what was its structure.
* **Visual arrangements:**
  * P1 made a few extra lines behind the paragraph he was just working with. In the debriefing he stated that he did so in order to visually separate the existing and the new paragraph to facilitate his work.
  * P4 arranged the screen layout so that the target document window and the source article window were side-by-side.
* **Window switching:**
  * All users were often switching to the source document for a reference.

3.2 Modification to text

* **Typo corrections:**
  * P1, P5, and P6 were correcting mistakes by pressing the backspace key.
  * P1 erased the entire word containing a typo and wrote it again correctly.
* **Splitting and merging paragraphs:**
  * P1 merged two paragraphs of text which had an extra empty line between them.
* **Splitting and merging sentences:**
  * P1 split a sentence in two by removing the conjunction "a" *(and)*, then made the first letter of the second sentence upper case.
  * P1 merged two sentences in one, by a comma ",", then made the first letter of the second sentence lower case.
* **Complying with the typographic standards:**
  * P1 added missing space after a full stop.
* **Using a portion of the source text:**
  * P2 copied and pasted words "spisovatel Nikos Dimou" *("writer Nikos Dimou")* from the source article, then added the verb "říká" *("says")* in order to complete a sentence.

* P1 copied and pasted a few words from the source article, then adjusted their formatting.
* **Declension and gender corrections:**[1]
  * P3 copied and pasted words "spisovatel Nikos Dimou" from the source article, then modified their declension case in order to match the grammatical context at the destination.
  * P3 changes the gender of an adjective "popsáno" *("described", neut.)* → "popsána" *(fem.)*
* **Using synonyms:**
  * P1 was frequently reformulating the statements, often replacing words with their synonyms.

4. DISCUSSION AND CONCLUSION

This study was our first look at the process of text editing that will help redesigning (augmenting) the set of available text editing actions. We identified a number of text editing actions that were routinely performed by the users but that were not directly implemented by the word processing environments. They were to be achieved by a sequence of finer actions (e.g. merging two sentences would require navigating to the end of the first, deleting the full stop and the space, and making the first letter lower case).

This presents an obstacle to any motor-impaired user which is forced to select a number of partial actions: The ability to quickly select the desired character or action by people with motor impairments is limited by the particular input channel they use.

In order that a word processing environment is a useful tool and not an obstacle to the user, the environment must adopt to user's style of work. Typical operations must be readily available.

The findings presented in this paper are a result of a work in progress. Immediate follow-up will be the investigation of the actual frequency of the actions in order to optimize the hierarchy of text editing actions, as presented to the users of input devices with limited set of input signal.

5. ACKNOWLEDGMENTS

This research is a part of the project TextAble, financially supported by the Ministry of Education, Youth and Sports of the Czech Republic, funding PROGRAM LH – KONTAKT II.

6. REFERENCES

[1] I.S. Mackenzie and T. Felzer. SAK: Scanning ambiguous keyboard for efficient one-key text entry. *ACM Trans. Comput.-Hum. Interact.* 17(3):1-39, July 2010.

[2] D. J. Ward, A. F. Blackwell, and D.J.C. MacKay. Dasher—a data entry interface using continuous gestures and language models. In *Proc. of UIST '00*, pp. 129-137. ACM, 2000.

[3] D. H. Mo and I. H. Witten. Learning text editing tasks from examples: a procedural approach. *Behaviour & Information Technology.* 11(1):32-45, Taylor & Francis, 1992.

[4] E. Missimer and M. Betke. Blink and wink detection for mouse pointer control. In *Proc. of PETRA '10*, Article 23. ACM, 2010.

---

[1] Though these corrections were specific to the Czech language, similar operations can be identified in other languages as well.

Preliminary Evaluation of Three Eyes-Free Interfaces for Point-and-Click Computer Games

Javier Torrente[1], Eugenio J. Marchiori[1], José Ángel Vallejo-Pinto[2], Manuel Ortega-Moral[3],
Pablo Moreno-Ger[1], Baltasar Fernández-Manjón[1]

[1] Complutense University of Madrid
Department of Software Engineering
and Artificial Intelligence
{jtorrente, e.marchiori, pablom,
balta}@fdi.ucm.es

[2] University of Oviedo
Department of Computer Science
Asturias, Spain
vallejo@uniovi.es

[3] Technosite, (Fundosa-ONCE Group
ONCE)
R&D Department
mortega@technosite.es

ABSTRACT
This paper presents a preliminary evaluation of the perceived entertainment value and ease of use of three eyes-free interfaces for point-and-click games. Interface 1 (I1) uses a web-like cyclical navigation system to change the focused interactive element. Interface 2 (I2) uses a sonar to help the user locate interactive elements with the mouse. Interface 3 (I3) interprets natural language commands typed in by the player. Results suggest that I2 adds more entertainment value and is appropriate for experienced players. Players find I1 is the easiest to use while I3 seems more adequate for users with little gaming experience.

Categories and Subject Descriptors
H.5.2 [**Information Interfaces and Presentation**]: User Interfaces – *auditory (non-speech) feedback, graphical user interfaces (GUI), natural language, screen design*;

Keywords
Accessibility, audio 3D, eyes-free games.

1. INTRODUCTION
The use of computer and videogames is rising quickly, not only for leisure but also for serious purposes such as advertising, education or health. As a side effect, the demographics of people who play games are increasingly more heterogeneous in gender, age and gaming habits (e.g. casual gamers vs. hardcore gamers).

However, videogames can pose significant accessibility barriers for people with disabilities. As their importance grows, so does it their potential for becoming a source of digital divide. Although research on accessibility in games has grown in recent years [3, 4], how to design universally accessible games remains an unanswered question. Therefore, it is necessary to investigate new interfaces that improve the accessibility of games taking also into account the current diversity of gamers, as not all the interfaces are appropriate for all sorts of players.

The purpose of this study is to investigate accessible interfaces that deliver the best game experience to screen reader (i.e. blind) users with different gaming habits.

This study is part of a more ambitious project aiming to integrate these interfaces into the eAdventure game authoring tool [1]. This would help to increase the accessibility of games produced with

eAdventure by cutting down development costs as developers could reuse accessible interfaces more easily. The focus in on point-and-click adventure games, although the studied interfaces and their results may be repurposed to suit other genres.

2. INTERFACES DEVELOPED
The three interfaces here presented use sound to convey information, combining text-to-speech with sound effects. However, each interface supports user input in a different way.

2.1 Cyclical navigation system (Interface 1)
With this interface, the interaction is similar to browsing the web using a screen reader. Available interactions in the scene are structured in a two-level focus cycle that can be navigated with left and right arrow keys. The first level contains the interactive elements on the scene (characters, objects, exits, etc.). The second level contains actions related to each element (e.g. talk to, grab, etc). To access the second level, the user hits the action key. To return to the first level, the user hits the cancel key. The specific keys for action and cancel can be customized.

2.2 Sonar (Interface 2)
The purpose of this interface is to guide the player in finding interactive elements with the mouse, instead of using the keyboard. Thus users can explore the game scenario independently and at their own pace without using vision. The scene can be examined through a 3D positional audio system. In this system, each interactive element is configured to emit a different sound [2]. Altering the intensity and pitch of the sound provides information about the position of the interactive element relative to the mouse cursor. The intensity of the sound increases inversely to the distance from the mouse cursor to the element. Pitch is used to provide information about the vertical position of the mouse pointer (high pitch denotes that it is near an element, while low pitch denotes that it is far from it).

2.3 Natural language commands (Interface 3)
With this interface interaction is articulated through short natural language commands that the user types. After the command is introduced, the system tries to interpret it and match it to one of the available interactions in the scene, using a regular grammar that defines the structure of supported commands and a thesaurus of synonymous based in a previous work [1]. The user receives audio feedback about the results of this matching and if it has succeeded, the interaction is triggered.

In contrast to interface 1, in this case the interactions available are not directly revealed to the user, but instead the player has to find them out by test-and-error of different commands. Nonetheless, the user can use some basic commands that are always available to get a textual description of the scene.

3. PRELIMINARY EVALUATION
3.1 Method and Settings
The three interfaces were evaluated by two screen reader (i.e. blind) users. They were asked to play three short games that were set up each with one of the interfaces. The users had different gaming habits: while user 1 was a casual gamer with little gaming experience, user 2 played games frequently.

The users completed the evaluation in independent sessions of 60 minutes, where two observers were present at all times. They were exposed to each game for about 10 min. After that, they rated two aspects of the interfaces using a 1-7 Likert scale:

a) Ease of use, defined as the ability of the interface to allow players to explore the game scenes, find interactive elements and trigger desired interactions with minimum effort.

b) Entertainment potential, defined as the ability of the interface to make the game interesting and appealing for the user.

Finally, they were asked to discuss with the observers which was the best overall interface for games in their opinion.

3.2 Games used
The games used had a similar design, with similar number of scenes (around 4), game mechanics and interactive elements (7-10), but a different story.

In each game the player was set out to solve a crime by inspecting the crime scene and surrounding areas while finding and collecting evidence. After interacting with elements in the scene new clues were unveiled. Some of them were deliberately designed to mislead the player, making the crime more difficult to solve to keep the player interested.

Each game started with a short explanation of the situation and basic instructions about the interaction and the interface.

3.3 Results and Discussion
3.3.1 Ease of Use
Both users reported interface 1 (cyclical navigation system) as the "easiest" to use (see Table 1).

Table 1. User rates for the ease of use of each interface

	User 1	User 2
Game 1 (cyclical navigation)	7	7
Game 2 (Sonar)	5	6
Game 3 (Natural language commands)	3	5

This data is backed up by the analysis of the game completion times (Table 2), as game 1 took less time for both users regardless of their gaming habits.

These results reflect the fact that interface 1 is more familiar for screen reader users and all interactions can be reached within a minimum number of keystrokes.

Table 2. Completion times for each game and user

	User 1	User 2
Game 1 (cyclical navigation)	4.30 min	3 min
Game 2 (Sonar)	11 min	8 min
Game 3 (Natural language commands)	7 min	6 min

3.3.2 Entertainment
Both users agreed in rating interface 2 (sonar) as the most fun (Table 3). Looking at the completion times, it is probably the most challenging - it took both users more than twice as much time to complete game 2 compared to game 1. The increased challenge can make the experience more engaging.

Table 3. User rates for the entertainment value

	User 1	User 2
Game 1 (cyclical navigation)	3	6
Game 2 (Sonar)	6	7
Game 3 (Natural language commands)	4	6

3.3.3 Overall evaluation
Users disagreed on which interface provides the best overall experience. User 1, considered as "non gaming expert", preferred interface 3 (commands), while the "gaming expert" user preferred interface 2 (sonar). User 1 commented that interface 3 (natural language commands) was probably more adequate because it is more interactive and fun than interface 1 (web-like navigation) but easier to use than interface 2 (sonar). User 2 leaned towards interface 2 because it provided more challenge than any of the others. This suggests that users appreciated the potential of interface 2 (sonar) for games, but it may be appropriate only for experienced gamers seeking new experiences.

4. CONCLUSIONS AND FUTURE WORK
The results of the evaluation conducted are promising, but the small number of users (2) prevents extracting final conclusions. In the future it is necessary to conduct research with a higher number of screen reader users and with higher exposure times to the games.

5. ACKNOWLEDGMENTS
The Spanish Ministry of Science (TIN2010-21735-C02-02), the European Commission (519332-LLP-1-2011-1-PT-KA3-KA3NW, 519023-LLP-1-2011-1-UK-KA3-KA3MP, FP7-ICT-2009-5-258169), the Complutense University (GR35/10-A-921340) and the Regional Government of Madrid (eMadrid Network - S2009/TIC-1650) have partially supported this work.

6. REFERENCES
[1] Torrente, J. et al. 2009. Implementing Accessibility in Educational Videogames with <e-Adventure> *First ACM international workshop on Multimedia technologies for distance learning - MTDL '09* (Beijing, China, 2009), 55-67.

[2] Vallejo-Pinto, J.Á. et al. 2011. Applying sonification to improve accessibility of point-and-click computer games for people with limited vision. *25th BCS Conference on Human-Computer Interaction* (Newcastle Upon Tyne, UK, 2011).

[3] Westin, T. et al. 2011. Advances in Game Accessibility from 2005 to 2010. *Universal Access in HCI, Part II, HCII 2011*. LNCS 6766, (2011), 400-409.

[4] Yuan, B. et al. 2010. Game accessibility: a survey. *Universal Access in the Information Society*. 10, 1 (Jun. 2010), 81-100.

Accessible Collaborative Writing for Persons Who Are Blind: A Usability Study

John G. Schoeberlein
Towson University
7800 York Road
Towson, Maryland 21252-0001
(410)931-3537
jschoe4@students.towson.edu

Yuanqiong Wang
Towson University
7800 York Road
Towson, Maryland 21252-0001
(410)704-2104
ywangtu@gmail.com

ABSTRACT

Collaborative writing applications are widely utilized in organizations to co-author documents and jointly exchange ideas. Unfortunately, for persons who are blind, collaborative writing applications are often difficult to access and use. Therefore, this paper presents the results from several usability studies that examined how visually able persons and persons who are blind interact with collaborative writing applications, and the accessibility and usability issues they encounter.

Categories and Subject Descriptors

K.4.2 [**Computers and Society**]: Social Issues – Assistive technology for persons with disabilities.

Keywords

Blind, collaborative writing, accessibility, usability, universal usability, human-computer interaction, Microsoft Word, Google Docs.

1. INTRODUCTION

Collaborative writing is a collaborative technology utilized to co-author documents and to exchange ideas and comments. Unfortunately, for persons who are blind, their inability to access and use collaborative writing applications hinders their performance by requiring them to take extra effort to determine the changes and comments made to a document [5, 6]. In order for persons who are blind to participate in collaborative writing, it is critical to examine and understand their access and use issues.

2. RELATED RESEARCH

Several studies have been conducted in regard to collaborative writing environments. Researchers surveyed respondents on the access and use of electronic documents [3], conducted automated examinations of Google Docs [7], and conducted screen reader examinations of Google Docs [1, 2]. Additional research is needed to examine collaborative writing environments in regard

to co-editing text synchronously, collaborative writing tasks such as adding, changing or deleting text and comments, and comparing these results between visually able persons and persons who are blind in order to identify ways to improve accessibility and usability.

3. RESEARCH METHODOLOGY

The Researchers recruited the participants for the baseline usability studies from the Members of the National Federation of the Blind (NFB) [4] and Students from local Colleges and Universities. Seven (7) participants were visually able and five (5) participants were blind with no residual vision.

The first collaborative writing usability study session was conducted in March 2012, with visually able participants. The second and third collaborative writing usability study sessions were conducted in April and May 2012, with persons who are blind with no residual vision.

The baseline usability study sessions began with a brief introduction of the purpose of the study, followed by the signing of an informed consent form. Each participant completed a pre-study questionnaire to collect background information about the participants. Following the completion of the pre-study questionnaire, each usability study session was conducted based on the collaborative writing tasks which included opening a document, initiating change tracking, adding, deleting and changing text of a document, adding a comment, and searching, accepting and rejecting changed text throughout the document. Each participant examined and edited the document, "*Amendments of the United States Constitution.*" During the usability study session, the researcher recorded task performance (complete or incomplete), task completion time (time to complete) directly next to each task on the task list. Audio, video and researcher notes were collected. Following the usability study, a brief post-study questionnaire was collected on the task experience and opinions of likes and dislikes, and how to improve the interfaces of Microsoft Word and Google Docs. Each baseline usability study session ran for 90 minutes per participant.

4. RESULTS

4.1 Task Mean and Standard Deviation

Based on the baseline usability studies conducted, the participants who are blind were out-of-range when compared to visually able participants (averaged 252.6 +- 99.84 minutes versus 120 +-34.64 minutes) when adding changes to a Word Document. Other tasks where the participants who are blind were out-of-range when compared to visually able participants included: deleting text (averaged 68 +- 28.85 minutes versus 42.85 +- 16.03 minutes); changing text (averaged 71 +- 39.11 minutes versus 38.57 +-

14.63 minutes); adding comments (averaged196 +- 98.72 minutes versus 42.85 +- 16.03 minutes); searching for all com ments (averaged 155 +- 67.82 minutes versus 51.42 +-14.63 minutes); accepting a change (averaged 73 +- 14.83 minutes versus 42.85 +- 16.03 minutes); and accepting/rejecting rem aining changes (averaged 249 +- 120.38 minutes versus 47.14 +- 16.03 minutes).

The participants who are blind tend to take longer to complete most of the tasks. Within the participants who are blind group, the performance varies more when com pared to the visually able group especially for tasks that requires the ability to identify and compare the changes with the original wording. W ithin the participants who are blind group, those who had less experience took more time to complete most tasks.

4.2 Collaborative Writing Experience

The visually able participants agreed (71.9%) or strongly agreed (28.1%) that M icrosoft Word's interface was clear and understandable, and agreed (57.1%) or strongly agreed (42.9%) that the interactions with Microsoft Word were flexible. Whereas, participants who are blind disagreed (40%) that Microsoft Word's interface was clear and understandable, and a lower percentage of participants who are blind strongly agreed (20%) or agreed (40%) that the interactions with Microsoft Word were flexible.

Visually able participants' disagreed (57.1%), when asked if the Google Docs' interface was clear and understandable, and disagreed (74.1%), when asked if the Google Docs' interface was flexible. Visually able participants' disagreed (42.9%) and strong disagreed (14.3%) when responding to the statements, "*I feel the tasks were easy to c omplete,*" and "*I was able to complete the tasks without any problems .*" The visually able participants' disagreed (14.3%) and strongly disagreed (14.3%) that Google Docs improved their collabora tive writing perform ance, and disagreed (28.6%) and strongly disagreed (14.3%) that Google Docs would be their choice when collaborative writing in the future. The five (5) participants who are blind did not examine Google Docs, since they experienced accessibility issues in the past and did not utilize Google Docs.

4.3 Discussion

The data presented shows that there are usability issues associated with both Microsoft Word and Google Docs, and that interface design improvements are needed.

In regard to Microsoft Word, ther e were issues related to the list of revisions. The inability of pa rticipants who are blind to understand the context of revisi ons and comments, and their inability to understand the presence of these revisions and comments within the sentence and paragraph was a common concern voiced by these participants. In order to pres ent the context of comments and revisions, addition interface tools should be added to present the sentence or paragraph where a change or comment exists. In order to improve the awarenes s of the revisions and comments, two possi ble views should be presented, one view without the revisions in cluded (prior view) and another view with the revisions (resulting view). This way, persons who are blind could listen to or m anually read with the Braille keyboard the differences within a sentence or paragraph. While interacting with Microsoft W ord, participants who are blind could not directly access menu items for accepting or rejecting changes, finding the next change, and finding the next comment. The

participants who are blind had to parse the m enu structure with the tab key and listen for the proper menu item. Direct key press access would improve the access time to these features and should be programmed directly into Microsoft Word.

In regard to Google Docs, there were issues related to the slow response and repainting of the in terface. The slow response time and repainting the interface would be im proved by improving the network bandwidth and the amount of memory of the computer. This issue is more a result of environm ental factors, such as the network and com puter memory and not necessarily an interface design issue. Revisions are s aved in tim e increments, so the visually able participants could not accept or reject a specific revision, but had to accept or reject a group of revisions. To improve the Google Docs interface in regard to revisions, each revision should be saved independent from other revisions, and all changed text should be appropriately identified on the current revision.

5. CONCLUSION

This paper presented the results from several usability studies that examined collaborative writing applications for accessibility and usability issues. The participan ts who are blind encountered usability issues when interac ting with Microsoft W ord. The visually able participants en countered usability issues with Google Docs, and preferred Microsoft Word for collaborative writing. Additional research w ill be conducted to exam ine an accessible prototype for collaborative writing currently under development.

6. ACKNOWLEDGEMENTS

The authors would like to thank the Members of the National Federation of the Blind.

7. REFERENCES

[1] Buzzi, M.C., Buzzi, M., Leporini, B., Mori, Giulio, Penichet, V. 2011. Collaborative Editing for All: The Google Docs Example, LNCS, 6768 (2011), 165-174..

[2] Buzzi, M.C., Buzzi, Mori, Giulio, M., Leporini, B., Penichet, V. 2010. Accessing Google Docs via Screen Reader, LNCS, 6179 (2010), 92-99.

[3] Doringo, Martin, Harriehausen, B. 2011. Survey: Improving Document Accessibility from the Blind and Visually Impaired User's Point of View, LNCS, 6768 (2011), 129-135.

[4] National Federation of the Blind. (2011). http://www.nfb.org.

[5] Schoeberlein, J., Wang, Y. (2011). Examining the Current State of Group Support Accessibility: An Expanded Study, Communications in Computer and Information Science. (2011), 173, 389 - 393.

[6] Schoeberlein, J., Wang, Y. (2011). Examining the Current State of Group Support Accessibility: A Focus Group Study, Universal Access In Human-Computer Interaction. 6768 (2011), 272-281.

[7] Schoeberlein, J., Wang, Y. (2009) Evaluating Groupware Accessibility. LNCS. 5616 (2009) 414-423.

E-Arithmetic: Non-Visual Arithmetic Manipulation for Students with Impaired Vision

Nancy Alajarmeh
New Mexico State University
Department of Computer Science
Las Cruces, NM 88003

nalajarm@cs.nmsu.edu

Enrico Pontelli
New Mexico State University
Department of Computer Science
Las Cruces, NM 88003

epontell@cs.nmsu.edu

ABSTRACT

In this paper we present a web-based system that enables children with impaired vision to handle basic arithmetic knowledge: addition, subtraction, multiplication, and division. Taking into consideration the accommodation of varied levels of vision disability—minor to severe—the new system provides an electronic auditory alternative to the currently used tools.

Categories and Subject Descriptors

H.5.2 [**Information Systems**]: Information Interfaces and Presentation—*User Interfaces*.

Keywords

Arithmetic Skills, Math Accessibility, Assistive Technology.

1. INTRODUCTION

Proficiency in mathematical skills determines the potential fields of education and future career [1]. Early mathematics education begins with attention primarily paid to arithmetic skills. Young children who are visually impaired are challenged in handling arithmetic manipulation. First, pencil and paper do not exist in their world, which makes it difficult to grasp and navigate a problem structure. Second, those young students lack the ability to access the visual simulation of problems which is essential to capture all aspects of a problem. Third, arithmetic problems require careful organizing skills which in turn affect final answers; unfortunately, organizing skills are compromised by vision disability. Students who are visually impaired must be able to perceive a problem in all its parts; more efficient ways are needed to enable students to access problems entirely or partially, locate where they are working, undo or redo certain actions to correct mistakes with minimal effort, and retrieve the original problem's details any time during manipulation. In addition, students with impaired vision need electronic platforms that enable them to handle arithmetic problems and catch up with the technological revolution in education. This revolution necessitates shifting into using computers for different tasks.

2. E-ARITHMETIC MANIPULATION SYSTEM

Similar to the vertical layout sighted users use to carry out arithmetic calculations using paper and pencil, E-Arithmetic is a web-based system that comprises four modules for addition, subtraction, multiplication, and division. E-Arithmetic aims to facilitate non-visual arithmetic manipulation for students in

elementary school at minimal cost, time, and effort. The basic structure of E-Arithmetic is a grid on which students place their numbers for manipulation with the support of non-visual navigation controls: aural feedback, hot-access keys, and special sounds. E-Arithmetic gives options to access the problem's parts any time during manipulation without losing track of navigation. Besides, E-Arithmetic facilitates easy recovery from mistakes, and it maintains the initial problem's information. In using E-Arithmetic, young students who are visually impaired can save:

- Resources: no waste of special paper needed to run a Braille writer, especially when a mistake is made.

- Efforts: no need to redo the whole work from the beginning when a little mistake is made, e.g., using the abacus.

Another goal of E-Arithmetic is to help students with impaired vision to do arithmetic manipulation on computers. This keeps them up to date with current trends in education: more reliance on web resources and online learning platforms. E-Arithmetic prepares students to deal with more interactive computer-based frameworks for mathematics manipulation. The following sections describe the four basic modules of E-Arithmetic; more advanced features and modules will be added later such as: decimals and fractions.

2.1 Addition Module

The addition module, showed in figure 1, allows students to carry out addition problems with at least two numbers. By default two rows are given; each row is divided into cells, where students fill their digits in to form entire numbers. The module also provides a row on top for the carryover, and another row on the bottom for results. Navigation is made through hot-access keys, with verbal output for the content of each cell when students navigate over that cell.

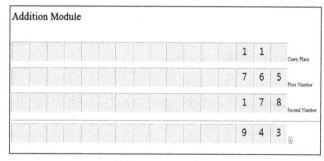

Figure 1. Addition module

Arrows are used to navigate in four directions. A special sound is played to indicate the limit of navigation when the edges are reached. Special sounds, similar to Windows system sounds, are also played when a student navigates through the carryover row or the result row. At any time by speech output, a student can read the digit of the active cell, the entire number that the active cell belongs to, or the entire problem's numbers. A special key can be invoked to let students know where exactly they are; which row and which column. Another special key allows students to move from a column to the one on its left. This allows easier navigation than arrows especially when a student finishes manipulating a certain column and is ready for the next. When students need to carry a digit from a certain column, they use a special key that leads them to the top row of the column to the left. The navigation is then returned back to the point where they were previously. Students can edit the content of any cell, and they can invoke the undo option. In addition, a hot-access key can move the cursor to the very first digit of the first number. This helps if at any instance students feel they are lost somewhere in the workspace.

2.2 Subtraction Module

This module allows students to subtract a number from another. Students are given three rows: two for the problem's numbers and one for the result; no further rows can be added. The navigation and controls are similar to those of the addition module. However, there is no carry operation, and there is a borrow operation. The borrow operation is invoked by a special hot-access key when a cell is active, which makes it blank and ready to receive a new value from the student. In the meantime, the original cell to its right becomes of length two to accommodate a new value.

2.3 Multiplication Module

In this module more controls and navigation hot-access keys are provided to deal with the complexity of multiplication problems that are longer and more alignment-sensitive. Multiplication problems have addition problems embedded, and they require a student's memory of the multiplication tables. Students find two rows for the numbers to be multiplied, a carryover row on top, a row for the intermediate results. More rows can be added upon requests by invoking a hot-access key. Students navigate by either arrows or keyboard keys. Keyboard keys from "Y" through "]" correspond to the digits of the first number. Keyboard keys from "G" through """ correspond to the digits of the second number. Digits are spoken out when keys are hit. Students read the corresponding numbers using the keyboard. Then they type their intermediate results. Every time students finish with an intermediate row, they can add another one underneath it with the farthest right cell skipped. This helps students align their intermediate results. When a new row is appended, the carryover gets reset with all blank cells. Once students finish the intermediate results rows, they request an additional row for the final result that allows adding the intermediate results rows similar to the addition module.

2.4 Division Module

This module has a level of complexity that results from the long division complexity that includes multiple steps, multiplication, subtraction, division skills, and the alignment of digits at each step. Students place their digits on the Divisor-Dividend row; hot-access keys help students go directly to the required location to either type or read. Students then start typing their results either on the Quotient row or on the intermediate rows. Every time students finish multiplying a Quotient's digit by a Divisor's digit, they request a new row to carry out the subtraction for that step. They keep doing the same procedure until solving the problem. Hot-access keys help students focus on the Quotient, Dividend, and Divisor for reading or editing. In addition, hot-access keys allow students to mark the location of the digits required for problem solving to help them figure out which digit is to be used next for division.

3. METHODOLOGY AND TESTING

A study was conducted to compare using E-Arithmetic to using the abacus and Braille Writer to manipulate arithmetic problems. Thirteen visually impaired students with an average academic achievement in mathematics participated. Experiments were conducted on different days with at least six problems for each skill. Students were given a demonstration in advance on how E-Arithmetic works. In each experiment, participants were asked to solve the given arithmetic problems by two approaches: the first day with either the Abacus or the Braille writer, and the second day with E-Arithmetic. After our experiments, we came up with the following observations:

- **Ease of Use and Navigation**

For familiarity reasons, it took participants longer to work on the first couple of problems in each skill compared to later problems. It took participants time to figure out the proper use of the hot-access keys, and how to invoke the options E-Arithmetic offers. Then participants became familiar with E-Arithmetic. Navigation controls, hot-access keys and alert sounds, were intuitive and easy to grasp. Compared to learning how to solve arithmetic problems using the abacus, the mathematics teacher noticed that E-Arithmetic took less time.

- **Speed and Accuracy**

Compared to using the Braille writer, a time consuming tool, students achieved better time working on E-Arithmetic especially on problems of the subtraction and division types. However, time was similar to that when working on the abacus. For lacking visual memory, blind participants needed more time than other students. The accuracy of their solutions was good. Students found addition and subtraction modules easier to manage than multiplication and division modules. This is related to the complexity of multiplication and division problems. However, time and accuracy improved on the second day of the experiments when students became familiar with E-Arithmetic features especially in the division module.

- **Recovery and Error Correction**

E-Arithmetic allowed easier recovery from mistakes through the use of the undo function, and editing any cell's content. In contrast, when students used the Braille writer, they had to redo their work entirely, wasting resources and time. Retrieval of the original problem's numbers was possible when a Braille writer was used; however, when students decided to work on the problem again, they had to start over in a new space. With the abacus there was no way to recover from mistakes unless students remembered exactly what recent movements they made, which is not an easy job. Retrieval of original numbers was not possible except by using memory, or if they had recorded them on an embossed sheet.

4. REFERENCE

[1] A. Karshmer, G. Gupta and E. Pontelli, "Mathematics and Accessibility: a Survey", in *Proc.9th International Conference on Computers Helping People with Special Needs*, Vol. 3118, Paris, France, 2004, pp.664-669.

A Music Application for Visually Impaired People Using Daily Goods and Stationeries on the Table

Ikuko Eguchi Yairi
Sophia University,
7-1, Kioicyo, Chiyodaku, Tokyo, Japan, 102-8554
+81-3-3238-3280, i.e.yairi@sophia.ac.jp

Takuya Takeda
Sophia University,
7-1, Kioicyo, Chiyodaku, Tokyo, Japan, 102-8554
+81-3-3238-3280, taktakeda@yairilab.net

ABSTRACT Music applications, like a GarageBand, have become more popular today because they afford intuitive comfortable visual interface for users to play, remix, and compose music. But visually impaired people have difficulties to use such a software application. Therefore, this paper introduces a novel music interface for visually impaired people using daily goods and stationery on the table. An experimental system was developed with Kinect for AR marker and gesture recognition, and with sounds of three instruments, the piano, the guitar and the percussion. Five blind young people participated in the evaluation of right combination of the goods. The results shows that the proposed interface is effective both single use and collaborative work.

Categories and Subject Descriptors

H.5.2[User Interfaces]: *Interaction styles.*

Keywords

Visually impaired people, Music application, AR marker, Kinect.

1. INTRODUCTION

Toward the upcoming ubiquitous computing and networking era, the digital divide problem of visually impaired people seems to become more serious today. Recent music applications, such as GarageBand on Mac and reacTable[1], could be ineffective for visually impaired people because of these rich intuitive comfortable visual interfaces and interactions. Our research goal is to propose the novel musical application using commodities at home for them. The idea is so simple that string objects, such as yarn, ropes and chains, help users to trace and adjust the positions of clip objects with AR marker on the table. The positions of clip objects are equivalent to musical note, and string objects are equal to phrase. This paper introduces our experimental work and evaluation with single user and two users.

2. DESIGN OF THE APPLICATION

We started this research from interviews of blind people and a teacher who developed and researched assistive applications for visually impaired students. They similarly indicated the difficulties to learn music because of the hurdle to memorize phrases or read music score with braille, and also because of the embarrassment of making funny sounds. It seems that visually impaired people are more interested in music applications than in real musical instruments, but there are few visually impaired people who master computer music applications. Agendas for designing the music application from the interviews are as follows; (1) composing music without memorizing or reading musical scores is a much-needed application for visually impaired people contrary to our expectation, (2) user friendly interface without making funny sounds helps visually impaired people to

enjoy the music application with others without embarrassment. What is such a user-friendly interface of music composing application for visually impaired people? We have focused on the importance of their rich touch experiences. Tangible interface using graspable objects is a good idea, but gestural interface without any visual feedback could not be comfortable for visually impaired people[2]. For helping intuitive understanding of composing mechanism, we employed the method of laying out tangible objects on the table. A vision sensor detects the positions of the objects, and the detection results are directly changed into musical score. As the objects, daily goods and stationeries are familiar enough for users to try out the application without embarrassment. After many trials, clip objects, such as paper clips, binder clips and clothespins, with AR marker, and string objects, such as yarn, ropes and chains, to help users to trace and adjust the positions of clip objects in Fig. 1 are seemed to be practical and promising for our music application. An experimental system was implemented using Kinect, ARToolkit, OpenCV and MIDI interface on Visual C++. Users can compose the piano and the guitar melody under continuous replay of the percussion sounds. To change the tempo of the percussion, users attach an AR marker with rubber band on their wrist and make waving gesture.

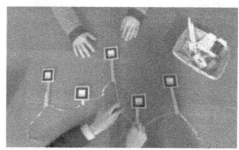

Fig. 1 A cooperative work image to compose music, using clip objects with AR markers and a string object.

3. SINGLE USER EVALUATION

Two male and three female blinds, aged 18 to 33, and all with some experiences of playing music, participated in the single user evaluation. The experiment was consists of three parts: (exp.1) composing without string objects within 10 minutes, (exp.2) with string objects within 20 minutes, and (exp.3) with favorite clip and string objects within 10 minutes.

Fig.2 is a comparison example of clip objects layout between exp.1 and exp.2. All examinees used wider area of the table, and were able to find more suitable melody with string objects than without them. Fig.3 is an example of a female examinee's changes of string objects in exp.2. She finally chose a chain as a string object and finished composing. In exp.3, all examinees answered the chain as the best string object. Large clothespins were the best clip object for three female, and small clothespins were the best for two male. The string objects helped them a lot to find clip objects, especially the texture of the chain perfectly suited to adjust clip objects as they liked. All participants commented that the application was so simple and satisfying to compose preferable music.

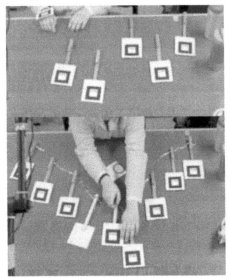

Fig. 2 The effect of string objects on clip objects' positions, upper: without string object, and lower: with string objects.

Fig. 3 Changes of the string object, (1)yarn, (2)paper clips, (3)a chain, (4)completion.

4. TWO USERS EVALUATION

Five blinds mentioned previously and one sighted male aged 22 participated in this evaluation, and were divided in three couples of a male and a female. The experiment was to compose music with favorite clip and string objects by two users within 10 minutes. All couples chose clothespins and chains.

Fig.4 is a Kinect't recognition output on two users' collaborations of composing music. AR marker worn on users' hands, which have the function for checking the musical note of the indicated clothespin, are equally detected as AR makers on clothespins. White dots and lines are optical flow for the recognition of hand waving gesture which has the function to up/down the tempo of percussion.

The first couple was close friends with lively communications and influences on each behavior during the experiment. They composed two phrases of the guitar and the piano, and were satisfied with their music. The second couple was not friends but knew each other with reserved communications. They divided composing area on the table into left and right parts and did not get involved in each others' composing. But they commented that the collaboration for composing was amusing. The third couple was first meet, and the male was the sighted. The male was an active helper for the blind female with lively communications. The female commented that the communications for collaborative composing was a pleasurable experience. From this experiment, it was confirmed that our proposed interface was effective to help users' collaboration of composing music in laying out objects on the table and also in the communication.

Fig. 4 A gesture and AR markers recognition result on the two users collaboration experiment.

5. CONCLUSION

This paper introduced our idea for the musical application interface for visually impaired people. The interface using daily goods and stationeries could be useful and fun for all people to compose music.

The experimental system employed a string object for the expression of the musical phrase, and clip objects with AR markers for the expression of the musical notes. As a future work, we would like to implement the application without AR markers. The information of colors, the size and shapes of the clip objects will be the important elements for nuanced music performance.

6. ACKNOWLEDGMENTS

We are deeply grateful to all participants of our experiments and Prof. Makoto Kobayashi at Tsukuba University of Technology. This work was supported by Scientific Research (C) (General) No.23500155 from the MEXT, Japan.

7. REFERENCES

[1] S. Jordà, et al., "The reacTable: exploring the synergy between live music performance and tabletop tangible interfaces", In Proc. of TEI '07, ACM Press, 2007, pp. 139-146.

[2] N. Rasamimanana, et al., "Modular musical objects towards embodied control of digital music", In Proc. of 'TEI 11, ACM Press, 2011, pp. 9-12.

A Feasibility Study of Crowdsourcing and Google Street View to Determine Sidewalk Accessibility

Kotaro Hara, Victoria Le, and Jon Froehlich
Human-Computer Interaction Lab
Computer Science Department, University of Maryland
College Park, MD 20742
{kotaro, jonf}@cs.umd.edu; vnle@umd.edu

Figure 1. Using crowdsourcing and Google Street View images, we examined the efficacy of three different labeling interfaces on task performance to locate and assess sidewalk accessibility problems: (a) *Point*, (b) *Rectangle*, and (c) *Outline*. Actual labels from our study shown.

ABSTRACT

We explore the feasibility of using crowd workers from Amazon Mechanical Turk to identify and rank sidewalk accessibility issues from a manually curated database of 100 Google Street View images. We examine the effect of three different interactive labeling interfaces (*Point, Rectangle, and Outline*) on task accuracy and duration. We close the paper by discussing limitations and opportunities for future work.

Categories and Subject Descriptors

K.4.2 [**Computer and Society**]: Social Issues-Assistive technologies for persons with disabilities

Keywords

Crowdsourcing accessibility, Google Street View, accessible urban navigation, Mechanical Turk

1. INTRODUCTION

The availability and quality of sidewalks can significantly impact *how* and *where* people travel in urban environments. Sidewalks with surface cracks, buckled concrete, missing curb ramps, or other issues can pose considerable accessibility challenges to those with mobility or vision impairments [2,3]. Traditionally, sidewalk quality assessment has been conducted via in-person street audits, which is labor intensive and costly, or via citizen call-in reports, which are done on a reactive basis. As an alternative, we are investigating the use of crowdsourcing to locate and assess sidewalk accessibility problems *proactively* by labeling online map imagery via an interactive tool that we built.

In this paper, we specifically explore the feasibility of using crowd workers from Amazon Mechanical Turk (mturk.com), an online labor market, to label accessibility issues found in a manually curated database of 100 Google Street View (GSV) images. We examine the effect of three different interactive labeling interfaces (Figure 1) on task accuracy and duration. As the first study of its kind, our goals are to, first, investigate the viability of reappropriating online map imagery to determine sidewalk accessibility via crowd sourced workers and, second, to

uncover potential strengths and weaknesses of this approach. We believe that our approach could be used as a lightweight method to bootstrap accessibility-aware urban navigation routing algorithms, to gather training labels for computer vision-based sidewalk accessibility assessment techniques, and/or as a mechanism for city governments and citizens alike to report on and learn about the health of their community's sidewalks.

2. LABELING STREET VIEW IMAGES

To collect geo-labeled data on sidewalk accessibility problems in GSV images, we created an interactive online labeling tool in Javascript, PHP and MySQL, which works across browsers. Labeling GSV images is a three step process consisting of *marking* the location of the sidewalk problem, *categorizing* the problem into one of five types, and *assessing* the problem's severity. For the first step, we created three different marking interfaces: (i) *Point*: a point-and-click interface; (ii) *Rectangle*: a click-and-drag interface; and (iii) *Outline*: a path-drawing interface. We expected that the *Point* interface would be the quickest labeling technique but that the *Outline* interface would provide the finest pixel granularity of marking data (and thereby serve, for example, as better training data for a future semi-automatic labeling tool using computer vision).

Once a problem has been marked, a pop-up menu appears with four specific problem categories: *Curb Ramp Missing, Object in Path, Prematurely Ending Sidewalk,* and *Surface Problem.* We also included a fifth label for *Other.* These categories are based on sidewalk design guidelines from the US Department of Transportation website [3] and the US Access Board [2]. Finally, after a category has been selected, a five-point Likert scale appears asking the user to rate the severity of the problem where 5 is most severe indicating "not passable" and a 1 is least severe indicating "passable." If more than one problem exists in the image, this process is repeated. After all identified sidewalk problems have been labeled, the user can select "submit labels" and another image is loaded. Images with no apparent sidewalk problem can be marked as such by clicking on a button labeled "There are no accessibility problems in this image." Users can also choose to skip an image and record their reason (*e.g.,* image too blurry, sidewalk not visible).

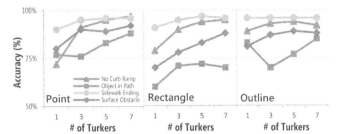

Figure 2. The number of turkers per image vs. accuracy for each of the three labeling interfaces. Note that the y-axis begins at 50%.

3. STUDY METHOD

To investigate the feasibility of using crowd workers for this task, we posted our three labeling interfaces (*Point, Rectangle,* and *Outline*) to Amazon Mechanical Turk. Crowd workers ("turkers") could complete "hits" with all three interfaces but would see each image at most once. Before beginning the labeling task with a particular interface, turkers were required to watch the first half of a three-minute instructional video. Three videos were used, one for each condition, which differed only in the description and presentation of the corresponding labeling interface. After 50% of the video was shown, the labeling interface would automatically appear (thus, turkers were not forced to watch the entire video).

Each labeling interface pulled images from the same test dataset, which consisted of 100 GSV images. These images were manually scraped by the research team using GSV of urban neighborhoods in Los Angeles, Baltimore, Washington DC, and New York City. We attempted to collect a balanced dataset. Of the 100 images, 81 contained one or more of the aforementioned problem categories. The remaining 19 images had no visible sidewalk accessibility issues and were used, in part, to evaluate *false positive* labeling activity.

To evaluate turker performance, we created baseline label data by having each of the three authors independently label all 100 images in each of the three interfaces. Inter-rater agreement was computed on these labels at the *image* level using Fleiss's kappa for each interface. More specifically, we tested for agreement based on the absence or presence of a label in an image and not on the label's particular pixel location or severity rating. We found moderate to substantial agreement [1] (ranging from 0.48 to 0.96). From these labels, we created a majority-vote "ground truth" dataset. Any image that received a label from two of the three authors was assigned that label as "ground truth" (Table 1).

	No Curb Ramp	Object in Path	Sidewalk Ending	Surface Problem
Point	34	27	10	29
Rectangle	34	27	11	28
Outline	34	26	10	29

Table 1. Frequency of labels at the *image* level in our ground truth dataset based on a "majority vote" from three trained labelers.

4. ANALYSIS AND RESULTS

We posted our task assignments to Mechanical Turk in batches of 20-30 over a one week period in June, 2012. In all, we hired 123 distinct workers who were paid three to five cents per labeled image. They worked on 2,235 assignments and provided a total of 4,309 labels (1.9 per image on average). As expected, the *Point* interface was the fastest with a median per-image labeling time of 32.9 seconds (*SD*=74.1) followed by *Outline* (41.5s, *SD*=67.6) and *Rectangle* (43.3s, *SD*=90.9). When compared with our ground truth dataset, overall turker accuracies at the *image* level were: 83.0% for *Point*, 82.6% for *Outline*, and 79.2% for *Rectangle*.

		No Curb Ramp	Object in Path	Sidewalk Ending	Surface Problem	Overall
Point	Precision	0.90	0.53	0.80	0.76	0.71
	Recall	0.82	0.93	0.73	0.93	0.87
Rectangle	Precision	0.85	0.48	0.80	0.59	0.63
	Recall	0.85	1.00	0.73	0.71	0.84
Outline	Precision	0.89	0.47	0.89	0.71	0.67
	Recall	0.91	0.93	0.73	0.89	0.89

Table 2. Precision and recall results for the three labeling interfaces based on majority vote data with three turkers compared to ground truth. "Object in path" is consistently the worst performing label.

We also explored accuracy as a function of the number of turkers per image and as a function of label type. To do this, we calculated four different turker-based majority vote datasets for each interface based on four different turker group sizes: 1, 3, 5, and 7. Group membership was determined based on the order of completion for each hit. The results are shown in Figure 2. Note that, again, we perform these comparisons at the *image* level rather than the individual label level and that we again ignore severity. These calculations are left for future work.

We did, however, employ an additional evaluation method by calculating the precision and recall rate of each interface, where:

$$Precision = \frac{True\ Pos}{True\ Pos + False\ Pos}, Recall = \frac{True\ Pos}{True\ Pos + False\ Neg}$$

True positive here is defined as is providing the correct label on an image, *false positive* is providing a label for a problem that does not actually exist on the image, and *false negative* is *not* providing a label for a problem that *does exist* in the image. Our results are presented in Table 2. Both high precision and recall are preferred. The precision rate for *Object in Path* and *Surface Problems* are relatively low for all three interfaces. This indicates that turkers are making false positive decisions for those labels—that is, they tend to use these labels for things that are not actually problems.

5. DISCUSSION AND CONCLUSION

In this paper, we explored the feasibility of using crowd-sourced labor to label sidewalk accessibility problems from GSV images. We showed that untrained crowd workers can locate and identify sidewalk accessibility problems with relatively high accuracy (~80% on average). However, there is a clear problem with turkers *overlabeling* images (*i.e.,* we had a high false positive rate). In addition, there is a non-trivial number of bad quality workers—11 out of 123 had an error rate greater than 50%. In the future, we plan to explore automated methods of quality control to identify and expel poor quality workers programmatically. An additional limitation lies relates to using GSV as a data source: often times GSV images can be rather old (the average age of our images were 2.9 yrs) and some images are distorted due to sun glare or blurriness. Finally, sidewalks are not always visible in GSV. They can be blocked by cars, trees, guard rails or other obstacles. A future study emphasizing breadth is needed to determine the magnitude of this problem.

6. REFERENCES

[1] Landis R. J. and Koch G. G. 1977. The measurement of observer agreement for categorical data. Biometrics 1977; 33:159 –74.

[2] Public Rights-Of-Way Access Advisory Committee (PROWACC). 2007. Special Report: Accessible Public Rights-of-Way Planning and Design for Alterations, http://www.access-board.gov/ prowac/alterations/guide.htm

[3] U.S. Department of Transportation, Designing Sidewalks and Trails for Access, http://www.fhwa.dot.gov/environment/ bicycle_pedestrian/publications/sidewalks/index.cfm

Replicating Semantic Connections Made by Visual Readers for a Scanning System for Nonvisual Readers

Debra Yarrington
Dept. of Computer and Information Science
University of Delaware
Newark, DE 19716

yarringt@eecis.udel.edu

Kathleen McCoy
Dept. of Computer and Information Science
University of Delaware
Newark, DE 19716

mccoy@cis.udel.edu

ABSTRACT

When scanning through a text document for the answer to a question, visual readers are able to quickly locate text within the document related to the answer while simultaneously getting a general sense of the document's content. For nonvisual readers, however, this poses a challenge, especially when the relevant text is spread out or worded in a way that can't be searched for directly. Our goal is to make the scanning experience quicker for nonvisual readers by giving them an experience similar to that of visual readers. To do this we first determined what visual scanners focused on by using an eye-tracker while they scanned for answers to complex questions. Resulting data revealed that text with loose semantic connections to the question are important. This paper reports on our efforts to develop a method that automatically replicates the connections made by visual scanners. Ultimately, our goal is a system that replicates the visual scanning experience, allowing nonvisual readers to quickly glean information in a manner similar to how visual readers glean information when scanning. This work stems from work with students who are nonvisual readers and is aimed at making their school experience more equitable with students who scan visually.

Categories and Subject Descriptors

K.4.2 [Computing Milieux]: Computers and Society – social issues –Assistive technologies for persons with disabilities.

Keywords

Text Scanning, Word Clustering, Natural Language Processing, Assistive Technology

1. INTRODUCTION

When visual readers want to answer a question by reading a document, they are able to quickly scan through the document and concentrate their reading in areas of the document most relevant to the question. For someone who uses a screenreader this is not possible. Instead an expert screenreader user will listen to the document at a very high rate of speed. However, having a screenreader read a document takes significantly longer, and is very different from a visual scanning experience. Nonvisual

reader also can't quickly re-locate information once they've gone past it. Moreover, visual readers scanning through a document in search of the answer to a question glean not only the answer to the question, but also other information including the general topology of the document, especially as related to the question. Our goal is to create a system that gives nonvisual readers information similar to the information visual readers get.

2. Process

In the development of a scanning system for nonvisual readers, clearly a critical step is working with these readers to develop an interface that delivers scanning information in the most useful manner to screenreader users. Before that work can begin we must (1) determine what in a document "catches the eye" of a visual scanner searching for a question's answer, and (2) determine how a computer system can identify and replicate that process.

For (1) we have recorded eye-tracking data while visual readers scanned through documents for the answer to a question. This paper focuses on (2). Future work will focus on the user interface.

2.1 Scanning Data

Work on stage 1 is reported in Yarrington and McCoy, 2010. Briefly, we had subjects scan through 10 documents for answers to complex questions (one per document) while being tracked by an eye tracking device. After scanning, subjects were able to answer the question correctly 86% of the time. Informal analysis of the data revealed that subjects seemed to spend more time on places in the document with words that were somehow semantically related to the question. For example, eye gaze analysis showed that cumulatively, subjects focused longest on the paragraph with the answer for 7 of the 10 documents even though there was no direct word correlation between the paragraph containing the answer and the question. Our immediate goal is to automatically replicate these semantic connections so that they can be used in a user interface to conveying relevant information. To do this we apply natural language processing techniques to score semantically related words. Because a paragraph is a unit that can be identified by most screenreaders, we use the scores of words to rate paragraph importance. For evaluation purposes, we gauge the reliability of our system by how well it accurately identifies the paragraph most focused on by the subjects in the scanning experiment.

2.2 Making Semantic Connections

Our previous work (Yarrington & McCoy, 2010) discussed two baseline methods. Here for the baseline we turn to the fields of open domain question answering and query biased text summarization to borrow from their methods of forming semantic relations.

2.2.1 Baseline

In question-document pairs, we took the question's nonfunction words, expanded that set of words by using WordNet (Felbaum, 1998) to include their synonyms, hypernyms, and hyponyms, then counted each of these words' occurrence in each paragraph in the document in order to rank the relevance of paragraph. The words were weighted using a variant of TF-IDF (Salton and Buckley, 1988), in which the paragraphs are equivalent to documents in the typical use of TF-IDF. Thus the number of paragraphs a word occurs in is considered the document-IDF, and the number of times a word occurs in a particular paragraph is considered the document-TF. This weighted words related to the document's topic lower than those unique to a particular paragraph's topic. We refer to this weight as "document TF-IDF".

This baseline method's ability to identify the paragraphs focused on by subjects when scanning was poor. (See Table 1, column 2). Studying the results suggested that the visual scanners made looser semantic connections than those identified using WordNet relations. We thus attempted to find looser semantic connections.

2.2.2 Semantic Connections Using the WWW

Out intuition was that we might identify loosely related words by finding words that are often discussed with the words in the question (e.g., "leash" is often discussed with "dog"). We call a set of such related words a word cluster and we use Web searches to identify a word cluster related to a question.

In our approach we did a Google search (www.google.com) using all the nonfunction words in a question. The search resulted in a list of URLs and accompanying snippets of text. For snippets that contained either all or most of the original nonfunction words, we located the snippet(s) within its associated Web page and added the 50 nons top words above and below the snippet to a word cluster. While this gives us the words discussed with the question words, intuitively some of these words are more important than others with respect to the question. Clearly words occurring most frequently are more important and thus we kept a count of the number of times each word occurred in the texts around any of the snippets. But, we also used a term akin to indirect-document-frequency by counting the number of times a word occurred in approximately 11000 random Web pages. Again, intuitively we give words that rarely occur in other pages more weight. We call the weighting of words in the cluster the global-TF-IDF weight.

In looking at the highly-rated words in our cluster, they do indeed seem to have a semantic relationship with the question. With this, we then attempted to use each question's word cluster (weighted for significance using the global-TF-IDF weights) to rank the paragraphs' relevance within a document. To eliminate "noise", we ordered the cluster words by their global-TF-IDF weight, and eliminated the bottom 75%, thus using only the top 25% most relevant words to rank the paragraphs in the document.

The method we used was to rank each sentence in the document, then use the top 25% most relevant sentences to rank paragraphs. Specifically, we took each sentence in the entire document and gave it a relevance score by matching the words in the cluster to the words in the sentence, weighted by multiplying its document TF-IDF weight and its global TF-IDF weight. The sentences were then ordered based on their relevance score. Because sentences with lower relevance scores provide little useful information, we used only the sentences with the top 25% relevance score. Those sentences were ordered, and given a number based on the inverse of their ranking. Then each paragraph's relevance score was calculated by adding the number assigned to each sentence belonging to that paragraph.

So, for example, each sentence in a document with 37 sentences is given a relevance score. The top 9 are saved. The sentence with the highest relevance score is given a 9, the sentence with the second highest gets an 8, etc. A paragraph's relevance score is calculated based on the scores of its sentences. So if a paragraph holds sentences ranked 1,2, and 7, it is given a score of 9+8+3, or 20. These scores were used to rate the relevance of each paragraph.

Results show that for 5 of the 10 questions, the paragraph ranked most relevant was the one most focused on during the scanning experiments (see Table 1 column 3). This is noteworthy because in 2 of the questions, the paragraph most focused on was not the paragraph with the answer. Thus results suggest this method is making the same type of semantic connection people make.

Table 1: Rankings of paragraphs most focused on using both the baseline method and the word clustering method.

	Baseline ranking of paragraph most focused on	Word clustering ranking of paragraph most focused on	Total # paragraphs in document
Q1	4	1	11
Q3	8	1	14
Q7	6	1	14
Q10	5	1	15
Q9	11,15*	1,2*	30
Q8	5	4	13
Q6	7	5	10
Q2	2	6	15
Q4	12**	7	12
Q5	4	10	25

*For Q9, 2 paragraphs tied as the most focused on. Our method ranked those 2 paragraphs as the first and second most relevant.
**9 of the 12 paragraphs tied for least relevant

3. FUTURE DIRECTIONS

Ultimately the goal is to incorporate a method for making appropriate semantic connections into a user interface. We will work closely with nonvisual readers to determine the best way to convey relevant information. For instance, if we know we have a reliable method for establishing semantic connections, we may then for each paragraph convey the sentence(s) within the paragraph ranked as most relevant, allowing the user to choose where to expand their focus.

4. REFERENCES

[1] Felbaum, C. 1998. *WordNet an Electronic Database*, Boston/Cambridge: MIT Press.

[2] Salton, G. and Buckley, C. 1988. "Term-weighting approaches in automatic text retrieval." Information Processing & Management, 24 (5): 513-523.

[3] Yarrington, D. and McCoy, K. 2010. "Automated Skimming in Response to Questions for NonVisual Readers." NAACL: SLPAT Workshop, Los Angeles, Ca.

It Is Not a Talking Book; It Is More Like Really Reading a Book!

Yasmine N. El-Glaly
Computer Science
Virginia Polytechnic Institute
and State University
Blacksburg, VA 24061, USA
yasmineg@vt.edu

Francis Quek
Computer Science
Virginia Polytechnic Institute
and State University
Blacksburg, VA 24061, USA
quek@vt.edu

Tonya L. Smith-Jackson
Industrial and Systems
Engineering
Virginia Polytechnic Institute
and State University
Blacksburg, VA 24061, USA
smithjac@vt.edu

Gurjot Dhillon
Industrial and Systems
Engineering
Virginia Polytechnic Institute
and State University
Blacksburg, VA 24061, USA
gurjotsd@vt.edu

ABSTRACT

In this research we designed, developed, and tested a reading system that enables Individuals with Blindness or Severe Visual Impairment (IBSVI) to fuse audio, tactile landmarks, and spatial information in order to read. This system renders electronic text documents on iPad-type devices, and reads aloud each word touched by the user's finger. A tactile overlay on the iPad screen helps IBSVI to navigate a page, furnishing a framework of tactile landmarks to give IBSVI a sense of place on the page. As the user moves her finger along the tangible pattern of the overlay, the text on the iPad screen that is touched is rendered audibly using a text-to-speech synthesizer.

Categories and Subject Descriptors

H.5.2 [**Information Interfaces and Presentation**]: User Interfaces – *interaction styles, auditory feedback.*

Keywords

Spatial Cognition, Blindness, Active Reading, Touch Devices.

1. INTRODUCTION

Books and documents are designed for sighted people. Walter J. Ong in his highly influential "Orality and Literacy: The Technologizing of the Word" [6] observed that before the invention of printing, all literature or inscribed cultural knowledge was designed for aural consumption. As such, the entire structure of ancient writing was tailored to aural comprehension, employing concomitant mnemonic structure and aural aids like rhyme, meter, and alliteration. The reverse of this observation is that after printing, literature has become a visual medium, and the necessary mnemonic and structural aids for non-visual consumption are deemphasized. Document organization and page structure provide readers with embedded spatial information that makes refresh of context easier and faster. Page layout is biased toward readers with visual capabilities to interpret certain information based on this spatial-visual layout. This bias is not only in the external structure of the information. It is deeply embedded in the way the information is encoded in the first place. Even theories used to design information displays emphasize encoding and mapping as interdependent visuo-spatial representations [1]. The title of this paper highlights the difference between the popular audio reader and active reading. Audio readers cannot address the spatial bias we have identified. Audio format provides IBSVI with information in the form of linear stream that overloads IBSVI's working memory and obliterate spatial layout, leaving IBSVI with no spatial reference while reading. Commercial solutions for screen reading such as VoiceOver or JAWS do not address the

spatial access of pages adequately [7; 8]. Our research is motivated by these observations to address the bias of information encoding and presentation. We address how IBSVI may be enabled to access spatial information in reading materials without visual cues, how such enablement may utilize other senses such as aural and tactile senses to access spatial information in printed material. Furthermore, we explore how to design such an audio-tactile device to enable spatial reading for IBSVI, what technologies are needed and how to test it.

2. RELATED WORK

In 1824, Braille transformed text into raised dot patterns laid out spatially on paper. The problem with Braille code is that only 10% of people with blindness in the USA can read Braille [9]. More importantly, Braille books are large in size and cumbersome to handle. Transforming Braille to the digital form has been done by refreshable Braille display [2; 4], and by display of virtual Braille dots [5]. These high cost technologies solved the portability and mobility problems of Braille books, however they eliminated the capability of Braille to provide spatial referencing because the size of the displays is relatively small.

3. APPROACH

We designed and developed a Situated Touch Audio Annotator and Reader (STAAR) for IBSVI by employing an iterative design-implement-test approach in our development efforts. STAAR comprises a static overlay with a tactile pattern over a standard Apple iPad device. The overlay serves as a tactile landmark pattern to help the IBSVI to navigate the iPad surface. A text document is mapped spatially on the iPad display. As words are touched, the system renders the words audibly by using speech synthesizer. Fusion of the words and location of the text takes place in the mind of the reader as she touches and hears. The tactile patterns will ground and map a mental model of how information is located and organized in the document being read.

3.1 The Reader Interface

The reader interface is made up of three general interaction areas: the vertical ruler area, the reading area, and the buttons area (Figure 1.a.). These three areas are delineated for the IBSVI in the tactile overlay and in the underlying system design. The ruler is designed to help the user to locate and situate themselves with respect to the text lines in the reading area. When the user's finger traverses along the vertical ruler, she will hear an audible cue whenever the finger is in line with a line of text. The central area that covers about 90% of the iPad screen, which is surrounded by a red rectangle is the reading area. At the bottom of the interface there is a consistent place for the user to locate the system's interaction buttons. The function of these buttons is to navigate the rendered document by page and by chapter. The tactile overlay (Figure 1.b.) function is to provide IBSVI with landmarks for reading and following straight lines of text, and landmarks for interaction with fixed-location virtual buttons. More importantly, it provides IBSVI with landmarks as a mental reference for location awareness to maintain place on a page.

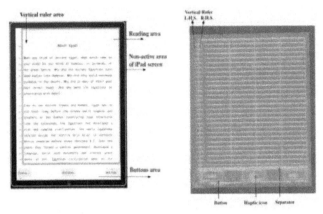

Figure 1. Left: The reader interface. Right: The overlay.

3.2 The Reader System

We built the reader system on the iPad platform. A page description is developed to facilitate the interaction with the different page elements such as words, lines, and white spaces. The reader system handles different interaction mechanisms and gestures. We found that groups of IBSVI users need to rest their palms or use two fingers on the iPad screen to provide a spatial reference for their hands while they are reading lines on the page. Hence, the reader system is designed to track the number, position, and direction of touches, and then to interpret these data to obtain an understanding of the real meaning of the user's touch intent. Finally, an audio cues module was developed to generate audio feedback according to the user's finger movement. Foe example, we found during the pilot studies that when IBSVI tried to explore a page without having any visual cues, she needed an information reference substitution. Hence, we added sonification to the reader system to convey white space, line finding, line ending, and skipping a word.

4. STUDIES

The cycles of the STAAR have three major studies of different kinds and for different purposes. The first one is actually a series of pilot studies. Each pilot study gave us further insight on how to better improve the system. When no more significant feedback was obtained from the pilot studies, we tested the system in a short-term usability study. Sixteen IBSVI were recruited for the cycle 2 study. We prepared 8 articles of one page length to be read in different conditions. The usability metrics employed were scenario completion, errors, time on task, and mental workload that is measured by NASA Task Load Index [3]. The results of cycle 2 study showed that STAAR can be operated by IBSVI, but is not functional enough to help with knowledge transfer. This study allowed us to determine the effective parameters for the overlay and the appropriate density of text that can be rendered on the iPad screen. The findings of the cycle 2 study were incorporated into the design for the third design cycle. We then designed a longitudinal study in which we seeded IBSVI with the device for a longer period of use. The goals of cycle 3 study were to investigate the effect of experiencing STAAR for longer time on the users' performance. For this study, we recruited 5 IBSVI. The results showed that STAAR at this stage was both operational and functional. We found that participants were able to develop a mental model of how to fuse multi channel information in order to read using their spatial, aural, and tactile capabilities. Participants better understood the auditory signals and reacted faster to them over time. They were able to read and understand the reading materials. Moreover, participants were able to catch up with their mistakes e.g. if a user skipped a line she can guess that it happened and can go back to find the correct line in sequence.

5. CONCLUSIONS

In this paper, we introduced a novel way of reading for IBSVI that makes use of their spatial, auditory, and haptic capabilities. STAAR has the advantages of being portable and digital as in audio reading medium. At the same time IBSVI can read at her self-pace similar to reading Braille. Results showed that STAAR is usable by IBSVI with different reading "backgrounds" (e.g. Braille, Audio books, or non active readers). STAAR encourages IBSVI to perform active reading. STAAR is still a rich environment for further improvements e.g. speech improvements and enabling zooming for IBSVI.

6. ACKNOWLEDGMENTS

This research is supported by the National Science Foundation under Grant No. IIS1117854. Any opinions, findings, and conclusions or recommendations expressed in this material are those of the authors and do not necessarily reflect the views of the National Science Foundation.

7. REFERENCES

[1] BADDELEY, A.D. and HITCH, G.J., 1974. Working Memory. *The psychology of learning and motivation 8.*

[2] BROWN, C., 1992. Assistive Technology Computers And Persons With Disabilities. *Communications of the ACM 35*, 5, 36-45.

[3] HART, G. and STAVELAND, L.E., 1988. *Development of a Multidimensional Workload Rating Scale: Results of Empirical and Theoretical Research, in Human Mental Workload.* Elsevier, The Netherlands.

[4] HEADLEY, P.C., HRIBAR, V.E., and PAWLUK, D.T.V., 2011. Displaying braille and graphics on a mouse-like tactile display. In *Proceedings of the The proceedings of the 13th international ACM SIGACCESS conference on Computers and accessibility* (Scotland, UK2011), ACM, 2049584, 235-236.

[5] LAVESQUE, V., PASQUERO, J., HAYWARD, V., and LEGAULT, M., 2005. Display of virtual braille dots by lateral skin deformation: feasibility study. *ACM Trans. Appl. Percept. 2*, 2, 132-149.

[6] ONG, W.J., ORALITY, 1984. Literacy, and Medieval Textualization. *New Literary History 16*, 1, 1-12.

[7] PETIT, G., DUFRESNE, A., and ROBERT, J.-M., 2011. Introducing TactoWeb: A Tool to Spatially Explore Web Pages for Users with Visual Impairment Universal Access in Human-Computer Interaction. Design for All and eInclusion, C. STEPHANIDIS Ed. Springer Berlin / Heidelberg, 276-284.

[8] PICCOLO, L.S.G., MENEZES, E.M.D., and BUCCOLO, B.D.C., 2011. Developing an accessible interaction model for touch screen mobile devices: preliminary results. In *Proceedings of the Proceedings of the 10th Brazilian Symposium on on Human Factors in Computing Systems and the 5th Latin American Conference on Human-Computer Interaction* (Brazil2011), Brazilian Computer Society, 2254474, 222-226.

[9] STEPHANIDIS, C., 2009. *Universal Access in Human-Computer Interaction. Applications and Services: 5th International Conference, UAHCI 2009, Held as Part of HCI International Applications, incl. Internet/Web, and HCI)* Springer.

MeetUp: A Universally Designed Smartphone Application To Find Another

Nara Kim
Department of Computer Science and Engineering
University of Washington
Seattle, WA 98195 USA
narakim@cs.washington.edu

Matt Moyers
Department of Computer Science and Engineering
University of Washington
Seattle, WA 98195 USA
mmoyers@cs.washington.edu

ABSTRACT

A universally designed mobile application, MeetUp, that assists users to meet up is designed and implemented for blind and sighted users. The Android application MeetUp was originally designed for blind users, but a visual interface was added so it could become usable by sighted users as well. The system design and user interactions with the application are described.

Categories and Subject Descriptors

K4.2 [**Social Issues**]: Assistive technologies for persons with

General Terms

Human Factors, Design.

Keywords

Blind, accessibility, way-finding, navigation.

1. INTRODUCTION

People with visual impairments experience challenges in finding another person at a general meeting location. Without extra help, knowing great detail about the meeting location appears to be required before they leave [7]. However when the meeting place is a large area such as a park, a shopping mall, or a convention center, difficulty of the task is even greater. The same problem arises among sighted people when they meet at a location both parties have never been to.

Mobile platform provides us with GPS, accessibility via vibration and verbal feedback, mobility and network access to facilitate communication among users. These features paired with its mass adoption led us to utilize mobile platform.

Sharing one user's location with another is a popular feature in commercial systems often called "check-in." Yet the lack of detail on each user's location does not alleviate the problem.

We explore a way to give routing information to users dynamically. As each user moves, their location is updated and shared with their friend. We built a universally designed prototype in the Android operating system and tested with blind and sighted users.

2. RELATED WORK

Many mobile applications exist providing location and routing information to the user. Popular GPS applications and devices can tell users when to turn and how to navigate the streets to a

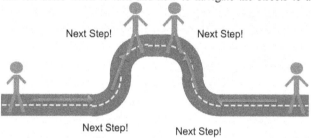

Figure 1. MeetUp enables two people to find one another.

fixed location. Others also provide accessible interfaces targeting blind or low vision users [9].

One emerging commercial feature often called "check-in" allows users to tag their location at a point in time. This "check-in" feature can be found in Facebook, Foursquare, and Google Latitude [2,3,4]. Google Latitude also supports a routing feature that gives one user a route to where someone last checked in. Once again this routing information is based on a fixed destination location. Our solution does not require checking-in, but automatically updates routes as people move to meet each other.

Some navigation solutions for blind people involve special purpose wearable computers to get location information [8]. What sets our system apart is we attempt to give this functionality on a mainstream device (smartphone) that users already have and are familiar with.

3. MEETUP CLIENT APPLICATION

We developed an Android application, MeetUp, that updates routes based on two moving targets (source and destination) and provides routing information to the user such as distance, cardinal direction, and relative direction at turning points. The typical workflow of MeetUp is for one user to choose a person to meet with, wait for that person to reciprocate, and get direction information. While MeetUp is getting location information from each user, routes are calculated and updated as needed. When the route becomes small, within talking distance, MeetUp notifies the user. When you have arrived, MeetUp terminates and stops the flow of location information.

3.1 User Interface

The user interface was constructed as a simple list of buttons, each of which can be selected by double tapping. Each screen has verbal instructions and verbal feedback for each UI element. For example in Figure 2 distance, duration, and a list of steps is shown and each item's text is spoken to the user when a finger is hovered on it.

The UI starts off at the contacts screen where the user selects a person to meet up with. This brings the user to the communication screen, where he or she can call or text the user before activating MeetUp. When the user starts MeetUp, the other user will be notified to start as well. This notification consists of verbal and vibration feedback. No location information is shared until both users choose each other to meet up with. Once MeetUp has been activated the direction screen is displayed. Here the user has many ways to gather information about the route he or she must take to get to their selected person. The application provides street name, plus cardinal direction, relative direction, and magnitude about the route as well as a visual map, which displays both users current location. It also provides vibration feedback when the user should move on to the next step. Each screen is updated as needed to display the most up to date routing information as they navigate to each other.

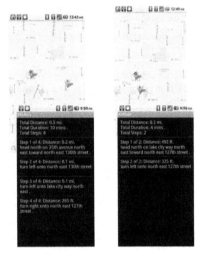

Figure 2. GUI Interface showing the transition from different points in the route.

One design challenge we encountered was how to provide routing directions to users with visual impairments. We consulted with a blind user, Peggy Martinez. The pattern feedback method in Azenkot *et al.*, which outputs a sequence of vibrations that symbolizes a relative direction, was presented. However, GPS accuracy during testing was less accurate, and this caused the user to turn to at incorrect locations. Pattern by itself was insufficient for our needs. Peggy discussed what visually impaired users would expect in these situations. So, we paired pattern with verbal information from the direction screen. The verbal information provides the user with relative directions as well as street names and estimated distance to the turn. This allowed the user to rely on his or her senses to conduct the turn.

If for any reason a completely new route is detected, a long vibration is given to the user. He or she can now use the direction screen to gather information on the new route.

3.2 System

The System consists of two components, a Client and the Server as shown in Figure 3. The server provides a means for the each phone to communicate with one another. The Client is responsible for two things, sending user's current location to the server periodically and refreshing routing data when needed. To accomplish this, the client application uses the internal GPS or Network information for user's current location and Google Maps for routes. To keep location data accurate between phones, every time the internal GPS reports a new location, the client sends it to the server. Refreshing the routing data is done as needed.

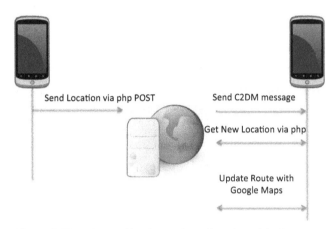

Figure 3. How the application updates location with the server

If the user goes off the provided route, a new route is fetched from Google Maps using their API. One problem that occurs, infrequently, is the route between the two users is different. To resolve this problem the server is contacted and one route is chosen for the users to follow.

4. ACKNOWLEDGMENTS

The authors thank Peggy Martinez, Richard Ladner, Alan Borning, and Shiri Azenkot for their assistance on the project.

5. REFERENCES

[1] Azenkot, S., Ladner, R.E., and Wobbrock, J.O. 2011. Smartphone Haptic Feedback for Nonvisual Wayfinding. ASSETS 2011. 181-182.

[2] Check in with Google Latitude. 2011. http://googlemobile.blogspot.com/2011/02/check-in-with-google-latitude.html

[3] Facebook. 2011. http://www.facebook.com/about/location

[4] Four Square. 2012. https://foursquare.com/app/autocheck_for_ios

[5] Garmin eTrail. 2012 http://www8.garmin.com/outdoor/eTrail/index.html

[6] Karimi, H. 2011. Universal Navigation on Smartphones. Springer Science+Business Media LLC.

[7] Passini R., Proulx G. 1988 Wayfinding Without Vision. 2, March 1988. Sage Publications, Inc.

[8] Ran, L. Helal, S., Moore, S. 2004. Drishti: an integrated indoor/outdoor blind navigation system and service. Page 23. IEEE Computer Society Washington, DC, USA 2004.

[9] Sendero Group LLC. 2012. http://www.senderogroup.c

Gesture Interface Magnifiers for Low-Vision Users

Seunghyun "Tina" Lee[1] and Jon Sanford[1,2]

[1]Center for Assistive Technology and Environmental Access, College of Architecture,
Georgia Institute of Technology, Atlanta, GA, USA
[2]Rehab R&D Center of Excellence, Atlanta VAMC
tinalee@gatech.edu, jon.sanford@coa.gatech.edu

ABSTRACT

This study compared different types of magnification and navigation methods on low-vision handheld magnifiers to determine the feasibility of a touch screen gesture interface. The results show that despite the fact that participants had no experience using gestures for magnification or navigation, participants were more satisfied with them. Gestures were faster and more preferred than the indirect input methods for pushing a button or rotating a knob, which had previously been familiar to participants from other electronic device interfaces. The study suggests that the use of gestures may afford an alternative and more natural magnification and navigation method for a new user-centric low vision magnifier.

Categories and Subject Descriptors

H.5.2. Information interfaces and presentation: User Interfaces–input devices and strategies.

Keywords

Low vision video magnifier, gesture.

1. INTRODUCTION

Existing low vision video magnifiers utilize similar types of *indirect* (i.e., require mental translation between hand and screen) input mechanisms on magnification (e.g., push button, rotate knob) and navigation (e.g., move magnifier, slide gesture) methods. However, studies [2,3] have shown that because indirect inputs require users to translate the physical distance moved to the virtual distance moved on a screen, they may further complicate reading tasks, particularly among older people with vision loss who also commonly have diminished working memory, selective attention, and motor control [1,5].

In contrast, studies [2-4] have shown that *direct* inputs (e.g., touch screen) which have no intermediary provide less physical and cognitive demand than indirect inputs. Despite the use of indirect inputs and the availability of direct gesture inputs (e.g., pinching a gesture on touch screen) for magnification and navigation, no studies have directly evaluated the effects across different indirect and direct magnification and navigation input controls on reading performance for people with low vision.

The purpose of this study was to investigate the effects of different direct (pinch gesture) and indirect magnification (push button) and navigation (move magnifier, slide gesture) methods to determine the feasibility of a touch screen gesture interface.

2. METHODS

Twenty low-vision adults (9 female; 11 male) from the Center for

the Visually Impaired (CVI) who were prescribed magnifiers for reading participated in the study. The age range was 30-63 years with a mean of 46.9 years. All participants were native English speakers with reading fluency, and who did not have experience using any of the test devices (i.e., SmartView Pocket, Amigo, iPodTouch).

The SmartView Pocket by Humanware is a handheld video magnifier with a 3.6" LCD display that provides magnification from 3x - 9x by pushing increase or decrease (-/+) button located next to the display. The Amigo by Enhanced Vision has a 6.5" LCD display and provides magnification from 3.5x - 14x by rotating a knob located on the side of the unit. The iPodTouch by Apple has a 3.5" Multi-touch display. This Multi-touch provides magnification by two finger pinch gesture and navigation by one finger slide gesture on the touch screen (See Figure1).

Magnification gesture	Navigation gesture
"Two finger pinch"	"One finger slide"

Figure 1. A sample of finger gestures

To control for the effect of window size, the Amigo with a 6.5" LCD display was mounted as a 3.5" display like the other two handheld devices. Table 1 shows the characteristics of all of the test devices.

Table 1. Test devices

	SmartView Pocket	Amigo	iPodTouch
Magnification input controls	"Pushing" a button (BUTTON)	"Rotating" a knob (KNOB)	"Pinch" gesturing on a touch screen (PINCH)
Navigation input controls	Movement with tilt (MWT)	Movement without tilt (MWOT)	"slide" gesturing on a touch screen (SLIDE)
Screen size	3.5"	3.5" (6.5")	3.5"

The Task was adjusting the desired magnification and reading aloud a medicine label (e.g., "Adults and children 4 years of age and older- chew one tablet daily*"). To control the learning effects, three devices and labels were randomly selected per participant. After the training, participants were asked to 1) adjust the magnification until he or she reached their desired level of magnification with the testing devices, 2) read aloud labels using each of three video magnifiers, 3) rate their ease of use, ease of understanding, and satisfaction of each magnification and navigation methods, and 4) ranked order the preference of the magnification and navigation methods on reading.

3. FINDINGS

The findings of this study suggest that direct gesture type magnification and navigation methods are potentially more effective methods of input for the low vision participants. Surprisingly, despite the fact that participants had no experience using gestures for magnification or navigation, they were faster and more satisfied when using a gesture on magnification than the indirect input methods, pushing a button or rotating a knob, which had already been familiar to them from other electronic devices.

A repeated measures analyses of variance (ANOVA) was used to examine significant differences in task performance, subjective ratings on ease of use, ease of understanding, satisfaction between magnification and navigation input controls. Magnification adjustment speed showed a statistically significant difference (F $(2,20)$=3.324, $p < .05$) between the direct PINCH control (mean = 11.46 seconds) and both the BUTTON (mean = 15.99 seconds) and KNOB (mean = 17.0 seconds) controls (see Figure 2). Paired-samples t-tests revealed that participants adjusted the magnification significantly faster using direct PINCH method compared to either the BUTTON (t (19)=3.171, $p < .01$) or the KNOB (t (19)=2.215, $p < .05$). This is strong evidence that such gesture inputs may be a viable candidate as a magnification method for low vision users.

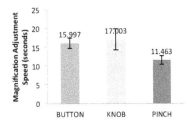

Figure 2. Mean magnification adjustment speed. The error bars show standard error of the mean.

Reading speed showed no statistically significant difference among types of input controls. However, we found that participants read faster using the device with slide gesture than those requiring the device to be moved.

Participants rated pinch gesture as a magnification method significantly higher than either the button or the knob on satisfaction. There was a statistically significant difference (F $(2,20) = 4.099$, $p < .05$) among BUTTON (mean = 3.95), KNOB (mean = 4.15), and PINCH (mean = 4.70) types. Participants also rated slide gesture as a navigation method significantly higher than either the button of the knob on ease of use, ease of understanding, and satisfaction. There were significant differences among all 3 controls for 'ease of use' (F $(2,20)$ =4.659, $p < .05$), 'ease of understanding' (F $(2,20)$ = 3.435, $p < .05$), and 'satisfaction' (F $(2,20)$ = 8.688, $p < .001$). The design of new devices might consider adopting the slide gesture for the navigation method.

More than two-thirds (n = 13) of participants preferred the PINCH gesture the most followed by 25% who preferred the BUTTON and 10% who preferred the KNOB as a magnification

method (see Figure3). Participants' comments included: "It's very unique, it's different than other devices", "very easy to do once I learn", "easier to magnify using fingers than other devices", and "pinch gesture seems more accurate than button." Remarkably, 85% (n = 17) of participants preferred the SLIDE followed by 10% for MWOT and 5% for MWT as a navigation input control (see Figure 4). Some of their comments were "very easy to move with one finger", "I am totally satisfied with this", "I just need to move my finger.. Just so easy."

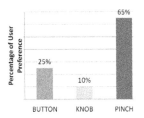 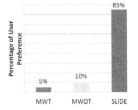

Figure 3. User preference of magnification input   **Figure 4. User preference of navigation input**

The limitations of this study were a lack of control over other physical characteristics of devices such as screen resolution, brightness, and different ergonomics of device. However, in this study, we focused on comparing of input controls of magnification and interaction of navigation rather than comparing the devices themselves. Overall, the data suggests that gestures could be a viable alternative input control on magnification and navigation for a new user-centric low-vision video magnifier. Our study is an important step forward in proceeding to the next step of developing a gesture-based interface.

4. ACKNOWLEDGMENTS

We thank all the low vision users who participated in our study and support from the Center for the Visually Impaired (CVI) and Atlanta VA Rehabilitation R & D Center for Vision Loss.

5. REFERENCES

[1] Charness, N., Holley, P., Feddon, J., & Jastrzembski, T. (2004). Light Pen Use and Practice Minimize Age and Hand Performance Differences in Pointing Tasks. *Human Factors: The Journal of the Human Factors and Ergonomics Society, 46*(3), 373-384.

[2] McLaughlin, A. C., Rogers, W. A., & Fisk, A. D. (2009). Using direct and indirect input devices: Attention demands and age-related differences. *ACM Trans. Comput.-Hum. Interact., 16*(1), 1-15.

[3] Rogers, W. A., Fisk, A. D., McLaughlin, A. C., & Pak, R. (2005). Touch a Screen or Turn a Knob: Choosing the Best Device for the Job. *Human Factors: The Journal of the Human Factors and Ergonomics Society, 47*(2), 271-288.

[4] Stößel, C., Wandke, H., & Blessing, L. (2010). Gestural Interfaces for Elderly Users: Help or Hindrance? In S. Kopp & I. Wachsmuth (Eds.), *Gesture in Embodied Communication and Human-Computer Interaction* (Vol. 5934, pp. 269-280): Springer Berlin / Heidelberg.

[5] Walker, N., Philbin, D. A., & Fisk, A. D. (1997). Age-Related Differences in Movement Control: Adjusting Submovement Structure To Optimize Performance. *The Journals of Gerontology Series B: Psychological Sciences and Social Sciences, 52B*(1), P40-P53.

3D Point of Gaze Estimation Using Head-Mounted RGB-D Cameras

Christopher McMurrough, Christopher Conly, Vassilis Athitsos, Fillia Makedon
Department of Computer Science and Engineering
The University of Texas at Arlington
Arlington, Texas
{mcmurrough, cconly, athitsos, makedon}@uta.edu

ABSTRACT

This paper presents a low-cost, wearable headset for 3D Point of Gaze (PoG) estimation in assistive applications. The device consists of an eye tracking camera and forward facing RGB-D scene camera which, together, provide an estimate of the user gaze vector and its intersection with a 3D point in space. The resulting system is able to compute the 3D PoG in real-time using inexpensive and readily available hardware components.

Categories and Subject Descriptors

H.5.2 [**User Interfaces**]: Input devices and strategies; I.4.8 [**Image Processing and Computer Vision**]: Scene Analysis—*object recognition, range data, sensor fusion*

General Terms

Design, Human Factors, Experimentation

Keywords

Eyetracking, assistive environments, multimodal systems, human-computer interaction

1. INTRODUCTION

Eye gaze interaction has been shown to be highly beneficial to people with physical disabilities. In the case study presented in [3], 16 amyotrophic lateral sclerosis (ALS) patients with severe motor disabilities (loss of mobility, inability to speak, etc.) were introduced to eye tracking devices during a 1-2 week period. Several patients reported a clear positive impact on their quality of life, resulting from enhanced communication facilitated by the eye tracking devices.

While the utility of gaze interaction has been demonstrated, existing eye gaze systems suffer from some limiting constraints. In general, they are designed for interaction with fixed computer displays or 2D scene images, and the 2D PoG of these systems does not directly translate into the 3D world. An accurate estimate of the 3D user PoG within an environment is clearly useful, as it can be used to detect user attention and intention to interact [1]. For example, knowledge of the user 3D PoG could be used to identify objects of interests for manipulation by an assistive robot. An

intelligent wheelchair could also utilize 3D PoG as a primary data modality for assisted navigation.

Furthermore, existing systems tend to lack mobility, and the mobile 3D PoG tracking systems that have been proposed in literature suffer from their own limitations. The head-mounted multi-camera system presented in [4], for example, gives the 3D PoG relative to the user's frame of reference, but does not map this point to the user's environment. Finally, the high monetary cost and proprietary nature of commercial eye tracking equipment limits widespread use. This has led to interest in the development of low-cost solutions using off-the-shelf components.

We propose a novel head-mounted system that addresses the limitations of current solutions. First, an eye tracking camera is used to estimate the 2D PoG. An inexpensive RGB-D scene camera is then used to acquire a 3D representation of the environment structure. Finally, we provide a process by which the 2D PoG is transformed to 3D coordinates.

2. EYE TRACKING CAMERA

The system eye tracking feature is accomplished using an embedded USB camera module equipped with an infrared pass filter. The user's eye is illuminated with a single infrared LED to provide consistent image data in various ambient lighting conditions. The LED also produces a corneal reflection on the user's eye, which can be seen by the camera and exploited to enhance tracking accuracy. The LED was chosen according to the guidelines discussed in [2] to ensure that the device could be used safely for indefinite periods of time. The image resolution of 640x480 pixels and frame rate of 30 Hz facilitate accurate tracking of the pupil and corneal reflection using image processing techniques which are further discussed in section 4.

The eye camera is positioned such that the image frame is centered in front of one of the user's eyes. The module can be moved from one side of the headset frame to the other so that either eye can be used (to take advantage of user preference or eye dominance), while fine adjustments to the camera position and orientation are possible by manipulating the flexible mounting arm.

3. SCENE RGB-D CAMERA

Information about the environment in front of the user is provided by a forward facing RGB-D camera, the Asus XtionPRO Live. This device provides a 640x480 color image of the environment along with a 640x480 depth range image at a rate of 30 Hz. The two images are obtained from individual imaging sensors and registered by the device such that each color pixel value is assigned actual 3D coordinates in space. This provides a complete scanning solution for the environment in the form of 3D "point clouds", which can be further processed in software. The completed headset is shown in Figure 1.

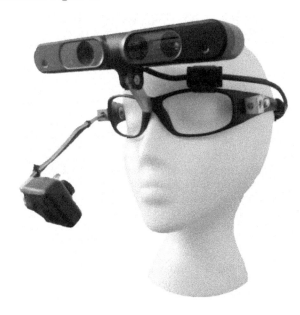

Figure 1: Headset with eye and scene cameras

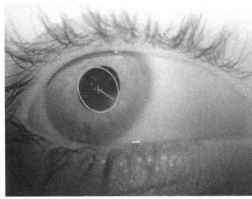

(a) Eye image with difference vector

(b) Scene image annotated with PoG

Figure 2: Mapping of gaze vector to scene

4. POINT OF GAZE ESTIMATION

An estimate of the user PoG is computed using a modified version of the starburst algorithm presented in [6]. This algorithm creates a mapping between pupil positions and 2D scene image coordinates after a 9 point calibration procedure is performed. During the pupil detection phase of the algorithm, an ellipse is fitted to the pupil such that the ellipse center provides an accurate estimate of the pupil center. The center of the infrared corneal reflection is detected during the next phase of the algorithm, which is then compared to the pupil center to acquire a difference vector. The resulting difference vector is then used to interpolate the 2D PoG in the scene camera, as shown in Figure 2. The 3D PoG can be obtained easily from the 2D point by looking up the 3D coordinates of the pixel in the point cloud data structure provided by the RGB-D camera. Exploitation of the RGB-D point cloud structure removes the need for stereo eye tracking during 3D PoG estimation as used in [4, 5].

5. CONCLUSIONS & FUTURE WORK

The resulting headset provides valuable information on user intent to designers of assistive systems. The low-cost approach will enable the inclusion of 3D PoG in a wide variety of applications. Future work will explore the use of 3D PoG for control of electric wheelchairs and service robots in assistive environments.

6. REFERENCES

[1] D. Milner and M. Goodale. *The Visual Brain in Action*. Oxford University Press, Oxford, UK, 2nd edition, 2006.

[2] F. Mulvey, A. Villanueva, D. Sliney, R. Lange, S. Cotmore, and M. Donegan. D5 . 4 Exploration of safety issues in Eyetracking. Technical report, Communication by Gaze Interaction (COGAIN), 2008.

[3] V. Pasian, F. Corno, I. Signorile, and L. Farinetti. The Impact of Gaze Controlled Technology on Quality of Life. In *Gaze Interaction and Applications of Eye Tracking: Advances in Assistive Technologies*, chapter 6, pages 48–54. IGI Global, 2012.

[4] F. Pirri, M. Pizzoli, and A. Rudi. A general method for the point of regard estimation in 3D space. In *CVPR 2011*, pages 921–928. IEEE, June 2011.

[5] K. Takemura, Y. Kohashi, T. Suenaga, J. Takamatsu, and T. Ogasawara. Estimating 3D point-of-regard and visualizing gaze trajectories under natural head movements. In *Proceedings of the 2010 Symposium on Eye-Tracking Research & Applications - ETRA '10*, volume 1, page 157, New York, New York, USA, 2010. ACM Press.

[6] D. Winfield and D. Parkhurst. Starburst: A hybrid algorithm for video-based eye tracking combining feature-based and model-based approaches. *2005 IEEE Computer Society Conference on Computer Vision and Pattern Recognition (CVPR'05) - Workshops*, 3:79–79, 2005.

Displaying Error & Uncertainty in Auditory Graphs

Jared M. Batterman and Bruce N. Walker
Georgia Institute of Technology
School of Psychology
Atlanta, GA, USA
+1 (404) 894-826
jmbatterman@gatech.edu, bruce.walker@psych.gatech.edu

ABSTRACT

Clear representation of uncertainty or error is crucial in graphs and other displays of data. Error bars are quite common in visual graphs, even though they are not necessarily well-designed, and often are not well understood, even by those who use them often (e.g., scientists, engineers). There has been little study of how to represent uncertainty in *auditory* graphs, such as those used increasingly by students and scientists with vision impairment. This study used conceptual magnitude estimation to determine how well different auditory dimensions (frequency, tempo) can represent error and uncertainty. The results will lead to more effective auditory displays of quantitative information and data.

Categories and Subject Descriptors

H.1.2 [**Models and Principles**]: User/Machine Systems—*Human factors; human information processing*; H.5.1 [**Information Interfaces and Presentation**]: Multimedia Information Systems—*Audio input/output*; H.5.2 [**Information Interfaces and Presentation**]: User Interfaces—*Auditory (non-speech) feedback; user-centered design*; J.4 [**Computer Application**]: Social and Behavioral Sciences—*Psychology*

Keywords

Sonification, Magnitude Estimation, Auditory Display

1. INTRODUCTION

Certainty is rare in the natural world, and even more so in the scientific realm. Representations of uncertainty are found not just throughout scientific literature, but also in weather reports, economics, and mathematics graphs (Constantinescu et al., 2010; Gilboa, Postlewaite, & Schmeidler, 2008). Whereas the graph and display type may vary, what does not change is that it is often presented solely visually. Unfortunately, representing data (and uncertainty about data) just visually has limitations.

First, it makes the data inaccessible to individuals with visual impairment, who still lack sufficient access to a wide array of data. It is imperative that any new measure of uncertainty be made available to them.

Secondly, current representations fail to take advantage of the unique display capabilities of other sensory modalities, most notably the auditory system. For example, research has demonstrated that relative to the visual system, the auditory system has superior temporal processing ability and pattern recognition capacity (e.g., Flowers & Hauer, 1992).

Finally, current representations of uncertainty are not well understood, even by those who utilize them for a living. In a study by Belia, Fiddler, Williams, and Cumming (2005), participants (all authors of scientific journal articles) were tasked with looking at a graph depicting two mean data points with bars representing either the Standard Error of the Mean (SEM) or a 95% Confidence Interval (CI) extending above and below them. They were asked to move one of the data points until they reached the point that the two means were judged to be just significantly different at the $p<0.05$ level. Those in the CI condition were overly strict, positioning the means too far apart; while those in the SEM condition were too lax, positioning the means too close together. When asked about their reasoning for their responses, 61% of participants gave statistically inaccurate explanations. These results are unsettling, and demonstrate the need for a better, more efficient, and more accessible way to display uncertainty.

Another issue with current representations is that there is nothing inherently uncertain about them. Thus, it would be difficult to design a new way to convey uncertainty without first finding out what makes something uncertain to begin with. In order to determine how changes in a stimulus (e.g., an increase in pitch) translate into changes in perceived uncertainty, we utilized the conceptual magnitude estimation procedure developed by Walker (2002) to determine an ideal auditory representation for uncertainty. However, unlike the pure tones utilized in Walker's (2002) experiments, we utilized white noise to convey uncertainty instead. We anticipate this mapping will be utilized in a large range of tools and devices, many of which use pure tones to convey other information (e.g., data values).

Furthermore, many displays of uncertainty also represent (or are similar to representations of) error. Due to this, we also tested error as a conceptual dimension to determine if its mappings were similar to those found for uncertainty.

2. Methods
2.1 Participants

Thirty-five undergraduates participated for extra credit in an introductory psychology course.

2.2 Stimuli & Apparatus

Stimuli were presented over Bose Quiet Comfort 2 headphones. They consisted of the same frequency and tempo dimensions utilized by Walker (2002). There were 20 stimuli, 10 for the frequency set and 10 for the tempo set. The sounds in the frequency set were played at 60 bpm and consisted of bandpassed white noise centered at 100, 200, 300, 400, 800, 1000, 1400, 1800, 2400, and 3200 Hz. This was done utilizing the LS Filter plugin, which created a bandpass filter around each of the specified central frequencies with a 6 dB decay per octave. The sounds in the tempo set were played at 1000 Hz and consisted of tempos of 45, 60, 105, 150, 210, 270, 420, 500, 550, and 600 bpm. All stimuli were then adjusted to ensure equal loudness utilizing the ReplayGain plugin.

Trials were presented via a graphical user interface (GUI) programmed in MatLab version 2011b, modeled after Walker (2002). It included a display of the conceptual data dimension (either error or uncertainty) which remained static throughout the study, a button to play the stimulus, a text box to enter numeric values, and a "Next Trial" button.

2.3 Design & Procedure

Conceptual dimension (error or uncertainty) was a between subjects variable; trial block was within. Participants received 4 trial blocks (2 using the frequency stimuli and 2 using the tempo stimuli) presented in a random order, with a short break between blocks. In each block, each stimulus was presented in pseudo random order (randomly selected from one of several pre-generated random ordered lists) to avoid order effects.

Participants received both written and oral instructions detailing the procedure and giving an overview of the interface. After all 4 blocks were completed; participants were debriefed and asked to fill out a short demographics survey.

3. Data Analyses

Data were coded for consistency and it was assumed that participants would conform to a consistent mapping for a given data dimension, but if they did not, their data were excluded from analysis (see Walker, 2002).

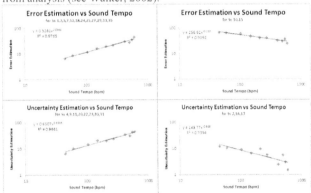

Figure 1: Geometric means of estimated values versus the tempo of the stimuli. Axes are in log units. Participants whose responses contributed to the means are indicated above each plot. The slope of the fit line is given by the exponent of x in the equation on each plot (adapted from Walker, 2002).

Participant data were then split by mapping polarity (positive or negative). In a positive mapping polarity, participant estimates of error or uncertainty increased as pitch or tempo increased. In negative mappings, increasing pitch/tempo led to decreased estimates of error/uncertainty. Geometric means were calculated for each data/display pair and plotted against stimulus values. We then calculated the slope of the best fit lines, their r^2 values, and the standard errors of the mean (see Walker, 2002).

For *error*, there was a strong positive mapping for tempo, with 12 participants giving a positive mapping (m = 0.67; SE_M = 0.53; r^2 = 0.98) and only 2 giving a negative one (m = -0.34; SE_M = 256.62; r^2 = 0.91). There was also a strong positive mapping for tempo in the *uncertainty* dimension with 8 participants giving that mapping (m = 0.65; SE_M = 0.65, r^2 = 0.97) and 3 giving a negative one (m = -0.62; SE_M = 149.77, r^2 = 0.71) (see Figure 1).

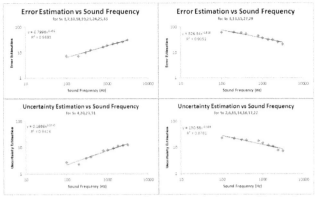

Figure 2: Geometric means of estimated values versus the frequency of the stimuli.

Unlike the tempo data, the frequency data were not the same across conceptual dimensions. For *error*, there was still a fairly strong positive mapping with 9 participants giving that mapping (m = 0.45; SE_M = 0.80, r^2 = 0.97) and 5 giving a negative one (m = -0.32; SE_M = 326.34, r^2 = 0.91). However, for *uncertainty* there was a strong negative mapping, with 7 participants giving that mapping (m = -0.34; SE_M = 130.58, r^2 = 0.88) and 4 giving a positive one (m = 0.53; SE_M = 0.19, r^2 = 0.94) (See Figure 2).

4. Conclusions

The strong positive mappings for tempo in both the error and uncertainty dimensions suggest that representations in both dimensions can be scaled in the same manner. Second, the opposite frequency mappings for error and uncertainty need to be taken into account, especially when designing error bars and confidence intervals for auditory graphs. Third, the overall success of this study further supports the methodology proposed by Walker (2002) as a tool to develop optimal sonifications. Future work includes extending the study to include visually impaired participants to determine if they have similar mappings to those discovered in the sighted population. This will allow us to design universally usable uncertainty representations that are both superior to the current (inaccessible) versions and more versatile (and cheaper) than currently available tactile graphics.

5. REFERENCES

[1] Belia, S., Fidler, F., Williams, J., & Cumming, G. (2005). Researchers misunderstand confidence intervals and standard error bars. *Psychological Methods, 10*, 389-396.

[2] Constantinescu, E. M.; Zavala, V. M.; Rocklin, M.; Lee, S.: & Anitescu, M. (2010). A Computational Framework for Uncertainty Quantification and Stochastic Optimization in Unit Commitment with Wind Power Generation. *IEEE Transactions on Power Systems, 26(1),* pp. 431-441.

[3] Flowers, J. H., & Hauer, T. A. (1992). The ear's versus the eye's potential to assess characteristics of numeric data. Are we too visuocentric? *Behavior Research Methods, Instruments, & Computers, 24,* 258-264.

[4] Gilboa, I.; Postlewaite, A.W.; & Schmeidler, D. (2008). Probability and Uncertainty in Economic Modeling. *Journal of Economic Perspectives, 22(3),* pp. 173-88.

[5] Walker, B. N. (2002). Magnitude estimation of conceptual data dimensions for use in sonification. *Journal of Experimental Psychology: Applied, 8,* 211-221. DOI: 10.1037/1076-898X.8.4.211

Visualizations for Self-Reflection on Mouse Pointer Performance for Older Adults

Jasmine Jones[1], Steven Hall[2], Mieke Gentis[2], Carrie Rennolds[2]
Chitra Gadwal[1], Amy Hurst[1], Judah Ronch[3] , Callie Neylan[2]
UMBC Human-Centered Computing[1], Visual Art[2], Erickson School of Aging[3]
1000 Hilltop Circle, Baltimore, MD 21250
{jasmin3, haste1, mieke1, rcar1, cgadwa1, amyhurst, ronch, neylan}@umbc.edu

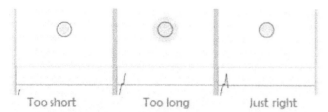

Figure 1. "Target Graph" Visualizing the duration of individual mouse clicks with a bulls-eye visual metaphor.

ABSTRACT

Aging causes physical and cognitive changes that influence how we interact with the world around us. As personal data becomes increasingly available from a variety of sources, older adults can use this information to better understand these changes and adapt. Our project explores information visualization as a tool to help older adults interpret and understand their own personal data. To test this concept, we created visualizations of a user's pointer performance metrics to help demystify problems in real-world mouse use. In a user study conducted with older adults with a range of computing experience, we learned that visualizations such as these can be a highly engaging information medium for this population. This paper presents our design process and recommendations for creating reflective visualizations for older adults.

Categories and Subject Descriptors

K.4.2 [Computer and Society]: Social Issues—assistive technologies for persons with disabilities; H.5.2 [Information Interfaces and Presentation]: User Interfaces—user centered design

Keywords

Older adults, visualization, personal informatics, pointing, reflection

1. Introduction

The field of informatics is rapidly innovating ways to effectively present data to people about all aspects of life, from one's health to one's energy use. Older adults, aged 65 and older, are a unique population when it comes to how they access and interpret information. They are typically juggling several different types of data from a variety of differently prioritized sources. They are also diverse in their familiarity with computing technology and digital data tools. Understanding the information needs and

ASSETS '12, Oct 22-24 2012, Boulder, CO, USA
ACM 978-1-4503-1321-6/12/10.

practices of older adults and developing solutions to help them leverage their personal information is a necessary and intriguing research problem.

There is growing interest in collecting and reflecting on personal data in everyday life [3]. Information visualization may be an engaging way to facilitate this self-reflection. The vision for these visualizations is to include the individual in the analysis of their own data (even non-experts), so they may contribute their contextual knowledge and gain a better understanding of their behavior. We explored this question through the example of mouse pointer performance data, which is currently widely used by accessibility researchers to understand computer usability issues.

In this project, we prototyped visualizations designed to enhance the ability of older adults to reflect on their mouse pointer performance. We conducted a user study with a variety of these visualizations to gauge older adult's responses to visualizations of personal data. This paper summarizes our prototypes, process, and major insights gained in this project.

2. Reflecting On Mouse Pointer Use

We designed visualizations to help older adults understand performance measures related to the mechanics of mouse pointer use. Many older adults have difficulty physically interacting with a mouse, which can be a significant barrier to computer access. While adaptive software can help, real-time feedback about pointer performance may reduce the confusion and frustration often accompanying pointer errors and even enable users to compensate with manual adjustments. We chose this scenario because we believed it would be interesting and relevant to older adults and would avoid a lengthy, burdensome data collection period.

We developed several visualizations for this scenario. "Target Graph" (Fig. 1) was designed to help users understand mouse-click timing. With the visual metaphor of a bulls-eye, this real-time visualization showed users how long each of their mouse button presses lasted, compared to the duration needed for a click to be recognized. The second visualization, "Session Graph" (Fig. 2) took a higher level view of the data by displaying a side by side comparison of all clicks recorded in a session of computer use and in multiple sessions. This visualization used a familiar bar chart layout to show mouse performance metrics such as click duration and the occurrence of clicking errors over time. The larger time scale of the Session Graph was designed help users identify problematic patterns and possible causes. The third visualization, "Venn Graph" (Fig. 3) is an aggregate overview of all clicks recorded during a session of computer use. With this alternative overview, viewers can see the distribution of activity in different types of applications and, when used in concert with the other visualizations, better understand their behavior overall.

To create these visualizations, we integrated the parallel

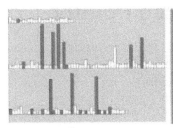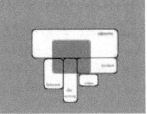

Figure 2. "Session Graph"; Figure 3. "Venn Graph"
High level views of mouse clicks over time in a use session

iterative development models for Visualizations [3] and Personal Informatics Systems [4]. First, we derived the following basic requirements from previous studies on developing technology for older adults: immediate utility, familiarity, and simplicity [2]. The visualizations were built in Processing, a rapid prototyping tool for real-time, interactive visualizations [*www.processing.org*]. We used an existing dataset of pointer performance data from Hurst, et al. [1] as a development base.

For immediate utility, we chose a use case of personal importance to older adults and focused each visualization on helping users identify and explain possible pointer problems. For familiarity and simplicity, we based the visualizations on visual metaphors, as explained above, that we think supported older adults' mental models of their computer use. Evaluating the design and usefulness of these visual metaphors is an area of further research.

3. Insights from the User Study

The goal of our user study was to determine whether older adults would consider visualizations of their personal data to be a tool of interest to them, and to gather their feedback on real-world examples. The interview was composed of an introduction to information visualization, a technology demo, and a feedback session. First, we explained the concept of information visualization and walked participants through analyzing and interpreting example visualizations of several different types of personal information, including mouse use[1], energy consumption [*visualization.geblogs.com*], health condition [5], and mood [*www.moodscope.com*]. Then we asked participants to rank the visualizations and indicate which features they preferred and disliked. The study was set up in this way to accommodate older adults who had limited experience with information visualization and to encourage conversation about the potential of visualizations rather than fixating on only the use case.

We interviewed four regular computer users and conducted a group demonstration for a class of twelve beginning learners and their teacher. Participants' ages ranged from 65 to 80, and none reported a serious disability that disrupted their computer use. From these conversations, we gathered three major recommendations to benefit our understanding of older adults' interaction with personal information and visualizations.

1) Simplicity is the preferred trait, although the definition of simplicity can vary. Each of the four interview participants were asked to rank the visualizations by preference. Of the mouse use visualizations, they all preferred the Session Graph because it was the easiest to "see the important information right away." Another favorite was a visualization of a person's positive and negative emotional states over a month-long period. Although the design was visually complex and required a lengthy explanation, the participants immediately began to recognize familiar mood

patterns and hypothesize about the cause. We believe that this visualization was well-received despite its complexity because it corresponded with the existing visual models that the participants held. In addition, the layout allowed viewers to ignore aspects of design that added complexity and unnecessary information.

2) Even in an experimental setting, the data must matter to the participants. All the participants were eager to interact with the visualizations, but they tended to be less enthusiastic about visualizations from undesirable scenarios. Notably, the participants ranked the health visualization lowest in preference, although it was visually appealing, explaining that it represented an undesirable condition and they never wanted to have to use it. Remaining aware of this "interest bias" will help researchers discern between general problems and individual preferences in designs for older adults.

3) The social aspect of personal information and visualization remains a question that needs further investigation. When the interview participants were asked whether they would share visualizations of their personal information with others, they all said no. However, one participant added that, as a caregiver, she would like to see her ward's information to provide better care. Similarly, the teacher of the computer class was eager to incorporate the visualizations into her lessons to help her better address the needs of individual students and more closely track their progress.

4. Conclusion

In this project, we developed visualizations for reflection on mouse performance for a target population of older adults. To evaluate this research direction, we conducted a qualitative user study to gather initial reactions and feedback to visualizing personal information, including mouse use and other types of personal data. Based on the results of this study, we believe that carefully designed visualizations can be a promising method of making personal data accessible to older adults. Our participants found visualizations appealing and engaging and were enthusiastic about the potential of using visualizations for self-reflection.

5. Acknowledgements

We would like to thank all of our participants and our colleagues from UMBC's Project 2061 seminar. This work was supported by a grant from the CRA-W Collaborative Research Experience for Undergraduates.

6. References

[1] A. Hurst, J. Mankoff, S. Hudson. Understanding pointing problems in real world computing environments. In Proc. Of ASSETS 2008, ACM Press (2008), 43.

[2] C. Leonardi, C. Mennecozzi, E. Not, F. Pianesi, M. Zancanaro. Designing a Familiar Technology for Elderly People. In Gerontechnology, 7(2):153, 2008.

[3] I. Li, A. Dey, J. Forlizzi. A Stage-Based Model of Personal Informatics Systems. In Proc. of CHI 2010, ACM Press (2010), 557.

[4] T. Muzner. A Nested Model for Visualization Design and Validation. In IEEE Transactions on Visualization and Computer Graphics, 15(6): 921- 928, 2009.

[5] Y. Sota, K. Yamamoto, M. Hirakawa, S. Doi, and Y. Yamamoto. 2011. Support of self-management for chronic kidney failure patients. In Proc. of VINCI 2011. ACM Press (2011), Article 6.

Accessible Skimming: Faster Screen Reading of Web Pages

Faisal Ahmed
Stony Brook University
Computer Science Department, Stony Brook, NY 11790-4400
faiahmed@cs.stonybrook.edu

ABSTRACT

Sighted people know how to quickly glance over the headlines and news articles online to get the gist of information. On the other hand, people who are blind use screen-readers to listen through the content narrated by a serial audio interface. This interface does not give them an opportunity to know what content to skip and what to listen to. In this work, I present an automated approach to facilitate *non-visual skimming* of web pages.

Categories and Subject Descriptors

H.5.2 [**Information Interfaces and Presentation**]: User Interfaces; H.5.4 [Information Interfaces and Presentation]: Hypertext/Hypermedia – *navigation.*

General Terms

Human Factors; Experimentation; Design.

Keywords

Skimming; Assistive Technology; Blind; User Interface; Screen Reader; Web Browser; Audio Interface; Accessibility.

1. INTRODUCTION

In our information-driven web-based society, we are all gradually falling "victims" to *information overload* [2]. However, while sighted people are finding ways to sift through information faster, Internet users who are blind are experiencing an even greater information overload. These people access computers and Internet using screen-reader software, which reads the information on a computer screen sequentially using computer-generated speech. So, they either listen to all of the content or listen to the first part of each sentence or paragraph before they skip to the next one. In this work, I design a novel skimming algorithm, outline a non-visual skimming interface, and report on our user study with 23 screen-reader users. The results demonstrate that the resulting algorithm for automatic summarization can be successfully used for non-visual skimming.

2. BACKGROUND AND RELATED WORK

When sighted users look at a random web page, their quick eye movements, called saccades, help them get a quick overview of the page and find what they need. The structure and formatting of the page further helps them find the information relevant to their goals. In most web pages, this still leaves them a lot of content to read through, imposing a *heavy cognitive load* [6]. But again, saccades help speed up reading and reduce the cognitive load. The process of quickly glancing over the textual content with the goal of picking up the gist of the content is called *Skimming*.

Screen readers [4, 5, 7] are assistive technology software that narrate the content of the screen using text-to-speech and allow users to navigate through the content marked up by HTML tags for headings, paragraphs, links, buttons, etc. Because of the low bandwidth of a serial audio interface and the fact that one has to hear the information before deciding if it is relevant, people who are blind spend considerably more time identifying the information they need [3]. A little has been done to develop an effective method for skimming, so that blind people could process information faster.

The JAWS screen-reader has a naive implementation of "skimming" [4] that allows users to read the first line or the first sentence of each paragraph. This methodology still does not offer a truly functional tool for skimming, and does not follow the same skimming process employed by sighted people. Our earlier experiment with 20 people [1] reported the usability of non-visual skimming in listening-and-comprehension and in search scenarios. To simulate skimming, we used several variations of human-generated summaries. These experiments demonstrated that skimming enabled people who are blind to read faster while maintaining high level of comprehension and retention.

Visual skimming is akin to the extractive summarization, because when people scan the text they take it as it is. Interviews with 20 screen-reader users [1] also suggested that the extractive summarization approach that preserves the original content is the most suitable technique for enabling non-visual skimming.

3. OVERVIEW OF OUR APPROACH

3.1 Skimming Algorithm

At a high level, our summarization algorithm works as follows.

Firstly, every sentence is parsed to extract grammatical relations amongst its words. Secondly, a lexical tree based on these relations is constructed, where each node of the tree represents a word in the sentence. Thirdly, for every word in this tree, its grammatical (i.e., POS tags) as well as structural features (related to in-degree/out-degree, etc.) are extracted. These features are given to a trained classifier to determine whether or not to include the word in the skimming summary. Finally, a subtree consisting of the selected words is constructed. This subtree represents the summary that users interact with via a non-visual interface.

3.2 Skimming Interface

Summarization by itself does not satisfy the need for skimming; for screen-reader users, reading a summary is more like reading a separate, albeit shorter, narrative. Therefore, we designed an interface that allowed screen-reader users to switch seamlessly between reading the skimming summary and the original web page preserving the current reading position. This feature helps emulate the behavior of experienced sighted readers who usually can scan quickly and then, at any point, slow down to read the text regularly.

The skimming interface was integrated into our Non-Visual screen-reading platform, which is a Java application that enables a screen reading interface for the Firefox web browser. It supports all the typical navigation shortcuts available in the mainstream screen-readers such as JAWS [4], e.g., paragraph / sentence / word / character navigation, pause / resume, etc.

A shortcut (e.g., Shift+S) lets the user toggle between skimming mode and full text mode. The skimming interface can be invoked on any web page content regardless of its length as long as the content is organized in sentences (e.g., snippets of news articles along with headlines), but lists of links that can be found in menus, on the other hand, should be read in their entirety.

4. USER STUDY

The Disability Resource Center at the Arizona State University helped us recruit 23 participants (7 male and 16 female) who were blind and well-versed in the use of screen readers, with JAWS as their primary screen reader. To evaluate the interface and the underlying algorithm, the participants were asked to perform three tasks in two different scenarios: listening-and-comprehension and searching. For each of the three tasks the participants were using one of the three different kinds of content: Gold-standard (human-generated) summary (G), Skimming summary (S), or the original text of the articles (F).

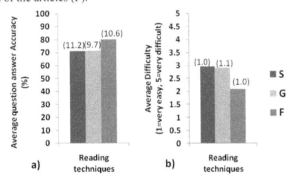

Figure 1. a) Average accuracy and b) Average difficulty (St. Dev.) of question answering with S, G and F

5. HYPOTHESES TESTING

We formulated a series of specific hypotheses to analyze the results of the study. The major hypotheses accepted based on the statistical significance tests are presented below:

H1: After listening to summaries S and G, subjects can answer reading-and-comprehension questions equally well (Figure 1a).

H2: Subjects perceive question-answering tasks to be of the same difficulty after listening to G and F or S and F Figure 1b).

H3: Subjects find information faster while skimming with G/S, than when using screen-reader navigation shortcuts (Figure 2a).

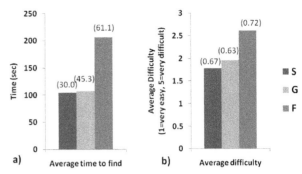

Figure 2. a) Average time and b) Average difficulty in the searching task using skimming vs. regular shortcuts

H4: Subjects perceived ad-hoc searching to be more difficult compared to using skimming S or G (Figure 2b).

H5: Subjects were not able to distinguish between human- and computer-generated summaries.

We observe no difference in performance on these tasks between groups of subjects: **H8:** who lost eyesight before age 20 and those who lost later, **H9:** belonging to different age categories, **H10:** with different comfort level with computers.

6. CONCLUSION AND FUTURE WORK

The approach presented in this work can summarize one sentence at a time without the dependence on the entire document. It can extract meaningful word combinations from most sentences and preserve the original order of the extracted text. All these properties make this summarization approach more suitable for supporting a non-visual skimming interface. Our experiments provide evidence to the claim that non-visual skimming can enable screen-reader users to browse textual content faster.

This work opens the possibilities to further accelerate non-visual skimming by varying the compression ratio of summarization. Skimming can also be extended to touch interfaces. Armed with the ability to change the amount of information as necessary, people who are blind will be able to battle the information overload and cognitive load more effectively, while enjoying the speed-reading commonly used by sighted readers.

7. ACKNOWLEDGEMENTS

Research reported in this paper was supported by NSF Awards IIS-0808678 and CNS-0751083. I am also thankful to my advisors, Dr. I.V. Ramakrishnan and Dr. Yevgen Borodin.

8. REFERENCES

[1] Ahmed, F., Y. Borodin, Y. Puzis, and I.V. Ramakrishnan, *Why Read if You Can Skim: Towards Enabling Faster Screen Reading*, in *W4A*. 2012.

[2] Berghel, H., *Cyberspace 2000: Dealing with Information Overload*. COMMUNICATIONS OF THE ACM, 1997. 40(2).

[3] Borodin, Y., J.P. Bigham, G. Dausch, and I.V. Ramakrishnan, *More than meets the eye: a survey of screen-reader browsing strategies*, in *W4A*. 2010, ACM: North Carolina. p. 1-10.

[4] JAWS, *Screen reader from Freedom Scientific*. 2011. freedomscientific.com

[5] NVDA, *Non-Visual Desktop Access*. 2011. nvda-project.org

[6] Sweller, J., *Cognitive load during problem solving: Effects on learning*, in *Cognitive Science*. 1988.

[7] Window-Eyes, *Screen Reader GW Micro*. 2010. gwmicro.com/Window-Eyes.

Accessible Web Automation Interface: A User Study

Yury Puzis
Stony Brook University
Stony Brook, NY, 11794, USA
ypuzis@cs.stonybrook.edu

ABSTRACT

With the growth of the Web as a platform for performing many useful daily tasks, such as shopping and paying bills, and as an important vehicle for doing business, the Web's potential to improve the quality of life of blind and low-vision users is greater than ever. However, the growth of sophistication of Web applications continues to outpace the capabilities of tools that help make the Web more accessible. Web automation has the potential to bridge the divide between the ways visually impaired users and sighted users access the Web, and enable visually impaired users to breeze through Web browsing tasks that beforehand were slow, hard, or even impossible to achieve. Typical automation interfaces require that the user record a macro, a useful sequence of browsing steps, so that these steps can be replayed in the future. In this paper, I present the results of evaluation of two web automation user interfaces that enable web automation without having to record macros. The experiments suggest that the approach has the potential to significantly increase accessibility and usability of web pages by reducing interaction time, and by enhancing user experience.

Categories and Subject Descriptors

H.5.2 [**Information Interfaces and Presentation**]: User Interfaces; H.5.4 [**Information Interfaces and Presentation**]: Hypertext/Hypermedia – *navigation*

General Terms

Human Factors, Experimentation, Design

Keywords

Web Accessibility, Blind Users, Low-Vision users Web Browser, Screen Reader, Macro Recorder, Macro Player, Non-Visual, Audio Interface.

1. INTRODUCTION

Visually impaired users rely for browsing on screen-readers [1-4], assistive tools that narrate the content of the screen. Screen-readers enable sequential navigation over the content and provide access to hundreds of shortcuts that can speed the navigation for an expert user on a website he/she uses on a regular basis. In most cases, however, users rely on screen-reader's sequential interaction mode, in which they have to listen to one piece of content at a time. Moreover, the highly interactive and dynamic design of the modern webpages leads to a situation in which the visually impaired user might never find important content because it has dynamically, and *silently* appeared in an already reviewed part of a webpage. As a result, visually impaired users spend significantly more time on seemingly simple online tasks than sighted users.

Web automation has the potential to make web browsing much more accessible and usable. Most existing automation tools employ the approach of recording, and later replaying a sequence of browsing actions (macro). Web automation with macros, however, (a) requires creating, managing, finding and invoking macros at the proper time,

(b) lacks the flexibility necessary to allow the user to deviate from the prerecorded macros, or to choose between several options in each step of the transaction, and (c) does not address the need of the visually impaired users to find non-interactive content, e.g. an article, a form submission error notification, etc. Those characteristics make the canonical approach to web automation too limiting to be useful for visually impaired users.

2. PRIOR WORK

The earliest approach required *handcrafting* a script to customize the behavior of the browser. The second approach to handcrafting is employing a graphical user interface to specify a macro, such as in Montoto at.el. [5]. The handcrafting approach requires learning the tool(s) used to create the macros: the syntax, the semantics, and the necessarily sophisticated user interfaces (with their own accessibility and usability problems).

The *Programming by Demonstration* [6] approach enables the user to perform and record a sequence of actions. This is the approach taken by the majority of end-user automation tools. Most existing Programming by Demonstration approaches are *explicit* [7]: the user is required to manually start and/or stop the macro recording process. This means that the user needs to manipulate the browser and the screen-reader into a state when the recording can be started, execute the actions flawlessly, terminate the recording at appropriate time and save it under a recognizable name. *Implicit* approach (this work) shifts the burden of the above decisions (except demonstrating the actions) from the user to the automation tool.

If the macro was executed without step-by-step feedback then the user may have to spend time and effort exploring: What webpage is now open? Where is the screen-reader's virtual cursor? Has the macro executed correctly? etc. Moreover, if the user is not able to easily deviate from the original recording, the smallest change in user preferences or webpage design can render the macro useless.

Unlike the "macro" approach, my approach does not require handcrafting or explicitly recording or replaying macros. Instead, every user action is recorded automatically, and the contextually relevant browsing actions are suggested to the user (upon his/her request) based on a statistical model of his/her prior actions. In my prior work [8], I evaluated a conceptual design of an accessible web automation interface that used hardcoded, webpage-specific rules to simulate automatic inference of suggestions. I subsequently built a fully functional system that uses a computational model to generate the suggestions based on the history of browsing actions. While the description of the model is not in scope of this paper, I report on the new experiments with a much improved user interface.

3. USER INTERFACE

The Assistant interfaces (A and B) were built on top of the Capti web browsing application, which has a standard screen-reader interface (akin to JAWS). The design is based on the guidelines for an accessible web automation interface [8, 9].

The workflow of the Assistant user is: (a) while browsing, query for useful suggestions (c) examine the suggestions using the standard interface provided by the browser and the screen-reader, with the Assistant providing voice feedback where appropriate (in addition or instead of the screen-reader feedback), (d) confirm execution of one of the suggestions, or ignores them and continue browsing, (e) optionally verify that the action was executed correctly by listening to the feedback provided by the Assistant, and/or examining the webpage. The following two interfaces implement this workflow:

Assistant A. The S and Shift+S keys are used to navigate to the next and the previous page elements for which an action is suggested. This interface is based on the standard screen-reading interface for navigating among elements of a particular type, e.g., B and Shift+B for buttons, A and Shift+A for links.

Assistant B. A single shortcut is used to toggle on/off the "suggestions" mode, in which the user can use standard screen-reader shortcuts, but navigation is only allowed among the suggestions of the Assistant, making the rest of the content "disappear" for the blind screen-reader user. If user's current position is not associated with a suggestion (because the mode was just turned on, or the suggestions changed), the user is immediately taken to the suggestion topologically following the current position. If there is no such suggestion, the user is taken to the suggestion topologically preceding the current position. This interface is similar to the HearSay layer interface [10], e.g., layer of links or layer of dynamic changes.

Any interaction with any element on the webpage may update the current suggestions. When the user navigates to an element for which there is a suggested action, the system will follow the standard screen-reader prompt applicable to the element with a terse description of the suggested action. The user can invoke the suggested action by pressing the Ctrl+Space shortcut, or interact with the element using the screen-reader commands (e.g. type in a new value into a textbox). When the action is executed the system will voice a confirmation, update its suggestions, and allow the user to continue browsing.

For example, let us say that the page contains a large number of elements, of which the 5th one, a textbox, and the 32nd one, a button, are associated with a suggestion. If the user's current reading position is on the 10th element, then pressing S will navigate directly to the button, while pressing Shift+S will navigate to the textbox. If the textbox is labeled "First name", it has no value, and the suggested value is "John" then the system will announce "Textbox 'First name' blank. Suggestion: John". Pressing Ctrl+Space will update its value, voice "Textbox 'First Name' John", and update the suggestions.

4. EVALUATION
4.1 Methodology
I tested the effectiveness of the Assistant interfaces (A and B) in a user study with 19 visually impaired screen-reader users performing tasks on web pages with and without the help of the Assistant. The participants consisted of 58% males, and were on average 54 (std. dev. 12) years old. The participants rated their level of computer experience at "not comfortable" (0%), "mildly comfortable" (0%), "comfortable" (26.3%), "very comfortable" (57.9%), and "expert" (15.8%). All the participants used JAWS before, and 90% use it as their primary screen-reader.

The participants were asked to perform 6 browsing tasks, each associated with a different website: (1) ebay.com, (2) hilton.com, (3) tigerdirect.com, (4) amazon.com, (5) monster.com, and (6) yelp.com. Of the chosen websites 80% of the participants had prior experience with amazon.com and 20% with ebay.com. Participants were asked to perform the tasks using 3 different user interfaces: the baseline screen-reader without automation, Assistant A, and Assistant B. Each system was evaluated with 2 consecutive tasks. I counterbalanced the tasks order, the system order, and task-to-system assignment. For each task I measured the completion time (or recorded a time-out if the participant exceeded 10 min.). The tasks that timed-out were not included in quantitative results computation.

The experiment was designed to evaluate the following hypothesis: visually impaired users can complete tasks significantly faster when using the Assistant (A / B) than when using a standard screen-reader.

4.2 Results
All participants completed all tasks with Assistants A & B within the given time constraints (10 minutes). Four of the participants were not able to complete 1 task (a different task in each case, total of 4 tasks) using the standard screen-reader interface.

Average time (standard deviation) to complete each task with Assistant A was 153 sec. (71 sec.), for Assistant B was 142 sec. (53 sec.), and for the standard screen-reader was 426 sec (132 sec.). One-way ANOVA test (alpha = 0.001) shows statistically significant result ($p<0.0001$) and Tukey's Multiple Comparison Test showed statistically significant difference between Assistant A and the standard screen-reader, as well as between Assistant B and the standard screen-reader ($p<0.0001$). The one-tailed t-test (99% confidence interval) for all tasks shows that both Assistant A (t=8.9, df=41) and Assistant B (t=11, df=45) provide statistically significant ($p<0.0001$) speed improvements when compared to a standard screen-reader. This corroborates the hypothesis.

Of the 6 websites used in the experiment only amazon.com was very familiar to most of the participants (80% used it on a *regular* basis). This resulted in improved time performance when using screen-reader without automation. However, even in this case both Assistants A and B provided statistically significant speedups when compared to the standard screen reader. This reinforces the hypothesis.

5. CONCLUSION
In this paper, I described an accessible web automation interface for step-by-step automation of repetitive web browsing actions. The proposed design significantly improves the speed of interaction of visually impaired screen-reader users with the Web. The usability of the two user interfaces was also evaluated, and showed significant *differences* between the two interfaces. Those results will be reported in future work. Both interfaces received highly positive feedback and *no negative comments* from the participants. The participants made a large number of suggestions and provided ideas for future improvements.

6. REFERENCES
1. JAWS, Screen reader from Freedom Scientific, 2011.
2. Geoffray, D., The internet through the eyes of windows-eyes, in CSUN, 1999.
3. NVDA. Non-Visual Desktop Access. 2012. Available from: http://www.nvda-project.org/.
4. VoiceOver, Screen reader from Apple, 2012.
5. Montoto, P., Pan, A., Raposo, J., Bellas, F., Lopez, J., Automating Navigation Sequences in AJAX Websites, in ICWE 2009, Springer-Verlag: San Sebastian, Spain. p. 166-180.
6. Cypher, A., Halbert, D.C., Kurlander, D., Lieberman, H., Maulsby, D., Myers, B.A., Turransky, A., eds. Watch what I do: programming by demonstration. 1993, MIT Press. 652.
7. Leshed, G., Haber E.M., Matthews, T., Lau, T., CoScripter: automating & sharing how-to knowledge in the enterprise, in CHI 2008, ACM: Florence, Italy
8. Puzis, Y., Borodin, E., Ahmed, F., Melnyk, V., Ramakrishnan, I.V., Guidelines for an accessible web automation interface, in ACCESS 2011, ACM: Dundee, Scotland, UK. p. 249-250.
9. Puzis, Y., Borodin, Y., Ahmed, F., Ramakrishnan, I.V., An intuitive accessible web automation user interface, in W4A 2012, ACM: Lyon, France. p. 1-4.
10. Borodin, Y., Bigham J.P., Raman, R., Ramakrishnan, I.V., What's new?: making web page updates accessible, in ASSETS 2008, ACM: Halifax, Nova Scotia, Canada.

Detecting Hunchback Behavior in Autistic Children with Smart Phone Assistive Devices

Shu-Hsien Lin
Department of Electronic Engineering
Chung Yuan Christian University,
Taiwan
ctjh881414@gmail.com

ABSTRACT

The research target in this case study was an autistic student at a special education school, who often unconsciously became hunchbacked during group activities or when not talking to people. We designed a system for hunchback detection using smart phone. Combined with an assistive T-shirt, the system could detect whether his/her back was hunched. Through this demonstration, we showcased the potential of using smart phones to develop simpler and more effective assistive devices for people with disabilities.

Categories and Subject Descriptors

H.5.2 [**Information Interfaces and Presentation**]: User Interfaces–*Evaluation/methodology, User-centered design, Prototyping, Screen design*; K.4.2 [**Computers and Society**]: Social Issues–*Assistive technologies for persons with disabilities*

General Terms

Design, Experimentation, Human Factors

Keywords

Autism, assistive technology, hunchback, accelerometer

1. INTRODUCTION

Recent technological advancements in smart phones have resulted in economical handheld devices with integrated voice activation, image processing, and motion sensor functions. Specialized technological assistive devices for people with disabilities often cost upwards of one hundred thousand USD. In this study, we focus on using equipment that is relatively affordable compared to specialized assistive devices. With customized program system, this equipment can enable people with disabilities to manage their daily work or rectify stereotypical behavior [1]. This case study was conducted in collaboration with the Kaohsiung Municipal Renwu Special Education School (KRSES) in Taiwan with the goal of designing a technological assistive device that enables autistic children to train or remind themselves to improve their hunchback behavior.

The participant in this case study was an autistic student at the KRSES. The student often exhibited unconscious hunchback behavior during group activities and when not engaged in conversation, as shown in Fig. 1. Special education teachers were required to monitor his condition and remind the student to straighten his back. Thus, we attempted to develop an appropriate assistive device for children exhibiting hunchback behavior to correct this stereotypical behavior and reduce the workload of

teachers. To understand the actual needs more comprehensively, we conducted site visits to the special education school. After conducting multiple field observations and one-on-one interviews with the participant, we discussed our observations with special education teachers, and proposed using a motion sensor on a smart phone to detect hunchback behavior. This would provide an extremely economical assistive device with significant effectiveness. Through this demonstration, we showcased the potential of using smart phones to develop simpler and more effective assistive devices for people with disabilities.

2. SYSTEM IMPLEMENTATION

The system uses the sensor device on a smart phone with a modified assistive T-shirt, as shown in Fig. 2, for operations. This "assistive T-shirt" was simply with a sewn-on pocket that could carry a mobile phone. The student was instructed to wear the assistive T-shirt, and the occurrence of hunchback behavior was determined by the smart phone's accelerometer. Using a smart phone provides the following two benefits: First, the currently available wearable assistive devices for hunchback correction tend to cause physical discomfort to wearing in hot weather. By contrast, because they are lightweight and convenient, the use of smart phones can increase the wearer's comfort when combined

(a)   (b)

Figure 1. Case student: (a) when aware of others' attention or when others were paying attention; and (b) obvious hunchback when no one is believed to be paying attention

Figure 2. Assistive T-shirt

with light cotton assistive vests. Second, the design and appearance of this system is neither obtrusive nor unusual; thus, it does not attract unwanted attention to the wearer during group interaction.

Regarding the entire system, in addition to identifying hunchback behavior using sensors, we also designed many relevant mechanisms to satisfy various contexts, scenarios, and demands for a certain venue. Those functionalities include assessing whether the user is hunched over, bowing, or sleeping on the stomach or in a prone position. Furthermore, because the smart phone used in this system was placed in proximity to the user's back, we set the smart phone to remain in flight or airplane mode, where all communicative functions are blocked, in consideration of the potential health effects of electromagnetic waves from the communication functions. This also reduces electricity wastage and unnecessary interference during hunchback detection.

A diagram of the system usage scenario is shown in Fig. 3. First, we defined the angle and alarm sensitivity settings. The angle function also allowed for customized angles in addition to the pre-defined angles of 45° and 60°. By pressing the "set" button when the user is in a hunchback position, a specific hunchback alarm angle can be set.

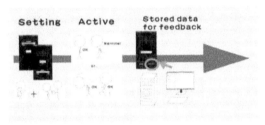

Figure 3. Usage scenario diagram

3. EXPERIMENTAL RESULTS

The experiment participant was a student with multiple disabilities enrolled in the vocational high school division of the KRSES. The student was diagnosed with mild mental retardation and moderate autism and had basic movement or action and language capabilities. Additionally, he was already exhibiting mild scoliosis caused by hunchback behavior. The experiment fields or venues were a computer classroom and a general classroom at the school.

We divided the experiment process into a baseline phase and an intervention phase. During the baseline phase, which lasted for one week, we observed from the sidelines and did not interfere with the student. We found the hunchback conditions of the student to be very severe. When adopting a sitting posture during classroom instruction, the student would often exhibit a hunchback because he was daydreaming or inattentive. The teacher had to constantly remind the student to remain upright.

During the intervention phase, the student's behavior was corrected or mediated using the assistive device. The planned duration of the intervention phase was 3 weeks. According to the student's state on a particularly day, we consulted with the teacher whether it was suitable to conduct the experiment. Overall, the experiment was performed for 6 days. In the first week, we selected the gentler 45° hunchback standard for the student to wear the device. On the first day, we found that the student was not comfortable wearing an assistive device. However, with the encouragement of the teachers and a period of adaptation, the

student gradually became accustomed to wearing the assistive device by the second day. In addition to attempting to remain upright to reduce the alarm sounds, data in Fig. 4 (a) shows that the student's hunchback behavior improved significantly. At the second week, we applied the stricter standard of 60° for the settings of the assistive device. Through observation, we not only found that the student had greater difficulty adapting to the stricter setting during the three days of testing but also the improvement was not as significant compared to the first week, as shown in Fig. 4 (b). Feedback from the teacher indicated that when the student was wearing the assistive device, his sustained alertness developed into focused attention when studying and active interaction with classmates, which gradually reduced his tendency to daydream.

The recorded user data allow the teacher to review the student's hunchback detection behavior for the entire day. Through the intervention of the assistive device, the workload of the teacher was reduced. Because the system replaced the original verbal reminder, the teacher was no longer required to remain at the student's side providing constant reminders. The student could also improve their sense of honor and achieve self-training using this assistive device, which effectively corrected hunchback behavior.

During the experiment, we encountered a number of interesting phenomena we had not anticipated during the design phase. Vibrations were used as the alarm for hunchback behavior in the initial design. However, we found that the student was not sensitive to the vibration of the smart phone on his back, and even regarded the vibrations to be a comfortable massage. Therefore, the student did not correct their hunchback behavior. Consequently, we changed the alarm to gentle classical music; however, this was no more effective than the vibration alarm. Finally, we changed the hunchback alarm to a high-decibel, monotone sound of a cat meowing. When the alarm was emitted during classroom instruction, nearby classmates reminded the student to adjust his posture if he had not corrected it immediately. Through the assistive device, the student's classmates could assist the special education teacher by providing reminders.

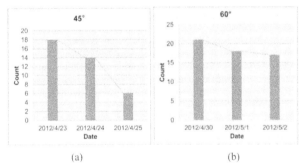

Figure 4. Number of detected (a) 45° hunchback incidents (b) 60° hunchback incidents

4. REFERENCE

[1] Yao-Jen Chang, Shu-Fang Chen, Zhi-Zhan Lu An Accelerometer-based Handheld System to Reduce Breaks in Performance of Young Adults with Cognitive Impairments, *Research in Developmental Disabilities*, Vol. 32, Iss. 6, 2011. pp. 2530-2534.

Detecting the Hand-Mouthing Behavior of Children with Intellectual Disability Using Kinect Imaging Technology

Tzu-Wei Wei
Department of Electronic Engineering
Chung Yuan Christian University,
Taiwan

weitzuw@gmail.com

ABSTRACT

Research indicates that approximately 17% of individuals with intellectual disability engage in hand-mouthing behavior. The proportion is even higher among those with extremely severe intellectual disability. Stereotypic and excessive hand-mouthing behavior may lead to an unpleasant odor, lesions of the skin and muscular tissues, and infections. Typically, a substantial amount of staff intervention is required for a special education teacher to correct hand-mouthing behavior. However, this results in prolonged treatment periods and has negative effects on the students' learning and interaction with their peers, which leads to barriers in their social integration. In this study, we applied Kinect imaging technology to detect children's hand-mouthing behavior. This method enables rapid verification of the hand mouthing intervention strategies proposed by special education teachers, thereby reducing students' hand-mouthing behavior and facilitating individual learning.

Categories and Subject Descriptors

H.5.2 [Information Systems] Information Interfaces and presentation; User Interfaces: Prototyping.

General Terms

Experimentation, Human Factors.

Keywords

Hand mouthing behavior ,Severe intellectual disabilities, Kinect

1. INTRODUCTION

1.1 Problem and Motivation

Hand-mouthing behavior refers to the repetitive behavior of placing one or more fingers into the mouth, which causes the face and hands to be wet with saliva. Researchers have shown that stereotypic behaviors interfere with attention, learning, and social interactions. There are numerous ways to reduce or eliminate stereotypic behaviors, such as exercise as well as providing an individual with alternative, more socially-appropriate, forms of stimulation. Some self-stimulatory behaviors occur in inappropriate times or locations. Teachers or parents can teach him to do so at a more appropriate time and place. Self-stimulatory behaviors can also be replaced by constructive alternatives through proper interventions. As a stereotypic behavior, hand mouthing is commonly observed among individuals with intellectual disability. According to previous studies, approximately 17% of individuals with intellectual disability engage in hand-mouthing behavior [1]. The more serious the intellectual disability, the higher the frequency, extent, and severity. Hand mouthing results in saliva being present on a person's hands and face, causing an unpleasant odor or stench, which subsequently affects his or her interpersonal relationships. Furthermore, hand mouthing leads to swelling of the hands and infections; long-term and high-frequency hand mouthing can even result in skin ulcers and tissue damage to the hand [2]. Therefore, hand mouthing is considered a self-injurious behavior. However, in special education schools, the correction of hand mouthing can consume a significant amount of staff intervention and increase the workload of special education teachers. This results in compromised teaching quality and prolonged hand mouthing correction training, which negatively affects the children's learning and interaction with their peers.

To reduce the hand-mouthing behavior of students with intellectual disability and improve the efficiency and quality of the special education, we developed a software application for detecting children's hand-mouthing behavior. This application can be used with the teachers' instructional strategies, reduce teachers' workload, and accelerate the hand mouthing correction training process to improve the efficiency of the children's learning.

1.2 Background and Related Work

In Taiwan, every special education teacher teaches up to 3.7 students on average. Because of the diverse characteristics of the students, the teachers can only provide instruction to one student at a time. Previously, during self-care behavior training sessions, special education teachers were required to develop a number of instructional intervention strategies in response to various scenarios, and actually experiment with these strategies to verify their feasibility. Generally, these experiments were video recorded for later review, and the data obtained from these recordings would be tabulated for analysis. However, such experimentation could consume a significant amount of time and effort. Therefore, to reduce the workload of special education teachers, we propose a system for detecting hand-mouthing behavior and automatically recording the process.

Special education teachers may adopt these instructional intervention strategies to guide students through their self-care and work. The suitability of these intervention strategies may vary depending on the scenario. By combining the proposed system with intervention strategies, the feasibility of the strategies can be verified more rapidly. Therefore, the proposed system can not only reduce the teachers' workload but also shorten the duration of treatment to correct students' hand-mouthing behavior.

2. SYSTEM DESIGN

The system proposed in this study was based on the Kinect, a motion-sensing device developed by Microsoft. Kinect has been successfully employed as assistive technology [3]. To accelerate the verification of teachers' instructional strategies and reduce the duration of treatment to correct students' hand-mouthing behavior, we developed a hand-mouthing detection and recording system using Visual Studio 2010, which can be run on a Windows 7 operating system. Based on the position coordinates of the right hand and head, as sensed by the Kinect, the system detects whether the observed cases are engaging in hand mouthing. If such behavior is detected, the system records the time and duration of the hand-mouthing behavior to inform the teacher remains of the hand-mouthing situation. For convenient operation of the system, we held lengthy discussions with special education teachers, performing adjustments and modifications that incorporated the suggestions they provided, to ensure that the system interface and functionality were adapted to the needs of special education teachers.

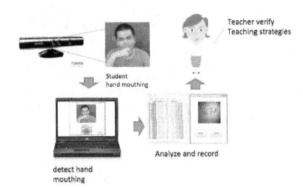

Figure 1. Hand mouthing detection system

3. EXPERIMENT

3.1 Experiment Setting

Throughout this study, we cooperated with a special education school to interact with the actual targets of the proposed system in context. Traditional human judgments were employed as the criteria to compare the data collected by the system and to verify the system practicality. At the experimental location, a video camera, Kinect motion-sensing device, and laptop computer were placed on a desktop, and the study participant was instructed to sit on a kinder chair. The Kinect was connected to the laptop computer, on which the system developed in this study was installed. The observers taped the entire experimental session. These recordings were then reviewed subsequently to obtain manual data using the partial-interval recording in special education, which is we separate our total observation time into several pieces with same interval, 5 sec in this study, and when participant has the hand mouthing behavior one time or more than one time in the interval, we judge that hand mouthing behavior is happened one time in this interval.

To minimize the errors of human observation in the experiment, two observers who had undergone a consistency test before the observation and had achieved an observational consistency score of 100%, were assigned to observe and record. Observational inconsistencies between the observers and the researchers were resolved through discussion and reexamination of the video recordings. The results of the discussions were then compared to the data captured by the system to determine the precision and recall rates of the system.

3.2 Participant

The study participant was a fifth grade student at an elementary school, who was identified through an evaluation process to have multiple disabilities, including extremely severe intellectual disability and physical impairments. The participant was a wheelchair user with minimal self-care skills and, thus, depended on staff assistance. Because of a history of high-frequency hand mouthing, the participant exhibited swelling and inflammation of the hands, particularly the right hand.

3.3 Result

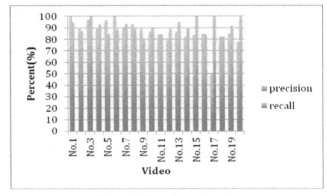

Figure 2. Experimental result

During the experiment, 20 video recordings, which corresponded to 20 files, each lasting 3 min for a total of 60 min, were obtained. The observations and recordings obtained by the researcher and two observers were compared with the data captured by the system to determine the precision and recall rates. As shown in Fig. 1, the average precision rate was 86.5% and the average recall rate was 90.9%, both exceeding 80%.

Through the detecting and recording functions of the system developed in this study, we anticipate substantial reductions in teachers' workloads, the time required for special education teachers to verify their instructional strategies, and the duration of treatment to correct students' hand-mouthing behavior.

4. ACKNOWLEDGEMENTS

I would like to thanks Dr. Lee from Kaohsiung Special School.

5. REFERENCES

[1] Rast, J., & Jack, S. (1992). Mouthing. In E. A. Konarski, J. E. Favell, & J. E. Favell (Eds.), Manual for the assessment and treatment of the behavior disorders of people with mental retardation (pp. 1–11). Morganton, NC: Western Carolina Center Foundation.

[2] Realon, R. E., Favell, J. E., &Cacace, S. (1995). An economical, humane, and effective method for short-term suppression of hand mouthing.Behavioral Interventions, 10, 141–147

[3] *Yao-Jen Chang, Shu-Fang Chen, An-Fu Chuang, A Gesture Recognition System to Transition Autonomously Through Vocational Tasks for Individuals with Cognitive Impairments,*Research in Developmental Disabilities*, Vol. 32, Iss. 6, 2011. pp. 2064-20

Face Tracking User Interfaces Using Vision-Based Consumer Devices

Norman Villaroman
Brigham Young University
Provo, Utah
normanhv@byu.edu

ABSTRACT

One form of natural user interaction with a personal computer is based on natural face movements. This is especially helpful for users who cannot effectively use common input devices with their hands but have sufficient control of their heads. Using vision-based consumer devices makes such a user interface readily available and allows its use to be non-intrusive. This user interface presents some significant challenges particularly with accuracy and design. This research aims to investigate such problems and discover solutions to creating a usable and robust face tracking user interface using currently available technology. Design requirements were set and different design options were implemented and evaluated.

Categories and Subject Descriptors

H.5.2 [**Information Interfaces and Presentation**]: User Interfaces – *Input devices and strategies.*

K.4.2 [**Computers and Society**]: Social Issues – *Assistive technologies for persons with disabilities.*

General Terms

Design, Human Factors

Keywords

Face, Detection, Tracking, Accessibility, Depth, Perceptual User Interface, Consumer Devices, Assistive Technology

1. INTRODUCTION

With all the advancement in computing hardware and technology over the years, the ubiquitous mouse and keyboard have remained largely unchanged, proving the usefulness of such simple hand-manipulated input devices. These devices, however, do not cater to those who, for various reasons, do not have full control of their hands. While a number of other input modalities may be available to such users (e.g. voice or movement of other body parts), the modality covered by the user interface in this study is that of natural head and face movement captured by consumer imaging and/or depth sensing devices.

A primary problem of face tracking user interfaces is accurate translation to computer input. In the first place, natural face movement does not span a large region of interest on a 640x480 imaging sensor. At the same time many applications today are made for or are more effectively used in high resolution screens. To top it all off, feature detection and tracking algorithms are, by nature of the technology and for various reasons, not very accurate. This accuracy problem makes or breaks this user interface. It is important that the implementation for such an interface be robust because as a naturally learned one, erratic responses can quickly and easily make it unacceptable.

In the following sections, the implementation of various vision-based face tracking user interfaces is discussed as well as some statistical results obtained. Plans for upcoming usability tests are also discussed. There is a great deal of research done, particularly in an application that depends on immense topics in multiple disciplines. While such review has been accomplished, an entire section on it cannot be included here because of prescribed limits but some will be mentioned throughout this paper. A few related works that will be noted now include similar research by Varona et al., the results and methodologies of which partially differ from those of this research.[2,6] The literature review done shows that this application has yet unresolved challenges. Advances in research and technology that address them are evaluated in this research.

2. IMPLEMENTATION

2.1 Design Requirements

To establish usability standards, the following design requirements were set to guide the implementation.

- For complete independence, aside from the initial hardware and software installation, normal usage should not require the intervention of a helper.

- Assuming an already running system, face movement controls the starting and stopping of the interface.

- Normal operation should be robust to some variance in the exact location of the user's face. Where necessary, calibration should be automatic or require only minimal effort.

- The interface input is completely controllable by natural face movements that do not require the movement of the torso.

- The face detection and tracking should be robust and accurate enough that it doesn't require multiple or prolonged attempts to accomplish simple input operations.

Keyboard functionality will be provided by an on-screen keyboard. The keyboard can be turned on manually by having the face point to an area below the screen for a few seconds. Pointing to an area right (or left) of the screen for a few seconds turns the cursor control on and off. Where necessary, the sides of the screen will serve as calibrating edges should the calculated cursor points be moved to an awkward location relative to the user's face.

2.2 Development Framework

The target system of control is a personal computer running Windows 7. The application was written in C++. A Kinect sensor was used where a depth sensor was needed. Development and testing were done on a machine with an Intel® Core™ i5-2500 (3.3 GHz) CPU and 8GB of memory. Tests done thus far have been with a user placed approximately 24" from a 23" screen (at a resolution of 1920x1080) where the sensor is also located.

2.3 Implementation Options

The components of the input data flow in this interface can be organized as described in Figure 1.

User Input
User actions to be treated as input

Input Technology
Hardware and supporting software to capture raw input data

Retrieval of Feature Characteristics
Algorithms that perform feature detection and tracking

Processing of Feature Data
Algorithms that translate feature data into computer input

Computer Input Behavior
How the computer should respond to processed input data

Figure 1. Input components by data flow

For each component, various options were considered and studied in regard to their ability to improve robustness and usability. A necessarily brief discussion for each follows.

For cursor control in the user input component, the major options studied are 1) "absolute pointing" where the 3D face location and pose determines the cursor point and 2) "location only", where the horizontal and vertical location of a face feature is projected onto a point on the screen.

For input technology, both regular imaging cameras and consumer depth sensors were used. The use of color and depth images separately and on their own were studied which also confirmed that the use of both color images and depth provides the best of both worlds and compensates for the weaknesses of the other.

Various detection and tracking algorithms were studied for applicability in a face tracking user interface. [4,8,9] Some implementations also provided a library or a codebase that served as the main detection and tracking engine for the interface. These include SeeingMachine's faceAPI [5], the recently released Microsoft Face Tracking SDK [3], and the head pose estimation using random forests of Fanelli et al. [1] Another option currently being investigated is the tracking capabilities provided by the Iterative Closest Point algorithm in a similar way it was used in a 3D modeling and animation application by Weise et al.[7]

As expected, the retrieval of feature characteristics produce point estimates that tend to be noisy for various reasons. A few methods were studied that can help reduce this noise. The Kalman filter was found to be an appropriate and effective method in dealing with such noise, disagreeing with a previous work.[6]

Computer input behavior determines how the cursor moves given the final calculation of feature data. The two options studied include 1) placing the cursor at locations directly calculable from the feature data and 2) moving the cursor in the direction and with velocity that are calculable from the feature data.[2]

Other techniques were also used that helped improve accuracy, but which are not discussed here for brevity.

3. EVALUATION

Much of the evaluation at the time of this writing has been from single user testing and statistical analysis. The purpose of the latter is to obtain a quantifiable measure of the spread of the cursor points produced by a face that was stationary for 5 seconds using the different options discussed in Section 2.3. The spread is an indication of usability because it is directly related to the user's ability to accurately target screen elements. Some of the results obtained are presented in Table 1.

Table 1. Standard deviation in the horizontal and vertical axes (screen pixels, rounded to the nearest integer)

	Location only[†]		Absolute Pointing[†]	
	--	Kalman	--	Kalman
Depth only[‡]	29, 20	21, 14	59, 16	14, 11
2D only[‡]	14, 5	9, 2	18, 13	7, 10

† See Section 2.3 for definition
‡ "Depth only" - Fanelli's head pose estimation. "2D only" - faceAPI.

Efforts are underway to organize formal usability tests with individuals who are in the target user group. The tests will have measures for the following:

- The speed at which certain normal computer-based activities can be accomplished. These activities include basic computer operations, sending an email, browsing a social media website, and playing multimedia content.
- The usability of the implemented interfaces compared to each other and to solutions currently used by the subjects.

4. CONCLUSION AND FUTURE WORK

Certain combinations of implementation options provided a sufficiently robust user interface that will be used in upcoming usability tests. The recentness of the release of the MS Face Tracking SDK prevented its full investigation and inclusion in the study done thus far but which is currently being pursued. The work already accomplished provided crucial insights in the robust design of face tracking user interfaces using consumer devices.

5. REFERENCES

[1] FANELLI, G., WEISE, T., et al., 2011. Real Time Head Pose Estimation from Consumer Depth Cameras. In *DAGM'11*, Frankfurt, Germany.

[2] MANRESA-YEE, C., VARONA, J., et al., 2006. Towards Hands-Free Interfaces Based on Real-Time Robust Facial Gesture Recognition

[3] Articulated Motion and Deformable Objects, F. PERALES and R. FISHER Eds. Springer Berlin / Heidelberg, 504-513. DOI= http://dx.doi.org/10.1007/11789239_52.

[4] MICROSOFT *Face Tracking*. http://msdn.microsoft.com/en-us/library/jj130970.aspx (Last Accessed: Jun 2012)

[5] MURPHY-CHUTORIAN, E. and TRIVEDI, M.M., 2009. Head Pose Estimation in Computer Vision: A Survey. *Pattern Analysis and Machine Intelligence, IEEE Transactions on 31*, 4, 607-626. DOI= http://dx.doi.org/10.1109/tpami.2008.106.

[6] SEEING MACHINES *faceAPI*. http://www.seeingmachines.com/product/faceapi/ (Last Accessed: May 2012)

[7] VARONA, J., MANRESA-YEE, C., et al., 2008. Hands-free vision-based interface for computer accessibility. *Journal of Network and Computer Applications 31*, 4, 357-374. DOI= http://dx.doi.org/10.1016/j.jnca.2008.03.003.

[8] WEISE, T., BOUAZIZ, S., et al., 2011. Realtime performance-based facial animation. *ACM Trans. Graph. 30*, 4, 1-10. DOI= http://dx.doi.org/10.1145/2010324.1964972.

[9] YILMAZ, A., JAVED, O., et al., 2006. Object tracking: A survey. *ACM Comput. Surv. 38*, 4, 13. DOI= http://dx.doi.org/10.1145/1177352.1177355.

[10] ZHANG, C. and ZHANG, Z. *A Survey of Recent Advances in Face Detection*. Microsoft Research, 2010. http://research.microsoft.com/apps/pubs/default.aspx?id=132077 (Last Accessed: June 2012)

`Kinempt: A Kinect-based Prompting System to Transition Autonomously Through Vocational Tasks for Individuals with Cognitive Impairments

Yu-Chi Tsai

Department of Electronic Engineering
Chung Yuan Christian University,
Taiwan

youji32@gmail.com

ABSTRACT

Kinect is used as assistive technology for individuals with cognitive impairments to achieve the goal of performing task steps independently. In a community-based rehabilitation program under the guidance of three job coaches, a task prompting system called Kinempt was designed to assist two participants involving pre-service food preparation training. Results indicate that for participants with cognitive disabilities, acquisition of job skills may be facilitated by use of Kinempt in conjunction with operant conditioning strategies.

Categories and Subject Descriptors

H.5.2 [Information Interfaces and Presentation]: User Interfaces–Evaluation/methodology, User-centered design, Prototyping, Screen design; K.4.2 [Computers and Society]: Social Issues–Assistive technologies for persons with disabilities

General Terms: Experimentation, Human Factors.

Keywords

Task prompting, Cognitive impairments, Kinect.

1. INTRODUCTION

1.1 Problem and Motivation

The research was started with an aim to use wireless pervasive computing as a measure to increase social connectedness and improve the quality of life for the majority of otherwise-employable persons who remain unemployed, rarely access appropriate community services, and are socially isolated. Persons with cognitive impairments tend to be viewed as unemployable and systematically excluded from labor markets. However, this assumption has been challenged recently after the development of community-based rehabilitation (CBR), and supported employment services in particular. With sufficient and appropriate support on the job, many people with developmental disabilities and cognitive impairments are capable of participating in the world of work to various levels, which not only provides them with financial support but also opportunities for social connection. In other words, employment services for persons with mental disabilities play a key role in the process of social integration for them.

1.2 Background and Related Work

The proliferation of mobile compact computing devices such as palm size PDAs enables a new platform for personal prompting and cognitive aides [1, 3]. PDA-based prompting is especially useful for task engagements that require constant moving, such as janitorial tasks, food preparation, parking patrol. Previous work on task prompting using PDAs relied on "Wizard of Oz" approaches [1], user self-conscience [3], or constant time delay (CTD) [2] in order to send the prompts.

2. SYSTEM DESIGN

2.1 Uniqueness of the Approach

The proposed system for vocational task prompting, called the Kinempt (a portmanteau of the words "kinetic" and "prompt"), is based on Kinect. Based around a webcam-style add-on peripheral for the Xbox 360 console, Kinect enables users to control and interact with the Xbox 360 without the need to touch a game controller, through a natural user interface using gestures. The device comes with an RGB camera and a depth sensor, which provide full-body 3D motion capture capabilities.

Using Kinect means that the users need not be bothered with sensors that can be intrusive and that the prompting system can save the user from carrying a handheld device. The design draws upon the usability studies of interfaces by people with cognitive impairments, and the requirements based on interviews with job coaches at rehabilitation institutes. In the Kinempt system, open-source PC drivers are used to identify gestures. A mini notebook computer running an in-house developed task prompting software is set up to work with Kinect. The sequence of user gestures is compared step by step to the sequence of vocational task analysis. If steps in the task analysis are not followed, the Kinempt system will raise an alert. Use of this technology can free a job coach or trainer from the burden of having to constantly stay with users for pre-service vocational training.

The Kinempt system shows step-by-step instructions of routine task steps in a vocational job. The Kinect sensor keeps track of the hand and wrist joints and checks whether they move in and out the designated position required by a task step. Both correct and incorrect task steps are identified by the Kinempt system.

2.2 Prompting Sequences

In the beginning, the users are assigned the tasks by the job coaches. The descriptions of the task steps are input to the PC and stored as routines. A computer screen shows the just-in-time instructions in text and picture, for example "Get a cup of pineapples." and "Get half a cup of shrimps." Each task instruction is matched with a task step so that it can be followed to fulfill an order. "Hands busy, eyes busy" users during task engagement alternatively rely on voice instructions as task prompts. See Figure1 for our system being used by a participant.

Figure 1. Experimental field simulation

3. EXPERIMENT

3.1 Setting of the Kinempt System

The Kinempt system was deployed in a local pizza chain store that spared non-business hours for the short order food preparation training of adults with cognitive impairments. Kinect transmitted the target response signal to a mini Asus EeePC notebook computer, a mini host installed with Kinempt software and built-in Microsoft Windows XP Home Edition. Benefiting from its low power consumption (saving up to 60% in energy consumption), small size and low price, it is convenient to develop as the computer for the disabled. The computer sent video signals to a 42-inch LCD screen to display vocational task steps.

3.2 Participants

Considering our long-term relationship with supported employment agencies, we primarily recruited participants who were already working in the sheltered workplace (Table 1). The job coaches who participated in the supported employment programs selected two participants for our experiment. With long term observation, three job coaches decided that Jill and Ann were more ready to participate in experiments than the other trainees were. The names of participants described in this paper have been changed to protect their privacy. The profiles of the two participants are summarized in Table 1.

Table 1. Profiles of two subjects

Subjects	gender	age	Disabilities
Ann	F	35	schizophrenia, affective disorder
Jill	F	29	schizophrenia

3.3 Result

We conducted experiments for a month and a half. Before the experiment was performed, and after receiving the consent of family members, we explained the assistive device and provided operating instructions. The researchers accompanied the students throughout the entire experiment to handle the emotional problems encountered and reduce as much of the frustration felt by the students when using the assistive devices. This also increased the students' willingness to use the assistive devices.

The two participants Jill and Ann repeated the experiment for 35 days. To prevent participants from fatigue, one session was performed each day. The 35 sessions were divided into three phases: baseline, intervention, and maintenance. In the baseline phase, participants read instruction sheets and then performed

food preparation. No technology was employed. In the intervention phase, participants used our prompting system to perform task steps. In the maintenance phase, participants backed off to the same instructional method as in the baseline.

Jill's data (Fig. 2) show that correctness remained between 70% and 80% during the baseline period. After intervention with the assistive device, correctness reached 100%. After the assistive device was withdrawn, the data remained the same as that during the device intervention period.

Ann's data (Fig. 3) show that correctness stayed between 70% and 90% during the baseline period. After intervention with the assistive device, correctness also increased to 100%. During the maintenance period, the data remained the same as that in the device intervention period.

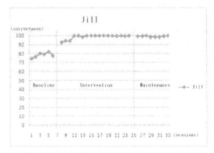

Figure 2. Jill's experimental data

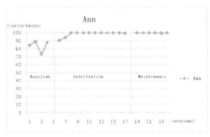

Figure 3. Ann's experimental data

These results indicate that the Kinempt task prompting system was effective for training and enhancing the two participants' work capabilities. Using this system can assist job coaches by enabling participants to start rapidly in the workplace during pre-service training. This allows a smooth transition into future vocational tasks, providing stable employment.

4. REFERENCES

[1] McKay Moore Sohlberg, Stephen Fickas, Pei-Fang Hung, Andrew Fortier, "A Comparison of four prompt modes for route finding for community travelers with severe cognitive impairments," Brain Injury, Page: 531 – 538, January 2007.

[2] Tony Gentry, Joseph Wallace, Connie Kvarfordt, Kathleen Bodisch Lynch, "Personal digital assistants as cognitive aids for individuals with severe traumatic brain injury: A community-based trial," Brain Injury, Page: 19 – 24, December 2007.

[3] Mike Wu, Ron Baecker, Brian Richards, "Participatory design of an orientation aid for amnesics," Proceedings of the SIGCHI conference on Human factors in computing systems, Page: 511 – 520, 2005.

Reusable Game Interfaces for People with Disabilities

Javier Torrente

Complutense University of Madrid

C Profesor Jose Garcia Santesmases sn, 28040 Madrid, Spain.

+34 649001538

jtorrente@acm.org

ABSTRACT

Computer games are a very popular media today, spanning across multiple aspects of life, not only leisure but also health or education. But despite their importance their current level of accessibility is still low. One of the causes is that accessibility has an additional cost and effort for developers that is in many cases unaffordable. As a way to facilitate developers' job, this work proposes the creation of s pecialized tools to deal with accessibility. The hypothesis defined was that it was possible to produce tools that could reduce the input needed to adapt the games for people with special needs but achieving a good level of usability, resulting in a reduction of the cost and effort required. As game development tools and approaches are heterogeneous and diverse, two case studies were set up targeting two different platforms: a high level PC game authoring tool, and a low-level Android game programming framework. Several games were developed using the tools developed, and their usability was tested. Initial results depict that high usability levels can be achieved with a minimum additional input from the game author.

Categories and Subject Descriptors

H.5.2 [**Information Interfaces and Presentation**]: User Interfaces – *auditory (non-speech) feedback, graphical user interfaces (GUI), natural language, screen design*;

Keywords

Accessibility, audio 3D, eyes-free games.

1. BACKGROUND AND MOTIVATION

Computer and video games have became a very popular kind of media, being part of m odern culture. Besides, current uses of games have escaped the boundaries of l eisure, as they are being applied to improve education [4], for advertising or health [1].

But games can be a significant source of di gital divide, as their current level of accessibility is low, with a small number of titles coping with the needs of pe ople with disabilities [6, 7]. The improvement of a ccessibility in games should be a priority to prevent the exclusion of a broad sector of our population from the ever-growing number of activities related to digital games.

The poor level of accessibility is not motivated by a single cause. Nevertheless, one of the most important is that improving game accessibility has a cost for de velopers, not only in economic investment but also in time and effort. From a t echnical perspective, accessibility increases the development time as new modules have to be created, such as in-game screen readers or speech input processing units. Moreover, from a design perspective accessibility demands dealing with alternative interaction paradigms or adapting parts of t he content. Game

developers live under great pressure as they are immersed in a highly competitive and risky industry where the production of each title requires huge investments. From this perspective, accessibility is unlikely to get to the top on their priority list.

Hence one of t he approaches to improve the accessibility of games is to make dealing with accessibility easier for developers. If the cost of introducing accessibility is low in economic terms, but especially in effort and time needed, the chances of accessibility would raise substantially.

Tools to support developers should be created, not to be distributed as independent products, but integrated into the development environments developers use every day (e.g. Unity or Eclipse). Thus impact achieved would be maximum.

Ideally, tools provided for developers should automate design and implementation tasks related to accessibility. For example, having alternative interaction modules that can be configured for players with different abilities and integrated into the games with minimum effort would be a valuable asset for developers.

But to get to that point it is necessary to reach a higher level of abstraction and generalization of c urrent game accessibility design guidelines [3, 7]. A growing body of research is exploring how to make games more accessible [6], but solutions proposed are usually focused on particular examples and they do not scale easily to fit other titles. It is necessary to conduct research that, building upon recent breakthroughs and successful stories on game accessibility, comes up with accessible interfaces that are general enough to be reused for di fferent games but specific enough to be implemented into mainstream game creation tools.

An additional challenge comes from the diversity of environments and tools used by game developers, such as high-level authoring tools for creating levels or s cenarios, where visual interfaces predominate, or l ow-level programming environments and libraries where code is the key. For example, tools like Unity or Eclipse can be used for ga me development, but they have very different characteristics.

The goal of the work presented was to investigate accessible interfaces that could be integrated into game development tools of different kind. First, several configurable interfaces were developed for a serious games authoring tool with a very high level of abstraction. Second, a low level programming library was developed for accessible mobile games.

2. HIGH-LEVEL APPROACH: A SERIOUS GAMES AUTHORING TOOL

The first approach was centered on t he eAdventure game authoring tool [5, 8]. This tool is oriented to educators so they can create their own educational games. The tool interface is simple, with a high level of a bstraction as programming is completely hidden from the end user. The strategy used in eAdventure to reduce the complexity of the tool is to narrow the type of games that can be produced to a limited number of genres. As opposed to more complex tools, like Unity, which allows development of a wide range of games, eAdventure allows development of only 2D, single player, adventure games.

Besides, many aspects of the games are preconfigured, although the user can perform some tweaks. This is the case of the interaction. By default, interaction is point-and-click, and these are the controls used:

- Mouse movements to explore the scene. When an interactive element is found, visual feedback is provided (the mouse pointer changes and a brief text is displayed).

- Mouse left button clicks: trigger interactions with some elements or makes the player's character move to the given location.

- Mouse right button clicks over interactive elements: display a contextual menu with available actions, if more than one.

Three alternative interaction modules that overrode the default point-and-click interaction were developed for eAdventure. These modules targeted three profiles of players: 1) screen reader users (i.e. blind), 2) players with limited vision that use high contrast settings, and 3) players with motor impairments in hands that use voice recognition software. Configuration of t he interfaces produced was straightforward as game authors only needed to introduce a few parameters and some additional content as alternative descriptions. The eAdventure accessibility module, using these settings, was able to generate the interfaces required automatically for the game being produced.

These interfaces were evaluated by creating a serious game: "My first day at work". The goal of the game was to facilitate access to the labour market for pe ople with disabilities. The game and its accessible interfaces were evaluated by 15 people with different motor, visual, and cognitive disabilities. In this study two parameters were analyzed for each of the interfaces: usability and enjoyment. Participants played the game for a n hour a nd the sessions were video recorded for pos t analysis. The videos are currently being examined to complete the study. However, through a preliminary analysis two main findings can be outlined. First, most of t he participants were able to complete the game without additional support from researchers, which is an indicator of high usability levels. Second, it seems that enjoyment experienced by participants vary depending on t heir gaming habits and experience, as participants who played digital games more frequently found the interfaces less appealing.

This suggested that the game experience was different for users with a similar disability but different experience with digital games. Nonetheless, it is unclear if this issue is caused by the interfaces used or by other factors, such as the game story or mechanics. To further explore this aspect, a second case study was conducted. This study targeted profiles of pl ayers sharing a common disability but with different gaming experience. The disability profile selected was screen reader users. Three interfaces were developed. The first one allowed interaction through short text commands. The second interface was similar to Web interaction, allowing users to browse through the elements and GUI controls with the arrow keys and use an action key (e.g. Enter) to trigger interactions. The last interface was the most innovative, being a 3D sonar that helped users in locating the

elements with the mouse. These interfaces were evaluated by a limited number of users. Initial results seem to confirm the initial hypothesis, as users with higher gaming experience preferred the most challenging interface (the sonar) while novice users preferred the text commands interface.

The main limitation of all the interfaces developed for eAdventure is that they were designed for a specific type of game and could only be used within the eAdventure platform. A similar approach could be applied to other tools, whereas it is inapplicable to games where interaction is a key part of the game experience.

3. LOW-LEVEL APPROACH: ANDROID FRAMEWORK FOR ACCESSIBLE GAMES

As a second approach, a framework was developed to facilitate development of 2D accessible games for s creen reader users in mobile devices. Android was chosen as application platform, as at the time of the start of the project it was a less accessible platform than its competitor, iOS. The outcome was a number of l ibraries and classes that could be integrated into Android game development projects. This framework is available for download from its Google Code repository [2].

Using this framework, four accessible games were produced. Three of them are available at Google Play. Currently the usability and accessibility of t he games is being evaluated with end-users.

Compared to approach 1, this solution allows for de veloping games of di fferent types, as adopting a low level strategy adds flexibility and scalability. While in approach 1 only point-and-click adventure games could be created, with this approach a minesweeper, a p oint-and-shoot game, a snake-like game and an interactive fiction game were developed. Besides, this approach is less platform dependent, as it could be reused in any Android project while interfaces developed in approach 1 c ould only be used within the eAdventure authoring tool. However, the cost of producing games in approach 2 w as higher as the setup of t he interfaces required coding, which is a significant drawback.

4. REFERENCES

[1] Arnab, S. et al. 2012. *Serious Games for Healthcare: Applications and Implications*. IGI Global.

[2] Blind Faith Games project: *http://en.blind-faith-games.e-ucm.es*.

[3] Grammenos A. Savidis, & C. Stephanidis, D. 2007. Unified Design of Universally Accessible Games. *Universal Access in Human-Computer Interaction. Applications and Services*. S.B./ Heidelberg, ed. 607–616.

[4] Johnson, L. et al. 2012. *NMC Horizon Report: 2012 Higher Education Edition*. Austin, Texas: The New Media Consortium.

[5] Torrente, J. et al. 2010. <e-Adventure>: Introducing Educational Games in the Learning Process. *IEEE Education Engineering (EDUCON) 2010 Conference* (Madrid, Spain, 2010), 1121–1126.

[6] Westin, T. et al. 2011. Advances in Game Accessibility from 2005 to 2010. *Universal Access in HCI, Part II, HCII 2011*. LNCS 6766, (2011), 400–409.

[7] Yuan, B. et al. 2011. Game accessibility: a survey. *Universal Access in the Information Society*. 10, 1 (Jun. 2011), 81–100.

[8] eAdventure website: *http://e-adventure.e-ucm.es*.

Wii Remote as a Web Navigation Device For People with Cerebral Palsy

Nithin Santhanam

Swanson School of Engineering

University of Pittsburgh, Pittsburgh, PA 15261

nis57@pitt.edu

ABSTRACT

This study evaluates the use of the Nintendo Wii remote relative to the standard wireless mouse as a web navigational device. Nine participants with cerebral palsy performed three typical web tasks. Six of them showed improved task times using the Wii remote. With suitable customization available from freely available software, the Wii remote shows promise to be a flexible and inexpensive alternative.

Categories and Subject Descriptors

H.5.2 [**Information Interfaces and Presentation**]: User Interfaces

General Terms: Human Factors

Keywords

Web accessibility, customization, user study.

1. INTRODUCTION

In spite of the abundance of tools and techniques available to improve web accessibility for people with visual and motor impairments, customizable and inexpensive options remain elusive. Due to the wide spectrum of conditions manifested, it is difficult to mass produce devices to meet the needs of all people with cerebral palsy. An earlier work [1] reported on the use of IBM accessibilityWorks software add-on [2] to Firefox browser to provide software customization options such as text enlargement, and large cursors. In the current work, the use of the popular gaming device Wii remote as an alternative for the wireless mouse is being explored. *IBM accessibilityWorks was used for both Wii remote and wireless mouse as support software and hence not a focus of this paper.*

There has been little research into the viability of the Nintendo Wii Remote (Figure 1) as an internet accessibility tool. It is a familiar household device, with positive associations. Due to the number and locations of the buttons and the motion sensing function it offers, Wii remote allows considerable customization when used as an input device. This study posits that the Wii remote or similar devices have the ability to be an effective internet browsing tool and compares the ability of a group of people with cerebral palsy to complete a set of Web tasks using a mouse and using a Wii remote.

Figure 1: Wii Remote

2. THE USER STUDY

2.1 Participants

There were 12 participants (5 male, 7 female). Eleven were wheelchair users. All had cerebral palsy, with vastly differing abilities. Most had some level of visual impairment. Each participant had some computer and web experience and all typically used the mouse to access the web.

2.2 Modification of the Wii Remote

In its normal usage, the Wii remote is simply a camera that senses infrared light and sends information such as its coordinates, button clicks, etc. to the Wii gaming system. It is well known that the Wii remote can be programmed for novel uses through its Bluetooth interface [3], thus allowing the Wii remote to communicate with a laptop computer by wireless. A highly customizable program to exploit the various buttons, controls and rich motion sensitive gestures of the Wii device is available online [4]. Using this program, any keyboard function could be mapped to any Wii remote control. Based on a preliminary assessment, two configurations were selected for this study (see Table 1). Configuration 1 exploits the motion sensing aspect of the remote to control the cursor and Configuration 2 uses the directional pad on the top of the controller to move the cursor. B-button (on the back of the Wii remote) was disabled in both configurations, since pilot testing showed it was often pressed accidentally. These two options gave enough flexibility for the participants to choose one of the two configurations based on their preferences. Having multiple setups is useful, since there is a wide spectrum of abilities among people with cerebral palsy.

Table 1: Mapping of the Wii controls

Wii Controls	Configuration 1	Configuration 2
Directional pad	Scroll	Cursor movement
A	Select	Select
+ and -	Magnification	Magnification
Home	Browser home	accessibilityWorks
1	accessibilityWorks	Scroll Up
2	Disabled	Scroll Down
Motion Sensing	Cursor Movement	Disabled
B (on the back)	Disabled	Disabled

2.3 User Tasks

Three typical user tasks involving websites, Facebook, Amazon and Fandango were defined. They covered key aspects of effective web browsing experience, representing a variety of core skills needed such as clicking, cursor movement, reading and scrolling. Typing actions were executed using the on-screen keyboard [5], which required clicking.

2.4 Methodology

The sessions took place at a United Cerebral Palsy center computer lab normally used by the participants for web browsing. Participants used a 24" screen attached to a laptop with Windows 7 operating system, an on-screen keyboard and a standard wireless mouse. A digital audio recorder and a screen recorder were used to record the session with each user, facilitating detailed analysis later. Each person chose one of the two configurations (shown in Table 1) based on his/her comfort. For the users of Configuration 2 who were not able to hold the Wii remote, it was attached to a wooden board using Velcro. Each user performed a set of 3 tasks twice, with a standard wireless mouse and then again with the Wii remote. The order of conditions was counterbalanced. The participants were free to stop during the trial whenever they chose. When a participant was unable to complete a task, the experimenter stopped the session and did not present the more difficult tasks. Participants were allowed to complete their tasks if they appeared confident. With this data, we measured the impact of the use of the Wii remote on the ability of the users to perform the tasks.

3. RESULTS

3.1 Qualitative Analysis

Of the 12 participants, three were unable to complete any of the tasks with the mouse or the Wii remote. Of the remaining nine, seven participants used Configuration 2, while two used Configuration 1. One of the participants was not able to do any of the tasks with the mouse and then proceeded to complete all of the tasks with the Wii remote. This was one of the highlights of the entire study. Conversely, all nine participants were able to use the Wii remote. Specifically, the Wii remote allowed the participants to sit comfortably in the wheelchair instead of having to exert a lot of effort in maneuvering to fit to the mouse environment. Small refined motions such as scrolling with a mouse wheel or a track ball were not necessary with either Wii configuration. Although Configuration 1 required good hand coordination for cursor movement, only a small wrist motion was necessary in comparison to larger hand movements with the mouse. Configuration 2 was particularly beneficial since it required just the use of a single finger for cursor movement and selection. This is due to the proximity of the directional pad to the A button.

3.2 Quantitative Analysis

Table 2 shows the statistics gathered for all 9 participants. As seen in the values of medians, inter-quartile ranges (IQR) and the p-values from the Wilcoxon sign rank test, the differences between the Wii-remote and mouse are not statistically significant. Given the efficiency and familiarity of the mouse, this is encouraging. Furthermore, a careful observation of the data reveals that there are two distinct groups of people: users who took less time using the Wii remote and users who took less time using the mouse. Table 3 shows the statistics for just the 6 users who benefited from the Wii remote. Of these six, 5 used Configuration 2 and 1 used Configuration 1. The median task times are smaller and the inter-quartile ranges are less spread out for the Wii remote compared to the mouse. In addition the p-values of the Wilcoxon

Table 2: Analysis of task times of nine users

Task	Wii: Median (IQR)	Mouse:Median (IQR)	p-value
1	168 (132-270) sec	153 (141-244) sec	0.374
2	167 (147-245) sec	173 (74-218) sec	0.296
3	123 (73-184) sec	160 (128-241) sec	0.110

sign rank test confirm that the Wii and the mouse data are different and significant. For the group of six participants who did better with the Wii remote, paired t-test across all the tasks shows that mean task time for the Wii remote was less than the mean task time for the mouse by 99 seconds with a p-value of 0.004.

Table 3: Analysis of task times of six users

Task	Wii: Median (IQR)	Mouse:Median (IQR)	p-value
1	175.5 (150-270) sec	206.5 (153-380) sec	0.046
2	159 (147-245) sec	198 (173-334) sec	0.028
3	106.5 (57-184) sec	200.5 (128-330) sec	0.028

4. CONCLUSION

This paper describes a study to assess the use of the Nintendo Wii remote in lieu of a traditional wireless mouse for nine users with cerebral palsy, performing common web tasks. Using qualitative and quantitative methods, it has been shown that the Wii remote can have a beneficial impact on a significant fraction of the users. Even though this study preselected two specific Wii remote configurations, users can easily customize the Wii remote buttons as they wish to have an inexpensive, yet flexible interface for web browsing. While more studies are needed, the current results are promising.

5. ACKNOWLEDGMENTS

The author thanks the participants and staff members at the United Cerebral Palsy Center in Suffolk, NY. This study was done under the guidance of Dr. Shari Trewin, Mr. Cal Swart and Dr. P. Santhanam of IBM Research, as a part of the Yorktown High School Science Research program.

6. REFERENCES

[1] N. Santhanam, S. Trewin, C. Swart and P. Santhanam, "Self-selection of Accessibility Options", in the Proceedings of the 13th International ACM SIGACCESS Conference on Computers and Accessibility (ASSETS 2011), October 24-26, 2011, Dundee, Scotland, pp. 277-278.

[2] V. Hanson, J. Brezin, S. Crayne, S. Keates, R.Kjeldsen, J. Richards, C. Swart, & S. Trewin, (2005) Improving Web accessibility through an enhanced open-source browser, *IBM Systems Journal*, 44(3), pp. 573 - 588.

[3] Johnny Lee (http://johnnylee.net/projects/wii/)

[4] A. L. Murgatroyd, Wii Remote Mouse Application, available as a free download at http://home.exetel.com.au/amurgshere/wiimouse.phtml

[5] Click-N-Type Virtual Keyboard available as a free download at http://cnt.lakefolks.com .

Author Index

www.ingramcontent.com/pod-product-compliance
Lightning Source LLC
Chambersburg PA
CBHW080353060326
40689CB00019B/3988